CURRENCY CONVERTIBILITY IN EASTERN EUROPE

JOHN WILLIAMSON
Editor

Institute for International Economics

JOHN WILLIAMSON, EDITOR

Currency
Convertibility In
Eastern Europe

INSTITUTE FOR INTERNATIONAL ECONOMICS
WASHINGTON, DC
September 1991

INSTITUTE FOR INTERNATIONAL
ECONOMICS
11 Dupont Circle, NW
Washington, DC 20036-1207
(202) 328-9000
Telex: 261271 IIE UR
FAX: (202) 328-5432

C. Fred Bergsten, *Director*
Linda Griffin Kean, *Director of
Publications*

The views expressed in this publication
are those of the authors. This
publication is part of the overall
program of the Institute, as endorsed by
its Board of Directors, but does not
necessarily reflect the views of
individual members of the Board or the
Advisory Committee.

"Liberalizing Foreign Trade in a
Socialist Economy: The Problem of
Negative Value Added" by Ronald I.
McKinnon is adapted and abridged with
permission from chapter 12 of *The Order
of Economic Liberalization: Financial
Control in the Transition to a Market
Economy.* Copyright © 1991 The Johns
Hopkins University Press.

Printed in the United States of America
95 94 93 92 91   5 4 3 2 1

Library of Congress Cataloging-in-
Publication Data

Currency convertibility in Eastern
Europe/John Williamson, editor.
Includes index.
    ISBN 0-88132-144-3 (cloth)
    ISBN 0-88132-128-1 (paper)
    1. Currency convertibility—Case
studies. 2. Money—Europe,
Eastern—Case studies. 3. Monetary
policy—Europe, Eastern—Case
studies. I. Williamson, John,
1937–   .
HG3851.C77   1991
332.4′56′0947—dc20   91-29947
                                 CIP

Dedicated to the memory of

Alfred Herrhausen

1930–1989

whose tragic death deprived the Institute
of one of the most respected and dedicated members
of its Board of Directors,
and whose devotion to the liberation
of Eastern Europe and the Soviet Union
helped inspire this study.

Contents

Preface *C. Fred Bergsten*   ix

1 **Introduction**   *John Williamson*   1

2 **The Views of Two Finance Ministers**   7
Price Liberalization and Currency Convertibility:
Twenty Days After   *Václav Klaus*   9
The Transition to a Market Economy:
An Austrian Perspective   *Ferdinand Lacina*   14

3 **How Quickly Should Convertibility Be Introduced?**   19
Convertibility: An Indispensable Element in the Transition
Process in Eastern Europe   *Jacques J. Polak*   21
The Place of Convertibility in the Transformation Process
Friedrich Levcik   31
Comment   *Domenico Mario Nuti*   48
Discussion   56

4 **Managing the Transition**   61
Convertibility in Eastern Europe Through a Payments Union
Jozef M. van Brabant   63
Liberalizing Foreign Trade in a Socialist Economy
Ronald I. McKinnon   96
The Transition to Convertibility in Eastern Europe:
A Monetary View   *Peter Bofinger*   116
Comments   *Peter B. Kenen*   139
Dariusz K. Rosati   142
John Flemming   146
Discussion   149

5 **Three Pioneers**   153
Poland   *Andrzej Olechowski and Marek Oleś*   155
Yugoslavia   *Ljubiša Adamovich*   169

East Germany   *Wolfgang Schill*   181
Comments   *Benedikt Thanner*   197
           Karol Lutkowski   200
           John K. Thompson   204
Discussion   211

6   **The Next Candidates**   **215**
Czechoslovakia   *Jaromír Zahradník*   217
Hungary   *Lajos Bokros*   226
Comments   *Miroslav Hrnčíř*   234
           Gabor Oblath   237
           Marie Lavigne   241
Discussion   246

7   **Future Candidates**   **251**
Bulgaria   *Ventseslav Dimitrov*   253
Romania   *Lucian C. Ionescu*   264
Comments   *Todor Valchev*   272
           Eduard Hochreiter   274
Discussion   276

8   **The Soviet Union**   **279**
Convertibility of the Ruble   *Boris Fedorov*   281
Toward the Convertible Ruble: The Case for a Parallel Currency
   Andrei I. Kazmin and Andrei V. Tsimailo   294
Comments   *Richard N. Cooper*   310
           Guzel Anulova   315
           Michael R. Dohan   318
           Richard Portes   328
Discussion   332

9   **Panel Discussion: Lessons From the Past
    and Strategies for the Future**   **337**
           Helmut Kramer   339
           Andrzej Olechowski   342
           John Williamson   344
           Boris Fedorov   347
           Flemming Larsen   349
Discussion   354

10 **The Economic Opening of Eastern Europe**   **361**
    John Williamson

References   **433**

Appendix
    Conference Participants   **445**

Index   **449**

Tables
Chile: profile of tariff reform, 1973–79   105
Reserves-imports ratios in selected European countries, 1989   130
Poland: retail prices and nominal exchange rates, 1980–89   159
Poland: official external reserves, 1980–89   159
Poland: zloty and foreign-exchange deposits as shares of total bank
    deposits of households, 1980–89   160
Poland: official and free market exchange rates, 1980–89   160
Poland: selected economic indicators, 1990   165
Poland: balance of payments in convertible currencies,
    1989 and 1990   166
Yugoslavia: selected economic indicators, 1980–89   170
Yugoslavia: monthly price indices, 1989–90   173
Yugoslavia: exports and imports, 1990   176
East Germany: selected economic indicators, 1985–89   192
East Germany: exchange rates and trading volumes in the market
    for East German marks, 1985–90   193
Czechoslovakia: selected economic indicators, 1985–90   219
Hungary: selected economic indicators, 1981–90   229
Bulgaria: selected economic indicators, 1980–89   258
Romania: selected economic indicators, 1980–90   270
Population, per capita income, and openness to trade of selected
    European countries   365
CMEA trade, 1987   366
External debts of the Eastern European countries, 1990   372
Estimated effects of shifting to world prices on the 1989 terms of
    trade and dollar values of trade balances of five Eastern European
    countries   372

Figures

Production of finished goods under socialist production and
under free trade   100

Effect of interim tariff protection during the transition to free trade   108

East Germany: selected economic data, 1990   194

Romania: macroeconomic and structural reforms from a financial
and banking perspective   270

Local-currency prices of traded goods under alternative schemes   398

Preface

The peaceful revolutions in Eastern Europe and the continuing political and economic crisis in the Soviet Union are among the most dramatic events of our time. A central element of the transformations in most of these countries has been a total reversal of economic policy from central planning to a market orientation. Because of the momentous importance of these changes not only for the peoples of these countries but for the rest of the world, the Institute has embarked on a series of analyses of key aspects of these historic transformations. Our May 1991 study by Susan M. Collins and Dani Rodrik, *Eastern Europe and the Soviet Union in the World Economy*, was a pioneering attempt to measure the impact of the region's liberalizations on world trade and capital flows.

The present volume, *Currency Convertibility in Eastern Europe*, analyzes the external aspects of the economic policies that are being adopted by these emerging market economies. The currency issue is the centerpiece of this dimension of their reforms and is thus the focus of the volume. A cardinal question is whether, and under what circumstances, countries should opt for a "big bang" strategy as have Poland and Yugoslavia or one of gradualism as did Western Europe after the Second World War.

The volume is based on a conference hosted and financed by the Austrian National Bank in Vienna in January 1991. In addition to analyzing the several conceptual approaches to economic opening, the volume includes studies of each of the countries of the region. A summary of its findings and policy recommendations was published by the Institute in June 1991 under the title *The Economic Opening of Eastern Europe*. We appreciate the advice provided to the author by study groups of experts that met in Washington and Vienna, and the suggestions made by members of the business community at a session hosted by Morgan Guaranty Trust in New York. The Pew Charitable Trusts supported John Williamson's research and the remainder of the project.

The Institute for International Economics is a private nonprofit institution for the study and discussion of international economic policy. Its purpose is to analyze important issues in that area, and to develop and communicate practical new approaches for dealing with them. The Institute is completely nonpartisan.

The Institute was created by a generous commitment of funds from the German Marshall Fund of the United States in 1981 and now receives about 12 percent of its support from that source. In addition, major institutional grants are being received from the Ford Foundation, the William and Flora Hewlett Foundation, the William M. Keck, Jr. Foundation, the Alfred P. Sloan Foundation, the C. V. Starr Foundation, and the United States–Japan Foundation. A number of other foundations and private corporations are contributing to the highly diversified financial resources of the Institute. About 12 percent of those resources in our latest fiscal year were provided by contributors outside the United States, including about 2 percent from Japan. No funding is received from any government.

The Board of Directors bears overall responsibility for the Institute and gives general guidance and approval to its research program—including identification of topics that are likely to become important to international economic policymakers over the medium run (generally, one to three years), and which thus should be addressed by the Institute. The Director, working closely with the staff and outside Advisory Committee, is responsible for the development of particular projects and makes the final decision to publish an individual study.

The Institute hopes that its studies and other activities will contribute to building a stronger foundation for international economic policy around the world. We invite readers of these publications to let us know how they think we can best accomplish this objective.

C. FRED BERGSTEN
Director
September 1991

1

Introduction

Introduction

John Williamson

Eastern Europe is engaged in a conscious attempt to reform its economic system. The scope of this change is without historical precedent, save perhaps when Eastern Europe itself moved in the opposite direction and implanted a socialist system. It has often been remarked that all the existing literature about intersystem transition reflected that earlier experience and dealt only with the transition to socialism. Therefore when the countries of the region decided that socialism had failed them and they wished to make the opposite transition to a market economy, there was almost nothing on which to draw. This book is a contribution to the literature that has sprung up to fill this void following the demonstration of demand.

One conspicuous feature of the reform process in Eastern Europe is that it involves integrating these emergent market economies into the global economy. A necessary condition for such integration is establishment of the convertibility of the local currencies. Indeed this is the policy measure on which attention rapidly focused after the pioneering decision of the Polish authorities to make convertibility of the zloty an integral feature of their "big bang" on 1 January 1990. Accordingly, the Institute for International Economics, in association with the Austrian National Bank, convened a conference intended to examine the modalities of establishing convertibility. The proceedings of that conference, which was held in Vienna in January 1991, are reported in this volume.

It rapidly became apparent that one could not sensibly discuss currency convertibility in isolation from the rest of the process of economic opening, or indeed from the rest of the process of economic reform. Hence the present volume deals also with such topics as the relationship of convertibility to the reform process in general, the type of exchange rate policy needed to sustain convertibility, and the case for temporary abridgment of the full force of convertibility by transitional protection.

The volume starts in chapter 2 with the texts of two after-dinner speeches delivered during the conference. The first is by Václav Klaus, Finance Minister of Czechoslovakia and the architect of the Czechoslovak reform program. He

3

describes the state of the program at the time of the conference, which came just twenty days after the country had made its currency convertible. Czechoslovakia was also then in the midst of a vigorous public debate on the merits of a voucher scheme designed to promote rapid and "democratic" privatization. As the chief protagonist of that scheme, Minister Klaus was surely gratified by its parliamentary approval some five weeks later.

The second speech in chapter 2 is that of Ferdinand Lacina, the Austrian Minister of Finance. Austria has perhaps done more than any other Western country to develop retraining programs to provide Eastern European policymakers with the new skills they will need to operate market economies efficiently: indeed, the fact that our conference was held in Vienna under the joint sponsorship of the Austrian National Bank reflects the country's commitment to this cause. Austria's lengthy effort to catch up with the rest of Western Europe, a task that was completed only in the 1980s, provides an admirable perspective from which to survey the task of reform on which its neighbors, including its onetime partners in the Hapsburg Empire, have now embarked. Austria's own approach to convertibility was decidedly gradual, but Minister Lacina argues for caution in drawing policy lessons from historical experiences in which circumstances differ so sharply.

The next chapter contains two papers that discuss this key question of the appropriate speed at which to introduce convertibility. Jacques J. Polak argues that an early move to something close to current account convertibility[1] is an indispensable element of the reform program, while Friedrich Levcik argues the case for gradualism. As in later chapters, the main papers are complemented by comments from discussants and a summary of the subsequent conference debate.

Chapter 4 contains three papers, each of which advocates a particular policy during the transition period. Jozef M. van Brabant presents his proposal for a Central European Payments Union modeled on the European Payments Union of postwar Western Europe. Peter Bofinger argues that the Eastern European countries need firm and credible monetary discipline right from the start, and contends that they could best get this by joining a European monetary union, if one is there to be joined. Ronald I. McKinnon argues for a significant level of

---

1. The definition of convertibility is discussed at length at the beginning of chapter 10. Suffice it to say here that, except where indicated otherwise the word as used in this book refers to something close to the concept of current account convertibility embodied in the IMF's Article VIII. This concept involves any agent, domestic or foreign, having the right to convert the domestic currency into a foreign currency at the official exchange rate in order to complete a current account transaction (the purchase of goods or services from abroad, including the remittance of profits earned on direct investment); it does not imply the right to convert in order to export capital. The concept of "internal convertibility" used by many of the Eastern European contributors limits the right of conversion to domestic residents, and thus does not include, in particular, any right to remit profits through the official market.

trade protection for existing industries on a transitional basis, to give enterprises a chance to adjust, rather than for going straight to something close to free trade. Needless to say, all three prescriptions proved controversial.

The next four chapters deal with the past experiences and present policy options of four groups of countries. The first group consists of three "pioneers" that had already established convertibility when the conference was being planned: Yugoslavia, Poland, and the former East Germany. The second group consists of those countries seen at the time of the conference as the "next candidates" for convertibility: Czechoslovakia, which as noted above took the step of making the koruna convertible only a few weeks before the conference, and Hungary, which has still not made a formal declaration of convertibility but has already proceeded a long way in that direction. This is followed by a chapter on the "future candidates" of Bulgaria and Romania. The last of the four chapters deals with the Soviet Union. All of the authors in these four chapters are (past or present) senior officials or leading academics in the countries involved, or both. Apart from Boris Fedorov, the former Finance Minister of the Russian Republic, their names are not yet widely known in the West, but some of them surely will be before long.

Chapter 9 contains the proceedings of the panel discussion that concluded the deliberations of the conference. The final chapter consists of my summary and synthesis of the conference; it was published separately in May 1991 as volume 31 in the Institute's POLICY ANALYSES IN INTERNATIONAL ECONOMICS series.

Western economists who have had the privilege of getting involved in the policy debate in Eastern Europe have, I think, been impressed by the way in which their Eastern European counterparts have measured up to their historic challenge. The present volume is certainly not offered as a textbook to instruct Eastern Europeans in Western wisdom on the art of managing a market economy: on the contrary, I suspect they will learn more from each other's experiences than from the West. But one of the great things about the new Europe is that we are increasingly less conscious of whether we are Easterners or Westerners. If Western research institutes like ours can help Eastern Europeans learn from one another, and in the process help Westerners keep abreast of developments in that region, we shall be well content.

2

The Views of Two Finance Ministers

The Views of Two Finance Ministers

Price Liberalization and Currency Convertibility: Twenty Days After

Václav Klaus

On 14 May 1990 the Czechoslovak federal government accepted a blueprint for the restructuring of the Czechoslovak economy. This document, entitled "The Strategy of Radical Economic Reform," outlined the necessary measures, and their sequence, for the transformation of the economy into a modern market system similar to those of Western Europe. The approval of the plan by the Federal Parliament in September constituted a victory for the real reformers in Czechoslovakia and for believers in a market economy and economic liberalism, it marked an end to the disputes between radicals and gradualists in the government.

Throughout 1990 one reform measure after another was implemented, and the last vestiges of a centrally planned economy, of its institutions and of its irresponsible economic policies, have been abolished. There have been some notable successes in this campaign; however, there have also been some delays and half-measures. The successes include:

- Reversal of the inflationary monetary and fiscal policies of the former regime, and their replacement with restrictive policies based on a budget surplus and on a minimal rate of growth of monetary aggregates;

- Cuts in subsidies to both producers and consumers (including the abolition of all state subsidies on food products);

- Liquidation of many of the institutions of the central planning regime (including the State Planning Commission, the Federal Price Board, and several branch ministries);

Václav Klaus is the Minister of Finance of the Czech and Slovak Federal Republic.

- Preparation of a completely new legislative framework suitable for a market economy and based on private enterprise.

However, the reforms have not yet been totally successful in the rapid initiation of privatization; in the demonopolization of basic industries, wholesale organizations, and services; or in the abolition of all existing bureaucratic obstacles to economic freedom and private initiative.

The economic situation in 1990 was complicated by a set of unfavorable external factors: the increase in the price of oil; the dismantling of trade, pricing, and payment arrangements within the Council for Mutual Economic Assistance; and the disintegration of the Soviet economy and of Soviet markets. Nevertheless, if one takes into consideration the significant domestic changes and uncertainties and the rapid, unexpected disruption of Soviet oil supplies (which fell by 20 percent), the preliminary results of the reforms in terms of current macroeconomic performance are relatively acceptable:

- Real GNP decreased by only 3 percent;

- Inflation accelerated, but only to 10 percent on an annual basis;

- Nominal personal income grew by 8 percent to 9 percent;

- Unemployment was held to around 0.5 percent of the labor force;

- The federal budget stayed in surplus throughout the year;

- The level of foreign indebtedness did not increase, as the balance of payments deficit was financed by means of domestic reserves, which, however, reached dangerously low levels.

On the other hand, Czechoslovakia's economic performance in the last weeks of 1990 was worse than these annual figures suggest; in particular, the rate of inflation rose to more than 18 percent in the fourth quarter.

Crucial Steps in the Original Reform Package

Czechoslovakia's radical economic reform program sought to implement the following four basic measures in a very short period of time:

- Lifting of price controls and price liberalization;

- Rapid and massive privatization of state firms;

- Foreign trade liberalization;

- Internal (i.e., resident) convertibility of the koruna.

The decision to undertake this reform strategy rapidly and in this sequence was based on two deeply held convictions on the part of the Czechoslovak reformers. The first was that central planning and a free market cannot coexist without further destabilizing the already unstable economy. The second was that, because of the relative economic weakness of the government and the vested interests of government bureaucrats (as postulated by the arguments of the public choice school), the central authorities do not have the ability to organize economic life in an appropriate manner or to guide state firms toward rational economic behavior.

The opposition to radical reform, at least in Czechoslovakia, has not come up with any concrete proposals for an alternative solution to the crisis. Instead it has limited its arguments to stressing the social costs of the rapid economic changes undertaken by the reform strategy.

It is generally accepted that the lifting of price controls on the one hand and privatization on the other represent the two most difficult operations in the whole process of transition to a market economy. The Czechoslovak reformers have understood that privatization must occur at the beginning rather than at the end of the restructuring process and, even more important, must be decentralized and not organized by a bureaucratic organization of the Treuhandanstalt type as in the former East Germany.

In Czechoslovakia privatization is divided into two parts. The so-called small privatization (of services, shops, restaurants, and other small enterprises) has been conceptually, legislatively, and even organizationally prepared and is to start at the end of January 1991. The privatization of large enterprises, based on a mixture of standard and nonstandard methods (the latter including a voucher scheme, which will play an important role in the process) is in the final stage of debate in the Federal Parliament, and as of this writing is expected to be approved in a few days' or weeks' time.[1]

The introduction on 1 January 1991 of internal convertibility of the koruna, based on the determination of a realistic exchange rate (after three successive devaluations in January, October, and December 1990) and backed by the extremely important financial support of the International Monetary Fund and the European Community, seems to be a rather standard operation. It is hoped that the new exchange rate will be viable and will play a positive role as a nominal anchor for the economy, stabilizing—together with restrictive macroeconomic policies—the level of domestic prices. In addition, a temporary import surcharge on consumer-goods purchases should help to curtail imports and to balance the current account. The situation seems to be under control, and as of this writing there has been no dramatic loss of reserves since the introduction of convertibility.

---

1. The small privatization program was begun on schedule, and the larger privatization program was approved in February 1991.

Price Liberalization

Also on 1 January 1991, a far-reaching price liberalization was introduced, accompanied by:

- Restrictive monetary and fiscal policies aimed at cutting aggregate demand;
- Partial price regulation, with maximum prices for a very limited number of commodities, obligatory cost-price calculation guidelines for another group, and, for a third group, the obligation to announce price rises of more than 20 percent or 30 percent (not more than 10 percent to 15 percent of all goods and services are subject to such regulation), with only *ex post* controls;
- Foreign trade liberalization;
- Wage regulation based on tentative agreements with trade unions about the size and schedule of wage increases;
- Lagged indexation of social benefits.

As of this writing, after three weeks of price liberalization, it is possible to draw some preliminary conclusions.

First, some monopolistic producers and especially wholesalers tried to misuse their market power and to refute the validity of basic economic laws by excessively increasing their prices at the very beginning of the program. These abuses were visible mainly in the food products industry. However, the demand constraint (along with the well-stocked refrigerators of most Czechoslovak consumers) began to push prices down again, and the monopolists soon discovered that their power was limited.

The behavior of producers helped to counter this behavior of wholesale firms. Many private firms, agricultural cooperatives, and even various state firms decided to bypass the monopolistic wholesalers and go directly to the consumers. This was an important change.

Since 1 January prices have been very volatile and have been fluctuating daily; it is therefore very difficult to calculate a reliable aggregate price index. Also, because of inefficiencies in markets and the lack of horizontal information, prices have differed from place to place. This has helped to divert popular discontent from the government (and the radical reformers) and direct it toward various monopolistic producers and wholesalers.

The price jumps evidently shocked the public, but its reaction has so far been unexpectedly cautious. There have been no strikes or demonstrations, and there has been no panic shopping, which would demonstrate a worsening of inflationary expectations. It is fair to argue that the authorities' estimates of repressed inflation were not far off the target, and one may be mildly optimistic that the first potential crisis period is over and that efforts may now be concentrated on other targets, in particular on privatization.

Lessons To Be Learned

To date Czechoslovakia's economic transformation is going according to plan and without major surprises or disappointments. What have we learned from this experience so far?

In the very first weeks and months of the reform process I repeatedly stressed—in accordance with the standard theoretical literature—the problem of the appropriate sequencing of reforms. I have to admit that I considered the sequencing question to be of the utmost importance. Now, after a year in which the Czechoslovak economy has been largely reformed—indeed transformed—I no longer mention the sequencing issue at all. I am deeply convinced that the idea of sequencing is just a technocratic or rationalistic notion based on unrealistic beliefs in social engineering, in scientific control of the reform process, and in the fine tuning of reforms.

Clearly the transformation of a centrally planned economy is a complicated, multidimensional social process, with its own dynamics and with very different time requirements for various reform measures. It would be very nice to be able to control this process and dictate the sequencing of economic reforms. However, to our great regret, such mastery of the transformation process must be relegated to the realm of utopian dreams and theoretical simplifications. The breakup of monopolies and the transformation of property rights prior to price liberalization is a rational textbook proposal, but economic, social, and political pressures may dictate something else. The only prescription that must be followed for successful institutional and systemic change is macroeconomic stabilization based on prudent macroeconomic policies. This is undoubtedly the main message we can deliver. Or, to put it slightly differently, we have to rely on orthodox methods of economic stabilization.

The Transition to a Market Economy: An Austrian Perspective

Ferdinand Lacina

The establishment of currency convertibility is but one element of the restructuring process in the countries of Eastern Europe, and one that must be carefully planned so as to fit coherently within a well-defined program of economic transformation. The transformation of a centrally planned economy into a market economy characterized by a decentralization of decisionmaking is largely uncharted territory. The proper functioning of a market economy depends on a specific infrastructure of property rights, regulations and regulatory bodies, corporate and labor laws, procedures for settling disputes, and so on. Much of this infrastructure is embodied in institutions, but important elements of it are embedded in social traditions and in conventions of business practice. These elements vary both in style and in terms of their relative importance from country to country. Therefore, beyond certain core elements, no single, homogeneous model of a market economy exists. As the Economic Commission for Europe has put it, considered as a policy objective, "the transformation of a centrally planned economy into a market economy is more a statement of general principle than a detailed programme of action."

Of course, when it comes down to restructuring a given economy, at a certain period of time, and in a specific international environment, just such a detailed program of action is needed. The sequencing of reform steps, which depends on the micro- and macroeconomic setting of the country in question, is of crucial importance.

The range and seriousness of economic problems facing Eastern Europe vary considerably from country to country. There are macroeconomic imbalances of varying degrees, and there are marked differences in the inflation rate, in the level of foreign debt, and in the size of the current account deficit. Thus, the reconstruction and transformation program has to be tailored to each country according to the economic conditions prevailing there. No general solution is applicable.

The introduction of realistic exchange rates and the move toward currency convertibility form a crucial element of any comprehensive reform program. In this context the question of whether currency convertibility should be introduced

Ferdinand Lacina is the Minister of Finance of the Republic of Austria.

suddenly, at the beginning of a reconstruction program, or gradually is hotly debated among economists. The experience of the Western European countries seems to argue in favor of a gradual approach, but one should be cautious in drawing general conclusions. The dismantling of exchange controls in the Western European countries took place in a particular economic environment, internally and externally, which is not the same as that facing the Eastern European countries today.

A fundamental difference between the transformation problems facing the reforming countries today and those facing the Western European countries after the Second World War is that the former have to reconstruct market economies from first principles whereas the latter could rebuild on existing market foundations. True, in the immediate postwar years the Western European economies were highly regulated—the legacy of the direct controls used to mobilize resources during the war. The level and composition of production and consumption were controlled through a set of instruments including price restrictions, import licenses, direct allocation of foreign currency and raw materials, and rationing of consumer goods. Nevertheless, beneath the surface of the wartime controls the basic features of a market economy survived. As soon as the shortages were overcome, largely through the support of the European Recovery Program, and as the regulations of the war economy were dismantled, the Western European countries embarked on a dynamic recovery process, taking advantage of the incentive structure of the existing market system.

In contrast, policymakers in the reforming countries of the former Eastern bloc are faced with the much more difficult task of creating the complex infrastructure of a modern decentralized economy where it did not exist before. The retreat of central planners and the elimination of bureaucratic controls are not a sufficient basis for the emergence of efficient markets. To transform centrally planned economies into market economies, institutional changes are needed on a very broad front. These include, among other things:

- Reform of the price-setting mechanism;

- The introduction of an efficient tax system;

- Reconstruction of the banking system;

- The establishment of capital markets;

- The construction of a social security system; and

- The liberalization of foreign trade.

The move toward currency convertibility for current account transactions is an instrument for the integration of the reforming Eastern European economies into the world trading system. It can help in replacing the system of relative prices inherited from the era of central planning, which often did not reflect the true scarcity of available goods and services. Currency convertibility and trade liberalization are necessary to increase competition in domestic markets, because the size distribution of enterprises in many sectors of the reform economies otherwise favors monopolistic behavior.

On the other hand, the introduction of currency convertibility and the exposure of the reforming economies to international competition can be risky for many firms in these countries, whose competitiveness appears to have deteriorated considerably over the last decade. The efficiency of productive capital and especially the marketing organization and skills of enterprises in the reforming countries are inferior to those of their Western competitors. A decrease in production and an increase in unemployment are therefore the likely result of introducing currency convertibility.

Economic reforms and liberalization measures tend to generate political resistance, because the immediate costs are usually perceived more clearly than the long-run benefits. If the speed of adjustment to the new economic environment, to the new mode of production, is too long, political instability can result. To prevent such an outcome in Eastern Europe, Western support, including both technical and financial assistance, is needed.

Technical assistance, which involves training managers and public officials as well as supplying expertise in specific technologies, is of the utmost importance. Both the Austrian government and other Austrian institutions, such as the Austrian National Bank, actively support such activities. Besides this bilateral effort, Austria is an outspoken advocate of the enhanced engagement of such international organizations as the International Monetary Fund, the World Bank, and the Organization for Economic Cooperation and Development, among others.

Financial assistance to the reforming countries will also take several forms. Currency stabilization loans can enhance the credibility of efforts to introduce convertibility. Balance of payments financing is indispensable when the level of foreign-exchange reserves is inadequate. Foreign direct investment can play a vital role in the transformation process, especially in the establishment of high-technology operations supervised by modern management techniques. Direct investments can be linked to debt-equity swaps, thereby reducing the level of foreign debt.

A precondition for foreign direct investment on a larger scale seems to be the radical improvement of transport and telecommunication systems and the material infrastructure as a whole. The European Bank for Reconstruction and Development intends to devote two-fifths of its resources to this end, and the World Bank is already active in this respect.

The European Community announced in mid-January 1991 that it will provide financial support to improve the power-generating system of Czechoslovakia. This support is highly commended. Austria, too, is prepared, on a bilateral basis or in cooperation with the World Bank or other multilateral organizations, to supply technical and financial assistance to increase the efficiency of energy production and consumption in Eastern Europe. Such support is urgently needed not merely on economic grounds but also for the sake of reducing the risks to our common environment.

The countries of the former Eastern bloc are in the process of transforming their economies into market economies. As we have seen in the last few years, political and economic developments in these countries are interdependent: the success or failure of economic reform programs depends on the will to undertake political reforms. The democratization of the former Eastern bloc countries was a precondition for the launching of the economic reform initiatives. If the restructuring program should fail, it would increase the risks of social unrest and political instability in these countries. Therefore, it is the responsibility of the Western community to support the transition process by all possible means. As it has in the past, Austria will contribute its share toward this end.

3

How Quickly Should Convertibility
Be Introduced?

How Quickly Should Convertibility Be Introduced?

Convertibility: An Indispensable Element in the Transition Process

Jacques J. Polak

The Slow Move Toward Convertibility After World War II

Convertibility did not in general receive a high priority in the early years of postwar economic reconstruction of the countries of Western Europe. True, these countries' membership in the International Monetary Fund obliged them to pursue as a long-term aim the convertibility of their currencies—with that term modesty defined in the Articles of Agreement as convertibility with respect to transaction on current account. But by 1952—five years after the IMF began operations and seven years after the end of the war—none of the countries in question had a convertible currency, and all became subject to the obligation to consult the IMF annually on the "further retention" of such payments restrictions as they still maintained that were inconsistent with the provisions on convertibility in the Articles of Agreement. Although some countries, such as Belgium, Germany, and the Netherlands, adopted foreign-exchange and trade practices in the early 1950s that were close to convertibility, it took until 1958 for most European OECD countries to adopt *de facto* convertibility, and until 1961 before they took the formal step of accepting the obligations of IMF Article VIII.

Convertibility for Eastern Europe

There is much evidence that the countries of Eastern Europe see the adoption of convertibility—or at least a major move in that direction—as a more important

Jacques J. Polak is President of the Per Jacobsson Foundation and a former Executive Director of the International Monetary Fund.

ingredient in their catching up with the industrial economies of the West than the latter viewed this step forty years earlier.

In discussing this question from the broad point of view of the most desirable economic policy, it is not particularly useful to separate the two aspects—payments and transactions, or the IMF aspect and the GATT aspect—of an inconvertible regime. Obviously, both need to be addressed *pari passu* to establish a meaningful degree of convertibility; the benefits of convertibility are derived from a combination of "financial" and "commodity" convertibility (Gilman 1990). In the planned economies, currencies are said to lack internal or commodity convertibility if holdings of domestic currency do not constitute effective purchasing power over domestic goods and services, in the sense that most domestic transactions require the purchaser to have not only money but also a purchasing permit of one sort or another. Similarly, for convertibility for international transactions to be economically meaningful, holders of domestic currency must be able freely not only to pay for foreign goods and services but to import those goods and services in the first place.

Although some of the early enthusiasm for convertibility in Eastern Europe may have derived from a general desire to restore respectability to their currencies, it is the commodity aspect, rather than the financial aspect, of convertibility that is of greatest relevance in welfare terms. The main reason to allow foreign goods to come into a country relatively freely is to subject domestic producers to competition from abroad and, in the process, to "import" a system of economic pricing. The price system the Eastern European countries inherited at the time of transition lacked all economic rationale, and there was only very limited domestic competition.

Given the central importance of establishing a rational system of pricing in the Eastern European countries, convertibility must not be delayed in time or qualified in scope to any important extent. The development of new export markets cannot start until existing factories shake off their past and adjust both their techniques of production and their pricing to available niches in world markets. And neither foreign nor domestic entrepreneurs will invest in new factories for exports until the cost level of domestic suppliers is brought down to competitive levels. Thus, "commodity convertibility" is not an optional feature of the transition process that can be introduced gradually as conditions improve. On the contrary, it is in the nature of a precondition for a balanced economy to be able to take off.

Acceptable Limits to Convertibility

Even though at least some of the countries of Eastern Europe are now moving toward convertibility, no one expects them to turn into instant Hong Kongs.

Some qualifications to the freedom to convert or to import, as well as some mitigation of the competitive impact on the pricing of goods, services, and assets, may well be acceptable if in this way other objectives of policy, such as equity or stability, can be more fully attained.

Many countries that have accepted IMF Article VIII still practice some restrictions on imports. As long as these restrictions are limited in scope, they do not greatly qualify the proposition that these countries' economies are exposed to the fresh winds of international competition that convertibility in the broad economic sense is designed to provide. Most Western European countries also limited the ability of residents to invest abroad for many years after 1961; indeed France and Italy maintained certain restrictions on capital movements until 1989. The experience of the last thirty years has shown that some degree of capital liberalization for business and banking is an essential accompaniment to the liberalization of trade; on the other hand, restrictions on, for example, the right of individuals to invest abroad certainly do not interfere with a country's reaping the economic benefits of convertibility. Restrictions on the availability of foreign exchange for personal travel, although they curtail transactions listed in the current account, are also a tolerable deviation from full convertibility. Such restrictions may find their justification either in the social motive of avoiding conspicuous foreign consumption (as would import restrictions on luxury items) or in the economic one of preventing capital export from taking place under another name. Both types of restrictions were used in Western Europe for many years after the adoption of convertibility.

Clearly, then, convertibility does not have to be 100 percent pure to be economically meaningful in the sense that it broadly provides the economy with the signals necessary for its integration into the world economy. There is a question, however, as to how far most Eastern European countries (or, for that matter, the Soviet Union) are still able to stop their residents from engaging in restricted transactions once the countries have legalized domestic markets in foreign currency. If residents badly want foreign exchange for purposes of capital flight or travel and cannot get it from official sources, they can buy it in that market, driving up the unofficial exchange rate. This will undermine the policy of using the official exchange rate as a nominal anchor (to prevent which the government may begin to sell official exchange in the free market), and it almost certainly will divert some export proceeds from the official to the free market.

Convertibility and Payments Unions

Would the adoption of a payments union among the countries of Eastern Europe be compatible with the attainment or maintenance of convertibility? The answer depends to a large extent on the purposes for which such arrangements would be introduced and on the role that mutual credit arrangements would be expected to play in them.[1]

Five Central American countries, all of which had accepted convertibility under Article VIII, introduced a kind of payments union among themselves in 1961 (the Central American Clearing House). The arrangement was limited in scope, however; it left countries complete freedom whether or not to channel intraregional payments through their central banks into the clearinghouse. For those payments that were centralized into the clearinghouse, credit and debit balances were netted out multilaterally, but debtors were allowed only a one-week grace period before they had to settle in full with the clearinghouse in dollars, which the latter then used to pay the creditors.

Under the mini-umbrella provided by these arrangements, the participating countries moved some distance toward the liberalization of trade among themselves, without however raising tariffs or import restrictions against other trade partners. Arrangements of this nature are of minimal economic effect, in particular if the group's intratrade is small compared to its total trade. The saving on reserves achieved by clearing payments on all intratrade rather than making *and receiving* payments on a transaction-by-transaction basis can at most be a trivial economy on float. It is not for such insubstantial reasons that groups of countries have often been encouraged to start payments unions—originally in Europe and later in many other regions such as South America, the ECAFE (Economic Commission for Asia and the Far East) region, West Africa, and now Eastern Europe.

There have been wide economic differences from country to country in all the regions for which payments unions have been proposed.[2] Mainly for this reason, with the exception of the highly successful European Payments Union (EPU) and the minimal arrangement in Central America, all past discussions on payments unions have failed to lead to agreements. Typically, the countries with stronger economies and currencies lacked interest in arrangements that would impel them to extend credit to, and practice trade discrimination in favor of, participating weaker countries. The negotiation of EPU nearly faltered on the same obstacle, with Belgium the main holdout. The origin and characteristics of that payments union deserve attention as background for the consideration of a possible payments union for Eastern Europe.

---

1. The latter point is stressed in a 1962 report by two IMF economists prepared at the request of the Center for Latin American Studies (CEMLA) of Mexico City (Keesing and Brand 1963).

2. For an extensive description and analysis of the discussions in Latin America from 1956 to 1962, and a good summary presentation of the European Payments Union, see Keesing and Brand (1963).

The European Payments Union

Soon after the war, countries in Western Europe began to conduct trade on the basis of bilateral payments arrangements. These arrangements provided for bilateral "swing" credits that could remain outstanding until reversed by a trade balance in the opposite direction, and full settlement, beyond that swing, in gold or dollars. Frequently, however, the swings did not alternate, and by 1947 most of the credit margins had been exhausted and intra-European trade was grinding to a standstill. If imports by, say, the Netherlands from Belgium had reached the point where they required full payment in dollars, the Netherlands would stop importing from Belgium because there were always more urgent imports from the dollar area.

The seizing up of intra-European trade produced a series of makeshift arrangements in 1948 and 1949, as well as a long-drawn-out process of innovative thinking, in Europe and in Washington, and negotiation that led by mid–1950 to the creation of the EPU. With its accompanying trade arrangements, the EPU provided for a sharp reduction of quantitative restrictions on intra-European trade; monthly multilateral settlements of European surpluses and deficits, with partial settlement in credit up to an agreed quota for each country and full settlement in dollars beyond the quota; and a capital contribution from the Economic Cooperation Administration (ECA) to cover any dollar shortfalls that might result from the EPU paying out more than it received.

Although the IMF opposed the EPU (as did the US Treasury—its proponent in the US government was the European Recovery Administration, the Marshall Plan agency), its motivation goes in a sense back to the position that the IMF itself took in 1946 with respect to the initial par values for members' currencies. The approach then taken was that, for these war-torn countries, par values need not be equilibrium exchange rates; the only requirement was that the rates chosen (which for almost all countries were the rates adopted by them at the end of the war) should not impede the recovery of exports. Trade restrictions rather than the exchange rate were counted upon to keep imports within the importing countries' ability to pay.

The plans for the EPU were designed with this same approach in mind. It was assumed that countries in Europe would for a long time need to restrict their imports from the dollar area. The "dollar shortage" was widely believed to be a permanent feature of the postwar period. But this was seen as no reason for these countries not to buy freely from each other; if they all moved together, they should be able to liberalize trade among themselves, provided there were new, multilateral swing credits and a supply of outside dollars to pay what were called the "structural creditors" in the group. Marshall Plan money was available for this purpose; without this money the EPU could not have been created (it was, indeed, difficult enough to create it *with* outside money).

By the time the negotiations on the EPU were finally concluded in early 1950, a major step had already been taken to bring the dollar shortage to an end. The devaluation of the pound sterling by over 30 percent in September 1949, immediately followed by devaluations (some smaller) of the other European currencies, abolished in one sweep the overvaluation of the European currencies—and, some would argue, brought about the overvaluation of the US dollar. But at the time neither European governments nor the ECA took this view (Kaplan and Schleiminger 1990, 20).

This change in underlying conditions was one of the reasons the EPU could be abolished in 1958, with a smooth introduction to *de facto* convertibility. Another reason was the sharp increase in European reserves, itself in part due to the adjustment of exchange rates, which allowed countries to take more risks with import liberalization on a worldwide basis.

Important Differences Between Western Europe 1950 and Eastern Europe 1990

In two respects, the situation in 1990 in Eastern Europe was quite different from that in 1950 in the so-called nondollar area. The first difference relates to the worldwide shift in attitudes regarding the relative merits of price signals versus governmental allocation decisions; the second is the relative size of the nondollar area in 1950 to the relevant Eastern European area in 1990.

Differences in Attitudes Toward Economic Policy

The Western European countries, emerging from their widespread wartime trade and foreign-exchange shortages of essential commodities, designed their trade and foreign-exchange policies on the implicit assumption that the government would decide the nation's import and export priorities, allocate scarce imported and domestic raw materials, and regulate consumption by rationing and investment by permit. Under this approach, the role of the exchange rate was downgraded (not only by the governments but also, as we have seen, by the IMF) to not being a serious obstacle to exports, and convertibility remained at best a far-off target. Although the Western European countries moved a considerable distance away from these beliefs in the course of the 1950s, they continued to dominate thinking about development economics in the Western world until well into the 1970s. Only the 1980s—indeed the late 1980s—saw the breakthrough on a broad front of an essentially nondirigiste approach toward the solution of what had seemed the intractable problems of the heavily indebted countries in Latin America and the retrogressing economies of Africa. This new approach is characterized by the revival of respect for market-clearing prices, in particular the real exchange rate, combined with a healthy skepticism with respect to the ability of governments to decide economic priorities—or to run businesses (Williamson 1990).

The Eastern European countries have had their own experience with guidance by the all-too-visible hand of the bureaucratic apparatus, and at least some of them have reacted by positing convertibility as a high-priority objective. In the difficult economic circumstances of the transition, and before productive efficiency can be raised, a counterpart of convertibility must be a low- to-undervalued currency that makes imports expensive and export activity especially profitable. The two Eastern European countries that have come forward with the clearest choices on transition policies, Hungary and Poland, have both set their exchange rates so as to err, if at all, in the direction of undervaluation. They have also liberalized imports. In Hungary, 90 percent of convertible-currency imports are now free of licensing obligations. In Poland, economic organizations have the right to purchase foreign exchange without limitation to finance imports and to cover certain other external obligations (Economic Commission for Europe 1990).

Thus, for these two countries at least, the trade arrangements that would have to accompany a regional payments union would amount to retrogressive steps on the road to convertibility. The aim of such arrangements is to encourage intratrade by reducing the "hardness" (a term much used in connection with the EPU) of the means of payments. Since importers must pay the domestic-currency counterpart of the foreign-exchange cost of imports whatever the source, they are not affected by intergovernmental arrangements in the region to soften the cost of imports by means of partial settlement in credits. To translate official discrimination among currencies into discrimination by importers according to country of origin, it is necessary to establish a discriminatory regime of import permits. Imports from outside the region must be restrained by licensing, whereas imports from within the region can be left free (as was mostly the case among the participants in EPU) or subject to a less restrictive regime of licensing. Whatever is done, therefore, the trade objectives of a regional currency union cannot be met without a restrictive system of licensing imports from outside the region.

Advocates of a currency union tend to concentrate their attention on the benefits that countries within the region will get from the extra demand that each thus receives from its neighbors. The Economic Commission for Europe (1990, 146) argues that "regional trade is going through an unnecessarily sharp contraction" and that means must be found "to facilitate that level of CMEA [Council for Mutual Economic Assistance] trade that needs to be maintained in the short run until either the CMEA integration mechanism can be reformed or the reforming members can redirect a substantial part of their trade to market economies."[3] But this, of course, is only one side of the coin. To the extent that licensing of imports from outside the region is maintained, intensified, or reintroduced for the purpose of channeling more import demand at higher cost inside the region, the economic benefits that were expected from convertibility and trade liberalization will be lost.

Even if restrictions on hard-currency imports were accompanied by a liberalization of trade within the region, there would be a large net loss of competitive pressure. More "competition" from other countries with unrealistic price structures and specialized, monopolistic industries that have grown up under the aegis of CMEA planning is no substitute for the market impulses that only the West can provide. (There is a major difference here from the situation in Western Europe in 1950, where liberalization within the region was expected to realize a good deal of competitive pressure and thus to help prepare countries for convertibility on a worldwide basis.) A credit union in Eastern Europe that would sacrifice the element of worldwide competition would put a brake on the speed of transition—not to mention the cost of the restrictive mechanism itself and that of the resulting misallocation of resources.

Differences in Economic Size

The nondollar area for EPU purposes included at the time not only Europe but the entire sterling area, the French franc area, the Belgian franc area, and the guilder area. Intratrade accounted for some 70 percent of trade by the EPU countries, as against some 10 percent or 20 percent for the five Eastern European countries that might qualify for an Eastern European payments union, or EEPU (Bulgaria, Czechoslovakia, Hungary, Poland, and Romania). It is true that these countries' total intra–CMEA trade was much higher: about 40 percent for Hungary, Poland, and Romania, and between 70 percent and 80 percent for Czechoslovakia and Bulgaria (1988 figures). But more than half of this was, for all countries, with the Soviet Union, and East Germany was the next-largest trade partner. The former East Germany has become part of the deutsche mark zone, and the Soviet Union would, for many reasons, not fit into an EEPU. It would dominate such a union; it has not yet developed the enterprises that could trade directly with foreign enterprises; and as the exporter of oil and other primary

---

3. The Commission also points out that there are strong technical reasons for certain CMEA trade flows to continue as before, such as the continued "demand for spare parts, components, maintenance and service to keep the obsolete machine park running (Economic Commission for Europe 1990)." Insofar as trade within the area is essential to importing countries, it would not of course need extra help from a discriminatory currency arrangement.

products, now to be sold at world market prices, it would likely be a structural creditor in any arrangement with Eastern European countries of which it formed a part (Kenen 1990).

Given the relative trade magnitudes among the five potential candidates for an EEPU, the disadvantages mentioned would almost certainly outweigh the advantages that each participant would receive in terms of discrimination in its favor by the other countries. The fact that the comparable balance of advantages and disadvantages in the EPU was on the whole favorable for its participants carries no message for Eastern Europe.

The small proportion of these countries' trade taking place within the region being considered for a payments union has other negative implications for such a union. These implications are related to the credit arrangements, which, as noted, are a crucial component of an effective payments union.

Ex ante, the mutual credit lines would allow each country to take greater risks in liberalizing intratrade, because if a deficit arose, only part of it would have to be settled in dollars. A more comfortable balance between a country's stock of reserves and potential need for it can, however, also be achieved by a reinforcement of the country's reserves (e.g., by means of a stand-by arrangement with the IMF), especially if the area to be covered accounts for only a rather small proportion of the country's trade.

Ex post, partial settlement in credit relieves the pressure on deficit countries, but the burden of this is borne by the surplus countries—unless the arrangement is supported by an outside source of foreign exchange. Among a small group of countries (even one excluding the Soviet Union), the probability that some will be structural creditors and others structural debtors in the region is of course great. Providers of outside money to the region would have to ask themselves two questions: first, do they want to encourage a system of regional discrimination by providing the indispensable outside finance? and second, do they see a convincing reason to channel their aid, through a payments union arrangement, toward the region's structural creditors?

Attempts to seek balance within such a small group would also encourage fresh trade distortions. The EPU, on the other hand, covered such a large proportion of the trade of all its members that a deficit within the group plausibly carried with it the presumption of excess domestic demand, and hence the need for adjustment. There could be no such presumption among a small group of Eastern European countries. To start a payments union among them would set the scene for an inherent conflict of objectives. On the one hand, to make the payments union "work," the aim would have to be to balance trade within the region. On the other hand, to foster efficiency (and ultimately full convertibility) trade flows should be allowed to respond to the forces of demand and supply.

Conclusions

The past forty years have seen a major shift in the attitude of countries, in the West and the East, toward the conduct of economic policy. Much greater emphasis is placed now on market-clearing prices, for both commodities and foreign exchange, than was the case when the EPU was conceived. This learning process received an extra fillip as the sad state of the economies of Eastern Europe was revealed. If the countries in transition toward market economies are serious in their desire to become associated, in one form or another, with the European Community, they will want to adopt as soon as possible the types of economic policies that fit with those pursued by the present EC members. A payments union heavily relying on credit to promote discrimination against imports from outside the group would not fit well into the policy approach now prevailing in the West.

The success of the EPU in the 1950s is of little relevance to the current problems of the countries in Eastern Europe, because the EPU arrangements were applied in an economic region that was many times larger (as measured by its intratrade) than the Eastern European region. Thus, problems of trade with the "outside world" that were manageable—though by no means unimportant—in the case of the EPU would be likely to prove highly disruptive in a payments union for a small group of countries in Eastern Europe.

The Place of Convertibility in the Transformation Process

Friedrich Levcik

The move to convertibility is an integral part, but only a part, of the complex process of transforming a centrally planned economy into a market economy. Convertibility is a notion essentially associated with the efficient working of a market economy. It makes little sense in a centrally planned and administered economy, where the central authorities decide what imports are necessary for plan fulfillment and what has to be exported (supplemented if need be by credits) to finance the imports. The aim of this paper is to show that the process of transformation toward a market economy has to be well under way, and the essential elements of a market economy must be already actually functioning, before the attainment of even a restricted form of convertibility can be meaningful.

In addition, in discussing the different approaches to the transformation process in Eastern Europe, one has to consider that political, social, and economic processes and forces have been unleashed in these countries that cannot be stopped or reversed by arguments of rationality, that is, by a sober evaluation of the advantages and disadvantages of alternative strategies. Under the impact of these processes and forces, the old system of controls is breaking up (although this breakup is further advanced in some countries than in others) without being immediately replaced by a functioning set of new controls. This vacuum of order goes hand in hand with increasing shortages in the supply of consumer goods, open and repressed inflation, and growing disorders in interfirm transactions. Under these circumstances, discussions about the essential remedies become personalized and emotionalized.

The winners of the day are those who promise to shorten the transition to a prosperous market economy, even at the price of a significant drop in economic activity, in the standard of living, and in employment levels during the transition. Those who advocate a more reasoned, gradual approach to the manifold steps of transformation are immediately labeled as conservative, as unwilling to hand over the old bureaucratic controls, and on the whole as hindering the transition to a market economy. Moreover, in some countries such as Bulgaria and Romania the political battle between the old and the new social forces is still undecided,

Friedrich Levcik is Director of the Vienna Institute for Comparative Economic Studies.

and steps essential for stabilizing the economy and for getting meaningful economic reforms under way are being postponed or subordinated to the imperatives of the political struggle. The question of the choice of strategy for establishing currency convertibility must therefore be discussed, not only as an integral part of the overall systemic changes, but also within the context of the existing economic, political, and social pressures in the individual countries.

Convertibility: Part and Parcel of Economic Liberalization

What the countries of the region are striving for is not unrestricted convertibility in the sense that their currencies should be freely exchangeable for another currency for whatever purpose (Bergsten and Williamson 1990, 1). In fact, only a minority of countries around the world—for practical purposes only the Western developed market economies—enjoy unrestricted convertibility for capital exports as well as for trade in goods and services. Rather, in the medium term, most countries of the region are aiming for a situation where domestic firms will have the right to buy foreign currency at the official exchange rate in order to import goods or services from abroad.[1] Firms would have to sell the foreign-exchange proceeds from their exports to the banks at the official exchange rate, and the freedom of nonresidents to hold the domestic currency abroad and to trade it on foreign-exchange markets would be restricted. However, special regulations would allow nonresidents to transfer earnings on their investments and eventually to repatriate their capital at the official exchange rate. Resident households with a pent-up demand for foreign travel would still be limited in their access to foreign currencies at the official exchange rate (Köves and Marer 1990, 2).

Achieving even such a restricted form of current account convertibility in a transforming post-Communist economy is far more difficult and involves greater risks, than, for example, the classical transition to convertibility seen in Western Europe and Japan after World War II or the more sudden transition to convertibility in some developing countries in the more recent past. Although the latter never experienced the institutional arrangements of a fully centrally planned economy, there are some similarities between them and the post-Communist countries of Europe. One similarity is the high degree of state control of economic activity, especially that pertaining to foreign economic relations. Both groups have also exhibited a substantial degree of macroeconomic instability—of disequilibrium in domestic and external markets leading to inflation and balance

---

1. Some of these countries—in particular the Soviet Union—have not yet even defined the concept of convertibility they are aiming at.

of payments difficulties. In some instances the two groups of countries have or had in common a huge external debt.

Yet the differences between the Eastern European countries and certain other countries at the time of their transition to convertibility are much greater than any similarities. When the Western European countries freed themselves from the exigencies of the war economy with its restrictive state regulations and controls, they could rely on existing private ownership structures, which were immediately adaptable to market signals at home and from abroad. They also had, from prewar days, corporate and tax laws as well as such institutions as stock exchanges and chambers of commerce, which (sometimes after some adaptations) could immediately be set to use in the new competitive environment.

Even so, in most of the Western European countries a gradual transition toward convertibility became feasible only after their war-damaged economies had been rebuilt, after equilibrium in the domestic market had been attained by a strict stabilization program, and after the scarcity of tradeables in foreign trade had been overcome (Rieger 1989, 3). At the same time, external conditions were favorable to an export-oriented policy (essential for maintaining convertibility at a given exchange rate), because their exports could easily be absorbed anywhere in the free world.

In the present-day countries of Eastern Europe, on the other hand, state ownership in production, banking, and domestic and foreign trade prevails in the early stage of transition; private ownership, before the 1989 revolutions, had been restricted to the fringes of the economy and hemmed in with discriminating rules. Even where these have been dropped, the private sector remains in an infantile stage. Industrial production is still concentrated in huge state enterprises, and the banking system and most enterprises engaged in foreign trade are still state owned.[2] Competition from within or abroad is practically nonexistent (Levcik 1990, 4).

The state enterprises have been geared from their creation toward plan fulfillment rather than toward achieving and maximizing profits in a competitive environment. They are accustomed to being automatically provided by the state bank with the financial means for fulfilling the plan or a state order, even when previous loans cannot be serviced. These soft budget constraints, buttressed by the maxim of maintaining full employment, precluded, under the old regime, the closing down of inefficient and heavily indebted enterprises. Yet at the same

---

2. Under the previous regime only specialized foreign trade organizations, and later some state enterprises in the productive sector, were allowed to engage in international trade. Even though these restrictions have been abolished and private firms are now allowed to participate in trade, the majority of firms remain state owned.

time there were no institutional provisions for creating new, innovative firms outside the established organizational structures.

Even since the abolition or fading away of the central plan, the behavior of these leviathans and of the old organizational structures has not changed decisively. One reason for this inertia is the absence of a legal, accounting, regulatory, and institutional framework commensurate with the functioning of a market economy. Another, even more important barrier is the system of state-regulated prices. This system embodies large price distortions, levying exorbitant taxes on some goods and services while granting extremely varying subsidies on others. Under these conditions, where the control mechanisms of the planned economy have ceased to function but have not yet been replaced by the new controls of the market, macroeconomic instabilities inherent in the old system come into the open and increase.

Last but not least, the centrally planned economies have developed over time certain social value conceptions that large sections of the population would like to preserve even after the transition. These include automatic employment security, regardless of the efficiency and viability of the employing enterprise, and the guarantee of stable state-regulated and state-subsidized prices, at least for basic needs. The abandonment of these cherished values, though a necessary accompaniment of the transition, is itself a shock that the population will absorb only gradually.

Making Convertibility Meaningful

The question of liberalizing prices and introducing even a limited (i.e., current account) form of convertibility, accompanied by a substantial devaluation of the currency, has to be judged in the light of the systemic characteristics of the post-Communist economies just outlined. Can one expect that free prices and a sufficiently devalued, convertible currency alone—even if accompanied by an austere monetary and fiscal policy—will do the trick? Can one rely on the market to bring out the right incentives and to set the economy, after some calculated initial sacrifices, on the path to prosperity? Are the central authorities sufficiently reconstructed, and are they competent to carry out a consistent macroeconomic policy? Can they implement such a policy, even if correctly designed, without a reformed banking system? How will state enterprises, which were formed and operated under completely different conditions and which have developed certain behavior patterns over time, react to a new environment that combines foreign competition and hard budget constraints with adverse macroeconomic conditions? How can the private sector expand under the burden of harsh macroeconomic austerity measures? How can privatization of state property proceed when the net worth of individual firms cannot easily be determined?

What new laws are necessary to give businesses and investors at home and from abroad safe and predictable conditions for operation? And what new laws and institutions must be created to protect consumers against price rigging, and to assist employees displaced from plants that have been closed down?

Questions such as these—and there are many more—are enough to show that price liberalization and convertibility require the fulfillment of many other conditions that cannot be fulfilled overnight. The listing by Lipton and Sachs of the elements necessary for the "big bang" in Poland (quoted in Bergsten and Williamson 1990, 44–45) either disregard some of the issues or play down the complexity of some of the conditions, which in the case of Poland were met only on paper. In fact, with the exception of a falling rate of inflation and a balance of payments surplus (a questionable advantage for an impoverished country undergoing transformation), one can detect few signs of improvement in Poland a year later. Indeed the external surplus was achieved mainly by a severe curtailment of imports, and in the last months of 1990 by growth of exports as well (Laski 1990, 5). Meanwhile, for 1990 as a whole, Polish GDP was down by at least 13 percent and real wages fell by 28 percent. Poverty is spreading, and increasing numbers of Poles are trying to escape the misery by emigrating or by engaging in black marketeering or even in crimes abroad. In the expanding private sector, new service firms dominate while new manufacturing firms are in the minority.

The essential elements of the transformation to a market economy are the following:

■ Macroeconomic stabilization: the establishment of appropriate macroeconomic frame conditions for executing an anti-inflationary fiscal and monetary policy, for supporting structural changes, and for developing a social safety net;

■ Systemic change,[3] including primarily institutional changes guaranteeing property rights, together with de-etatization and demonopolization, to promote the extensive spread of private property;

■ Liberalization of the economy by establishing market-determined prices and freeing foreign trade (especially imports) through the introduction of currency convertibility.

All three elements have to be solved as interlinked parts of a single process. Only if the establishment of currency convertibility is conceived as an integral part of

---

3. It is the presence of this element that distinguishes the transformation process in the former centrally planned economies from the otherwise similar process undertaken in other countries that have sought to integrate their economies into the world trading system.

the transformation and is introduced along with these other elements can one assume that the main goal, which is to integrate the country efficiently into the world trading system, can be achieved.

Macroeconomic Stabilization

To enable the central authorities to execute a consistent macroeconomic policy, some essential preconditions pertaining to the role and functions of the various administrative departments must be met. The responsibility of the ministry of finance must be increased, in the first instance by limiting or abolishing the tasks and duties of the planning board and of the industrial branch ministries. Indeed these ministries will become redundant altogether. In drafting a budget that is, to the extent possible, balanced, new rules have to be developed by which lower administrative units (especially in countries with federal constitutions) will have their own budgets and their own budgetary incomes. A new tax system suitable to a market economy has to be created, with *inter alia* a value-added tax, corporate taxes, and personal income taxes. Social security contributions must be separated from the tax system and incorporated into a separate social security system.

The banking system must be reformed by establishing an independent central bank and several commercial banks acting under the monetary control of the central bank, but otherwise guided in their activities only by their own profit-making interest. For the banks to play that role, means have to be found by which they can be freed from bad loans and endowed with the necessary initial capital. To lay the foundations of a capital market, stock exchanges have to be founded where they do not yet exist, and bonds, stocks, and other instruments have to be legalized.

Besides the creation of appropriate macroeconomic frame conditions, policies supporting structural changes must be put in place, along with labor and social policies to provide a social safety net for those adversely affected by the other reform measures. Without these and related reforms of the central administration, the intent to practice a consistent and prudent macroeconomic policy will remain a hopeful wish.

According to an official blueprint of the economic reforms to be introduced in Czechoslovakia in January 1991 (Federal Government of the Czech and Slovak Federal Republic 1990), just getting the macroeconomic frame conditions of the reform under way will require that some twenty new laws, or extensive amendments to existing laws, will have to be drafted, accepted by the administration, and passed by the Parliament. It goes without saying that the legislative part alone will take some time. Even once the laws have been enacted, some further time will be needed before the new institutions can be set up, and it will be longer still before they will be able to perform according to the legislators' intent.

Systemic Change

The crux of systemic change lies in the treatment of property rights. In place of monolithic state ownership, a decentralized ownership pattern of private, cooperative, state, and municipal entities, all with equal rights and responsibilities, and acting in a competitive environment, will have to evolve to make a market economy work.

As the process of privatization is at best a medium-term task, one school of thought believes that one can relegate privatization to a later period, after the establishment of free prices and current account convertibility (Bergsten and Williamson 1990). Others, wary of the likely dysfunctional and perverse responses of unreformed state enterprises to market signals, seek to speed up privatization by extravagant schemes. For example, some have suggested distributing national property to citizens free of charge in the form of coupons. Distribution of ownership in this manner, however, would in no way immediately change the behavior pattern of the former state enterprises, nor would it give rise automatically to Schumpeterian entrepreneurship—the will and competence of gifted individuals to initiate innovations and accept risk, enriched by organizational and marketing abilities—which is sorely lacking in the post-Communist economies (Lavigne 1991).

Meaningful change in this direction could perhaps be expected when the shares that can be "bought" with the distributed coupons become sufficiently concentrated in the hands of a few emerging capitalists able to exercise their property rights by controlling and, if need be, changing the management of specific enterprises. But even this short-cut method of privatization would take some time. If the coupons are declared nonnegotiable, the process of concentration of shares would be prolonged. Even if, on the other hand, they are negotiable, those who attempted to hoard coupons could justly be accused of insider trading, since only those with advance and inside knowledge would have the incentive to collect coupons from other citizens at a nominal sum, and then to exchange them for large amounts of shares of a specific enterprise with bright prospects. Even in this case an established capital market would be necessary, and capital markets take time to establish.

In most of the countries of the region, enterprises engaged in trade, catering, hotels, handicrafts, and personal services were concentrated under Communist rule in cumbersome and bureaucratic state or municipal organizations. These can be privatized rather quickly by selling individual establishments at auction to the highest bidder. At the same time the creation of new private firms and their unhindered entry into the market have to be fostered by a set of financial incentives (tax relief, favorable credit terms, etc.) and infrastructural backing (e.g., accounting standards, and organizations to perform R&D and provide sourcing and marketing support).

Some scholars and policymakers view privatization as the single solution to all of the issues concerning systemic change. It might be said that their paradigm of desirable or even necessary ownership patterns is biased by ideology no less than was that of the Marxist-Leninists. Whereas the latter believed that only the primacy of state ownership with *ex ante* coordination by the central plan could safeguard socialism, the former believe that only a maximum of private owner-ship can safeguard the functioning of a market economy.

Yet the systemic changes necessary for a successful transition amount to more than mere privatization. A process of demonopolization and de-etatization of the existing enterprise structure will have to precede privatization. Most of the former state enterprises will have to be turned into joint-stock companies, with the shares held initially by the state. They will have to operate under the supervi-sion of boards of trustees recruited from experts committed to the principles of a market economy, and under the general control of a public trustee board whose independence from the government of the day has to be safeguarded. The principal task of these boards will be to demonopolize these enterprises (some of which are organized as trusts, corporations, or so-called combinates, which are a highly integrated form of industrial enterprise designed to avoid interfirm buying and selling to the extent possible) wherever this will support competition. The boards will also work out consolidation programs and new business strate-gies that will make these enterprises, or the viable parts of them, competitive and profitable. The firms will have to work within hardened budget constraints, under the threat of bankruptcy if results are not seen within the fixed consolida-tion period.

Foreign direct investment could speed up this process for those enterprises that have passed through at least part of the period of consolidation and show viable prospects for future development. In any case it seems advisable to priva-tize only consolidated enterprises. Therefore the post-Communist economies seem to be condemned to pass through a transition period characterized by a sizable sector of de-etatized but still publicly owned firms (Dietz et al. 1990, 8).[4] Market-conforming behavior on the part of these enterprises can only be

---

4. Even in the reunited Germany, where the strong West German economy exercises an overwhelming pull in the direction of consistent market behavior upon the former East Germany, "the German State will remain for many years [in addition to agricultural and forestry land and other specific property items] also the owner of significant industrial aggregates. To be sure, involuntarily, because nobody is keen on it" (Detlev Rohwedder, Chairman of the Berliner Treuhandanstalt, in an interview in *Wochenpresse* [Vienna,] no.46, 15 November 1990).

expected if they have to operate in a competitive environment and are receiving correct market signals, in particular prices that reflect true scarcities.

Liberalization

This brings us to the related but separate issue of economic liberalization, by which is meant the freeing of the economy from state-determined prices with arbitrary cost and price ratios, and from insulation, by a nonconvertible currency and tight import controls, from prices prevailing in the market economies. Market-determined prices that reflect scarcity and currency convertibility, allowing trade to proceed on the basis of comparative advantage, are in this respect the final aim of the countries of the region in transforming their economies into full-fledged market economies. Obviously the freeing of domestic prices must precede the freeing of imports and the establishment of even restricted current account convertibility. It is true that import liberalization is a powerful instrument for generating competition and for helping to improve the domestic price structure. Still, it hardly makes sense to introduce convertibility in a situation where arbitrary price structures, with separate price circuits for wholesale, retail, agricultural purchase, and foreign trade prices (indeed with differing price regimes within the region itself) are still intact. It seems, therefore, indispensable to implement a domestic price reform to deregulate prices altogether before introducing currency convertibility.

Can domestic price liberalization be introduced at one stroke? It has been done in the former East Germany, as we know, with disastrous results for the population, although there the adverse effects have been cushioned by huge gifts from the West German government, which it has been willing to offer as the price of German unity. The other countries of the region can hardly expect any similar level of outside support. Under more realistic circumstances, domestic price liberalization has to involve doing away with price subsidies at each of the price circuits mentioned—if necessary by changing some of the price subsidies into income subsidies. In addition, these separate price circuits must be linked by unifying, to the extent possible, the existing turnover tax rates (later to become value-added taxes). Further, the legal and organizational instruments needed to execute a prudent fiscal and monetary policy have to be put in place. The process of de-etatization and demonopolization of state enterprises, and of establishing a functioning and expanding private sector, ought also to be well under way, to ensure the presence of a sufficient range of independent economic agents when prices are freed to be determined by the market. Once the most important preconditions have been met, the bulk of domestic prices ought to be freed at one stroke.

With the advent of economic liberalization, employees and households will lose some of their most cherished value preferences, namely, automatic employment security and stable, subsidized prices for basic needs. Of course, they will eventually adopt the value perceptions of citizens in a market economy, but in the meantime they must be safeguarded by a set of social measures against the hard consequences of the changeover to market-determined prices. It is not sufficient to legislate entitlements to unemployment benefits; at a minimum, unemployment insurance has to be introduced and agencies have to be set up to administer the unemployment insurance program, provide for job placement (mainly in an expanding private sector), and operate retraining facilities. At least for the underprivileged sections of the population, compensation schemes for the inevitable rise in prices have to be prepared. The financial means for these social measures have to be earmarked in an already constrained—and if possible balanced—budget. In the process of wage bargaining, independent trade unions should be allowed to function as responsible partners.

The Case for a Gradualist Approach to Convertibility

If the reforms described in the preceding section are necessary to make currency convertibility work, then even current account convertibility cannot have a top priority in the sequence of economic reforms. Rather it must be concluded that the introduction of currency convertibility belongs to a later stage of the transformation process. Yet another question is whether, once these conditions (which are by no means an exhaustive list) have been met, current account convertibility (at least) should be introduced at one stroke or in stages.

There is something to be said for a prompt move to current account convertibility, provided the other conditions have been fulfilled. Domestic relative prices can be improved, and foreign competition in the small and medium-sized economies of the region will become a powerful instrument for increasing competitiveness in the exposed sector of the economy. Also, the risks of dysfunctional or perverse supply responses of the state sector become smaller once de-etatization and demonopolization have been accomplished and an expanding private sector is exacting some competition. Hard budget constraints imposed by a functioning macroeconomic policy may curb the inclination of former state enterprises to take the easy route to labor-management harmony, meeting all wage demands and either passing the resulting cost increases on in the form of higher prices or borrowing the shortfall from the state bank.

On the other hand, given that fulfilling all the other conditions will take quite some time, why not also introduce convertibility in stages, *pari passu* with the other transformation measures? The main objection to a gradual approach, not only to convertibility but to the entire transformation process, is the claim that it has been tried time and again and that it has not worked. Today this objection is being voiced even in Hungary, even though, in my opinion, this is just the direction in which the Hungarian government is going.

There is, however, a fundamental difference between gradualism hesitatingly attempted by a Communist government, and gradualism undertaken after the Communists have lost their unlimited power and the conditions for democracy have been established. Once a democratic legislature has been elected, a democratic government committed to freedom and to establishing a market economy has been created, and the bureaucratic power of the Communist Party has been broken, the remaining stumbling blocks are the competence of the government in mastering the process of transformation, the maintenance of a majority in parliament that supports the government in its reforms, and the trust of the population that this process will eventually improve their standard of living.

The aim of those Communist regimes that attempted economic reforms was not to transform the planned socialist economy into a market economy but to make the socialist economy work more efficiently while retaining its essential features. The same is true of their attempts to improve the central plan, to blend plan and market, or to establish some kind of market socialism. In any event, all these attempts were subordinated to the principle of preserving the rule of the Communist Party. Given these constraints, gradually and often haphazardly introduced reform measures were bound soon to run into trouble. They invariably made the governments that initiated them go back on their promises, either because initial successes made further, more risky reforms unnecessary in the government's view, or because the reforms were abandoned as soon as they ran into difficulties.

In the wake of the popular revolutions of 1989, however, most of the countries of the region are determined to fundamentally change their economies into market economies of a Western type, with at least substantial private-property rights, free product and factor markets, and integration into the world economy. Yet while there seems to be broad agreement in most of these countries about the eventual destination of the transformation process, there is far less agreement on how that goal is to be reached.

One can certainly agree with the critics of gradualism if one means by that term the attempts of governments to postpone necessary reforms or to implement them in only partial or piecemeal fashion (see Federal Government of the Czech and Slovak Federal Republic 1990, 6). Under those circumstances economic and social conditions will only become increasingly destabilized, without any positive responses emerging. A gradual approach to the transformation process can be conceived of in a more rational way, however.

First, there has to be a clear understanding within the government about the final aim of the reform, which is to change the economy into a market economy of a Western type, with all its positive and negative characteristics. This understanding must extend to the government's constituencies and the public at large, as well as to the trade unions and other groups with specific interests. Arriving at this shared understanding can be complicated by the fact that these post-Communist governments are in many cases coalition governments composed of groups with differing beliefs and creeds, and united only by their hostility to Communism.

For some time one can leave open the issue of what kind of Western market economy one is aiming at: a laissez-faire type after the American pattern, a welfare state of the European variety, or a more patriarchal model as in Japan. But this issue too will have to be settled soon after the transformation process is under way.

Next there has to be an understanding that one has to deal with three interlinked but distinct elements of reform. As defined earlier these are a set of macroeconomic frame conditions, systemic and institutional changes, and liberalization of prices and trade.

Then a timetable for the entire transformation process has to be worked out, taking into account that, for each of the three essential elements of the transformation, several things have to happen. First a legal base has to be established; then institutions must be set up to implement and execute the new laws, which also have to be tested in practice; and finally the individual stages within each of the three essential elements of the transformation have to be dovetailed with the appropriate stages of the other elements of the process. It would far overreach the scope of this paper to try to enumerate the individual stages within each of these parts of the transition, or to describe their synchronization with the corresponding stages of the two other parts. In any case, the conditions prevailing at the outset differ considerably from country to country, necessitating a different emphasis and timing for each stage of the process.

A sober assessment of the many measures to be undertaken at each stage of the transformation process indicates that one should think in terms of a transition lasting several years, rather than in terms of a "big bang" that immediately puts the market in operation, quickly setting things right after some initial difficulties and hardships that one has to take in stride. So far there is no empirical evidence that after such a big bang, with many legal, regulatory, and institutional conditions still unmet, the self-healing forces of the market can lead a former planned economy back to self-sustained growth and eventual prosperity. Similarly dramatic transformations have been attempted in certain developing countries, where some market features and private ownership structures were already present. Even there the monetarist advisers of those countries failed to achieve the primary objective of breaking inflation for any sustained period of time, not to mention setting these economies on the path of sustained growth.

On the other hand, there are strong arguments for compressing the stages of the transformation process into as short a time horizon as will allow an orderly rather than a chaotic advance toward a functioning market economy. There are several dangers involved in spacing out the reforms: the instability of a system where the old controls have ceased to function and the new ones have not yet got into their stride; the growing impatience of the population; the opportunity that delay presents to the old, defeated forces to marshal resistance; and the lack of trustworthiness that gradualism often conveys to the "free world" (meaning here the IMF and the World Bank). There is some truth in these arguments against a gradual approach, but they have to be weighed against the risks of an ill-timed big bang at a time when the social fabric of the new democracies remains fragile.

Together these pros and cons suggest the following principles for the sequencing of transformation measures:

- Each stage of the process should embody as much simultaneity as popular forbearance, budgetary restrictions, skilled labor constraints, and foreign-exchange considerations allow.

- Each stage should follow the previous stage as quickly as the above-mentioned constraints allow (Marrese 1990, 9).

In countries where the governments are still in full control of the transformation process, one could perhaps draw up a workable timetable of three to five years, leading, one hopes, to the operation of the basic elements of a market economy, though very likely still with some props. It may take another five years before such countries could qualify for membership in the European Community.

The questions to be answered next are the following: At what stage of such a timetable should current account convertibility be introduced? And should it be done at one stroke or gradually and in stages? It seems clear from the preceding that first of all one must have at one's disposal the essential tools to operate a prudent anti-inflationary fiscal and monetary policy, as well as to implement a social policy that will soften the impact of the opening of the economy. Among the macroeconomic tools needed are effective budgetary controls, a rational tax system, and an already functioning two-tier banking system with independently acting commercial banks, relieved to the extent possible of past bad loans. An effective social policy will require such institutions as unemployment insurance, job placement services, and retraining centers.

To make all these tools available to the authorities, extensive legislation will have to be undertaken beforehand. In the meantime the privatization of small businesses (especially in commerce and services), of apartments and houses, and in some cases of land should be already near completion, to ensure a sufficient number of decentralized economic agents capable of operating and of competing on the market. De-etatization and demonopolization of state enterprises ought to be well under way, with most of them already converted into joint-stock companies. The domestic price structure ought also to be liberalized by successively cutting subsidies on wholesale and retail prices and by applying, as far as possible, unified turnover tax rates.

It follows that the liberalization of foreign trade, and especially of imports, should not be attempted before certain preliminary measures are taken. In the initial phase a split market for imports might be advisable, with an official commercial exchange rate applying to some imports and a free-floating rate to the rest. Which imports would be subject to the official rate may vary from country to country, but one could envisage essential materials and fuels falling in this category (to cushion the impact on the price level of manufactures), as well as some machines and equipment purchased on credit terms, where one could expect fast returns from increased competitive exports. Importers of other goods would have to buy foreign currency for their essential imports at the free-floating rate, as would individuals for tourism (Sulc 1990, 10).

Exporters would be entitled to retain a certain fixed percentage of their export proceeds for their own use. They could use the foreign currency for their own import needs, or to open a free currency account at the bank, or they could sell it at the going exchange rate at currency auctions to be held periodically. If the retention quota is sufficiently large, these currency auctions could exert a downward pressure on the exchange rate in the parallel market.

The principal argument against the introduction or subsequent increase of the system of foreign-exchange retention accounts and currency auctions is that it complicates the exchange rate system (Wolf 1990, 11). If the government wishes to avoid these complications, it can instead go the traditional route (used by the Western European countries after World War II) of relaxing import controls in stages, by gradually increasing—*pari passu* with the increase of exports—the number of items in the open-license category. For imports in this category, foreign exchange at the official exchange rate would be automatically available.[5]

Yet another approach to the gradual liberalization of foreign trade is that put forward by Ronald McKinnon (chapter 4, this volume). McKinnon's proposal

---

5. Some measures will have to be taken to prevent the total disruption of mutual trade flows among the former CMEA countries during the transition to hard-currency accounting at current world market prices. Faced with the pressing need to husband their scarce resources of convertible currencies, these countries may find it necessary to lower mutual trade flows below the level that would be considered rational. To avert such a development, an Eastern European payments union, anchored in a Western currency or in the ecu, could be set up as a multilateral clearing system, where balances could be settled at least partly in hard currency. For a discussion of the problems of such a union see the paper by Jozef M. van Brabant (chapter 4, this volume).

calls for a series of "cascading" tariffs, designed to enable enterprises to be sheltered for a limited period by prohibitive custom barriers to allow them a chance to adjust to competition.

At a later stage of the transformation process, when foreign trade and especially imports have been liberalized to a substantial degree, and *pari passu* the other essential elements have started to exert their effects on the behavior of economic agents, the time will come to introduce current account convertibility. The gradual approach will have prevented to some extent the adverse consequences of opening an unprepared economy at one stroke. One can also hope to have avoided a sudden and substantial devaluation of the currency, with its attendant risks of either starting an inflationary spiral or—through the application of draconian budgetary and monetary constraints—throwing the economy into deep recession. It is also probable that, with gradual strengthening of the country's export potential, the eventual introduction of current account convertibility—after, say, three years—will mean a less drastic devaluation than would have been needed had one aimed at convertibility too soon.

Available Strategies

The choice of transition strategies is not always under the authorities' control. As noted at the outset, in most of the countries of Eastern Europe processes and social forces have been unleashed that cannot easily be stopped or reversed by rational argument. It is very likely that only in Hungary and Czechoslovakia is it still realistic to plan for a fast but orderly, step-by-step transformation to a market economy.

Hungary, which has already traveled some way along the road to a market economy, has over the years accumulated a set of experiences some of which favored its transition and others of which had to be abandoned. However, its room for maneuver is hemmed in by its large external debt. Nevertheless, according to the President of the Hungarian National Bank, György Suranyi, Hungary seems to be well placed to achieve current account convertibility in the foreseeable future by continuing the gradual approach that it has already pursued for some time.

In the middle of 1991 a free currency market will be established in Hungary. The commercial banks will be entitled to buy and sell foreign exchange at an exchange rate that will be adjusted daily. They will also be allowed to operate on international credit markets. All this is possible because the balanced supply situation on the domestic market has contributed to a substantial narrowing of the difference between the official exchange rate of the forint and that on the parallel market.

In 1990 Hungary achieved a surplus in its hard-currency merchandise trade of almost $1 billion—the largest in its history. In addition, Hungary enjoyed a surplus in tourism of $400 million.[6] Including interest payments on the external debt, Hungary's current account in 1990 should show a surplus of $100 million to $200 million (Richter 1991, 13). The further devaluation of the forint by 15 percent at the beginning of 1991 is intended to compensate for the higher rate of inflation in Hungary than in the West, and for the deterioration in the terms of trade due to the switch to world market prices and settlement of trade with the East in convertible currencies.

In Czechoslovakia, the instability experienced initially at home and in foreign economic relations is far less pronounced. However, its leadership and its academic economists have had little practical experience with reform measures and still entertain many illusions about the possibilities of introducing rapid changes. Czechoslovakia has worked out, apparently with the support of the IMF and the World Bank, a basically reasonable and consistent program of transformation (Federal Government of the Czech and Slovak Federal Republic 1990). However, by proceeding to the liberalization of prices and simultaneous introduction of current account convertibility at one stroke, at an early stage before some other essential elements of the reform are already functioning, they seem to be unrealistically speeding up the transition process. Czechoslovakia thus seems headed for a big bang.[7]

With all the reservations mentioned, if a gradual approach is indeed attempted in both Hungary and Czechoslovakia, it should, in my opinion, get full support from the West.

In the other countries of the region, the determination of the optimal approach to economic transformation is far more complicated. Poland has already opted for and implemented the big bang approach. There the discussion should rather concentrate on alleviating the adverse consequences of the shock program that were unforeseen by its designers at home and in the IMF. (Similar considerations pertain to the territory of the former East Germany.) In Bulgaria and Romania the political issues are not yet resolved. Until a consolidation of political decision-making in the hands of a clear majority, determined to move on to a market economy, has occurred, it will be difficult to develop consistent programs of stabilization, systemic change, and liberalization.

In the Soviet Union the possibility of an orderly, gradual transformation process has been frittered away by the half-hearted, conceptless, and piecemeal

---

6. György Suranyi in *Neue Zürcher Zeitung*, 12 December 1990.

7. First-quarter 1991 results for Czechoslovakia indicate that this prediction, originally made in October 1990, was correct: industrial production was down by 12 percent and industrial employment by 8 percent, and the consumer price index rose by more than 50 percent.

introduction of unconnected reform measures, constrained in addition by ideological taboos; for example, well into 1990 privatization to any meaningful extent was not even being considered in any of the official reform programs. Meanwhile a process of political and economic disintegration has set in, and it is becoming increasingly difficult to design any program that has a chance of combating the deepening crisis using measures applicable to the Soviet Union as a whole (Havlik 1990). In the Soviet Union, then, as in Bulgaria and Romania, the political issues will have to be resolved before meaningful progress toward a functioning market economy can be hoped for.

Comment

Domenico Mario Nuti

The usual role of a discussant is to stir up controversy, but the two papers in this chapter appear to take positions that are so far apart that instead I shall try to be conciliatory. When and how fast should currency convertibility be introduced in the Eastern European economies? Friedrich Levcik's answer is that it should be introduced fairly late in the process of transition to a market economy, which process should take place gradually over a period of three to five years; another five years will be needed before these countries become eligible for EC membership. According to Jacques Polak, convertibility should come early and fast, almost as fast as advocated by Czechoslovak Finance Minister Václav Klaus, who said in his oral presentation at the conference, "There is no convertibility problem—all there is to do is declare it."

Although the two papers appear to be far apart, they are in fact quite complementary. Polak treats the Eastern European economies as if they were ordinary less developed countries, whereas Levcik addresses precisely their system-specific features. However, there remains an irreducible difference between them: that difference concerns the costs involved in speeding the course of transition, which Polak neglects and Levcik strongly emphasizes.

Some reflections on the nature of money in the traditional Soviet-type system and on the very important consequences of its lack of convertibility should help to highlight both the need for and the difficulties involved in establishing convertibility. Three main preconditions to convertibility can be inferred, and a rush to convertibility before they are satisfied involves specific costs, which neither EPU–type arrangements (considered by Polak) nor a parallel currency (see below) can really alleviate. Convertibility, like most reforms, should be thought of as an investment—a good one, but, like all investments, in need of finance.

The nature of money in a Soviet-type system can be understood by an analogy. Imagine a lottery where tickets give a recurring entitlement to weekly prizes, with a probability p of winning a prize at each draw. The tickets are similar to British premium bonds but differ from them in three respects: they are not redeemable; winning tickets get a prize equal to their face value instead of a multiple of it; the probability p decreases over time. Only a fool would actually buy such tickets, for at best one would only recover one's stake.

Domenico Mario Nuti is Professor of Political Economy at the University of Siena (Italy) and an Adviser to the Commission of the European Communities. The views expressed in this paper do not necessarily reflect those of the Commission of the European Communities.

Now, however, imagine an economic system in which these lottery tickets are used as money, in fact the only money for the payment of weekly incomes, with only winning tickets giving access to the purchase of goods and services, at prices that are pre-fixed in terms of the units in which the tickets are denominated. Sellers, by law but grudgingly, pass on the winning tickets they receive to the lottery organizers in exchange for new lottery tickets. People who do not have winning tickets to spend can still exchange their nonwinning tickets for goods and services at a price approximating $1/p$ of the price applied to winning tickets. Tickets may instead be deposited, in which case they do not take part in the draw but receive an interest paid in additional lottery tickets; the rate of interest is lower than the rate at which the probability p of a prize falls over time.

Lottery tickets in general, and especially those of this peculiarly unattractive kind, are very bad candidates for fulfilling the role of money. They lack all the desirable attributes of money, such as certainty of current purchasing power, stability of that power over time, and liquidity; even if they were decreed to be legal tender they would presumably be increasingly replaced by better candidates, such as nonperishable divisible objects with a more certain and stable purchasing power, from cigarettes to hard foreign exchange. Nobody ever designed such an absurd, grotesque monetary system. Yet the system described is precisely equivalent to a traditional monetary system of the Soviet type, with $p = (1 - h)$, where h is the domestic currency overhang expressed as a share (increasing over time) of the total quantity of money.[1]

Rubles, the Romanian leu, and the Bulgarian leva[2] increasingly resemble such lottery tickets, and are progressively being displaced by dollars, deutsche marks, and packages of Marlboros, with unlucky holders having to part with more notes than the lucky ones have to pay for their purchases. The Czechoslovak koruna, the East German mark, and the Hungarian forint never moved quite as far in

---

1. Some may regard this characterization as an exaggeration of the defects of monetary systems of the Soviet type, but in fact Soviet-type money is even worse than this analogy indicates, in several respects. First, in the actual Soviet system, enterprises can only spend money if it is accompanied by plan documents approving the transaction; it is in this sense that Joseph Berliner talks of a "documonetary" system in the socialist economies. Second, there are two separate circuits for interenterprise transactions and for payments to and from the population; these are, at least in theory, strictly insulated from each other. Third, on the very day this comment was presented, the Soviet authorities confiscated high-denomination (50 and 100 rubles) banknotes beyond a small personal allowance (200 rubles, although this was later raised in some of the republics). The effect of this, in terms of the lottery analogy, was to inflict large, random, negative prizes on the holders of these peculiar lottery tickets.

2. Until the IMF–backed Bulgarian stabilization program of February 1991. In April 1991 the Romanian monetary overhang also decreased following price increases and devaluation.

that direction, whereas the Polish zloty—until the 1990 stabilization—went even further: in Poland repressed inflation at times coexisted with open hyperinflation.

The monetary arrangement just described has nothing whatever to do with socialism—it is a policy-related, not a system-related phenomenon—except that it has been associated for so long with the socialist system as to be difficult to separate from it. The policy in question is a lethal combination of monetary indiscipline, due mostly to overambition and to the lack of any prior consensus about the allocation of available resources, and to a misguided, blind, and obtuse commitment to price stability at all costs. This policy is ultimately responsible for the Soviet and Eastern European economic catastrophe: for the endemic and growing shortages; for queueing and empty shops, black markets, corruption, and the emergence of a mafia; for near-famine conditions in some areas; and for the disintegration of both the CMEA and the Soviet Union itself. None of this would have happened if the ruble had been a hard and convertible currency.

To turn a centrally planned economy, with its state enterprises executing central commands and its banks issuing the equivalent of Monopoly money, into a market economy, the peculiar lottery tickets have to be turned into ordinary money as we know it, and enterprises have to be transformed from administrative agencies into profit-maximizing, entrepreneurial entities. Levcik deals with the difficulties of consolidating money and reforming enterprises. Polak takes it for granted that in Eastern Europe "money" is money and "enterprises" are enterprises, and hurries on to the next stage, that of convertibility.

For any exchange rate policy to be effective, let alone for convertibility[3] to work, three preconditions must be satisfied: first, there must be market-clearing prices (i.e., no shortages, or what is sometimes called commodity convertibility) under nonhyperinflationary or at least not excessively inflationary conditions; second, there must be no generalized subsidies on tradeable goods and services; third, there must be a significant price elasticity of demand and supply. Failure to satisfy the first two conditions explains why transferable-ruble balances were

---

3. I refer to convertibility by residents for current account transactions, what in Poland and Czechoslovakia is now called "internal convertibility"; this differs slightly from the IMF Article VIII definition, which includes also debt service. Here it is worth noting that the specific features of Eastern European experience have led to a change in conventional terminology, for "internal convertibility," "resident convertibility," and "commodity convertibility." Normally, countries treat nonresidents at least as favorably as residents, and therefore internal convertibility presumes external convertibility; however, in Eastern Europe nonresidents may be subject to stricter conditions than residents. Usually commodity convertibility is understood to include convertibility also into imported commodities, i.e., to imply internal convertibility other than financial convertibility; in Eastern Europe, on the other hand, the frequent presence of a monetary overhang leads to use of the term "commodity convertibility" to indicate simply the lack of such an overhang and the presence of market-clearing prices. Jacques Polak uses the traditional terminology, whereas Friedrich Levcik and I follow the more recent usage peculiar to Eastern Europe.

never transferable even within the CMEA, let alone convertible: shortages create a sellers' market in which enterprises have no incentive to export; subsidies lead to a transfer of domestic resources abroad through the export of subsidized goods, which are all the more likely to be in shortage; thus the prospect of exporting goods that are subsidized or in short supply leads to the imposition of export bans or quotas, and the transferability of ruble balances becomes subject to negotiations over the kinds and quantities of goods that might be purchased with those balances.

The third precondition—responsiveness of demand and supply to price changes—is necessary for currency devaluations to improve the trade balance rather than merely worsen the terms of trade, under conditions in which world demand for domestic exports is not perfectly elastic. In turn, the price elasticity of supply and demand is bound to be very low when enterprises can obtain *ex post* and ad hoc compensatory subsidies and confiscatory taxes.

The first two conditions were satisfied by the price liberalization and macroeconomic stabilization plans of December 1989 in Yugoslavia, of January 1990 in Poland, and of January 1991 in Czechoslovakia; in East Germany they were satisfied by replacement of the existing currency with deutsche marks and the *de facto* unification already with West Germany on 1 July 1990. The third condition has also been partly satisfied by the stabilization plans, because the price elasticity of demand must have been enhanced by the budgetary and monetary restraint implemented through those plans. Elasticity of supply, however, has been present to a lesser degree in these four countries, but with substantial differences among them: considerable elasticity of supply exists in Poland, which has a large private sector in both agriculture and nonagricultural activities; the same is true in Yugoslavia because of a longer-standing market tradition, even though the private sector's share of the economy is lower than in Poland.[4] Supply is less elastic in eastern Germany. In Czechoslovakia the likelihood of a strong supply response is open to question, because of the lack of both a private sector and a market tradition.

Thus, if Minister Klaus can assert that all one has to do to introduce convertibility is to declare it, without worrying about sequencing, it is because, as John Williamson quipped, Czechoslovakia has in fact already done what it takes beforehand—and, one might add, because Klaus is optimistic about the likely supply response. Hungary is progressing more slowly toward convertibility but is almost there, and has perhaps come the furthest among the four countries

---

4. There is a theoretical presumption that Yugoslav worker self-management might induce supply rigidities or even perverse responses to price changes due to the temptation of value-added-per-worker maximization; however, this theoretical prediction has never been conclusively proven empirically.

toward fulfilling the third precondition because of its greater progress toward freeing enterprises from central control and toward privatization.

In all of these countries this elasticity of response can be enhanced by privatization programs, by liberalization of the housing market, by increasing labor mobility, by improving transport and communications facilities, by encouraging competition, and by investment in capacity restructuring. However, these are time-consuming endeavors; even privatization, which many think could be done instantaneously by distributing state capital freely to all citizens, takes time to have an effect and cannot be expected to enhance price elasticity until financial markets are well established and functioning effectively.

In Romania, Bulgaria, and the Soviet Union, none of the three preconditions listed above are anywhere near being satisfied, although the first two might be approached soon in Bulgaria, when the stabilization plan currently under negotiation with the IMF is implemented.[5] Until recently the authorities persistently refused to raise prices, on the ground that inflation is not socially acceptable, but consumers in these countries can no more be protected from the fallout of monetary explosions than they could be protected from the fallout of the Chernobyl explosion. Quite perversely, in both the Soviet Union in 1990 and Romania in 1991, price increases were announced long beforehand, inducing panic buying, and then were withdrawn and postponed, but without also withdrawing the compensatory wage increases, which indeed took place in advance of the price hikes. The effect was to increase the monetary overhang at every step along the way. Eventually, however, any government standing between the irresistible force of monetary expansion and the immovable object of fixed prices is going to be crushed.

A distinctive feature of these three economies, which is present to a lesser extent in the other four, is the deeply rooted economic inertia in their state sectors. All studies of prereform Eastern European state enterprises stress their rigidities, their risk aversion, their hoarding, their cult of gross physical indicators (*kult vala* in Russian) and neglect of net monetary results, and their reluctance to innovate and to adjust to changing economic conditions. In the state sector— which is still extremely large everywhere in the region—this kind of behavior cannot be changed at a stroke, and indeed it may be made worse by managers' uncertainty about the timing and mode of their enterprises' privatization, or about how their performance might be assessed, penalized, or rewarded in the future. The turmoil of shock treatment will shorten their time horizon, and the high rate of return on inventories (both financial and in terms of the production

---

5. A Bulgarian stabilization program was in fact implemented in February 1991; some reduction of subsidies and of the monetary overhang also occurred in Romania in March-April 1991.

flexibility they afford) may continue to favor speculative hoarding relative to production.

The only managerial inducement to maximize profits in the not-yet-privatized state enterprises is the hope of a merger or joint venture with or sale to a foreign company; even then managers' efforts may be diverted to stripping the enterprise's assets rather than to maximizing the return on those assets. It is precisely this economic inertia, visible in the conspicuously absent or weak supply response at least in the first stages of current stabilization and reform plans, that distinguishes the Eastern European countries from ordinary developing economies undertaking similar programs of stabilization, deregulation, privatization, and trade liberalization. This critical difference is well understood in Friedrich Levcik's paper, and totally neglected by Jacques Polak. This neglect is, one hopes, not terribly important in the cases of Poland, Czechoslovakia, Hungary, and Yugoslavia; it is undoubtedly unwarranted in the cases of Romania, Bulgaria, and the Soviet Union.

Ultimately, the question "How fast can convertibility be introduced?" has two answers. The first answer is that it can be introduced as fast as the three preconditions listed above—equilibrium, absence of subsidies, and a significant degree of price elasticity—can be met. In heavily indebted economies, such as Poland, Hungary, Bulgaria, and the Soviet Union, equilibrium must mean also debt rescheduling or relief (or both) and external support of the move to convertibility on a scale sufficient to allow some accumulation of hard-currency reserves instead of their depletion, and to lend credibility to the maintenance of convertibility once it is introduced. The first two preconditions can be implemented quickly through a stabilization plan; the third, especially on the supply side, is time-consuming and sensitive to the sequencing of reforms. Price inelasticity of supply is the main reason for the Polish recession and stagnation in 1990–91 and will be, unless Klaus's optimism is right, the main reason for a Czechoslovak recession in 1991.

The second answer is that it depends on how high an adjustment cost one is willing or able to accept. The faster the rush to convertibility, the higher the cost. A relatively rapid move to convertibility increases the share of low-positive-value-added activities that have to be run down, and increases the impact on the terms of trade, price elasticities being lower in the short than in the longer term. Hence, the faster the move to convertibility, the greater the domestic-currency undervaluation necessary to ensure its credibility.[6]

---

6. In Poland the undervaluation was overdone by setting the nominal rate of exchange at the level prevailing in the free market; nevertheless the sustainability of that rate in spite of a point-to-point rate of inflation for 1990 as a whole of 249 percent reflects the increasing credibility of the permanence of convertibility during the year.

Could intra–Eastern European cooperation through an Eastern European Payments Union similar to the postwar European Payments Union in the West (see the paper by Jozef van Brabant, chapter 4) reduce this cost? Jacques Polak seems to underestimate its potential. Reserve savings would be "trivial," as he suggests, only for an unchanged level of trade, but in fact trade would be expanded by such an arrangement. Intra-area trade is low only if the Soviet Union is left out. Surplus countries will have no incentive to join only if they are operating at full capacity. This is not the case with the Soviet Union (although arguably the Soviet Union does operate at full capacity of its productive system as a whole, in the sense that there is no lack of demand). The main arguments against an EPU–type arrangement are that there is no demand for it on the part of any of its potential members, and that the external aid and finance necessary to induce the Soviet Union (as a prospective structural creditor)[7] to participate in such a scheme are unlikely to be forthcoming. Assuming that these objections can be overcome, the scheme does not deserve to be dismissed too easily; the alternative suggestion of a customs union also presumes a convertible currency and therefore is not a true alternative to convertibility with or without an EPU–type arrangement.

A much less plausible alternative is popular in the Soviet Union and is put forward in this volume by Andrei I. Kazmin and Andrei V. Tsimailo (chapter 8). This is the introduction of a parallel convertible currency alongside the ordinary ruble, first in selected areas or sectors but eventually pervading the whole economy, gradually and painlessly replacing the old inconvertible ruble. This approach is clearly rooted in the monetary stabilization that took place under the New Economic Policy in 1922–24, based on the chervonets (a gold- and commodity-backed monetary unit equivalent to 10 prewar gold rubles, with limited convertibility).

There is neither theoretical nor historical justification for a parallel convertible currency—as distinguished from the partial use of foreign exchange in domestic transactions, which may be a necessary evil in conditions of hyperinflation. Theoretically the case for such a device implicitly rests on the presumption that there is a positive supply response to be obtained from economic reform, but that that response is only available for a slow diffusion of reform measures via the growth of a parallel monetary circulation. Moreover, in order to wipe out the monetary overhang, that supply effect must be not only positive but greater than the current inflationary gap. Such an expectation has no foundation.

A new parallel currency with a fixed exchange rate would have the same effects as dollarization of the economy, whereas a floating parallel currency

---

7. In 1990–91 the prospect of the Soviet Union being a substantial structural creditor has been reduced by the Soviets' inability to deliver fuels and other materials to Eastern Europe in the quantities expected (and contracted).

would have an arbitrary value determined solely by the monetary authorities; in any case its conditions of issue are not clear. Admittedly some resources may be derived from the resulting seignorage, but until the economy is successfully stabilized, the national monetary authorities are bound to lack the necessary credibility.[8]

The new currency would need a one-to-one reserve backing (or more, to cover possible fluctuations in the value of hard-currency bonds, as used to be required to back the sterling convertibility of the national currencies of the British colonies). Interest-bearing liabilities denominated in convertible but not very credible rubles would have to offer an interest rate differential sufficient to induce substitutability with hard-currency deposits. These are hardly foundations for substantial seignorage.

The stabilization of the ruble through the introduction of the chervonets under the New Economic Policy was accompanied by hyperinflation and the demise of the old ruble, the sovznak, and there is no reason to suppose that this would not happen again today. There simply are no costless paths to convertibility.

The costs of speedier convertibility, and more generally of a speedier transition to a market economy, are necessarily the object of a political assessment, but they cannot be ignored. We cannot argue with people or governments that assign a low weight to such costs, but we can and must argue—joining Friedrich Levcik—with those who are prone to neglect such costs or at least the necessity of investigating them more thoroughly. The additional cost of a speedier convertibility may be regarded as an investment, if it is expected to lower the overall longer-run costs of transition to the new regime. Indeed, the whole reform process can be regarded as an investment, since the longer-term benefits of reform are not in doubt, whereas the initial economic deterioration caused by drastic reforms has been seen only too frequently. But we know from investment theory that even good investments, with large positive present values relative to the initial outlay, should not necessarily be undertaken unless there is unrestricted access to credit at the discount rate used to calculate such present values. This applies especially to indivisible projects, which systemic replacement and currency convertibility must be. Unfortunately, the fruits of investment in reform and in a speedy move to convertibility are not easily appropriated by investors, and therefore these projects are not easily bankable, even with the IMF, the World Bank, and the European Bank for Reconstruction and Development. However, this is not an argument against reform, or against convertibility; rather it is a strong case for aid.

---

8. It is rumored that in 1990 in Leningrad, when food rationing was introduced, more coupons were distributed than were covered by current supplies, so that there was not only a ruble overhang but also a rationing coupon overhang. Given such behavior by the authorities in the recent past, would investors be indifferent between holding hard currency and holding convertible rubles, or between deposits denominated in either?

Discussion

Richard Portes claimed that Friedrich Levcik's oral presentation had been unreasonably critical of economists, who are not as a group guilty of inconsistency in their recommendations. It is not true that, in urging convertibility for the Eastern European currencies, Western economists are calling for changes more drastic than they would support for their own countries: most Western European economists would, for example, favor complete dismantling of the Common Agricultural Policy. The very existence of a literature on sequencing shows that economists are alert to the need for a form of gradualism, involving *inter alia* introduction of a social safety net before other labor market policies are changed. It is the politicians, not the economists, who have given in to demands for restitution, which is a disastrous mistake economically.

A big bang is not merely wrong, according to Portes, but infeasible as well. Indeed all the really important questions are those of sequencing: where convertibility comes in the sequence, how it relates to other economic measures, and how to avoid economic irrationalities such as setting up foreign-exchange auctions before proper financial controls on enterprises are in place. The difficulty with gradualism lies in its lack of credibility, as shown by the history of failed reform efforts, and the way it allows opposition to build up. Thus, a central issue is how the introduction of convertibility can help to build credibility.

Finally, Portes argued that Mario Nuti needed to distinguish between market-clearing prices and macroeconomic equilibrium: the former could exist without the latter, with positive inflation offset by a crawling devaluation.

Susan Collins argued that one of the long-term objectives of the transition is industrial restructuring, and that a necessary precondition to structural changes is establishment of a set of relative prices from the world economy that can guide those changes in an efficient direction. Restructuring needs to be distinguished from short-term concerns about the adjustment process and the unemployment that may be created during the transition. One can expect the absorption of labor in expanding industries to take longer than the demission of labor from industries being phased out, but one of the lessons of theoretical trade work is that it is necessary to target policies to the particular issue. Hence if the concern is about transitional unemployment, the appropriate policy is not to adjust the prices of goods but to target the problems of the unemployed directly, for example by retraining.

Collins challenged Nuti's assertion that the costs of a big bang necessarily exceed those of a gradual approach, on the ground that one needs to look at total costs over time. The immediate costs of a big bang are perhaps bound to be larger, but they need to be weighed against the longer-run costs, inherent in a more gradual adjustment, of delaying the benefits of restructuring.

Miroslav Hrnčíř agreed that the issue was how to compare the costs and benefits of alternative transition strategies, recognizing not only short-term but also longer-run impacts. The discussion often tends to concentrate on the stabilization and liberalization processes only, reflecting the debate on the stabilization programs in some Latin American countries. However, the process of transition in the former centrally planned economies has more dimensions than in those countries. The aim is not only to stabilize and deregulate the economy, but also to introduce basic institutional and systemic changes. To make those changes effective, a longer time horizon is required. Consequently, alternative options regarding the speed (fast or gradual) arise only with regard to certain elements of the transition process, notably macroeconomic stabilization and price, foreign trade, and foreign-exchange liberalization.

It is therefore no surprise that Poland, having implemented its big bang, is still facing the transition problems of the longer run, inherent particularly in the restructuring and privatization processes. As those institutional, regime changes require more time, a certain lag between the macro and the micro dimensions of the transition is experienced in all the reforming countries.

The following inferences should be drawn. First, to shorten the lag and thus decrease the costs, the institutional and systemic changes should be introduced and promoted from the very beginning of the transition. Second, the relative costs and benefits of faster as opposed to more gradual options are conditioned by the specific features of each country, and could therefore hardly be assessed in a general way.

Rouben Indjikian reinforced Hrnčíř's argument that the fundamental need was to make basic institutional changes as quickly as possible, so as to induce rational economic behavior. In his own country, the Soviet Union, basic institutional change is still lacking. One does not need much time to demolish the central planning system and the branch ministries, and to establish proper macroeconomic management based on conventional monetary and fiscal policies (although radical change in a large country like the Soviet Union needs Western technical assistance to help modify macroeconomic management). The micro changes will come at a different pace, which will depend on how quickly agents can adapt. This contrast between macro and micro is crucial in assessing the desirable pace of change.

Jean-Pierre Patat criticized Jacques Polak's view that it is desirable to choose an undervalued exchange rate. Even if undervaluation is necessary initially, it should be resisted in the longer term. In the present world situation, a weak currency brings more disadvantages than benefits, particularly in the form of inflation, especially if demand for imports is inelastic. The stimulus to exports is brief and artificial, and confined to goods with low value added. The policy weakens the more promising part of the manufacturing sector and traps the country in a cycle of ever-decreasing living standards. It would be better for

Eastern Europe to form a payments union and link its currencies to the European Monetary System, if necessary with a large fluctuation margin.

John Williamson said he was a little taken aback at Nuti's initial contrast between the arguments of the two papers. Many of the things that Levcik had argued for spacing out should indeed be done gradually, but nevertheless there is a core of measures that would seem to be best undertaken simultaneously. These may include macroeconomic stabilization, if that is not already in place, but will certainly include price liberalization and, to complement that, commodity convertibility, hard budget constraints, and current account convertibility (to provide competition to discipline domestic prices). The initial discipline may not be very tough, but some discipline needs to be present, and would seem to be best undertaken simultaneously.

Williamson also challenged Nuti's elasticity condition. In the most favorable case, where both foreign elasticities are infinite, the condition for the balance of payments to improve is not that the sum of the remaining elasticities exceed unity but that they exceed zero; that condition is always met. This does not mean that devaluation has no cost, since it does worsen inflation. The right criterion for picking the exchange rate is whether it is sufficiently competitive to stimulate the growth of exports. As Polak had explained, that was the question asked in Western Europe immediately after the war.

Dariusz Rosati agreed that Poland had gone through a big bang with regard to price liberalization and macroeconomic stabilization, but he pointed out that prior to 1990 it had already passed through some preliminary stages with regard to convertibility. Export retention quotas had been introduced in 1982, and by 1989 over 50 percent of import demand was determined in a decentralized way. (This did imply different implicit exchange rates among enterprises, however.) He also argued, echoing Hrnčíř, that the benefits of introducing convertibility quickly rather than slowly could depend on a country's particular situation. Immediate convertibility does risk short-run costs from some agents being driven out of business, but it promises quicker benefits from better resource allocation. Which is the best policy will in general depend on the discount rate used to weigh future benefits against immediate costs, as well as on the magnitude (which is country-specific) of those benefits and costs. Poland had had little choice but to act quickly; Czechoslovakia has a greater range of choice, but its policymakers should be aware of the credibility risk of excessive gradualism.

Thomas Lachs, in his capacity as chairman, offered a resolution of the difference between Levcik and Portes. Perhaps it is that Western politicians long ago learned to disregard the advice of their economists, whereas in Eastern Europe politicians still believe they must follow this advice!

Replying to the discussion, *Mario Nuti* thought that, if Williamson were right about the elasticity condition, it would be implausibly easy to satisfy. After saying initially how far apart the two papers were, he had in fact gone on to argue that they were really complementary. He accepted Portes's point that macroeconomic stability was different from having market-clearing prices. On the point made by Susan Collins regarding the intertemporal trade-off, implying that reform should be regarded as an investment, he argued that the mere existence of a positive present value did not imply that the reform should be undertaken, because reform is not a bankable project against which one can borrow (except perhaps from the new European Bank for Reconstruction and Development).

Friedrich Levcik welcomed Nuti's conciliatory approach of treating the two papers as complementary. However, he thought that solution was perhaps too easy, because too many Western economists are following Polak in treating the countries of Eastern Europe as though they were normal developing countries that face no special difficulties in freeing everything, liberalizing all prices, and establishing convertibility instantaneously. The evidence that this is the mainstream thinking is that no one had yet referred to the Hungarian case; instead all the references were to Poland. Hungary has pursued reform gradually, but now has a much more solid private sector than that in Poland; in Hungary most prices and imports are already liberalized.

Levcik rejected Williamson's argument that all the price liberalization needed to be done on a single day rather than over a longer period. Of course reforms need to be dovetailed, but they can still be spaced over time. Czechoslovakia risked losing the advantages of its favorable starting point through its excessive haste in liberalizing before a number of preconditions had been met. Levcik endorsed Nuti's preconditions for convertibility.

4

Managing the Transition

4

Managing the Transition

Convertibility in Eastern Europe Through a Payments Union

Jozef M. van Brabant

The ongoing economic transformations of Eastern Europe are expected eventually to yield full-fledged market economies. Before they reach that stage, which will certainly include some measure of currency convertibility, many changes in economic policies, institutions, instruments, and structures need to be carried out. The range of minimal requirements is considerable, beginning with the establishment of the rudiments of markets for goods, services, labor, and capital; opening up these heavily protected economies to foreign competition, including competition from other countries in the region; establishing some measure of current account convertibility; and putting in train the prerequisites for pursuing balanced macroeconomic policies. The transition to a market economy is bound to be protracted and painful, regardless of the imagination of policymakers in the area and the amount of international financial and technical support that can be mustered in the process.

One area in which adjustment is proving to be painful is in the difficulties caused by payments imbalances in clearing current trade. These countries presently face two kinds of payments imbalances. One stems from the impact of the crisis in the Persian Gulf, which has made it more difficult for Iran, Iraq, and Syria to service their debts to Eastern Europe or to fulfill their current commitments under existing clearing arrangements. In addition, the rise in oil prices, the loss of exports to Iraq, and the reduced levels of demand in the West for products from Eastern Europe have curtailed earnings. I shall not deal with these

Jozef M. van Brabant is a staff member of the Department of International Economic and Social Affairs of the United Nations Secretariat in New York. The opinions expressed here are those of the author and do not necessarily reflect those that may be held by the United Nations Secretariat.

issues here because as this volume goes to press it appears that the effects will either be short-lived or need to be resolved through structural adjustment finance.

The other type of payments imbalance emanates from the shift in traditional transferable-ruble trade and payments regimes in Eastern Europe and the desire of the reforming countries to divert trade to the West; this shift will be accompanied initially by terms-of-trade losses. To address this type of payments imbalance, I advocate the creation of a payments union, here referred to as a Central European Payments Union (CEPU). Barring a quick dash to sustainable convertibility and the diversion of intraregional commerce to the West without substantial terms-of-trade and export revenue losses, I see such a facility as an indispensable instrument of the reform process. It would guide the reforming countries toward currency convertibility; it would buttress intraregional economic collaboration based on the fuller exploitation of comparative advantage, possibly through some form of economic union; it would foster the structural adjustment process while minimizing its social costs; and it would prepare the countries for participation in the global economy on market terms.

The basic features of such a payment mechanism are as follows:

- It would be set up for a fixed duration, perhaps a single negotiated term of about five years.

- Technical clearing tasks would be entrusted to an existing institution such as the Bank for International Settlements (BIS). Participants would grant each other unlimited credit until net balances are periodically reported to the clearing agent; with modern telecommunications this could be executed on a daily basis. If so, only the clearing agent would levy interest charges. These would essentially be those prevailing in international markets, or perhaps slightly higher for creditors than debtors to encourage surplus countries to hold their balances on deposit with the union.

- Transactions would be limited to those incurred on current account, excluding debt-service obligations. Both debts and current imbalances in transferable rubles existing prior to the inception of the union would be worked off outside it, given the disarray in transferable-ruble prices at which these imbalances were originally incurred, or be revalued at more realistic prices.[1] But there are also convertible-currency debts that should preferably be addressed outside the payment framework; otherwise the pressure to divert intraregional surpluses to settle external deficits would be uncontainable. Given the present widely distorted relative prices, it may be desirable initially to let most noncommercial transactions be conducted through a parallel market.

---

1. If the Soviet Union were to join such a union, it might be useful to include the renegotiated imbalances, since they would bolster the financing capabilities of the union.

- The settlement and surveillance mechanisms should guarantee that, on balance, the demand for resources from the central fund for the orderly conduct of trade decreases over time as a steadily rising proportion of the cumulative imbalance is paid in convertible currency.

- The European currency unit (ecu) would be the unit of account of the CEPU.

- Settlements of net imbalances would consist of a combination of loans and payments within the provisions of an overall quota against which participants could draw. The quota would be based on some share of past trade volume and would be divided into multiple tranches of various degrees of hardness. There would also be an asymmetry for creditors and debtors to encourage intraregional exports. Asymmetry would apply in two ways. One is that the combination of currency payments and loans would differ depending on the size of the imbalance relative to quota. Also, the combination of currency payments and loans, for any imbalance relative to quota surpassing some minimum tranche, would contain more currency for the creditor than for the debtor.

- To make such a scheme manageable in the sense defined, there must be external financial support as well as supervisory authority; both would be provided by European institutions or bodies functioning under their aegis. External finance will be required to support asymmetric settlement. Tight supervision is desirable to "manage" the financial resources to maximum effect in terms of clearing intraregional trade, but also to ensure that the facility promotes market-oriented reform commitments, including domestic price liberalization, and a significant relaxation of the presently prevailing trade and foreign-exchange controls.

- The capital required to support the scheme would be a function of the number of participants, the degree of stringency with which settlement would be enforced, and the likely size of the imbalances of the reforming countries. It would not, in any event, be very large.

- Membership would be open to all countries of Eastern Europe that adopt credible market-oriented reforms. Under certain conditions, this might include Yugoslavia or its successor republics as well as the Soviet Union or its successor republics.

The rest of this paper will be devoted to explaining the rationale for this scheme. The first section will specify precisely what I mean by convertibility. The minimum requirements for marketization and for the shift to current account convertibility, given the legacies of central planning, are considered in the next section. The third section looks at the problems now besetting the more radically reforming countries in Eastern Europe. In the fourth section I examine ways in which critical elements of past economic cooperation could be stabilized through the formation of some economic union among the reforming countries. Aspects of the prevailing external payments problems are highlighted in the fifth section. How a payments facility with Western financial and advisory support could ease the transition is the subject of the next two sections. Whether participation in such a union should be allowed strictly on the basis of economic merits or also invoke the politics and techniques of transition is considered in the concluding section.

On Currency Convertibility

Convertibility can be a very powerful tool in the expeditious implementation of sound economic policy under proper conditions. Because most Eastern European commentators on the subject generally fail to specify all of the key parameters when they endorse the move toward convertibility, their policy stance is open to multiple interpretations, all legitimate but none authoritative. This uncertainty is especially pronounced when the objectives of ongoing policy discussions, long-term policy goals, and emerging institutions are in considerable flux. To avoid erroneous evaluations, observers should not entertain unrealistic policy options that promise swift changes in the model and development strategy of the former centrally planned economies.[2] To see why this is so, a succinct perspective on the legacies of central planning and the traditional trade and payments framework of the Council for Mutual Economic Assistance (CMEA) may be useful.

Before entering into these problems and examining the requirements for sustaining currency convertibility, an operational definition of what policymakers may be envisaging will prove useful. This is by no means obvious (Brabant 1987a, 365–59; 1989c; 1990a). For practical purposes, I shall use as a criterion the definition embodied in Article VIII of the International Monetary Fund's Articles of Agreement, in which convertibility is limited to current account convertibility. Under this definition, convertibility simply means the ability of some class of holders of a country's currency to exchange it for another or into goods on demand. I have deliberately specified "some class" among the holders of currency to remain realistic, but I am not imposing any restriction on the ability of that class to convert its money holdings. Let me explain these qualifiers.

---

2. This attitude is by no means limited to Eastern European observers. Even for the very orthodox planned economy it is as meaningful to affirm that convertibility is impossible as it is to assert (Colombatto 1983, 488) the converse. Indeed there is no systemic impossibility of establishing some highly circumscribed form of convertibility by legal means (see Altman 1962, 367). Simply declaring convertibility is, however, quite different from using it as a credible and sustainable policy instrument.

For most countries since World War II convertibility essentially has meant what is stated in Article VIII, section 2, of the IMF's statutes: "no member shall, without the approval of the Fund, impose restrictions on the making of payments and transfers for current international transactions" (IMF 1978, 29).[3] The three operative qualifiers need to be interpreted (Gianviti 1989, 270). International transactions are those between residents of different countries. Restrictions are present when a country by administrative decision denies or curtails a request for foreign exchange for a proper international transaction (Edwards 1985, 390–91) without the IMF's concurrence. Finally, "current" refers to payments for foreign trade, other current business, and normal short-term banking and credit facilities; for interest on loans and net income from other investments; of moderate amounts for amortization of loans or for depreciation of direct investments; and moderate remittances for family living expenses (Gianviti 1989, 271). Precisely what "moderate" means in this context is left unspecified.

By a recent count, 67 members of the IMF (of the total of 152 members at the end of 1988) fall under Article VIII's regime, although some resort *de facto* to multiple exchange rates (IMF 1989, 568ff.). Many countries apply convertibility to residents, too: of the IMF members subscribing to Article VIII, only 52 are listed as not having current account and 30 as not having capital account restrictions (for resident-owned funds) as defined by the IMF.[4] In other words, few countries allow their currency to be converted on demand for whatever purpose a holder may entertain; a few more, but still a minority, maintain current account convertibility without restrictions. Against this backdrop, one could term the Polish zloty convertible since 1990, even though that distinction applies only to resident merchandise and related transactions by duly registered businesses other than those conducted in transferable rubles or on other clearing accounts. Private individuals can resort to a parallel market that is linked to the official one at the central bank's discretion, but the peg is neither instantaneous nor complete.

There are cogent political and economic reasons why the currencies of Eastern Europe have remained inconvertible for so long (Brabant 1987a, 236–44 and 357–74). Under orthodox central planning, economic resources are distributed only with the explicit approval of the relevant planning authorities. Because the

---

3. Prior to the Second Amendment of the Articles of Agreement, the IMF considered a currency to be totally convertible if it could be used without restriction of a currency character for any reason whatsoever; it could be exchanged for any other currency without restriction of a currency character; and it could be used or exchanged at its par value, or at a rate of exchange based on the par value, or at some legal rate of exchange defined in any other way considered desirable (Gold 1971, 1–2). This definition still holds, except for references to "par values" (François Gianviti, personal communication, 23 October 1990).

4. Lebanon, Maldives, and the former Arab Republic of Yemen (IMF 1989, 570–73) are under the regime of Article XIV, yet apply no restrictions on current or capital account.

plan is the motive force of resource mobility, money cannot command goods and services within the enterprise sector. Goods inconvertibility prevails because the holder of a currency balance must generally pass through the planning hierarchy and obtain clearance before being granted title to mobilize the balance to acquire inputs, and can only acquire those inputs explicitly approved by the planning authorities. Likewise, an enterprise with a money balance cannot normally acquire other currencies without first obtaining the approval of the banking, trading, or planning authorities.

Before the seminal changes of 1989, planners in the Eastern European countries only rarely considered scrapping the major components of the material-technical supply system in favor of genuine wholesale trade. Those that have meaningfully devolved central decisionmaking have by necessity created some range for real markets to emerge. But it has proved rather cumbersome to introduce convertibility for such restricted markets. Commodity convertibility remains highly confined as long as the planner can preempt the decisionmaking process by allocating goods directly rather than through some market. Hence, substitute solutions have traditionally been preferred.

Marketization, Transition, and Convertibility

To assess the requirements for making functional use of a convertible currency, it is necessary to understand the trade and payments regimes of a stereotypical planned economy and its interrelations with other economies within the former CMEA system.[5] Listing the key peculiarities may suffice to illustrate the breadth of the chasm to be jumped in moving toward convertibility.

National Trade and Payments Regimes

National trade and payments regimes in the centrally planned economies follow logically from the way in which the policymakers in these economies have conceived their orthodox economic model and development strategy, both in the original Stalinist version and in the reform attempts undertaken since the late 1950s. The strategy of development aims, among other things, at full employment, rapid socioeconomic growth, extensive industrialization in breadth as the foundation for steady economic development, and substantial domestic policy autonomy in support of elaborating a mostly self-contained economy.

---

5. For a more detailed description see Brabant (1987a, 1987b, 1989a).

For most of the postwar period, such a development strategy was predicated on establishing the Soviet prototype economic model. Three of its many components are critical to the trade and payments regimes. First, central planning in physical detail takes the role elsewhere played by orthodox macro- and microeconomic policies. Indirect coordination is hence deliberately disregarded in resource allocation. Second, most economic decisions are channeled through a complex, highly bureaucratic hierarchy in which economic considerations form but one set of motivations for administrators, not to mention trade union and party interest groups. Finally, in both the model and the strategy the domestic economy is separated rather rigidly from foreign influences.

Integral to this model is the more or less complete disjunction of the domestic economy from external influences by means of special instruments and institutions. Trade decisions are formulated through planning institutions and instruments rather than based on real scarcity indicators. As a result, external economic relations do not form a coherent component of the traditional planned economy. Trade levels tend to be well below what is considered normal for countries of similar size and level of development. There are in addition biases in the commodity composition and geographical distribution of trade compared with what would have emerged in a market economy.

The organizational disjunction between domestic and foreign economic activities is accomplished through the creation of a state monopoly of foreign trade and payments. This embodies total control of central agencies over strategic trade and foreign-exchange decisions, including commercial policy and the determination of the fundamental directions for development. Institutionally, the monopoly consists of various organizational and financial ministries as well as separate foreign trade organizations. The latter purchase domestic products destined for export and sell earmarked imports at domestic fiat prices. Differences between domestic prices and foreign prices converted at the official or the commercial exchange rate, both of which are artificial, are offset through the so-called price equalization account, which is a component of the central-government budget.

Because trade eludes the complete control of one planning center, planners attempt to gain greater stability in the domestic economy by forecasting trade flows as accurately as possible. They seek to do so through detailed bilateral trade and payments agreements constructed around relatively stable, if artificial, prices (Brabant 1987b). These organizational accommodations partly account for the geographical bias in the trade orientation of these economies. Because of the subdued role of money, key features of the trade model are the use of multiple exchange rates, which reflect multitiered domestic price systems; currency and commodity inconvertibility as the counterpart of planned resource allocation; bilateralism to facilitate foreign trade planning; and exchange controls to insulate domestic from foreign markets.

In this standard planning model, macroeconomic decisionmakers and especially enterprise managers are poorly informed about the real cost of their import substitution policies, in part because they remain physically removed from trading markets. When growth flags, central planners have a natural predisposition to push trade as a prop for domestic growth. In facing up to the multiple opportunities in the domestic and foreign trade sectors, policymakers begin to explore new decision criteria and organizational forms to stimulate more efficient trade relations, but they do not completely abandon their autonomous economic policies. Thus, the link between domestic and foreign prices remains highly tenuous and discrete, and pseudo-exchange rates (called currency coefficients, multipliers, reproduction coefficients, transaction rates, and so on) are just that: poor substitutes for an effective exchange rate. It is only when policymakers seek comprehensive decentralization that an environment can emerge in which there is room for indirect coordination, including coordination in trading matters through current account convertibility.

The Transferable-Ruble Trade and Payments Regimes

The establishment of close economic ties among the countries of Eastern Europe after World War II motivated these countries to create trade and payments regimes in support of their inward-oriented development. Within this shelter, rules for trading and payments differed sharply from those prevailing elsewhere. Key to these arrangements were fairly detailed bilateral agreements as intrinsic parts of the domestic planning of the CMEA economies rather than an agreed regionwide policy.

The CMEA trade and payments regimes consisted of formal multilateral settlements of bilateral imbalances, with the transferable ruble as the accounting unit, but with bilateral accounting of real trade flows kept intact; the creation of the transferable ruble, the establishment of nominally multilateral settlement procedures, and the management of short-term credit at one regional bank (the International Bank for Economic Cooperation in Moscow), while maintaining the *caesura* between monetary and commodity transactions; coordination of investment intentions and the promotion of joint investment financing through another regional bank (the International Investment Bank in Moscow); the introduction of a relatively autonomous and stable price regime in CMEA trade, but with actual transaction prices set bilaterally; and the elaboration of multiple exchange rates for various transactions that were, at best, poorly interlinked. The CMEA mechanism never embodied agreed-upon macroeconomic policies for the region as a whole, nor was it ever operated automatically. Because of the centrality of bilateralism, economic cooperation could be fostered only within the context of concrete bilateral intergovernmental arrangements. Certainly, in some cases individual firms cooperated without administrative intermediation. But governments had to make explicit arrangements for such limited links to emerge.

This passivity of the CMEA remained intact until the regime began to unravel in 1990 and died officially in 1991. Only in late 1987 did signs of change begin to emerge. Discussions went on until late 1989 but eventually foundered (Brabant 1990c, 1991a). Beginning in January 1990, a new reform commission tried to redefine the CMEA in a major way, but this renewed attempt at regional collaboration failed to get under way because of deep-seated opposition, especially in the radically reforming countries (Brabant 1991d, 1991e).

Marketization and Convertibility

Comprehensive marketization is contingent on transforming existing enterprises into autonomous agents subject to market-based incentives. Such agents can emerge only from the creation of domestic markets with flexible prices and quantities, including a direct link to world prices through trade liberalization. This is critical to usher into these economies the discipline of market competition, including the threat of domestic or foreign takeover. It also enables the country to import an adequate relative price system for traded goods. Through factor price adjustments, these prices will eventually influence the relative prices of most nontraded goods as well.

Such an environment requires a markedly different style of managerial behavior from that of the economic and organizational models tried earlier. Time is therefore required to engineer such a structural shift. Because of the continued importance of intraregional relations, the shift in managerial behavior in the reforming countries will require adjusting not only to competition in world markets but also to the dysfunctional legacies of CMEA trade and payments.

The power of currency convertibility in formulating and implementing economic policy derives from the flexible access to markets it provides, thereby promoting wider competition on the basis of scarcity indicators. To foster this broadened competition, convertibility is inalienably bound up with the existence of markets, whose operations are guided and coordinated through macroeconomic policies. As such, the automatic and anonymous clearing of some class of transactions, such as by firms, improves resource allocation. This is especially important for countries whose economic structure is highly monopolized and whose small market size does not permit near-atomistic competition among domestic agents. How this potential could best be exploited and to what degree the reforming countries of Eastern Europe are prepared to modify their policies are separate issues, however.

Convertibility as defined cannot be embraced without effective market-oriented reforms. Key elements of a market environment, especially wholesale trading and flexible prices, are present in some countries of Eastern Europe but only in rudimentary form. They can only be established over time and require perseverance to cushion the adverse socioeconomic costs of adjusting to competition. Furthermore, markets in these countries are far from integrated, in foreign trade as in other respects. To sustain such a regime at a fairly predictable exchange rate, the authorities must secure approximate current account equilibrium with the reserves on hand, including calls on foreign loans. That is, the demand for and supply of foreign exchange must balance at least over the medium term. It would therefore seem realistic to envisage a convertible currency emerging only after a substantial transition phase, during which the price regime is rationalized and trade is liberalized to permit global competition. For the latter to emerge, a stable domestic economic environment is a necessary condition. The time required depends on the distance to be covered and the ability and determination of the leadership to foster market-oriented reforms.

There are many paths to convertibility. Four basic variants may suffice for the purposes of this paper. Most spectacular is the big bang approach, which simply unleashes market forces at once in the expectation that both demand and supply will be sufficiently elastic to respond appropriately to the newly created market incentives. Poland and Yugoslavia took this route in 1990,[6] as did Czechoslovakia in 1991, at least for merchandise and related transactions by residents other than those conducted in transferable rubles or on many other clearing accounts.[7]

The opposite of the big bang approach is a gradual progression toward convertibility, in the first instance for current account transactions. This approach essentially seeks to put in place, after monetary stabilization, genuine wholesale

---

6. Note that both did so under the extraordinary circumstances of runaway inflation, a crisis of confidence in the political leadership, and all but complete destabilization of their economies and societies. Furthermore, this action was taken after decades of tinkering with various kinds of reforms and some liberalization of prices, foreign-exchange allocation, and competition. Both made the move with substantial external support and with domestic agents holding sizable foreign-exchange reserves. The costs in terms of unemployment, inflation, a sharp recession, destruction of liquid wealth held in local currency, an inelastic supply response, and other indicators has been very substantial. Furthermore, in both countries the pace of inflation picked up once again during the second half of 1990. Yugoslavia was forced to devalue the dinar in December 1990 and reimposed some exchange controls in late 1990 and early 1991 (another sharp devaluation was enacted in April 1991). In contrast, Czechoslovakia is moving to convertibility in an environment that, by and large, is still that of strict central planning and with most of its trade having been conducted in transferable rubles for a long period. The short-term costs of adjustment in relative terms are likely to exceed those of either Poland or Yugoslavia.

7. Following the unsettled state of economic and political affairs since mid–1990 and the sharp devaluations in December 1990 and April 1991, Yugoslavia has for all practical purposes abandoned convertibility of the dinar.

trading at flexible prices and to relax the foreign trade regime to allow competition between domestic as well as foreign agents.

A specific variant of this route, which the Soviet Union seriously considered for a while, is the creation of a parallel currency for use in one sheltered segment of the economy where "hard" economic conditions prevail. The link between the hard- and the soft-currency sectors (the internal exchange rate) would be comparatively flexible to enable policymakers to control to some degree the shift of resources under the pull of convertibility according to a set schedule. But this can be adhered to only by tolerating a fluctuating internal exchange rate that may eventually completely erode the value of the soft currency. As such, it provides an alternative to rapid inflation or outright monetary confiscation prior to macroeconomic stabilization. But experience shows that a parallel currency is not likely to delay those events for very long or to mitigate their cost.

Finally, convertibility can be achieved through a cooperative arrangement that takes the form of a payments facility. There are many possible variants. The ideal one would comprise nearly universal membership, as in the IMF. For Eastern Europe, a payments union such as enacted through the European Payments Union (EPU) for Western Europe after World War II would appear to be quite promising, even though the initial conditions are very different (Brabant 1991b, chapter 4).[8] In some sense, the payments union approach combines elements of the three preceding approaches. It multilateralizes intragroup trade through the big bang, creates a dual market for foreign exchange (hard currency and clearing claims), and gradually shifts domestic resources and macroeconomic policies by upholding certain rules on international payments with implications for the management of the participating economies. The central purpose is to accommodate bilateral imbalances by transforming them into multilateral ones and ensuring the manageability of net surpluses or deficits vis-à-vis the group. "Manageable" in this context means that the facility should have sufficient funds to finance the imbalances and ample supervisory clout to guide partners into mutually reinforcing behavior, so that trade imbalances do not get out of hand either by remaining too small to invoke surveillance for as long as exchange controls remain in effect, or by becoming so large, because of trade liberalization, that the agreed-upon surveillance mechanism in fact breaks down.

A regional payments union for parts of Eastern Europe could be one critical instrument on the way to currency convertibility. It could help these countries revamp their regional cooperation as a buttress for the transition to effective

---

8. Some suggestions to enact "soft" convertibility, for example through one of the predecessors to the EPU (notably Finebel—consisting of France, Italy, the Netherlands, Belgium, and Luxembourg), for Eastern Europe ignore the fact that relative prices in these countries are still very heavily distorted. Any attempt to swap soft-currency balances under these circumstances is bound to founder.

decentralization and marketization. The next section elaborates on the considerations that underlie this proposal (see Brabant 1990b, d, e, f, g; 1991a, b, c) and what its realization would entail in terms of capital needs, the mechanics of clearing, and surveillance.

Aspects of the Problems of Transition

The sudden eruption of hostilities in the Persian Gulf in mid–1990 drove world energy prices up once again, this time with wider repercussions for Eastern Europe than in past crises. Iraq owes several Eastern European countries a substantial debt, which was to have been amortized through oil shipments. Iraq was also their largest trading partner among the developing countries (and an outlet for their arms production), and has provided a venue for invisible earnings of some magnitude. The crisis enabled Iran and Syria in particular to divert oil deliveries that had been earmarked for clearing on favorable terms for Eastern Europe.

The crisis has affected Eastern Europe through direct and indirect terms-of-trade and export revenue effects as well. The bottom line, if the effects of the crisis persist for some time, will be a marked import gap that simply cannot be financed under prevailing circumstances. The need for massive and rapid adjustment policies, with dire consequences for levels of economic activity and living standards as well as for the orderly transition to markets in Eastern Europe, would seem to be the more likely outcome.

In what follows, I examine what might be undertaken for and by Eastern Europe if the main consequences of adjustment to market conditions emanate from the domestic transition process itself, the shift in CMEA trade and payments regimes, and the desire of some countries to raise the level of their economic interaction with the West even if at the express expense of intraregional trade.

Economic relations within Eastern Europe have recently been considerably burdened by two developments. One is that since about mid–1989 these countries have been experiencing severe problems in clearing their reciprocal trade. Commitments made in past trade agreements have been increasingly flouted, in part because shifts in the terms of trade have made it difficult for potential surplus countries to maintain the flows to which they had committed themselves. Unanticipated developments in output levels and shifting export priorities, including those with respect to Soviet energy, have further aggravated bilateral imbalances. As a result, several countries have been reluctant to incur intraregional surpluses and have inaugurated unprecedented domestic policies to stem exports to the transferable-ruble area.[9] Together these have jelled into a major

---

9. Poland provides a striking example. As of 1 June 1990, it raised its exchange rate against the ruble from 2,100 to 1,000 zloty, yielding an implicit ruble-dollar exchange rate of 9.5

hurdle, especially in relations with the Soviet Union, because it continued to be very cumbersome to mobilize transferable-ruble surpluses.[10] Rather than extend nearly interest-free loans at a time of sizable external payments pressures with the market economies, the potential surplus countries have on the whole decided not to live up to their obligations. The result in 1989 was a gradual contraction of intraregional trade. This has been sharply accentuated since early 1990 as a result of the newly negotiated trade protocols and disagreements about what to do about intraregional commerce.

Relations have also been strained for practical reasons on account of diverging economic mechanisms. Reforming countries that seek to steer their economy rapidly according to market criteria have encountered problems in dealing with partners that, by and large, still adhere to detailed administrative planning. Inasmuch as these economies are heavily interdependent, they can gradually reserve more room for autonomous microeconomic decisionmaking, coordinated through proper macroeconomic policies, only if relations with partner countries are also placed on a solid economic footing.

Unfortunately, even the most critical questions of how to effectively buttress intraregional cooperation in the CMEA context remain unresolved, even though a major restructuring of the organization had been announced for 1989 (Brabant 1990c, d, e; 1991d, e); instead the CMEA and its associated trade and payments framework collapsed by default. In the meantime, intraregional trade has been needlessly compressed simply because some countries do not wish to accommodate payments imbalances.[11] Also, the unconventional way in which intraregional relations are still being conducted weighs heavily on the pace and direction of the more ambitious national economic reforms. For that reason, some reforming countries prefer to reduce their heavy dependence on intraregional relations and place the remainder on a convertible-currency footing. This gives rise to two vexing conundrums, namely, how to accomplish this diversion and how best to transform trade flows that used to be denominated in transferable rubles.

Trade diversion would be very costly in the short run, given that these countries are tightly interlinked—roughly 40 percent to 80 percent of their overall trade

---

rubles to the dollar for transactions outside the trade protocol as compared to 4.5 (the rate introduced in January 1990 for all transactions) for goods included in the trade protocol, as compared to 2.2 in early 1989, 2.5 at midyear, and 3.2 in December 1989. For a while (30 July until 24 September 1990) that cross rate was reduced to 19 rubles to the dollar, and for a few days it was even compressed to 95 to the dollar.

10. The transferable-ruble regime disappeared finally in January 1991. However, as of mid-1991, many transactions continue to be undertaken on clearing account that, as in the case of Poland, are still referred to as "transferable-ruble" transactions. Also, at least Hungary and Poland continue to quote exchange rates for the transferable ruble.

11. Note that trade has eroded also because the reforming countries are weeding out unprofitable trade lines—in itself a desirable phenomenon.

in 1989 was cleared with each other.[12] Also, the economic structures in place, including the capital stock, can be redesigned for Western markets and many of the skilled workers retrained in support of such a renovated production profile only at a high cost. Much of this capital would need to be scrapped altogether in the event of a substantial diversion of trade in the short to medium run. Furthermore, the transportation infrastructure (including railroads, oil and gas pipelines, roads, electrical power grids, and ships) is overwhelmingly inwardly oriented. The alternative is gradually to amortize those assets that still produce competitive goods for Eastern markets but for which there is little, if any, demand elsewhere, and to retrain employees over an affordable period of time.

Even if these countries wanted to incur such a cost now because they thought it politically opportune to pursue this goal assiduously, for practical purposes the adjustment could only be absorbed over time. There remains a considerable demand, for example, for spare parts, components, maintenance, and service to keep the obsolete machine park running. Also, unloading and processing facilities for critical fuels and raw materials are simply inadequate to accommodate trade diversion in the short run.

Even if a dramatic change in the geographical distribution of trade were to be an explicit policy objective in its own right, the paramount technical issue of how to deal with intraregional relations in the interim remains to be addressed. This invokes concerns about the transition away from the trade and payments regimes typical of the CMEA. In considering the switch to world prices and convertible currencies in intraregional trade, it is important to distinguish transactions among reforming countries from those conducted with unreformed partners. Only if firms in market-oriented countries, once domestic prices are aligned with those observed in East-West trade (to avoid excessive and macroeconomically undesirable arbitrage), can negotiate prices and quantities on the basis of their own profit motive can one properly speak of market-clearing prices being applied. World prices will filter through into the reforming domestic economy and should therefore guide the microeconomics of profitable trade. Firms in such an economy should not be concerned about the selection of exchange rates and the settlement of imbalances, both of which are tasks for macroeconomic management.

Placing such trade on a dollar cash basis invokes two apprehensions in the short run. One stems from the need to increase the size of transaction balances of scarce foreign exchange (about which more below). The other arises from the distinct possibility that the country may exacerbate its deficit. This surge in the

---

12. Trade data at official exchange rates, especially of reporters that then still adhered to notional exchange rates (mainly Bulgaria and the Soviet Union), tend to overstate the CMEA's share. Even if corrected for that distortion, Eastern Europe remained quite dependent on intraregional trade.

demand for foreign currency can be met only by running an export surplus at some point. The severity of both policy concerns can be eased through some multilateral clearing scheme that enforces the discipline of moving steadily toward convertible-currency trading relations.

Firms cannot conduct transactions with Eastern countries that do not even remotely strive for genuine markets unless agents in the unreformed country can freely set prices and quantities[13]—an unlikely event. The prices at which such transactions take place must of necessity be negotiated, or at least approved, usually at a fairly high administrative level.[14] There may be a desire to emulate world prices. But the current debate on doing so in the former CMEA revolves entirely around "imputed" prices that have little to do with underlying scarcities, including those in the reforming countries themselves. Most often the imputation process involves documenting prices charged by leading Western firms: for example, a price quoted for a tape recorder produced by Philips or Sony would be taken as the "indicative" world price of a Soviet tape recorder, perhaps after some adjustments for the most overt design and performance differentials. This has in the past given rise to numerous disputes, which have needlessly burdened intragroup economic relations (Brabant 1987b, 113–30).

More fundamental than short-term dependence is the presence of static comparative advantages in Eastern Europe. Some of these have been exploited only marginally, owing to the peculiar institutional and policy features of central planning. Firms acting on their own account would presumably identify trading opportunities and capitalize on them. There would seem to be ample scope for scale economies, for example, for manufactured consumer goods as well as foodstuffs. Furthermore, as a result of national reforms and structural change, dynamic comparative advantages are also bound to crystallize. These economic opportunities should be fully exploited. For that to happen, proper institutions, trade policies, and commercial policy instruments are urgently required to guide agents in choosing activities in which they hold or hope soon to have true

---

13. Under those conditions there is no reason to inhibit economic agents in reforming countries from exploiting the temporary benefits accruing from artificial trade pricing in the partner economy. But authorities should, of course, be apprehensive about potential imbalances that may drain scarce foreign exchange. A proper exchange rate policy may help to elicit more rational microeconomic behavior vis-à-vis the distorted partner market. But suppressing the export surplus through wild exchange rate changes, as in Poland, or through administrative means, as in Hungary, may bankrupt firms that under the reformed principles of the domestic economy would be economically viable.

14. Certainly (notably in Hungary), firms were actively involved in CMEA trade negotiations and may have introduced their microeconomic interests into the process. However, inasmuch as the framework of trade (including volume, broad commodity composition, and trade and payments conditions) is set at a high administrative rung and partner enterprises as a rule do not possess this latitude, the trade deals negotiated yield scarcity prices only by fluke.

comparative advantage. By gradually accommodating change through economic discipline, processes that are hard to justify on solid economic grounds must be phased out quickly.[15] Others that are warranted on comparative advantage grounds are in need of more suitable accommodation than has been accomplished thus far.

As matters stand in early 1991, the prospects for buoyant intraregional trade are worse than they have been for the past three years. Switching to convertible-currency settlements and world prices, however eminently desirable to foster marketization, was from the beginning bound to lead to sizable terms-of-trade effects, mainly because of the sharp rise in the real dollar price of Soviet energy.[16] In addition, Soviet imports of below-standard Eastern European manufactures would probably be cut and their real price lowered, certainly over time.[17] For Eastern Europe's exports, the effect of the regime shift would probably be larger for quantities traded, given that the devolution from central to enterprise purchasing is likely to result in a demand shift, than for "real" prices on the ground that in the short run many exports are required to maintain machinery of Eastern European provenance. How large the effect in the end would be is something that has vexed many economists; it has also been a natural bone of contention among politicians.[18]

Regardless of how sizable the reversal might have been on account of the switchover by itself, the sharp contraction in exports to the Soviet Union and

15. This is not to say that such activities should be suppressed forthwith. The reforming economy may find it cheaper to subsidize such production over some period of time than to provide welfare benefits in a situation where supply is rather inflexible and the threat of chronic unemployment is serious.

16. Note that, at the official exchange rate, the price of Soviet oil until August 1990 exceeded the corresponding world price. But at any of the dollar-ruble cross rates adopted by the other Eastern European countries, the price of Soviet oil was but a fraction of the world price. Thus, if in 1989 Soviet oil had been priced at what the Soviet Union on average obtained in East-West trade, Eastern Europe would have had to pay from $4.6 billion to $7.1 billion more, depending on the cross rate.

17. Commentators often exhibit confusion in estimating the "real" cost of the price adjustments. The extra cost of oil and raw materials is usually figured by taking the difference between actual dollar cost at a realistic exchange rate of the ruble to the dollar and presumed world prices. For Eastern European exports of manufactures, however, the cost is usually seen as the difference between rubles earned and the "real" world prices that the Soviet Union, after conversion, is willing to pay. Of course, the difference between the dollar cost and the presumed world price should be included on both sides of the equation.

18. Concrete data on the various factors involved in such a reversal are, unfortunately, not available. Estimates tendered before the runup in oil prices ranged between $1.5 billion and $2.5 billion for Czechoslovakia, $0.5 billion and $2 billion for Hungary, and $0.8 billion and $4 billion for Poland; the higher estimates entail sizable deficits with the Soviet Union. However, the methodology of these estimates leaves a lot to be desired.

the sudden deterioration in Eastern Europe's terms of trade with the world could not but entail sizable deficits with the Soviet Union, provided that the latter can maintain its traditional exports and that the deficits can be financed. Without some mechanism in place to accommodate those deficits, Eastern Europe cannot avoid an austerity that will rob the structural reform program of most of its buoyancy. Even if there were no deficit with the Soviet Union, because of the latter's inability or unwillingness to maintain exports, Eastern Europe would have to sustain equivalent deficits with other markets, unless severe austerity measures curb import demand.

In connection with the shift in the CMEA's trade and payments regimes, it is worth noting also that even if a major reversal in imbalances could be staved off, the proposal to move to imputed world prices and surrogates for convertible-currency settlement is not very attractive on three grounds. Rebilateralization of trade relations, in some cases down to interfirm barter, signals a retrogression in regional cooperation (de Vries 1969b) that should be discouraged by all means. Furthermore, utilizing imputed prices that have little to do with underlying economic scarcities is a halfway solution, if that. These prices are likely to emanate from laborious bilateral negotiations involving the kind of "advanced haggling" that has been a hallmark of the intransparency of intraregional relations.

Another question in this connection is what to do with the imbalances that are bound to arise at some point. Although the issue has been debated, to my knowledge no clear-cut solution is in place. Clearly, imbalances resulting from trade conducted at relative prices that have little to do with actual East-West prices will be offset in dollar payments only with the greatest reluctance. As a result, bilateralism will compress trade to the export capacity of the weaker partner. It will simply defer the core problem of the transferable-ruble regime to another currency unit and the bilateral level—on the whole a regression in thinking, if perhaps not in trading practices. Certainly, the reforming countries are considering conducting as much as possible of their own intraregional trade in a transparent manner. But several instances of exchange controls or bilateral agreements for one type of transaction or another are known to exist. In relations with the Soviet Union a plethora of ad hoc arrangements have been negotiated. It might have been more productive to adhere to the existing trading and payment system, to smooth imbalances in a mutually satisfactory manner through quantitative controls, and to relax this regime when some segments of the Soviet economy have been placed on a genuine economic footing.

The Desirability of Economic Union

The alpha and omega of the transferable-ruble regime has been market separation, price equalization, and bilateral trade and payments agreements. These run counter to the very essence of the present reform's intentions and must therefore be tackled head on. But the issues at stake cannot satisfactorily be resolved unilaterally. Individual countries can funnel the rationality emerging in their domestic economies into trade negotiations as much as possible and take advantage of opportunities for reform among themselves (see Brabant 1990f), but this is not an ideal solution. The embedded constraint is important because Western and Eastern sources or destinations of traded goods and services for now are not simple substitutes. It is also crucial because intraregional trade is being burdened by disagreements that cannot soon be resolved (Brabant 1991a).

In this connection, it needs to be recognized that several Eastern European countries are now wedded to pursuing radical economic reform. Their reciprocal relations could increasingly be conducted by firms whose behavior is guided by the profit motive, provided a solution can be found for the payments imbalances that may emerge as these countries move toward full-fledged markets. The argument for greater regional cooperation in Eastern Europe could be markedly strengthened if the Soviet Union or its principal successor republics became fully committed to market-oriented reform. If Yugoslavia's dash toward convertibility were to falter,[19] its trade relations (or those of its successor republics) with Eastern Europe, which have been substantial, could be included in some regional arrangement. This state of affairs offers the international community a unique opportunity to look for a near-regionwide solution that will eventually prepare both old and new countries for regular participation in the multilateral global trade and payments networks.

Throughout the recent debates on regional cooperation, little thought has been given to introducing tiered integration in Eastern Europe. Most observers consider advocacy of such integration *after* the seminal political and societal transitions that have occurred in Eastern Europe to be an emanation of professional obtuseness, to put it mildly. But that position is often based on a questionable reading of what Eastern European economic collaboration has been—and even more what it could be—all about (Brabant 1990e, 1990g). Given the emerging problems of transition at a time of deep economic crisis, the fluid environment could have set in motion serious discussions on revamping regional cooperation within a full-fledged constitutional framework similar, for example, to the Treaty of Rome. By separating the judicial, legislative, and executive aspects of regional integration through an overall constitutional framework, the boundaries within which individual members could advance their own causes would be clearly demarcated. A fairly flexible arrangement would then enable some countries the opportunity to move forward with integration more rapidly than others without harming the latter's fundamental interests (Brabant 1989b).

---

19. After the two sharp devaluations of December 1990 and April 1991, this state of affairs has slowly been recognized.

Arguments in favor of reviving regional cooperation can be based on ordinary customs union theory, trade theory, transitory comparative advantages, the underdeveloped nature of trade in these countries, and other grounds. I will not elaborate on these points in great detail here (see Brabant 1991b), but the essence should be invoked as a key input in my advocacy in the next section of a regional payments union to weather current problems.

I find the peremptory rejection of Eastern Europe as a viable trade horizon for competitive economies an odd position. These may be poor economies, but in competition with each other (Lipton and Sachs 1990, Sachs 1990) they could nonetheless yield sizable trade—the example of the Benelux countries in the postwar period immediately springs to mind, although its market size was then at best one-third that of any Eastern European union.[20] The case can be made even more compelling by reaching beyond that stylized model, for Eastern Europe cannot yet access the global competitive framework on an equal footing. This is so because Eastern Europe's productive capacity is geared largely to intraregional trade. Many of these products either find little demand in the West or encounter obstacles in penetrating markets there. The former case pertains in particular to capital goods and many consumer durables; the latter applies, for example, to products that are "managed" in world trade or by the Common Agricultural Policy of the European Community. Several countries are only now seeking to normalize their relations within the framework of the General Agreement on Tariffs and Trade. Attempts to switch markets would hence result in trade destruction rather than trade diversion.

Certainly, Eastern Europe's potential for trade and specialization in the near term comes nowhere near that of the most vibrant global markets. Yet each of these countries must possess comparative advantages over the others that have not so far been fully exploited. Certainly, revamping trade and payments regimes on economic grounds, with independent firms conducting the transactions, would lead to a different level, commodity composition, and geographical orientation of commerce as economic restructuring eliminates trade based on administratively assessed advantages. But such restructuring should not altogether eliminate that trade. It fact, it might significantly increase trade among these countries, given that in the past their trade was radially linked to the needs and potentials of the Soviet economy and based on administrative criteria that distinctly favored producer goods. Likewise, economic reforms that succeed in generating factor-productivity growth should yield dynamic comparative advantages. I certainly see no reason to ignore these potentials.

---

20. Of course, in the late 1940s the Benelux countries ranked among the more developed countries in the world, unlike Eastern Europe at this juncture.

The economic merits, perhaps as distinct from current foreign policy considerations, of an Eastern European Economic Union[21] are fairly obvious. Eastern Europe would stand to gain from actively pursuing regional integration through some form of economic union. Finding the proper ways and means of exploiting such comparative advantages should rank high among the priorities of policymakers. These countries' trade with each other now consists essentially of manufactured goods, which previously were not subject to tariffs. Certainly as newly applied by Hungary and Poland,[22] most-favored-nation tariffs on this trade are fairly high (on average some 25 percent). Czechoslovakia started to apply its tariff to Eastern European trade in 1991 and has already instituted a 20 percent surcharge (on import value) mainly for consumer goods. Relations with the former East Germany are now subject to the external tariff of the European Community, which is low on average but not for many exportables of direct interest to Central Europe. Furthermore, that trade is now subject to many quantitative restrictions applied by the Community. This rise in import prices and loss in export markets are adding to the incremental restrictions on traditional trade within Eastern Europe.

There is ample room for building up scale economies, albeit in products that for now are difficult to market in the West, but not only because of their inferior quality. Such effective regional specialization would enable these countries to maintain fairly buoyant trade levels while they rapidly restructure their economies to reflect intraregional as well as world demand. On the basis of normal customs union considerations, some form of economic union for Eastern Europe would primarily avert trade destruction in the short run and be trade creating in the longer term. It would not divert trade because the underlying structures of these countries are mostly competitive rather than complementary, because flexible trade among the group as well as with outside partners has been hampered for systemic reasons, and because there is not much in the way of imports from the outside that can be diverted to the members of the group. These countries would therefore stand to reap substantial economies of scale. In addition, such a union in Eastern Europe would strengthen the market orientation of these economies and enable them to restructure their economies in a more

---

21. Such a suggestion is not new. But earlier proposals (see Brabant 1976, 1989a; Machowski 1973) either were anchored to the central planning framework after the decentralization attempts of the 1960s had been reversed, or referred (Wandycz 1970) to efforts of the interwar and immediate postwar years.

22. Effective 1 July 1990, Poland suspended or sharply reduced its tariffs. A new schedule was to have been in place by 1991. However, this target could not be met because of the political situation in late 1990 and the fact that Poland is currently renegotiating its accession conditions to the General Agreement on Tariffs and Trade. In any case, the suspension and reduction of import duties have been extended into 1991.

orderly fashion and at a lower short-term sociopolitical cost than if such adaptations were to be forced upon them through direct competition in world markets. Without such accommodation, the likely prospect of active trade destruction should be carefully evaluated.

Perhaps even more important, greater intragroup cooperation would in all likelihood elicit considerable Western support, for two reasons. On the one hand, it would postpone the diversion of substantial trade to Western markets. This would be difficult to accommodate in the short run, given the Community's other priorities (such as realizing the unified market, further integrating the southern European members, assimilating the former East Germany and future new members, and coming to grips with those standing in line for membership), which aggravate the Community's already sizable adjustment burden. Also, in this way it might be easier to change Eastern Europe's economic structures so that the reforming countries can eventually be fully integrated as market economies. Because of the time gained, orderly accession deliberations could be scheduled for later in the decade. In other words, economic union should not be seen as an alternative to joining "Europe." Quite the contrary, I see it essentially as a temporary stage to facilitate the transition phase, in terms of both the time required and the costs incurred in the process, toward eventually becoming fully integrated members of a united Europe, perhaps around the turn of the century.

A customs union requires at least a transferable currency. If the reforming countries cannot sustain convertibility, there might be room to consider how best to provide the financial support and supervisory discipline to guide the process toward more robust convertibility in conjunction with the pursuit of other objectives.

External Payments Problems and a Payments Union

Arguably the most critical problem on the way to market orientation and a convertible currency is the foreign-exchange constraint. In some countries, this stems from the inability to raise sufficient export revenue to satisfy import demand at desired levels of economic activity and welfare. In others, the constraint is compounded by the need to service substantial external debts. This situation is being exacerbated by several untoward developments, in trade with both the other ex–CMEA members and in world markets, as discussed previously. Because of the scarcity of foreign exchange, these countries are quite reluctant to earmark it for payments that used to be defrayed in transferable rubles.

Second, the foreign-exchange constraint is being exacerbated by the expected sharp deterioration in Eastern Europe's terms of trade, mainly with the Soviet Union, as a result of switching to world prices in 1991. Certainly, at any realistic ruble-dollar cross rate, the effective price of imported fuels and raw materials will surge. In addition, prices of manufactures in terms of raw materials and especially fuels have recently been slipping. If such a trend were to be superimposed upon the switch away from the transferable ruble, the import shock could be devastating. In the short run, the prices of many manufactured exports may be stabilized because these products are required to maintain the machine park, or in view of acute shortages of consumer goods in the partner country. But to the degree that import demand is increasingly formed by independent firms rather than trade bureaucracies, a considerable shift in the composition of demand is bound to ensue. Partly because of this exacerbation of the foreign-exchange constraint, the useful switch to world prices and convertible currency is being undermined by the perceived need to revert to bilateral solutions at imputed world prices. This is not a very promising avenue toward constructive reforms.

The region's current account problems do not stem solely from shifting terms of trade and trade regimes, however. The dramatic change in the composition and level of demand for manufactures exported by Eastern Europe may also pose a burden. This arises, as already noted, in the first instance from demand shifts, as import selection is increasingly devolved to firms acting in their own interest, and away from the bureaucrats. Also, the prospect of a faltering pace of economic activity in Western Europe may adversely affect the pursuit of radical economic reform.

Demand for foreign exchange is also surging because of the replacement of transferable-ruble clearing for noncommercial transactions by a partly cash-based payment system. Because of the limited form of convertibility being pursued, many noncommercial payments will by necessity be eliminated, thereby impeding the flow of peoples and ideas in Eastern Europe and complicating transfers of pensions, grants, alimony, scholarships, royalties, and the like.[23]

These foreign-exchange constraints may nip in the bud the process of moving toward genuine markets, including limited convertibility, because the austerity required to equilibrate the external accounts in such circumstances is bound to be unpopular. The populations of these countries are unlikely to shoulder a big bang approach voluntarily as long as domestic economic activity avoids receding into chaos, with runaway inflation, stalemated policymaking, unserviceable foreign debt, an inability to progress with reform, and other factors that made the Polish and Yugoslav experiments initially acceptable. Some gradualism would therefore commend itself.

---

23. Because of the disarray in relative prices, I would not recommend that such transactions be immediately included in multilateral clearing. It would be preferable for now to handle these flows through a parallel market as in Poland. This may yield sizable arbitrage gains, but there is no reason to excise such operations altogether.

Given this reality, it might be useful to rethink the experience with the EPU after World War II. Of course, the plight of the reforming countries in Eastern Europe differs in many respects from the situation in Western Europe in the 1950s. But there are also undeniable parallels. One is the nature of the payments constraint. The EPU alleviated the acute dollar shortage, which was hampering recovery in Western Europe, in the context of the broader aims of the Marshall Plan.[24] To avoid chronic payment problems, these countries found it necessary to manage trade through a wide spectrum of exchange and trade controls, including formal bilateralism (de Vries 1969a, 1969b). The dollar shortage and European bilateralism tended to inhibit the mutually reinforcing benefits from buoyant intragroup trade. The EPU was created precisely to bolster such opportunities by eliminating bilateralism. Another essential ingredient was the starting capital contributed by the United States. By requiring that intraregional payments be increasingly effected in fungible assets managed through the EPU (Kaplan and Schleiminger 1989; Tew 1967, 109–23; Triffin 1957, 168ff.), Western Europe returned to current account convertibility around 1958.

A clearing institution with some supervisory muscle would seem to offer a useful intermediate policy choice in the direction of convertibility for reforming countries. It would also help to promote other desirable objectives of reform. Membership should initially be limited to market-oriented countries, chiefly Central Europe. It is there that the political and social consensus on moving toward pluralism through some market-based economic framework, however vague at this stage, is more pronounced than, say, in the Balkan countries, including Yugoslavia for now. But the CEPU could expand its membership as other countries in the region adopt similar reforms to enhance their integration into the world economy. This would be particularly pertinent if the Soviet Union were to embrace marketization wholeheartedly or if it were to adopt a weak confederal status with several republics pursuing market orientation. The same would hold in the event of a fragmentation of Yugoslavia or the reimposition of exchange controls on commercial transactions.[25]

The core short-run objective of a payments union for Eastern Europe is not so much to bolster the opportunities for trade through multilateral arrangements as was the case for the EPU. Rather it is to obtain support for revamping and restructuring intraregional commercial relations on the basis of rational economic decisions while structural adjustments are being sought at a measured pace. One

---

24. Economic historians and others (Diebold 1988; Hogan 1987; Knapp 1981; Milward 1987, 1988, 1990; Wexler 1983; Wood 1986) have been waging an at times acrimonious debate on the role of US assistance in Europe's economic recovery. But this is not the issue here.

25. This materialized with the devaluation of December 1990 and has since been exacerbated.

obstacle to fostering such a transition is precisely the shortage of foreign exchange. It needs to be reemphasized that any clearing scheme that does not allow for the rapid emergence of more rational trade—and domestic—prices will undermine any kind of multilateral clearing, regardless of how sophisticated the technical accommodations laid down may be.[26]

Conceptual and Technical Aspects of Clearing

The key features of a CEPU as I envisage it were set forth in the introduction to this paper. But there remain many grave questions in connection with the proposal: How long will it take to reach convertibility? How much capital support is required? What proportions of loans and payments could bolster trade? How much discrimination for intraregional trade is required, and to what degree might it inhibit moving toward convertibility with the West? What conditions need to be met to ensure that the clearing agency can operate in a stable environment? What is to be done with the inherited imbalances, including those incurred on account of voluntary and other loans? Who will set the macroeconomic adjustment policies, and how are they to be enforced? At what interest rates should the accounts be kept? What could be done with the capital resources available when the clearing fund's rationale evaporates?

Some aspects of these questions are of a highly technical nature and can be settled only through negotiation. Others, however, can be addressed with a view to specifying the most desirable characteristics of the CEPU (Brabant 1990g, 1991b).

The duration of the clearing mechanism depends on how soon the reforming countries will be able to support convertible-currency trade, given the size of the adjustment cost and how quickly it can be borne. Eastern Europe needs not only to innovate market-oriented reforms but also to restructure its external trade and payments, almost literally from the ground up (Brabant 1990d). The task of maintaining economically warranted trade, while effecting radical changes in its commodity composition in line with comparative advantages, is daunting. The assignment is made even more complex by the fact that the rational restructuring of the domestic economy can proceed only by revising the traditional pricing mechanism and ensuring that the necessary changes materialize by knitting meaningful linkages between the domestic and external sectors. This is a very tall order indeed, even under favorable domestic and external circumstances.

---

26. Indeed, disparities among relative prices not justified by some scarcity criterion have been the bane of previous attempts at multilateralizing Eastern Europe's trade and payments (Brabant 1987a, 273–78).

Nobody knows how long it will take to cement in the foundations for convertible-currency trading based on the self-motivated behavior of economic agents now operating under central policy guidelines. Some policymakers are optimistic and would like to dollarize all of their trade in two to three years. Others are more cautious. Perhaps a common commitment by the reforming countries to reach convertibility by, say, the mid–1990s could offer an acceptable compromise. I suggest such a fixed target because the EPU's experience with successive two-year renewals proved not to be the most constructive solution. If countries want to move toward convertibility faster than originally forecast, they should be enabled to do so, of course. This could perhaps be combined with the upward revision of the currency share of payments.

The technical aspects of the clearing fund and what needs to be safeguarded against to prevent its premature demise are comparatively simple. The BIS, which was the EPU's accounting agency, could be entrusted with the CEPU's technical accounting once an agreement is reached on an acceptable mode of clearing. This would necessarily involve negotiations about the respective shares of convertible-currency payments and loans to be extended to surplus and deficit members relative to some mutually agreed-upon financing quotas. In the EPU, the shares of payments and loans varied with the degree to which agreed-upon quotas were utilized at the reporting date for imbalances; this would also be a desirable feature of the CEPU. The precise shares would need to be negotiated, of course (see below). Over time, the EPU's requirements on actual convertible-currency settlements for a given use of quota increased to at least 75 percent (Triffin 1957, 170–72), and 100 percent at the conclusion of the facility at the end of 1958.

Any possible clearing scheme suffers from a fundamental weakness due to asymmetries. To require in principle that all countries balance their current account within the clearing system is tantamount to assuming that they balance at the same time their accounts with other partners. Without this, participants are tempted to utilize any surpluses they generate to offset deficits with outside trade partners. On the other hand, countries in deficit with the clearing agency would not want to repatriate their outside surpluses.[27] This necessitates discriminatory adjustment policies as well as access to trading under the payments arrangements.

In the case of the EPU, this temptation was on the whole not very significant for several reasons. One was the size of intragroup trade. Most participants conducted the bulk of their external commerce with other participants, after the

---

27. The criticism that any regional payments union addresses the "wrong" balance of payments, in the sense that what matters is the global balance, has merits but only if *ex ante* and *ex post* notions are kept apart. If payments outside the union are in balance, then it is the regional balance that may pose a bottleneck in attempts to enhance regional cooperation. It is in this sense that my proposal should be understood.

currency devaluations of 1949 buttressed the recovery process in Western Europe. Furthermore, by the early 1950s, these countries had considerable reciprocal trust and confidence, and therefore on the whole observed the agreed rules scrupulously, although not without some cajoling by the guarantor (Kaplan and Schleiminger 1989). As a result, each was willing to pay some price to make the transition toward currency convertibility work. This helped the EPU to reach consensual solutions to otherwise intractable technical problems. Also, trade with third countries was overwhelmingly with the United States, and hence in a convertible currency. This country had been one of the main sponsors of the EPU to begin with and had little interest in draining its own currency from the fund.

Critical in this respect was the fact that the United States explicitly allowed Western Europe to discriminate against dollar trade through the payments mechanism rather than through a plethora of nontransparent trade policy instruments. Similar support for the CEPU, this time extended on behalf of the European Community, would be very important indeed. Some positive discrimination in currency matters, rather than through tariffs, quotas, or even more onerous trade policy instruments, would unquestionably also help to solidify the foundations of the economic union and persuade potential members that it would be in their own interest, including in their endeavor to link up with the European Community, to first transit through the economic union. Inasmuch as the reforming countries are not willing or able to conduct their mutual trade in convertible currency at once and cannot divert their trade without sustaining measurable terms-of-trade and export revenue losses, the discriminatory features of a payments union would not inhibit countries, such as Poland, with domestic convertibility from extending it. Instead of the licensing currently required for a plethora of bilateral deals, the licensing of trade and payments with any reforming country in the context of the payments union would simply apply to the transactions not yet conducted in convertible currency and not yet slated to be included in such settlements.[28] Discrimination through currency would hence be aiming at averting trade destruction rather than encouraging trade diversion; in fact, after the slashing of imports from convertible-currency partners in the 1980s, there is not much trade left to be diverted to intraregional trade.

Are the conditions under which the EPU succeeded likely to be replicated in a CEPU? Given the present disarray in Eastern Europe, these countries are hardly

---

28. My disagreement on that score with Jacques Polak (chapter 3) stems from his apparently assuming either that the reforming countries have a licensing-free system for all trade or can divert all of their trade subject to licenses to convertible-currency trade. If this were so, a discriminatory regime for import permits would therefore be required if these countries were to join a payments union. However, neither of these assumptions applies, as I have tried to demonstrate here and elsewhere (Brabant 1991b, chapter 7).

imbued with a great deal of mutual trust. Such trust may emerge once the uncertainty about where to go from here, including in the Soviet Union, dissipates. This lack of confidence is much less pronounced for some of the smaller Eastern European countries, however. Thus, a CEPU would cater to shared political interests and commitments to making the arrangements work, even though the degree of overt commonality for now remains rather shallow. Lingering social and political revendications even within that subregion may pose unusual obstacles, but these could be overcome through concerted policy action.

The severe debt problems of some of the reforming countries, including most notably Hungary and Poland, could undermine the CEPU scheme from the very beginning by tempting them to earmark surpluses for servicing obligations with outside partners. It would therefore be useful to find a way to permit these countries, at least for now, to focus on current trade (and perhaps services other than on debt account), while the seemingly intractable problems caused by their inherited external debts are addressed through other means. I have no ready suggestion as to what could be done. However, the East-West assistance efforts that are now coming to fruition may well embody a greater degree of political capital and potential commercial interest in a pragmatic solution entailing a substantial write-off of the debt. This should ensure the separability of the stock of debt from current payments for trade and services other than debt service, as underlined by the rescheduling of a considerable portion of Poland's official debt to the Paris Club.[29]

Even if a solution can be found for the inherited imbalances, Central Europe's major external payment flows are chiefly with nonparticipants in the CEPU, if the Soviet Union is not a member. The key partner in the East is the Soviet Union, with which, beginning in 1991, trade is conducted at imputed prices through a mixture of barter, clearing, and payments. Western Europe constitutes the key Western partner. Trade with the latter might tempt participants to erode the clearing fund's base by appropriating surpluses to pay for outside deficits. Only concerted action on the part of major Western partners, through the surveillance exercised in the CEPU's context, could help to stem that tide. Even granting these obstacles to a successful CEPU, I still consider it useful to explore the possibilities of setting up a capital fund from which reformers in Eastern Europe could find support for transiting in a relatively short period of time to current account convertibility. This could usefully be arranged within the context of the

---

29. See *International Herald Tribune*, 17–18 February 1990, 15; and 23 January 1991, 9. On 15 March 1991, Poland obtained relief of about 50 percent of its external debt from the Paris Club; it obtained further bilateral relief from France, Germany, and the United States and is hoping to negotiate similar relief of its commercial debt with the London Club.

assistance currently provided, for example, by the Group of Twenty-Four. The sums involved are not at all substantial.

German unification poses its own problems. For one, the former East Germany was Eastern Europe's second-largest trading partner. Its industrial prowess, though trailing behind that of most industrial economies, was nonetheless intimately linked to Eastern Europe's needs. At the very least, the other Eastern European countries continue to need parts, components, and maintenance of the existing machine park. This could have been met only if the German unification had not forcibly precluded gradualism in restructuring the former East Germany's industry. At the time of monetary union in mid-1990, it could have been take care of.[30] It is now too late to seek an accommodation for East Germany's part of the trade of a united Germany within the CEPU. In consequence, that trade is also being eroded for lack of means of payment.

There are, of course, other issues to be resolved, such as the currency unit of the CEPU and the exchange rates to be used. There is no ideal solution, given that Western exchange rates are flexible, Eastern European currencies are generally inconvertible, and there is simply no ideal—let alone any fixed—exchange rate that could be selected for managing the CEPU. A pragmatic solution therefore recommends itself. One such solution would place the ecu at the heart of the CEPU. The ecu is attractive because it is becoming the invoicing currency of a rising share of Eastern Europe's trade. It is also more stable than most currencies, including the dollar, especially because West Germany has long pursued a policy of low inflation. Furthermore, the ecu does not depend solely on one country's national monetary policy, and it plays a key role in the integration of the European Community, membership in which is coveted by the Eastern European countries. In that sense, the ecu should be as attractive, especially for the creditor, as dollars were in the EPU. The members of the CEPU themselves would have to take care, for the time being, of managing the rates at which their external trade gets translated into domestic currency. This solution would invite CEPU participants gradually to manage their foreign-exchange regime in tandem with that of the European Monetary System and to subject it increasingly to the latter's discipline. Of course, such a choice would invite the Community to assume a major role in financing the CEPU's initial capital and seeing to its success over a fairly protracted period of time (Brabant 1991c).

Setting up a payments union with an operational surveillance mechanism is not at all straightforward. In my view, this poses the core issue of making a CEPU work (Brabant 1991b, chapter 6). Aside from the many technical issues involved

---

30. One possibility would have been for West Germany to guarantee existing contracts, as it did for East German-Soviet relations. It could have arranged for full payment in deutsche marks for German exporters and importers of duly identified "Eastern" goods, while settling these claims with the Eastern European partners through the payments union.

(including those of the prior debt, the existing short-run imbalances, funding, credit quotas, the duration of clearing, the technical clearing agency, interest to be charged, and exchange rate guarantees), exercising surveillance is by definition a political matter. The clearing scheme has to ensure that payments imbalances remain manageable while the countries promote more rational trade and domestic prices. The latter task will be daunting enough for the smaller countries of Eastern Europe; it will be a Herculean effort to exercise proper surveillance over Soviet marketization. Nonetheless, I deem it politically wise and economically farsighted to conceive the clearing union with the Soviet Union counted in, but to make effective application subject to the adoption of credible market-oriented reforms either by the union or by key republics. Fragmentation of the ruble market would indeed entail settlement problems among the republics (and between them and Eastern Europe) that are similar in nature to external-payment problems. Their scale could not but magnify the external constraints of the reforming countries far beyond those deriving from switching to world prices and modified convertible-currency settlements.

The Costs of Funding a CEPU

Would a payments union be very expensive? Although many variables cannot now be quantified, any set of reasonable assumptions suggests that the capital requirements of a CEPU would be rather modest. Precisely how modest depends critically on what is to be accomplished. The central guideline should be how best to ease the payment problems of the participating countries while also nudging policymakers into adopting proper macroeconomic policies, so that over the time period envisaged the groundwork for sustainable current account convertibility will be laid.

Even if agreement on these principles can be reached, predicting the size of the imbalances to be financed through a payments union for economies that are now in the process of restructuring themselves is an impossible task. Nonetheless, it may be useful to recall that intraregional imbalances have traditionally been a small share of turnover.[31] True, the lifting of bilateral constraints on trade among countries that increasingly devolve decisionmaking to accountable agents cannot but precipitate greater intraregional imbalances. Changing behavioral

---

31. Eastern Europe's trade at prevailing exchange rates amounted to some $82 billion in 1989, whereas half of the sum of imbalances totaled some $4 billion, largely on account of the Soviet Union. The volume of trade among Czechoslovakia, East Germany, Hungary, and Poland in 1989 was roughly $16 billion, with half of the absolute imbalances vis-à-vis the group amounting to less than $300 million. The imbalances actually to be financed would be smaller, owing to offsetting service and so-called noncommercial imbalances, whose magnitudes are not known.

relations render it difficult to estimate the financial requirements of a payments union.

Even so, it is instructive to have some anchor for the magnitude of capital support that may be required, as it undoubtedly would prove very difficult to revise the capital base periodically. One starting point could be the financial requirements of the application of similar parameters as those initially used for the EPU if recent imbalances among various combinations of potential CEPU participants had been settled through a payments union. The EPU's initial parameters were essentially that up to 60 percent of quotas based on 15 percent of visible and invisible transactions among the EPU members in 1949 could be utilized as credit. Furthermore, credit was available symmetrically for the first 20 percent of cumulative imbalances, including those brought into the EPU from previous years, at the end of each month. Beyond that, creditors had access to currency and credit for 50 percent, yielding a maximum of 60 percent of credit claims. Similarly, for each tranche of 20 percent beyond the first, deficit countries had to pay 20, 40, 60, and 80 percent in convertible currency (or gold at the time), again yielding a maximum of 60 percent credit. Imbalances surpassing quotas, in principle, had to be settled fully in convertible currency, although this sanction was only rarely imposed.[32] Outside resources were required because deficit countries' imbalances could be spread over up to $n - 1$ members of the union, possibly remaining within the first tranche, while the single creditor would surpass that tranche, thus laying a net claim on convertible-currency payments; also the principle of "last in, first out" in determining the particular tranche necessitated outside financing. The actual capital brought into the EPU was nominally $350 million, but in fact was much smaller because (notably) Belgian and UK participation could be secured only through outright compensation for initial positions.

It should in principle be easy to compute both the quotas and the kind of imbalances that might have had to be supported, thus yielding some indication of the capital required, if trade among the Eastern European countries for some recent years had been settled through a payments union. Actually, matters are not that simple if only because of insurmountable statistical problems.[33] For these and other reasons, I have computed the quotas on the basis of half of the reporter and mirror statistics of the various countries ranked in alphabetical order for

---

32. Instead, financial diplomacy persuaded even reluctant creditors to be accommodating. Also, extra resources were funneled to debtors from outside the union. For details, see Kaplan and Schleiminger (1989) and Milward (1990).

33. Especially important in this regard are the facts that current exchange rates are disequilibrium rates and that cross rates to convertible currencies are far from even approximately uniform. Also, data for invisible trade are unavailable and mirror statistics are irreconcilable.

1989 and an average for 1987–89.[34] I computed these quotas for several combinations of Eastern European countries, including Czechoslovakia, Hungary, and Poland with (EE4) and without (EE3) the former East Germany, each of those groups with the Soviet Union (EE4 + S and EE3 + S), and Eastern Europe as a whole (Bulgaria, Czechoslovakia, East Germany, Hungary, Poland, and Romania) with (EE7) and without (EE6) the Soviet Union. Finally, quotas equal to 5, 10, 15, 20, and 25 percent of turnover in 1989 and the average of 1987–89 turnovers were computed. Imbalances for 1989 and averages for 1987–89 were utilized for clearing within the above two alternative quotas. I shall detail here only some of the magnitudes obtained.

Using 1989 trade data both for imbalances and quotas equaling 15 percent of trade turnover, net claims on the payments union in 1989 would have been on the order of $6 million for EE3 and $1.7 billion for EE7; the comparable data for the three-year averages would have been $20 million and $706 million, respectively. Under less generous quotas with 1989 as reference, claims on funding rise to $15 million for EE3 and to $1.8 billion for EE7 in the case of a 10 percent quota; the corresponding data for a 5 percent quota are $17 million and $1.7 billion. The latter decrease is due to the fact that countries hit their absolute quota ceiling earlier and would therefore have had to provide 100 percent convertible-currency payments. Under the most liberal quota (25 percent), claims on outside funding decrease to zero for EE3 and to $1.3 billion for EE7; the corresponding data for a 20 percent quota are zero and $1.5 billion.

The claims established with reference to the averages for 1987–89 are naturally slightly different. Under the more stringent requirements, drawings on the capital fund rise to $24 million for EE3 and to $769 million for EE7 in the case of a 10 percent quota; the corresponding data for a 5 percent quota are $22 million and $926 million. In this case, a decrease in calls on the capital fund results from the fact that the imbalances in 1987–89 were smaller than those of 1989. Under the most liberal quota, the claim on the capital fund decreases to near zero for EE3 and to $275 million for EE7; the corresponding data for a 20 percent quota are $10 million and $490 million.

Claims on the union when imbalances for 1989 are settled against quotas computed for 1987–89 are, of course, slightly larger. They range from zero and $14 million for EE3 under the most generous and the most restrictive quotas, respectively, to $1.2 billion and $1.7 billion under the most generous quota and the 10 percent quota, respectively.

From these hypothetical computations, two suggestions emerge. One is that imbalances relative to overall trade in the late 1980s were small even in the most unbalanced year. This is unlikely to remain so once trade liberalization in the

---

34. For a detailed discussion of the methodology and results, see Brabant (1990g, 1991b).

payments union gets under way and firms are called upon to capitalize on their perceived comparative advantages. This would call for a generous capital fund. Second, the Soviet Union is *the* major unbalanced economy in the region and was in substantial deficit in 1989. That, too, is unlikely to recur in the near future, owing to the gains in the terms of trade with Eastern Europe in any case and with the rest of the world if fuel prices remain high in the aftermath of the Persian Gulf crisis. However, it is impossible to establish the magnitude of future imbalances with the Soviet Union, given the uncertainties surrounding future Soviet export levels and changes in world prices. Under the circumstances, to make the payment scheme attractive and afford leverage over the transition phase, the more liberal quotas and capital fund might be set *ab initio* with a corresponding increase in the advisory role of the body entrusted with surveillance.

Conclusions

Because several Eastern European countries are resolutely determined to move toward a market orientation, there is now a good chance that their mutual economic relations can soon be conducted at market-clearing prices by enterprises in a competitive environment linked to global trade. For such decentralization and trade liberalization to work well, macroeconomic authorities need to take care of exchange rate and settlement matters. This condition would be satisfied if trade, including intraregional trade, were placed on a convertible-currency footing or if economically warranted intraregional trade could be diverted to the West without significant terms-of-trade or income effects; in the latter event, intraregional trade could be reconstructed later on. If these desirable features cannot be attained, I deem it useful to liberalize trade through a regional or subregional integration scheme. Any such union can function well only if there is a transferable currency. Attaching a transitional mechanism for moving toward currency convertibility to the economic union would offer a temporary alleviation of foreign-exchange constraints. Such a solution could usefully be explored in the context of Western assistance efforts.

The comparatively small amount of outside capital required to operate a CEPU needs to be placed against the backdrop of the constructive benefits such a clearing scheme is likely to yield. Perhaps most important, aside from achieving currency convertibility and phasing in trade liberalization, it would help to avert destruction of intraregional trade, especially if the CEPU were attached to some form of economic union. Also, it would assist participants with the industrial restructuring that is to be undertaken in any case. Furthermore, it would transfer assistance in a form that least interferes with the emerging economic incentives for microeconomic agents and the macroeconomic framework being elaborated.

Moreover, it would ease the pressure on Western European markets to accommodate significant trade diversion from Eastern Europe. Finally, it could reduce the magnitude of the contraction in levels of activity in Eastern Europe during the restructuring process, given supply rigidities there. In my view, these potential benefits are of some consequence.

Regardless of how far the reforming countries may want to move by themselves, they will remain very dependent on trade with the Soviet Union for years to come. At present only poorly transparent trade and payment arrangements are in place to substitute for the defunct transferable-ruble regime. Better arrangements can crystallize only when the Soviet Union aims its reform at market guidance. That, unfortunately, is not yet in sight.

Acknowledgment

I am most grateful to Jacques J. Polak for his efforts to extract for my benefit a contemporary interpretation of the IMF's rules, as earlier done by J. Gold (1971), through the good offices of François Gianviti, legal counsel at the IMF.

Liberalizing Foreign Trade in a Socialist Economy: The Problem of Negative Value Added

Ronald I. McKinnon

In the wake of their remarkably swift adoption of free trade with full current account convertibility in 1990, both East Germany and Poland have experienced rapid industrial decline. Enterprises in an astonishing variety of manufacturing and agricultural industries turned out *ex post facto* not to be internationally competitive. The collapse of many enterprises and whole industries in these countries suggests that there are practical limits to how quickly currency convertibility and free arbitrage between domestic and foreign markets for goods and services can be achieved in a liberalizing socialist economy.

At first glance, the great difficulty East Germany and Poland have had in expanding their export activities and creating new ones as their old import-substitution industries contract seems to refute the Ricardian law of comparative advantage. The Ricardian model assumes that, under conditions of free trade or of economic autarky, all goods are, or can be, produced according to predetermined production technologies from basic labor. Even if average labor productivity is low, therefore, under free trade the comparative efficiency of at least some major domestic industries will soon assert itself if the real wage is set sufficiently low (i.e., if the real exchange rate is sufficiently devalued). Some reasoning such as this apparently lay behind the willingness of the Polish and German policymakers to move so quickly toward unrestricted foreign trade.

This paper will argue that production in a typical socialist economy does not fit this Ricardian model based on predetermined labor coefficients. Instead, goods are produced from intermediate inputs such as fuels and other materials as well as from labor and capital, and there is a substantial array of possibilities for combining these various inputs. In this substitution model, technological capabilities—including labor productivities at the time of liberalization—are conditioned by the preexisting structure of protection. I will attempt to show that, if

Ronald I. McKinnon is William Eberle Professor of International Economics at Stanford University. This paper is a shortened, adapted version of chapter 12 in The Order of Economic Liberalization: Financial Control in the Transition to a Market Economy, *to be published by the Johns Hopkins Press in September 1991.*

this *implicit* protection in the traditional Stalinist economy is taken properly into account, then no matter where the exchange rate is set, most manufacturing and food-processing industries will not necessarily be viable under free trade at preexisting combinations of factor inputs: indeed in the short run these industries might well exhibit negative value added at world market prices. The presence of industries with these characteristics calls for a more gradual program of trade liberalization than has been implemented in Poland and East Germany. An appropriate program would be one based on temporary tariff protection and the repricing of material inputs so as to winnow out those industries that cannot survive in the long run under free trade from those that can.[1]

Implicit Protection in the Traditional Stalinist Economy

In the traditional Stalinist economy, for which the Soviet Union will serve here as the leading prototype, virtually all domestic production of more or less finished goods—those sold directly to consumers or sold back to industry as plant and equipment—is insulated from foreign competition. Because the domestic currency is inconvertible into foreign exchange on current account, protection for domestic manufacturers—including those of processed agricultural goods—is automatic: the state trading agency can refuse to authorize competing imports unless there are pronounced domestic shortages of similar products. Although there are no formal tariffs or quota restrictions, the *implicit* rate of protection is very high; the result is as if quantitative restrictions had virtually eliminated competitive pressure from abroad. At some equilibrium exchange rate (to be discussed below), domestic prices for finished goods—after discounting for their normally poorer quality in the protected setting—are typically higher than those of their foreign counterparts. Thus, in its general repercussions on economy-wide resource allocation, this price wedge is similar to the effect of a high tariff on the importation of competing finished goods.

At the same time, exports of energy, raw materials, and limited amounts of manufactures (largely military equipment in the Soviet case) are largely determined centrally by a "vent-for-surplus" doctrine. That is, once the planners have

---

1. Behind the scenes in this paper is the presumption that the liberalizing socialist economy has strong domestic fiscal and credit controls in place that prevent enterprises from overbidding for scarce resources (Lipton and Sachs 1990). Thus, the national government need not resort to blocking the cash balance positions of enterprises—i.e., to commodity inconvertibility (Williamson 1990)—in order to prevent domestic inflation. To avoid this syndrome of commodity inconvertibility, however, the whole structure of domestic taxation and money and credit may have to be reformed at the outset of the liberalization (see McKinnon 1991a, 1991b.) Here I simply assume that liberalization has proceeded to the point where enterprise money can be spent freely for domestic purposes.

determined that domestic "needs" for, say, energy at low domestic prices have been more or less satisfied, the residual (which has been quite large in the Soviet case) is sold abroad at much higher world market prices. The effect of these controls on exports is similar to an export tax on energy that drives its domestic price below that paid by foreign buyers.

Primary products subject to implicit export taxation may amount to a substantial share of total exports in the Soviet Union. For example, energy in all forms, together with nonfood raw materials which were similarly "taxed," accounted for over 60 percent of Soviet exports in 1989, and over 75 percent if one omits "protected" military sales from the export base. In order to approximate how these relative prices in the Stalinist economy differ from those prevailing the world economy, therefore, let us partition the tradeable goods produced and consumed into two categories: finished goods, which are largely manufactures and processed foodstuffs, and material inputs, which are largely energy products and nonfood raw materials. For modeling purposes, we may assume that all finished goods are largely import substitutes or imports and are not exported, whereas material inputs are either exported or used up in the domestic manufacture of finished goods. Reinterpreting the notation and methodology of Tan (1970):[2]

(1) $\quad Z_i = Z_i(L_1, L_2, \ldots, L_n; M_1, M_2, \ldots, M_r)$

where the L_i's refer to primary factors such as labor or land, and the M_i's are intermediate material inputs. In considering the production choices facing industry i (figure 1), however, let us dispense with all but one intermediate input, M, and one domestic factor, L. We can then denote value added in domestic prices of finished-goods industry i as:

(2) $\quad V_i = P_i Z_i - P_m M$

where P_i and P_m are the domestic-currency prices of the finished product and the material input, respectively. In other words, the value added by the domestic factor is simply gross value minus the cost of intermediate inputs. The normal

---

2. Tan was concerned with the structure of differential tariffs in developing countries where finished goods—largely consumer manufactures—received high tariff protection but intermediate inputs entered duty free. For purposes of this analysis I treat the taxed export good as the relevant intermediate product. However, for the smaller Eastern European economies where material inputs are imported, one might want to introduce a subsidized importable as a third commodity in the analytical model, as in McKinnon (1966).

presumption is that value added at domestic prices is positive.[3] But what determines the relative prices of Z_i and M in domestic commodity markets, and how is that linked to domestic factor costs?

The Coefficient of Protection for Finished Goods

Consider relative commodity prices first, presuming that one unit of the domestic currency exchanges for one foreign. Because we are dealing with an economy that is a small part of the world economy, foreign-currency prices (denoted here with asterisks) are fixed. Let t_i represent the implicit tariff protecting domestic production of the finished product. This tariff is defined as the gap between the foreign and the quality-adjusted domestic price, such that:

$$(3) \quad P_i = (1 + t_i)P^*_i$$

Similarly, let t_m represent the implicit export tax on material inputs, such that:

$$(4) \quad P_m(1 + t_m) = P^*_m$$

In order to see the divergence between domestic relative prices and their foreign counterparts, divide equation (3) by equation (4) and rearrange to get:

$$(5) \quad P_i/P_m = (1 + t_i)(1 + t_m)(P^*_i/P^*_m)$$

Equation (5) captures the dual aspect of the overall protection of the gross output of finished goods: the effect of restricting competing imports *and* of subsidizing the use of material inputs. Indeed, from Lerner's symmetry theorem (Lerner 1936), we know that restricting imports and taxing exports have "equivalent" protective effects in long-run equilibrium (this is worked out more fully in the presence of intermediate products in McKinnon 1966). For industry i, we thus define the overall coefficient of protection to be:

$$(6) \quad 1 + \tau_i = (1 + t_i)(1 + t_m)$$

---

3. In any market economy, positive value added at domestic prices is a necessary condition for the firm to exist—although by no means a sufficient condition to ensure profitability. In a socialist economy, in extreme cases one could imagine a degree of public subsidy that enabled an enterprise to keep going even when it was not covering the costs of its material inputs. But I am ruling out this unlikely possibility.

Figure 1 Production of finished goods under socialist production and under free trade

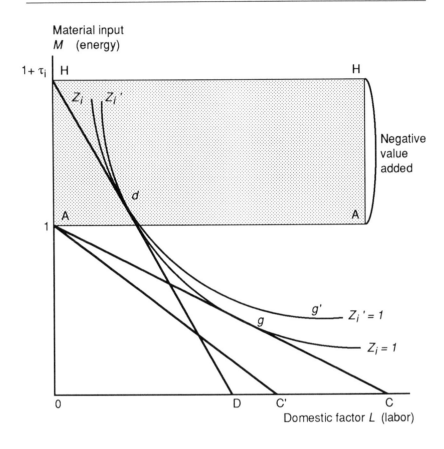

On the vertical axis of figure 1, the coefficient of protection shows the domestic relative price of finished goods in terms of material inputs. To better interpret figure 1, however, let us first consider domestic value added at world prices:

(7) $V^*_i = P^*_i Z_i - P^*_m M$

From equation (5), we can rewrite V^*_i in terms of domestic prices to get:

(8) $V^*_i = [P_i Z_i - (1 + t_m)(1 + t_i)P_m]/(1 + t_i)$

Although we presume that V_i remains positive, there can be *no presumption that domestic value added at world prices is positive.* Indeed, if either t_m or t_i is sufficiently high, and if the relatively cheap M is substituted for other factors of production, equation (8) tells us that $V'_i < 0$.

These relationships are depicted in figure 1, which is a modified version of that used by Tan (1970). For a "typical" finished-goods industry i (which is assumed to be one of many similar manufacturing activities in the socialist economy), the unit isoquants Z_i and Z_i' portray alternative possibilities for substituting the tradeable material input for the domestic factor of production in the long run (i.e., not taking transitional adjustment costs into account). The distance OA on the vertical axis represents the quantity of material inputs that is equivalent to one unit of finished goods at world prices. For example, at the hypothetical free-trade equilibrium at point g, where the new budget line AC (whose slope now reflects the relatively higher world cost of energy in terms of labor) is tangent to the unit isoquant Z_i, one unit of final output could buy OA in material inputs.

Going one step further, we can scale our measure of output in figure 1 so that one unit of the finished good is worth just $1 of foreign exchange: the unit isoquants Z_i or Z_i' then denote just $1 worth of finished good i. Similarly, we can scale our measure of material inputs on the vertical axis so that one unit of, say, energy is worth just $1: the distance OA in figure 1 is 1. Then, under the preexisting system of implicit protection, equation (5) tells us that the *domestic* relative price of the final output in terms of material inputs—the distance OH in figure 1—is simply our coefficient of protection $1 + \tau_i$. The higher domestic price of finished goods compared with that prevailing on world markets (and compared with the price of material inputs) reflects both the implicit export tax on material inputs and the implicit tariff on competing imports.

The Overuse of Material Inputs and the Shoddy Product Syndrome

Under protected domestic prices, all feasible input combinations (feasible in the sense that domestic value added is positive in the production of one unit of finished goods) must lie below the horizontal line HH in figure 1. Below HH, the domestic value of finished-goods output exceeds the domestic cost of the material inputs used in their production.

At world relative prices, on the other hand, all feasible input combinations must lie below AA if domestic value added is to be positive. Indeed, all production points in the shaded area lying above AA in figure 1 show negative value added at world prices. For example, point d is profitable under the existing mantle of protection: the budget line HD (whose slope shows relatively cheap energy and expensive labor) is just tangent to the unit isoquant Z_i (or its alternative Z_i'). Nevertheless, d shows negative value added if the final output is to be sold, and material inputs are to be purchased, in unrestricted world markets.

Why is this phenomenon of negative value added at world prices probably commonplace in Soviet (and Eastern European) industry? First, as drawn in figure 1, the relative prices of energy and other material inputs to most sectors of the Soviet economy have been kept very low, causing them to be used intensively. In addition, the old Stalinist system of rewarding managers by whether they fulfill gross output targets encourages them to waste material inputs. Shmelev and Popov note:

> According to the calculations of the Soviet Institute of World Economy and International Relations, we [in the Soviet Union] use 1.5 times more materials and 2.1 times more energy per unit of national income than the United States. . . . Our agricultural production is 15 percent less than the United States but we use 3.5 times more energy. (Shmelev and Popov 1989, 128)

Second, the Stalinist planning system based on gross output targets tends to produce manufactured or processed outputs of uncertain quality: "The quality of Soviet produce appears to have been declining steadily since the 1960s, as a result of permanent excess demand, regardless of technical progress" (Aslund 1989, 76). For an example, take a common household product like detergent that is introduced at a certain benchmark standard. The (protected) domestic producer will have a continual incentive to degrade product quality if, by so doing, more units can be produced. After users complain, the enterprise might get permission to introduce a new and "improved" benchmark detergent at a higher price, for which it gets more weight in its gross output target than for the unimproved product.[4] Then the slippage in quality begins all over again. I will call this reiterative process the "shoddy product syndrome."

In figure 1, the shoddy product syndrome affects the position of the unit isoquant because material inputs at world prices—or, equivalently, units of foreign exchange—are the numeraire by which final output is measured. The shoddier the product, or the more uncertain the product quality, the further from the origin will be the unit isoquant—say at Z_i' rather than Z_i. In the sudden East German trade liberalization of 1990, for example, the adverse signaling from simply knowing that a good had been produced in East Germany was sufficient to induce East German consumers to reject it in favor of a higher-priced West German good. This increased the distress in East German industry.

In a sudden move to free trade at *any* exchange rate, therefore, a finished-goods industry chosen at random is likely to show negative cash flows under the

---

4. This absence of a market test for valuing final outputs is one important reason why the growth in Soviet GNP may have been significantly overstated in the postwar period. The continual decline in product quality did not reduce measured GNP, while the continual introduction of "new and improved" products was allowed to increase it.

preexisting combination of factor inputs and low valuation of the finished product in world markets. A devaluation coinciding with the move to free trade would simply raise material input prices in tandem with the prices of shoddy finished goods. In the short run, before input combinations and product quality can be adjusted, negative value added persists. The result is wholesale industrial collapse, the effect of which on the overall economy is all the greater given that manufacturing absorbs a much higher proportion of the labor force in the Soviet Union than in the United States (Shmelev and Popov 1989).

The Adjustment Problem

If the exposure of socialist industries to world prices leaves them incapable in the short run of producing goods with positive value added, is it possible that those industries can be made viable at some long-run free-trade equilibrium? Returning to the substitution model of figure 1, suppose our putative reformers observe the "protected" starting point d, a combination of output and inputs with negative value added at world market prices. The reformers do not know whether industry i (and similar finished-goods industries) will be capable of ultimately shifting away from its current heavy dependence on material inputs while improving product quality, and thus become profitable under free trade. At the outset it is uncertain whether industry i is on an "efficient" unit isoquant such as Z_i, or on an "inefficient" unit isoquant such as Z_i', since both isoquants run through point d. In the former case, output at world prices is ultimately sustainable at point g. In the latter, the best industry i can hope to manage in the long run, after energy becomes more expensive, is a production point like g', where the value of gross output remains less than the total cost of production.

Notice that the long-run viability of industry i depends not only on its production efficiency (i.e., whether it is on unit isoquant Z_i or Z_i') but also on the prevailing costs of the domestic factors of production after a new free-trade equilibrium is established. Suppose labor is the principal domestic factor of production. Then the budget line AC shows the real wage (in terms of material inputs) to be sufficiently low under free trade that point g tangent to Z_i is profitable. However, if the equilibrium real wage is higher, so that AC' is now the relevant budget line for producing one unit of the finished good, then industry i will not be profitable under free trade. AC' lies to the left and below Z_i. The real wage in long-term equilibrium facing any particular industry i will be the outcome of a complex macroeconomic interaction as *all* industries liberalize simultaneously.

This example illustrates a fundamental uncertainty about substitution in production, product quality, and equilibrium real factor costs when all industries are finally liberalized in the long run. Given this uncertainty, can the reformers devise a system of *interim* protection at "correct" relative input prices that initially sustains the profitability of most existing finished-goods production, but that when systematically reduced over several years allows market mechanisms to phase out inefficient finished-goods industries, while encouraging "learning by doing" in others so that they eventually thrive under free trade?

From Implicit to Explicit Tariff Protection: The Case of Chile

The trade liberalization in Chile after 1973 was, until the Polish and East German experiences of 1990, perhaps the most comprehensive and draconian of modern times.[5] Chile's tariff and foreign-exchange policies after 1973 provide useful clues of what to do, and what not to do, in a similarly comprehensive trade liberalization program in a socialist economy like the Soviet Union's.

In 1973, Chile protected its finished-goods producers with very high formal tariffs. These averaged over 90 percent, with some going as high as 500 percent (table 1). However, these numbers conceal the fact that much protection in Chile in 1973 was in the form of nontariff barriers. Quota restrictions and absolute prohibitions on imports of finished goods were commonplace, along with restrictions on the export of food and industrial raw materials. In addition, the government refused to allocate foreign exchange for imports that did not suit its immediate social objectives, and it set multiple exchange rates across different categories of imports and exports to such an extent that many tariff rates themselves had become rather meaningless.

The Chilean liberalization of foreign trade in 1974 and 1975 set out, first, to unify the exchange rate so that all exporters and importers transacted at the same rate; then to convert all quota restrictions into some rough tariff equivalent, lumping similar commodities together in the same tariff category; and then to move to unrestricted foreign-exchange convertibility on current account. The net effect of these first steps taken in 1974 and 1975 was to convert implicit protection by direct controls into explicit protection by tariffs. These remained very high, as table 1 shows, but by 1976 this conversion was virtually complete. Only then did the government proceed to phase out the explicit protection over a period of several years by reducing the high tariffs, in preannounced small steps, to converge upon a modest, uniform import tariff at a prespecified future date.

In the event, Chile speeded up this process slightly and converged to a uniform 10 percent tariff on all imports by July 1979 (table 1), with no other significant

---

5. Edwards and Edwards (1987) put the remarkable empirical details of the Chilean reforms into a solid analytical perspective.

Table 1 Chile: profile of tariff reform, 1973–79 (percentages)

Period		Average nominal tariff rate	Maximum nominal tariff rate[a]
1973	July–December	94	500+
1974	January–June	80	160
	July–December	67	140
1975	January–June	52	120
	July–December	44	90
1976	January–June	38	70
	July–December	33	60
1977	January–June	24	50
	July–December	18	35
1978	January–June	15	20
	July–December	12	15
1979	June 30 onward	10[b]	10

a. With a few exceptions for some automotive vehicles. Small cars could be imported at the standard tariff rates.

b. Of the 4,301 commodities or tariff lines that are classified for customs purposes, only 12 are exempt from any duties.

Source: Central Bank of Chile.

import restrictions. The uniform tariff was justified on revenue grounds, and from Lerner's symmetry theorem we know that such a tariff is equivalent to a 10 percent tax on all exports in long-run equilibrium.

Note that after 1973 Chile also removed all controls and other significant taxes on exports per se. However, in parallel with what should be the case for the natural resource–based exports of the Soviet Union, the Chilean government continued to tax the profits and other economic rents associated with natural resource–based industries rather systematically. For example, in the copper industry, which dominated Chile's exports much as petroleum now does the Soviet Union's, the government retained ownership and control of a number of major mines, and concessions given to private mining companies—whether international or domestic—were rather carefully taxed. The important point for our purposes, however, is that these were "profits" taxes rather than export taxes. Hence, after liberalization, they did not drive a wedge between the price faced by domestic users and that faced by foreign buyers of exportable material inputs—unlike in the Soviet energy industry today.

In summary, in difficult political circumstances, Chile in late 1973 eschewed the cold-turkey approach to free trade adopted by Poland and East Germany in 1990. Instead, Chilean producers of finished goods were allowed some years in which to adjust. The one major mistake the Chilean policymakers made was to allow excessive capital inflows, which forced a severe overvaluation of the Chilean peso in 1978–82 and caused widespread bankruptcy in the newly opened tradeable-goods sectors (McKinnon 1991a, chapter 6). Despite this early trauma, Chile's trade liberalization and its political commitment to free trade have been successfully sustained into the 1990s.

A Transition Parable for Soviet Foreign Trade

Suppose the spirit of the deliberate, staged Chilean approach to free trade could be depicted within the confines of our two-commodity substitution model. How might an "idealized" transition from socialism to free trade be worked out?

In the Soviet case, the authorities got off on the wrong foot in 1989 by decentralizing foreign-exchange contracting by domestic enterprises before their budget constraints were hardened so that domestic commodity prices could be decontrolled, and before the regime of multiple exchange rates was unified. In 1990, hundreds of individual exchange rates, ranging from the old official rate of 0.64 rubles to the dollar to more than 20 rubles, continued to proliferate. Thus, as a practical matter, the Soviet government might have to recentralize foreign-exchange allocations until the domestic financial controls necessary for supporting a market economy have been established (McKinnon 1991b) and until the exchange rate is unified.

But how should this unified nominal exchange rate be set when unrestricted commodity or financial arbitrage with the outside world does not yet exist? We know that the price of exportable material inputs—inclusive of the huge energy sector—must rise sharply relative to domestic factors of production, including labor. Moreover, the ruble prices of these fairly homogeneous material inputs can be directly compared to those prevailing on world markets, which are typically quoted in dollars. Thus, the ruble-dollar exchange rate can be set according to a limited version of the principle of purchasing power parity as follows.

Take the prevailing domestic wage level in rubles as a starting point. Then estimate the average increase in the relative price of energy (and other material inputs) against wages that would prevail in long-run equilibrium if the economy were to move toward free trade. Accordingly, adjust the domestic ruble price of energy (and other material inputs) sharply upward, doubling or trebling it in terms of wages at the outset of the trade liberalization process. In figure 2, the slope of the budget line BB', running through the old production point d, now represents this higher price of energy relative to labor, whereas HD, also running through d, represents the old budget line when energy was underpriced.

Simultaneously, to make the new ruble price level for material inputs effective, set the exchange rate in rubles to the dollar to equate the average domestic price of material inputs to that prevailing in world markets. This new unified exchange rate should now apply to all current account transactions, on both the import and the export sides, for material inputs, finished goods, and services. Once established, this nominal ruble-dollar exchange rate will be invariant to further ups and downs of world prices for material inputs. At the fixed exchange rate, continual minor changes in the domestic ruble prices of individual material inputs (and other tradeables) will keep them aligned with their counterparts on world markets.

What have we accomplished by this exercise in exchange rate unification? First, the implicit export tax on energy and other material inputs has been eliminated as their ruble prices rise sharply to world levels. (Note, however, that the revenue position of the government would be greatly enhanced if it retained a full claim on the profits or surpluses generated by natural resource–based industries at the higher domestic prices.) In the short run, producers in industry i would have an immediate incentive to begin economizing on energy and other material inputs.

Second, this nominal exchange rate is now capable of sustaining the real purchasing power of domestic money in terms of material inputs—a very broad class of primary commodities produced, traded, and consumed throughout the economy—once full current account convertibility is achieved. This potentially stable "real" exchange rate also provides a benchmark for converting the implicit tariff protection associated with quota restrictions and the existing system of exchange controls into explicit tariff-equivalents. That is, the authorities may now calculate the t_i's sufficient to keep most finished-goods manufacturing in existence—such a calculation requires a stable real exchange rate if effective protection by tariffs is itself to remain operative at some prespecified level.

For finished-goods industry i in figure 2, the vertical scale at point H shows the coefficient of protection, $1 + \tau_i$, prior to this elimination of the domestic subsidy to the use of material inputs. This total implicit protection depends on the preexisting implicit tariff on imports of finished goods and on the old input subsidy. As before, the resulting budget line for producing one unit of finished good i at point d is HD, whose steep slope reflects the low prices of energy and other material inputs relative to that of domestic labor.

After the prices of material inputs increase to world levels, however, explicit tariff protection from competing imports of finished goods has to be adjusted upward to its old implicit rate if industry i is to survive. Suppose t_i' is the new explicit tariff needed to keep industry i in business once exchange controls are removed and current account convertibility is achieved. Then $t_i' > t_i$. To

Figure 2 Effect of interim tariff protection during the transition to free trade

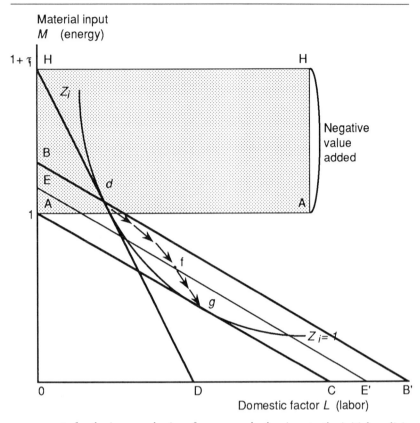

Material input
M (energy)

compensate for the increased price of energy and other inputs, the initial explicit tariff has to be somewhat higher than the previous quality-adjusted differential between the foreign and the domestic price of finished good i. The vertical distance AB in figure 2 shows the level of this new (hypothetical) explicit tariff relative to the (newly increased) prices of material inputs. Insofar as the domestic price of material inputs now equals the world level of $1, AB also represents the actual ad valorem tariff needed to protect the domestic industry. BB' is the corresponding new budget line just sufficient to sustain production at point d (i.e., at the old combination of domestic factors and material inputs). BB' is flatter than the old budget line HD, reflecting the higher price of material inputs relative to labor. Because the price of material inputs has also increased relative to that of finished goods, the distance AB is correspondingly less than AH.

But this is not the end of the parable. Because the slope of the new budget line BB' is flatter, it now cuts the unit isoquant Z_i at point d rather than running tangent to it. This induces the managers of industry i to raise profits by employing more domestic factors and reducing energy dependence—in other words, to start moving along the new budget line from d in the direction of B' as fast as the equipment of the enterprise permits. The great advantage of raising material input prices rather sharply at the outset of the trade liberalization is that firms immediately see the "right" relative factor costs; this induces them to economize on material inputs, exports of which will then slowly increase.

Nevertheless, our controlled liberalization differs from a strategy of jumping directly to free trade. Under immediate free trade with no interim protection for domestic finished goods, industry i would face budget line AC in figure 2, which does not support existing production at point d. Because under free trade the world market would bid material inputs and energy away from domestic uses, exports of these would jump sharply and so cause the collapse of most domestic manufacturing and goods-processing activities.

That said, interim tariff protection as in our parable should be implemented in a way that leaves no doubt in the minds of domestic industrialists, merchants, and farmers that the economy will eventually move to free trade, as in the final stage of the Chilean program. Simultaneously with the introduction of explicit tariff protection for finished-goods industries, the liberalizing socialist government could announce that the higher tariff rates would be scaled down by small steps until, say, ten years hence all rates have converged to some low, uniform level. Further reductions in this resulting "revenue tariff" would then depend on the government's fiscal position.

Figure 2 nicely illustrates the nature of this declining tariff protection in smoothing the transition to free trade. Starting with the high explicit tariff equal to the vertical distance AB, the relevant budget line supporting production at point d is BB'. Some years later, formal tariff protection for our representative finished good is reduced to AE so as to support production at point f along the new budget line EE'. Finally, tariff protection for finished-goods industries is phased out altogether. The relevant budget line becomes AC—that prevailing under free trade. (For diagrammatic simplicity, figure 2 does not show the process ending with a low revenue tariff, and I have simply assumed that the initial guess of the authorities in raising the price of material inputs relative to domestic factors turns out to be correct in free-trade equilibrium.)

During this transition, which is successful in the particular case of industry i in figure 2, the combination of factor inputs for producing one unit of the finished good shifts along the locus shown by the arrows from d to f to g. Only at the beginning point d and the endpoint g are these production combinations actually on the unit isoquant Z_i. That is, the unit isoquant traces out efficient production points *in long-run equilibrium* after the industry has had the necessary time to rebuild its capital stock and restructure its labor force to adjust to the change in relative prices. The other points on the locus dfg are above the efficient long-run unit isoquant, and their "excessive" use of material inputs and domestic factors represents the real (social) costs of the transition. These costs are covered by the interim tariff protection and thus are shifted to the final users of the finished goods.

Even so, the change from implicit quota restrictions and import prohibitions to explicit tariff protection could benefit users of finished goods. First, even with high tariffs, the new threat of import competition would curb the monopoly power of concentrated domestic manufacturers. Manufacturing industries in the Soviet Union, for example, are indeed highly concentrated. One hundred percent of Soviet sewing machines are produced by a single state enterprise; the same is true for such diverse goods as tram rails, locomotive cranes, and cooking equipment. All hydraulic turbines produced in the country come from a small number of plants run by a single government ministry; the same can be said for tin plate production and certain consumer goods such as color photographic paper and freezers (*The Economist* 1990, 67). Second, the shoddy product syndrome would be immediately alleviated; the worst domestic products would not survive in the face of even modest competition from abroad. Indeed, the successful transitional production locus *dfg* in figure 2 implicitly incorporates improvements in product quality.

A Generalized Cascading Tariff?

These advantages from the move to explicit tariff protection presume that the government does not precisely tailor individual tariffs to keep each finished-goods producer in business at the outset of the liberalization. Rather, the vertical distance *AB* in figure 2 is best interpreted as simply a representative initial tariff—a common levy—that applies to imports of all finished goods within a given category. However, following the Chilean experience and that of other primary products–producing countries such as Canada, which once had quite high tariffs, one could instead start off with fairly broad tariff categories: a "cascading" tariff scaled downward according to the distance from the final consumer and the degree of manufacturing complexity. Ranked from highest to lowest, a single tariff rate could apply to each of the following or similar categories:

- Consumer durables: automobiles, home appliances, and so forth;

- Consumer nondurables: such as textiles and highly processed foods;

- Capital goods and manufactured intermediate products; and

- Industrial materials and basic foods.

The highest tariff in the first category could be over 100 percent, depending on how one computed the average survival capability of enterprises in these industries after the prices of material inputs have been raised sharply; the lowest tariff would be the final uniform tariff of, say, 10 percent, on imports in the last category. To the extent possible, the government would set a simple, across-the-board "yardstick" tariff in each category. Not only would this general approach weed out the most inefficient producers at the outset, but rent seeking by individual industries petitioning for protection geared to their own specific needs would be minimized.

Then, over perhaps a 10-year interval (the period adopted for tariff reduction in the 1988 Canada–US Free Trade Agreement), the rates in the first three categories would be gradually but firmly reduced to those prevailing in the fourth category—again without accepting any special pleas for exceptions. In order to facilitate adjustment in his own mix of inputs and outputs, each producer should know what cumulative tariff reductions[6] he will face at the end of every year until virtual free trade is established.

A cascading tariff schedule, but one that is not adjusted downward, is often used by developing countries to protect their infant finished-goods industries. In our transition parable the purpose is quite different: to make explicit and then phase out already very high levels of implicit protection for domestic manufacturing. Moreover, given the degree of uncertainty as to which firms will ultimately survive the opening of the economy, it is simply not feasible for those firms that would be viable in the long run to jump immediately to free trade and to cover their early losses and transition costs by borrowing. Indeed, such massive borrowing by socialist enterprises would undermine the hard budget constraints, based on limited access to external capital, that are essential for achieving domestic financial control (McKinnon 1991a, 1991b). Instead, temporary tariff protection, which increases the internal cash flows of manufacturing firms, is fully consistent with keeping self-finance as the main source of financing for liberalized enterprises in a transitional socialist economy.

Are Foreign Capital Inflows Necessary?

Because a properly orchestrated move to free trade presents no inherent problem of foreign-exchange shortages for the Soviet Union, our parable of step-by-step trade liberalization did not discuss the role of capital flows from abroad. Quite the contrary, the country abounds with energy resources and other material

---

6. The authorities would not, however, have to reveal the exact dates on which tariffs would be discretely adjusted, which would invite inventory speculation. Continual adjustment by very small amounts to yield a prespecified cumulative change would be much preferred.

inputs that are overused at home. Thus, the elimination of implicit export taxes should allow exports to increase rather easily. Indeed, flooding the economy with foreign exchange by borrowing abroad could well worsen the adjustment problem. Domestic finished-goods industries would face additional competition from "subsidized" manufactured imports that reduced their international competitiveness (McKinnon 1973).

Are there circumstances where one might want to mitigate this seemingly harsh judgment against heavy reliance on foreign capital inflows to ease adjustment to free trade? Unlike the Soviet Union, some of the smaller countries of Eastern Europe are not particularly rich in natural resources that are easily traded internationally. Worse, their extensive manufacturing and agricultural industries have also become addicted to cheap material inputs, particularly energy. Before 1990 at least, the close trade links among the countries of Eastern Europe simply extended the ambit of the old Stalinist industrial system. Through the trading apparatus of the CMEA, the Soviet Union sold relatively cheap energy and other material inputs to the smaller Eastern European economies in return for manufactured goods of a lesser quality than those traded in Western markets. In fact, the extensive trade among the CMEA countries (see table 2 in chapter 10 of this volume), albeit largely bilateral in nature because of the absence of a freely convertible trading currency, also included the exchange of (shoddy) manufactured goods through direct bargaining by state trading agencies.

The problem for the former CMEA countries in adjusting to full-scale trade liberalization with the West is obvious. The smaller countries that have little to export in the way of primary products (what we have been calling material inputs) will find themselves faced with an immediate shortage of foreign exchange. First, they stand to lose the subsidies on their Soviet-produced material inputs: Soviet authorities will no longer be willing to accept their manufactured products at very favorable terms of trade. Second, the syndrome of negative value added at world market prices means that these countries cannot sell their manufactures, without significant improvements in product quality, to the West. In effect, they are currently producing at a point like d in figure 1, but where the vertical axis showing material inputs now reflects actual imports rather than potential exportables as in the Soviet case. Hence, a highly industrialized country like Czechoslovakia, about 80 percent of whose exports went to other socialist economies in 1988 (table 2 in chapter 10, this volume), faces an immediate foreign-exchange shortage from the collapse of the CMEA trading umbrella.

In a general-equilibrium model based on just two highly aggregated commodities, the Stalinist system of protection under the prototypical "Soviet" case can be distinguished from the prototypical "Czechoslovak" case. In the Soviet case, exports of primary materials are heavily (albeit implicitly) taxed, with the domestic government collecting the tax revenue, whereas potential imports of finished manufactures face very high (implicit) tariffs. In the Czechoslovak case, imports of material inputs such as energy are subsidized by an outside agent (the Soviet Union), and so are exports of finished manufactures subsidized[7]: first by the cheap energy inputs, and second insofar as they can be unloaded in other CMEA countries.

The distinction between these two cases is important. In the Soviet case, a natural method of easing the transition to free trade is to impose temporary explicit tariffs on competing imports of finished manufactures, as sketched above, in order to give domestic producers of these goods time to adjust as prices of energy and material inputs increase to world levels. But that would be insufficient in the Czechoslovak case. Czechoslovak producers of finished goods need some temporary protection in their export markets when their energy subsidies are removed. Moreover, even if such export subsidies to Czechoslovak manufactures were allowed under the General Agreement on Tariffs and Trade, they would be a big drain on the Czechoslovak government's budget. Perhaps a return to CMEA arrangements for some years into the transition would be a partial solution.

However, converting the CMEA into a full-fledged common market with convertible currencies and a common external tariff (on the model of Western Europe) seems completely out of the question (Schrenk 1990). This is a much more difficult task than reforming each socialist economy individually. Nevertheless, apart from the scheme for tariff-based liberalization sketched above, continuing the bilateral exchange of manufactured products through state trading agencies on an interim basis could be helpful for some years before each socialist economy is fully liberalized. Very likely, however, the net debits or credits arising out of bilateral imbalances in such trade would have to be settled in convertible Western monies rather than inconvertible rubles as is presently the case.[8]

To proceed with the main task of liberalizing its foreign trade with the West, therefore, a smaller Eastern European country might well require some carefully crafted bridging finance from an international agency, such as the European Bank for Reconstruction and Development set up in 1990. However, the conditionality imposed by this agency for lending the money might well follow our parable sketched above and reflected in figure 2: a discrete increase in the domestic price of energy and other material inputs to world levels, coupled with conversion from implicit protection through exchange controls to an interim system of explicit protection for finished goods through tariffs or special export subsidies. At the beginning of such a liberalization, with otherwise free convertibility on current account, the agency might well provide the foreign exchange necessary

---

7. I am greatly indebted to Peter Kenen for suggesting this point to me.

8. The possibilities for hardening the transferable ruble, making it convertible into Western monies, are discussed in McKinnon (1979, chapter 3).

for, say, Czechoslovakia to continue buying material inputs until its manufactured exports become more competitive in world markets.

However, accepting official bridging finance based on strict conditionality is *not* tantamount to a general relaxation of controls over private capital movements. Only after the domestic capital market is fully liberalized, with unrestricted borrowing and lending at equilibrium domestic interest rates, should the socialist economy's currency be made convertible into foreign exchange on capital account. Many years hence, individuals and enterprises—including joint ventures with foreign firms—could be allowed to choose freely between domestic and foreign sources of finance. But this is the last, rather than the first, step in the optimum order of liberalization.[9]

Conclusions

In the traditional centrally planned Stalinist economy, protection for domestic manufacturing is almost entirely implicit. Through exchange controls and the apparatus of state trading, disguised subsidies to users of energy and other material inputs are coupled with virtually absolute protection from competing foreign manufactures. Although no formal tariffs appear in any legal codes, the implicit structure of tariff equivalents "cascades" downward from very high levels for the domestic production of finished consumer goods through manufactured intermediate products to industrial raw materials and energy, whose production is negatively protected because of implicit export taxes (or import subsidies).

This highly cascaded structure of implicit tariffs in socialist economies raises the level of effective protection in finished goods to the point where most manufacturing exhibits negative (or very low) value added at world market prices. In such circumstances, a precipitate move to free trade could provoke the collapse of most domestic manufacturing industries no matter at what level the exchange rate is set, and no matter that some of this industry might eventually be viable at world market prices.

Thus, reforms to make commercial policy more explicit should accompany efforts to make the currency convertible on current account. This paper has suggested the simultaneous tariffication of quantitative restrictions on competing imports and the elimination of implicit export taxes on energy and material inputs as the economy moves quickly to a market-based system. Once made explicit, the highest tariffs in the cascade can then be phased down step by step to a low, uniform level over a preannounced 5- to 10-year time horizon. The

---

9. That the international convertibility of the ruble on capital account comes last rather than first in the optimum order of economic liberalization is well recognized by Aganbegyan (1988, 25–44) and is discussed at some length in McKinnon (1991a).

newly marketized economy would then converge to free foreign trade at a more deliberate pace that better recognizes the problem of overcoming distortions from the preexisting system of protection.

Acknowledgments

The author would like to thank John Hussman, Peter Kenen, David Robinson, John Williamson, and Michael Treadway for their help in preparing this paper.

The Transition to Convertibility in Eastern Europe: A Monetary View

Peter Bofinger

This paper discusses alternative options for the transition to currency convertibility in Eastern Europe. It analyzes the issue of convertibility not in isolation but from the perspective of an exchange rate regime that is compatible with the requirements of the transformation process. The rationale for this approach is quite intuitive: problems of convertibility can be assessed in a meaningful way only if it has been decided in terms of which other assets, at which exchange rate, and under which other institutional arrangements (intervention facilities, rules for exchange rate adjustment, etc.) the national currency will be made convertible. These issues will be addressed primarily under the criterion of monetary stability. It will be shown that all solutions that provide a stable "nominal anchor" for the transformation process will also enhance the microeconomic efficiency and competitiveness of the former socialist economies.

The focus of the paper is on the Eastern European countries, with the exception of the Soviet Union. Because of the economic and political weight of this country, its integration in the world economy will require an international effort similar to the foundation of the Bretton Woods system in 1944.

After a short survey of the status quo in the section that follows, subsequent sections present the options for the exchange rate regime and convertibility as well as the interrelationships between the two; the main criteria for the evaluation of exchange rate and payments arrangements; the role and the scope of monetary policy in the transformation process; the case for a fixed exchange rate peg of the Eastern European currencies vis-à-vis the European currency unit (ecu); and alternative institutional arrangements for enhancing the credibility of the exchange rate peg. The concluding section discusses the real-sector requirements for and the adjustment costs of a fixed exchange rate regime.

The Status Quo in Eastern Europe

The exchange rate and payments arrangements of the Eastern European countries are presently in disarray. At the supranational level, the Council for Mutual

Peter Bofinger is an Economist at the Landeszentralbank Baden-Württemberg, Stuttgart (Germany). This paper is part of research conducted under the auspices of the Centre for Economic Policy Research's project on The Transition from Socialism. *All opinions expressed are those of the author.*

Economic Assistance (CMEA), which had been nothing more than a bookkeeping institution to record politically determined foreign-exchange transactions, ceased to have any economic significance after 1 January 1991. Since that date payments among these countries have had to be made in convertible currencies and on the basis of world market prices. At the national level, widely diverging policies toward currency convertibility can be observed. Some countries still maintain a strict isolation of their economies from international interference. Their currencies are inconvertible, their official exchange rates politically determined and, because a multitude of product-specific coefficients apply, void of any economic significance. Poland, Yugoslavia, and Hungary have undertaken courageous steps toward the unrestricted convertibility of their currencies, which in the first two cases was based on a fixed peg of the national currency to a stable foreign currency. Czechoslovakia introduced current account convertibility for enterprises at the beginning of 1991. A central feature of the present initiatives in this field is that there is neither a coordinated approach among the individual countries for their transition to convertibility, nor a conceptual framework for the final integration of the Eastern European currencies with the European monetary order or with other international monetary arrangements. The transition to convertibility requires solutions for both issues. Some degree of coordination within the present CMEA area is necessary to avoid the negative effects of disintegration. Clarification of the final aim of monetary integration is indispensable to identifying adequate intermediate steps leading to this objective.

The Options

The search for a currency order in Eastern Europe that is compatible with a market economy (or with the transitional phases of the transformation process) encompasses two general tasks: the choice of an exchange rate regime and the choice of the desired degree of convertibility. The two are interrelated. The basic options for the exchange rate regime include:

- Flexible exchange rates for all the currencies of Eastern Europe vis-à-vis all other countries;

- A fixed exchange rate regime within Eastern Europe (or a subgroup of these countries), with flexible rates vis-à-vis the rest of the world;

- Fixed exchange rates between the Eastern European currencies and the ecu, with possibly a specific international solution for the ruble.

The form and the degree of currency convertibility are a second determinant of the international monetary integration of a country. For the following it is assumed that convertibility is defined according to Article VIII, section 2(a) of the IMF Articles of Agreement, which means unrestricted payments and transfers for current international transactions. Because an inconvertible currency is incompatible with a stronger international integration of the Eastern European countries, only two options have to be considered:

- Regionally unrestricted convertibility;

- Convertibility of the Eastern European currencies within Eastern Europe (or parts of it) combined with inconvertibility vis-à-vis the market economies.

The latter could be realized by establishing a multilateral payments union for Eastern Europe (Kenen 1990; Bofinger 1991; Brabant, this chapter).

The interrelationship between the exchange rate regime and the desired degree of convertibility can be demonstrated by analyzing the rationale for restrictions on international current transactions. As the example of the European Payments Union (Kaplan and Schleiminger 1989) shows, the case for regional solutions rests on the assumption of structural and unsustainable current account deficits of the union's member countries in their transactions with the outside world under unrestricted convertibility. Thus, the question arises whether the Eastern European countries (or a group of these countries) would experience permanent current account deficits, not financed by private capital flows, if their currencies became freely convertible. However, a forecast of structural current account deficits can only be made if one knows the exchange rate regime, the rates themselves, and the rules for their adjustment.

In a regime with freely flexible exchange rates the need for payments restrictions or a payments union is absent.[1] Even under fixed rates the balance of payments is not determined by exchange rates alone. Additional assumptions about the future stance of fiscal and monetary policies are necessary.[2] On the whole, it does not seem possible to make a case for convertibility restrictions (or a regional payments union) without clarifying the underlying exchange rate regime and the role of macroeconomic policies. An approach along these lines is adopted in the next section.

---

1. See Kaplan and Schleiminger (1989, 357): "Ingenious as was the EPU's automatic mechanism, it was obviously time-bound to an era of fixed exchange rates. . . ."

2. Aggregate current deficits are identical with the sum of individual current deficits. If a permanent aggregate current deficit arises and is not financed by private capital flows, there must be lenders present that are not guided by market criteria. Normally this is the central bank financing either government deficits or private deficits that do not find private creditors, or both.

The Criteria

The future exchange rate and payments regime of Eastern Europe has to be considered an integral part of the process of economic transformation. Thus, the criteria for its evaluation have to be consistent with the micro- and macroeconomic requirements of the transition process.

Among the microeconomic aspects, a more intensive international integration of Eastern Europe should contribute to:

- Creating undistorted price relations within national economies, and between them and the existing market economies (static integration effect);

- Enlarging hitherto relatively small markets and enhancing the degree of competition in them, which has been very low in the past because of the presence of large, monopolistic state enterprises (dynamic integration effects);

- Establishing a framework that will secure a larger inflow of foreign direct investment; and

- Achieving a level of the exchange rate that is compatible with the international competitiveness of the Eastern European economies.

Among the macroeconomic aspects, the international opening of Eastern Europe can contribute to the process of transformation by providing a stable nominal anchor in the form of a peg of the national currency to a stable foreign currency. Later this argument will be elaborated in detail. It will be shown, however, that the requirements for macroeconomic stability will also enhance the microeconomic efficiency of the Eastern European economies.

The Role and Scope of Monetary Policy in the Transformation Process

To clarify the macroeconomic contribution of the exchange rate regime to the process of economic transformation, a more intensive discussion of the role and the tasks of monetary policy is required. This is not an easy task, because economists and politicians admittedly know very little about the role of monetary policy in the transition from socialism. This gap in our knowledge may be due to the piecemeal nature of past reform efforts, which did not change the traditional role of money and monetary policy in the centrally planned economies: there money mainly serves as a lubricant of real-sector processes, financial links between the enterprise sector and private households are nonexistent—the money supply is "dichotomized," to use the expression of Wolf (1985)—and because prices are centrally determined, macroeconomic stabilization of the price level is not necessary.

In the emerging discussion elaborating the role of monetary policy in the transition from socialism (see Sokil and King 1989, Hinds 1990, and Nuti 1990a), two interrelated questions are of central importance:

- At which stage of the reform process are appropriate instruments and institutions for implementing firm monetary policies required?

- What strategy should central banks in Eastern European countries pursue in order to provide a stable monetary environment for real-sector reforms?

The Inflationary Impact of Real-Sector Reform

Although there is still no consensus among economists on the optimal sequencing of reforms, the importance of a firm monetary and fiscal framework at a very early stage of the reform process is now increasingly acknowledged (see, e.g., Sokil and King 1989, 19; Camdessus 1990; Kloten 1990; and Nuti 1990a). In fact, the 1980s provide impressive evidence of the inflationary impact of economic transformation. An analysis by Wolf (1990) shows that economic reform in China, Hungary, and Poland not only failed to stimulate structural change and growth but also caused high inflation, large current account deficits, and a high level of external indebtedness (Organization for Economic Cooperation and Development 1990). In Poland, inflation turned into hyperinflation; at the end of 1989 the annual inflation rate was 640 percent. Yugoslavia, which embarked relatively early on a process of economic transition, had an inflation rate of 2,700 percent at the end of 1989.

The inflationary consequences of real-sector reform are due to several factors. First, reform of the enterprise sector leads to increasing public-sector deficits, which are financed by the central bank. As McKinnon (1989) points out, the greater autonomy of enterprises over their own funds considerably reduces the revenue of the public sector, which in the past was financed mainly by direct contributions from enterprises and which lacks a comprehensive system of indirect and direct taxes.

Second, an integral element of price liberalization is the removal of subsidies on food and other consumer goods. Given downward price inflexibility of non-subsidized goods, these measures will lead to an overall increase in the price level, which in the centrally planned economies has been held almost constant for decades. Although liberalization per se only implies a transitory impact on the inflation rate, under the conditions of economic restructuring this shock tends to be translated into a permanent increase of the inflation rate and an ensuing wage-price spiral. In the past, the inflationary impact of reforms was due not only to different indexation mechanisms (Commander and Coricelli 1990, 32) but also to the relatively low bargaining power of enterprise managers (Bauer 1990, 20) in connection with "soft budget constraints" and the dismal incentive structure of self-managed enterprises.[3] The high degree of monopolization (Hillman 1990, 60) and the widespread existence of sellers' markets allowed enterprises to match the higher wage bill by raising their prices.

A third cause of inflationary tensions after price liberalization is the existence of a monetary overhang, which is regarded as a typical concomitant of the central planning process.[4] This excess supply of money becomes virulent as soon as traditional forms of rationing at administratively set prices are replaced by the market mechanism. Although the price shock caused by the spending of excess money balances is also of a transitory nature, in the specific environment of a transforming economy one has to expect that it will lead to a permanent increase in the inflation rate. In principle, forced savings could be reduced by a currency reform to adjust the money stock to money demand at an unchanged price level. However, as the reduction of East German savings in the process of German monetary unification shows, such measures are extremely unpopular (Nuti 1990a, 17). Thus, governments will hesitate before deciding on a general reduction of savings accounts.

The Real Costs of Inflation

In an economy undergoing transformation, the welfare costs of inflation are higher than in market economies, where an efficient allocation of resources already exists. Among the various components of these costs (for a survey see Garfinkel 1989), the reduced information content of relative price changes seems to be a serious problem for the Eastern European countries with their already extremely distorted price structures. The blurring of relative and absolute price changes makes it difficult for enterprises to find out the relative price structure and to discover a basis for specialization that is compatible with a competitive

---

3. See Hinds (1990, 35): "If workers do not believe in the seriousness of the government's stabilization program, their best bet is to keep on increasing their wages to maintain or improve their acquisitive power vis-à-vis the rest of the economy. If they become convinced that the government is serious, and their company faces bankruptcy (or that they may be fired), their best bet is again to increase their wages to extract as much as they can from the enterprise before they become unemployed."

4. See Wolf (1985). According to Walras's law the excess supply of money mirrors rationing on goods markets (Commander and Coricelli 1990, 3). Hinds (1990, 5) shows that a rationing system can only achieve its objectives if the supply of the composite money exceeds the supply of rationing entitlements.

environment. Additional welfare losses are created if inflation leads to the hoarding of goods, which aggravates the prevailing shortage situation and the real costs associated with it (e.g., long queues, black markets). High inflation also causes a reduction of real money balances; the suboptimal use of the national money leads to inefficient barter transactions and reduces seignorage. This creates additional incentives for the government to accelerate the increase of prices (Dornbusch 1990). In the end, inflation has enormous costs or, as Dornbusch (1990, 27) has put it, "In the process of high inflation all institutions melt."

The inflationary momentum of real-sector reform and the high social costs of inflation call for a stable nominal anchor as an element of the stabilization program in the more "advanced" Eastern European countries and as a monetary framework for countries just embarking on the path of economic transformation. The main question is, therefore, What kind of monetary policy is required under the specific conditions of economic transformation? Compared with the industrialized market economies, central banks in Eastern Europe face two serious problems: a very low credibility of their noninflationary policies, and a high degree of instability in both the financial and the real sector.

The Credibility Problem of the Central Bank

A major problem facing any attempt to achieve a noninflationary policy in an Eastern European country is the low credibility of the central bank's monetary policy in the transition phase. In countries with a rather long history of inflation (Hungary, Poland, Yugoslavia), it is in general very difficult to break the inertia of inflationary expectations (Bauer 1990, 25). An important reason for the low reputation of central banks in all the Eastern European countries is their insufficient control over the asset side of their balance sheets (Sokil and King 1989, 19). This can be changed only if large parts of the enterprise sector are privatized—which is identical with a substitution of "soft" budget constraints by stringent bankruptcy laws—and if the high degree of monopolization is reduced by more liberal foreign trade regulations. Present conditions, characterized by intensive interfirm credit creation, where the central bank is sooner or later obliged to provide the credit the enterprise sector needs,[5] are incompatible

---

5. Hinds (1990, 36) gives a good description of the failure of restrictive monetary policies in an environment that includes state-owned enterprises and foreign trade restrictions. A restrictive central bank lending policy first leads to increasing indebtedness between firms. The velocity of money rises. This process is facilitated by the high degree of monopolization in Eastern Europe. Suppliers and buyers are dependent on each other, which forces creditors to lend even to bad debtors. If this process of interfirm credit creation proceeds to its logical conclusion, the central bank has no alternative but to give in. If it sticks to its original policy stance, it will cause the bankruptcy of profitable as well as unprofitable firms.

with a noninflationary monetary policy. In this respect, the strong interdependence between micro- and macroeconomic efficiency becomes quite evident.

As the work of Barro and Gordon (1983) demonstrates, a noninflationary policy that the private sector regards as noncredible is associated with output losses. Depending on the social welfare function of the country, this outcome can be worse than an inflationary policy that is fully anticipated. Even after substantial privatization and trade liberalization, it will be difficult for any Eastern European central bank to establish by itself a reputation for being stability-minded. It cannot be excluded that the central bank will have to produce some periods of surprise deflation in order to convince private agents of its anti-inflationary stance.

In the case of Israel's successful Shekel Plan, real interest rates had to be kept at high levels for more than eight quarters to break the prevailing inflationary expectations (Barkai 1990). Given the relatively low living standards in Eastern Europe at present,[6] this price might be too high in the short term (Dornbusch 1990, 38), with the consequence that inflation becomes a long-term problem. Thus, the credibility problem facing noninflationary policies in Eastern Europe calls not only for far-reaching real-sector reforms but also for a mechanism to tie the hands of the central bank in a credible way in order to generate the expectation of low inflation among private market participants.

The Strategy Problem: Limitations of Domestic Monetary Policy Targets

A second group of problems for monetary policy during the transition process arises even if central banks are absolutely independent and even if their policies are credible. Operational difficulties are caused by the extreme instability of almost all the parameters needed to determine domestic targets for monetary policy and to assess their actual stance. For a policy of monetary targeting (with flexible exchange rates vis-à-vis foreign currencies), a stable trend path of potential output and of the velocity of money is required. In addition, the central bank has to determine a minimum inflation rate that it regards as compatible with price stability or that it will tolerate in order to avoid unacceptable unemployment risks.

The determination of the trend growth rate of potential output is impaired by the fact that the capital stock and capital productivity are strongly affected by the transformation process. The opening of national markets to the world market

---

6. See Institute for International Finance (1990), which comes to the conclusion that the former socialist European countries have living standards well below those of most market economies.

may necessitate the closing of at least some production plants and investments in others to ensure their competitiveness. On the other hand, the replacement of the central planning mechanism with the incentives of the market process and the economies of scale achieved by a better integration in world markets can considerably improve the productivity of capital. Both effects, which are difficult to quantify *ex ante*, will lead to substantial breaks in the time series used to estimate the trend growth of potential output.

A specific requirement for a policy of monetary targeting is a reliable long-term trend of the velocity of money. During the transformation phase, however, a high degree of instability of this parameter is to be expected. The creation of a private commercial banking system and private financial markets, the increasing responsibility of enterprises over their financial funds, and the introduction of modern payments systems and techniques will lead to relationships between money and nominal variables that can be quite different from past values. Currency substitution between national currencies and the deutsche mark or the dollar, which are intensively used as parallel currencies in some socialist countries, is an additional source of instability of the velocity of money. The definition of a nominal quantity-of-money path as a nominal anchor for real-sector reform is also impaired by the fact that successful stabilization will increase the demand for money and thus reduce its velocity (Nuti 1990a, 10).[7]

A third determinant of monetary targets is a target inflation rate that the central bank can tolerate. As already mentioned, a temporary increase of prices is a normal consequence of the liberalization process and should not be resisted by means of monetary policy. The experience with the Austral and Shekel plans shows that it is not easy to forecast the change in the price level required after the removal of subsidies and by the transition from central planning to market-determined prices. If the monetary overhang is not reduced by a currency reform, an additional adjustment of the price level will be required. This effect is difficult to quantify. It depends crucially on estimates of the equilibrium money demand, which are not easy in an environment containing black markets, parallel currencies, and strong shifts in all behavioral patterns.

In sum, the reform process is associated with a high variance of potential output, velocity, and price-level forecasts. This creates serious problems for a strategy that uses a preannounced monetary target as a nominal anchor for the stabilization process. The same applies to any kind of interest rate policy. During the transformation period, the interest rate will be even more misleading as a monetary target than it is in market economies. The real interest rate is extremely difficult to determine under the conditions of a widespread price reform; moreover, because of real-sector instability, variations in the growth rate of output

---

7. Barkai (1990) has demonstrated this for Israel.

do not necessarily indicate a response to monetary policy. It is not even clear whether the real rate of interest should be positive or negative during the transition process (Nuti 1990a, 15).

The strategy problems associated with domestic intermediate targets of monetary policy do not mean that it is impossible to pursue a restrictive monetary policy on the basis of such aggregates. The difficult diagnostic problems suggest, however, that a central bank that wants to succeed with its stabilization policy will have to apply a policy with a restrictive bias in order to compensate for possible forecast errors. Thus, the overdose of restriction that is associated with the strategy problem causes specific real costs, which have to be added to the real costs of the credibility problem.

A Solution to the Strategy Problem: Nominal Exchange Rate Targets

The specific conditions of economic transformation create a serious dilemma for monetary policy. On the one hand, they require a very stringent macroeconomic framework from the outset. On the other hand, as we have seen, they make it almost impossible for a central bank to build up the necessary reputation and to develop a monetary policy strategy based on targets for a monetary aggregate or interest rates.

Alternative solutions to the credibility problem are discussed in the next section. Here we analyze whether a nominal exchange rate target could provide a better anchor for real-sector reforms policy than a domestic intermediate target with flexible exchange rates.

Drawbacks of Flexible Exchange Rates

The strategy of an exchange rate peg to a stable monetary unit provided by one or several foreign central banks is suggested above all by the literature on exchange rate policies for developing countries. The past shows no examples of developing countries that have floated successfully and independently on a sustained basis (Collier and Joshi 1989). The failure of a strategy of flexible rates in this context—which is identical with domestic intermediate targets of monetary policy—is commonly attributed to the inadequate development of domestic financial markets and their lack of integration with world markets. It is argued that a responsiveness of short-term capital flows is required as a stabilizer for temporary disturbances in the trade balance (Wickham 1985). In this respect, financial markets in the Eastern European countries are not very different from their counterparts in most developing countries. Another argument against floating exchange rates (and domestic policy targets) is the very small size of almost all the former socialist countries—except the Soviet Union and, possibly, Poland—which suggests that they do not constitute an optimum currency area.[8]

The Exchange Rate as Nominal Anchor

Using the exchange rate as an intermediate target of a noninflationary monetary policy requires the definition of a nominal exchange rate target. The nominal anchor role of an exchange rate peg precludes any kind of adjustable or crawling peg, which could be made identical with a real exchange rate target. It is also evident that a peg to a stable monetary unit can only be used as an instrument of domestic macroeconomic stabilization if restrictions on foreign trade—including restrictions on capital movements for current transactions and the practice of several exchange rates and of a multitude of differentiated currency coefficients (Daviddi and Espa 1989)—are abolished. Thus, the strategy crucially depends on unrestricted convertibility for international current transactions.[9] With this degree of convertibility, arbitrage of goods and services links domestic prices and the domestic price level to international prices and price levels. In contrast to the gradual approaches adopted in the past, this strategy provides not only a stable price level but also a nondistorted price structure from the outset. Seen from this perspective, a "heterodox" strategy achieving open markets, price liberalization, and a stable macroeconomic framework simultaneously seems again to be necessary. Its risks can be reduced by starting with an exchange rate that undervalues the domestic currency. If the initial price and wage level is too low, it can be raised in the adjustment process. Such a transitory rise in the price level will not lead to permanent inflation as long as the central bank sticks to its exchange rate

---

8. McKinnon (1963) argues that the currency of a small, open economy, which fluctuates against all other currencies, might be substituted in its monetary functions by foreign currencies. Exchange rate fluctuations lead to variations in the domestic prices of tradeables. Because monetary policy can only influence the price of nontradeables, an unstable exchange rate would lead to a high price level and price structure variability in such an economy, which would undermine the monetary functions of the domestic currency.

9. This would be compatible with Article VI, section 3, of the IMF Articles of Agreement: "Members may exercise such controls as are necessary to regulate international capital movements, but no member may exercise these controls in a manner which will restrict payments for current transactions. . . ."

target. An undervalued currency would also reduce the problem of the monetary overhang.[10]

Given the large share of intra-CMEA trade in these countries' total trade and the present inconvertibility of bilateral surpluses, the implementation of a currency peg and convertibility would be facilitated if all the Eastern European countries adopted this strategy at the same time. Such a coordinated transition to convertibility would avoid the disintegrating tendencies associated with the present national initiatives toward convertibility.

The main problem with nominal exchange rate targets is their limited credibility.[11] As Dornbusch (1990, 35) points out, stabilization on the basis of a fixed exchange rate will sooner or later call for a devaluation if it is not possible to stop inflation completely. A delayed adjustment would cause an overvaluation, the expectation of a devaluation, and the need to keep real interest rates very high to ward off speculative attack. In the end, an exchange rate crisis could lead to a collapse of the exchange rate arrangement. Portes (1990, 13) concludes that other anchors in addition to the exchange rate are required to make a regime change credible and effective. The following subsections discuss the possibility of enhancing the credibility of nominal exchange rate pegs by alternative institutional approaches.

The Ecu as a Pivot

The ecu has an advantage over all national currencies in that it offers a multicurrency peg. It is thus identical with an effective exchange rate target and eliminates the disturbances that might arise if the currency of a single-currency peg shows strong variations against third currencies. Although there would be no choice of the pivot, if the Eastern European countries participate in the European Monetary System (EMS) or a European System of Central Banks (ESCB), the ecu could be a candidate also for a unilateral exchange rate peg, especially as it has been given very positive treatment by the Eastern European countries in the past (Bartha 1989). In addition, the ecu has an advantage over any "tailor-made" basket, reflecting the exact foreign trade structure of a specific country, in that it is already traded in highly developed financial markets. The share of foreign trade of the individual Eastern European countries covered by the currencies making

---

10. If the exchange rate that guarantees international competitiveness does not suffice to reduce the monetary overhang, in some countries a currency reform might be required. To mitigate its political impact, a currency reform could be combined with the privatization of state-owned enterprises.

11. Nuti (1990b, 181): "In Poland today the choice of a fixed nominal exchange rate in the presence of uncontrolled hyperinflation makes no sense at all."

up the ecu basket—now about one-third of their trade to all non-CMEA countries—could rise considerably if several Eastern European countries adopted an
ecu peg simultaneously; it has already increased with the implementation of
German monetary unification.

In sum, a credible nominal exchange rate peg could serve as an effective
intermediate target for monetary policy in the Eastern European countries. It
considerably reduces the strategy problem facing monetary policy during the
transition process and the associated real costs. The question remains whether
an institutional arrangement can be designed to guarantee the credibility of such
an anchor.

Solutions to the Credibility Problem

Domestic Prerequisites

It has become evident that the low credibility of monetary policy in Eastern
Europe has important domestic causes. Credibility can be enhanced—and the
output costs of disinflation policies reduced—above all by changes in national
central bank statutes. These would include establishing the independence of the
central bank's governing board from political instructions, long-term appoint-
ments for the governors, and strict limitations on central bank lending to the
government. Central bank autonomy would have to be supplemented by measures to establish hard budget constraints for the enterprise sector; these would
take the form of bankruptcy laws combined with privatization and an opening
of national markets.

These changes on the domestic scene would have to be supplemented by an
adequate exchange rate regime, which can further increase the credibility of
monetary policy and its exchange rate peg. An ecu peg for the Eastern European
currencies could be achieved by any of three different institutional approaches:

- A unilateral peg to the ecu without any support from the EC countries themselves (the "Austrian model");

- Membership in the exchange rate mechanism (ERM) of the EMS, including
  participation in Stage I or II of the transition process to European economic
  and monetary union (EMU).

- Full transfer of all monetary responsibilities to an ESCB, which implies absolutely fixed rates between member currencies or a complete substitution of
  the ecu for the national currency (this solution would be a European analogue
  to German monetary unification [GMU]).

Because of political objections to the implementation of either of the second two solutions and a possible further delay in the implementation of an ESCB, synthetic arrangements that would function in a relatively similar way will also be discussed.

A Unilateral Peg to the Ecu

From an institutional point of view, the easiest way to implement an exchange rate target for the Eastern European currencies would be through a unilateral decision by the government to peg its currency to the ecu. A central bank only has to announce a rate at which it will buy and sell the national currency against the ecu. This approach, which is identical with the peg of the Austrian schilling to the deutsche mark, does not require formal approval by the European Community.[12]

From the perspective of credibility, a unilateral exchange rate peg is superior to domestic policy targets as it defines the "rules of the game" in an easily observable way. Private agents need only look in the newspaper to check whether the central bank is sticking to its anti-inflationary target. As the work of Barro and Gordon (1983) shows, submitting monetary policy to such rules tends to enhance the reputation of the central bank. In an environment of widespread real- and financial-sector instability, monetary targets or interest rates would make it very difficult for private market participants to assess the actual monetary policy stance.

Credibility problems remain, however, as a one-sided exchange rate arrangement of this kind is typically characterized by a strong asymmetry. Adjustment following any real or financial shock has to borne by the pegging country alone: interventions affect only its monetary base and its foreign-exchange reserves. The shocks would have no repercussions on present EMS member countries, as long as the Eastern European countries use ecu commercial bank deposits for their interventions.[13] Although a certain asymmetry of fixed rate arrangements is essential in order to discipline countries with an inflationary policy stance, all multinational fixed exchange rate systems in the past offered at least some buffers

---

12. The peg to the dollar adopted by Poland in January 1990, which stabilizes the zloty at a rate of 9,500 to the dollar, differs from the strategy suggested here, as the exchange rate for private households' transactions is still freely flexible.

13. The macroeconomic effects of intervention would be similar to those of the so-called intramarginal interventions in the EMS before the Basel-Nyborg Agreement of September 1987. Until that date, the credit facilities of the Very Short-term Financing Facility could not be used for these interventions. Thus, intervening countries had to use Eurocurrency deposits held with private commercial banks, which led to a similarly unequal distribution of the burden of the adjustment. See Bofinger (1989).

to provide for a more symmetrical response in situations involving short-term shocks. It is evident that a one-sided exchange rate commitment, especially one made by a country with weak economic performance, is bound to provoke speculative attacks. Thus, its realization depends crucially on the stance of monetary policy and the level of foreign-exchange reserves. In the literature (Grubel 1971) the ratio of reserves to imports is normally regarded as an important criterion for reserve adequacy.

To assess the adequacy of the reserves of the Eastern European countries, one can compare their ratio of reserves to imports with the corresponding figures for EMS member countries. As a rough estimate, one can assume that the reserve need for a country adopting a unilateral peg will be considerably higher than that of countries participating in the EMS, which have access to the very ample credit facilities of that system. Data for the EMS (table 1) show that countries with "weaker" currencies, such as Spain and Italy, hold significantly higher reserve stocks than do countries with stronger currencies. The reserves-imports ratios of the Eastern European countries would thus have to be compared with the 35.7 percent ratio of Italy or the 68.8 percent ratio of Spain. As the table

Table 1 Reserves-imports ratios in selected European countries, 1989 (percentages)

Country	Foreign-exchange reserves as share of imports
Bulgaria	31
Czechoslovakia	26
Hungary	19
Poland	53
Romania	27
Soviet Union	48
Yugoslavia	34
Belgium	12.4
Denmark	23.5
France	15.8
Germany (West)	25.3
Ireland	24.8
Italy	35.7
Netherlands	18.0
Spain	68.8

Source: Organization for Economic Cooperation and Development, *Financial Market Trends,* and International Monetary Fund, *International Financial Statistics,* various issues.

shows, the reserves-imports ratios of Hungary, Czechoslovakia, Romania, and Bulgaria are below the Italian level, although those of Poland and the Soviet Union are higher. None of the Eastern European countries has a reserves-imports ratio as high as that of Spain.

A second difference between a unilateral peg and formal EMS membership is the procedure for exchange rate adjustments. According to EMS rules, appreciations or depreciations of individual currencies require the consent of all participants. Thus, the EMS rules entail tying the hands of the national authorities, which is an essential element in enhancing the credibility of the exchange rate commitment. Under a unilateral peg, changes in the exchange rate target are entirely at the discretion of the pegging country, and therefore the target is less credible. This also implies a relatively high need for foreign-exchange reserves.

From the point of view of the EC countries, the extreme asymmetry of this arrangement has the advantage that it would not interfere with the functioning of the EMS or the process of monetary coordination in Stages I and II of the enhanced integration process. Matters would be different if the Eastern European countries chose a peg to a national European currency, for instance the deutsche mark. In that case, interventions as well as the buildup of reserves could have undesirable effects on EMS cross rates.

In sum, the asymmetry of a unilateral peg of the Eastern European currencies to the ecu confirms the skepticism of most economists about the anchoring role of nominal exchange rate targets. The lack of credit facilities and of sufficient reserves makes such arrangements prone to speculative attacks and impairs the credibility of the stabilization effort even if it is supported by domestic reforms that enhance credibility internally. The less ambitious Polish example shows that an exchange rate peg that is supported by a high level of foreign-exchange reserves and a very stringent monetary policy can contribute at least to a temporary stabilization of the economy. It remains an open question whether the severe output loss caused by this therapy (a reduction of real GNP by 25 percent and of real incomes by 30 percent in 1990) could have been avoided by choosing a more credible nominal anchor for the stabilization program.

Participation in the Exchange Rate Mechanism of the EMS

The main difference between a unilateral ecu peg and membership in the ERM is that the latter would provide access to the EMS's credit facilities and the common decisionmaking process on realignments. In addition, because of the bilateral intervention rates of the system, the peg would not be a direct ecu peg, but a peg to each of the currencies of the system (a "parity grid").

Membership in a European Central Bank System

The recent monetary union (Bofinger 1990b) between the two Germanys is a model for a third approach to the transition to convertibility. It is identical with the general framework suggested here in that it abolished all restrictions for international transactions and established a fixed peg to a stable foreign currency. It differs from other strategies, however, in that it completely replaced the East German currency with that of West Germany. This immediately transferred the high credibility of the Bundesbank's monetary policy to the area of the former East Germany. Thus, a credible monetary framework could be established from the very outset of the economic transformation without incurring the output costs associated with the time-inconsistency of monetary policies. This is reflected by the fact that there is no currency-specific risk premium on interest rates in East Germany. The strategy of German monetary union (GMU) also reduced the costs related to the strategy problems of monetary policy during the transition process: because of the relatively small economic weight of the former East Germany—its GNP is about 10 percent that of West Germany—the Bundesbank's monetary targeting is not seriously impaired by forecasting errors for economic aggregates (potential output, velocity of money) in the former East Germany.

Despite the many country-specific elements of the German solution, one has to ask whether a similar approach could be adopted by the other Eastern European countries. The European analogue to GMU would be membership of the Eastern European countries in a European Monetary Union (EMU), with the transfer of all responsibilities in the field of monetary policy to the emerging European System of Central Banks.[14] The complete renunciation of national monetary autonomy may seem radical from the present point of view. However, as the following quote from John Stuart Mill shows, the idea was quite common even before the era of the international gold standard, when central bank policy mainly consisted in the maintenance of gold convertibility:

> So much barbarism, however, still remains in the transactions of most civilized nations, that almost all independent countries choose to assert their nationality by having, to their inconvenience and that of their neighbours, a peculiar currency of their own. (Mill 1848, 176)

There are several important differences between membership in a monetary union and the two other strategies for an ecu peg. First, as already mentioned,

---

14. In the following, it is assumed that the ESCB will be constructed according to the proposals of the Delors Committee (Committee for the Study of Economic and Monetary Union 1989).

monetary union is identical with the surrender of national monetary autonomy to a European institution. If the common central bank system is federatively structured, the national central banks could be maintained in a legally independent form, as the US Federal Reserve Banks are, but all measures concerning the conduct of monetary policy would have to be decided by the ESCB council. According to the blueprint of the Delors Committee, this transfer of monetary responsibilities implies that national central banks would no longer be entitled to lend to their respective national governments. For the Eastern European countries, membership in the ESCB would result in the introduction of a hard budget constraint for the government. It would also limit the credit available to the commercial banks, as their refinancing would be decided at the European level as well. Restrictions on government lending and commercial bank refinancing would also spell the end of the soft budget constraints enjoyed by enterprises in these countries. Thus, EMU membership could only be achieved if it were accompanied by far-reaching internal reforms, which have already been mentioned.

A second difference is that, in contrast to a unilateral peg or ERM participation, exchange rates in a monetary union are irrevocably fixed. This means that the choice of the peg has more far-reaching consequences than under the other two options. It also means that the exchange rate cannot be used as an instrument of adjustment.

For the Eastern European countries, ESCB membership would have the advantage that they would obtain a stable monetary unit and a credible monetary framework for the process of real-sector reform. In contrast to a strategy of national monetary targeting or an (adjustable) exchange rate peg, the substitution of the domestic currency by the ecu would definitively rule out inflation emerging in Eastern Europe, as long as the policy of the ESCB Council is not inflationary. ESCB membership would therefore be the most credible approach to a noninflationary policy in the transition period. The irreversibility of the regime change, which is associated with the transfer of monetary responsibilities to the ESCB and the conversion of all financial stocks and flows from the national currency into ecus, would send an obvious signal to private market participants to adjust their inflationary expectations at once. This strategy would thus prevent the output loss and the emergence of a risk premium on interest rates (Dornbusch 1990, 34) associated with a noncredible exchange rate peg or a noncredible policy of monetary targeting. A further advantage of an absolutely fixed rate is that it would avoid real overvaluation, which in the literature is expected to occur in cases where capital account liberalization precedes import liberalization (Edwards 1989).

For the present EMS countries, membership of the Eastern European countries in EMU would pose fewer risks than their participation in the ERM. The transfer of national monetary responsibilities to the ESCB can be regarded as credibly tying the hands of the Eastern European governments, which would strongly enhance their commitment to a stable monetary environment.[15] It would prevent the dilemma that could arise for a national central bank during the transformation process. Although one has to expect that national interest groups will try to exert political pressure on the ESCB, this institution will be in a much better position to resist the demand for accommodating policies than any national institution. Some operational problems might arise for the present EMS countries, as the monetary management of the ESCB would become more difficult with the enlargement of the EMU to include the Eastern European countries. To evaluate its impact, it seems useful to compare the economic size of these countries with the size of the present ERM member countries: the aggregate GNP of Bulgaria, Czechoslovakia, Hungary, Poland, Romania, and Yugoslavia was about $400 billion in 1988, whereas that of the ERM countries was about $4,650 billion. The ratio of the two groups' GNPs is thus almost identical to that of the two Germanys before unification.[16] Given the relatively small economic weight of this group, the specific instabilities in the real and financial sectors of these economies (see above) would not seem not to endanger the process of monetary management in the EMU as a whole.

An Eastern European Central Bank System

From the perspective of establishing a noninflationary monetary framework for the transformation process, the EMU solution is superior to other approaches as it solves both the strategy problem and the credibility problem of monetary policy in Eastern Europe at relatively low real cost. In addition, it does not entail inflationary risks for the other European countries. The solution has several potential political drawbacks, however. First, it is not clear at what date an ESCB will be established; it is evident that the more reform-minded Eastern European countries need a stable monetary framework as soon as possible. Second, membership in a European monetary union cannot be separated from participation in its twin, European economic union. Participation of the Eastern European countries in this endeavor would have many economic and political ramifications

---

15. On this and other techniques for making commitments more credible see Kronman (1985).

16. In comparison, the population of the Eastern European group is about 100 million, or one-third the population of the ERM countries (300 million).

beyond the field of monetary policy—including fiscal policy,[17] regional policy, competition policy, and democratic accountability—which might be an impediment for the realization of such a monetary strategy. Thus, one has to ask whether a substitute for EMU participation could be devised.

For the countries that have already undertaken significant reforms, one might consider a politically independent Eastern European System of Central Banks (EESCB), which would be designed according to the Delors Committee's blueprint. Its council would be composed of the national central bank governors and of the members of an EESCB board. Its credibility could be increased by including representatives of international organizations (the IMF, the World Bank, or the European Community) in the EESCB Council. The system would issue a common currency, which might be called the East ecu, and which would be defined in the same way as the ecu of the European Community.[18] It would be the main task of the EESCB to pursue a monetary policy guaranteeing that its ecu notes are quoted at par with the ecu of the Community.

Compared with independent national central banks, an Eastern European currency union would have the advantage of being even less subject to pressures from national interest groups. The currency reform that would be required to translate all monetary stocks and flows from the national currency into East ecus could be used to reduce existing monetary overhangs in an indirect way. A common currency for Eastern Europe would also avoid the potential problem of currency instability between Eastern European currencies. The pooling of national reserves in a common institution would allow a better defense against speculative attacks. Nevertheless, support from the EC central banks might be necessary, above all the provision of credit facilities for foreign-exchange interventions. Membership in the EESCB would be open to all Eastern European countries (including the Soviet Union or its republics) as soon as they fulfill the criteria for an efficient monetary policy (including privatization, hard budget constraints, and fiscal consolidation).

---

17. A difficult issue is that of the coordination of fiscal policies in a monetary union. A matter of particular controversy is whether stringent rules or upper limits on national government deficits are required in order to prevent an excessive government debt on private markets. This topic has been discussed intensively since the Delors Committee's suggestion of a very far-reaching transfer of budgetary responsibilities to the Council of Economic and Finance Ministers (ECOFIN). An answer to these questions depends on the assessment of the market's ability to discipline overexpansionary national fiscal policies by imposing credit rationing or, at least, a risk premium on interest rates. Analysis of this subject would go beyond the scope of this paper. However, especially in the context of the Eastern European countries, a declaration by the European Community that a fiscally imprudent state will not be bailed out seems to be useful. See Bishop et al. (1989).

18. A similar approach was adopted by the members of the Latin Currency Union founded in 1865, which defined identical gold and silver coinage standards for the members' national currencies (all of which were called "francs").

Implications for Real-Sector Reform

Sequencing of Reforms

As the preceding sections have shown, setting price stability as a priority in the transformation process allows one to identify the reforms required in other fields in order to implement an ecu peg. Thus, establishing this fixed point facilitates the discussion of the optimal sequencing of reforms.

Participation in the institutional framework of a European (or East European) Central Bank System requires complete autonomy of national central banks from the instructions of their governments and necessitates a complete separation of central bank and commercial bank functions. This institutional setup would also enhance the credibility of central banks pursuing a unilateral ecu peg or participating in the EMS.

Because a strict limitation of central bank lending to the government is an indispensable precondition for all pegging strategies, a large part of the enterprise sector has to be privatized, and hard budget constraints have to be established. This supports the view of Hinds (1990, 1) "that the introduction of market forces in these economies should be centered on large-scale privatization of means of production." The Shatalin Plan in the Soviet Union explicitly adopts this form of sequencing.

The nominal anchor function of the exchange rate peg necessitates the removal of all restrictions on capital movements and on the free exchange of goods and services. The abolition of trade restrictions and the restoration of convertibility at the same time provide a solution to the problem of monopolization by exposing domestic enterprises to international competition. Thus, it is not a sequencing of reforms that is required but a more or less simultaneous achievement of price liberalization together with the creation of the constituent elements of a market economy.

Real Costs of a Noninflationary Monetary Framework

It has been shown that a stable monetary framework has important real advantages. It either avoids the real costs that are caused by strategy problems and by a noninflationary policy that lacks credibility, or it avoids the welfare costs of high inflation, which can be quite significant. However, most observers agree that all forms of shock therapy have significant real costs, too. Ideally, one would have to compare these costs of rapid adjustment with the benefits of having a stable and credible monetary unit. Unfortunately, the theoretical basis for evaluating the adjustment costs caused by differences in the pace of transformation is not very well developed.

The real costs of a rapid monetary integration were intensively discussed in the debate on GMU. It was argued that the irreversible locking of exchange rates could lead to an overvaluation of the East German currency, especially as the post–GMU productivity of East Germany is difficult to evaluate *ex ante*. Thus, given downward inflexibility of nominal wages, the integration process could result in a noncompetitive enterprise sector and high unemployment. However, fundamental trade theory shows that absolute cost differences are not relevant for foreign trade and that an exchange rate can always be found that guarantees foreign trade on the basis of comparative cost advantages. This argument calls for an ecu exchange rate that undervalues the currencies of the Eastern European countries. The temporary reduction of real incomes might be accepted by the population if they obtained in return a freely convertible currency, which considerably increases the spectrum of available goods. As basic microeconomic theory demonstrates, the welfare loss due to such a negative income effect can be at least partly compensated by a positive substitution effect. In the ensuing adjustment process, trade unions and employers can find a level of wages that is competitive. In the setting of EMU, a possible upward adjustment of wages does not entail the risk of permanent inflation, as the overall price level is tied to the ecu price level in Europe. In contrast to GMU, the leeway for a temporary undervaluation is higher in the case of Eastern Europe, because of the much weaker labor mobility between these countries and the European Community.

A second argument against GMU—and the rapid achievement of monetary unions in general—rests on the assumption that the denomination of wages in the same currency will lead to a rapid harmonization of the wage level throughout the union. This tendency could in effect be observed in the wake of GMU. However, it might have been difficult to avoid it under any other arrangement, because under a fixed exchange rate system East German workers—at least those who know how to use a pocket calculator—could always have calculated their relative wage compared with that prevailing in West Germany.

The real costs of monetary union could also rise over time if differences in productivity growth are not matched by differences in wage increases. It is argued that the absence of the exchange rate as an adjustment variable can cause unemployment. This assumes that workers can be easily persuaded to take a real wage reduction in the form of a devaluation that reduces their real incomes by changing the terms of trade. In principle, this argument is based on a belief in money illusion. However, in an environment with rational expectations it will not be possible to achieve permanent real effects by adjusting a nominal variable. Accordingly, after the reduction of real incomes through devaluation of the currency, workers will demand higher nominal wages, restoring the initial mismatch of wages and productivity.

Of course, this short summary of arguments against a rapid currency unification does not suffice as a comprehensive analysis of the real costs of shock therapies. However, a complete analysis of the real costs and benefits of alternative transformation strategies is beyond the scope of this paper.

The Convertibility Problem: What Remains?

This paper has shown that the issue of convertibility poses a host of difficult conceptual problems, and that declaration of convertibility is not enough to make a currency convertible. The move to convertibility has to be embedded in an overall strategic concept for the future integration of the Eastern European economies into the West. The most important question concerns the choice of an exchange rate regime that is compatible with the overall requirements of the transformation process. The criterion of a stable monetary framework calls for unlimited convertibility for current account transactions and a fixed exchange rate of the Eastern European currencies vis-à-vis the ecu. This arrangement will also foster the restructuring of the real sector as it enhances the degree of competition and sets the right price signals at the microeconomic level. As the experience in Latin America shows, the main problem with exchange rate pegs is their limited credibility. Several solutions to this problem have been discussed. Besides internal efforts to increase the effectiveness of monetary policy and intervention facilities from EC central banks, supranational solutions (EMU membership or the creation of an independent EESCB) should be sought to tie the hands of monetary policy as far as possible. This will reduce the real costs of establishing central bank credibility, which in Eastern Europe with its low income levels might otherwise be prohibitive.

With stable monetary policies a major cause of unsustainable current account deficits will be removed. A relatively low (i.e., undervalued) exchange rate for the East European currencies vis-à-vis the ecu will be an additional factor contributing to balance of payments equilibrium in the newly liberalizing countries. Thus, the potential risks of permanent balance of payments problems in Eastern Europe under full convertibility are not exogenous to the transformation process. They depend on the concrete strategies chosen for the reform of the national and the international monetary sector. The institutional framework suggested here does not seem to require the safeguard of convertibility restrictions. On the contrary, convertibility for current transactions is an important element of the overall transformation strategy.

Comment

Peter B. Kenen

The papers in this chapter agree on one vital point. A rapid transition to current account convertibility would help the countries of Eastern Europe restructure their economies. To join the world economy and thus use their domestic resources most efficiently, they must adopt world prices. They should import those prices, however, not try to emulate them. Bureaucrats cannot be expected to behave like Walrasian auctioneers.

This is easy to say but hard to do. Who will decide how the economy is going to adopt world prices? Where will they get the capital they need to implement their decisions? In my view, too much of the debate about privatization has focused on ownership rather than control. I understand the symbolic and political importance of shrinking the public sector, but I also believe that more must be done to nourish the private sector. Furthermore, the very conditions that call for comprehensive domestic reform make it hard to liberalize trade and payments and thus to import the world prices on which domestic reform should be based. Finally, the external environment facing the countries of Eastern Europe is becoming less favorable and less stable.

Jozef van Brabant examines these problems in the first half of his paper and offers some proposals for solving them in the second half. Unhappily, the two halves don't fit together. In fact, some of the problems listed in the first half make it impossible for Eastern Europe to adopt the solutions proposed in the second half.

In 1989, when the governments of Eastern Europe and the Soviet Union began to discuss reform of the CMEA system, many economists asked what these countries might learn from the experience of Western Europe after the World War II. The analogy was far from perfect, but there was an important similarity. The CMEA system was based on the use of the transferable ruble, which was not really transferable, and the CMEA countries sought therefore to balance their trade bilaterally, not multilaterally. This had likewise been the case in Western Europe, where trade was governed by bilateral agreements until 1950, when the European Payments Union (EPU) was created. It was therefore quite natural to ask whether a payments union like the EPU might be used to multilateralize trade and payments among the CMEA countries.

Some of us had doubts about the analogy, even before the collapse of the CMEA system. The economies of Western Europe in the late 1940s were market economies with fairly coherent prices. Although they were distorted by trade

Peter B. Kenen is Professor of Economics and International Finance, and Director of the International Finance Section, at Princeton University.

and domestic controls left over from the war, those prices could be used to measure profitability and impose market discipline. The governments of Western Europe were deeply committed to trade liberalization, and the clearing and credit arrangements of the EPU did not lead them to discriminate more sharply against the outside world. Furthermore, the EPU did not set the pace for trade liberalization; that was left to the Organization for European Economic Cooperation (OEEC). The gradual hardening of EPU settlements should be seen as a measure of its members' progress toward current account convertibility; it was not what made them forgo trade controls or discrimination against dollar goods. Finally, the EPU covered a very large fraction of its members' trade, including its trade with the whole sterling area, whereas a Central European Payments Union would cover a rather small fraction of its members' trade. The figures cited by Brabant are misleading because they include trade between Eastern Europe and the Soviet Union (and they are based on official exchange rates); this trade accounts for much of the region's total trade.[1]

With the collapse of the CMEA system, moreover, the analogy has broken down completely. There is no need to multilateralize transferable-ruble settlements because there are no longer any such settlements. In brief, the Central European Payments Union is a solution in search of a problem.

There are, of course, plenty of serious problems. There is the enormous shift in the terms of trade against Eastern Europe resulting from the shift to trade at world prices. There is also the disintegration of the Soviet economy, which is disrupting trade with Eastern Europe's largest partner. If the Soviet Union were willing to form a payments union with the countries of Eastern Europe, they would find it easier to cope with these hard problems. But there is no visible support for this solution in Eastern Europe or the Soviet Union, and even if there were such support, an economic obstacle would stand in the way: countries that expect to be structural creditors in a payments union will not want to join the union. This problem arose in 1950, during the EPU negotiations, when Belgium expected to be a structural creditor; Marshall Plan money was used for side payments to buy Belgium into the EPU (see Kaplan and Schleiminger 1989).

The same problem is sure to arise in trying to design a payments union for Eastern Europe, even without the Soviet Union. In Brabant's own words:

> Rather than extend nearly interest-free loans at a time of sizable external payments pressures with the market economies, the potential surplus countries have on the whole decided not to live up to their obligations

---

1. Using trade data based on official exchange rates, Brabant finds that trade within the CMEA area accounted for 40 percent to 80 percent of its members' total trade in 1989. Using data supplied by the Economic Commission for Europe, based on a uniform exchange rate of $0.50 to the ruble, one obtains smaller numbers for trade among the five potential payments union members. These range from about 15 percent for Czechoslovakia to less than 10 percent for Bulgaria and Romania. See Kenen (1991).

A Central European Payments Union would make this problem somewhat less serious, inasmuch as settlements with surplus countries would be made partly in convertible currencies, just as they were in the EPU. To that same extent, however, the payments union would be less helpful to deficit countries (or would have to have more capital of its own to bridge the inevitable gaps between its hard-currency payments to surplus countries and its small hard-currency receipts from deficit countries).[2]

Brabant wants the countries of Eastern Europe to form a customs union as well as a payments union (and he would even allow them to intensify their trade controls against the outside world). A customs union, he says, would not cause much trade diversion; as Eastern Europe's imports from the outside world have fallen to rock-bottom levels, there isn't much trade to divert. Nevertheless, a customs union would cause trade creation because the economies of Eastern Europe are currently competitive but potentially complementary. Finally, Brabant believes that a customs union would help to multilateralize trade in Eastern Europe and discourage the use of negotiated prices that have no relationship to world prices.

Unfortunately, the low level of trade with the outside world and the possibility of complementarities within the Eastern European economies do not tell us very much about the amounts of trade diversion and trade creation that would result from a customs union. These have to be measured by comparing trade under a customs union with the trade that would take place without discrimination against the outside world. The welfare effects of a second-best regime must be defined with reference to the corresponding first-best regime, not with reference to the current third-best regime, especially when everyone agrees that the third-best regime is very close to being the worst of all possible worlds. It does not make much sense, moreover, for the countries of Eastern Europe to invest in exploiting the complementaries afforded by a customs union if the union itself is going to be a temporary way station on the road to membership in the European Community. This would involve a costly two-step process: restructuring production to participate effectively in the customs union, then restructuring all over again in order to exploit the opportunities afforded by EC membership. To put the same point more generally, a customs union for Eastern Europe might turn out to be a move away from the basic objective, which is the rapid liberalization of trade and payments with the outside world, culminating in current account convertibility, in order for Eastern Europe to import world prices and thus reallocate resources most efficiently.

---

2. A Central European Payments Union would also ameliorate the problem by allowing a member to use a bilateral surplus with one partner for meeting bilateral deficits with other partners. As Brabant notes, however, the most worrisome deficits are with the market economies, not with the other Eastern European countries.

If the ultimate aim of these countries is EC membership, we should perhaps be looking for interim arrangements involving the Community, including credit arrangements linked to the use of IMF credit. The countries of Eastern Europe badly need balance of payments financing, but they need it from the outside world, not from one another.

Comment

Dariusz K. Rosati

These three interesting and insightful papers broaden significantly our knowledge of the problems of the transition from central planning to a market economy. All three authors support the idea of currency convertibility in the Central European economies, and all argue that convertibility can only be introduced gradually.

Jozef van Brabant's paper discusses the need for and possibilities of establishing a multilateral payments facility in the form of a Central European Payments Union (CEPU). The paper starts by recalling the characteristic deficiencies of the traditional CMEA trade regime, and suggests that full current account convertibility is not feasible at present in many of the former CMEA countries because of structural and institutional constraints. He then offers three supporting arguments for his proposal.

The first is a historical argument referring to the successful functioning of the European Payments Union in the 1948–58 period in Western Europe. Brabant sees far-reaching analogies between the economic situation of the Western European countries in the early postwar period and the present economic conditions of Eastern Europe. A payments union, he argues, was then and could again be a means to alleviate a shortage of foreign exchange in a situation of chronic balance of payments deficits, and a way station on the road to full convertibility of domestic currencies.

Historical analogies may, however, be deceptive. In the late 1940s and early 1950s most of the Western European countries already had a rational price structure in place, and comprehensive markets for products and resources already existed. The EPU was essentially meant to allow for mutual trade expansion by overcoming the liquidity shortage. The assumption was that Western Europe as a region did not have to run a structural balance of payments deficit. In contrast,

---

Dariusz K. Rosati is Director of the Foreign Trade Research Institute, Warsaw, and a Professor in the Warsaw School of Economics.

the former CMEA member states' fundamental task is to restructure their economies profoundly and to change existing trade patterns accordingly; thus, trade diversion seems to be at least as important a goal for them as trade creation. But to accomplish this restructuring, developed market institutions (including an undistorted price system) and a strong private sector are necessary. These are missing in Eastern Europe for the time being. Furthermore, the smaller CMEA countries are likely to develop structural deficits with the Soviet Union and with the West alike, if they are to avoid a very deep recession in the early stages of the transformation. Thus, the present situation of the CMEA countries differs significantly from that of the Western European countries some 40 years ago.

The economic argument for a CEPU is derived from the principle of comparative advantage. Brabant argues that the reduction of intra–CMEA trade, due primarily to the apparent shortage of foreign exchange, may also lead to a discontinuation of (or sharp fall in) economically justified trade, thus resulting in a loss of welfare. Although this possibility cannot be dismissed, it is difficult to explain why this should not happen also in trade with the Western economies—which has always been settled in convertible currencies—and therefore why one should not envisage a similar trade-supporting mechanism for trade with the West. Under Brabant's proposal, the CEPU would create an additional incentive for intra–CMEA trade, discriminating against trade with the Western countries and slowing down the process of necessary restructuring. Thus, the economic argument calls rather for more capital inflows to Central Europe to maintain and expand welfare-increasing trade, and not for the introduction of an additional trade-distorting mechanism in the form of a geographically limited payments union.

The financial argument for the proposal relies on the proposition that the CMEA countries will suffer from a chronic foreign-exchange shortage for many years to come. A CEPU, with a substantial financial contribution from the European Community, would therefore provide a convenient mechanism to overcome this constraint. This may be true indeed, but it may also be argued that the present foreign-exchange shortage results from inefficient foreign-exchange allocation schemes, distorted prices, overvalued exchange rates, and wrong monetary policies. The recent experience of Poland demonstrates that the dollar shortage syndrome may quickly disappear after restrictive financial policies are introduced and consistently pursued.

Thus, none of Brabant's three arguments are really convincing. But what is perhaps more important is that his proposal may have simply come too late to be taken as a realistic alternative. Poland introduced so-called internal convertibility of the domestic currency back in January 1990, and Czechoslovakia has followed in 1991. Thus, for these countries, a CEPU would not be an intermediate step toward convertibility, but rather a step backward. The other former CMEA countries, except for the Soviet Union, have not expressed an immediate interest in establishing a multilateral payments facility for the purpose of intra–CMEA trade financing.

In the case of Poland, the share of the CMEA countries in total trade declined substantially from 46 percent in 1988 to 31 percent in 1990; the share of the Soviet Union was reduced from 24 percent to 18 percent. To create a CEPU to accommodate the needs of one partner only (the Soviet Union) is not a very appealing proposition for the other countries; on the other hand, to create it only for the smaller ex–CMEA countries does not make much sense, as their mutual trade is relatively small.

Peter Bofinger's paper puts the convertibility issue within the broader framework of stabilization policies and institutional reforms during the transition to a market economy. Convertibility is seen here only as an endogenous policy measure, dependent on the optimal foreign-exchange regime to be adopted in the process of transition. The author considers inflation to be the main danger in the transition, and he argues that monetary policies cannot be very effective in curbing inflation because of the high volatility of key parameters (money velocity, real income, expectations) and the low credibility of the central banks in these countries. Under these circumstances, a stable exchange rate provides the only reliable nominal anchor in the stabilization process. Thus, the best solution for the Central European countries (excluding the Soviet Union) is to peg their currencies to the ecu. Such a regime, accompanied by restrictive monetary policies (including positive real interest rates), ensures that the exchange rate will serve as an effective protection against inflation.

This proposition, which seems quite compatible with the standard IMF approach to stabilization, is certainly based on powerful economic logic, but the empirical evidence on the anti-inflationary power of such policies, observed in several countries, raises some concern.

First, the increase in inflation that is likely to occur during the initial phase of stabilization should be seen in large part as a corrective price increase rather than an autonomous phenomenon. It substitutes for shortages, thus eliminating repressed inflation, and the overall inflationary disequilibrium is likely to fall rather than increase, contrary to Bofinger's warning.

Second, to adopt a fixed exchange rate right at the beginning of the stabilization program may be inefficient and even counterproductive, if prices are not liberalized first. Under such conditions, the initial devaluation must be large enough to anticipate the corrective inflation resulting from price liberalization; but, as the Polish stabilization demonstrated, the extent of the corrective inflation may be difficult to predict. The initial overdevaluation leads invariably to a contraction of output due to structural rigidities in the economies in transition, and has a substantial inflationary impact as well, through an increase in the prices of imported inputs. The use of a fixed exchange rate as a nominal anchor may therefore be less anti-inflationary than expected, and at the same time more contractionary than expected. The costs of this option should be weighed against the benefits, and it may well be argued that fixing the exchange rate should be postponed until price liberalization is completed and the bulk of the pass-through effects have been absorbed. In such a case, the whole concept of a nominal anchor is open to question, and a more flexible approach may be needed, with restrictive monetary and fiscal policies the main anti-inflationary instruments during the initial phase of stabilization.

In discussing the possibilities for currency convertibility in Eastern Europe, Bofinger stresses that the credibility issue can be solved through adopting an exchange rate peg. Three institutional approaches are evaluated: a unilateral peg to the ecu, membership in the EMS, and full transfer of all monetary responsibilities to a European System of Central Banks. However, the second option is not feasible economically, and the third is politically unrealistic; thus, a unilateral peg to the ecu is perhaps the best immediate solution.

McKinnon's paper discusses the case within which distorted producer prices lead to immiserizing trade. Using a two-goods, two-inputs model of production and trade, McKinnon explains how production with negative value added (at international prices) could occur in industries making intensive use of local inputs (e.g., energy) with artificially low domestic prices. Under such conditions a devaluation coupled with trade liberalization (which is a necessary component of standard stabilization programs) leads to further welfare losses, as the cost of tradeable inputs increases even further. The solution is temporary protection through tariffs, which allow the value-subtracting industries to restructure, substituting other inputs (especially labor) for those that had been used excessively.

McKinnon's analysis is interesting, but it applies only to the very special case of an economy with two distinctive features: overuse of locally supplied tradeable material inputs in manufacturing, and domestic prices for those inputs that are severely distorted with respect to both international prices for the same inputs and the prices of other inputs (including labor). Only the Soviet Union broadly fits this pattern; it does not describe the Central European countries, which have undertaken a number of partial reforms in the past and in some cases (such as Poland and Hungary) have already removed the worst distortions. Empirical studies of the Polish economy suggest that in 1986 there may have been some industries with low-value-added production, but only a few cases of negative-value-added production (in the food processing sector) were observed.

This observation is confirmed by the behavior of the external sector in the Polish economy during the recent stabilization. The initial sharp devaluation was accompanied by extensive trade liberalization, which in the presence of a negative-value-added syndrome should have led, according to McKinnon, to a "wholesale industrial collapse." In fact, Polish exports increased in 1990 by 14 percent in real terms, and although total industrial output declined by 23 percent, bankruptcies of enterprises were few.

McKinnon's suggestion of temporary tariff protection to allow for orderly restructuring is in fact close to the familiar infant-industry argument for protection, and suffers from similar weaknesses. On what grounds should it be decided that a given industry or sector deserves protection, and at what welfare cost to the country as a whole? What is the guarantee that the tariffs will indeed be scaled down in the future? It has been recognized that the determination of governments to adhere to a rigorous tariff reduction plan usually diminishes over time, as political pressures and rent-seeking lobbying increase. Furthermore, the welfare costs of protection may be substantial, in particular in a reforming economy, where a thoroughgoing restructuring is needed.

One more point with reference to McKinnon's model is that, since this is not a general-equilibrium model, nothing can be said about the responses of the supply of other inputs, especially labor. But it may be assumed that the input substitution process would lead to increases in wages and other input prices, with the final proportions of inputs being less labor-intensive than expected. It should be noted that wages in Central and Eastern Europe have long been very low by international standards.

An important conclusion that may be drawn from McKinnon's analysis is that one of the first things to be done in the transformation process is to remove domestic price distortions. Then a devaluation is necessary to improve the relative prices of tradeables, and selective tariffs may be applied to facilitate industrial restructuring.

Comment

John Flemming

Ronald McKinnon makes a case for transitional protection to deal with a set of problems he associates particularly with the existence, in the planned economies of Eastern Europe, of industries with negative value added at world prices. This set of problems arises particularly from the inefficient use of underpriced energy.

The case for some kind of transitional relief is, however, more general. Low- as well as negative-value-added industries are threatened by a rapid move to world prices, which would not enable them to pay conventional wages. Whether such industries should cease operations depends crucially on how rapidly the resources thereby released would be reabsorbed into expanding

---

John Flemming is Chief Economist at the European Bank for Reconstruction and Development. At the time of the conference he was an Executive Director of the Bank of England.

industries. Some pessimism on this score may well be warranted. The reemployment of labor in particular is relevant both for economic efficiency and on distributional grounds.

A second consideration is that such an industry, if it continues as a going concern and keeps its labor force intact, may constitute a better foundation for the construction of new, viable industries than any greenfield. Whether this is the case, of course, is, like the speed of reabsorption of labor, an empirical question; however, it is particularly likely to be the case where the key change required relates to the design and marketing of the product.

My own view that these arguments carry substantial weight is reflected in the recommendations in the Houston Summit report on the Soviet Union (IMF et al. 1990) that temporary export taxes be imposed on energy (after a very substantial immediate rise in its domestic price) and temporary import taxes on certain imported goods. These taxes would have the kind of cascading structure advocated by McKinnon in order to approximate a uniform degree of effective protection in the successive stages of the industry in question.

I have suggested elsewhere (Flemming 1990) a temporary tax at the enterprise level on deviations of value added per man-hour from the national average. This proposal is designed to redistribute the quasi-rents incidental to the radical change in the structure of prices without substantially weakening the price signals and incentives for the reallocation of resources. The main reservation I have about such schemes is whether the rapid phasing out of taxes required by the last consideration is compatible with the maintenance of demand for products whose price (or quality) can be expected to be lower (higher) in a few years' time.

Jozef van Brabant's paper considers a similar case for transitional measures, with the added feature that countries should not resort to devices that, as a side effect, would reduce trade among the countries of the region. I agree with this point. To the (probably considerable) extent that the previous distortions in each country were the same, any set of temporary import and export taxes that might be adopted should be operated on a common basis as in a customs union.

It may be for this reason that Brabant seems to prefer discrimination through a payments union, for which there may be other arguments in the aftermath of the disintegration of the CMEA. However, I find much validity in Jacques Polak's arguments (chapter 3, this volume) against a Central European Payments Union. Some of the political arguments against the "ghettoization" of countries seeking association into the Western trading system would, of course, apply equally to a payments or a customs union. This may point to the need for a transitional tax on deviation in value added per man hour, which meets much of McKinnon's case (although there may be an argument for a cutoff at negative value added) without distorting or disrupting international trade.

Peter Bofinger puts the payments and convertibility question in the context of the monetary arrangements required for the stabilization of planned economies making the transition to the market. I am sure that he is right to reject monetary targetry in this context. Less radical reforms in the United Kingdom have destabilized velocity enough to undermine the feasibility of a broad money target. And uncertainty about the rate of change, and even the measurement and definition of the price level in the transition from nonclearing markets, makes the interest rate an unreliable indicator. Thus, the use of the exchange rate as an anchor, which always has merits for small, open economies, has particular usefulness in this case.

Given the difficulty, demonstrated by Poland and Yugoslavia among others, of choosing an initial level of the exchange rate, the credibility of an *exogenous* transitional crawl may well be higher than that of a rate that is fixed from the beginning. It is only an *endogenous* crawl that involves a target real exchange rate. Bofinger's emphasis on credibility is surely right, but how credible can a fixed rate be when the initial inflation rate is substantially higher than that of the reference currency? Although in the presence of capital inflow controls a fixed rate may prevent overvaluation as a result of capital inflows as the world becomes convinced of the economy's prospects, it does not rule out a cumulative loss of competitiveness if inflation takes time to fall into line—time that a crawl might give.

Given the location and aspirations of the Eastern European economies, I agree that the question of links to the ecu, the ERM, and the ESCB naturally arises. However, it is less clear to me how much credibility would be gained by the fuller institutional development that Bofinger advocates.

Discussion

Richard Portes remarked that, partly swayed by the arguments of Peter Bofinger and Peter Kenen, he had changed his mind on the merits of a payments union. Whereas before he had been agnostic on the issue, he was now persuaded that the proposal was neither politically feasible nor economically justifiable and should be buried. That would allow discussion to focus on the serious options for regional cooperation, such as that for a customs union. The primary problems of Eastern Europe are those of structural transformation, not of intraregional payments imbalances. Moreover, a payments union that excluded the Soviet Union would hardly be worth the effort, while one that included it would face the problem of persistent intraunion imbalances—a problem that caused a great deal of trouble in Belgium's relations with the EPU.

Portes also addressed the question of whether Ronald McKinnon's problem of negative value added is empirically important. Dariusz Rosati had mentioned some Polish studies on the issue, and there are others in progress. But Portes argued that it probably *is* more important than those studies seem to imply. How much of the existing capital stock is currently earning positive quasi-rents at world prices? The CEPR (1990) study of the impact of the Eastern European transformation on Western Europe assumed that the answer to that question is zero. That may be extreme, but it is not obvious that the right answer is greater than 20 percent or 30 percent. If that is true at current low wages, then there are a lot of industries that are creating negative value added.

Hans Genberg declared himself puzzled at McKinnon's argument that even industries with negative value added should be phased out gradually. It reminded him of the old story about the company that lost money on each sale but hoped to make it up in volume. Keeping industries with negative value added operating did not seem any more sensible. Even industries with positive but low value added ought to be phased out quickly if the alternative is a short period of unemployment followed by absorption into industries with much higher returns.

On the question of a payments union, Genberg recalled that the EPU is not the only historical precedent for such a venture. There have been many other attempts to create such institutions, for example in Central America, in Africa, and in Asia; in each of these cases the experience was much less positive than that with the EPU. He suggested that these precedents might give more guidance as to what could be expected in Eastern Europe.

Genberg expressed his sympathy for Bofinger's argument that a fixed nominal exchange rate could provide credibility and an anchor for monetary policy. One problem, however, had been touched on too briefly, namely, how to determine the initial exchange rate at which to fix. Establishing the credibility of a fixed exchange rate raises two problems. The first is a flow problem: how do you prevent the government from creating too much money? The other is a stock problem: how do you get the initial exchange rate right, so that there is no inherited monetary overhang? If you get it wrong, enormous adjustment problems can be created. For example, a 50 percent overdevaluation could require a 50 percent differential inflation; how can inflation of that magnitude be explained to the population as a necessary part of the adjustment process, and must that not undermine credibility?

Lawrence Brainard also focused on the issue of credibility. He suggested the need for a sufficiently long-term view of its determinants in order to know what standards to recommend and what speed of adjustment to choose. Experience in the Western Hemisphere indicates the danger of jeopardizing credibility not just through failure of the central bank to maintain convertibility, but also (as can be seen in the United States) through failure to fulfill another important central bank responsibility, which is to regulate banks effectively. Similarly, both Mexico and Brazil show that benefits achieved by pegging the currency at an appropriate level and adopting world market prices can be threatened if the credibility of the central bank is undermined by "black holes" in the commercial banking system. If enterprises in Eastern Europe come to discover that they will be bailed out by the government whenever they lose money, the mere establishment of convertibility will not suffice to sustain central bank credibility and avoid the emergence of Latin American–style inflation.

According to *Marie Lavigne,* the main problems in Eastern Europe are, as Portes suggested, real rather than monetary; hence the principal aim should be to create a customs union or free trade area for the region. This proposal often encounters the objection that a dismantling of regional trade barriers would invite excessive purchases of goods from the residents of neighboring countries, but this would hardly be possible unless there were something wrong with exchange rate policy! Lavigne expressed her skepticism regarding arguments that the region had already committed itself to trading multilaterally at world prices with convertible currencies, so that such arrangements were superfluous or even a step backward. One still heard assertions that dollars were certainly not going to be wasted on buying goods from neighboring countries. Hence there is still a problem of how to conduct regional trade, and one cannot bury the subject yet.

Ljubiša Adamovich supported the gist of Portes's remarks and expressed his disagreement with attempts to take the Eastern European countries back to some kind of reservation, in the form of a payments union or anything else. This is not what the countries want; rather they seek to be integrated into the mainstream of the world economy. Ten years ago there were similar attempts in the ECDC (Economic Cooperation among Developing Countries) talks: make the poor work with the poor so that they can get rich! Eastern European countries cooperating with one another away from the technological frontier would not have much of a chance at successful development either. Psychologically, people in the region are ready to step into the mainstream, even if it is risky.

Mario Nuti argued that there had been confusion between negative value added and negative profits. Doubtless the former does exist—as in the production of aluminum in both Czechoslovakia and Poland, where the energy used up costs more at international prices than the value of the output, or in some pharmaceutical processes. But these cases are exceptional. Were they not, the reduction in output and employment in Poland would have led to an *increase* in value added and living standards. Hence analysis cannot be based on the conjecture that people are so silly as to persist in operating systems that create widespread negative value added. The systems are inefficient and there are no automatic responses, but eventually even planners learn to weed out activities that subtract value.

The ultimate argument against the CEPU is that there is no demand for it. It should nonetheless not be dismissed as lightly as it is now, since a payments union does not preclude making progress toward convertibility in other ways.

Reinforcing Nuti's opening point, *Jan Kregel* argued that asking whether existing capital equipment will still be in use in a few years' time is *not* the same as deciding whether value added is positive or negative. What we should be asking is whether the existing enterprises will still be in operation. To ask the question in terms of capital equipment is to rule out the possibility of corporate reorganization that might allow the existing assets to be used in a different way. Portes was essentially ruling out that possibility. Kregel argued that a CEPU could be thought of as a way of granting enterprises a grace period that would permit such corporate restructuring.

Replying to the discussion, *Peter Bofinger* agreed with John Flemming that one could have a crawling peg rather than a fixed exchange rate, but he insisted that it was vital that the rate of crawl be determined exogenously and not as a function of the rate of inflation. He also agreed with Rosati and Flemming that the exchange rate peg should be chosen after price reform rather than before; this would still help ensure that a transitory price shock did not get translated into a permanent increase in the rate of inflation. Genberg was right to point to the difficulties of choosing an initial exchange rate peg; those difficulties had led Bofinger to advocate initially choosing a rate that was clearly undervalued, and to rely on a credible anchor to limit the subsequent price increase to no more than the economy can afford. Finally, Bofinger accepted that black holes in bank balance sheets require bank restructuring before a stable monetary system can be established.

John Williamson, who had presented McKinnon's paper in the latter's absence, commented that the essential feature underlying McKinnon's policy conclusion was the past underpricing of energy and materials, not their local availability. Poland had suffered from that as much as the Soviet Union. If there are no possibilities of improving the performance of industries that produce negative value added at world prices, then clearly Nuti and Genberg were right to argue that the best thing to do is to close them down as quickly as possible. But McKinnon argues that it is possible to adapt, given time; that is surely a possibility, although we lack much evidence as to whether it applies to an empirically important class of cases. Williamson also noted that the difference between negative value added and negative profits can be easily seen in McKinnon's figures: at point A the two are identical since there is zero input of intermediates, but elsewhere the two differ, since value added is negative above line AA whereas profits are negative above the isocost line. In the long run one would want to exclude all points of negative profit as well, but in the short run there is a much stronger case for maintaining at least some of the production that generates negative profits (the low-value-added cases), since it will be impossible to transfer all workers to new activities quickly.

Jozef van Brabant emphasized that the payments union proposal was conceived as a mechanism to help the reforming countries to establish market conditions among themselves. The Flemming-Portes proposal to create a customs union among these countries was fine, but it would require a transferable currency, which they presently do not have. It was because of this need that he had argued that, as long as there is no convertibility in the Eastern European countries, and as long as it is impossible to divert their trade to Western markets without a strong terms-of-trade cost, a customs union will require something like a payments union. A payments union would be better than the old-style transferable-ruble bilateralism, and much better than the new-style barter or convertible-currency arrangements, since it would force economic agents to make a profit; and it will remain better than the alternatives until genuine and multilateral (including intra–Eastern European) convertibility is present.

Brabant explained that his purpose is not at all to petrify existing economic structures. Certainly the unjustified trade created by forty years of CMEA should be dispensed with, so that initially there will be a sharp and justified decline in intraregional trade. But the further compression of regional trade due to political obstacles, customs duties, and lack of a payments mechanism is destroying trade without justification. Brabant had no trouble accepting that with transparent markets and convertibility a payments union would be redundant, but the problem is that these countries do not have these advantages. Creating conditions in which microeconomic agents are able to work on their own account rather than having to worry about intracountry settlements is pro-market, not the converse.

Brabant agreed with Nuti that there is currently no demand for the idea, and with Portes that it is politically infeasible. Nonetheless, the proposal has some inherent logic, and if the dash for convertibility fails, there will be a danger of reversion to all sorts of bilateral arrangements. The CEPU might then come back into demand.

5

Three Pioneers

5

Three Pioneers

Poland

Andrzej Olechowski and Marek Oleś

Poland in the 1980s: A Centrally Commanded Economy

Like all the other socialist economies of Eastern Europe, the Polish economy in the 1980s was to a large degree centrally commanded. However, the degree of this control was gradually relaxed in a series of systemic reforms during the course of the decade. Liberalization was implemented in a context of soft and inconsistent macroeconomic policies resulting from a fear of social unrest. As a result of these policies, in 1988 and 1989 the economy was in a state of chaos, with a large monetary overhang, inflation running at 20 percent to 30 percent per month, budget deficits of over 8 percent of GDP, decreasing production, stagnating foreign trade, several different (implicit and explicit) exchange rates, and a large foreign debt.

The Official Foreign-Exchange System

Prior to 1982 the typical productive enterprise in Poland was insulated from world markets, its inputs and outputs were subject to central allocation and price controls, and its growth and development plans required official approval and allocation of the necessary means. In particular, enterprises did not have the right to initiate export or import transactions on their own but were obliged to use the services of the state foreign trade organization (FTO).

Andrzej Olechowski is First Vice President of the National Bank of Poland. Marek Oleś is Director of the Foreign Department of the National Bank of Poland. The views expressed in this paper do not necessarily represent those of the National Bank of Poland.

Social unrest and the emergence of the Solidarity trade union led in 1982 to the implementation of several economic reforms, based on the principles of self-dependence, self-financing, and self-government of enterprises. One of these reforms allowed enterprises to obtain licenses to conduct foreign trade operations, provided that exports accounted for at least 25 percent of the enterprise's total sales or amounted to more than 1 billion zlotys, and that the enterprise had staff with sufficient expertise in foreign trade transactions.[1] In another reform, producers were no longer required to use the services of only one specialized FTO but were allowed to select from among several FTOs for the handling of their overseas trade. The 1982 reforms also opened the door to the establishment of joint-stock companies with the participation of industrial and foreign companies as shareholders. Several FTOs were transformed into such companies, thus giving producers some influence over their strategies and operations.

In Poland during this period, FTOs actually took title to the goods they traded and resold them to the final purchaser. It was the FTO's responsibility to market the product, set its price, and arrange for all the details of the transaction. There was no direct connection between buyer and seller in a financial or a commercial sense.

To export or import any given product a license was needed. The objective of export licensing was to ensure sufficient supply for the domestic market as well as to avoid what the authorities feared would be cutthroat price competition among Polish enterprises on export markets. Exports were allowed only when the licensing authorities (the Ministry for Foreign Trade and the Planning Commission) were assured that domestic needs were adequately covered. Given Poland's low share of international trade (less than 1 percent of total world exports) and thus the highly elastic demand for Polish goods, FTOs were in constant search for products that could be sold abroad. The purpose of the import licensing regime (which operated using three types of licenses: open, general, and specific) was to ensure balance of payments stability.

Export prices were set by the FTOs at the level needed to make the deal. Although they tried to get the best price possible, the FTOs had a tendency to undercut the market to gain entry—a quite understandable trading practice given Poland's minor position in most markets. The price the FTO paid the domestic producer was, as with other domestic transactions, determined in one of three ways: by administrative decision, by regulation, or by contract. Administered and regulated prices applied to raw materials and semifinished products and accounted for some 40 percent to 45 percent of exports and imports. A special facility called an equalization account was maintained through which taxes were

---

1. This reform led to an increase in the number of licensed foreign traders from 109 in 1982 to 232 in 1983, 289 in 1984, and 361 in 1985.

collected on products for which subsidies had been paid in cases where the administered export price was lower than the domestic price.

Exporting producers were eligible for reductions in income and so-called excess wage taxes. The latter gained importance in the second half of the 1980s, when the government was seeking to mitigate growth in wages. An additional incentive to exports was provided by a system of special export bonuses granted by the Ministry for Foreign Trade, which were exempt from income and wage taxes. These bonuses were available only to producers that did not benefit from subsidies—that is, whose goods were sold in export markets at prices that were higher than their costs and than corresponding domestic prices.

Before the 1982 reform, FTOs paid producers in domestic currency. From 1982 on, however, exporters (initially the traders, but later also the producers themselves) were given so-called retention quotas, which entitled them to purchase foreign exchange up to a fixed percentage of their export earnings. The right to repurchase, and later to retain, part of their export earnings proved to be probably the most effective incentive to export. Imports financed from enterprises' own foreign-exchange accounts increased rapidly from some 3 percent of total imports in 1982 to 15 percent in 1985 and over 50 percent in 1989. The rules governing retention quotas were gradually relaxed—by 1989 exporters could keep their quota earnings in bank retention accounts denominated in foreign exchange, could spend those earnings on almost any kind of imports, could use them to pay for domestic goods, or could exchange them for zlotys either at the official exchange rate or at a rate determined in regular foreign-exchange auctions. Since the retention quotas were not uniform but varied with the degree of processing of the exported product and with some other variables, in effect each exporter (or group of exporters) faced a different exchange rate for its export earnings.

Foreign exchange for imports came from either an enterprise's own foreign-exchange account, a cooperating enterprise's account, or centrally allocated funds. Foreign-exchange auctions, which became especially popular in 1989, were another option. Requests for foreign exchange out of centrally controlled resources had to be approved by the Planning Commission (since 1984 by the Ministry for Foreign Trade) and the foreign exchange purchased at the official rate.

Formally, all transactions were carried out at the official exchange rate, which was set periodically by the central bank, the National Bank of Poland. The reform plan provided for a so-called submarginal exchange rate, that is, that rate which secured the profitability of 75 percent to 85 percent of hard-currency exports. In fact, that target was rarely met—for fear of increasing inflation, the zloty was kept overvalued throughout the 1980s, with the possible exception of two short periods following devaluations in 1987 and 1988 (table 1).

The policy of an overvalued exchange rate, the predominance of domestic targets, and the treatment of the external sector as a residual resulted, as one would expect, in a dramatic shortage of foreign reserves and a structural balance of payments deficit. This development is documented in table 2.

The Parallel System

In Poland, in contrast to some other socialist countries, individuals and households have for some time been allowed to own foreign exchange and deposit it in interest-bearing accounts in selected Polish banks. As the real interest rate on zloty deposits was negative from about 1974 on, foreign exchange (in particular the dollar) became the most popular financial asset—on 31 December 1989 savings denominated in foreign exchange accounted for over 66 percent of total household savings in the banks (table 3). Large amounts of foreign currencies were also used as a means of payment in several retail chains that sold for foreign exchange products otherwise not available in Polish shops; foreign currencies were also widely used in transactions of larger value between individuals (real estate, cars, etc).

In addition to these uses of foreign exchange, it should be noted that the available data do not reflect holdings of foreign exchange by individuals in the form of cash. Its size can be only approximated, but it is believed that this component of the financial assets of households was in the range of $3 billion to $3.5 billion by 1990.

Obviously a large (and efficient) market existed to intermediate between demand and supply. Although it was illegal to sell or buy foreign currencies, the prohibition was never seriously observed, and a large number of curbside dealers operated. That market was legalized as of January 1990, when the establishment of so-called *kantors*, or licensed foreign-exchange dealers, was allowed.[2]

Accelerating inflation and market segmentation rapidly increased the discrepancy between the official and the free market exchange rates; the free market rate was also subject to volatile short-run speculative movements (table 4). At the same time, however, the free market rate became an important and popular institution, an indicator of the state of the economy, while the dollar became the only stable reference point in an otherwise rapidly changing economic environment.

---

2. Private *kantors* existed in 1989 under individual foreign-exchange permits. The legal status of these and other buyers and sellers of currencies was comprehensively addressed only in 1990 under the new foreign-exchange law.

Table 1 Poland: retail prices and official nominal exchange rates, 1980–89 (1980 = 100)

	1980	1981	1982	1983	1984	1985	1986	1987	1988	1989
Retail prices	100.0	121.1	247.6	300.6	345.1	396.9	466.4	584.4	942.6	3,240.6
Nominal exchange rate[a]	100.0	111.9	185.0	199.3	247.7	315.7	379.5	583.8	958.4	3,696.4

a. Period average for the zloty-dollar exchange rate.

Source: National Bank of Poland.

Table 2 Poland: official external reserves, 1980–89 (millions of dollars except where noted)

	1980	1981	1982	1983	1984	1985	1986	1987	1988	1989
Gross official reserves	430.6	465.8	835.3	954.0	1,294.8	1,059.3	886.6	1,682.9	2,244.2	2,503.2
Imports in convertible currencies[a]	8,154.0	5,793.0	4,275.0	3,890.0	3,944.0	4,032.0	4,281.0	5,123.0	6,307.0	7,335.0
External reserves as months of imports	0.6	1.0	2.3	2.9	3.9	3.2	2.5	3.9	4.3	4.1
Prepaid letters of credit[b]	0.1	104.1	408.9	510.3	499.3	270.3	282.4	540.0	631.3	476.6
Gold[c]	303.3	188.0	188.5	188.8	188.8	188.9	188.9	188.9	189.0	189.0

a. Payments basis.

b. Included in the definition of gross official reserves.

c. Valued at $400 per ounce.

Source: National Bank of Poland.

Table 3 Poland: zloty and foreign-exchange deposits as shares of total bank deposits of households, 1980–89
(percentages)

	1980	1981	1982	1983	1984	1985	1986	1987	1988	1989
Zlotys	91	77	84	79	78	74	65	50	32	34
Foreign exchange[a]	9	23	16	21	22	26	35	50	68	66

a. Converted at the free market zloty-dollar exchange rate.

Source: National Bank of Poland.

Table 4 Poland: official and free market exchange rates, 1980–89 (zlotys per dollar)

	1980	1981	1982	1983	1984	1985	1986	1987	1988	1989
End of period										
Official rate	50.0	55.8	86.4	98.4	126.2	147.9	197.6	315.5	503.0	6,500
Free market rate	125.0	488.0	430.0	699.0	656.0	664.0	862.0	1,300	3,380	7,454
Ratio of official to free market	2.5	8.7	5.0	7.1	5.2	4.5	4.4	4.1	6.7	1.1
Average										
Official rate	46.0	51.5	85.1	91.7	114.0	145.2	174.6	268.5	437.2	1,700
Free market rate	125.0	286.2	396.9	585.2	637.6	651.1	747.8	1,030	1,979	5,565
Ratio of official to free market	2.7	5.6	4.7	6.4	5.6	4.5	4.3	3.8	4.5	3.3

Source: National Bank of Poland.

The Polish Economy on the Brink: 1989

Poland's exchange rate policy in the late 1980s has to be seen in the context of the overall economic policy pursued in that period. Expansionary monetary and fiscal policies, stagnant production, unfavorable developments on the external side of the economy, and accelerating inflation were the predominant features of the economic situation at the end of 1989.

The balance of payments in convertible currencies deteriorated dramatically. The trade surplus in convertible currencies in 1989 ($240 million) was near its lowest level of the decade. This outcome was magnified by lower-than-expected net private transfers and a historically high deficit on the services account—all this despite a series of significant devaluations of the zloty against the dollar in the second half of 1989.

These devaluations were, of course, strongly connected with Poland's accelerating inflation, but that was not their only rationale. The ground was being prepared for the elimination of price controls and the reorientation of exchange rate policy. The exchange rate, which at the beginning of 1989 was slightly above 500 zloty to the dollar, was set in June at 835 zloty to the dollar, and at the end of 1989 at 6,500 zloty to the dollar.

The Introduction of Convertibility: 1990

The stabilization program initiated in January 1990 established the exchange rate as one of two nominal anchors of the Polish economy. The zloty was made convertible for current account transactions. The market for foreign exchange for payments and transfers for current transactions was unified at an exchange rate of 9,500 zloty to the dollar, with some exceptions related mainly to transfers of foreign exchange by individuals.

Several considerations were taken into account in determining the new exchange rate. Among these were expected high inflation in January through March 1990, and the need to compensate exporters for the phasing out of the remaining indirect and direct export promotion measures; a margin was also set to allow for maintenance of the competitiveness of exports (in terms of labor costs for the whole of 1990). Competitiveness was also to be ensured by the second and more important anchor of the stabilization program, a near freeze on nominal incomes, to be enforced by a highly restrictive wage tax policy. The exchange rate resulting from these considerations was not significantly different from that prevailing in the free market, but was somewhat higher than the rates prevailing in the foreign-currency auctions, and much higher (46 percent) than the official rate in December 1989.

Equally important was a change in the exchange rate system. The policy of setting the external value of the zloty in terms of a basket of currencies was abandoned, and instead the zloty was fixed against the dollar. Fluctuations against other convertible currencies were to be accounted for on a weekly basis according to movements in cross rates. A peg against the dollar was considered most appropriate for "psychological" reasons, as it provided a stable exchange rate against a currency that accounted for more than 50 percent of Polish exports and imports in convertible currencies and was the currency most commonly used in foreign-exchange transactions between individuals. Another reason was the relative weakness of the dollar on international money markets at the time.

The New System

The new exchange rate regime was introduced together with sweeping systemic, legal, and institutional changes affecting foreign trade and financial flows. First, regulations governing the right to engage in foreign trade were greatly simplified and liberalized. Any natural or legal person wishing to engage in foreign trade can now do so without any particular authorization.

Second, foreign trade restrictions were almost completely eliminated. All quantitative restrictions on imports from the convertible-currency area were eliminated, and a unified customs tariff for commercial and personal imports was introduced with a temporary surcharge for certain consumer goods. This surcharge was eliminated by mid–1990. At the same time customs duties were eliminated, lowered, or suspended for a very large number of imported items in an effort to strengthen import demand for investment and intermediate goods. The number of exported commodities subject to quotas was reduced by almost half.

Third, the foreign-exchange system was reorganized. All export proceeds in foreign exchange are to be surrendered to the licensed banks (so-called foreign-exchange banks) in exchange for zlotys. The banks in turn resell the foreign exchange to the central bank, which manages the country's external reserves. Importers (which could be any natural or legal person wishing to import goods "and associated services") can purchase unlimited amounts of convertible currencies from the foreign-exchange banks. The National Bank of Poland is to provide these banks with the necessary foreign exchange.

Fourth, all other foreign transactions linked with a transfer of foreign exchange require permits, in the form of a general, open permit by the Ministry of Finance or an individual authorization from the central bank. Regulations concerning capital transfer have also been liberalized, but in a more limited way. For example, enterprises can freely extend commercial credits and receive short- or medium-term loans up to the amount of $500,000. Credits with longer maturities or in higher amounts require individual permits (which in 1990 were given by the central bank in liberal fashion). Similarly, Polish enterprises can open accounts with foreign banks under an individual foreign-exchange permit issued by the central bank.

Fifth, households retain the right to hold assets in foreign exchange. They are free to buy and sell foreign exchange on the parallel market through the *kantors*, which operate on the basis of individual permits. Individuals are quite free to use these assets as they see fit, although there are restrictions on the amount of cash that may be directly taken abroad.

Enterprises may maintain their deposits denominated in foreign exchange after 2 January 1990, but no new deposits may be made. Outstanding balances may be spent on imports or converted into zlotys. In the course of 1990 these balances decreased from $2.7 billion to slightly more than $0.5 billion. Indirect export incentives have been eliminated, together with the central allocation of imports and foreign exchange.

Initial Results

The stabilization program launched in 1990 was a clear break with the past and a course for which there were no obvious precedents. Past experience offered little guidance as to how the economy would perform. For this reason, the new exchange rate policy—even in the context of a tight monetary and fiscal stabilization program—was widely considered to be an extremely risky endeavor. It was feared that the phasing out of the direct controls that remained at the end of 1989 and the possibility of an outburst of consumer import demand would result in a large increase in the current account deficit, which would undermine the stability of the exchange rate and the overall credibility of the program.

These expectations were partly reflected in the balance of payments projections for 1990, which called for a trade deficit of $0.8 billion and a current account deficit of $3.0 billion. A stabilization fund of $1.0 billion was made available by the Western governments to support the liberalization of the foreign-exchange policy and bolster its credibility. Transitory pressure on the official exchange rate was expected at the beginning of the program, as was a temporary drop in foreign-exchange reserves.

The early results of the stabilization program have been different in many respects from what was expected (tables 5 and 6). The exchange rate policy proved of decisive importance for the outcome in the external sector of the economy, which in 1990 can be considered the most successful part of the stabilization program. Although it is extremely difficult to assess its quantitative impact on trade flows (mostly because of structural changes also occurring during the period), the real depreciation of the zloty and the stable nominal exchange rate were certainly the predominant factors behind a remarkable export performance. The sharp decrease in domestic demand was only of secondary importance.

In the case of imports the dominant factors were the drop in production, the high cost of domestic lending, and the presence of large (in many case excessive) stocks of intermediate goods. The removal of import restrictions started to have an impact only in the fourth quarter of 1990. It was also at that time that the distribution system recovered from its initial collapse due to inadequate capitalization and institutional changes. Finally, the positive effects of regulatory changes (the elimination of central allocation, access to foreign trade, etc.) on export and import performance do not need to be elaborated.

Capital flows differed little from those in 1989. Inflows of medium- and long-term capital remained very low because of weak investment demand. The large increase in net short-term capital reflects increased export activity, the liberalization of foreign-exchange transactions, and the technical inadequacy of the interbank settlements system. Finally, the increase in transfers is partly in line with the tendency of the last decade, and partly reflects assistance received from Western governments.

Prospects for the Polish Economy

The overall success of the stabilization program will depend on the continuation of the current foreign-exchange policy through 1991. The ability to maintain a stable nominal exchange rate will in turn depend critically on incomes policy. Other important elements that will need to be addressed include:

■ The shift to convertible currencies in trade with the former CMEA countries. Poland is faced with a decline in import demand in these countries due to the inferior standards of many of the goods (especially manufactures, traditionally exported to them) as well as to domestic developments within certain of these countries (such as the unification of Germany). On the other hand, many of the prices of goods traded with the CMEA countries were very low compared with world prices, and thus Polish exporters should remain competitive even after the introduction of payments in convertible currencies.

■ Although Poland's generally tight macroeconomic policy will not be changed, there will be important institutional changes and restructurings. In particular, an accelerated pace of privatization, the launching of restructuring programs, and major improvements in the banking sector are to be expected. These will result in strengthened investment demand. The impact of this development on the exchange rate will depend on the inflow of foreign capital, in the form of both credits and direct investment.

Table 5 Poland: selected economic indicators, 1990 (percentages)

	Jan.	Feb.	Mar.	Apr.	May	June	July	Aug.	Sep.	Oct.	Nov.	Dec.
Inflation rate[a]	79.6	23.8	4.3	7.5	4.6	3.4	3.5	1.8	4.6	5.7	4.9	5.9
Change in money supply[b]	32.6	5.8	6.8	6.6	6.0	5.8	9.4	8.5	5.0	4.6	5.5	1.6
Change in nominal wages[c]	2.5	15.4	40.1	−8.8	−3.8	1.1	10.8	4.8	7.9	13.6	10.5	47.5
Unemployment rate[d]	0.4	1.1	2.0	2.6	3.3	4.2	5.2	6.1	6.9	7.5	8.1	8.3

a. Change from previous month, as measured by the retail price index.

b. Change from previous month; includes "A" accounts and enterprises' "M" accounts.

c. Change from previous month, in five main areas of the socialized sector.

d. As percentage of total employment at the end of 1989, private agriculture excluded.

Source: National Bank of Poland.

THREE PIONEERS   165

Table 6 Poland: balance of payments in convertible currencies, 1989 and 1990 (millions of dollars)

	1989	1990 I	II	III	IV	Total
Current account balance	-1,843	181	948	712	-1,173	668
Exports	8,342	2,408	2,816	3,172	3,794	12,190
Imports	8,330	1,684	1,725	2,258	4,459	10,126
Trade and nonfactor services balance	12	724	1,091	914	-665	2,064
Interest receipts	382	114	116	166	185	581
Interest payments	3,469	1,076	830	979	1,025	3,910
Of which paid:	1,066	114	80	146	90	430
Net interest	3,087	-962	-750	-833	-935	-3,480
Unilateral transfers	1,232	419	571	611	328	1,929
Capital account, long- and medium-term	-2,843	-1,292	-846	-1,395	-785	-4,318
Credits received	-2,870	-1,288	-855	-1,396	-795	-4,334
Drawings	226	53	61	85	100	299
Repayments	3,096	1,341	916	1,481	895	4,633
Of which paid:	497	61	66	63	141	331
Credits extended	48	-7	9	1	10	13

Other financial operations, net	−12	3		0	0	3
Short-term capital, net	−25	−1,206	−693	−305	−99	−2,303
Errors and omissions	−256	397	−113	104	−325	63
Overall balance	−4,958	−1,920	−704	−884	−2,045	−5,553
Gross official reserves	−259	−333	−1,020	−1,496	392	−2,457
Liabilities	215	11	124	129	0	264
Debt relief[a]	2,089	5,832	1,539	2,086	1,274	10,731
Change in arrears	2,913	−3,590	61	165	379	−2,985
Memorandum: change in other nonfinancial assets of the banking system		−1,300	−555	−299	42	−2,112

a. Includes converted obligations.

Source: National Bank of Poland.

One of the most important measures yet to come will be a further liberalization of capital flows. The question that remains unanswered is how quickly this process should move forward. On the one hand, liberalization may need to be gradual, in tandem with the slowing down of inflation. On the other hand, a gradual approach could be self-defeating, if its effect is to retard the opening and adjustment of the Polish economy.

Yugoslavia

Ljubiša S. Adamovich

Convertibility of the dinar has been given a central role in Yugoslavia's fight against hyperinflation. In the reform program adopted by the Yugoslav federal government in December 1989 (Federal Executive Council 1989, 439), the new dinar was made fully convertible for current account transactions; this extended to the right of citizens to use dinars to buy foreign exchange from Yugoslav banks for any purpose. It was declared that for the first six months of 1990 the dinar would be pegged to the deutsche mark at an exchange rate of 7 to 1 and would fluctuate with the mark against all other currencies.

The government's reform program aimed to continue to liberalize imports as well as the system of foreign exchange. At the same time, the policy of export promotion and protection of the national economy was to be supplemented by stimulation of structural changes and new investment in the Yugoslav economy. Another important goal was to buy back a considerable part of the country's foreign debt.

The Yugoslavian Federal Executive Council (FEC) anticipated that the reforms would result in a fall in GNP in 1990 of about 2 percent from its 1989 level (selected indicators for the Yugoslav economy are presented in table 1). Personal consumption would have to be cut by about 0.5 percent, and real personal incomes would have to fall by 2.5 percent, while exports of goods and services would have to increase by 8 percent. Exports to countries with convertible currencies would have to be increased by 10 percent. Meanwhile imports of goods and services were expected to increase by 16 percent in total, and by 17 percent from the countries with convertible currencies (Federal Executive Council 1989, 452). A current account surplus of about $220 million was expected for 1990. The Law on Foreign Trade in Goods and Services, which went into effect on 1 January 1990, provides for a high degree of import liberalization, thus completing the policy framework for a rapid entry of the Yugoslav economy into the world economic system.

These reforms are evidence that Yugoslavia's answer to the dilemma of how to introduce convertibility has been to adopt a "big bang" approach similar to that in Poland, rather than the more gradual approach practiced by the Western European countries in the past, Hungary more recently, and possibly the Soviet

Ljubiša S. Adamovich is Chairman of the Department of International Economics, University of Belgrade, and a Research Adviser at the Institute for International Politics and Economics, Belgrade.

Table 1 Yugoslavia: selected economic indicators, 1980–89

	1980	1981	1982	1983	1984	1985	1986	1987	1988	1989
Population (millions)[a]	22.3	22.5	22.6	22.8	23.0	23.1	23.3	23.4	23.6	23.7
Industrial production (volume, 1980 = 100)	100	104	104	106	112	115	119	120	119	120
Agricultural production (volume, 1980 = 100)	100	101	109	107	109	100	112	107	101	106
Cost of living index (1980 = 100)	100	140	185	260	400	694	1,313	2,892	8,522	115,208
Official exchange rate, end-year (dinars to the dollar)	29.30	41.82	62.48	125.67	211.75	312.80	457.18	1,244.4	5,210.8	118,160
Net foreign indebtedness[b] (billions of dollars)	17.3	19.5	18.5	18.7	18.3	17.9	18.4	19.5	16.8	15.2
Trade (billions of dollars)										
Current account balance	−2.3	−0.8	−0.5	−0.3	0.5	0.8	1.1	1.2	2.5	2.4
Exports[c]										
Total	9.0	10.9	10.2	9.9	10.3	10.6	10.3	11.4	12.7	13.5
Eastern European clearing	3.3	4.4	3.3	3.6	3.6	4.1	3.8	2.9	3.0	2.8
Other clearing	0.05	0.5	0.8	0.4	0.5	0.5	0.5	0.3	0.2	0.2
Convertible-currency area	5.7	6.4	5.9	6.3	6.6	6.5	6.5	8.5	9.7	10.6
Imports[c]										
Total	15.1	15.8	13.3	12.2	12.0	12.2	11.7	12.6	13.2	14.9
Eastern European clearing	3.6	3.9	3.6	4.0	4.2	3.9	3.3	3.1	2.9	2.8
Other clearing	1.0	0.9	0.8	0.5	0.7	0.5	0.5	0.4	0.1	0.1
Convertible-currency area	11.3	11.7	9.6	8.1	7.8	8.2	8.4	9.5	10.2	12.0

a. Estimated at mid-year.

b. Until 1981, short-term commercial credits (as part of total credits) excluded three-month commercial bank deposits. After 1986, data are expressed at current exchange rates.

c. Data for 1987, 1988, and 1989 are expressed at current exchange rates.

Sources: Federal Statistical Committee (1990); National Bank of Yugoslavia (1989).

Union in the future. One year later, it is possible to begin to evaluate the relative merits of shock therapy versus gradualism in the case of Yugoslavia. Fighting hyperinflation, which in December 1989 reached 60 percent per month, and achieving the convertibility of the dinar proved to be extremely ambitious goals and exacted a very high price, at least in the short run. In judging the results of Yugoslavia's reform program, however, it is essential to remember the unique economic, social, and political characteristics of the country, and to take note of several indispensable conditions for the success of convertibility that appeared to be met in Yugoslavia's case but, as it turned out, were not.

First, the convertibility of the dinar was not supported by stable economic performance. Instead of a mere 2 percent decrease in GNP as projected, the decrease suffered for the whole of 1990 will turn out to have been between 9 percent and 10 percent—this after almost a decade of near stagnation. Thus, the current FEC will be able to claim two ignominious records: before the reforms were adopted it achieved the highest level of inflation in Yugoslavia's history, and since then it has presided over the greatest one-year decrease of GNP recorded in Yugoslavia since World War II.

Second, inflationary pressures still have not been brought under control. Instead of falling to the officially projected rate of about 13 percent in 1990, inflation remained high at almost 130 percent for the year as a whole (December to December). That level of inflation may be counted as progress compared with the hyperinflation of 1989, but it is far from the goal established in the reform program, and it represents the ruin of one of the most important anchors of the reform.

Third, the FEC was unable to win the consensus of all six constituent republics for the implementation of its program. The lack of broad popular support for the present regime is vital to an understanding of the current economic and political crisis in Yugoslavia. One of the most important aspects of the economic reforms being attempted in Yugoslavia is that they have not been accompanied by social and political changes as dramatic as those in the other socialist and former socialist countries. This has been one very important reason why many observers and analysts have questioned the quality of economic reform in Yugoslavia.

This feature of economic reform in Yugoslavia can be explained by the unique development history of the socialist system in Yugoslavia. Since 1948, when Joseph Stalin broke with Yugoslav leader Marshal Tito, Yugoslav society has been gradually introducing a number of changes into its version of the Soviet economic model. Without entering into a detailed analysis of those innovations, one can describe their common denominator as a slow introduction of democratization, which has made the rule of a one-party system easier to bear than in other socialist countries. Despite its questionable economic efficiency, the system of worker self-management has democratized economic life in a number of ways and has brought about a broader involvement of various social groups in public life than has been seen in other socialist countries. This is one of the most important distinguishing features of the socialist system in Yugoslavia.

In addition, the Yugoslav system is characterized by the presence, if on a limited scale, of small private businesses and private farms, and the freedom of individuals to travel and work abroad as well as the freedom and the right to hold savings and checking accounts both in nonconvertible domestic currency and in convertible foreign currencies. All this has contributed both to improvements in the standard of living as well as to greater respect for human rights.

These and many other factors are helpful in understanding why the changes taking place in Yugoslav society in the period from 1988 to 1990 did not provoke serious social controversies and tensions. Even the ethnic unrest, it is safe to say, is the result primarily of emotional factors rather than of the presence of significant economic disparities between ethnic groups. However, given these ethnic problems, which are the most important ones facing today's Yugoslavia, it is hard for the FEC to get social consent on any economic program of a federal character.

Fourth, consensus has also been missing among the trade unions, enterprises, and the government on how to apportion consumption. This explains why the federal government has been unable to keep not only budgetary but also general public-sector expenditures under control. Personal incomes have also been allowed to grow beyond what was provided for in the plan. At the same time the share of investment in GNP has fallen. The cumulative result has been a level of inflation that is 10 times higher than anticipated by the FEC. Once inflation was out of control, pressures on the fixed exchange rate regime increased, and it proved impossible to keep the exchange rate at 7 dinars to the mark.

Thus, it seems that the expectation of the FEC that the consistency of its reform program would outweigh the lack of social consensus proved overly optimistic. Even the FEC itself, succumbing to temptation, increased budgetary expenditures and resorted to deficit financing. All this is not to say that, had there been a social consensus, all of the parties sharing in the consensus would have respected their obligations. But the fact that there was no social consensus made it much easier for all potential participants to behave more like free riders than as parties to an agreement.

Fifth, a lack of discipline in monetary policy has been the largest single contributor to the failure of the reforms. Given that the anti-inflationary program consisted primarily of monetary measures, failure to control the money supply in general and mistakes in the timing of monetary measures in particular had a serious negative effect. The FEC applied a more restrictive monetary policy during the first six months of 1990 than in the second half of the year. One has the impression that the FEC tried to overuse monetary policy to compensate for the lack of a unique and single Yugoslav fiscal policy and a coordinated policy of income distribution.

Finally, the six constituent republics deserve negative marks for their lack of cooperation with the federal reform program. The federal government was unable to impose fiscal and monetary discipline upon the republics. This fact is not widely publicized, and that explains among other things why the constituent republics have been able to shift the blame for the failures of economic reform to the FEC, when at least an equal share lies with the republics themselves.

A Successful Start

During the first half of 1990 the reform program seemed to be meeting with great success. The prospects for convertibility, in terms of the most important short-run indicators such as control of inflationary pressure, looked very good. The early results of the shock therapy can be seen from the monthly data on price increases in 1990 (table 2). The relatively quick success of the reforms in the first half of 1990 did not turn into a more stable achievement, however, not

Table 2   Yugoslavia: monthly price indices, 1989–90
(1989 average = 100)

Month	Retail prices	Cost of living	Wholesale prices[a]
1989			
December	377	384	380
1990			
January	534	528	468
February	606	595	504
March	638	618	516
April	656	645	514
May	658	658	513
June	656	652	510
July	670	663	514
August	683	675	520
September	731	727	543
October	791	793	587
November	815	818	606
December	836	846	n.a.

n.a. = not available.

a. Manufactured goods only.

Source: Institute of Statistics, Federal Office of Statistics, Belgrade.

only because of the failure of monetary policy but also because it was not followed by needed structural changes in the productive sector. This has given rise to one of the most important contradictions in the Yugoslav economy, namely, a stable exchange rate of the seemingly convertible dinar under conditions of rising internal prices of goods and services (except for those items still under official price controls). In practical terms, this meant that the purchasing power of the mark and other convertible currencies on the Yugoslav market was starting to diminish. At the same time, the personal incomes of those employed in the public sector were increased by almost 100 percent in terms of the mark. These changes have been taking place despite the fall in GNP noted earlier of about 10 percent.

Thus, shortly after the first impressive results of convertibility had been recorded, clouds started to gather over the reforms. Shock therapy seemed to be good at bringing quick and impressive results, but the durability of those changes was another question. The most favorable effect was the end of hyperinflation and the achievement of a relatively stable price level. Until August, there was no problem in keeping the exchange rate fixed and the dinar convertible. Price stability and the freedom to buy and sell foreign currencies contributed to a temporarily high level of Yugoslavians' confidence in and support for the program. The best evidence of this support is the fact that foreign-exchange reserves were on the rise until the month of August.

It was only in September that a renewed jump in prices signaled the possible beginning of a new wave of inflation. That trend continued in the months that followed, increasing the pressures, particularly from the export sector, for devaluation. The federal government resisted that pressure until the end of December 1990, when it yielded to the inevitable and accepted a 22 percent devaluation to 9 dinars to the mark. Needless to say, the fact that inflation had reached, by the end of 1990, nearly 130 percent on a year-to-year basis, instead of the planned 13 percent (corrected during the year to 20 percent), imposed a need to revise many other basic indicators for the Yugoslav economy for 1991.

At the end of June 1990, Prime Minister and head of the FEC Ante Markovich gave a speech to both houses of Parliament proudly claiming that inflation was under control and practically down to the level considered socially acceptable in the developed countries; that the black market for foreign currencies had practically disappeared overnight upon the establishment of convertibility; and that foreign-exchange reserves had reached $8.7 billion and were expected to approach $10 billion by the end of the year. Markovich also rightly claimed that the foreign debt had been diminished by about $2 billion and that foreign trade in goods and services, both exports and imports, was expanding. He declared that, according to the IMF, practically all conditions had been fulfilled for external convertibility of the dinar in accordance with Article VIII of the IMF's Articles of Agreement.[1]

---

1. *Politika* (Belgrade), 30 June 1990.

It is quite possible that this optimistic outlook and the favorable results of the first several months led the FEC to adopt overoptimistic expectations for the rest of the year, and convinced them that the best policy in the area of foreign exchange was to stay the course and keep the exchange rate at 7 to the mark, at least until the end of 1990.

Shadows over Success

The favorable prospects for the Yugoslav economy seen in the spring of 1990 contributed enormously to the popularity of the FEC and its chairman Markovich. The maintenance of a fixed exchange rate, the control of inflation, and the restoration of a domestic market well supplied with both domestic and foreign consumer goods created a very optimistic social atmosphere. In many ways that favorable economic climate was, at least from the short-run point of view, a very happy counterbalance to the continuing ethnic strife.

It remains to be seen, however, to what extent the FEC's policies helped to diminish other tensions in Yugoslav society during 1990. Not only does the Yugoslav market remain well supplied, but the combination of an already-higher standard of living than in the rest of Eastern Europe, together with the reform program itself (including the convertibility policy), has made conditions in Yugoslavia in no way comparable with those in the rest of Eastern Europe and the Soviet Union.

It is important, however, to recall that every form of therapy, including shock therapy, has its cost. The establishment of convertibility in Yugoslavia has been directly tied with the anti-inflationary program, part of which has involved the freezing of prices in several sectors and industries. In some of these, such as iron and steel, the price freeze has brought the industry almost to the point of collapse.

Another dangerous area has been foreign trade relations. The level at which the exchange rate was fixed proved insufficiently stimulating to exporters given rising internal prices. At the same time, the fall of production in general and of manufacturing in particular diminished the volume of goods available for export, and the overvaluation of the dinar made imports all too attractive for both enterprises and individuals. As table 3 shows, the value of exports for the first nine months of 1990 was 11 percent higher than in the same period of 1989, whereas total imports for the same period were 26 percent higher.

Despite the overvalued dinar, then, exports did not fall but actually rose. This can be explained at least in part by reduced internal demand and the growing liquidity problems of buyers on the domestic market. Even though domestic prices for many goods were higher than those abroad, many Yugoslav firms wanting to purchase those goods were unable to provide prompt payment.

Table 3 Yugoslavia: exports and imports, 1990 (1989 = 100)[a]

Month	Exports	Imports
January	155	182
February	102	120
March	108	117
April	125	136
May	104	126
June	111	133
July	129	113
August	102	125
September	88	113
January–September	111	126

a. The base for each month is the corresponding month of 1989.

Source: Ekonomska politika (Belgrade), 22 October 1990.

Pressure for cash, mainly for urgent expenditures such as payrolls, prevailed in the business decisions of many Yugoslav firms to sell abroad rather than at home.

This policy, which often meant exporting even at a loss, contributed to growing losses in the Yugoslav economy as a whole—part of the price for the reform program in general and of convertibility in particular. Although it is far from easy to arrive at a relatively precise accounting of the losses to the Yugoslav economy, it is safe to estimate that the losses due to the overvalued dinar were between $2 billion and $5 billion.

The falling trend in exports observed in August and to an even greater extent in September indicates that the federal government failed to control the money supply properly; with the more relaxed monetary policy many enterprises, instead of exporting, turned again to domestic buyers. The fact that the trade deficit for the first nine months of 1990 reached a level of $2.3 billion is the best proof available that monetary policy was less restrictive in the second half of the year than in the first six months.

It remains to be explained why the FEC concentrated its economic reform efforts in the first half of the year, and then in the second half turned its attention to intensive political activity. The federal cabinet and its chairman, showing a kind of self-promotion seen only in Yugoslavia, decided to organize a political party of their own, called the Alliance of Reform Forces. Although it is true as a rule that the cabinets of all countries are formed on the basis of political and party affiliations, Yugoslavia has produced the extraordinary spectacle of a federal government organizing its own political party while running the country. By his involvement in efforts to create his own political party, Markovich's image as a politically unbiased expert has been tarnished. The fact that, when free, demo-cratic, multiparty elections were held during 1990 (and witnessed by interna-tional observers, including members of the US Congress), the new party failed to gain popular support indicates that most of the voters were confused by this double role.

One serious political handicap for the program of convertibility in Yugoslavia has been its timing. Convertibility was introduced in the year in which Yugosla-via's first multiparty elections were held. The resulting political pressures together with the inheritance of the socialist economy, characterized among other things by soft budget constraints for businesses, made it very difficult for the FEC to establish monetary discipline. It has been especially difficult when the govern-ments of all six Yugoslav republics preferred to have higher levels of employment and production so as not to lose votes to the opposition. Therefore, in practically every one of the six Yugoslav republics, the regional governments did their best not to conform to the monetary discipline upon which the FEC insisted.

In an effort to preserve convertibility, the FEC devalued the dinar toward the end of December 1990. By itself, however, that step was not very promising. The essential conditions for a lasting convertibility are control of the money supply and stable prices. The price for achieving these conditions is a further decrease in production and further changes in the structure of the Yugoslav economy. During the adjustment process a functioning social safety net has to be elaborated; otherwise social conflicts could take place. These conflicts were held at bay during 1990, partly because the FEC did not insist upon a restrictive monetary policy, and partly because in a period of ethnic resurgence in all parts of the country, growing nationalism has replaced the socioeconomic aspects of life as the issue of primary concern.

Convertibility became a central priority of Yugoslav economic reform at a time when Yugoslav society found itself overburdened with establishing the various elements of a pluralistic society, including in particular pluralism of markets, pluralism of ownership, and pluralism of political parties. Although political pluralism is not a matter of direct concern for economic reform, as a symbol of the process of democratization it is indispensable in creating a sociopolitical climate in which economic changes can take place. Therefore, political pluralism has been socially and legally accepted as an integral part of the economic reform package.

Unfortunately, in real life the priorities were reversed. Pluralism of political parties seemed to be the easier achievement. Whatever their regional differences and ethnic rivalries, the tribal chieftains in all of the regions of Yugoslavia seemed better able to provide noisy and colorful ethnic and political festivals than to deal with the very complex economic issues they face—better, in other words, at providing circuses than at providing bread. Needless to say, Yugoslavia has no monopoly on this style of politics. But sooner or later economic issues are going to come to the fore.

Effects on Individuals

One unique feature of convertibility in Yugoslavia is the fact that only individual citizens have been given the opportunity to buy foreign currency on capital account. Business firms have not been allowed to convert their dinars into foreign currency or to hold balances in foreign-exchange accounts at will. They are, however, able to use their dinar assets to buy foreign currency for the purpose of settling their current transactions. Whereas such treatment of business transactions is more or less similar to that of firms in the market economies, the extensive freedoms given to individuals in regard to convertibility are relatively unusual. Apart from Yugoslavia, such arrangements are found only in the industrial countries.

It would be reasonable to expect that, under conditions such as those prevailing in Yugoslavia, most domestic savings by individuals would be held in foreign-exchange accounts. But in fact, after an initial wave of demand for foreign currency, not only did the owners of saving accounts not convert all of their savings into foreign currency, but instead there has been a tendency for individuals to bring hoarded foreign exchange to be deposited in the banks. As a result, the foreign-exchange reserves of the country actually increased during the first seven months of 1990.

Some experts claim that establishing the convertibility of the dinar was premature and a serious mistake on the part of the FEC. It is my belief, however, that both the FEC and the population at large had overoptimistic expectations that monetary policy would remain under control, and that the FEC would be able to stay the course of restrictive monetary policy—one of the most important anchors of the entire program. The relatively stable retail prices in the second quarter of 1990, following the unavoidable price adjustments of the first quarter, acted like a sedative: it was only after inflationary pressures revived in September 1990 that the sedative effect passed and the changing of bad dinars for healthy marks and other currencies started to exert strong pressure on foreign-exchange reserves. This led, toward the end of the year, to the establishment of limitations on the amount of foreign currency that individual citizens could buy, as well as to the devaluation of the dinar.

Convertibility, despite its relatively short duration, has had a beneficial effect upon the population at large. Domestic wages and salaries have been increasing, and Yugoslav citizens are able to use part of their savings in dinars to be converted into foreign currencies. In practical terms, this has provided some protection from inflationary pressures and thus has increased the real value of the currency.

A question that arises from Yugoslavia's experience with convertibility is the following: on the assumption that the FEC anticipated what actually happened, is it possible that it deliberately used the introduction of convertibility to privatize, as it were, foreign exchange, by allowing citizens to use their private savings in dinars to buy foreign exchange from the official reserves? If, on the other hand, the government was taken by surprise by these developments, more serious questions arise about its professional expertise, which would seem to be much below the average for the nation as a whole.

A second question is directly associated with the first: if Yugoslavia does achieve external convertibility, will internal convertibility survive in its present form, or will it be nullified along with the right of citizens to hold foreign-exchange accounts? In the latter case, would the foreign exchange held in individuals' accounts have to be given back to the National Bank (in other words, to the state) in exchange for dinars (as in countries that enjoy full convertibility, where there is no need for the existence of parallel private accounts)? Obviously even a weak signal in this direction could provoke a lack of confidence and a rush to withdraw foreign exchange from the banks. On that basis there is reason to be concerned about the government's decree of 29 December 1990, which limits the amount that individuals traveling abroad may withdraw from their foreign-exchange accounts to DM1,000 (or the equivalent in other currencies).

By introducing convertibility at a fixed exchange rate, which had to be supported by restrictive monetary policy as well as by the liberalization of prices and foreign trade (particularly imports), the FEC tried to create a framework within which business enterprises would be pressed to increase their efficiency or to adopt various other changes, in order to intensify the process of adjustment in the Yugoslav economy. Had all aspects of this framework been maintained, an inevitable part of the structural adjustment process would have been some serious social problems. By refusing to face those problems and instead postponing the moment of truth, the Yugoslav government has, without intending it, postponed the process of adjustment as well.

It is important to realize that federal regulations have given enterprises the opportunity to generate additional financing for their survival by transformation of their property, through various schemes ranging from employee stock ownership plans to sales on the capital markets. The fact that, in practical terms, each of the six republics is now trying to postpone the process of property transformation suggests that the new, democratically elected politicians are unwilling to part with the monopolistic power of the state. Thus, there are some fairly close connections among the lack of perseverance in monetary policy, the almost complete absence of progress in the reform of property ownership, and the pressures upon the exchange rate and foreign-exchange reserves.

Conclusions

The program to establish convertibility of the Yugoslav national currency, although long overdue, was also too optimistic when finally implemented. The process of transforming a nonconvertible into a convertible dinar encountered many difficulties, some of which could have been expected, but many of which could not. It was necessary actually to embark on the introduction of convertibility in order to make the various hidden difficulties become apparent.

The fact that the convertibility program called for declaring the external convertibility of the dinar in September 1990, the very month in which inflationary pressures reappeared, accounts for Yugoslavia's decision to postpone its application to the IMF for acceptance into the family of nations with convertible currencies. The main real and legal obstacle to achieving full convertibility is the potential danger of reintroduction of foreign-exchange restrictions.

Despite the often-vocal criticism of the FEC and its reform program, including its plan to establish convertibility, it is hard to imagine a theoretical and practical alternative set of principles and policies. There have been a number of barriers to the program's success, including that of the introduction of external convertibility, most of which are outside the government's control. Among these barriers, the most important ones have been the lack of political consensus about the functioning of the single Yugoslav market; the absence of any real connection between personal incomes and productivity; loss of demand in some of the strongest markets for Yugoslav goods and services, such as the Soviet Union and Iraq; the postponement of privatization; and the lack of budgetary discipline, resulting in continued extremely high costs of social overhead.

In addition, some of the criticisms directed against the reform program were based on unwarranted expectations that the program could fight inflation, establish convertibility, and stimulate new investment all in the same short period of time. If the Yugoslav experience has shown anything, it is that establishing convertibility can be a much more troublesome proposition than either the theoretical models or countries' ambitious economic policy programs typically acknowledge.

East Germany

Wolfgang Schill

In July 1944, when 45 nations agreed at Bretton Woods to establish the International Monetary Fund and drafted what became its Articles of Agreement, fulfillment of the terms of Article VIII, which defined and called upon members to achieve currency convertibility, was not seen to be an extremely high priority. Indeed, almost all of the member countries applied comprehensive foreign-exchange controls and restrictions in the early years after World War II. It would take most of the Western European countries 10 to 15 years to apply *de facto* convertibility even to current transactions. And it was only very recently that some important EC countries (e.g., France and Italy) finally agreed to liberalize capital transactions completely (see Bergsten and Williamson 1990).

Given this history, it is extraordinary that the urgent desire for a convertible currency appears to have contributed substantially to the peaceful revolution in East Germany in 1989.[1] Yet one of the slogans most often shouted by the hundreds of thousands of East German demonstrators in those weeks and months was, "Kommt die D-Mark, bleiben wir; kommt sie nicht, gehen wir zu ihr" ("If the deutsche mark comes to us, we will stay; if it doesn't, we will go to it").

A straightforward interpretation of the events and the popular mood that ultimately led to the unification of the two Germanys on 3 October 1990 would indeed suggest that the demand for convertibility played a decisive role in and even triggered the revolutionary events. It could be argued, however, that what the East German people were striving for was not just convertibility in the strict, technical sense of Article VIII, but rather something like a "freely usable currency," as defined in Article XXX(f). At the moment only the US dollar, the pound sterling, the French franc, the yen, and the mark are "freely usable" in this sense. On 3 October 1990, the people of the former East Germany joined this exclusive club, with all of its privileges and obligations.

The option enjoyed by the East Germans is clearly not available to the other former socialist countries in Eastern Europe, and one might wonder whether

---

1. In this paper, and throughout the volume, "East Germany" refers to the state that was the German Democratic Republic (GDR). References to "eastern Germany" denote the territory of the former East Germany, which is now part of the united Germany.

Wolfgang Schill is an economist at the Deutsche Bundesbank. The opinions expressed are those of the author and do not necessarily reflect those held by the Deutsche Bundesbank.

the opportunity to achieve only a more restricted form of convertibility would mobilize people to a similar extent. Nevertheless, the example of German economic, monetary, and social union (GEMSU) can contribute to a more informed discussion about the most appropriate strategy for transforming the former centrally planned economies into market economies. Even though East Germany is a unique case and not a model for the other countries of the region, the strategy chosen by the German authorities should not be neglected in the often-puzzling debate over gradualism versus radicalism in reform measures.

In this paper it is argued that the German strategy was ultraradical but took place under unique circumstances. To explain what "ultraradical" and "unique circumstances" mean, the first section of the paper attempts to summarize the major arguments of the gradualist and radical approaches, after which the second section describes the measures taken by the German authorities in more detail. The third section then assesses the special features of monetary union in the German context and discusses the general role of the exchange rate regime during the transitional phase. The fourth section reports on the initial effects of GEMSU, and potential conclusions about the alternative routes to a market economy are drawn in the concluding section.

Gradual Versus Radical Strategies

For proponents of the radical school (see, for example, the paper by Jacques J. Polak in chapter 3 of this volume), convertibility usually means current account convertibility—holders of domestic currency must be able freely to use that currency to pay for and import foreign goods and services. They consider this limited form of current account convertibility to be much more important for Eastern Europe today than it was for Western Europe in the 1950s, for two reasons. First, it is urgently needed as an economic policy instrument to subject domestic producers to competition from foreign suppliers and promote market-based pricing in the former socialist economies, which have inherited a price system that lacks all economic rationale. Second, it will enable the former socialist countries to break with existing protective practices and price distortions so as to allow exports to rise and foreign as well as domestic entrepreneurs to invest in the reformed economy.

A necessary counterpart of convertibility, in this view, is an undervalued currency, to stimulate export demand and dampen import demand. The attempt instead to revitalize intra-area trade through an Eastern European payments union is opposed, mainly because concentration on intraregional trade would delay market-oriented restructuring, retard adjustment, and perpetuate the ongoing misallocation of resources due to wrong relative prices. Only the intensification of trade with the more competitive Western countries can ultimately lead to an integration of Eastern Europe into the world economy. In addition, the set of potential members of such a regional arrangement (Eastern Europe except for the former East Germany and the Soviet Union) would be too small for an effective payments union in several respects; comparisons with the European Payments Union of the 1950s are therefore inappropriate.

In the gradualist view (see, for instance, the paper by Friedrich Levcik in chapter 3), convertibility in a socialist economy is a meaningless concept unless the transformation toward a market economy is well under way and its essential elements are already functioning. Compared with Polak's position, Levcik's concept of current account convertibility (also restricted to convertibility on current account transactions) is more an economic objective than a policy instrument. The presence at the outset of many obstacles to convertibility—among them the complete lack of any market experience, a highly distorted price system, the lack of control mechanisms to replace the rejected central planning mechanisms, the continued presence of state monopolies, and certain social values and expectations—argues that a gradual transition toward convertibility will become feasible only after a number of preconditions have been fulfilled. Free prices and a sufficiently devalued currency alone will not set the economy on a path of growth and prosperity. Only by integrating currency convertibility into an overall process of transformation, and by timing it appropriately with other essential elements, can one expect a successful integration of these countries into the world economy. According to Levcik, currency convertibility is therefore not a top priority, but should rather be considered at a later stage of the transformation process.

Levcik argues that gradualism undertaken by a democratic government committed to freedom and market principles differs fundamentally from the hesitating reform attempts of Communist governments still in power. Whereas the latter will most probably increase instability, the former can establish the basic elements of a market economy within three to five years, thereby providing for a large degree of current account convertibility.

The Strategy of GEMSU

Neither Pure Shock Treatment nor Sophisticated Gradualism

The overall strategy of GEMSU essentially rested on four pillars:

- *A new monetary regime.* The former East Germany was furnished with a convertible currency overnight on 1 July 1990. It did not need to establish convertibility for its own currency, the East German mark or ostmark. Since that day the West German deutsche mark has been the only legal tender in the former East Germany, and responsibility for internal and external monetary policy has been transferred to the Deutsche Bundesbank. At the same time, East Germany gained full access to Western goods markets and to a developed and functioning banking system and capital market, but lost the exchange rate as an instrument of adjustment.

■ *A new economic regime.* With the entry into force, on 1 July 1990, of the Treaty between the Federal Republic of Germany and the German Democratic Republic, the latter adopted all the major laws of the Federal Republic, or adjusted its own legislation accordingly. Overnight, the East German economy adopted a degree of liberalization of its goods, labor, and capital markets (except for certain transitional regulations) identical to that prevailing in West Germany.

■ *A new social regime.* The former East Germany introduced a social security system modeled on the West German one, with West Germany contributing the necessary means of finance.

■ *A new political regime.* On 3 October 1990, political unification of the two parts of Germany took place. The economic, monetary, and social transformations just described were indeed only in anticipation of East Germany's constitutional accession to the Federal Republic.

If one compares these changes with the arguments and proposed strategies of the gradualist and radical schools, it becomes clear that the German approach does not match either completely. GEMSU was obviously not a gradual transition to a market economy, but rather a sudden and complete opening up of the economy, simultaneous with the transformation of all levels of economic, social, and political life. In this sense GEMSU was "ultraradical." Yet ironically, this ultraradical approach fulfilled at one stroke many of the conditions that gradualists usually consider indispensable for the transformation of a socialist into a market economy. Levcik's basic criticism of radical measures—that convertibility cannot be a meaningful concept unless the transformation is well under way and the essential elements of a market economy are already working—therefore does not apply to the case of GEMSU. However, the fact that these essential elements could be established in the former East Germany in a very short time must be viewed as owing to unique circumstances.

The Major Elements of GEMSU

After 1 July 1990, producers in the former East Germany were subjected to competition from West German and foreign suppliers in the most comprehensive way possible. On that date all import restrictions were abolished, and simultaneously the whole range of price subsidies and surcharges was eliminated at one stroke. These reforms go well beyond any conventional definition of shock treatment. The result of this external liberalization and price reform was an almost complete importation of the market-based price structure of West Germany for all traded goods. Subsidies on rents, household energy use, and public transport were kept in place but will be phased out gradually from 1991 onward.

The East German external trade system, formerly a state monopoly, was completely liberalized. All arrangements for intra-German trade were abolished, and a free external trading system was introduced, thus incorporating the former East Germany into the European Community. Special protection, however, was given to existing contracts and trade relations with partners in the member countries of the Council for Mutual Economic Assistance (CMEA). In particular, until the end of 1990, exports to Eastern Europe using transferable rubles were allowed, at an exchange rate of DM2.34 to 1. Regarding the existing liabilities of the former foreign trade monopolies to the CMEA countries, which these enterprises might be unable or unwilling to fulfill, an understanding was reached that these contracts would be fulfilled. This is part of the so-called protection of confidence accorded to trade relations between the former East Germany and its CMEA trading partners.

Simultaneously with the introduction of the deutsche mark as legal tender, the monetary system of East Germany was completely reorganized. Responsibility for monetary policy was transferred completely and in one stroke to the Bundesbank, so that the same conditions for monetary management now apply in all parts of Germany. Steps have been taken to ensure that the Bundesbank's successful policy of monetary stability can be continued in the extended currency area. A major prerequisite to enable the Bundesbank to fulfill its task of controlling money and credit creation was the establishment of a market-based banking system. In preparation for GEMSU, the East German parliament passed a law on 6 March 1990 that eliminated the central position of the former monobank, the Staatsbank. Several formerly specialized East German banks were merged into universal cooperative banks, while the municipal and rural savings banks, which formerly only took deposits, were allowed to operate as universal banks as well (for technical details see Deutsche Bundesbank 1990b, 23, and Lipschitz and McDonald 1990, 151–54).

Although one cannot yet speak of a fully developed banking system in East Germany, a structure similar to that in West Germany was set up in a very short time. Since 1 July 1990 all major West German banks and banking groups have established joint ventures with East German institutions, have opened up new branches in the now-unified banking market, or, in the case of savings banks and cooperative banks, cooperate closely with their Eastern counterparts. In addition, a number of foreign banks are now operating freely in eastern Germany.

The rapid establishment of a modern banking system was a prerequisite not only for monetary policy but also for monetary reform and currency conversion. After a lengthy political and public debate, all flows (wages in particular) were converted at parity into deutsche marks, and banks' liabilities were converted at an average rate of 1.8 ostmarks to 1 deutsche mark and other liabilities at a rate of 2 to 1 (for details see Deutsche Bundesbank 1990a). In order to balance the new deutsche mark assets and liabilities of the banks, an equalization fund was established.

Together with external liberalization and price reform, the currency and banking reform were the cornerstones on which the new economic environment in East Germany was built after 1 July 1990. The real economy faced full competition from the world market, and the relative prices of tradeables were adjusted immediately to market conditions. In the financial sector, too, full convertibility was introduced, the monetary overhang was by and large eliminated, and prices and instruments in the financial market reflected market conditions from the outset. All in all, one can only regard these changes as a genuine "big bang."

This radical opening of the East German economy, which went far beyond the textbook descriptions of shock treatment, was only possible within the framework of a more comprehensive approach. Many additional features were introduced at the same time to ensure that the rapid move to a market economy and full convertibility would not be jeopardized by inadequate economic, social, and political structures. Therefore, one could argue that the successful economic order of West Germany—the social market economy—was exported to East Germany (see Tietmeyer 1990).

To start with, the whole process of economic decisionmaking was decentralized substantially, and the authoritarian economic system was destroyed. These were replaced at all levels with structures corresponding to Western standards. Although one should not expect the new institutions to work as efficiently as their Western counterparts from the outset—because inefficiencies will continue for some time, because resistance from the old apparatus must be overcome, and because people's thinking and expectations need time to adjust to the new environment—the new system should nevertheless fulfill the minimum requirements, at least for the time being, and should improve its functioning rapidly. At the highest level, responsibilities were transferred to a newly elected federal government in Bonn, which can rely on a skilled public administration in fulfilling them.

At the level of the states (Länder), new democratic governments have been elected in the East, and the West German states will contribute to the establishment of a more efficient administration in their Eastern counterparts; in general, the same applies to lower levels of administration. Clearly, these are the effects of political union.

Second, in terms of economic union, East Germany has been furnished with the whole framework of laws, regulations, and administrative systems that are widely held to be necessary for the proper functioning of a market system. This applies to the tax system and to the goods and labor markets (including independent trade unions). In addition, a large degree of macroeconomic stabilization has been imported from West Germany. East Germany has gained indirect access to the West German tax base and its fully developed capital market, and does not face macroeconomic foreign-exchange bottlenecks; all of these factors should cushion any adverse initial developments.

Thus, the legal and organizational instruments needed for effective economic policies are in place. However, it is quite obvious that new rules and regulations are not sufficient by themselves to guarantee that an agent's behavior will conform to market requirements. The new trade unions will have to define their role, the new tax and corporate laws and regulations will have to be digested, and a new class of entrepreneurs will have to emerge. These developments, too, will take time, and meanwhile the people of East Germany must come to terms with the new system. The break with the past system in terms of rules and regulations must be followed by a quick break with old attitudes and behavior patterns.

Third, a new social security system has been established along the lines of the West German system. Pension payments have been put on a new basis, mainly reflecting general income developments in East Germany, and a comprehensive unemployment insurance scheme has been implemented. In the area of health insurance and services, a transition to West German systems and standards is taking place. East German residents will have to come to understand that social security is not something provided *ex nihilo* by the state, but is rather a function of what is produced in the economy. The present structures can be sustained in the medium term only if economic performance in the former East Germany comes into line with the level of social security desired.

Finally, privatization was dealt with in the framework of GEMSU by transforming East Germany's state-owned enterprises into joint-stock or limited-liability companies and creating a public trust corporation, the Treuhandanstalt, to take temporary ownership of and administer the state properties. This entity operates under an executive board and a supervisory council, recruited largely from high-level West German managers, public administrators, and other relevant groups. Assisted by Western accounting and managerial staff, the Treuhandanstalt has as its task to sell the viable enterprises as quickly as possible, to try to restructure enterprises that are encountering difficulties, and, finally, to close the operations of enterprises that prove unable to survive.

The Treuhandanstalt has to live up to huge expectations. Its main work is to transfer responsibility for the enterprises to private hands; it would overtax its resources to try to conserve a large part of the old industrial structures or to restructure all of the 8,000 companies presently under its umbrella. The indications are that the Treuhandanstalt has a good understanding of its primary job, but one should not expect the entrepreneurial landscape to look like that in West Germany very soon.

One important factor tending to slow down the process of privatization is the issue of property ownership. The treaty between the two German governments laid down certain basic principles in this area. With the exception of expropriations undertaken by the Soviet military government in 1945–49, expropriated or state-administered real estate or companies and participations are in principle to be returned to the previous owners (or compensation is to be paid). In particular, no real estate the property rights to which are unclear shall be sold before the expiration of an application period.

If the implementation of these guidelines proves to be slow, property issues will contribute to uncertainty and may delay private investment in the former East Germany. A rapid solution of property questions therefore appears to be a high priority.[2]

As a whole, the task of breathing life into new political, economic, and social structures and of overcoming privatization and property problems clearly has a time dimension, and no immediate adjustments can be expected. The architects of GEMSU have taken this time dimension into account. However, a peculiarity of GEMSU is that no predominant consideration was given to so-called sequencing problems: no comprehensive protection measures were taken to preserve East German companies until the social and economic fabric is working smoothly by Western standards. Instead, an effort was made to combine a radical opening of the economy with an immediate and simultaneous restructuring of the economic and social infrastructure. As will be shown below, this approach incurred substantial costs in terms of initial real output losses and substantial fiscal disequilibria, but it is expected that these costs can be recovered in the medium term.

Monetary Union and the Exchange Rate Regime During the Transition

Although GEMSU had a whole range of unique features, its most outstanding peculiarity was the incorporation of the East German economy into the currency area of the deutsche mark. It would, however, be somewhat misleading to view German monetary union predominantly within the usual framework of the relative advantages of exchange rate targets and domestic monetary targets, or

---

2. In April 1991 the federal government took measures to facilitate the transfer of property in cases where investment plans were being delayed by unsettled property issues.

to consider it as an example of how to solve monetary policy problems that might arise in the other reforming countries. One could even argue that monetary union between East and West Germany was not a monetary policy measure at all, but rather a political decision in the widest sense of the term.

As was mentioned earlier, a major aspiration of the East German population was to obtain a "fully usable currency," which implicitly meant a full integration of both economies. The West German government, in substance, had only two options: either it could decide in favor of monetary union and then develop a strategy to incorporate monetary union into a general framework for the transition, or it could decide against monetary union and put eastern Germany on a transitional track similar to that in Poland, Czechoslovakia, or any of the other former socialist countries. In essence, it was the real prospect of a not-too-distant political unification of Germany that finally led West German Chancellor Helmut Kohl, on 6 February 1990, to propose negotiations with the East German government about the establishment of monetary and economic union.

As a senior official of the Bundesbank and an active participant in the preparations for monetary and economic union wrote:

> In purely economic terms, a more gradual approach would surely have been preferred over the abrupt introduction of the D-Mark. As long as economic and structural conditions in the two parts of Germany differ as much as they actually do, exchange rate changes are indispensable to cushion the shocks according to conventional wisdom. In view of the political pressure, however, there was no time for the normal sequence of reform measures; the monetary union between the two German states could not wait for an adequate adjustment of the GDR economy to the performance standard in the Federal Republic. How great the need for action was is revealed by the fact that, from the opening-up of the Berlin Wall to the beginning of February 1990, i.e. in only three months, more than 300,000 residents left the GDR. A continuation of this emigration would have had incalculable economic and social consequences, not only in the GDR but also in the Federal Republic. (König 1990, 5)

Thus, it can be concluded that monetary union was not chosen because it was considered in some sense an optimal exchange rate regime. Rather, the exchange rate regime was determined by the political forces driving the country to political union. Political union called for monetary union and created the need for—or almost presupposed—economic and social union.

No such causality exists elsewhere in Eastern Europe. German monetary union can therefore hardly be regarded as a model for other countries. In terms of pure monetary policy considerations, the monetary union did, of course, solve the conventional credibility problems, and it allowed East Germany to import stable monetary conditions from West Germany. To focus only on the monetary and exchange rate implications of monetary union, however, would be to neglect the real causality and largely to ignore other substantial components of the reform package for East Germany (see Bofinger, chapter 4 of this volume).

Monetary policy in the other countries of Eastern Europe will have to cope with the credibility problem and deal with the question of which exchange rate regime could best be incorporated into the overall strategy of transformation. Conventional wisdom has it that exchange rate targets, particularly in smaller economies, can serve as a nominal anchor for monetary policy to enhance its credibility; the experience of Western Europe, however, also shows that the fixing of nominal exchange rates alone does not provide a sufficiently stable solution. As long as the authorities do not succeed in keeping domestic prices stable, they sooner or later face a trade-off between accepting a real overvaluation of their currency or losing credibility by realigning exchange rates.

A pragmatic solution for small countries seeking to cope with the risk of such an exchange rate trap is to adopt an ambitious crawling peg. That is, the authorities would forswear quasi-automatic accommodations to domestic inflation if developments get out of line. In the event of a devaluation of the home currency, they would accommodate only part of the inflation differential. This contrasts with a purely "permissive" policy of devaluation that sanctions every bit of misbehavior in incomes and fiscal policy. Such a policy would indeed be nothing but money illusion on the part of the policymakers, and would be bound to lead to a complete loss of credibility.

This solution allows the authorities to announce that they will stick to an exchange rate target, and thus demonstrate their determination to keep domestic price trends in line with price increases abroad. At the same time it would leave open the possibility of realigning the exchange rate in case the authorities broadly fail to keep foreign and domestic prices aligned.

The basic argument in favor of such an approach is that anchors other than the exchange rate are necessary in order to provide for a stable and effective monetary regime (see Portes 1990). Monetary policy alone can hardly do the trick; it has to be supported by incomes policy and fiscal policy. A monetary policy that is unable to overcome rigidities in incomes and fiscal policies in the short run can, however, employ a medium-term strategy of using the exchange rate to correct in a partial manner for massive misalignments in price competitiveness, without giving up its ambitions regarding price stability.

A strategy of this kind certainly is a tightrope: it involves determining how much "importation" of monetary stability via fixed exchange rates a country can afford at the expense of a loss of price competitiveness. But it must be judged in terms of the alternatives available, and not against some ideal state of the world. One alternative is a system of fully flexible exchange rates, which implies that a domestic anchor of monetary policy is available. A second is a system of rigidly fixed exchange rates, which increases the risk of overvaluation of the currency and its negative impacts on export performance.

Initial Results of GEMSU

Economic developments in both West and East Germany were strongly influenced by the completion of GEMSU and by political unification. Tables 1 and 2 and figure 1 provide some relevant data on developments in East Germany, although it must be mentioned that comprehensive and reliable figures are still lacking.

Since 1 July 1990 the population of East Germany has had a fully convertible currency and complete access to world goods markets; wages and social transfer payments increased considerably in the months thereafter. The improved purchasing power over Western goods and the availability of the whole spectrum of those goods led to a total neglect of locally produced goods; this, together with the breakdown of the command economies in other CMEA countries, triggered a drastic slump in production and employment in the former East Germany. From the fall of 1989 to the fall of 1990 industrial production fell by 50 percent. The number of unemployed rose to 642,000 by the end of 1990, for an unemployment rate of 7.2 percent. At the same time there were 1.8 million part-time workers.

In short, a painful process of adjustment and restructuring is taking place, in the course of which many enterprises are being and will continue to be forced out of the market. Although the signs are increasing that the economic situation might improve during the second half of 1991, unemployment in the five new Länder will remain high, and may temporarily rise even further. This continued weakness of demand for labor may occur even as output increases, reflecting the need to eliminate overstaffing and reduce the labor-capital ratio considerably. The extremely strong reaction of the real economy in the former East Germany underlines the fact that the need for internal adjustment has been greater there than in other formerly planned economies, because of the sudden and complete opening of the economy and the loss of the exchange rate as an instrument of adjustment. The only adjustment instruments now available are wage differentials and financial transfers from West Germany.

Although wage negotiations are still in progress in the former East Germany, and the risks are increasing that the resulting wages will not fully reflect productivity differentials,[3] massive government financial transfers from West to East are already being effected. For the time being, transfer payments are the main element bridging the gap between public expenditures and tax revenues in East Germany; this gap reflects the substantial start-up costs of the social security system (particularly to finance the high unemployment). The public-sector borrowing requirement in Germany will rise to a total of at least DM150 billion, or more than 5 percent of GNP, in 1991.

---

3. Wage settlements reached in the months following the conference tended to exacerbate such fears.

Table 1 East Germany: selected economic indicators, 1985–89

	1985	1986	1987	1988	1989
National income[a]	124.9	130.2	134.6	138.4	141.3
(1980 = 100)					
Consumer price index	107.1	106.9	107.4	109.8	112.3
(1980 = 100)					
Trade (millions of dollars)					
In nonconvertible currencies[b]					
Exports	9,798	9,657	12,932	16,261	16,127
Imports	9,246	9,839	12,882	15,445	14,958
Balance	562	−182	50	816	1,169
In convertible currencies[c]					
Exports	3,135	2,758	2,898	3,409	3,737
Imports	2,375	2,512	3,750	4,927	5,003
Balance	760	246	−852	−1,518	−1,266
Intra-German trade[d]					
Exports	2,594	3,153	3,696	3,861	3,830
Imports	2,684	3,434	4,097	4,114	4,308
Balance	−90	−281	−400	−253	−477
Gross external debt[e]					
(millions of dollars)	10,249	11,574	14,063	16,013	16,999
Official exchange rate[f]					
(East German marks	2.95	2.18	1.80	1.75	1.88
per dollar)					

a. In constant prices.

b. Trade with CMEA countries.

c. Trade with industrialized Western countries.

d. According to West German statistics.

e. In convertible currencies, according to BIS statistics (excluding liabilities vis-à-vis banks residing in the Federal Republic of Germany).

f. Annual averages.

Sources: Central Statistical Office of the German Democratic Republic, Statistical Office of the Federal Republic of Germany, Bank for International Settlements. The figures provided here have only limited reliability and may be distorted by unconventional accounting standards.

Table 2 Exchange rates and trading volume in the market for East German marks, 1985–90

Period	Exchange rate[a] Buy	Sell	Average[c]	Volume[b]
1985	18.0	21.0	19.5	
December				n.a.
1986	14.8	17.6	16.2	
December				n.a.
1987	12.0	14.6	13.3	
December				n.a.
1988	11.6	14.1	12.8	
December				n.a.
1989	10.5	13.0	11.7	
June				n.a.
October	9.6	12.1	10.9	n.a.
November	10.5	13.6	12.0	33
December	12.3	15.7	14.0	26
1990	12.8	15.7	14.2	
January				31
February	15.9	18.9	17.4	70
March	18.0	21.8	19.9	80
April	23.0	27.1	25.0	82
May	25.9	30.1	28.0	78
June	32.6	37.4	35.0	n.a.

n.a. = not available.

a. Monthly averages; in deutsche marks per 100 East German marks.

b. Sum of purchases and sales by major foreign-exchange bureaus and some banks in West Berlin and the Federal Republic; in millions of deutsche marks.

c. Average of buy and sell rates.

Source: Deutsche Bundesbank.

Figure 1   East Germany: selected economic data, 1990

New orders and output / New businesses registered

Period	Industry New orders (change in % from previous month)	Industry Output 1 (change in % from previous year)	Construction New orders (change in % from previous year)	Construction Output 2 (change in % from previous month)	Construction Output 2 (change in % from previous year)	New businesses registered (Thousands)
1990 1st qtr	.	− 2.7	− 4.5	.	− 14.0	16.9
2nd qtr	.	− 4.7	− 9.5	.	− 0.1	84.0
3rd qtr	.	− 44.5	− 48.1	.	.	96.4
March	.	1.2	− 4.1	.	− 13.7	.
April	.	− 0.7	− 3.9	.	− 4.6	p 12.9
May	.	− 5.1	− 9.0	.	− 6.7	p 16.8
June	.	− 6.6	− 15.5	.	11.3	p 54.1
July 8	.	− 34.9	− 42.1	.	− 15.0	35.8
Aug.	− 15.0	− 14.5	− 50.8	22.0	.	30.8
Sep.	− 8.3	2.2	− 51.1	34.4	.	29.8
Oct.	.	.	.	.	.	29.4

Labour market

Period	Persons employed in industry and construction (Thousands)	Persons employed (% from previous year)	Vacancies (Thousands)	Short-time workers 3 (Thousands)	Unemployed (Thousands)	Unemployment rate 4
1990 1st qtr	3,525	− 3.7	.	.	.	.
2nd qtr	3,332	− 9.2	67.2	.	83.3	1.0
3rd qtr	3,049	−17.0	27.0	1,295.0	308.9	3.5
June	.	.	41.4	.	142.1	1.6
July 8	3,138	.	27.7	656.3	272.0	3.1
Aug.	3,077	.	20.4	1,499.9	361.3	4.1
Sep.	2,934	.	24.3	1,728.7	444.9	5.0
Oct.	.	.	24.7	r1,703.8	r 536.8	6.1
Nov.	.	.	23.8	1,773.9	589.2	6.7

Retail trade, wages and prices

Period	Retail turnover 5 (% from previous year)	Wages 6 Industry (% from previous year)	Wages 6 Construction (% from previous year)	Producer prices of industrial products (% from previous month)	Cost of living index 7 (% from previous month)	Cost of living index 7 (% from previous year)
1990 1st qtr	7.0	4.2	4.6	.	.	.
2nd qtr	− 0.6	.	.	.	.	.
3rd qtr	− 45.0	.	.	.	.	− 4.7
May	2.9	17.4	24.5	.	.	− 1.7
June	− 9.1	.	.	.	− 10.6	− 12.1
July 8	− 44.0	.	.	.	7.5	− 5.5
Aug.	− 44.8	.	.	− 4.5	0.4	− 5.1
Sep.	− 46.1	.	.	.	1.8	− 3.4
Oct.	.	.	.	.	1.7	− 1.8
Nov.	.	.	.	.	0.1	− 1.9

* Data not fully comparable with the corresponding figures for West Germany. — 1 Gross output, adjusted for working-day variations. — 2 Adjusted for working-day variations. — 3 Including participants in retraining and further training schemes. — 4 Unemployed as a percentage of the total labour force; until May, calculated by the Bundesbank. — 5 At current prices. — 6 Monthly gross earnings per wage and salary earner. — 7 All households. — 8 Inception of the economic, monetary and social union. — p Provisional. — r Revised figures. BBk

Source: Deutsche Bundesbank.

It is obvious that deficits of that size are not sustainable (see also Jochimsen 1990, 13). Part of the cost of restructuring East Germany has to be borne—sooner or later—by the West German taxpayer or by the present beneficiaries of public spending. One message, therefore, of Germany's large borrowing requirement is that the sudden implementation of monetary union, convertibility, and openness of the economy requires that someone bear the costs of adjustment. West Germany was in a position to assume such a heavy financial burden temporarily: GNP growth and tax revenues had been unexpectedly high for several years; in 1989 the overall public-sector deficit amounted to only 0.3 percent of GNP; and the Federal Republic recorded an overall current account surplus of more than DM100 billion (4½ percent of GNP).

Partly because of strong import demand in East Germany, the trade and current account surpluses for Germany as a whole diminished sharply. The current account surplus will probably fall from DM104 billion in 1989 to approximately DM75 billion in 1990, and in 1991 a further drop to below DM50 billion is expected.[4] Thus, a substantial part of the higher demand for Western goods in East Germany has spilled over to Germany's Western trading partners.

Finally, the monetary aspects of GEMSU were positive. The effective conversion of the East German banking system's liabilities at an average rate of 1.8 to 1, roughly in line with the Bundesbank's proposal in the negotiations, led to an initial increase in the money stock of about 15 percent. Measured against the added production potential from East Germany (approximately 10 percent of the existing West German potential), the increase in the money supply seemed rather high. It must, however, be taken into account that the Bundesbank's measure of the money supply includes East Germans' savings deposits, which are repayable at any time. Since 1 July 1990 the residents of the former East Germany have had the entire spectrum of investment instruments at their disposal. One should expect them to adjust their portfolios, which at the time of monetary union consisted almost entirely of savings deposits, toward long-term, high-yielding, nonmonetary assets. Such a shift can already be observed, and after this adjustment is completed the expansion of the German money stock should be roughly in line with the additional production potential of the East German economy (see also Schlesinger 1990, 5–6).

One positive early result of monetary union was the absence of any surge in prices in East Germany after 1 July. Despite the abolition of subsidies for simple foodstuffs and a sharp correction in relative prices, the overall price level in deutsche mark terms was actually somewhat lower than that on an ostmark basis in the preceding year.

---

4. As this goes to press, the current account is expected to achieve near balance for 1991.

Potential Conclusions

On the one hand, the Eastern European countries in principle face similar problems and adjustment needs. Among these the most pressing issues are the integration of their relatively isolated economies into world markets, the liberalization of prices and the restructuring of relative prices, the decentralization of decisionmaking, the establishment of stable macroeconomic conditions, the privatization of state-owned enterprises, and the adjustment of individual citizens' behavior patterns to the prerequisites of the market economy.

On the other hand, the political, economic, and social conditions at the outset differ from country to country; these differences are probably the main reasons for the countries' divergent choices in the sequencing of their reform measures. The special features of GEMSU allow one to draw no strong conclusions from the German experience about the optimal speed of restructuring and the appropriate mix of policies. The fact that GEMSU could be implemented at a stroke permitted the former East Germany simply to avoid making such choices.

In more general terms, however, GEMSU can be considered an extreme example of a combination of external liberalization and domestic restructuring. Both components were regarded as complementary, mutually reinforcing elements of an overall restructuring process. A general message of GEMSU could therefore be that external liberalization is indispensable for breaking up a heavily distorted price structure and for putting an end to an immense misallocation of resources, and that an internal restructuring of political, economic, and social forces is necessary to support the importation of market mechanisms from abroad (see also Kloten 1991, 7). The problem of sequencing reform measures, particularly in the sense of fine tuning and social engineering, might well appear less pressing, if one also aims for a parallelism of external and internal adjustment to the greatest degree possible.

Although the Eastern European economies will have to show more flexibility in this respect, they will merely delay the costs of adjustment—in terms of production losses and unemployment—if they allow external or internal adjustment to proceed slowly. Only if rapid steps are taken can these costs be clearly associated with past Communist mismanagement, while the benefits of the restructuring in terms of new goods available, new opportunities, and better future perspectives can be attributed to the efforts of a government determined to push reform and adjustment.

Comment

Benedikt Thanner

Currency convertibility is usually treated in the context of traditional price theory, as a means of making the prices of domestic goods comparable to those of foreign goods, and thus, via liberalization of foreign trade, of anchoring the country in question more strongly within the international division of labor. To achieve this aim, price liberalization, as undertaken in Poland, and vigilance against inflation are necessary.

I believe, however, that this approach is too limited to allow an adequate discussion of the major problems of currency convertibility in the countries now undergoing the transformation to a market economy. From the outset, convertibility should be seen as a monetary concept; this is best achieved when convertibility is understood as the unrestricted capacity to pay in foreign currency. This at once involves the whole complex of a country's international position, which goes far beyond mere trade and commerce. Convertibility in this sense is an expression of the quality of the whole economy, especially its monetary policy, and is therefore nearly synonymous with international creditworthiness.

A planned economy and currency convertibility are mutually contradictory. Granting individual state-owned plants or citizens a certain degree of disposition over foreign exchange does not change this basic fact. Convertibility implies that foreign exchange can be used even by an enterprise that does not generate foreign exchange itself because of its domestic orientation. The real test of convertibility is whether foreigners are willing, at prevailing domestic interest rates, to invest money in the local currency, and, conversely, whether residents are allowed to place money in foreign investments.

Obviously my intention here is to move the argument away from the assumption that exchange rates are relevant only to trade or to real transfers of goods and services. If this assumption is not laid to rest, as often it is not by Eastern European economists, the danger arises of viewing the path to convertibility somewhat too optimistically. The paper on Poland seems to me to make this mistake in its abstraction from the question of foreign indebtedness.

To summarize, I think that many widely used definitions of convertibility are purely mercantilistic and based on a limited concept of money as merely a unit of account and medium of exchange. The third function of money, as a store of value or a medium of payment, is critical, especially in an international context.

Benedikt Thanner is Director of the Eastern Europe Department of the IFO–Institut für Wirtschaftsforschung, Munich.

Turning to the three countries under discussion here, I would like to suggest an important criterion by which to assess the efforts of countries to introduce convertibility, namely, whether such efforts are incorporated into an overall development strategy and theory. The achievement of convertibility cannot be seen as an end in itself; the goal is rather to lead the countries of Eastern Europe to a much higher level of economic development. In this context the experience of the Third World developing countries and the Asian newly industrializing countries, and that of West Germany after World War II, take on greater relevance.

It is obvious that Poland and the former East Germany as well as the former CMEA countries, including Yugoslavia (with some reservations), have been confronted, after the removal of the apparatus of the command economy, with the fact of their general noncompetitiveness. Thus, their future development is still a very uncertain proposition, to judge from the history of similar efforts in other parts of the world.

What is most interesting about this history—especially that of Japan, Taiwan, Korea, and West Germany after the war—is the fact that in none of these countries was the catch-up process accompanied by a rapid move to currency convertibility. Instead their developmental strategies can be largely characterized as a combination of restrictive monetary policy and selective protectionism, combined with a high propensity to invest and a strong export orientation. The key point is that success was achieved in these countries not in the main by external "help" or capital inflows but by a strategy of currency undervaluation (where possible with fixed exchange rates) combined with development of the domestic market. Countries like Japan and especially Taiwan actually delayed for some time (and some continue to delay) the full adoption of convertibility, despite their having achieved developmental "maturity" by certain objective measures. Japan indeed wanted for mercantilistic reasons to continue to maintain the relative undervaluation of the yen.

It is in this context that we must consider the efforts of Poland, Yugoslavia, and the former East Germany to achieve currency convertibility. Upon monetary union with West Germany, East Germany ceased to exist as an independent economic entity. On that date, East Germany's development problem became a West German affair. The two Germanys chose this route for a number of important reasons, foremost among them the impossibility of East Germany's maintaining any sort of monetary autonomy in light of its rapidly disintegrating state structures. It is of special interest to Poland, which is also using radical monetary measures, that the adoption of the deutsche mark as a common currency in the two Germanys led initially to the collapse of output in East Germany. The effect of this was to rob potentially viable East German enterprises of their sales and potential capital resources for investment. The local authorities in what was East Germany now receive very limited tax revenue, which means that the whole economy would be in a state of insolvency were it not for the compensating transfer of money from the west. Even these transfers are strongly consumption-based. The migration of the labor force continues—as is rational since there is a need for that labor in the west.

One can conclude from all of this that further attempts at currency unions between very differently structured countries in Western and Eastern Europe would face extremely difficult problems. In the case of the two Germanys, political imperatives inevitably dominated economic ones, and therefore politics must also face the consequences (i.e., large transfers from west to east) and cannot simply leave matters for market forces to sort out.

For Poland and Yugoslavia, a currency union–like linkage to the European Community would be a catastrophe, or at least impractical any time in the near future. This does not mean, however, that the contrary solution is automatically the correct one. The Polish economy, in my opinion, urgently needs both a currency-linked bonus of confidence from the Community as well as a pegged exchange rate against the ecu at as low a level as possible, such as already has taken place against the dollar.

I tend to doubt, however, whether Poland will be able on its own strength to maintain such a linkage. The undervaluation of the zloty has so far not been tied to a worsening of the current account balance, because plants have sharply reduced their production and have cut back on imports. There is undoubtedly a negative trade-off between rigid anti-inflationary policies and currency devaluation: increased imports are necessary for the revival of industrial production. Selective protectionism may be needed to prevent too much consumer purchasing power from flowing abroad. The country's limited means must be kept available for the expansion of export industries.

For Poland, full currency convertibility is a realistic goal only in the distant future. It is sufficient in the short term to detach the foreign indebtedness from current transactions with both Western and Eastern countries, and to establish a flexible link to the zloty, backed by the European Community, to a Western European currency (for example, the ecu). In addition, capital transfer is urgently needed to expand the country's infrastructure.

The case of Yugoslavia, in my opinion, shows the risks of an ill-considered currency linkage: the level of the exchange rate chosen was far from realistic; perhaps more important, the Yugoslav central government had lost its monetary sovereignty years before in the conflict with the constituent republics and the spontaneously developing private sector. Moreover, I think it is absolutely dangerous to connect anti-inflation policy with convertibility of the currency without the implementation of a market-oriented monetary constitution. Fighting inflation is a task for domestic policy. The Yugoslav example also shows that we are dealing here more with the situation of a developing country that had maneuvered itself some time ago into the unfavorable position of an "underdeveloped" trading partner. One need only mention in this context the notion of the "extended workbench." Poland and the other Eastern European countries must by all means avoid getting themselves into such a dependent position. Such a strategy in the medium and long term becomes a hindrance to development and, especially when accompanied by a deliberate strategy of undervaluation, leads to a transfer of resources abroad.

In conclusion I would like to address the indebtedness problem. In contrast to the developed industrial countries, Poland and Yugoslavia were unable to borrow in their own currencies. They therefore do not have at their disposal, as does for example the United States, the convenient instrument of devaluation to achieve a partial reduction of their indebtedness. On the contrary, currency devaluation under these circumstances leads to an upward valuation of the debt from a domestic perspective. This, in my opinion, is one of the main reasons why definitions of convertibility that are related purely to flows of goods and services are inadequate. Historically similar cases—not least that of postwar Germany— show that a more or less significant reduction of indebtedness is much more important for longer-term development than a permanent influx of foreign capital.

Comment

Karol Lutkowski

These three papers highlight some common aspects of the experiments in currency convertibility undertaken in Poland, Yugoslavia, and the former East Germany, and they draw some universally valid conclusions. However, I am impressed above all by the vast differences in historical circumstances and local conditions in the three countries. For this reason, I will confine my remarks to the one case that I can claim to know from direct experience, that of Poland.

On the whole, I share the assessment of Andrzej Olechowski and Marek Oleś that the rapid switch to convertibility of the zloty, implemented as part of a larger stabilization package, was of momentous importance to the Polish reform program and imparted an entirely new quality to the Polish currency. The trend toward a double-currency standard, with all its hazards, has been radically stopped and reversed, and inflation has been stabilized at a much lower rate than before. Although the shock therapy administered to the Polish economy brought

---

Karol Lutkowski is Adviser to the Minister of Finance and Professor of International Finance at the Warsaw School of Economics.

enormous social costs and a decline in the level of production and in living standards, the economy seems now to be on the right track. Poland can now expect to attain its ultimate goal of transition to a full-blown market economy, provided that internal and external circumstances permit the government to stick to its chosen course of action. I have no doubts about its intent to do so.

Nevertheless some aspects of the Polish experiment remain open to legitimate criticism; in my view Poland's choice of exchange rate policy is one of them. The purpose of introducing convertibility at the start of the reform process rather than later was, in Wolfgang Schill's formulation, to use convertibility as an instrument of economic policy to accelerate certain structural changes seen as necessary to increase the overall efficiency of the economy. The immediate aims were, first, to import a more rational price structure; second, to import more intense competitive pressures, which were missing internally because of the degree of industrial concentration; and, last but not least, to use the fixed exchange rate, at which the zloty was convertible, as a nominal anchor of monetary stability.

The function of the exchange rate as a nominal anchor was to assume overriding importance in the initial phase of reform, in view of the fact that the reform process was initiated under hyperinflationary circumstances. Breaking inflationary expectations was considered the most urgent concern, and modern theory suggested that a fixed exchange rate might be the appropriate tool for the job. The commonly accepted conviction in Poland is that the convertibility experiment, together with the radical opening of the economy, has turned out to be the most successful element of the new economic mechanism. Evidence of this is the stability of the exchange rate during 1990, the unexpectedly rapid growth of exports, and the remarkable (by historical standards) increase in the country's foreign-exchange reserves.

All this stands in sharp contrast with the fears voiced immediately before the start of the reforms, when convertibility was viewed as a particularly risky part of the project. Some believed that general conditions in Poland were not ripe for such a move; in fact, the stand-by agreement concluded with the IMF required Poland to keep its exchange rate fixed for a period not shorter than three months—the expectation was that it would be impossible to keep the rate stable for a longer period. As the exchange rate of the zloty has now been kept unchanged for more than a year, a feeling of satisfaction at the results may appear fully warranted. The results may also be interpreted as an encouraging signal to countries contemplating a similar move.

Although I agree with the authors' positive assessment of the Polish experiment in convertibility, the favorable results in the external sector were due not to foreign-exchange policy alone but to the implementation of the package as a whole, with all its mutually supporting elements. Foreign-exchange policy was merely one of these. In my view, the decision to fix the exchange rate at the level of 9,500 zlotys to the dollar—roughly a 50 percent devaluation—was probably the single most important error the Polish reformers made. It was probably a pardonable error given the lack of transparency in foreign-exchange matters at the outset. Still it is important to recognize, with the benefit of hindsight, that the devaluation was excessive.

The sharp devaluation contributed powerfully to the social cost of stabilization and created a misleading impression all around that Poland's external payments position was relatively comfortable. Instead of the moderate deficit anticipated at the outset, Poland's balance of trade for 1990 as a whole closed with a substantial surplus; this lowered the country's standard of living more sharply than was necessary. Incidentally, the hypothesis of negative value added in a country subjected to this type of shock treatment may be not far off the mark in Poland's case. For a time at least, Poland may have experienced such a phenomenon, when the impact of the devaluation on the terms of trade is taken into account. Thus, exchange rate policy in Poland contributed to making the cost of stabilization unnecessarily high.

Of course, one may argue that the increase in foreign reserves is a welcome development for a variety of reasons, especially at a time when the economy was being subjected to such unexpectedly violent shocks as the rise in oil prices and the breakdown of the CMEA payment mechanism. On the other hand, the reduction of consumption that took place in the meantime was not originally intended. In the Polish case, the extent of the devaluation decisively contributed to that effect by strengthening the price rise at the moment when prices were being liberalized and the zloty was made convertible.

This is an important point, because it seems to me that the same error is being repeated in other countries of Eastern Europe that have embarked, or are about to embark, upon a path of reform similar to Poland's. Why would other countries make the same mistake? One reason may be an unjustified and uncritical confidence in the indications provided by the parallel foreign-exchange market; a second may be the erroneous belief that the sharper the devaluation, the more credible and stable the resulting exchange rate will be. The truth of the latter proposition is far from obvious, especially if the moment of devaluation coincides with that of price liberalization in a situation of repressed inflation.

I fully agree, of course, that a country in such a situation typically has to devalue quite substantially. However, too great a devaluation will so intensify inflationary pressures as to require an excessively restrictive monetary stance to reach the stabilization target. I am afraid that a stable exchange rate and the introduction of convertibility may never become fully credible, even if both are maintained for quite a long time, if the price of the strategy is a prolonged and deep recession and a choking off of the growth process. Rightly or wrongly, there will always be a residue of uncertainty as to whether the government will be politically capable of staying the course under such circumstances, and the conviction that it will not may easily become a self-fulfilling prophecy. In the case of Poland, the critical early phase of the reform was passed relatively peacefully, thanks to an exceptional degree of popular support for the reform attempt at the outset, but such conditions may not always and everywhere be fulfilled.

On the use of the exchange rate as a nominal anchor: I do not question in general the usefulness of such an instrument in breaking the impetus of the wage-price spiral under hyperinflationary circumstances. Nevertheless, I am inclined to believe that the stable exchange rate of the zloty played that role in the Polish stabilization effort to a lesser extent than was intended, for two reasons. First, a firm commitment to keep the rate unchanged for any significant period was never formally made. Second, the sharpness of the devaluation itself could have undermined that role from the start: during the first few months of the stabilization exercise the zloty was predominantly under upward pressure on the market, so that the effort to keep it stable was actually a powerful *pro*-inflationary factor from the point of view of price dynamics. It is hard to see how it could have acted as an anchor of price expectations at the same time.

It is true that stabilizing the exchange rate helped to reverse the trend toward a double-currency standard, and in that sense it did play a positive role by strengthening confidence in the external value of the currency. But the same cannot be said with respect to the zloty's internal value, so that on balance the signals coming from the external sector could have been rather confusing. In any event, the stability of the exchange rate was supported by other anchors, first and foremost by the tough, tax-based wage policy and the generally restrictive macrofinancial framework, which probably were the decisive factors in bringing inflation down.

Although convertibility did help Poland "import" a rational price structure from the world market, I doubt whether it was equally successful in importing competitive pressure. Clearly, the excessive devaluation acted as a substitute for a high tariff barrier, although it also gave a strong impetus to exports. This was a positive thing in itself, although not necessarily an unmixed blessing under the circumstances, as mentioned above. The fact remains that, in the first quarter of 1990, imports were 30 percent lower than in the comparable quarter of the previous year. Thus, it is thinkable that, despite the sharp cuts in tariffs, the economy found itself effectively more isolated from outside competition than before, at least for a time. It was only in early 1991, one year after the start of the experiment, that outside pressure began to make itself felt, and the still-stable rate of exchange began to function as a price anchor of a sort. It should be noted, however, that this happened in the context of a rate of inflation almost three times as high as that targeted by the original program for 1990. It is unfortunate that Poland had to rely on inflation to reverse the initial error of an excessive devaluation, because stemming inflation at minimum possible social cost was precisely the top priority of the original program.

The introduction of convertibility, together with the rest of the radical reform program, has put the Polish economy on an entirely new and highly promising track. However, to err is human, and we should admit that some significant blunders have been committed in the process, not least in the sphere of exchange rate policy. One can only hope that Poland will be able to avoid another error in the future—that of clinging too long to an excessively rigid exchange rate mechanism after the nominal anchor has served its purpose.

Comment

John K. Thompson

Convertibility can play a decisive role in the transition to a market economy by opening the economy to international trade (and ultimately to international capital movements) and thereby giving an economy in transition direct access to powerful price signals.[1] This applies equally whether the country in question is pursuing a gradualist (currently only Hungary) or a radical approach (e.g., Poland and Czechoslovakia) to the transition. Economies in transition from socialism to a market economy are likely to introduce convertibility at an earlier stage of their reforms than are economies that already have functioning markets. The latter have already achieved market-based domestic prices and have achieved stabilization as closed economies, even if the domestic economy was protected and domestic prices deviated from international prices. In contrast, the former command economies find the absence of meaningful price signals and the lack of competitive pressure to be serious barriers to a speedy transformation.

The conceptual underpinning of convertibility as an instrument of systemic change is derived mainly from the traditional theory of comparative advantage and the gains from trade. In a small, open economy, the price of tradeable goods is equal to the international price times the exchange rate. Liberalization obliges domestic enterprises to deal at international prices; specialization in production ensures that firms are given powerful incentives to use resources efficiently.

1. Since this comment mainly discusses the opening of the economy to international trade in goods, the expression "trade liberalization" could be substituted for convertibility.

John K. Thompson is Senior Economist in the Financial Markets Division of the Organization for Economic Cooperation and Development and a Research Fellow at the Center for Russian and East European Studies at the University of Pittsburgh.

The change in relative prices is the most important result of the opening of the economy to competition, but the role that convertibility can be expected to play in the transformation is more complex. The process of systemic transformation can be conceived as operating on three levels simultaneously: in addition to the change in relative price signals, two other crucial aspects of the transition are macroeconomic adjustments and structural transformation.

Macroeconomic adjustment means the achievement of a level of aggregate demand in the economy that is compatible with economic equilibrium, by which is meant the growth of national income at the potential rate, price stability, full employment, and a sustainable balance of international payments. Given the great systemic distortions in the former planned economies at present, all macroeconomic indicators (real growth, inflation, employment, balance of payments) inevitably show great instability, and it will be necessary to accept great macroeconomic imbalances in the medium term in order to create the minimal conditions for a functioning market economy.

Structural changes arise from changes in the motivations and behavior of institutions and individuals in response to new systemic rules. Banks and accounting systems fulfill different functions in a market economy than in a centrally planned economy.

To understand the interactions of these changes, one should remember that the move from a centrally planned economy occurs when enterprises are expected to act in response to prices in a market rather than to commands in a planning hierarchy. Relative price signals become important at precisely that time when enterprises are required to operate as profit-maximizing firms in a market economy rather than to respond to commands and directives as under central planning. It is conceivable that firms could begin to operate as profit-maximizing entities under the old prices. But in fact the move to world market prices is likely to occur at approximately (and probably exactly) the same time as the change in systemic rules: this will occur at once if the country is pursuing a policy of radical shock therapy, or it will be phased in if the policy is one of gradualism. Thus, not only are firms expected to behave as profit maximizers, but the resulting prices will contain the best available information about opportunity costs worldwide.

In order for economic agents to respond to price signals, some minimum of the institutional features that characterize a market economy must be present. The creation of institutions and behavioral patterns that are responsive to market signals may be characterized as structural adjustment.

Individual policy measures and instruments often influence more than one of the three aspects of the transformation. For example, fixing the exchange rate influences relative prices (especially between tradeable and nontradeable outputs) and, by influencing real wages and real money balances, has powerful macroeconomic effects as well. The system of wage determination is first of all an institutional or structural phenomenon, but it also affects relative prices and macroeconomic performance. The removal of subsidies will affect relative prices but will also have significant macroeconomic effects by reducing public expenditure and by lowering real wages.

In the past few decades, analysis of policy has tended to stress the macroeconomic aspect of adjustment. It was, for example, assumed that one important purpose of devaluation was to improve the current account balance and to shift domestic production toward tradeables. In more recent years, economic adjustment policies, particularly some undertaken in cooperation with international financial organizations, have emphasized the necessity of having correct relative price signals as well. Important price relationships postulated were the real exchange rate, the real wage, the real interest rate, and the balance between rural and urban prices. It was frequently recommended that trade liberalization be undertaken at the same time as price reform. In making policy prescriptions, it was presumed that the profit-maximizing firm adjusts output to changes in relative prices and that wage demands will moderate as the unemployment rate rises. To the degree that firms and individuals deviate from this assumed pattern of behavior, however, underlying assumptions about likely reactions will not adequately explain observed behavior.

The system of central planning created an array of institutions and mechanisms designed to encourage economic agents to respond to central commands rather than to market signals. Thus, as the goal of systemic change is established, the functions of all the component parts of the centrally planned economy are changed. Banking, accounting, trade unions, and company law, to name a few, all must function differently in order to support the transition to a market economy. To the degree that agents continue to behave as before, the effectiveness of macroeconomic measures and relative price changes is dissipated.

To take one example, enterprises in most of the former centrally planned economies still do not face hard budget constraints. These enterprises are to a large degree motivated by factors other than profitability, such as maintaining relationships with traditional clients. Ownership of these enterprises is frequently unclear, and in many cases actual control has often drifted into the hands of workers' councils. Banks find themselves unable to enforce financial discipline on enterprises. High real interest rates and a concentration of bank credit in the least creditworthy firms are observed. In brief, a functioning market is largely absent.

The discussion to this point has mainly considered the effect of introducing world prices into a closed, formerly centrally planned economy at a given time. A second major point concerns the relationship between domestic inflation (changes in prices over time) and convertibility. (The conceptual question of whether one-time increases in the price level following price liberalization and devaluation should properly be termed "inflation" will not be pursued here.)

The simultaneous freeing of domestic prices and liberalization of trade implies that links between domestic and international prices will become closer. In fact, as the domestic prices of tradeables come to approximate the international price multiplied by the exchange rate, so increases in those prices will tend eventually to approximate the rate of change of the exchange rate. Changes in the nominal wage rate will affect the ratio between tradeables and the real wage.

Poland and Yugoslavia both decided to adopt convertibility at a time of high domestic inflation. In both cases, the annualized rate of inflation exceeded 1,000 percent at the time the economy was opened to trade. The availability of imported goods limited the capacity of domestic producers to increase prices, thereby mitigating price pressures. In Poland, hyperinflation existed alongside severe shortages; hence opening the economy not only slowed inflation but also alleviated the shortages. Additionally, by reducing real money balances, the surge of price increases following devaluation and price liberalization forced Polish households and enterprises to save—that is, to rebuild money balances—thereby reducing demand pressures. The large devaluation and resulting price increases also led to a sharp drop in the real wage.

Although the initial experience of these two countries indicates that the opening of the economy to trade has led to reduced inflationary pressure, their later experience shows that the introduction of convertibility by itself has severe limits as an anti-inflationary device. After the initial reduction in the rate of price increase, a reacceleration of inflation followed within a few months. In Yugoslavia, liberalization was not accompanied by sufficient discipline over bank credit expansion to restrain the growth of demand. Thus, it is clear that, at a minimum, the move to convertibility must be supported by appropriate demand management policies.

The Polish example is more troubling. The stabilization package of January 1990 was accompanied by a considerable tightening of fiscal and monetary policy. Nevertheless, after monthly inflation had been reduced from 70 percent in January to 1 percent to 2 percent around midyear, a distinct reacceleration occurred, with monthly rates of 5 percent (80 percent annually) registered near the end of the year. The fact that real national income contracted sharply and the current account balance improved dramatically strongly suggests that the deflationary macroeconomic measures were indeed powerful. However, the subsequent Polish experience suggests that even a resolute pursuit of restrictive macroeconomic policies and the introduction of world prices in the domestic economy may not be sufficient to achieve price stability.

This leads us to the first major conclusion of this analysis, namely, that the explanation for the resurgence of inflation may lie in the rigidity of economic structures. Many analysts tend to resist suggestions that structural rigidities, particularly in the wage and price formation process, may be a cause of inflation. However, even those holding strong monetarist views will recognize that the assertion that only excess demand can cause inflation is valid only if underlying structures and systemic rules are responsive to prices. If systemic rules are changed but economic structures do not change correspondingly, the potential for inflation can be very high.

To demonstrate that the problem may be more than a simple inability to control demand, it is useful to contrast the experience of the high-inflation countries of Eastern Europe with that of Hungary and Czechoslovakia, which have had relatively low rates of inflation. In the low-inflation countries, the initial result of the opening to international trade, which is usually accompanied by a removal of subsidies, price liberalization, and devaluation of the currency, is nearly always to increase the rate of inflation, even though the objective of the policy is to achieve better relative prices. The only means to change relative prices is by a general increase in the price level in which some prices rise faster than others. Additionally, in order to reduce real incomes so as to live within a tight balance of payments constraint, it is essential to reduce excess purchasing power with price increases.

Reflecting this process, the rate of inflation in Hungary has been moving upward since the mid–1980s, when it was some 5 percent to 10 percent, to more than 30 percent at present. Following the measures introduced at the beginning of 1991, Czechoslovakia too will have a rate of inflation exceeding 30 percent. The Czechoslovak authorities believe that this rate merely represents a correction following devaluation and price liberalization, and that in later periods inflation will fall. However, the experience of other former centrally planned economies is not especially encouraging. The Hungarians have been pursuing a policy of price liberalization since the mid–1980s, but no turning point in inflation is yet in sight. The available evidence does not yet prove conclusively the presence of a structural bias toward inflation, but thus far the preponderance of evidence points in that direction.

As was mentioned earlier, a change of behavior on the part of economic agents is now recognized as essential to transformation. The experience of the former centrally planned economies may well indicate that the structural rigidities that remain from the old central planning system, combined with the need to achieve good relative price signals, may impart a very strong inflationary bias to econo-mies in transition. For example, it is known that enterprises in these economies for the most part do not face hard budget constraints and do not pursue profit-ability as their most important objective.

The mechanisms that existed under the older central planning systems may have been adequate to contain demand pressures in some countries. For example, Czechoslovakia, a rather well-run centrally planned economy, appears to have prevented both open and suppressed inflation. However, the effectiveness of a given mechanism in containing inflation under a central planning system does not necessarily mean that the same country will succeed in stabilizing under an entirely different system.

If indeed a structural tendency toward inflation can be identified in the former centrally planned economies, it would appear inevitable that severe constraints will exist on the efficacy of aggregate demand management and policies to affect relative prices throughout the economy. In other words, it is quite possible that a serious imbalance may exist between the powerful price signals that arise when the economy is opened to foreign competition and the limited capacity of domestic structures to respond. Other things being equal, this would suggest that the gradualist rather than the radical approach is to be recommended, since the process of structural adjustment is by its nature gradual. Whereas powerful price signals can be introduced immediately, ingrained patterns of behavior take years, if not decades, to change. Moreover, the traditional measures used to produce good price signals (devaluation and price liberalization) tend to induce cost pressures, and rigid economies tend to be able to pass on higher costs rather easily.

This does not imply that policies at the level of the entire economy will be ineffective; quite the contrary, they are essential to the transformation. However, any recommended package of policy remedies for a former centrally planned economy should stress structural change to a higher degree than for a market economy. Moreover, until structural change has progressed significantly, the prospects for controlling inflation may not be especially promising.

My second major conclusion is that a structural tendency toward inflation, if eventually proven to exist in these countries, has serious implications for their exchange rate policy. In much recent discussion, the economies in transition have been advised to use the exchange rate as a nominal anchor for policy. This term contains considerable ambiguity. On the one hand, it may be simply an indication that the exchange rate is a more reliable guide to the short-term conduct of monetary policy than monetary or credit aggregates. (This argument may well be invalid, since these economies, which have only primitive money markets and still maintain tight controls on capital movements, are better equipped to control their aggregates than are most market economies.) The more significant meaning that may be drawn from the term "nominal anchor" is that the exchange rate should be held relatively stable for long periods in order to promote domestic price stability.

If this is what a "nominal anchor" means, then use of a nominal anchor may lead to unfortunate consequences in these economies. In particular, there is a clear trade-off between the objective of maintaining relatively cheap import prices and that of maintaining trade competitiveness.

My final conclusion concerns the appropriate exchange rate regime in economies in transition. A case can be made for an initial large devaluation to accompany convertibility, followed by a period in which the exchange rate remains unchanged, to generate expectations of relative stability. However, to conceive of the exchange rate as a nominal anchor in current circumstances will thwart several key objectives of the transformation. A country that has made the needed structural adjustments and has achieved general macroeconomic balance may consider adopting a fixed exchange rate. This is the solution that most Western European countries appear to be adopting at this time, but it is probably not an appropriate policy for the economies now in transition.

Given the strong capacity of these economies to pass on cost increases, and given the limited supply response, a large devaluation may well have a strong inflationary impact while producing limited behavioral change. At the same time, a policy of not adequately adjusting the exchange rate as time goes on may well create a set of inappropriate relative prices that would send false signals throughout the economy. As a result, the most appropriate exchange rate solution for an economy in transition may be a crawling peg, in which the exchange rate is adjusted by small amounts at frequent intervals in order to maintain international competitiveness. Such a mechanism is a temporary expedient, to be maintained only until underlying structures become more responsive. However, it has proven effective elsewhere in cases similar to those now found in the former centrally planned economies.

Discussion

Jozef van Brabant commented that all three speakers had addressed the financial conditions concerning trade between their country and the West, but had said little or nothing about those governing their trade with one another and with other countries of the former CMEA. He asked all three speakers to describe what had happened to the arrangements for trading in nonconvertible currencies that formerly existed within the CMEA, including the clearing arrangements previously maintained by Yugoslavia. Had those arrangements been abandoned or modified? How had the special arrangements to permit the maintenance of East German exports in 1990 been modified to cover the rest of Eastern Europe, as well as the Soviet Union, in 1991? What was happening to Polish trade with the former CMEA countries? Was it not true that traders were resorting to all kinds of arrangements, from strict interfirm barter to dealings in convertible currencies? Why was Poland refusing to allow its traders to pay for imports from Czechoslovakia in convertible currencies?

Michael Marrese questioned the meaningfulness of Wolfgang Schill's comparison of 1989 East German prices measured in East German marks with 1990 prices measured in deutsche marks, which was the basis for his claim that inflation in East Germany had been negative. To try and tease out the implications of the decision to unify the two German currencies at an exchange rate of 1:1, Marrese suggested comparing the actual situation with a hypothetical one in which political union had occurred without monetary union. There would thus have been two separate currencies but a single government, and a single Bundesbank running both currencies and lending its credibility to both. Now suppose that the exchange rate had been 4 East German marks to 1 deutsche mark instead of the actual 1:1. What would the implications have been for eastern Germany? Would real wages have been lower? Would the region have been a more attractive location for foreign investment?

Richard Portes asked for the empirical evidence supporting the Olechowski-Oleś claim that the export boom and positive balance of payments performance of Poland were primarily due to the competitive and stable exchange rate rather than to the domestic recession. He went on to mention the massive real appreciation (around 250 percent) that Poland had experienced since the beginning of 1990. Exports had gone on rising so far, but what sort of lag structure underlies that performance? Why had imports risen so much in the last quarter of 1990? Output did not appear to have risen, so could the answer be a fall in real interest rates or the end of destocking?

Portes also asked Karol Lutkowski to describe the mechanisms by which the excessive initial devaluation of the zloty could have caused stagnation. Was it the classical case of contractionary devaluation? Finally, he remarked that, after the experience of the last decade, many member countries of the European exchange rate mechanism would challenge Benedikt Thanner's assertion that anti-inflation policy had to be essentially domestic.

Lawrence Brainard suggested that the question on Poland could usefully be rephrased in the following terms: Is the exchange rate still the nominal anchor, and if so, what will the authorities do when the balance of payments deteriorates in 1991? While agreeing with Schill that the East German experience is not a model for other countries, Brainard argued that it is the only success we have so far, which explains why we are so interested in it. He asked Schill what, with the benefit of hindsight, he thought should have been done differently.

Klaus Schröder asked why Poland had chosen to peg to the dollar rather than to the deutsche mark or the ecu.

Replying to the discussion, *Andrzej Olechowski* agreed that the zloty had been devalued too much at the time of the stabilization; that would be difficult to deny, given that prices had risen by 250 percent since then. He explained that the exchange rate chosen nonetheless involved the *smallest* devaluation that anyone had mentioned in the discussions preceding implementation of the plan. For the future, he suggested that it would be desirable at some stage to move to a market-based system for determining the exchange rate, but he thought that the time had not yet come. For technical reasons, Poland was not yet ready to float, and there was still a need for a stable exchange rate to assist medium-term planning (the medium term being about three months in Poland). For psychological reasons, Poland was also unready to abandon the dollar peg in favor of a basket: the dollar had originally been chosen because almost 50 percent of Polish trade is conducted in dollars, and because every Pole knows what a dollar is, whereas few know what a currency basket is.

Was the exchange rate still playing the role of nominal anchor? Olechowski agreed with Lutkowski that it was only in the last few months that it may have begun to play that role, since it was only recently that it had begun to provide for effective competition from abroad. The reason for the sharp reduction in imports in early 1990 was not only the undervaluation of the zloty, but also the collapse of the distribution system. For example, imports of pesticides had for years been planned by a technical committee in the Ministry of Agriculture; this committee was disbanded as superfluous in late 1989, but it was not until January 1990 that someone realized that no alternative plans had been made to import pesticides. Only in the summer of 1990 had new wholesalers emerged in a number of sectors to provide alternative channels for distribution.

Wolfgang Schill started by responding to Brabant's question. Ruble-based trade had expired at the end of 1990, but trade with Eastern Europe would now benefit from improved credit facilities and guarantees, with the aim of sustaining trade in 1991. He accepted that there were problems in comparing this year's price level as measured in deutsche marks with last year's as measured in East German marks, but since the conversion ratio had been 1:1 he felt there was some logic in converting them on that basis also for the purpose of making intertemporal comparisons of price levels. What would have been the impact of a 4:1 conversion in place of 1:1? He assumed the question referred to the conversion of flow variables such as wages, pensions, and rents. The predominant opinion is that the exchange rate does not matter much so far as the flow variables are concerned. The conversion only determines the starting point for (for example) wage negotiations between employers and trade unions, and one could assume that the outcome of the bargaining process will be largely independent of the initial position.

What would he recommend doing differently with the benefit of hindsight? He indicated that he would not choose to change any decisions on the monetary side—either the transfer of monetary policy to the Bundesbank, or the conversion of stocks at an average rate of 1.8:1. He did believe that the real side of the East German economy could have been better prepared for restructuring, particularly by better educating the population to understand what changes would be necessary. He also believed that there might well have been a better way to privatize companies than to hand everything over to the Treuhandanstalt. What could certainly have been handled better was the fiscal problem: the deficit had grown excessively, partly as a result of the speed of the transition and the hurry to make decisions.

Ljubiša Adamovich remarked that for the past thirty years Yugoslav foreign economic relations had been dominated by the Soviet Union, Germany, and Italy. Brabant was right to point to the difficulties that had been created for Yugoslav exporters by requiring Soviet buyers to pay in convertible currencies; given such a choice, any rational Soviet importer would choose to buy Italian rather than Yugoslav shoes. Yugoslavia still had a couple of barter arrangements in effect, but they were being phased out, and he argued that their loss was a price worth paying for the rationalization of Yugoslav trade, which would yield long-term benefits.

6

The Next Candidates

6

The Next Candidates

Czechoslovakia

Jaromír Zahradník

The November 1989 revolution put an end to Czechoslovakia's flirtation with the idea of a market economy and to debates over to what extent market forces should be tolerated within the centralized system of economic management. In early September 1990 the Czechoslovak parliament approved a program of radical economic reform based on transformation to a market-oriented economy.

For almost forty years the role of money in Czechoslovakia has been predetermined by the central plan, with cash flows merely its passive reflection. Money, credit, interest, and exchange rates all acted merely as humble servants to His Majesty the Plan. What we Czechoslovak bankers are now experiencing in the wake of the Velvet Revolution is no less than the rebirth of money and banking, as monetary functions again begin to play an active role in the economy.

The experience acquired from the functioning, or rather the nonfunctioning, of the socialist countries' financial mechanism has taught these countries a valuable lesson: until the necessary prerequisites are established, these countries will never achieve currency convertibility, because convertibility is nothing but the reflection of an economy's level of development and of its domestic and external equilibrium. In other words, the path to convertibility is a matter of removing all deficiencies and obstacles to that development and of fundamentally transforming the economy. These deficiencies and obstacles include:

- Domestic and external disequilibria;

- Monopolies in various industries and an underdeveloped private sector;

- The obsolescence of a number of industries, an underdeveloped service sector, and obsolete banking methods;

Jaromír Zahradník is Deputy Governor of the State Bank of Czechoslovakia.

- Scarcities of raw materials and products;

- Wastage of energy and general inefficiency;

- Lack of capital and of foreign competition.

It is also important that the period during which the former system of management is dismantled be kept as short as possible; otherwise a further disruption of economic equilibrium and a further slowing of economic development are unavoidable.

The Czechoslovak Economy in the 1980s

The economic situation of prerevolutionary Czechoslovakia may be characterized as contradictory. There was a relatively low rate of inflation, ranging, according to estimates, from 3 percent to 5 percent per year (table 1). However, because of price rigidities and the inelasticity of other payment methods, it was impossible to identify the size of the inflationary gap solely in terms of price development. In fact, domestic market imbalances were usually translated into resource scarcities, in other words into an excess of demand on retail and investment markets. The price system was greatly distorted, and the relationship between foreign prices and domestic wholesale and retail prices was highly anomalous.

In external economic relations, there prevailed a massive disequilibrium in convertible-currency trade, as foreign-exchange receipts failed to cope with demand for imported products and for foreign exchange. Even so, Czechoslovakia managed to maintain a relatively low level of gross indebtedness (about $7 billion). On the other hand, exports of Czechoslovak products to the modest CMEA market brought in considerable profits and, along with low and falling raw materials prices, provided substantial foreign-exchange assets for the state. Although the quality of some Czechoslovak exports was below world market standards, those exports were nonetheless sufficient to pay for most of the country's raw materials imports. The transition to world prices and payments in convertible currencies means that Czechoslovakia now needs larger amounts of convertible currencies to pay for the raw materials imports that previously were paid for in transferable rubles.

In the second half of the 1980s, Czechoslovakia embarked on a program designed to encourage enterprises to pay greater attention to their foreign trade performance. A system of foreign-exchange accounts for manufacturing enterprises similar to that used in Poland in the early part of the decade was introduced. Under this system, exporters were allowed to retain part of their foreign-exchange receipts and deposit them in their own foreign-exchange accounts. From these

Table 1 Czechoslovakia: selected economic indicators, 1985–89

	1985	1986	1987	1988	1989	1990
Population (millions)[a]	15.5	15.6	15.6	15.6	15.7	15.7
Net material product (billions of current korunas)	556.3	570.1	583.3	606.4	618.1	673.3[b]
Consumer price index (1985 = 100)	100.0	100.5	100.6	100.7	102.1	112.3
Merchandise trade (millions of current dollars)						
In nonconvertible currencies						
Exports	7,783	9,202	10,645	10,017	8,769	5,744
Imports	8,202	9,812	10,791	9,549	9,043	6,457
In convertible currencies						
Exports	3,852	4,293	4,545	5,014	5,442	5,994
Imports	3,157	4,069	4,669	5,096	5,022	6,780
Current account balance (millions of current dollars)						
In nonconvertible currencies	−100	−300	430	1,152	500	−206
In convertible currencies	789	469	−59	−59	439	−1,105
Foreign indebtedness (millions of current dollars)	5,574	6,715	7,657	7,805	8,691	9,214
Exchange rates[c] (korunas per dollar)						
Official[d]	6.85	6.00	5.47	5.32		
Commercial[e]	17.18	15.00	13.68	14.36	15.05	17.95
Noncommercial	11.99	10.50	9.57	9.31	9.75	17.95

a. End of period. b. Preliminary. c. Period average. d. Discontinued as of 1 January 1989.
e. Until 31 December 1988, the commercial rate was the official rate multiplied by a coefficient for commercial payments. The commercial and noncommercial rates were unified on 8 January 1990.

Source: State Bank of Czechoslovakia.

they could pay for their imports at their own discretion. The rest of the foreign-exchange receipts were channeled to the so-called central foreign-exchange source, from which funds were appropriated according to the central plan.

This system increased the responsibility of enterprises for their exports and for their foreign-exchange allocation. The system was, however, complicated and ultimately unworkable. Although it had seemed a step in the right direction, it suffered from one serious defect: it failed to link the domestic currency, the koruna, with its foreign counterparts. There still existed entirely different domestic and foreign market prices, unrealistic exchange rates, different guidelines for domestic-currency and foreign-exchange lending, different interest rates, and different rules of access to koruna and foreign-exchange funds.

Laying the Foundation for Reform: Macroeconomic Measures

Following the November 1989 revolution, Czechoslovakia set for itself the goal of establishing a market-oriented economy with all its characteristic features, including currency convertibility. It would, of course, have been feasible to specify conditions under which the existing system of foreign-exchange accounts could have led to convertibility of the koruna. But that system by itself could not have led to the rapprochement and merger of domestic and foreign price relations. On the contrary, as the Czechoslovak experience has shown, it would have risked the dollarization of the economy. Indeed such a development would have been inevitable if major internal and external disequilibria had been allowed to persist.

Czechoslovakia's paramount aim for the year 1990 was therefore restoration of its economic equilibrium. This aim took precedence over the need to achieve economic growth. To this end, a restrictive financial and foreign-exchange policy was adopted, to reduce the aggregate demand of enterprises, individuals, and the state. Economic growth was adversely affected by the collapse of the former control and managing system and by rapidly changing external conditions, especially the disintegration of the CMEA market, the reunification of Germany, and the Persian Gulf crisis. To limit the impact of these influences, macroeconomic measures relying primarily on monetary instruments were adopted. The discount rate was gradually increased, and the koruna was devalued against the convertible currencies on three separate occasions during the year.

Although a modest surplus in the state budget was achieved, and although additional domestic credit to enterprises and households amounted to only 1 percent (limits for this credit for 1990 were from −1 percent to 2.6 percent), inflation nevertheless rose to 10 percent. Simultaneously, national income dropped by roughly 3 percent and domestic demand increased by about 1.6 percent. This higher spending was balanced by an increase in the external debt position. The trade balance with the convertible-currency countries showed a deficit of 1.1 billion korunas. The trade deficit with the nonconvertible-currency countries was 9.6 billion korunas, although there were large variations within this group (a surplus with the Soviet Union of 8.9 billion korunas, and a deficit with the former East Germany of 10.3 billion korunas).

The Introduction of Convertibility

The macroeconomic measures implemented during 1990 created generally healthy conditions for the realization of basic reforms beginning on 1 January 1991. These included:

■ Price liberalization;

■ The beginnings of privatization;

■ Foreign trade liberalization;

■ The implementation of internal convertibility of the koruna.

One of the milestones in Czechoslovakia's transition from a centrally managed to a market economy was the introduction of internal current account convertibility of the koruna on 1 January 1991. The move to convertibility is a natural part of the opening of the Czechoslovak economy. It will enable Czechoslovakia to create a true market environment for foreign exchange, although convertibility is to be restricted initially to residents and legal entities.

Under the Foreign Exchange Act, which went into effect on 1 January 1991, the foreign-exchange balances of all enterprises are to be sold to the banks for korunas at the market rate. The banks in turn are bound to meet foreign-exchange commitments resulting from the import of goods and services for their clients, in return for the equivalent in korunas. Foreign-exchange accounts of legal entities are banned. The new law affects not only state, cooperative, and municipal enterprises, but also private entrepreneurs and joint ventures with foreign capital participation. Individuals' access to foreign exchange is understandably limited at this point to purchases of 5,000 korunas.

In line with standard international practice, initial efforts toward convertibility will focus on the liberalization of the current account. At a later stage, capital flows (credits and foreign investments) will gradually be liberalized, as a stable market economy is created.

The introduction of internal convertibility was preceded by much debate over how to lessen the external and internal impact of liberalizing the foreign-exchange system. Attention was concentrated mainly on establishing an acceptable path of external indebtedness and on finding an exchange rate that would stabilize the balance of payments.

The first option considered was to increase the supply of foreign exchange and draw on foreign credit sources to obtain foreign-currency reserves with which to intervene in the internal foreign-exchange market. However, this would have created a considerable risk of a disproportionate increase in Czechoslovakia's hard-currency debt, which, in turn, could have restrained future economic development. Therefore it was necessary to treat Czechoslovakia's economic capacity as the deciding factor in introducing internal convertibility.

The second option was to seek equilibrium in the foreign-exchange market by limiting demand and reviving supply through devaluation of the koruna. The solution actually chosen attempted to strike a balance between an acceptable buildup of external debt and an appropriate degree of devaluation.

The appropriate level of the exchange rate, given the level of debt accumulation considered tolerable, became the object of heated discussion. A number of bases for determining the appropriate exchange rate were suggested. One proposed method was to base the exchange rate on the long-term production costs (in korunas) necessary to generate one unit of convertible currency; this method suggested a rate of approximately 16 korunas to the dollar. Calculations based on purchasing power parity suggested a rate of approximately 8 to 10 korunas to the dollar, whereas calculations based on marginal production costs put the rate at 30 to 35 korunas to the dollar.

It gradually became clear that adoption of an exchange rate that would achieve purchasing power parity would require a very tightly regulated policy. It would impose extreme hardship on Czechoslovakian citizens and would be inconsistent with the market-based distribution of foreign exchange. Consequently, the later discussion concentrated on the optimum degree of devaluation of the koruna.

In fact these discussions concentrated on the nature of the foreign-exchange mechanism. The achievement of a proportionate rate in the market became inevitable, as further developments also confirmed.

Unfavorable developments in Czechoslovakia's external liquidity position during the second half of 1990, together with a significant reduction in foreign-exchange reserves, contributed to the final decision regarding the initial exchange rate. These problems arose from both internal and external sources. Internally, entrepreneurs concerned about the long-term effects of devaluation tried to minimize the expected damage by withdrawing the remaining balances on their foreign-exchange accounts and accelerating their payments for imports. This development taught the Czechoslovak authorities a valuable lesson in the implementation of monetary and foreign-exchange policy, since it confirmed the existence of considerable sensitivity to any signs of a change in the new exchange rate. Externally, a larger number of investors ceased their dealings with Czechoslovak banks.

These factors merely accelerated the decision to bring the exchange rate into line with current market levels. Following a 55 percent devaluation of the koruna in October 1990, the exchange rate was finally fixed at 28 korunas to the dollar on 28 December 1990—a further devaluation of 17 percent. On the same date the separate tourist rate was abolished.

During 1990, Czechoslovakia's policies were oriented primarily toward finding a market level for the koruna that would secure equilibrium in the balance of payments. Given the considerable excess of demand over supply, and given widespread fears regarding the impact of price liberalization, a substantial devaluation was unavoidable. Beginning in 1991, however, policy is to be aimed at stabilizing the koruna and at reviving confidence in it in order to provide an anchor for prices.

Technical Aspects of Convertibility

In technical terms, since 1 June 1981 the exchange rate for the koruna has been linked to a basket of five freely convertible currencies. As of 28 December 1990 the relative weights of the basket currencies were as follows:

Deutsche mark	45.52 percent
US dollar	31.34 percent
Austrian schilling	12.35 percent
Swiss franc	6.55 percent
Pound sterling	4.24 percent

These weights are based on the estimated balance of payments turnover relative to each currency (excluding purely banking operations).

It is often suggested that the exchange rate of the koruna be pegged to some supranational monetary unit such as the European currency unit (ecu) or the Special Drawing Right (SDR), or to a single major currency such as the deutsche mark. Ultimately the decision comes down to whether the peg should reflect the closeness of the country's economic ties with a given country or countries, or whether it should simply be a mathematical reflection of cross rates against the freely convertible currencies, to ensure nominal stability for the koruna vis-à-vis the average of these currencies.

In the Czechoslovak authorities' opinion, linking the koruna to a single freely convertible currency or to a supranational monetary unit cannot be justified for macroeconomic reasons. Given the different currency weightings within the SDR and the ecu, on the one hand, and the koruna on the other hand, linking the koruna to either the SDR or the ecu would simply distort its value, since Czechoslovakia's economic and trade relations would no longer be accurately reflected.

Furthermore, it is important that the koruna be allowed to find its own level with regard to other currencies. The question of an acceptable level of foreign debt is relevant here and was considered in detail during the formulation of the IMF memorandum on future Czechoslovak economic policy.

In 1991 a deficit of $2.5 billion is forecast for Czechoslovakia's current account.[1] Together with private capital inflows and borrowings on the capital markets, this imbalance is expected to be financed by official sources of support such as the IMF, the European Community, and the World Bank. A certain portion of the IMF funds will be used to increase the gross level of foreign-exchange reserves, from the current $1.2 billion (four weeks' worth of 1991 imports) to $2.3 billion (1.7 months' worth of 1991 imports). By the end of 1991, foreign debt in convertible currencies (including borrowings from the IMF) should reach $12 billion,[2] or 37 percent of GDP, and debt servicing should reach approximately 11 percent of current account receipts.

On 7 January 1991 the Board of Executive Directors of the IMF approved Czechoslovakia's economic program. Part of this agreement includes a range of conditions on the disbursement of credit. The stand-by credit will be available for a term of 14 months and total 105 percent of Czechoslovakia's quota (i.e., SDR620 million, or $886 million at the then-current SDR–dollar exchange rate). A compensatory financing facility will be granted to a maximum of 82 percent of Czechoslovakia's quota (i.e., SDR439 million, or $692 million).[3] This sum is designed to cover the increased cost of oil imports and to compensate for a drop in exports. Further financial assistance is to be provided in the form of a so-called contingency element, to cover any further sudden increase in oil and gas prices. These funds will amount to a maximum of 25 percent of Czechoslovakia's quota (i.e., SDR147 million). The first disbursement is envisaged for 15 May 1991, should another oil price increase occur.

Other Reforms

The introduction of internal convertibility is being accompanied by certain other reforms needed to create a market environment. The most notable of these is price liberalization, since this will influence the basic relationship between supply and demand within the economy and will substantially limit the regulatory function of the state. The proportion of goods still subject to price regulation

---

1. As this goes to press, the projection for the deficit has been lowered to $2 billion.

2. As this goes to press, the foreign debt in convertible currencies is estimated at $11 billion.

3. This was raised in the months following the conference to SDR484 million.

comprises approximately 15 percent of total production. As soon as circumstances allow, further items will be removed from the list of regulated goods.

It is expected that the freeing of the majority of prices, a substantial rise in the cost of fuels and other raw materials, and movements in other world prices will bring about an overall price increase of some 25 percent in the first three months of 1991. However, as strict financial and incomes policies are introduced, the rate of inflation should drop to an annual rate of approximately 5 percent during the remaining months of the year. Thus, inflation for 1991 as a whole is expected to be around 30 percent.[4]

A further basic step is a change in property rights throughout the economy. Along with the creation of new laws and regulations governing property rights, broad programs of privatization of state property are being prepared, including the restoration of property to former owners.

The mechanism of internal convertibility for current account payments has been made possible by the creation of an interbank foreign-exchange market. In this market the forces of supply and demand are allowed free rein, as the varying foreign-exchange requirements of individual banks are met internally each day. The State Bank of Czechoslovakia (the central bank) acts as a special entity to which the banks sell their foreign-exchange surpluses. It also maintains equilibrium in the internal market by drawing on its own foreign-exchange reserves. Since the introduction of convertibility in January 1991 there has been no substantial increase in demand for foreign exchange. The full extent of intervention by the central bank from its foreign-exchange reserves has not exceeded the prescribed limits and has enabled the authorities to comply with the range agreed upon with the IMF.

---

4. Actual inflation in the first quarter came in at 41 percent; as this goes to press, inflation for 1991 as a whole is expected to be between 50 percent and 60 percent.

Hungary

Lajos Bokros

For more than twenty years Hungary has been considered a front-runner in implementing economic reforms in Eastern Europe. Yet in spite of comprehensive financial modernization in the areas of banking, capital markets, foreign investment, taxation, and public finance, the issue of currency convertibility as a cornerstone of establishing a market economy has never come up. Making the Hungarian forint fully convertible has always remained a somewhat vague and distant final goal to be achieved through consecutive reforms rather than taken as their starting point. The lack of adequate foreign reserves and the high level of foreign debt were universally accepted as completely impeding any meaningful step to ease tight centralization and control of foreign-exchange transactions.

In the wake of the historic changes that swept over Eastern Europe in 1989, the question of currency convertibility was suddenly pushed to the forefront by the pressing need to establish all the essential institutions of a market economy as quickly as possible. It was argued that the serious financial imbalances that had been an intrinsic feature of nearly all the centrally planned economies would be best cured by a shock treatment, including the imminent establishment of at least current account convertibility. In theory, currency convertibility seems to be an indispensable element of a successful shock therapy, since only a more or less stable exchange rate can provide the anchor needed to stabilize the price level and resist the mismanagement of aggregate demand after the once-for-all big leap in the adjustment of prices of goods and factors has been made.

Hungary has not only serious financial imbalances but also the highest per capita foreign debt in Eastern Europe. Yet Hungary has deliberately avoided implementing any form of shock treatment, and despite some political rhetoric on the surface, it has not set currency convertibility as an immediate goal. Although seemingly the most market-oriented of the former socialist countries, Hungary has opted for a rather conservative, gradualist approach, which often leaves the impression that real progress toward a market economy is lagging behind political expectations.

Lajos Bokros is Managing Director of the Capital Markets Department at the National Bank of Hungary and Chairman of the Budapest Stock Exchange.

The Need for Shock Treatment

Shock therapy as a one-time big step for restoring domestic financial equilibrium is a necessary adjustment measure in a situation characterized by the following features:

- Prices of important goods and factors are administratively set and do not reflect marginal cost and efficiency levels, leading to serious price distortions and misallocation of resources.

- As a consequence of these distortions and misallocations, the economy is characterized by serious shortages on the one hand, and substantial waste and underutilization of factors on the other; these deficiencies are not alleviated by foreign trade since imports are not liberalized.

- Shortages are accentuated by systematic government overspending, which is not—indeed can no longer be—financed by foreign borrowing; fiscal deficits are instead financed by unlimited monetary expansion, which creates forced savings and a massive monetary overhang.

- All this leads to an inflationary explosion where goods with fixed and very low, subsidized prices gradually disappear from official distribution channels to reappear in black or gray markets at prices many times higher than the official ones.

- The increasingly obvious dualization of the economy is reflected in a fast-spreading currency substitution, where the official legal tender is replaced by some well-respected hard currency as a means of transactions and saving.

- The official exchange rate becomes increasingly unrealistic and useless; the black market rate is a high multiple of the official one.

None of these factors are present in the contemporary Hungarian economy. Quite the contrary, the present situation shows almost all the features of a successfully applied shock therapy, with currency convertibility the only exception:

- Hungary started price liberalization well before the historic political changes of 1989, and through gradual deregulation achieved an almost complete liberalization of prices by the beginning of 1991, with more than 90 percent of not only producer but also consumer prices already free of controls.

- Import liberalization is already far advanced, with only 10 percent of imports on the list of restricted goods and services as of 1 January 1991.

- For more than twenty years, beginning long before prices and imports were liberalized, Hungary has avoided the emergence of a classic shortage economy, because government overspending was financed not by domestic monetary expansion but by massive foreign borrowing.

- The restrictive monetary policy of the last three to four years was quite successful in checking domestic demand and curbing inflation, which is clearly on the rise but has never got out of control (much of this inflation is in fact the result of the substantial reduction of subsidies).

- There is no monetary overhang waiting on the sidelines, ready to jump into the market at the first appearance of consumer goods. The problem is just the opposite: not an excessively high but an inadequately low level of domestic financial savings.

- The dualization of the economy and the crowding out of the domestic currency were largely avoided by the simultaneous application of price and import liberalization, restrictive demand management, and consecutive devaluations of the forint to maintain the competitive edge of exports over nontradeables. The difference between the official and the black market exchange rate is small, generally less than 10 percent to 15 percent.

Although Hungary's macrofinancial belt-tightening and gradual liberalization were not achieved without setbacks (for example, mismanagement of the tourist trade in 1989 was reflected in a sharp deterioration of the current account), it can be considered successful in the sense that there is no need for any shock treatment to restore domestic macrofinancial equilibrium. In fact, by simply closing the gaps in this tightly restrictive demand management, Hungary was able to improve its current account situation quite remarkably in 1990 (table 1). Compared with a $1.4 billion deficit on current account in 1989, a $200 million to $300 million surplus is expected when the data are in for 1990.[1] There are basically two factors behind this improvement: an administrative ban on nontargeted exports to the CMEA countries, mainly to the Soviet Union, and an administrative rationing of foreign exchange to households simultaneous with a substantial widening in scope of liberalized imports of consumer goods. The latter move has strengthened the position of the Hungarian currency considerably: in spite of its official inconvertibility it is one of the most highly valued currencies in Eastern Europe because of the availability of Western consumer goods in Hungarian shops.

Gradual Progress Toward Current Account Convertibility

The Hungarian currency has already reached a certain degree of convertibility even without any outright declaration. With import liberalization almost complete, the Hungarian forint is mostly convertible for domestic corporate entities wishing to buy foreign goods and services. Foreign clients, both corporations and individuals, have the right to maintain Hungarian forint accounts and use

---

1. The actual figure, which became available after the conference, was $127 million.

Table 1 Hungary: selected economic indicators, 1981–90

	1981	1982	1983	1984	1985	1986	1987	1988	1989	1990[a]
Gross domestic product (real) (1980 = 100)	102.9	105.8	106.5	109.4	109.1	110.7	115.2	115.1	114.9	113.0
Consumer price index (1980 = 100)	104.6	111.8	120.0	130.0	139.1	146.5	159.1	183.8	215.0	270.9
Trade (millions of dollars)										
In nonconvertible currencies[b]										
Exports		4,207	4,146	4,174	4,390	5,012	4,915	4,484	4,047	3,084
Imports		4,465	4,485	4,285	4,070	4,995	4,873	4,390	3,540	2,907
Current account balance		−235	−250	−28	390	133	201	233	866	n.a.
In convertible currencies										
Exports		4,831	4,832	4,916	4,188	4,186	5,050	5,505	6,446	7,063
Imports		4,163	4,059	4,025	4,060	4,668	5,014	5,016	5,910	6,118
Current account balance		−299	71	67	−847	−1,495	−876	−807	−1,437	127
Gross external debt (millions of dollars)										
In nonconvertible currencies		1,299	1,379	1,232	1,150	1,021	946	582	360	n.a.
In convertible currencies		10,215	10,745	10,983	13,954	16,907	19,583	19,602	20,390	21,132
Total		11,515	12,124	12,216	15,105	17,928	20,530	20,185	20,750	n.a.
Official exchange rate (forints per dollar)	34.3	36.6	42.7	48.1	50.1	45.8	47.0	50.4	59.1	63.2

n.a. = not available.

a. Preliminary.

b. Data for nonconvertible currencies cover only that part of CMEA trade and payments that were settled in nonconvertible currencies. Total CMEA trade and payments figures are not available.

Sources: National Bank of Hungary and Central Statistical Office of Hungary.

their claims for any current transactions. Convertibility of the forint was even extended to some capital account transactions as a result of new, liberal regulations on foreign direct and portfolio investments. Foreigners may repatriate not only profits and dividends but the proceeds of their invested capital as well should they sell their assets and want to leave the country.

Nevertheless, progress toward even current account convertibility is far from complete. Under current regulations the central bank, the National Bank of Hungary, has maintained comprehensive centralization and control over foreign-exchange transactions:

- Domestic nonfinancial corporations generally do not have the right to operate foreign-exchange accounts or even retain a portion of their export earnings in foreign exchange. Instead they are obliged to sell current hard-currency receipts to the central bank. The reason for this rather harsh measure is basically the necessity to maintain a relatively high level of foreign reserves in order to service the external debt; this debt service is managed exclusively by the central bank as a consequence of the earlier state monopoly over foreign borrowing.

- Decentralization of foreign-exchange transactions within the banking sector got under way only in 1990 and was extended to a limited number of institutions. The authorization of Hungarian-owned and joint-venture banks is quite uneven. The joint-venture banks have always had an almost unrestricted license to engage in foreign-exchange transactions of any kind abroad and to buy and sell almost unlimited amounts of forints to and from the central bank. Some of the Hungarian-owned banks were given licenses to engage in current foreign-exchange transactions of very limited scope (mostly related to foreign trade). Some of these banks also have the right to accept foreign-exchange deposits from foreign and domestic noncorporate clients. The Hungarian-owned banks are tightly controlled by the central bank and must run their foreign-exchange operations with very low working balances in cash at home and on deposit abroad.

- Hungarian citizens have very limited access to hard currency. They have the right to buy foreign exchange only up to the equivalent of $50 per year at the official exchange rate. It is still illegal to buy hard currency in any unofficial market or to accept any domestic payment in hard currency. Hungarians are prohibited from holding more than the equivalent of 5,000 forints in hard currency in cash. However, they may deposit unlimited hard-currency holdings in a legally accepted account with any of the authorized banks without declaring their origin. The purpose of this somewhat hypocritical and inconsistent regulation is to stimulate the growth of much-needed foreign reserves within the banking system while discouraging currency substitution—always a real danger in an inflationary environment, especially when expectations are running higher than the observed increase of the general price level.

It is clear, however, that further decentralization and liberalization of foreign-exchange transactions are not only desirable but unavoidable. Inconsistent regulation cannot be maintained for long; ordinary Hungarians are eager to gain easier access to hard currency for purposes of travel at least. Therefore the medium-term goal of the government should be (indeed realistically can only be) to establish current account convertibility covering all economic agents, both domestic and foreign, in a more or less unrestricted way. In addition, it is conceivable that nondebt capital imports and related transactions could be liberalized substantially for domestic nonfinancial corporations, and perhaps capital import transactions of all kinds could be allowed to the domestic financial sector. It is most likely that the Hungarian government will adopt the so-called standard gradual approach to convertibility followed by most of Western Europe after World War II.

The Polish and Hungarian Approaches Compared

In comparing the Polish big bang solution with the seemingly very conservative Hungarian gradualism one quickly realizes that the measures and their results are almost completely identical: both countries pursued fiscal and monetary austerity, the elimination of excess demand, liberalization of prices and imports, and deregulation and demonopolization of the state sector, among other policies. The only element missing from Hungary's approach—to its detriment—is currency convertibility. So, even if it is true that Hungary did not need shock therapy in order to restore domestic macrofinancial equilibrium, the question of why the Hungarian authorities considered currency convertibility largely unnecessary or impossible to reach is still valid.

My impression is that Hungary, unlike Poland, did not have to establish current account convertibility largely because inflation, although on the rise, has never really escaped control. Restrictive fiscal and monetary policy coupled with comprehensive price and import liberalization seemed to be sufficient to preserve and even strengthen the acceptability (i.e., the real currency status) of the forint. A very important difference between the two countries is that the Hungarian currency has never been so widely replaced by hard currencies in domestic transactions as the zloty was, since the supply of goods available for forints has always been maintained at an incomparably higher level than in any of the other centrally planned economies. Inflation of the forint has surpassed the double-digit threshold only as a consequence of the elimination of subsidies, the implementation of the value-added tax system, and the tightening of monetary regulation in order to slow the further increase of foreign debt.

The situation in Poland was quite the reverse: inflation reached levels of several thousand percent per year as a consequence of almost completely uncontrollable government overspending. There is much evidence that the degree of hardness of an otherwise soft, inconvertible currency is determined basically by two factors: the availability of goods and services in exchange for the currency and the expected level of inflation. It is very doubtful that the confidence of the Polish people in such an extremely substituted currency as the zloty was before the shock treatment of 1990 could have been restored had the Polish government not declared unrestricted current account convertibility.

It is equally important that the current account convertibility of the forint was not only unnecessary but until now almost completely impossible to achieve. Another marked difference between the Polish (and also the Yugoslav) and the Hungarian situation is that Hungary has never stopped servicing its very high level of foreign debt, and it is an unquestionable top priority of the Hungarian government to avoid any rescheduling. Given this imperative, the National Bank of Hungary has never been able to renounce its very tight foreign-exchange reserve management, and consequently the continued centralization of all export receipts has been unavoidable. In 1990 the current account showed a surplus for the first time since 1984; this achievement, coupled with a sharp increase in foreign investment in Hungary, has greatly helped to build up the country's foreign-exchange reserves. The example of Hungary shows very well that the generally accepted conditions of current account convertibility—current account equilibrium plus an adequate level of foreign-exchange reserves—really count only in a situation where the country in question is to continue servicing its foreign debt. For those countries that have already asked for rescheduling it is no longer necessary to centralize foreign-exchange receipts, and so they can much more easily afford to declare convertibility. This is especially so if the exchange rate is not fixed but flexible or at least pegged to another currency, with frequent timely adjustments if inflation is still substantial. By correcting the exchange rate, the monetary authorities can influence the level of reserves necessary to service the already-rescheduled part of the foreign debt, the amount of which depends very much on the willingness of the government itself to repay. In a highly indebted but still solvent country the situation is quite the opposite: the amount of reserves needed for timely debt service is determined exogenously. The monetary authorities of such a country have no choice but to maintain a high centralization of foreign-exchange receipts at least until an adequate level of reserves has been built up, mostly through current account surpluses and substantial nondebt capital imports.

Next Steps Toward Current Account Convertibility

In the second half of 1991 the National Bank of Hungary is planning to establish and manage a domestic interbank foreign-exchange market.[2] The central bank will largely renounce the mandatory surrender of foreign-exchange receipts and

---

2. The scenario described in this section is not the only conceivable one and by no means reflects any officially adopted policy of the National Bank of Hungary.

intends to rely mostly on purchasing the hard currency necessary for external debt service rather than any forced centralization. On the other hand, the National Bank will also give up its obligation to sell hard currency to corporate customers wishing to pay for their imports. Hard currency will be sold by the commercial banks in a much more businesslike manner. The aim is to retain the foreign-exchange reserves of the country within the monetary sector, but not necessarily in the central bank. Domestic resident entities—both corporate and individual—will have the right to hold hard-currency balances but also the obligation to maintain foreign-exchange accounts with the authorized banks. The most important change is likely to be that Hungarian enterprises will not be obliged to sell all their export receipts even to the banking sector; they will have the alternative to retain these receipts in domestic foreign-exchange accounts. The banks themselves will be authorized to buy and sell foreign exchange among themselves.

The National Bank of Hungary intends to play an active role in this domestic interbank foreign-exchange market. It may and surely will intervene in order to build up its own reserves and to protect a certain level of the exchange rate. Daily fixings are likely to determine the prevailing exchange rate for all transactions executed with clients outside the market. (Nonfinancial corporate and noncorporate clients will not have the right to trade foreign exchange directly among themselves.) Instead of a fixed exchange rate, the National Bank of Hungary will announce a band, and the daily exchange rate may in practice fluctuate between the upper and lower intervention points. If domestic inflation remains higher than in the countries that are Hungary's most important economic and financial partners, there will be adjustments of the band itself from time to time.

With import liberalization almost complete, it is obvious that nonfinancial corporate clients will continue to be able to buy foreign currency from the banking sector. This right, however, is unlikely to be extended to individuals before 1993. It is contemplated that truly unrestricted current account convertibility is feasible only after a comprehensive stabilization of the economy, which involves not only the restoration of domestic macrofinancial equilibrium but also a substantial drop in inflation and the start of a take-off period on the basis of a complete turnaround and modernization of the enterprise sector.

Full convertibility is unlikely to be adopted in the first half of the 1990s. The right of limited and controlled foreign borrowing may be extended to the banking system, but not to the nonfinancial corporate sector. Acceptance of foreign credit will continue to require central bank authorization on a case-by-case basis. The same individual consideration and discretionary regulation will apply to foreign investment into domestic instruments. Foreign investment will be directed mostly toward joint ventures and equity investment.

In the area of capital exports, only selected productive investments of Hungarian resident corporations might be allowed, strictly on the basis of their individual merit and dynamic impact on the balance of payments.

Comment

Miroslav Hrnčíř

These two papers provide a revealing examination of the progress achieved in Czechoslovakia and Hungary toward currency convertibility. I find their inclusion together in this chapter particularly interesting, because there are both important similarities as well as considerable differences in the approaches followed by the two countries.

Both Czechoslovakia and Hungary already maintain a certain degree of currency convertibility in practice, whether officially declared or not. Both also have a relatively good chance to proceed further and to achieve their ultimate aim of making their currencies convertible in accordance with IMF rules.

At the same time it is evident that the approaches of the two countries differ significantly. This provides us with an opportunity to evaluate the alternative approaches to currency convertibility identified and discussed in general terms in the previous sessions, using the experience gained so far in their implementation in the economies undergoing transition.

I will address three issues that the two papers have raised:

- How should one characterize the Hungarian and Czechoslovak approaches to convertibility as presented in the two papers?

- Do the two approaches offer a sustainable process through which currency convertibility can be reached?

- What are the benefits and costs of the alternative approaches?

Even though Hungary has not yet officially declared its currency convertible, Lajos Bokros presents evidence that there has been a gradual extension of at least some elements of currency convertibility for domestic enterprises and joint ventures, and to some extent also for foreign firms. He argues that Hungary is in fact quite close to satisfying the conditions under which limited convertibility on current account could be achieved. I find his arguments convincing.

The present state of affairs in Hungary was achieved through a number of successive steps toward import and domestic price liberalization, accompanied by successive adjustments in the exchange rate of the forint. It may therefore be concluded that the present favorable prospects for the official introduction of some degree of currency convertibility are the outcome of a longer-term, gradual process of adjustment.

Miroslav Hrnčíř is a Senior Research Fellow at the Institute of Economics, Prague.

Some aspects of the Hungarian path toward currency convertibility parallel the approach followed in Western Europe in the 1950s. The introduction of currency convertibility in Hungary, if it is accomplished, could therefore be taken as verifying the feasibility of the gradual approach in the previously centrally planned economies in transition.

The Czechoslovak case is different. There a limited form of currency convertibility on current account (for businesses but not for individuals or nonprofit institutions) was introduced simultaneously with domestic price and foreign trade liberalization at the beginning of 1991. This implies a radical, abrupt change in a country that, unlike Hungary, maintained an only slightly modified centrally planned economy, with foreign trade and foreign-exchange monopolies and administrative domestic pricing, until the end of 1989.

The Czechoslovak approach thus represents an attempt to introduce a certain degree of currency convertibility at the very beginning of the transition process, as an instrument within that process rather than its final result. In this way the case of Czechoslovakia offers some parallels to the Polish case.

In assessing Czechoslovakia's progress, however, it seems important to distinguish between the "nominal" and the "real" changes that have been accomplished. Proper functioning of the foreign-exchange market and of the exchange rate is likely to require a prolonged time horizon, as always with institutional and systemic changes.

I do not find entirely convincing Bokros's assessment that Hungary was not a classic shortage economy in the past, with no monetary overhang and no hot money. Even if those phenomena were less pronounced and less detrimental in Hungary than in some other countries, particularly in recent years, the arguments presented do not appear fully convincing. The shortage of domestic savings argued for Hungary is a common feature of all the transforming countries and does not preclude the existence of a monetary overhang. Given the existing rigidities, a savings shortage and a monetary overhang can and do coexist in the previously centrally planned economies.

The issue of the sustainability of progress toward currency convertibility is of crucial importance for both approaches. But it is evidently more crucial for Czechoslovakia, as commitment to an early convertibility, however limited, must be a credible commitment; any failure to establish credibility would be detrimental.

The minimum conditions to be met include both macroeconomic and microeconomic conditions. At the microeconomic level, a satisfactory standard of financial discipline is particularly important. At the macroeconomic level, aggregate demand must be under control, and there must be reasonable balance in foreign trade flows and in foreign-exchange payments, at least in the medium run (the flow issue), along with sufficient reserves (the stock issue).

In the Hungarian case the main constraint is the existing external debt, which is relatively high both in absolute volume and in per capita terms, and the need to service it. This seems to be the main reason behind the rather cautious approach of the Hungarian authorities to the official declaration of currency convertibility.

In Czechoslovakia, on the other hand, because of the uncertainties involved in the abrupt liberalization of both domestic prices and foreign trade flows, the current development of the balance of payments (the flow dimension) is likely to be of key importance and a potential constraint. Czechoslovakia ran a deficit on its current account already in 1990, and that deficit is expected to increase substantially in 1991.

A sustainable balance of payments position depends particularly on establishing a realistic, competitive exchange rate; given that convertibility is to extend only to trade flows and to be for residents only, the interest rate parity is of minor importance. The option of floating the currency might seem attractive, but there are strong arguments against such an approach, particularly in Czechoslovakia. Given the country's rather unstable transition situation and its thin foreign-exchange market, exchange rate misalignments are likely to be substantial. Instability of this key price would only undermine the main goal of the early introduction of currency convertibility, namely, to import a rational price structure and to discipline domestic agents, enterprises, and households, as well as the central authorities.

On the other hand, the Czechoslovak authorities did not feel the need (for stabilization reasons) nor were they willing (because of the uncertainties involved) to commit to a fixed exchange rate as a nominal anchor for a specified period. The government and the central bank declared their intention to maintain the exchange rate at the level at which it had been set, but did not commit themselves to maintain it for any specific period, nor did they exclude the possibility of adjustments.

Such a compromise solution was deemed to combine the positive elements of a stabilized "norm" with some flexibility to adjust if necessary. The intention was, of course, to make adjustments as infrequent as possible. No answer was given, however, to doubts about the credibility and anchoring capacity of such a solution.

Zahradník identifies the wide range of options considered for the initial level at which to peg the koruna. The rate actually adopted was 28 korunas to the dollar, which implied a substantial depreciation of the koruna (amounting to 90 percent in the commercial sphere) from the rates applied toward the end of 1989. To dampen import demand further, a special surcharge of 20 percent of customs value was applied to imports of consumer goods and foodstuffs.

At the same time, however, the new exchange rate has to be seen as a compromise solution. On the one hand, the inflationary impact is likely to be considerable, but on the other hand estimates of the current account deficit for 1991 are running up to $2.5 billion.

Sustainability thus presents two conflicting requirements. In the short run, sustainability requires a cautious approach and the adoption of various safety measures to avoid a foreign-exchange bottleneck. In the medium run, however, the disciplining effects of currency convertibility on economic agents should be as unobstructed as is feasible. This requires the elimination of various cushions and corrective instruments of protection.

Both of the alternative approaches to currency convertibility are evidently possible under present conditions in the two economies. Both have their own benefits and costs.

An early move to currency convertibility is expected to provide discipline through the introduction of foreign competition. It should also serve to counter-act the exercise of monopoly power by domestic producers and traders (which can be particularly strong in a small economy) by "importing" foreign price ratios and initiating the reallocation of resources toward the pattern expected in an open economy. There are, however, substantial risks and costs as well, particularly in the potential foreign-exchange constraint and in the impact of a substantial devaluation.

The cost-benefit ratios of the alternative options are difficult to evaluate. The crucial point is that convertibility is intertwined with all the other aspects of the transition strategy. Given the strategy chosen in Czechoslovakia, the introduction of at least some degree of currency convertibility at the very beginning of the transition process appears justified to make the whole strategy viable. In Hungary, on the other hand, the gradualist approach to currency convertibility seems to correspond with the quite different reform path being followed in that country.

Comment

Gábor Oblath

I should like to begin my discussion of these two informative papers with a personal statement. For reasons to be addressed below, I am a firm supporter of the gradualist approach to convertibility in Eastern Europe. I believe that anyone who has the patience to become familiar with the structural characteristics of, and the types of problems faced by, the contemporary Eastern European

Gábor Oblath is head of the Research Department at the Institute for Economics, Market Research, and Informatics (KOPINT-DATORG), Budapest.

economies—not to mention the social and political landscape within these countries—will think at least twice before advocating a shock approach to currency convertibility in Eastern Europe. Therefore, although I am far from impressed by present Hungarian economic policy in general, I do support Hungary's gradualist approach to the external liberalization of its economy.

A second preliminary remark: I believe that the focus of this conference on currency convertibility might cause us to miss the real substantive issue, namely, the opening of the Eastern European economies to the world economy. The moment one is willing to accept that not convertibility proper but external liberalization is the central issue, it becomes clear that the latter can be perceived and implemented only as a process. The opening of these economies might be rapid or slow, but it certainly implies some kind of structure or (to use the more popular term) sequencing. Currency convertibility, on the other hand, suggests the notion of a single step or act to be performed by economic policymakers. This notion is there in the back of our minds, even though we all know that "convertibility" means too many things and can have a variety of interpretations and cover a variety of actual practices. To concentrate on convertibility and neglect external liberalization would be to put the cart before the horse.

Let me illustrate my point with an example from the Hungarian and Czechoslovak experience. It is far from clear why and in what economically meaningful way one should consider the koruna a convertible currency since 1 January 1991 and at the same time consider the forint an inconvertible currency. If the koruna is convertible, then, according to the information given in Bokros's paper, the forint has been convertible for several years, even though the Hungarian authorities have not declared it as such.

Since I am not in a position to make substantive comments on the Czechoslovak paper, I will raise some questions here concerning the interpretation of the convertibility of the koruna. What type of restrictions still apply to imports and to which product groups? Without information on these issues, it is extremely difficult to have a clear view on the actual content and relevance of the declaration concerning resident convertibility in Czechoslovakia. To be sure, I have no doubts that genuine steps have been made to open up that country. But one would have to know much more about the limitations to the koruna's convertibility in order to judge how far the country has managed to get on the long road to external liberalization.

Turning to the paper on Hungary, I have no significant disagreement with either the analysis or the interpretation and outlook presented by Bokros. There is, however, one point on which our views seem to differ. I do not think that providing domestic corporations the legal right to hold foreign-currency balances really points toward establishing convertibility of the forint. Convertibility involves the freedom to convert domestic currency into foreign currency. Offering companies the opportunity to hold foreign-exchange accounts, by means of retention quotas or otherwise, is to be interpreted as partial compensation for the lack of this freedom. It therefore points toward the dollarization of the domestic monetary system rather than to its strengthening or to the establishment of genuine convertibility of the home currency.

My remaining remarks are partly amendments to the information and analysis presented by Bokros, and partly relate to aspects of the Hungarian experience and Eastern Europe's prospects for liberalization that have not been treated in his paper.

I agree with Bokros's arguments against introducing convertibility in the context of a shock treatment in Hungary. Shocks are certain to come anyway, mainly as a result of the switchover to convertible-currency payments in CMEA trade. This will amount to a bigger bang, both from the macroeconomic and the microeconomic point of view, than any shock economic policy can design. The trade and current accounts, together with the government budget, are going to deteriorate substantially. At the same time, companies whose exports are oriented toward the East will experience an extremely sharp reduction in the protection previously offered by the safe and relatively soft clearing arrangements among the Eastern European countries. Thus, the switchover to dollar payments within the CMEA amounts to a major external liberalization measure for both Hungary and the other Eastern European economies.

Past international experience should also call for some caution in the timing and sequencing of external liberalization in Eastern Europe. On the one hand, these economies have been much more closed off from external influences than any of the "strongly inward-looking" developing countries discussed in the international literature on foreign trade regimes. On the other hand, given Western Europe's experience of a 10- to 15-year process of establishing convertibility under substantially more favorable conditions, the pressure on Eastern Europe for an abrupt opening is at least questionable.

My other concern with external liberalization is related to its sustainability. It is relatively easy to initiate a major external liberalization, but, as indicated by the recent Yugoslav experiment at introducing convertibility, maintaining it is much more difficult.

From this perspective, even the Hungarian variant of the gradualist approach is not really comforting. Over a period of two years, 90 percent of Hungary's imports (65 percent to 70 percent relative to domestic production) have been exempted from all licensing. This represents a very swift movement to free trade, which raises the question of why and how this process was sustainable. In my view, there are two explanations, both equally important. First, the economy went into a recession; this held the demand for imports at a lower level, and raised exports to a higher level, than otherwise would have been the case. Second, there has been a "loosening up" of the domestic monetary system stemming from the extension of financial disintermediation, that is, the increase in the stock of unpaid bills among domestic companies. This phenomenon, which is characteristic not only of the Hungarian but also of the Yugoslav and, more recently, the Polish economy, amounts to money creation by enterprises. Since this means of "payment" cannot be used to pay for imports, domestic suppliers have had a rather strange but significant advantage over foreigners. This relative disadvantage of foreign suppliers is very likely to have contributed to the success (i.e., the sustainability) of import liberalization.

In spite of these restraining factors, imports from the West grew by $700 million (12 percent) in 1990. Meanwhile, exports increased by more than $1 billion (18 percent), but it is far from certain that this favorable export performance can be repeated in 1991, the year in which payments within the CMEA are to switch to a convertible-currency basis. Also in 1991, the proportion of liberalized imports is to increase from 70 percent to 90 percent. Therefore, the sustainability of liberalization is certain to become a serious question.

Conventional wisdom suggests devaluation in these circumstances. A 15 percent devaluation was indeed carried out in Hungary in early 1991, but this did not amount to a real depreciation of the domestic currency, and rightly so. Partly because of the low efficiency of monetary policy resulting from the interenterprise "money creation" mentioned above, and partly because of overheated inflationary expectations, devaluations are not likely to have lasting effects. Instead they are likely to contribute to inflation and to jumps in inflationary expectations.

Is there any way out of this spiral? I believe there is. If the preexisting nonprice (administrative, informal, and quantitative) restrictions on imports were replaced with temporary tariff protection—with the timetable for the gradual phasing out of the tariffs announced immediately—then the liberalization of imports could be accomplished in a sustainable and relatively noninflationary manner. This proposal might seem obsolete in Hungary, but it could prove relevant if the present level of liberalization of imports were jeopardized by either microeconomic disruptions or balance of payments constraints.

The proposal to combine liberalization of existing controls with a temporary increase in tariff protection was rejected by the Hungarian government, mainly because it had already declared to the General Agreement on Tariffs and Trade that there were no existing quantitative controls in Hungary. And of course there is no way that other countries are going to accept the replacement of nonexistent quantitative restrictions with tariffs. As already mentioned, I am uncertain about the relevance of this proposal for Hungary in 1991, but it might still be useful for other Eastern European countries attempting external liberalization. Be that as it may, an important lesson of the Hungarian experience is that misleading or outright false representations of the workings of one's foreign trade regime can backfire and block the implementation of otherwise rational steps leading to external liberalization.

The question has been raised whether liberalization in Hungary has increased the danger of providing additional inputs to activities with negative value added. I do not think so. Although external liberalization was implemented pragmatically, without serious theoretical support, energy and basic raw materials prices to producers were raised to world market levels in Hungary in the early 1980s, so that this was not really a danger.

To conclude, let me offer the proposition that the debate over whether to consider currency convertibility as a starting point for reforms or as their final objective may put the matter too starkly. Convertibility is, it seems to me, better understood as a by-product of the gradual and sustainable process of external liberalization of the Eastern European economies.

Comment

Marie Lavigne

These two papers and the others in this volume have clearly shown that there is no master blueprint for convertibility. The convertibility question may be broken down into three issues, on all of which both papers have something to say:

- Why should a country seek to achieve convertibility of its currency?

- How should convertibility be introduced and managed?

- How should countries proceed from the early stage of limited convertibility to full convertibility of their currencies?

It has sometimes been suggested that convertibility is first of all a "signal of quality"—of market-type sophistication. One might also speak of "monetary snobbery," by analogy with the term "technological snobbery" used long ago by Peter Wiles to describe the eagerness of planners in the Eastern bloc to get the most sophisticated equipment available from the West, even when domestic constraints (lack of materials, of training, etc.) prevented its efficient use. The drive toward convertibility in the former socialist countries takes the *present* situation of the developed market economies as its model and does not take into account either the past experiences of those economies or the present situation

Marie Lavigne is Director of the European Studies Center of the Institute for East-West Security Studies, Štiřín, Czechoslovakia, and Professor at the University of Paris (Sorbonne).

of most of the developing economies. Even so, a policy of prompt introduction of convertibility might be rational in view of the fact that several Western international organizations on which these countries rely for aid and financing—above all the IMF—insist upon it. Whether this advice is indeed justified is another question.

A second reason for introducing convertibility is to use the nominal exchange rate as an anchor in a macroeconomic stabilization policy. Here the Czechoslovak policymakers have obviously been influenced by the Polish example (although, as Andrzej Olechowski and Marek Oleś report in chapter 5 of this volume, in the Polish case there was not a complete consensus on the use of the exchange rate for this purpose). A question, then, for Jaromír Zahradník is, Why did Czechoslovakia's macroeconomic package use only two of the three anchors used in Poland (namely, the exchange rate and nominal wages), and omit the use of an explicit real interest rate policy? In Czechoslovakia, despite measures to raise interest rates in the framework of a tightening of monetary policy, real interest rates were still negative in early 1991 (the ceiling has been fixed at 24 percent, which is less than the rate of inflation). Did the monetary authorities decide from the outset to control monetary policy directly through credit restrictions? Or did they choose this approach after coming to a negative assessment of the Polish policy?

In this context, Lajos Bokros comes to the conclusion that convertibility is not an immediate goal for Hungary precisely because Hungary does not need shock therapy. Its domestic macroeconomic conditions are already stable, and hence there is no need to have a nominal exchange rate anchor as part of a domestic stabilization policy.

A third set of reasons for introducing convertibility is linked to foreign economic policy considerations proper. But these reasons plead in favor of easier access to foreign exchange rather than in favor of convertibility per se. Indeed, Gábor Oblath, commenting on Bokros's paper, said that he preferred to speak of liberalization rather than of convertibility.

There are actually three arguments for the introduction of convertibility as a component of a foreign economic policy of liberalization: first, to make hard currency available to all enterprises, and not only to those exporting on hard-currency markets; second, to build prospective Western investors' confidence by guaranteeing them easy repatriation of their profits and assets; and third, to provide an instrument for influencing the levels of exports and imports: even a partly convertible currency can be devalued to encourage exports and discourage imports, thus allowing for liberalization of foreign trade through the removal or reduction of tariffs, quantitative restrictions, and the like.

Bokros argues that all three aims have already been reached in Hungary, without the formal introduction of convertibility. Although they are forbidden to retain hard currency, Hungarian enterprises may buy the foreign exchange they need from the National Bank of Hungary (the Hungarian central bank). Foreign legal persons and individuals have the right to maintain forint accounts and to repatriate profits, dividends, and assets when they leave the country. Foreign trade has largely been liberalized: only 10 percent of imports are still restricted. All of this makes sense, but what is less clear is Bokros's statement that under Hungary's present conditions convertibility would even be dangerous—a position he then seems to retreat from in stating that the Hungarian government should (in the medium term) establish a more or less unrestricted current account convertibility. In the short run, Bokros argues, convertibility in Hungary is not only unnecessary but impossible, because the country is heavily indebted but still solvent and thus has to service its debt; therefore it has to centralize its hard-currency resources. A rescheduling country, according to Bokros, does not have to worry about debt servicing and may therefore much more easily declare convertibility. One wonders what the Polish experts would have to say about that.

Zahradník does not elaborate as much as does Bokros on the reasons for introducing convertibility; this is understandable given that Czechoslovakia actually introduced convertibility of the koruna on 1 January 1991. Zahradník instead dwells much more on the mechanisms for implementing and managing convertibility.

Both countries, although this chapter describes them as "the next candidates" for convertibility, have in fact introduced so-called internal convertibility on current account for residents, and in this regard they seem to stand not so far behind Poland. In both Czechoslovakia and Hungary the two questions that had to be solved were how to choose the initial rate of exchange (and later to regulate it), and how to control foreign-exchange operations.

The paper on Czechoslovakia, not surprisingly, goes into much greater detail on the first question than does the paper on Hungary, since Hungary settled the problem a long time ago. Both countries chose a fixed exchange rate pegged to a basket of currencies. Both (Hungary in 1976, Czechoslovakia in 1989) initially introduced a commercial exchange rate, calculated as the average amount of domestic currency needed to produced one unit of foreign currency through exports, and a tourist rate, calculated on the basis of the purchasing power parity of the domestic currency. The next step was to unify the two exchange rates— in Hungary this was done at the beginning of the 1980s. Finally, the exchange rate was brought close to the market rate through a series of devaluations. In Hungary such devaluations have occurred over the whole of the past decade, with the most recent one in January 1991. In Czechoslovakia, on the other hand, as Zahradník explains in detail in a most interesting part of his paper, these steps were taken over a much shorter period of time, resulting in a strongly devalued, unified rate in January 1991.

This last measure was preceded by a hot debate among Czechoslovak economists over the choice of measures on which to base the final exchange rate: the purchasing power parity rate, the average commercial rate, or the marginal commercial rate. The third solution was ultimately chosen, but this still required a choice between a "moderate" (i.e., 50 percent) and a "strong" (i.e., 80 percent) devaluation from the level of late 1990. The latter was chosen, for the same reasons that prompted a similarly strong initial devaluation in the case of Poland: the desire to head off expectations of a further devaluation, and the need to encourage exports and hold back imports without resorting to taxes and subsidies (although even this sharp devaluation did not prevent Czechoslovakia from imposing an "import surcharge" of 20 percent, which is not mentioned in the paper, presumably because it had not yet been introduced at the time the paper was written).

Both countries have chosen to limit individuals' access to hard currency; the regulations in Hungary are more liberal in that there are no limitations on hard-currency deposits held by individuals in the banks. Whereas the Hungarian authorities seem quite aware of the need for further liberalization of access to hard currency for individuals, their Czechoslovak counterparts seem less so, probably because the introduction of convertibility in Czechoslovakia is so recent. The Czechoslovak authorities probably expect that individuals' demand for hard currency will be held in check by the harsh austerity measures introduced on 1 January 1991, as increases in domestic prices erode the cash balances held by the population. Yet the question will have to be addressed in the future.

In both countries, resident enterprises have to surrender all of their hard-currency proceeds to the banks. In the case of Hungary, these proceeds must be turned over to the central bank; in this respect the Hungarian regime seems much less "decentralized" than that in Czechoslovakia, although this might be an illusion since in Czechoslovakia the commercial banks are much less independent of the central bank than in Hungary. Resident enterprises, including joint ventures and foreign companies, have the right to buy hard currency from the banks (from the central bank in Hungary). In Czechoslovakia this access is still limited to purchases of currency for commercial operations (i.e., current payments for imports of goods and services). Thus, free repatriation of profits earned in local currency by joint ventures does not yet exist in Czechoslovakia, unlike in Hungary, and the paper by Zahradník does not describe Czechoslovakia's future plans in this area.

The Hungarian paper is explicit about the next steps to be taken: a more liberal policy toward individual residents when the balance of payments situation permits (which might not be very soon); and a relaxation of the central bank's control of foreign-exchange operations, first through the creation of an interbank foreign-exchange market, rather than through liberalization of direct access of resident enterprises to foreign-exchange operations. This may seem a long way yet to go, but we have to remember that in some Western countries (France, for instance) full internal convertibility was not achieved until very recently. Full convertibility extending to the capital accounts will not be introduced for a long time in either country, as both authors confirm.

Neither paper looks at the convertibility concept from the point of view of the mutual convertibility of the currencies of the region itself. This topic has been addressed by Jozef van Brabant (chapter 4) in the context of his proposal for the creation of a Central Payments Union. I will not comment on the merits of that particular approach, but the stalemate in intraregional trade since the beginning of 1991, when it became obvious that the arrangements specified in 1990 were not working and that in fact mutual trade is *not* being conducted in hard currencies, demands that closer consideration be given to the question of mutual convertibility.

Intraregional trade is collapsing because, apart from some trade in high-priority items, none of the countries or their enterprises are willing to devote scarce hard currency to payments to a neighbor. Thus, the former payments system is being replaced mainly by barter. Tourist movements are affected as well, because beginning in 1991 Eastern European tourists traveling to other Eastern European countries must first buy hard currency and then exchange it for local currency— a practice that encourages black market trading and illegal private arbitraging operations. This situation also leads to the continuation of protectionist barriers for intraregional trade even as trade with the West is being liberalized. In such circumstances it is fair to ask why mutual convertibility of the domestic Eastern European currencies is not envisioned, preferably in a concerted way as was done in Western Europe in the 1950s.

Discussion

Andrzej Olechowski expressed puzzlement at Lajos Bokros's interpretation of the concept of shock therapy. What he himself understood by the term was a rapid removal of government-imposed controls and restrictions. To limit the effects of this liberalization on stability and welfare, some tightening of demand management is generally necessary. All restrictions involve costs in terms of growth and freedom of choice, so they should be removed; sometimes there may also be short-term costs of removing the restrictions, and these may be higher or even unsustainable at a particular moment, but that does not make removal of the controls undesirable. Hence there is no justification for such assertions as that current account convertibility is not necessary or is impossible; it may have been impossible to remove the controls until now because of short-term costs, but that does not make their removal any the less necessary.

Michael Marrese commented that 15 years ago the Hungarians had enjoyed a good press, which represented their situation as being better than the reality; today, in contrast, Bokros gave the impression that the Hungarian situation was much better than it was being represented in the press. But when Marrese had recently gone to Hungary and talked to Hungarians, they had told him that the situation was actually terrible. If one looks at Hungary's positive achievements thus far—price liberalization, something close to convertibility, sound fiscal and monetary policy, a growing private sector, elimination of most subsidies, not much unemployment, political freedom, some institutional reform—one has to ask, Why are things so bad?

John Thompson noted that during his presentation (chapter 5) he had concentrated on countries (Poland and Yugoslavia) that had started with a high rate of inflation and had tried to use the move to convertibility to stabilize prices. Here, in contrast, one had two countries that were starting from a position of reasonable stability and were seeking to liberalize, anticipating a burst of inflation in the process. This presents some interesting contrasts. A first issue, which Olechowski had already raised, is how to define "shock therapy." A few months ago this term was being defined in terms of Poland's actions in devaluing drastically, liberalizing its foreign trade, and unifying its exchange rate; now Czechoslovakia was doing all these things except the last, and this too was being defined as shock therapy. What did the panel think this term encompassed?

Thompson also asked Bokros how high he thought inflation would be in 1991, given that in 1990 it had been 30 percent and since then there had been another devaluation. Thompson observed that Hungary had never been particularly bothered about the nominal anchor concept, but had been ready to neutralize excess inflation through devaluation so as to maintain competitiveness. Was there any disposition to consider changing this policy? Finally, he asked whether this policy would still be feasible under the new, decentralized system of foreign-exchange management.

With regard to Czechoslovakia, what was the inflation outlook in the light of price liberalization, devaluation, and the oil price shock? Would it be feasible to maintain the exchange rate as a nominal anchor in the presence of the high inflation these were likely to generate? Thompson recalled Jaromír Zahradník's remark that a year ago Czechoslovakia was a fully centrally planned economy, and up to now it has surely made much less progress on the supply side than Hungary. Is it not therefore likely that the rigidities are much greater, and did that not imply that the inflation risk is much greater?

According to *Friedrich Levcik*, the description of the session, which bracketed Hungary and Czechoslovakia as "the next candidates," was misleading. In terms of their formal declarations they might be comparable, but the session had reinforced what everyone already knew, namely, that Hungary had made vastly more progress than Czechoslovakia in transforming a command economy into a market economy. Miroslav Hrnčíř had rightly pointed out that Hungary had made the systemic changes much earlier. The two cases were so different that he wondered whether it was useful to treat them together.

Levcik asked how much of Hungary's billion-dollar trade surplus in 1990 was due to an expansion of exports and how much to a policy of restricting imports. Who were the exporters who were demonstrating an ability to compete on the convertible-currency markets?

Levcik also asked Zahradník whether he thought that Czechoslovakia's public discussion of devaluation had been not only intellectually stimulating but also a good way to conduct policy. In his twenty years of living in the West, Levcik had noted many cases in which countries had devalued or revalued, but the central bank always denied, right up to the last minute, any intention of changing the exchange rate. The Czechoslovak exercise had prompted speculation by enterprises (accelerating import payments and lagging exports) and even encouraged additional buying by consumers who knew that prices would rise at the end of the year. Was that really wise?

Thomas Lachs, speaking from the chair, remarked that he took comfort in hearing praise for central bankers who lie.

Jozef van Brabant noted the similarity between Gábor Oblath's question regarding the licensing still practiced in Czechoslovakia and the question he himself had asked in the previous session. To what extent is there differentiated licensing as between trade with the convertible-currency countries and trade with other Central European countries that have also undertaken substantial trade liberalization, notably Poland?

Brabant also challenged Bokros's assertion that there had been no substantial discrepancy between the official and black market exchange rates for the previous 18 months: in November 1989 he himself had bought forints legally at 57 to the dollar, only to be offered a rate of over 100 to the dollar with no bargaining a little later on the black market. The narrowing of the differential was relatively recent, and one reason that it had narrowed subsequently was trade liberalization, which had made available foreign goods that Hungarians wanted to buy. He also asked whether Hungary's $200 million to $300 million trade surplus for 1990 was only with convertible-currency countries, or whether it was an overall balance of payments outcome. Finally, he questioned Bokros's reference to an administrative ban on nontargeted exports to the CMEA countries; presumably this referred to the omission of goods from "indicative lists"? That certainly applied to the Soviet Union; did it also apply to exports to the other Central European countries? That is, to what extent was there an exception to the 90 percent export and import liberalization for the other Eastern European countries?

Michael Dohan commented that all the discussions seemed to contain an implicit assumption that prices were going to increase. As one moves to a market economy, one expects prices to become more flexible and one hopes that efficiency will increase. Does this not create a potential for prices to *decrease?* Is there any evidence of prices having decreased in certain industries? And are there any instances of wages having decreased? Unless wages and prices are flexible, in the sense that they can decrease as well as increase, there is a built-in institutional bias toward inflation. Can one under those circumstances expect convertibility and a stable exchange rate to provide a nominal anchor?

John Williamson asked Bokros if he could describe the principles that underlay the process of gradual price liberalization in Hungary. When it is decided to liberalize another product, how does one decide that it should be product X rather than product Y? In Western Europe after the war, one started with inputs and then moved on to capital goods—roughly the reverse of the sequence proposed by McKinnon for determining the level of transitional protection. Given the existence of effectively functioning market economies, there was a presumption that this would not lead to any particular anomalies. But with soft budget constraints and negative value added, could this be assumed in Eastern Europe?

Replying to the discussion, *Lajos Bokros* addressed some of the many questions that had been directed to him. He said that avoidance of currency substitution had demanded that forint-denominated assets carry a higher effective interest rate than foreign assets. Even so, the Hungarian authorities had hesitated to abandon the requirement for mandatory surrender of export receipts. With regard to inflation, the latest estimate was that the consumer price index had risen by 27 percent in 1990 and was likely to rise by about 35 percent in 1991. He doubted whether it was possible to have much more liberalization until inflation had been brought under control, but unfortunately what was good long-run anti-inflation policy tended to have a strong short-run effect in increasing inflation. The foreign transfer amounted to 5 percent of GDP, and it was difficult to offset the resulting inflationary impact by a restrictive monetary policy. With regard to Michael Marrese's question, Bokros suggested that the real problem is that Hungarians always want to eat the goose that lays the golden eggs, as they had done by borrowing so much abroad. The loss of 5 percent of output in the foreign transfer in 1990 represented a very serious setback to living standards. Demand management had succeeded in suppressing demand not just through a very restrictive fiscal and monetary policy, but also by a very severe wage policy. Wages have not been liberalized in Hungary. This helps from the standpoint of macrofinancial management, but it has implied a very serious loss in real wages. Given that Hungary wanted to continue to service its foreign debt, it had no alternative but to tighten fiscal, monetary, and wage policies. A restrictive wage policy, Bokros argued, provided a better nominal anchor than a pegged exchange rate.

Hungary had devalued the forint by 15 percent only two weeks before the conference. This was quite a harsh measure, even though it neutralized only half the inflation of the previous year. The real questions concerned the supply-side response. Hungary had been lucky (compared with Czechoslovakia, for example) in that privatization had started as long ago as 1982. By 1990 the private sector accounted for more than 25 percent of GNP and 18 percent of the capital stock, and for the last decade the sector had been the only source of growth.

Hungary already had over 5,000 joint ventures with Western firms, more than all the other countries of the region combined. The sums of capital involved were relatively small, but foreign direct investment nonetheless already cumulated to over $1 billion. One other bright spot for the future was the growth in foreign portfolio investment on the Budapest stock exchange.

Gábor Oblath stated that the improvement in Hungary's 1990 trade balance had been composed of a $1.1 billion increase in exports partially offset by a $700 million increase in imports. Replying to Williamson's question, he commented that the basis for selecting products for liberalization was very pragmatic, but it was true that inputs, especially of goods that were not produced domestically, tended to be liberalized first, followed by some consumer goods to balance the market, and then capital goods. In January 1990 most categories of imports had been liberalized, the exceptions being certain consumer goods and food products making up roughly 10 percent of imports. But there was no clear theory underlying the exercise.

Jaromír Zahradník commented that he had been told that the one case in which it was permissible for a central bank governor to lie was when he intended to devalue. Since he was not a governor, he could state categorically that Czechoslovakia had no intention of devaluing. He admitted that conducting open discussions of devaluation during 1990 might have been an error, but some errors are unavoidable. Early in the year it was not clear whether or how the country would make the transition to a market economy, and in his view it was misleading to label the Czechoslovak program as a case of shock therapy. Several measures had been taken during 1990, so that the program was better considered a case of compressed gradualism. Of course he agreed that Hungary was ahead of Czechoslovakia in many respects, since Hungary had not had its reform efforts forcibly terminated in 1968.

With regard to exchange rate policy in 1990, the cuts in Soviet oil deliveries from September on had left Czechoslovakia little choice but to devalue (or revert to central planning). However, the devaluation had only occurred in October. Present expectations were for a price shock of 25 percent in the first quarter of 1991 following price liberalization, but after that it was anticipated that prices would increase no more than a further 5 percent or so through the rest of the year.

As in Hungary, wages were still under central control in the public (but not in the private) sector. Import licensing was now insignificant, but there was still some licensing on the export side to prevent a price explosion of some raw materials. The Czechoslovak authorities expected to eliminate export licensing by the second quarter of 1991. With regard to profit remittances, joint ventures had the same right of access to foreign exchange as any other Czechoslovak enterprise. The authorities were aiming to maintain the present exchange rate for at least several months, in order to reestablish confidence, and Zahradník saw no case for special treatment of joint ventures.

7

Future Candidates

7

Future Candidates

Bulgaria

Ventseslav Dimitrov

For many years Bulgaria regarded the convertibility of its national currency as a vague opportunity to be accomplished in some far-off future. From time to time (for example, in 1988), short-term political considerations have prompted some to create the illusion that a rapid move to convertibility was possible, even under the old socialist system, provided only the will was there. As one can imagine, however, this remained nothing but words.

The current situation, however, is completely different. Now everyone in Bulgaria is speaking of convertibility as of something both imminent and of great importance, although not everyone is clear about the market relations that will emerge or the amount of preparation that will be required.

It would be an illusion to believe that convertibility can be introduced outside the context of introducing market relations throughout the economy. The marketization of the Bulgarian economy is presently facing considerable difficulties, yet already various parties—even some who disagree on other key issues—are pressing for a rapid introduction of convertibility. These people continue to assume that, to make a currency convertible, it is sufficient that the officials responsible for the economic management of the country strongly desire it. Such pressures come even from some Western experts, who may understand very well the principles of operation of the market economies but are unfamiliar with the workings of the former socialist economies, which are characterized by a high degree of irrationality in both their structures and their functioning. Probably the degree of this irrationality has been highest in Bulgaria—in any case it has been much higher there than in Hungary, Yugoslavia, Poland, or Czechoslovakia,

Ventseslav Dimitrov is Chairman of the Banking and Financial Subcommittee of the Grand National Assembly of Bulgaria.

and it may be comparable with the degree of irrationality one observes in the Soviet Union.

The economies in question have a relatively low level of monetization; that is, the power of money in them is very small, and money operates only in a narrow field. This in turn creates great opportunities for distortions in price ratios.

Pressure is also exerted by some supporters of the superseded administrative economy. These individuals wish to integrate themselves quickly into the global economy in order to be perceived as legitimate when a large part of the nonmarket relations of the old system are preserved, and thus maintain their economic power.

A third group pressing for a quick shift to convertibility are Bulgaria's private businessmen, who naturally want to have the freedom to deal in foreign currencies and to have it now, because they see no reason why they should be obliged to hand over part of their foreign-currency earnings to the state (participation in the centralized distribution of hard currency was until the beginning of 1991 a privilege accorded only to the state-owned enterprises). They want to be free not only to import goods but also to export capital and to keep hard-currency deposits in foreign banks. Such freedom is clearly in their own interest, but it could wreak havoc not only economically but also politically, and thus postpone the beginnings of meaningful change in the system.

Yet another group in favor of convertibility consists of potential foreign investors in Bulgaria. Investing in Bulgaria is, after all, a reasonable proposition only if the national currency is convertible.

Convertibility and the Transition to a Market Economy

The question of whether to have a rapid or a slow shift to convertibility is intimately linked to the question of whether to have a rapid or a slow transition to a market economy. Even so, it is possible to separate the convertibility problem from that of the general evolution of the economy toward a market economy, and to ask at which precise point in the transition it is necessary to undertake some concrete steps toward convertibility. The first question, however, is more important and even fundamental. The second one is also important, but it is subordinate and second in significance.

The major problems that Bulgaria must solve in finding its way toward a market economy are the following:

- *Privatization.* At present about 95 percent of the country's economic assets are in the possession of the state. The problem is aggravated by the fact that these assets have been at the disposal not of some state authority but of the machinery of what was until recently the ruling party. This gives state property in Bulgaria a quite different character from state property in a normal market economy.

- *Demonopolization.* The power of Bulgaria's state monopolies is most conspicuous in the very important consumer-goods market. For example, one state company produces all of the country's meat and meat products, another produces all of its milk and dairy products, a third handles all tourism, and so on. If prices are eventually liberalized, as Bulgaria's limited experience shows (for example, in the case of fruits and vegetables in 1990), the monopolies will not be stimulated to supply more products; indeed production is likely to decrease as the prices and profits of the monopolies rise.

- *Reform of the tax system and the budget.* The greater part of the state's revenues come from taxes on the profits of enterprises. This is counterproductive. Incomes from capital are not created. At present over 90 percent of national income (i.e., net material product) is redistributed through the budget, thanks to the enormous subsidies and the huge and inefficient bureaucracy.

- *Remonetization of the economy.* Until January 1991 money had very little power to command goods and services in Bulgaria, and the monetary and banking system remained (and still remains) quite strange by Western standards.

- *Agricultural reform.* Bulgaria's farms, dominated by state cooperatives, are unable to provide enough food to sustain the population, even though Bulgarians have given lessons in agriculture to half of Europe in the past.

- *External debt.* Bulgaria has had difficulty in servicing its foreign debt, and as of early 1990 payments had been suspended for nearly a year.

- Other problems stem from a fundamentally wrong pattern of *international specialization,* with extremely tight links to the Soviet Union, and the presence of an enormous volume of inefficient productive assets whose products are not competitive on international markets. For such hard currency as it receives, Bulgaria relies mainly on countries like Iraq, Iran, and Libya.

All these circumstances, combined with the destruction of the old system, with the criminal inaction of the government during 1990, with the collapse of the CMEA, and with the crisis in the Persian Gulf, produced a quickly deteriorating economic situation in Bulgaria in the last months of 1990. Would it be correct in a situation such as this to proceed quickly to convertibility, as a condition and as a tool for the introduction of a market economy? Indeed is it possible at all? Unfortunately the answer is no.

The introduction of convertibility would mean acceptance of an exchange rate close to the present black market rate. That rate, thanks to the increasing deficit, the difficulties in supplying basic goods, the introduction of coupons (which means further demonetization), and the strong expectations for inflation instilled in the population by the previous government, together with the unceasing printing of bank notes, was at the end of 1990 about 20 leva to the dollar (see table 1). At this rate all of Bulgaria's exports would not be enough even to pay for the country's oil imports for the year, to say nothing of other imports. To put it another way, at the black market rate, the average wage in the country would be somewhere between 5 and 7 cents an hour.

For all these reasons, it seems reasonable to assume that the way to convertibility passes through the introduction of market relations, and the speed with which they are introduced will determine the speed with which Bulgaria moves in the direction of convertibility. When market relations come to exceed some critical mass, it will then be time to start to introduce some measures aimed at convertibility.

If we start from the assumption that convertibility is part and parcel of the move to a market economy, then all the basic and indispensable elements of market reform will also be indispensable conditions for the shift to convertibility. Among these are changes in the forms of ownership, demonopolization, agrarian reform, reforms in tax and fiscal policy, reforms in the system of pricing and in the labor market, and of course reforms in the monetary system. Since convertibility is an attribute of money, the focus of attention should be the creation of a money market, that is, a real market of money and capital, with the appropriate functions and institutions. This certainly does not mean that it would be possible to do without any of the other basic elements of market reform. Indeed the omission or postponement of even one of them would mean the failure or postponement of the whole reform.

Privatization

Privatization will both strongly enhance the Bulgarian people's motivation to work and at the same time contribute to decreasing the monetary overhang. Privatization and the enhancement of private property rights will serve in the first place as a powerful tool for attracting the savings of the population and directing them to productive activities. In terms of ownership of assets, the state is by no means poor. On the contrary, it is extremely rich, possessing title to practically all property, including municipal property. There is a great deal of property to sell off, and the process will not be complete by the end of the decade.

The most efficient course of action would be to start immediately with small privatizations: shops, restaurants, small hotels, and other facilities in the service sector, as well as small workshops and the like in the goods sector. Bulgarians will be inclined to buy such property because they can relatively easily estimate the expected profits. At this early stage of the transition they will be more prepared to buy a small shop than to enter into a partnership or buy shares in a corporation for the purchase of a chain of shops. Fears of uncontrolled inflation might work to encourage such direct investment, by creating a preference for holding physical rather than financial assets.

The privatization of large firms will work in the same direction, although its full effect is to be expected at a later stage of the reform. In both cases the following principle is valid: the greater the extent to which investors pay for their investments with cash, the better will be the effect on the economy. It is important to understand that the state or the municipality loses nothing in these sales. There exist unreasonable fears that the nation's assets will be sold at distress prices, or that the absence of a sound methodology for valuation of the assets will lead to their being sold for less than their worth. But if there is real competition among potential buyers, prices will be realistic.

The Tax System and the Budget

Fundamental transformation of the tax system and the budget is necessary if the economy is to function effectively on the basis of market principles, both from the point of view of the population and of businesses, and from the point of view of the state as well.

In preparation for the introduction of convertibility, a whole set of steps must be taken: expenditures must be reduced and a number of activities eliminated from the budget entirely; direct financing of the deficit and the debt via the monetary system must be abolished. The only way to do this, apart from privatization, is to issue sufficient state bonds to cover not only the current deficit, but a part of the accumulated debt as well. This debt, because of the unreasonable conditions in which it was financed, is constantly creating opportunities for irresponsible and uneconomic management, as money borrowed at very low interest, or none at all, never stimulates investment. In this sense the accumulated debt is pushing the economy in a direction away from convertibility.

Tax reform must reduce the tax burden on firms to an acceptable level. A value-added tax system and a progressive income tax must be introduced.

The effect of tax reform should be to transfer the tax burden from enterprises to the population, as the value-added tax will not only replace the present turnover tax, but will also take away some of the burden on enterprises stemming from the taxation of profits. The main burden will fall on the population, who ultimately pay the taxes in any case.

The Financial System

The changes needed in the financial system are closely related to the issue of convertibility. This does not mean, however, that the changes in this sphere are

Table 1   Bulgaria: selected economic indicators, 1980–89

	1980	1985	1986	1987	1988	1989
Population (millions)						
Total	8.86	8.96	8.96	8.97	8.98	n.a.
Employed	4.36	4.46	4.47	4.49	4.47	n.a.
Retired	2.04	2.12	2.25	2.29	2.33	n.a.
GNP[a] (billions of leva)	25.8	32.6	34.4	36.5	38.3	39.3
Balance of payments						
Nonconvertible currencies (millions of TR)						
Merchandise exports[b]	4,706	8,338	8,393	8,692	9,135	8,892
Merchandise imports	4,864	8,478	8,868	8,762	8,553	8,013
Current account balance	46	−61	−320	64	696	933
Convertible currencies (millions of dollars)						
Merchandise exports	3,338	3,307	2,656	3,277	3,539	3,138
Merchandise imports	2,532	3,694	3,488	4,232	4,511	4,337
Current account balance	907	−85	−715	−773	−840	−1,306
External debt						
In TR (billions)	0.82	1.42	1.59	1.45	0.58	−0.38[c]
In convertible currencies (billions of dollars)	4.2	3.2	4.7	6.1	8.2	9.2

Exchange rates (leva per dollar)[d]

Official	0.88	1.00	0.90	0.83	0.83	0.81
Commercial	1.01	1.15	1.35	1.24	1.64	2.02
Black market[e]	3.0–3.5		3.5–5.0			

n.a. = not available; TR = transferable rubles.

a. At current market prices.

b. All export and import figures are on an f.o.b. basis.

c. Net creditor position; the convertible-currencies figure for 1990 is $10.3 billion.

d. Exchange rate quotations are end-of-period.

e. This rate was reported to be 15 to 20 leva to the dollar in December 1990.

Sources: Bulgarian Foreign Trade Bank, World Bank.

sufficient for the introduction of convertibility. They must be considered as only a part, though a very important part, of the formation of the market.

The existing financial system in Bulgaria is underdeveloped by international standards. The major unsolved or only partly solved problems are the distribution of functions in the banking system, the relations between banks and other enterprises and between banks and the population, the structure of the banking system itself, the payment mechanism, relations with the rest of the world, the proper level of interest rates, and protection of the consumer.

The most serious problem at the moment is the need to eliminate the administrative functions of the Bulgarian banking system. In no other country do the banks perform administrative and supervisory functions to such an extent as in Bulgaria. The longer this system remains, the longer will be the delay in the introduction of convertibility. Convertibility is incompatible with administration by the banks.

Another serious problem is slow payments procedures: often payments between enterprises require 15 to 20 days to clear. The main reason is the form of payment. All such delays have a cost, which is usually borne by the bank. It is all the more strange, then, that it is the banks that usually cause these delays.

Recently, with the creation of a system of 70 independent banks, the process has become still more complicated, and the technical difficulties have increased. Yet even the new system as presently organized does not represent progress toward a system of commercial banks with branches throughout the country.

The problems involved in providing banking services to the population are no less serious. In most countries, households are the main source of savings. The same is true in Bulgaria, but there household savings are not normal savings. To a large extent they are forced savings and therefore represent deferred consumption that is simply waiting for an opportunity to be released.

Of the approximately 20 billion leva accumulated in the State Savings Bank, the population is using, in the form of various loans, about 5 billion leva. Until January 1991, as a rule, these 20 billion leva paid interest of 1 percent per year. The interest rate on loans to households ranged from about 3 percent (on loans for housing) to 7 percent (on loans for consumption). These rates have not been changed since the system was introduced in 1974 with a decision of the Council of Ministers. Reforms are expected in the near future. Mention should be made also of the more than 1 billion leva in installments for the purchase of cars, which money is kept separately in the State Savings Bank. The 15 billion leva in the State Savings Bank that is not lent to the population is lent to the National Bank of Bulgaria at 2 percent interest. The profit from this lending goes into the state budget. There it is considered to be a secure, preplanned income. The low rate of interest makes possible the inefficient use of this credit resource by the National Bank. Part of it is used for direct financing of the state budget deficit. In fact, for many years this financing has been calculated in the income part of the budget.

In the developed countries the direct financing of the deficit through the central bank is always considered to be inflationary. But it is an indication of the way of thinking of Bulgaria's pseudo-experts, including those who occupy the highest positions, that the current law of the budget assumes that, in order to limit the "credit resource," it is actually desirable that the excessive money in the National Bank be used for direct financing of the deficit. Clearly such a policy does serious harm to the basic economic interests of the population and is unacceptable in a market economy.

Of a similar nature is Bulgaria's policy regarding enterprises. Bulgarian companies are oppressed on the one hand by total state control, and on the other by the present credit policy. Payment of interest is considered first of all to be a means for retaining some income in the bank in order to pass it on to finance the budget. It is almost impossible for enterprises to earn interest on their deposits at rates higher than 1 percent. Yet they have nowhere else to keep their money. The result is a monopoly by the banking system, and through it by the budget, which both use to extort tremendous profits. Consistent with this is the provision in the budget law that levies taxes on the profits of the banks at a rate of 80 percent. Companies have no incentive under the present system to hold cash, and therefore it is natural that instead they prefer to keep their savings in the form of large quantities of materials (mostly raw materials) and products, thus creating shortages elsewhere.

Whereas in the developed countries the interest expense paid by banks on companies' deposits is usually about half or a third of the banks' interest income, in Bulgaria the same ratio is 1:50 or even 1:100. This situation is abnormal; what has been lost sight of is the fact that money does not belong to the state but is created to serve all economic agents.

The scant opportunities households and businesses have to earn interest on their savings, given the low rates paid and the high taxation of interest receipts, are a principal reason for the demonetization of the economy, for the emergence of overstocked inventories, for the tremendous amount of unfinished construction, and for the slow rates at which new production facilities are introduced—in a word, for what might be called the anti-economical approach to economic development. At the same time it is the reason for the scarcity of economic thinking in the country. This two-way relationship is extremely important because it reproduces itself on all levels.

To begin to solve these serious problems a redistribution of functions within the banking system is necessary. The National Bank of Bulgaria must limit its functions to those handled by central banks in the developed countries. It must not serve any longer as a principal conduit for most of the cash flows in the economy, skimming off whatever is necessary to support the state budget. The monopoly of the State Savings Bank in the mobilization of personal savings must also be eliminated. The provision of financial services to firms and households must be entirely in the hands of the commercial banks and other specialized financial institutions. The National Bank of Bulgaria should not perform such functions. The State Savings Bank will then find itself in competition and will have to increase the interest rates it pays in order to be competitive. This will eliminate the unnecessary segmentation of the financial market.

An advanced banking system is one of the great achievements of civilization, and if Bulgaria takes artificial steps to avoid adopting such a system, it will be the whole nation that suffers. The commercial banks occupy the key place in such a system. In 1989 there was a very unfortunate move to create as many new commercial banks as possible, even while retaining the existing local branches of the National Bank. This was unnecessary and even harmful, as it will considerably slow down progress toward the creation of a real money market. For a country the size of Bulgaria it is sufficient to have at most some 15 to 20 commercial banks. These should be universal banks, authorized to receive deposits and to make payments, and to trade in securities and in foreign currency (although the latter should probably be done only by the strongest banks).

The main concern of the new system should be the creation of an interbank money market. What is most important here is to allow free formation of interest rates on short-term interbank deposits. These rates must be free to fluctuate quickly according to changing conditions in the capital market. All other interest rates in the banking system will adapt to these interbank rates, which will set the ceiling for deposit rates and the floor for lending rates. Competition between the banks must be encouraged to make banking services cheaper and more efficient.

Toward this end, creation of a securities market is necessary. Of course, first it will be necessary to create the securities themselves. In this respect Bulgaria is again very much behind the other former socialist countries. And here too we must not subscribe to the illusion that merely revising legislation will automatically solve the problem.

Formation of appropriate financial institutions and markets in Bulgaria is a necessary condition for the success of general market reform. It is indispensable to price reform and free formation of prices. A commodity market cannot exist, nor can market prices emerge, until there is a well-developed financial sphere.

Epilogue: The Outlook for Reform in Early 1991

In December 1990 a new Bulgarian government was formed with ministers of the opposition heading the key ministries of finance and industry. On 1 February 1991 the most radical reform program yet undertaken in Eastern Europe was begun. Subsidies were cut and prices liberalized. In two months prices rose by about 350 percent to 400 percent. A new budget, which accorded with the recommendations of the IMF, was proposed. The interest rate charged by the (now independent) central bank to the commercial banks was sharply increased, first to 15 percent and later to 45 percent and eventually 52 percent. The rate of inflation was reduced to 10 percent by May.

The exchange rate was liberalized at the outset of the program, and the currency quickly depreciated to near the black market rate. In spite of the sharp initial price rise, however, the exchange rate then appreciated from 25 leva to the dollar to the range of 15 to 18 leva to the dollar by June 1991.

These first steps were taken without any support from the international organizations—the first IMF credit came in April. Subsequent steps called for by the reform program include the reshaping of the financial system and the tax system, and of course privatization. As a result of the program the outlook for Bulgaria in mid–1991 is much more optimistic than only a few months previously.

Romania

Lucian C. Ionescu

The Current State of Economic Reform

During the summer following the elections of May 1990, the Romanian government presented its strategic analysis of the reforms needed in Romania. On the
basis of this report, the Council for Reform, a new advisory body established in
July of that year, worked out a program for coordinating the reform projects in
the most important fields of economic and social activity.

Thus, in the second part of 1990, stress was laid upon creating the legislative
and institutional framework strictly necessary for the transition from the structures of a command economy to those of a modern market economy. The
State Enterprises Conversion Act (which covers the transformation of the state
enterprises into "autonomous" and/or trading companies) was adopted in
August and went into effect in September.

Also in September, a conference of the ministers responsible for economic
reforms from all the Eastern European countries took place near Bucharest.
These proceedings pointed out the importance and usefulness of such meetings
concentrated on analyzing problems of mutual interest. The findings of the
conference underscored the importance of country-specific conditions but also
the common problems raised by the process of transition to a market economy.
Special attention was paid to the Yugoslav and Polish experiments in currency
convertibility, which at that time seemed to have reached their climax.[1]

Romanian experts, who also benefitted from the experience of specialists from
the IMF and the World Bank, drafted a new Banking Activity Law and a new
Central Bank Law. The latter would radically reshape the National Bank of
Romania so that it can fulfill the role of an independent central bank in relations
with the commercial and investment banks.

After this promising start, the program met with resistance from the old, rigid
structures in the bureaucracy and in the still highly monopolistic enterprise

---

1. Since the beginning of 1991 difficulties have emerged in those countries in maintaining
current account convertibility at the chosen exchange rates; all future candidates for
convertibility will have to take these developments into consideration.

---

*Lucian C. Ionescu is an expert in monetary and financial affairs with the Romanian government's
Council for Reform.*

sector, where power remained concentrated in the hands of the ministries and the large state-owned enterprises. This prompted the government in October to speed up the process of economic reform. Consequently, at the beginning of November 1990 the first stage of price liberalization was enacted. This decision has roused an ardent controversy.

The balance sheet for the year 1990 shows mixed results for the government's economic reform program. On the one hand, it is incontestable that the government has firmly opted for a market economy, for privatization, and for the granting of extensive decisionmaking autonomy to enterprises. At the same time, the new Romanian Parliament has debated over 60 laws, the majority of which have been aimed at creating a socioeconomic environment suitable to a rapid and complete abandonment of the practices and mindsets of a centralized economy. The new legislation included laws governing privatization of state enterprises,[2] reform of the social safety net and the reintegration of unemployed workers into the labor force, public finance, antitrust, wages and salaries, commercial banking, the role of the central bank, foreign investment, and numerous other areas.

On the other hand, despite these efforts, 1990 ended with poor economic results (table 1): GDP was nearly 10 percent lower than in 1989, and both the budget and the current account recorded substantial deficits. The top priority in early 1991 is to finish the program of macroeconomic structural adjustment. Against this background, the transition to convertibility, which is closely correlated with the processes of privatization and liberalization of prices, is of crucial importance for the entire economic reform.

The Transition to Convertibility

For Romania, the working out of a viable model for convertibility should reflect both the specific conditions of the national economy and the impact of the international environment. It is of particular importance to plan for convertibility in the context of an increasingly unified European economy. Any new regime not only must take into account the experience and progress of the other Eastern European countries but must adopt a strategy that is compatible with the further evolution of the European Community and the European Monetary System.

For any country, and especially any European country, that wishes to develop into a modern economy, the transition to convertibility must go hand in hand with the adoption, domestically, of the monetary and financial structures and

---

2. As of July 1991 the proposed legislation on privatization was being hotly debated in the Romanian Parliament.

Table 1   Romania: selected economic indicators, 1980–90[a]

	1980	1981	1982	1983	1984	1985	1986	1987	1988	1989	1990
Gross domestic product (1980 = 100)	100.0	100.1	104.1	110.4	116.9	116.8	119.6	120.6	120.0	113.0	104.0
Industrial production (1980 = 100)	100	103	104	109	116	120	129	132	136	133	107
Consumer price index (1980 = 100)	100.0	n.a.	n.a.	n.a.	n.a.	126.9	129.1	129.7	133.5	134.3	n.a.
Trade (millions of current dollars)											
With CMEA member countries											
Exports	3,734	3,058	2,961	3,143	2,685	3,431	3,620	3,760	4,004	3,658	2,107
Imports	3,537	3,074	2,641	2,913	2,651	3,300	3,996	3,869	3,754	4,032	3,344
With all other countries[b]											
Exports	7,667	8,123	6,887	6,704	7,213	6,743	6,143	6,732	7,388	6,830	3,763
Imports	9,663	7,904	5,683	4,734	5,078	5,102	4,088	4,444	3,888	4,406	5,770
Exchange rate[c] (lei per dollar)	18.0	15.0	15.0	17.2	21.3	17.1	16.2	14.6	14.3	14.9	22.4

n.a. = not available.

a. The population of Romania as of 1 January 1991 was 23.2 million.

b. Includes East Germany.

c. Commercial rate, period average.

Source: National Bank of Romania.

institutions of a market economy, including a modern commercial banking system, non-bank financial institutions, stock and bond exchanges, and so on. On the external front, convertibility must accompany the process of integration of the economy into international trade and capital flows. Thus, sound management of the balance of payments is crucial both for the adoption of convertibility and for the continued credibility of a convertible currency. In the view of the Romanian central bank authorities, there are four principal ways by which Romania could make the transition to convertibility of the national currency.

The first involves an official commitment to a fixed exchange rate, using a tight connection with one of the main foreign currencies as a nominal anchor. This approach would require substantial foreign-currency and other financial resources—which Romania does not now have—to be used as a stabilization fund. Even if Romania could rely on some important credits, the utilization of such funds, especially for stabilization of the exchange rate, would conflict both with the need to keep the balance of payments deficit within bounds and with the acute necessities associated with implementing the macroeconomic structural adjustment program. At the same time, the continued existence of a distorted cost and price structure generates a major risk of purely speculative behavior emerging, which would amplify the economic and financial disequilibria.

The second scenario involves the transition to convertibility via an Eastern European payments union (see, e.g., the proposal by Jozef van Brabant in chapter 4 of this volume). Although such an institution has often been proposed during the last two years, the discussion has not yet passed the theoretical stage. The failure to move forward on this issue shows either the existence of divergent interests among the union's prospective members or the absence of a well-elaborated proposal that balances the interests of the Eastern European countries. The idea of an Eastern European payments union should be given further consideration, also taking into account the disintegration of CMEA and with it the elimination of the system of payments in transferable rubles. This situation is already creating serious financial difficulties for trade among some Eastern European states.

Third, an extremely interesting and attractive approach to the transition to convertibility would be to link the process in some way to the European Monetary System. This possibility deserves much greater attention not only from each of the countries involved, but also within a multilateral framework (such as the Eastern European payments union mentioned above). The interdependence between the economic and financial difficulties and the sociopolitical tensions that the Eastern European countries are facing highlights the need for a concerted approach to the problems of convertibility. However, it seems that the process of European reintegration is still in an incipient stage. Therefore it would be imprudent to rely on a solution involving the EMS becoming available in the near future. Even so, it is essential to prevent capricious events and temporary frictions from hindering cooperation at the European level.

Taking into account all of the problems and conditions that have been mentioned, the most realistic way for Romania to make the transition to convertibility is probably through a fourth route: this would involve a gradual but relatively fast process of bringing the official exchange rate closer to the market level, in tandem with the liberalization of prices and the consolidation of the new financial and banking system. Under Romania's present economic conditions, a sudden and radical transition to convertibility could have negative effects of an unforeseeable intensity and amplitude. The extremely distorted costs and prices inherited from the previous system, reflected in a six- to sevenfold overvaluation of the leu (according to data available at the end of 1990), present major risks. A sudden transition to convertibility at an exchange rate similar to that on the black market would result in a burst of inflation, with unfortunate sociopolitical consequences. However, the alternative of an official exchange rate subject to small but frequent changes would inevitably contribute to the emergence and strengthening of inflationary expectations.

Under these circumstances, the National Bank of Romania prefers a transition to convertibility through a two-tier system:

- A fixed official exchange rate that accepts the present overvaluation of the leu to be applied to trade in a small number of products considered vital for the Romanian economy, and

- A floating rate, closer to that prevailing in the black market, to be applied to all other products and services, with settlement in daily interbank auctions; the official exchange rate would gradually gravitate to this floating rate.[3]

In early 1991 Romania laid the foundations of a new interbank foreign-exchange market to which all economic agents will have access. Two sources are to be used to supply this market with funds: enterprises' retention accounts (in which enterprises will be allowed to retain 50 percent of their export revenues) and foreign-exchange auctions, to be organized on a regular basis.

The creation of a foreign-exchange market has three main objectives:

- Exporters will have the opportunity to credit to their accounts a part of the countervalue of their exports at the unofficial rate, which will be more

---

3. The interbank foreign-exchange market was effectively inaugurated in February 1991, with six commercial banks authorized to take part in daily auctions under the supervision of the National Bank of Romania. Between February and June 1991 the exchange rate determined in these auctions fluctuated between 180 and 200 lei to the dollar; in April the leu at the official fixed exchange rate was devalued by nearly 50 percent to a level of about 60 lei to the dollar.

advantageous than the official rate; this should stimulate production and exports.

- Importers will be able to purchase foreign merchandise either by using their own foreign-exchange accounts or by buying foreign exchange on the market with lei at the daily rate.

- Useful information will be obtained both with respect to trends in the free market exchange rate and with respect to the most efficient distribution of the scanty foreign-exchange resources of the country.

The experience gained from setting up and operating the foreign-exchange market, together with the expected improvement in economic performance, will permit the establishment of current account convertibility.[4]

Some Comments and Proposals

It is becoming increasingly obvious that the transition to currency convertibility in the Eastern European countries represents a decisive test of the viability of their programs of liberalization and modernization. Not long ago, convertibility was considered a result of reform, the fruit of successful economic development. Examples may be found among the Western European countries that adopted convertibility in the 1980s, such as Ireland, Spain, and Portugal. Lately, however, the big-bang approach, especially the Polish experiment begun in January 1990, has left its mark on scenarios regarding the transition to convertibility. Yugoslavia appears to occupy an intermediate position: after two unsuccessful attempts in the 1970s and 1980s, the present program, in effect since December 1989, has had remarkable success. In this area of policy, as in others, the optimum seems to lie between the extremes, somewhere in the temperate zone of economic

---

4. By the summer of 1991 Romania could be said to have laid the foundation for the establishment of convertibility. As Williamson notes in chapter 10 of this volume, "the freedom to buy imports at all, even if only at the severely depreciated rate set in the auctions, is the most important element of convertibility so this liberalization [by Romania] represents important progress." There have even been some signals, in particular from the National Bank, that the timetable for unification of the exchange rate may be speeded up, perhaps culminating by the end of 1991. However, considering that Romania is attempting to use the money supply and not (as in Poland) the exchange rate as the nominal anchor for the economy, a crawling peg approach may offer the best chances for success. Much depends on how quickly the supply side of the economy can be revived from its present faltering state.

and social life.[5] As Richard Portes recently observed at another international conference:

> [C]onvertibility is for these countries [of Eastern Europe] not simply a question of international macroeconomics, not a monetary issue. . . . It is central to the process of transformation and must be situated within that process in a way appropriate to the particular country concerned, which may depend heavily on whether it will be possible to *sustain* convertibility once introduced. Certainly, a forced retreat would be devastating to the credibility which is indispensable for any reform programme. (Portes 1990)

In my view the conditions necessary for the introduction and maintenance of convertibility include the existence of a sizable private sector, or at least the implementation of a broad and accelerated privatization process in a way that favors competition; liberalization of a majority of prices; progress of the banking system toward a status appropriate to a market economy with an ever-greater number of institutions involved in the setting up of monetary, foreign-exchange, and capital markets; structural adjustment of the production process so as to stimulate more efficient exports and to put a brake on inefficient imports; a favorable trend in the current account; the promotion of significant flows of foreign investment and financial assistance; and the presence of a sufficient volume of foreign-exchange reserves to maintain a stable exchange rate.

Of course, meeting these conditions, which are interdependent, raises problems of speed and quantity, as well as qualitative problems. A purely formal and superficial process of economic liberalization will in the end only bring economic and social chaos.

Beyond the internal aspects of transformation, which are specific to each country, the Eastern European countries face a series of economic and financial problems that should enhance their interest in the establishment of a payments union. I have doubts about the outlook for the new International Economic Cooperation Organization that is intended to replace the CMEA according to the statement made public at the beginning of 1991.[6] But I would underline the urgent necessity and the potential advantages of creating a foreign-exchange and financial union among the small and medium-sized countries of Eastern Europe.

Any such union would have to conclude special agreements with the Soviet Union, on the one hand, and with the European Community on the other. Of course, the two kinds of agreements would be quite different in nature.

---

5. The dramatic events of the summer of 1991, and especially the danger of civil war in Yugoslavia, have unfortunately confirmed the strong correlation between the economic and the social aspects of a country's historical evolutions.

6. Apparently for lack of interest, the new organization failed to materialize as planned upon the final abolition of the CMEA in June 1991.

A "payments union" is actually not the best term for the kind of organization I would most like to see established, taking into account the specific backgrounds of the individual Eastern European countries. The core of the union, as I have envisaged and repeatedly urged it, would be an interconnected banking and financial infrastructure. The jettisoning of the central planning system and with it the network of state planning committees at the heart of the CMEA creates the need for a new means of establishing coherence between the macro- and the microeconomy. In this a banking and financial system that is integrated at the national and the international (i.e., the European) level will play a crucial role and should serve as an essential "common denominator" (to use the OECD's term) for the Eastern European economies in transition.

We all know that the international situation, after a period of relaxation in the second half of the 1980s, has become tense once again under the impact of a succession of critical events, of which the Gulf crisis is only the most striking example. Under these conditions, European reintegration takes on new and vital significance, and I believe that an Eastern European payments union should be conceived and implemented as a way of approaching the structure and mechanism of the European Community. (I also support the notion that the ecu is the logical anchor for the Eastern European currencies.) To achieve this objective, the European Monetary System and the European Bank for Reconstruction and Development should each play a decisive role, and the IMF and the World Bank will have to become closely involved as well. These proposals are not meant to nurture the illusion of Europe as an "island of stability" in a stormy international ocean. Rather they are offered as part of a vision of a united Europe that could contribute, together with other countries and peoples, to the peace and prosperity of the world.

Comment

Todor Valchev

As these and the other papers in this volume have shown, economic conditions in the countries of Eastern Europe have a number of similarities but are by no means identical. In particular, the degree to which the preconditions for convertibility are presently met differs quite greatly from country to country. The situation in Bulgaria is very different from the situation in, for example, Hungary and Poland.

As Ventseslav Dimitrov has said, prices of goods and services in Bulgaria are now determined by the government. However, a sweeping liberalization of prices is planned for 1 February and will affect nearly all goods and services, including bread, meat, and milk and excluding only energy, coal, transport, and a very few other commodities and services.[1]

On 22 January 1991 interest rates in Bulgaria were raised quite sharply. The so-called basic rate was increased from 4.5 percent to 15 percent. As of this writing it is uncertain how the population will react to this increase. I would not be surprised if their reaction is a stormy one, because a lot of people will be affected by the higher interest rates on mortgages, which were raised from only 2 percent to 10 percent. Even this, I think, is low, but I do not expect the Bulgarian population to agree with me.

Meanwhile the budget deficit remains large. In 1990 it was 10 percent or 11 percent of GDP, but in the budget to be released in February 1991 it is expected to fall to the range of 4.5 percent to 5 percent of GDP. Under the old regime the central bank was strongly dependent on the government and financed its deficits.

Bulgaria has a huge external debt and absolutely no monetary reserves. The country also maintains a system of multiple exchange rates. For all of these reasons, Bulgaria appears far less ready for the introduction of currency convertibility than Poland, Hungary, Czechoslovakia, or Yugoslavia, and in some sense than Romania as well.

On the other hand there have also been some positive developments. A new government with a non-Communist prime minister came to power in December 1990. Bulgaria has become a member of the IMF and has signed an agreement with the European Community, which is Bulgaria's biggest trading partner in the West—much of that trade is with Germany. However, there has been a

---

1. This liberalization and other reforms were implemented on schedule (see chapter 10).

Todor Valchev is President of the National Bank of Bulgaria.

significant lack of progress in the negotiations with the advisory committee representing Bulgaria's bank creditors, but there is reason to hope that this stalemate will be broken.

Bulgaria's situation thus does not favor an immediate shift to convertibility. It seems to me that the best course of action for Bulgaria to take is to accept the terms of Article XIV of the IMF Articles of Agreement and not, for the time being, those of Article VIII. Meanwhile Bulgaria should start to prepare the foundations for the adoption of convertibility, using a gradualist approach as advocated by Friedrich Levcik (chapter 3) and others in this volume. Eventually it will be possible to introduce so-called internal convertibility, as has been done in Yugoslavia, Poland, and Hungary; only some years later should Bulgaria make the move to full convertibility in the sense of Article VIII.

Dimitrov's paper has given some sense of the complexity of the task of transforming the Bulgarian economy into a market economy. An important part of this transformation is the privatization of state enterprises. Unfortunately, much of the initial effort at privatization has resulted in the plundering of state property by those closely connected to the Party apparatus, who were able to buy up these assets at extremely low prices. The democratic opposition stopped this first attempt at privatization; privatization is to be resumed in March 1991, beginning with small businesses, under a different set of rules. A related question—and a very difficult one for Bulgaria—is reform of land ownership. There is as yet no consensus in the country on how to proceed in this area, and therefore it is likely that Bulgarian land will not be freely bought and sold for some years to come.

Another precondition for convertibility is reform of the monetary and credit system, leading to independence of the central bank, a system of market-oriented commercial banks, and later the development of stock and bond markets.

In the gradualist approach to convertibility that I would prefer to see implemented, the present multiple exchange rate system would be continued for a time, during which there would be regular currency auctions. When the exchange rate established in these auctions stabilizes, it will then be possible to unify the exchange rate. All foreign-exchange reserves would be concentrated within the central bank, and at that point it would be possible to introduce internal convertibility, and later full convertibility in the sense of IMF Article VIII.

What in fact is likely to happen is that the recent rise in interest rates will give the Bulgarian people an incentive to hold the national currency. This will be followed by the liberalization of prices planned for February 1991. After that internal convertibility will be introduced, with a floating exchange rate rather than the fixed rate that I would prefer. I would be delighted to see this approach succeed, but success seems doubtful in the early months.

Comment

Eduard Hochreiter

Ventseslav Dimitrov and Lucian Ionescu have presented two extremely interesting and stimulating papers. They describe the present stage of the reform process in their countries and offer their views on how and when convertibility of the Bulgarian lev and the Romanian leu could be achieved. At present both economies are besieged by massive price distortions, a significant monetary overhang, a lack of reserves, and, in the case of Bulgaria, an overpowering foreign debt. Institutional reforms are only in their infancy. Against this background, both authors conclude, and I concur, that at present the economic preconditions for currency convertibility are not met.

My remarks will concentrate on two important issues regarding currency convertibility. The first relates to the political preconditions for convertibility, and the second deals with the anchoring problem.

Whereas the focus of most of the papers in this volume has been on the economic preconditions for convertibility, I would like to stress that there are not only economic but also political preconditions for a successful move to convertibility. Without a political consensus, it is impossible to carry through the reforms necessary for the transition from a centrally planned to a market economy. Without a legitimate government to ensure the acceptance of reforms by the population, there can be no lasting reform. Looking at the two countries, I find that Bulgaria, after the change in its government at the end of 1990 and the "Agreement for a Peaceful Transition Toward Democracy" reached in January 1991, has gone further toward meeting the political preconditions than has Romania.

The long-term sustainability of convertibility, as Ionescu puts it, depends on the will of both policymakers and the population to achieve economic stability. This will is all the more important when the reforms are expected to lead initially to lower real incomes, reduced real wages, and mounting unemployment. This important point is noted by both authors. The point that remains to be emphasized is that, until very recently, this will on the part of policymakers and the public has not been clearly visible. As a consequence, uncertainty about the future economic development of these countries has been particularly great, raising the risk that the reforms will fail.

The second issue I would like to raise concerns one important aspect of convertibility, namely, the effect convertibility might have on the credibility of the domestic currency. In my view this issue merits particular attention, especially because all reform-minded countries start out with a more or less discredited

Eduard Hochreiter is Senior Adviser and Chief of the Foreign Research Division at the Austrian National Bank and Lecturer in International Economics at the University of Economics, Vienna.

currency. To build confidence, a credible, stability-oriented monetary policy is indispensable, and at the heart of such a policy is some form of nominal anchor. An appropriate nominal anchor is not a panacea, of course. In the long run, only sound economic policy as a whole can make credibility (and thereby the anchor) sustainable.

The nominal anchor that I favor for the countries of Eastern Europe is some form of exchange rate anchor. Leaving aside the question of which currency to choose for this purpose, I would like to look in a little more detail at whether reforming countries should opt for a fixed exchange rate anchor or for a crawling peg. My own preference is for a fixed exchange rate anchor, because it offers the best opportunity for a discredited currency to regain acceptance by the population and to eliminate the risk of high inflation. Furthermore, currency substitution can be at least substantially reduced—a sine qua non for any attempt at sound economic policies.

Pegging the exchange rate is likewise no panacea. Credibility over the longer term can only be built if the domestic economy validates the exchange rate level chosen. Most important in this respect is the development of wages. Therefore the sustainability of the exchange rate anchor depends to a large extent on its supplementation by a long-term wage anchor. In the case where wage rises are related to productivity advances, the maintenance of the peg does not lead to a loss of international competitiveness. It is this crucial connection on which economic policymaking ought to focus.

Ionescu advances some interesting proposals for a transitional arrangement. He suggests a temporary dual exchange rate arrangement, with one slightly overvalued exchange rate for vital imports and another, related to the black market rate, for all other transactions.

The reason given for this proposal is that the economic situation in Romania is so difficult, and the degree of uncertainty with regard to future economic developments so large, that it is impossible to guess at an adequate exchange rate. I personally think that Bulgaria is in a similar situation. In fact, Bulgaria introduced a "triple exchange rate arrangement" in May 1990, which could be adopted for the transitional phase in Romania as well.

I would like to close with some questions regarding this proposal. First, do the Romanian authorities envisage a clear and credible timetable for the phasing out of this arrangement, and what time horizon, if any, is envisaged? Second, how does one assess the danger of creating new or maintaining existing distortions in resource allocation? Finally, how does this proposal compare with McKinnon's temporary tariff proposal and the gradual removal of licensing procedures as applied by Hungary?

Acknowledgment

Efficient research assistance by Peter Backé is kindly acknowledged.

Discussion

Ileana Ionescu shared the view that it was premature to discuss such questions as a nominal anchor in a country like Romania, where the basic preconditions for a market economy had not yet been created. Romania was still far from achieving even commodity convertibility. In 1968, for every leu in circulation, there were goods and services produced with a value of 2.5 lei; at the beginning of 1990, annual production corresponding to every leu in circulation was 0.2 lei, and by the end of 1990 that had fallen to 0.1 lei. One cannot expect to have a credible monetary policy until one has a credible economy!

She also argued that the Polish big bang had not really been as radical a shock as outsiders seemed to think. By late 1989 the Polish economy had already undergone a series of reforms; by comparison the Romanian economy, like those of Bulgaria and the Soviet Union, was essentially unchanged from what it had been forty years before, with state monopolies of everything. A premature declaration of convertibility under such circumstances could be more costly than a well-prepared but delayed step: she recalled that in the 1920s the Soviet Union had lost 200 tons of gold in three days following a similar move, with dire consequences for the Minister of Finance. The sharp differences between different groups of economies in transition—Czechoslovakia, Hungary, Poland, and Yugoslavia on the one hand, versus Bulgaria, Romania, and the Soviet Union on the other—created fears that a revival of regional cooperation, whether through a payments union or otherwise, could lead to a repetition of the phony efficiency of the CMEA.

Romania was now trying to escape from its past mistakes and to face reality. It had already gone a long way toward unifying the exchange rate, and it had started devaluing to achieve a more realistic rate. The exchange rate was, however, still far from equilibrium, and few trade transactions were settled at the official rate, because subsidies still existed and prices were still controlled. Price liberalization was under discussion, but unless it could be accompanied by institutional reform, it was not clear that price signals would have profound supply-side effects.

John Flemming reassured Lucian Ionescu that the European Bank for Reconstruction and Development (EBRD) indeed intended to give priority to reform of the financial infrastructure of the economies in transition. Banking reform was a crucial element in reconciling the hardening of budget constraints with the attainment of monetary stability. The EBRD was committed to the private sector, which implied both privatization and the development of secondary markets in ownership claims (i.e., stock exchanges). The balance between a commercial banking system and stock exchanges nonetheless posed difficult questions, to which different solutions had been chosen in the Anglo-Saxon countries on the one hand, and Japan and the Continent on the other. The EBRD would have to develop its own position on that issue. In Britain there had recently developed considerable disenchantment with the Anglo-Saxon practice of restricting the role of bank finance to the provision of short-term, self-liquidating loans and leaving the control and monitoring of management to the stock exchange, where it was a public good and, like most public goods, undersupplied. Many of the mechanisms of privatization now under discussion in Eastern Europe seem likely to leave ownership even more fragmented, and hence pose even more of a problem of supervision and monitoring.

Flemming also responded to Eduard Hochreiter's comment about the crawling peg. Given the uncertainty involved in choosing an initial rate and the problem of maintaining a credible fixed rate between countries whose initial inflation rates were widely divergent, he saw attractions in allowing a limited initial period during which rates might crawl. This could in fact add to credibility and give adequate time to achieve convergence.

Replying to the debate, *Lucian Ionescu* underlined the breadth of support in Romania for the decision to move to a market economy. No political force in the country opposed it. Of course, there were many political disagreements about ways and means: Romanians had no desire to replicate the "consensus" that had existed under Communism. But there was widespread support for the fundamental lines that policy was now pursuing, and Ionescu invited skeptical Westerners to come and work to help build the new Romanian economy and see for themselves how private property rights were now being respected. The capital inflows that were so badly needed would in turn help to strengthen the political consensus.

Eastern Europe's most urgent need was the development of a financial and banking infrastructure adequate to the transition to a modern market economy. The creation of such an infrastructure not only is the principal condition for a viable payments union but would form the basis for a credible move to currency convertibility.

Ionescu concluded by stressing that the desire to build a united Europe was not restricted to Western Europe but extended also to the East, including Romania. Of course there were objective differences in conditions, both between West and East and within the East, but there was also a common need and desire to apply the principles of a market economy to the whole of Europe.

Ventseslav Dimitrov said that he did not believe in any consensus that embraced those who had been implicated in the previous regime. Prior to the last election in Bulgaria, the democratic opposition had joined the government in signing a document declaring a consensus on the need to create a market economy. The Communists had then exploited the situation, frightening the people with stories about the costs of a quick transition, about price increases and inflation, and so on. A new consensus had now been established, but this time the democratic forces remained vigilant against possible abuses.

So far as the credibility of the Bulgarian currency was concerned, Dimitrov agreed that its foreign-exchange value was currently unrealistic. It was possible to buy 20 bottles of beer with $1 swapped at the black market rate in Bulgaria. The Bulgarian authorities were planning to increase and ultimately free prices, but that would not solve the problem of credibility. They had intended to start with small privatizations, so as to mop up the monetary overhang, but that possibility had been spoiled by the asset-stripping practiced by the Communists when they were still in power in 1990. The agenda now had to be to end the budget deficit, eliminate the monetary overhang, implement a restrictive monetary policy, resume small privatization, make a start on demonopolization, and then move on to the privatization of large enterprises and the creation of a money market with positive real interest rates. But there is no time to sequence these steps properly, and the process might have to start with more administrative price increases.

In *Todor Valchev's* view, establishing the credibility of money in Bulgaria was going to require higher interest rates, a restrictive credit policy, an appropriate wage policy, a tight fiscal policy, and enough raw materials to get production up again. In reply to Hochreiter's question about the Bulgarian view on dual exchange rates, Valchev said that he had sympathized with that view two years before, when Bulgaria actually had three exchange rates. If reform had been started at that time it might have been possible to bring them together gradually, but he thought that under current circumstances there was little alternative to a rapid unification.

8

The Soviet Union

8

The Soviet Union

Convertibility of the Ruble

Boris Fedorov

Convertibility of the ruble, according to some economists, is the crucial reform that will give birth to a truly meaningful exchange rate. Other economists believe that convertibility can be achieved by government decision, and even offer precise timetables, usually on the order of 5 to 15 years. The present Soviet government seems convinced that convertibility is a cure-all for the economy and even issued an official statement to that effect. Several government bodies were instructed as early as 1987–88 to prepare detailed programs for the introduction of convertibility.

Unfortunately, convertibility of the ruble is at present neither a possibility nor a priority. It would be naive to try to introduce convertibility without at the same time drastically transforming the entire Soviet economy and introducing an economically rational system of institutions and laws. Any radical convertibility plan would have to confront a variety of limitations and peculiarities of the Soviet system and introduce a number of quite basic measures.

It must be assumed that, for the next few years, the basic features of the Soviet economy will remain unchanged. It will continue to be a one-sector economy, in which private, cooperative, and foreign business activities are negligible compared with those of the state. Money and material resources will continue to be distributed mostly vertically and by administrative decree, making it impossible for the ruble to perform the usual functions of a monetary unit. Foreign-exchange restrictions will continue to apply to practically all external transactions.

Meanwhile the Soviet economy remains flagrantly inefficient in the utilization of all types of resources. Many enterprises produce goods that cannot be consumed. Soviet workers lack motivation to produce, to increase their efficiency,

Boris Fedorov is a former Minister of Finance of the Russian Republic.

or to show initiative. Workers who do perform at levels above the average are commonly looked on with disfavor. The government is clearly losing control over the economy. Decentralization is being forced upon the economy much faster than new, efficient regulatory systems can be introduced.

The authorities are fairly strongly committed to developing alternative sectors of the economy and encouraging horizontal flows of resources, and to boosting general economic efficiency through decentralization, de-etatization, and demonopolization. However, the government will not, in the medium term, allow widespread bankruptcies of loss-making enterprises to occur or unemployment to rise to excessive levels.

The timetable for the introduction of convertibility must be such as to achieve tangible results within at most three to five years. The initial steps must be taken in the course of 1991 and must be sufficiently drastic to inspire hope for change in the population.

Definitions

Convertibility is not something that can be achieved by a single government decree. Rather, it is a feature of a certain type of market economy. There are widely varying degrees of convertibility. If by convertibility one means simply that an exchange of currencies is possible, then even a system of centralized currency administration can be said to offer convertibility. True convertibility, however, means a full-fledged link between the internal and the external market—in other words, an absence of restrictions at least on current account transactions, relatively free price formation internally, and openness of the economy to multilateral trade and foreign competition.

All of these are nonexistent in the Soviet Union and will be difficult to achieve. The Soviet government is not yet ready to manage the economy through indirect instruments; indeed few such instruments as yet exist. Decentralization of the economy has scarcely begun. The government's insistence on currency self-financing—that an enterprise should spend only as much foreign exchange as it earns—clearly shows that the marketization even of external economic relations cannot be too quick.

Convertibility also presupposes some kind of international use of the national currency or at least the guarantee that the currency can be exchanged. Yet at present it is illegal for persons not residing in the Soviet Union to earn rubles (although there are experiments in this direction); even if they acquired rubles they would have difficulty buying anything with them or selling them for foreign currencies. Given the ongoing shortages and the existing price and exchange rate distortions in the economy, if nonresidents were granted permission to use rubles, the result could contribute to the excess of purchasing power, which would be neither politically nor economically acceptable. Therefore external convertibility as practiced in the West is not an enticing option for the Soviet Union.

Convertibility in a narrow sense means the possibility (which, however, may not be widely exercised) of using the national currency for external payments. Hence, convertibility in a modern context boils down mainly to lifting exchange restrictions, at least those on current account transactions. In practice this means that nonresidents can legally accept rubles in payment for goods and services, and in turn use them for purchases or investments in the Soviet Union or sell them on the foreign-exchange market, and that residents can use rubles to pay for imports or buy foreign exchange.

Discussions of convertibility focus on various essential elements: a realistic exchange rate, a well-defined exchange regime, a strong exchange authority, and a developed internal exchange market. But in a wider sense convertibility requires a developed monetary and fiscal system and mainly market-based goods and financial flows. If money does not fulfill its most basic functions within the country of issue, it cannot be considered money in an international context. Thus, whereas for most countries convertibility is mostly a matter of developing and managing external economic relations, for the Soviet Union it is a question of how to make the ruble real money.

Thus, for the Soviet Union, solving the convertibility problem amounts to solving the problem of how to reform the economy in general. That is why any sensible program will address three major aspects of the problem:

- Developing a new model of economic policy, of the use of policy instruments, and of policymaking institutions and their interrelationships;

- Designing the specific elements of convertibility proper;

- The time element: how to introduce reforms in parallel, comprehensively, and quickly.

Each aspect involves setting priorities and specifying measures to be implemented at each stage. The complexity of the reforms and the uncertainties that will be encountered at each step along the way make it impossible to construct an exact timetable. But it is vitally important that the measures at least not contradict each other.

The time element is crucial. A comprehensive package of reforms should be embarked upon immediately to ensure that the principal institutional and legal structures are firmly in place by the end of 1991. Given the present process of decisionmaking in the bureaucracy and the Supreme Soviet, it would be utterly impossible to enact such a package through conventional channels. The only hope is for the President of the Soviet Union to make drastic decisions on his own. Even so, the political turmoil witnessed by the Soviet Union since the summer of 1990 suggests that convertibility could well become a politically unattainable goal.

Soviet bureaucrats often point to what they see as the absolute prerequisites that must be fulfilled before convertibility can be attained: increased export potential, adequate reserves, proper integration into the world economy, increased efficiency of enterprises, and the development of a qualified work force that is motivated to increase its productivity. All such talk reveals nothing but these officials' own paralysis of will, incompetence, and inability to act in an environment that is becoming more and more market-oriented. All the necessary reforms should be embarked on simultaneously and comprehensively. If we do nothing but wait for the situation to improve, things are bound to go from bad to worse.

General Reforms

The state's direct participation in production, trade, and banking must be ended as quickly as possible, to be replaced by a merely regulatory role in these activities. The only way to do this is by transforming the majority of state enterprises and banks into joint-stock companies and severing their direct links to government (leaving them with only the power to tax, elect managers, and distribute profits). The goal should be to convert to joint-stock companies, within three to five years, at least 75 percent of productive enterprises now owned by the state. The privatization process should go hand in hand with the elimination of monopolies and the breakup of huge industrial concerns.

The state in most cases would initially retain from 60 percent to 100 percent of the shares of these enterprises, although efforts should be made from the start to distribute shares to their workers, to other enterprises, and to the general public. It must be acknowledged, however, that not all of these firms are capable of being sold. To help smooth the transformation, no single individual should be allowed to own more than 5 percent to 10 percent of the equity in any single company.

The new joint-stock companies should be free from the outset in choosing what to produce, where to sell and at what price, and how much to pay their employees. Acceptance of state orders and state-established prices would be voluntary. At the same time, however, price controls in the economy generally will have to be retained and price liberalization allowed to proceed step by step, concentrating on certain sectors and making adjustments in cases of flagrant disproportion. The primary goal will be to cut costs and increase efficiency by increasing worker motivation and reorganizing the production process.

Inefficient enterprises should be closed, dismantled, broken up, leased, sold, or simply given away to other enterprises (whether domestic or foreign) or cooperatives. Individuals would be free to start up businesses in the form of either single proprietorships, partnerships, or corporations. Incentives should be offered to promote the creation of small businesses. Wholly foreign-owned enterprises should be legalized. What is needed is not a general law governing property rights but specific decrees covering a variety of activities.

Governmental Reorganization

The process of stripping the state of its role in productive activities will require radical changes in how policy is made. All branch ministries and second-tier Council of Ministries bodies (bureaus and commissions) should be eliminated. The remaining ministries should be made responsible for their own actions and granted enough authority to fulfill their responsibilities. They will have to learn to accomplish those responsibilities through indirect means instead of by decree. The State Planning Committee should be merged with the price committee (Goskomtsen) and certain other bodies to form a new Ministry of Economics, which would be responsible for overall structural and regional economic policy. At the same time, several new, independent agencies should be created under the Supreme Soviet and assigned the roles of securities market regulation, antitrust enforcement, and privatization and the management of the remaining state properties.

It is a fair guess that, without the appointment of several hundred or at least several dozen market- and internationally oriented people to very high government positions, the reforms are doomed. The present officials are incapable of changing their ways.

Market Infrastructure

Urgently needed are all the institutions and infrastructure of a market economy, including financial markets, commodities markets, and labor market and worker training institutions. A legal and regulatory infrastructure must be constructed to set out the "rules of the game" in the new economic environment. Some of the necessary laws have already been or are scheduled to be adopted (such as those on property and land ownership, leaseholds, and taxation), but many others are not yet even on the agenda. For the purpose of achieving convertibility, the most important of these are:

■ Drastic changes in the money-issue mechanism, including regulation of the money supply, the breaking of barriers between cash and cashless circulation, the reduction of cash circulation through development of a payments system, and the creation of new instruments that can be used for monetary regulation. All of these presuppose the creation of a strong, independent central bank (indeed this is more important in the Soviet Union than anywhere else), with jurisdiction over all monetary and foreign-exchange policy.

- Drastic changes in the system of budgetary financing, including total prohibition of central bank financing of budget deficits, securitization of the existing internal debt, and the creation of a debt management system.

- Drastic changes as well in the budget process itself, including cuts in the capital investment budget and the separation of the central government's budget from those of the republics and localities. For 1991 the budget deficit should be scaled down to a negligible amount. Legal limits on the budget deficit should be given serious consideration.

- Changes in the government's management of the economy. The government's task should be to influence broad economic aggregates through the use of such instruments as tax policy, interest rates, and subsidies; it should enforce the "rules of the game," breaking up monopolies and stimulating competition.

Dealing with Imbalances

During the transition to a market economy, the management of imbalances in the economy, especially the buildup of money balances held by the population, will be a critically important issue. Drastic measures will need to be taken to establish a policy of tight money, with higher interest rates and hard budget constraints, to link wages as closely as possible to results and to soak up excess liquidity.

The monetary overhang could be absorbed in part by radically reorienting the composition of imports to include more consumer goods, and by the sale of real and financial assets (land, buildings, stocks, bonds, insurance), with part of the monetary proceeds to be withdrawn from circulation. An international aid and loan consortium could perhaps be organized to obtain consumer goods for the Soviet market.

As a last resort, if conditions do not improve in the course of 1991, a temporary partial freeze on the deposits of both individuals and businesses may become necessary.

Exchange Reforms

The general measures just described are needed to create the foundations of a market economy in which convertibility of the ruble can be contemplated. But the attainment of convertibility will also require a number of changes in the foreign-exchange regime and in external economic relations generally.

Exchange Authority

No exchange mechanism is viable without a proper division of authority among various governmental and nongovernmental bodies. All duplication of functions must be scrapped and all unnecessary administrative bodies (such as the present State Commission for External Economic Relations) abolished.

Ideally, the central bank (Gosbank) should be responsible for all foreign exchange, foreign borrowing, and international investment matters, leaving authority for all trade-related matters to the Ministry for External Economic Relations. The Bank for External Economic Relations would become an authorized bank serving as an agent for the government. The Ministry of Finance would be responsible for the external payments position of the public sector and of the country in general.

The Exchange Rate

There is absolutely no doubt that the ruble will be devalued. However, the extent of the devaluation remains a matter for conjecture, since exchange controls still apply to 100 percent of transactions, economic agents are not yet free to make their own commercial decisions, and a free internal market does not yet exist even on paper. The exchange rate prevailing on the black market is not an accurate indicator of the implicit market rate, but mainly reflects prices of a limited range of consumer goods (mainly consumer electronics) that are in acute scarcity.

The first step will involve administrative setting of the exchange rate at a more realistic level—perhaps 3 to 6 rubles to the dollar. The commercial rate established in November 1990 of 1.8 rubles to the dollar was surely a step forward, especially in that at the same time differentiated currency ratios for different goods were finally abolished.

More important than the initial setting of the rate are certain principles of exchange rate management:

- There should be a unified commercial rate for all types of external operations (the present official rate could be maintained for statistical purposes and certain intergovernmental agreements with Third World countries);

- The exchange rate should be adjusted according to the state of the balance of payments;

- The system of hard-currency distribution and exchange controls needs drastic change in the direction of decentralization;

- A single exchange rate should be the common criterion for making trade decisions.

Thus, in the very near future, the Soviet exchange rate system could comprise an official rate (used only for limited statistical purposes), a unified commercial rate, and a free market and auction rate. The commercial rate would be fixed daily by the central bank on the basis of the balance of payments position. It would have the authority to change this rate within a 5 percent band without prior government approval. Free market elements in the form of an interbank market and auctions should be introduced immediately. Eventually the commercial rate and the free market rate should be merged.

It would be an absolute mistake to wait for any kind of price reform as a precondition for the introduction of a unified commercial rate. Prices will play a more important role when their liberalization is at last well under way, when market institutions have been created, and when exchange restrictions have been lowered.

Allocation of Currency

A major obstacle to progress is the present Soviet system of hard-currency allocation. This system wastes resources, is not linked to any realistic exchange rate, and instills no motivation or sense of responsibility in economic agents. Instead of the intermediation of markets there exist a number of bureaucratic go-betweens, which are in fact nothing more than parasites impeding rather than facilitating the flow of goods and money. Unless drastic measures are taken, this system will lead to national bankruptcy due to a wastage of currency revenues.

The only sensible path to convertibility involves gradually cutting back the proportion of hard-currency earnings that pass through the centralized distribution system: a reasonable goal would be to reduce that share from its pre–1991 level of 95 percent to 75 percent or even less in 1991.

The system of hard-currency retention was a mistake; it will have to be restricted initially and ultimately abolished. The system effectively denies access to foreign exchange and foreign technology to those enterprises that are not already in some way oriented to foreign markets. The result is economic stagnation. The system also induces exporting enterprises to import foreign consumer goods for their workers; this leads to a fragmented economy in which export enterprises and industries become islands of prosperity.

Export promotion policy should be practiced with an eye to maintaining a stable balance of payments and should be exercised principally via the exchange rate, certain forms of subsidy, and tax incentives. If the internal market remains distorted and uncompetitive overall, any forced promotion of exports would only be self-destructive, merely adding to domestic shortages.

The reformed system of hard-currency distribution should include:

- Sale of hard currency to those who have obtained import licenses at the official commercial rate (and possibly to foreign investors seeking to repatriate profits);

- The obligatory surrender (for control purposes) of most hard-currency revenues to authorized banks in exchange for rubles at the commercial rate;

- State centralization of hard-currency revenues earned by natural monopolies such as oil and gas production;

- Allocation of part of the hard-currency resources collected by the authorized banks for hard-currency loans to domestic borrowers and for sale by auction;

- Phaseout of the existing retention system.

In short, most hard-currency holdings of the state would be sold or lent at the official or the free market exchange rate. The use of hard-currency resources for budgetary expenditures would be limited mainly to social programs.

There would be a twofold division of the foreign-exchange markets: an official market, in which the state itself would buy and sell hard currencies through the central bank or other authorized banks at the official rate, in quantities determined by position of the balance of payments; and a free interbank market, so that the authorized banks themselves could use these resources efficiently while also hedging against risk. The latter would include a program of official auctions, at which centrally collected foreign exchange would be sold directly to all legal entities at the free market rate.

The task of the central bank would be to minimize the discrepancies among these different markets and exchange rates. All operations would be conducted through the authorized banks, although some sort of foreign-exchange trading and exchange rate fixings at the newly created Moscow International Stock Exchange could be envisaged during the transition. The official and free exchange markets would be merged as early as possible.

The system of foreign-exchange planning also needs to be modified, to separate official reserves from those of the authorized banks and other legal entities. The former should fall under the management of the central bank, one of whose roles would be to intervene when necessary on the free market. Centralized hard-currency revenues, for example those generated from oil exports, should be kept on separate accounts. They should be treated no differently from ordinary commercial accounts by the authorized banks, which would act as ordinary commercial banks in competition with each other.

Of utmost importance is reform of the system by which the Soviet Union borrows from abroad. This system is directly connected with the system of exchange distribution. All borrowings and their utilization are centralized, leading to utter inefficiency and lack of clear responsibility. By all accounts the Soviet Union stands on the verge of a major debt crisis calling for extreme measures:

- The power to borrow should be delegated, within certain limits and quotas, to those who are able to repay their loans;

- Centralized borrowings need to be cut radically, and those remaining effected, and the proceeds utilized, with the consent of the constituent republics (and in the future only for projects of major importance to the entire Soviet Union or to increase official reserves);

- Legal limits on the accumulation of total external debt should be set immediately;

- A system of exchange controls should be set up to regulate foreign borrowing, other capital flows, extension of guarantees, and so on.

Foreign-Exchange Controls

The introduction of a convertible ruble will initially require the creation of a comprehensive system of orderly foreign-exchange controls, whose gradual liberalization will constitute the transition to convertibility. The most important aspect of this system will be the payments regime, governing trade payments (subject to import licensing), noncommercial payments (subject to legal limitations), and investments (subject to foreign-exchange licensing). A medium-term target should be maximum possible liberalization of the trade and exchange regime for current account operations.

To regulate the new system, the necessary powers would be delegated either to the central bank or the Ministry of Finance, or to a totally new body. The former alternative is the preferred one, as it would contribute to enhancing the role of the central bank in the economy. Its powers would include, among others, the issuing of exchange licenses, administration of the obligatory surrender of foreign exchange, administration of currency auctions, the right to designate the currencies in which payments may be effected, and administration of the regime of resident and nonresident foreign-currency accounts.

Practical administration of the system would be in the hands of the authorized banks, each with a wide network of branches operating by virtue of an exchange license granted by the regulatory authority. Only these banks would be authorized to transact currency flows and foreign trade settlements. Licenses would also regulate dealings in foreign exchange, external borrowings and investments, and other types of payments by nonbank entities.

The obligation to surrender foreign-exchange earnings (i.e., to sell them to the authorized banks) would affect all currency revenues over and above present-day retention quotas.

The regulatory body would fix the rules governing interbank dealings in foreign exchange. Companies and individuals would be allowed to engage in foreign-exchange transactions only through the authorized banks or at auction. They would not be permitted to hold large amounts of foreign currency for longer than a month after its importation, nor would they be allowed to have foreign-exchange accounts abroad unless they are residing abroad for more than six months. All foreign-exchange earnings would be taxed.

Two major types of accounts would be established, for residents and nonresidents. Residents would be allowed to hold, within the Soviet Union, foreign-exchange accounts for purposes of retention, for currency bought at auction, or for currency borrowed for commercial purposes. All other foreign exchange would be sold to the authorized banks. Ruble accounts of residents would be convertible into foreign exchange only to the extent authorized by official import licenses or obtained at auction or on the interbank market through the authorized banks.

A free regime would be in effect for the foreign-exchange accounts of nonresidents. A wide range of instruments would be developed for purposes of nonresident investment in ruble-denominated assets. Nonresidents would have the opportunity to partake in currency auctions and other market activities, with the appropriate guarantees by the authorities.

The most important aspect of the exchange control system will be the payments regime. The central bank would have the power to manage exchange rate policy through changes in exchange and interest rates, intervention in the markets, credit policy, and actions affecting bank liquidity.

Controlling Currency Substitution

Energetic efforts should be made to prevent foreign exchange from being used as a means of internal payment—such substitution is increasingly becoming a threat to financial stability in the Soviet Union. Measures should be taken to stabilize the ruble, extending at least to a ban on foreign banknotes being used in substitution for rubles. Other means of substitution are also a threat, however.

Price and Currency Basis of Trade

In the interest of speeding up reforms, the Soviet Union must introduce world prices into the economy and develop the ruble into a hard currency as expeditiously as possible, so as to create a single criterion for external relations.

Attracting Foreign Capital

The introduction of convertibility will be much easier if foreign investment in the Soviet Union grows quickly to sizable proportions. For that to happen, comprehensive legislation liberalizing foreign investment is required, leaving only minimum formalities on the establishment of joint ventures and even wholly foreign enterprises and banks.

Inducements for foreign capital should consist not only of tax incentives and official guarantees but the promotion of an ever-increasing freedom of action on Soviet markets. A single government body to promote foreign investment should be created, to focus on development of infrastructure, work-force training, and assuring supplies and adequate transportation.

General Conclusions

The program outlined in this paper is daunting, yet convertibility of the ruble is quite feasible if a package of various economic measures is implemented in a coordinated and comprehensive way by leaders who have the skills, experience, and vision equal to the task. It is time for Soviet policymakers to stop theorizing and temporizing and to begin taking the first practical steps toward convertibility immediately. The main obstacles are internal, although reform of the trade and exchange regimes cannot be postponed.

Limited convertibility should be viewed neither as a panacea nor as a sacred and distant promised land that only our descendants will inhabit. The advantages of convertibility could all too easily become disadvantages in a mismanaged economy. The countries of the industrialized West have proved that convertibility can be achieved (even if not all of them have achieved it fully) and maintained for indefinite periods.

The convertibility package that the Soviet Union needs is one that includes measures of immediate impact, affecting the exchange rate, the foreign-exchange market, the division of authority, and the phasing out of restrictions. The introduction of long-overdue reforms in the foreign-exchange system will mean advancing at once to convertibility and using it as a policy tool. There can be no doubt that putting trade on a multilateral basis and adopting relatively flexible exchange rates will change the Soviet economy profoundly, provided enterprises are also made truly independent.

At the same time, however, it would be a mistake to think that convertibility, or for that matter foreign-exchange policy in general, is strictly a question for external economic policy. Such thinking is part of the existing problem in the Soviet Union, where artificial barriers between the external sector and the rest of the economy remain and sometimes even become stronger. Convertibility of the ruble will remain an economists' theoretical abstraction if budget, tax, banking, planning, distribution, monetary, and other major aspects of economic policy remain in their present state.

The Soviet Union's economic problems are rooted fundamentally in the internal sector, and the changes there must be sweeping. The first priorities involve simple things: turning the budget into a real budget, banks into banks, credit into credit, and interest rates into interest rates; and putting real curbs on the powers of administrators to make arbitrary decisions without regard to the interests of enterprises and citizens.

During the summer and fall of 1990, the naive euphoria that had prevailed with regard to the convertibility issue melted away as the real state of affairs began to dawn on the Soviet people. Promises of cure-all reforms began to command less and less belief, and no new bright ideas emerged. In 1990 there was an attempt to organize an essay competition on the subject of convertibility— it was a fiasco. The "winners" offered a variety of unsound solutions, and the jury, strangely enough, went for proposals, such as for dollarization, that were clearly misleading.

The declarations of sovereignty by various republics added a totally new dimension to the convertibility problem. There is now the possibility that a multiplicity of monetary units could appear, all of them mutually as well as externally inconvertible.

Meanwhile the Ryzhkov government persisted in offering general proposals that were absolutely unrealistic. Eventually the Gorbachev-Yeltsin 500–Days Plan brought a clearer perspective: only by means of a tough stabilization program will the ruble become convertible, first into goods and later into other currencies. Privatization, an internal foreign-exchange market, strict protection of the ruble as the only legal tender, and a comprehensive system of foreign-exchange management are the most important building blocks.

In early 1991 there were still no signs that a really viable stabilization package will soon be implemented. The Polish-Yugoslav approach seems to be the only remaining medicine, a form of shock therapy that will—perhaps—change the mindsets of our politicians and hasten economic reforms. This, of course, presupposes that the requisite political will and wisdom will be in adequate supply.

Toward the Convertible Ruble: The Case for a Parallel Currency

Andrei I. Kazmin and Andrei V. Tsimailo

Russia is a peculiar world where peculiar conditions of economic activities require peculiar instruments for maintaining equilibrium.

Nikolai Ogarev (1813–1877)
Russian writer, poet, and revolutionary

Current Account and Domestic Commodity Convertibility

With the end of the Cold War, political barriers to the integration of the Soviet Union and the Eastern European countries into the world economy have fallen. Economic obstacles, however, remain. Chief among these is the inconvertibility of the currencies of the former socialist countries, including the ruble.

Soviet as well as Western experts now generally agree that the problem of achieving convertibility does not admit of a separate, purely technical solution through the initiation of a free exchange rate for the ruble or the liberalization of trade restrictions. Even partial convertibility of the ruble (at least on current account) can be achieved only in conjunction with the transition from a planned to a market economy. Until the Soviet economy is administered by a system of market coordination of production and distribution, the ruble will continue to be used mostly as an accounting unit. As long as the ruble does not fulfill the basic functions of money even in internal transactions, it certainly cannot fulfill those functions in foreign trade. Therefore, current account convertibility of the Soviet currency requires guaranteed domestic commodity convertibility as well: the ruble must become freely convertible into goods and services throughout the territory of the Soviet Union.[1]

---

1. V. Belkin (1988) and A. Tsimailo (1989a and b) were the first Soviet economists to publish an advanced argumentation of this thesis. Some American economists (Bergsten and Williamson 1990; McKinnon 1989) have come to the same conclusions.

Andrei I. Kazmin is Senior Research Fellow at the Commission for Study of Productive Forces and Natural Resources, Moscow. Andrei V. Tsimailo is Head of Department at the Institute of Europe in Moscow. This paper is based on "The Program of the Transition to the Convertibility of the Ruble," prepared by V. Belkin and the authors for the Commission for Alternative Reform Projects, headed by A. Aganbegyan, in March 1990.

This does not, however, mean that the transition to current account convertibility must wait until commodity convertibility is fully assured. Instead, the best strategy for the transition to commodity and current account convertibility appears to be one in which the two are achieved in parallel through a series of orderly stages. Alongside the revival of the domestic market (now barely alive after sixty years of consistent suppression) and the reestablishment of the ruble's commodity convertibility, it will be useful to expand the current account convertibility of the ruble in a gradual manner, so that both processes interact and stimulate each other. The question is how in practice to accomplish this complicated task under the tremendous monetary overhang (consisting of cash as well as bank deposits) that now exists in the Soviet Union.

The Problem of the Monetary Overhang

The Soviet Union's attempts at economic reform since 1987 have already demonstrated a fundamental reality: under the pressure of the monetary overhang, softening of the plan constraints that prohibit any kind of free trade between enterprises is not by itself enough to cause the market (especially the wholesale market) to spring into operation. This is not a surprising revelation—because all of their payments continue to be automatically guaranteed by the state-owned banks or, rarely, the budget, these enterprises are not motivated to pursue any reductions in costs or improvements in product quality.

Thus, instead of the promised transition to free market trade, shortages of capital and consumer goods are becoming ever more acute. In addition to the huge reserves they have already accumulated, enterprises continue to enlarge their stockpiles of material resources as a precautionary measure as well as for use in direct barter. The result has been an absolute reduction of economic output followed by a nominal rise in private incomes and total destruction of the consumer market. According to an official statement by then–Soviet Minister of Finance V. Pavlov on 26 November 1990, the national income of the Soviet Union during the period from January through October 1990 decreased by 13 billion rubles, while total wages increased by 31 billion rubles.[2]

The rapid demonetization of the economy, coupled with suppressed inflation, seems to offer no chance of reestablishing commodity and current account convertibility of the ruble in its present form. At first glance there would seem to be no other way out of the crisis but instant elimination of the existing money overhang by means of shock therapy. The price to be paid for such a big-bang solution would be very high, but after demand is finally balanced with supply it

---

2. *Izvestia*, 27 November 1990, 2.

would then be possible to begin to rebuild the market and to restore commodity convertibility of the ruble.

Together with similar recommendations from a majority of Western experts, this radical approach came to dominate both the reform program advocated by Nikolai Ryzhkov and Leonid Abalkin (who later, as Prime Minister and Deputy Prime Minister, respectively, supervised the actual implementation of that program), as well as the rejected alternative project, the so-called 500–Days Plan presented by S. Shatalin. The main difference between the two was that, under the Ryzhkov plan, the government intends to reestablish monetary-commodity equilibrium through an instantaneous two- to threefold increase in prices,[3] together with heavy tax increases, whereas the Shatalin approach was based on a restrictive fiscal policy. The latter called for huge cuts in subsidies to unprofitable enterprises, in defense expenditures, in industrial construction projects, and in other budget items, followed by price liberalization.

The alternative project seemed to be the lesser evil, but its authors made the same mistake as the architects of the government's program. Both considered the achievement of demand-supply equilibrium and commodity convertibility of the ruble as preconditions for the transition to the market economy, rather than as its result.

Whatever the negative social consequences of the two plans, the maximum goal that either could hope to achieve is a general temporary reduction of the money overhang. The equilibrium reestablished in this way could not be sustained even in the short term, because state budget expenditures would also be multiplied according to the scale of the price increase, and this would lead the unreformed financial and credit system to reproduce the money overhang all over again. (This argument is supported by the experience of the regressive Soviet monetary reforms of 1947 and 1961.) Thus, the second mistake of the official transition program, as well as of the rejected alternative, is that it ignores the danger of constant destabilization of the ruble created by the administered financial and credit system itself, which in its essential elements remains unchanged.[4]

One must also take into account the fact that the immediate price increase called for under the Ryzhkov plan, with its provision for compensation to private consumers, would require a corresponding multiplication of the stock of money

---

3. This scheme became a reality on 2 April 1991 when it was implemented by a new Soviet government with Pavlov as Prime Minister.

4. Overcoming the inertia caused by the traditional inflationary policy of the Eastern European central banks is acknowledged by some Western economists to be one of the most difficult problems in the transition period (see Bofinger, chapter 4, this volume).

in circulation.[5] This is a second reason why the present money supply disproportion would surely be reproduced on an enlarged scale.

Unlike the Ryzhkov-Abalkin scenario, the Shatalin Plan would have sought
to restrain the money overhang by totally eliminating the fiscal deficit, which in
1990 reached 100 billion rubles, within half a year. That was too optimistic in
any case, but even within a more realistic time frame it would still be impossible
to achieve this goal while preserving the existing administratively prescribed ties
between enterprises until the end of 1991.[6] It is evident that these two targets
are mutually inconsistent. Either the old nonmarket system would end up being
saved, at the expense of the fiscal target, by the prolongation of budget subsidies,
or the traditional supplier linkages would be broken by the instant cancellation
of the state's financial aid to unprofitable enterprises. Given the extremely high
level of monopolization in the Soviet economy, the breaking of these linkages
would certainly result in a rapid fall in economic output and an inevitable
reduction of government revenue.

A second reason why the budget deficit cannot be reduced immediately is that
the Soviet Union faces enormous adjustment costs during the transition to a
market economy that only the state can bear. Huge amounts are needed for the
conversion of the military sector to civilian output and for the overall technological modernization of the economy; there are also the costs of reeducation and
support payments for those unemployed during the adjustment period, the need
to index payments to those on fixed incomes, and so on. And, of course, the
budget can be balanced and the ruble stabilized only when an effective tax and
credit system, suited to a market economy, has been created. Such a system
cannot be put in place all at once; indeed, its construction has just begun with
the adoption by the Supreme Soviets of the Soviet Union and of the Russian
Republic, in December 1990, of new laws governing the central bank as well as
commercial banks and the rest of the banking industry.[7]

The impossibility of eliminating the budget deficit immediately and of accomplishing a full-scale, instantaneous reform of the whole financial and credit system
leads to the conclusion that excessive monetary emission cannot be stopped in
the near future. Under these circumstances all attempts to restore equilibrium

---

5. The actual price increase implemented on 2 April 1991 was initially only partly compensated, but there is much evidence to suggest that it will eventually be compensated more
or less in full to calm social unrest.

6. According to President Mikhail Gorbachev's decree of 27 September 1990, an enterprise
that refuses to prolong its contracts with its administratively designated partners must pay
the local budget up to 50 percent of the value of the rejected contract (*Pravda*, 28 September
1990, 1). A later decree obliges state-owned enterprises to assure their traditional partners
that their 1991 deliveries to them will equal those of the previous year (*Pravda*, 15
December 1990, 1).

7. *Izvestia*, 18 December 1990, 3–4.

and the commodity convertibility of the ruble are bound not only to fail but to carry dangerous consequences in their wake. The present economic, social, and political situation in the Soviet Union requires that the transition to the market economy and the "hard ruble" be carried out under the inherited commodity-monetary imbalance, with no prospect of its rapid elimination.

We are convinced that the best way to solve this extremely complicated problem is to introduce, in parallel with the existing currency, a new and stable currency, which will not be used for financing of the budget deficit. The new currency should be introduced in tandem with the liberalization of prices and thus stimulate the establishment of the domestic wholesale market on a solid basis.

Why Is a Parallel Currency Needed?

The idea of establishing a parallel currency as an instrument of radical economic reform in the Soviet Union has been discussed for several years. A number of well-known Soviet economists, such as Oleg Bogomolov (1989) and Nikolai Petrakov (1990), support the idea in principle, although they may differ on the details of its implementation. For a short time at the end of 1989 and the beginning of 1990, the Soviet government also considered the idea, but never adopted it.[8]

That the idea of a parallel currency has for the present been rejected at the official level is insufficient reason, however, to dismiss it. It must be realized that the government has undertaken no serious analysis of the proposal. Indeed the rationale for introducing a parallel ruble has not been clearly understood within the government, and therefore the proposal has been ignored.

As was argued above, a stable parallel currency is needed first of all to create favorable conditions for the rapid transition to a market economy (especially the creation of a wholesale market) during the period when the state is not yet able, because of the inertial effects of the dying planned economy, to stop the emission of "old" rubles to finance the huge budget deficit. Thus, the creation of a parallel ruble would help the Soviet Union find a realistic way out of its present dilemma, in which market relations are not developing because there is no stable money, yet the ruble cannot be stabilized until the market starts to function.

The second basic argument in favor of a parallel currency stems from the fact that, during the transition to a market economy, the old administrative financial and credit system will have to be gradually replaced by a new, market-oriented

---

8. See Nikolai Ryzhkov's speech at the Second Congress of People's Deputies, 13 December 1989.

one. The same is true for price liberalization. It is much better to introduce a new, rational price structure consonant with world standards simultaneously with the initiation of a new, market-oriented currency that is absolutely independent from the influence of the existing financial and price system.

A gradual (that is, fast but orderly) transition to the new monetary and financial system, as well as to the new market price structure on the basis of a stable parallel currency, would cushion the adaptation of economic agents in the Soviet Union to the basic laws of market behavior. One can never forget that three generations of Soviet people have never lived under market conditions, and the present, soft ruble is unsuitable for providing successful reeducation in the ways of the market.

A third reason why a parallel ruble should be introduced is to substitute for the ever more widespread use of foreign currencies in internal transactions in the Soviet Union. The dollarization of the Soviet economy has been actively stimulated since 1990, when the government legalized foreign-exchange operations for enterprises in domestic trade, reopened the special shops that sell consumer goods for hard currency, and softened the restrictions on private hard-currency deposits.

The government has already declared that in 1991 the foreign-exchange regime will be liberalized to allow Soviet residents (but not private individuals) to buy and sell foreign exchange freely for rubles.[9] It is evident that this manner of introducing current account convertibility is doomed to fail because commodity convertibility of the ruble is not yet assured. As long as no wholesale-goods market exists in the Soviet Union, the freeing of the foreign-currency market will only result in further rapid depreciation of the ruble, which would be actively ousted by foreign exchange in internal circulation. Given that the monetary overhang will continue to rise because of the budget deficit, there is no free exchange rate of the ruble that would stabilize the unlimited demand for hard currency. Therefore, if a strong competitor to the dollar does not appear on the domestic market in the very near future, national control over money circulation and ultimately the whole economy will be totally lost.

In addition to these compelling reasons, a stable parallel currency is the only instrument that can help to normalize economic relations among the various republics and autonomous regions of the Soviet Union. This problem recently has become more acute as the tendencies toward regional separatism and autarky become more and more evident. These centrifugal forces already are a real threat to the future of the Soviet Union as a unified state. The Baltic republics have begun to establish customs controls on their borders, and in 1991 Estonia and

---

9. The opening of the foreign-currency exchange, expected to take place on 1 January 1991, was postponed until April.

Lithuania intend to issue their own currencies. In November 1990 the Ukraine, to protect its consumer market from the inflow of "empty" rubles from other parts of the Soviet Union, began issuing coupons to its citizens, which must be presented along with payment for the purchase of most goods. A similar plan is being worked out in Latvia. Meanwhile the rest of the Soviet republics (as well as several autonomous regions) have all adopted declarations of their sovereignty, which envisage the possibility of the establishment of separate monetary systems. Thus, the proposal to establish a parallel nationwide currency is one of great political as well as economic importance.

The Transition to Commodity Convertibility

The introduction of a parallel currency will not, of course, by itself guarantee success in attaining all of these critical objectives. Also needed is an effective mechanism for protecting the stability of the new money once it is established in circulation. The general scheme for the creation of such a mechanism is based on the plan for the transition to commodity convertibility and creation of a wholesale market worked out by V. Belkin of the USSR Academy of Sciences, in cooperation with P. Medvedev and I. Nit of Moscow State University, in 1986.[10]

According to this plan, the new currency, to be called the domestic convertible rouble (DCR), would be put into parallel circulation with the existing ruble simultaneously with initiation of the wholesale market. The new currency, which would be issued in bank deposit form only, not in cash, would be fully convertible for internal transactions.[11] The DCRs would be introduced into circulation in such a way that the first holders of the new currency would be those enterprises— whether state-owned, joint-stock, cooperative, or private—that produce goods or provide paid services for consumers within the Soviet Union or for export. Unlike the rubles presently in circulation, the money originating from these sources would thus be truly earned—the social need for the items sold by these enterprises would be confirmed by the very fact that they were freely purchased by final consumers in the Soviet Union or abroad. That is the reason why the new money could be used during the transition period as a specific wholesale currency in internal trade at legalized contract market prices.

---

10. For more detailed information (in English) about this plan, see Belkin et al. (1989).

11. The possibility of introducing a parallel currency in cash form as well increased significantly following the Soviet government's actions of early 1991, when, in addition to the price increases mentioned above, the government withdrew 50- and 100-ruble banknotes from circulation.

Besides these channels, the DCR would be put into circulation through special bank loans (guaranteed at a fixed proportion of state reserves of gold and hard currency) to enterprises that produce export and consumer goods on a purely commercial basis. In this way the inflow of the parallel currency would be regulated by the rational demands of economic turnover, and therefore, unlike the "old" rubles, this money could be spent freely by its owners.

Once launched in these limited sectors of the economy, the further expansion of the DCR would proceed in a self-regulating fashion—those enterprises serving the domestic consumer and/or the export market and receiving DCRs would pay their suppliers in the new currency. These suppliers in turn would be able to spend their DCR earnings freely, to purchase inputs on the wholesale market, pay wages, and so on. Through this process the DCR would eventually penetrate the whole economy.

To prevent confusion of DCRs with old rubles currently held in financial accounts, DCRs should be deposited in separate bank accounts (referred to here as free current accounts) governed by special rules fully compatible with market standards. These rules would exclude the traditional automatism of payments and bank credits under the administered system and protect the rights of economic agents to use money in their free current accounts without administrative restrictions. Bills of exchange, mortgages, and discount operations would be legalized in transactions using the DCR. However, any lending of DCRs to the treasury for the purpose of financing the budget deficit would be strictly prohibited. Together these measures would ensure the stability of the new currency.[12]

The proposed gradual replacement of the old monetary and credit system would not require the exchange of cash, since payments between enterprises in the Soviet Union are legally accomplished only by debiting and crediting bank accounts. Thus, the creation of a parallel currency for the wholesale market could be carried out without the issuance of DCR banknotes.

The increase in economic output that would be stimulated by the development of a commodity market using the DCR would surely in the end increase government revenue and (assuming reasonably sound fiscal management in the future) gradually eliminate the fiscal deficit. When this happens it will no longer be useful to continue the emission of "old" rubles, and therefore the necessity for parallel circulation of the two currencies and the coexistence of two monetary and credit systems would disappear. At that time the outstanding "old" rubles could be replaced by DCRs at an exchange rate determined by the market.

Apart from several superficial distinctions, the scenario just outlined would in essence mean the adaptation of the Soviet monetary reform of 1922–24 to

---

12. For a more detailed description of the parallel system of DCR payments and bank loans, see Kazmin (1989). An English version is provided in Belkin et al. (1990).

modern conditions. At that time depreciated settlement notes (sovznaks) were replaced by a stable currency, the chervonets, which played a decisive role in the success of the New Economic Policy. In the present context the replacement of existing cash rubles could not be allowed for social reasons. More important, however, as was explained above, such replacement would not generally be needed for economic reasons.

In studying the successful monetary reform of 1922–24, one must keep in mind that although chervonets were issued in cash, they were issued in large denominations and used mainly in wholesale trade—the use of cash was inevitable because at that time there was no developed clearing system backed by modern means of interbank communications. Today, however, the Soviet banking system has the technical capability to introduce a parallel, accounts-based system of payments and loans without the need to issue new currency in cash. Thus, the radical transformation of the entire monetary and credit system without the exchange of cash money can bring about the same results as the monetary reform of 1922–24. It would strengthen the ruble by ensuring its domestic commodity and external convertibility.

Principal Features and Methodology of the Transition to Current Account Convertibility

The proposed introduction of a parallel currency is aimed also at the transition to ruble convertibility for current international transactions, in other words at meeting the requirements of Article VIII, sections 2, 3, and 4, of the Articles of Agreement of the International Monetary Fund. During the transition period it is assumed that external convertibility would be partial: some restrictions on current payments and/or transfers would be maintained for certain types of transactions and certain economic agents. Such arrangements, together with an expressed willingness to lift the exchange restrictions at the end of the transition period, would be compatible with Article XIV of the Articles of Agreement of the IMF. According to established international practice, measures of trade regulation are not considered restrictions on payments (Gold 1978). Nevertheless, because of the impact trade restrictions have on payments and therefore on convertibility, eventual liberalization of the foreign trade regime is foreseen as well.

The following description of the mechanics of the transition to ruble convertibility applies only to the DCR unless otherwise stated. Only the DCR would enjoy partial (limited) convertibility from the very start of its introduction into circulation. This seems both possible and necessary. First, DCR convertibility, although limited, would stimulate the interaction between the domestic market and the world market, thus helping import a rational market price structure. This gives rise to the possibility, ultimately, of setting a uniform exchange rate that would reflect market-based price relations. Second, only the immediate introduction of limited convertibility for the DCR will halt the inflow of foreign currency for use in domestic payments. This inflow is now being stimulated, both explicitly and implicitly, to the detriment of the national monetary system and of the role of the present Soviet currency in the economy (see "Conclusions" below). Third, the attainment of limited convertibility would increase the credibility of and therefore the demand for the DCR. In line with the emission mechanism described above, this would mean a real and self-accelerating turn-around to meeting consumers' needs, as well as a more rapid transition to a market economy.

The possibility of introducing the DCR on a partial-convertibility basis from the very beginning is based to a great extent on the initially limited supply of new money as well as on maintaining this supply, through the comprehensive monetary mechanism described above, at the level required by the real needs of the market in formation. This has two important consequences. First, the new money would possess rather high, and initially possibly too high, commodity backing. Second, preliminary and very rough calculations suggest that the effective DCR demand for foreign currency would not be too high. From the DCRs held in their free current accounts (the accumulation of which would proceed in tandem with the filling of the market with goods), enterprises would have to pay salaries, taxes, and interest as well as purchase inputs. The purchase of inputs, to the extent that these are imported, would generate DCR demand for foreign currency. But the implementation of reasonable price and tariff policies (first and foremost in respect to raw materials and intermediate products) as well as the development of a wholesale market could significantly reduce that demand.

One of the key issues for the transition is how to establish a uniform ruble exchange rate, at least for current transactions. Under the existing structure of domestic prices and the existing administrative system of price formation it is impossible to calculate a "correct" basic exchange rate that would relate the purchasing power of the Soviet currency to that of its foreign counterparts at the macro level, and at the same time be economically reasonable for most foreign trade operations.

The aim of the transition is to create an environment in which prices are set predominantly by the market. Given the changes in existing domestic price structures that this implies, it seems that for some time to come it will be impossible to fix the exchange rate for the ruble for any extended period. On the other hand it would not be appropriate to let the ruble float freely, because during the transition period the old command-administrative system of price formation and resource allocation would coexist with the new market system. A compromise between these two extreme exchange rate regimes may be possible through the creation, for the whole of the transition period, of a dual exchange market, with dual (official and free) exchange rates.

The official exchange rate would be quoted daily by the State Bank. It would be pegged to a composite of currencies within determined margins of fluctuation. The maintenance of the official exchange rate within these margins would be achieved by the measures of market intervention traditional in the West. The official exchange rate could be changed from time to time if it is severely out of alignment with prevailing free market conditions.

In this respect the central element is the initial determination of the level of the exchange rate. As long as the exchange rate has not only to reflect purchasing power relationships (and to have an impact on them) but, first and foremost, to be a clearing market price for foreign exchange, it seems possible to determine the initial exchange rate of the ruble through large-scale currency auctions with the broad participation of all holders of DCRs.

The main feature of the proposed exchange arrangements is the obligatory repatriation and surrender, on the official or the free market, of export proceeds earned by Soviet residents. It would be possible to give exporters (in specified cases) the option of selling their foreign-currency export proceeds on either market. Exporters could also retain from 5 percent to 10 percent of the proceeds for final settlement of the deal. The obligatory surrender of foreign-currency export proceeds is not considered an exchange restriction. It helps to accumulate foreign currency in the banking system and therefore to increase the efficiency with which supply and demand are balanced on the market for foreign exchange.

The proposed mechanism is also aimed at eliminating the present orientation of enterprises toward "currency self-sufficiency" and at raising the share of foreign-currency proceeds that exporters may retain. The practice of self-sufficiency tends to transform the export sector into a relatively closed economic enclave and inhibits the efficient participation of the Soviet economy in the international division of labor. A number of ill effects have already resulted from this orientation. First, direct and indirect suppliers of exports come to demand foreign-currency payments for their deliveries, diminishing further the role of the national currency in the domestic payment system. In addition, suppliers, who are mostly monopolists on the domestic market, begin to delay deliveries or offer them at unrealistically high ruble prices, thus contributing to inflation. Second, the opportunities for participation in foreign trade are further diminished for those enterprises that produce mainly for the domestic (mostly the consumer) market and do not have any export potential.

The self-sufficiency of enterprises should be measured in national-currency terms, without drawing any distinction between foreign-currency and ruble self-sufficiency. Foreign trade transactions should be undertaken only where they have an economic effect measurable in DCRs. Obviously, the rate of exchange, the tariff regime, and the tax regime facing exporters all play an important role here. All of these as well as other instruments can be used by the authorities during the transition period.

The guiding principle of the proposed system of import payments is the decentralization of foreign-currency allocation and its conversion to a market basis. Any holder of DCRs would be able to convert them on the official or the free market into foreign currency and to transfer foreign currency abroad in payment for imports. Thus, the policy instruments used to affect DCR demand for foreign exchange would primarily include measures of foreign trade regulation. During the first phase the use of quantitative restrictions on imports and a more differentiated form of import licensing would continue. Initially there would be relatively little automatic granting of licenses. In the next phase a reduction of restrictions on foreign-currency conversion and transfer of DCRs would take place, mainly through the gradual replacement of quantitative restrictions by tariffs and through widening the list of imports exempt from licensing. A variety of other trade liberalization measures could also be implemented.

Connected with the option of surrendering foreign-currency export proceeds on either the official or the free market is the possibility of reverse conversion of DCRs. It is assumed that in most cases exporters who have sold their foreign-currency receipts at the official exchange rate would also have the right to buy foreign currency at that rate. Changes in the rules governing the types of transactions that must be settled on the official or on the free market could be used by the authorities as an instrument for regulating demand for foreign currency.

Imports paid for from foreign-currency accounts or DCR accounts with free conversion would be exempt from licensing. Payments for invisibles (i.e., shipping, insurance, and the like) connected with merchandise trade would be made according to the rules established for trade transactions.

Special regulations would govern the use of foreign currency and the conversion of rubles by individuals and other holders of cash. Although the basic strategy assumes the preservation of the existing supply of cash, the main exchange restrictions on ruble conversion for international current transactions would be maintained in this sphere, above all for Soviet residents, during the whole transition period.

The introduction of limited convertibility of ruble banknotes may be handled in the following manner. During the greater part of the transition period the existing system of nonconvertibility of cash rubles would be maintained. In the course of filling the domestic market with goods and services, achieving goods-monetary equilibrium in that market, and establishing predominantly market prices, restrictions on the sale of foreign currency for cash rubles on the free market could be liberalized (following the Polish model, for example).

At the same time it would be possible to use DCRs in quasi-cash form (e.g., credit cards) for domestic payments. DCRs of this kind would originate from foreign currency imported into the Soviet Union in cash form by Soviet or foreign residents as well as from foreign-currency accounts or DCR accounts with free conversion. A necessary evil in this case would be the creation of special shops trading in DCRs (or the existing hard-currency shops could be preserved and allowed to trade in DCRs). A rate of exchange between cash rubles and DCRs would inevitably appear. Nevertheless, the preservation of some form of hard-currency trade for individuals, at least for foreigners, also seems inevitable. The proposed scheme would at least promote the elimination of the use of foreign currency for domestic payments and at the same time reinforce the DCR.

Under the proposed plan, all payments in foreign currency on Soviet territory would be banned (how to deal with the increase in black market currency trading that would surely result is another issue), and limits would be set on the amount of foreign currency that may be bought with cash rubles and taken out of the country for the purpose of individual travel (later these limits would be raised).

Rules would have to be devised to govern the conversion of DCR–denominated profits earned by nonresidents in the course of their business activities on Soviet territory. It seems reasonable to assume that minimal restrictions would be sufficient to deal with this type of transaction. Freedom from restrictions in this area could become an important incentive for foreign investment in the Soviet Union.

Soviet residents would be allowed to open and use bank accounts of various types, including checking, savings, and term accounts, denominated either in foreign currency or in DCRs with free conversion. Deposits to these accounts could consist of foreign-currency transfers (other than export proceeds) as well as foreign currency in cash brought in from abroad. The withdrawal and use of funds from these accounts would be free of any particular regulation other than the general ban on the use of foreign currency for domestic payments.

Nonresidents would also be allowed to have accounts of various types either in foreign currency or in DCRs with free conversion. Regulation of withdrawals from these accounts would be the same as that described earlier.

During the transition period a gradual widening of access of foreign residents to the domestic wholesale market is assumed. To trade on this market, nonresidents would have to buy DCRs from authorized institutions, using foreign currency as payment. Reconversion of these DCRs into foreign currency could be made without restrictions up to the amount originally converted. All other DCR revenues held in nonresident DCR accounts would be converted subject to certain restrictions. Goods bought on the domestic market could be exported under existing export regulations. As a domestic market for securities denominated in DCRs developed, access of nonresidents to this market would become a possibility as well. Especially in the beginning, sales of securities to nonresidents would have to be restricted to long-term instruments—for example, bonds with a payoff period of not less than five years. Access to all of these markets, by encouraging nonresidents to exchange foreign currency for DCRs, would serve as an important additional source of foreign-currency supply on the internal market for foreign exchange.

At least for the duration of the transition period, the existence of a dual market for foreign exchange is foreseen. Throughout the transition period there would be strict regulation of which types of commodities could be traded and which types of transactions settled at the official as opposed to the free exchange rate.

The institutional structure of the market for foreign exchange under the proposed system would include the State Bank of the Soviet Union, the Bank for External Economic Relations, the commercial banks, and other financial institutions authorized to deal on the market for foreign exchange. In addition, a formal foreign-currency exchange should emerge from the regular foreign-exchange auctions to be established under the new system.

The State Bank is the main authority responsible for the formulation and implementation of monetary policy and foreign-exchange control. Among its tasks would be surveillance and regulation of the market for foreign exchange through the use (on the official market) of the same instruments commonly employed in other countries (open market operations, discount rate policy, reserve regulations, etc.); maintenance of the official exchange rate; regulation of the country's balance of payments; and management of gold and foreign-exchange reserves. The State Bank does not and would not engage in foreign-exchange transactions with Soviet residents other than the authorized institutions named above.[13] The authorized institutions would buy and sell foreign currency for DCRs on the official and the free market and would also hold positions in foreign currencies.

The main task of the Bank for External Economic Relations is to lend for export and import (mostly within the framework of large-scale state programs). It could also act as a guarantor of export and import credits.

An institutionalized foreign-currency exchange is another possible channel for trade in foreign currency. At the beginning of the transition, currency auctions would take the place of a formal exchange. As these became more regular and frequent (perhaps eventually being held on a daily basis), and as an institutional framework of brokers and dealers developed, an institutional foreign-currency exchange could ultimately emerge.[14]

One of the key elements of the transition to ruble convertibility is a sweeping reform of foreign trade practices aimed at the creation of a liberalized trade

---

13. Similar ideas were embodied in the Law on the State Bank of the Soviet Union adopted in late 1990 (*Izvestia,* 18 December 1990, 3–4).

14. The foreign-currency exchange that began operation in April 1991 could be used to fix the exchange rate of the DCR, in parallel to or instead of the currency auctions.

regime. Such a reform would involve the replacement of individualized licensing and quantitative restrictions on imports by tariffs, which would gradually be lowered and unified.

To stimulate exports, current export restrictions will have to be lifted, and a preferential regime will have to be created for imports of inputs needed for export production. Free economic zones should play an important role here.

Conclusions

Attempts to reform the Soviet economy will remain fruitless as long as Soviet policymakers fail to recognize the necessity of a gradual, staged transition to a market economy. We have sought to prove that the transition to current account convertibility of the ruble cannot be achieved in isolation from the achievement of commodity convertibility, which in turn must take place simultaneously with the formation of the domestic market. It is impossible in a relatively short period of time to eliminate the tremendous monetary overhang that now exists in the Soviet Union—the legacy of an outdated financial and credit system and years of huge budget deficits. In the presence of such an enormous overhang, the ruble in its present form has no chance of being restored even to domestic commodity convertibility, to say nothing of current account convertibility.

Given this dilemma, the transition to a market economy and ruble convertibility should be accomplished through the creation of a new, stable, parallel currency, the domestic convertible ruble. By pegging to one or a basket of hard currencies, the DCR will achieve limited convertibility from the very beginning. Along with the introduction of the DCR, a suitable market price structure should be gradually established. The temporary coexistence of the old (centrally planned) and the new (market) sectors of the Soviet economy will require dual price and monetary systems throughout the transitional period.

Epilogue

Since 1989 the convertibility issue has acquired vast political resonance in the Soviet Union—references to it can be found almost in every other speech of the newly elected deputies. Therefore in December 1989 the Second Congress of Peoples' Deputies obliged the Soviet government to elaborate as soon as possible a comprehensive program for the transition to convertibility. To date, however, no such program has been published.

Meanwhile a number of presidential decrees and governmental regulations concerning currency arrangements appeared in the second half of 1990. Some of them, and especially the Council of Ministers' Regulation of 4 August 1990

("On the Measures Aimed at the Formation of the Internal Foreign Currency Market"), can be regarded as first steps toward convertibility. Nevertheless the measures ordained in these regulations, which are predominantly of a technical character, are not linked—as we have argued they must be—to the formation of the domestic market or to restoration of the ruble's domestic monetary functions. Indeed some of them are actually aimed either at the preservation of the centralized distribution of foreign currency[15] or at further dollarization of the Soviet economy.[16]

Thus, it is clear that hardly any practical steps toward creating even the preconditions for a sound ruble have been taken. This, together with the evident widespread unpreparedness (not to mention the unwillingness) of an absolute majority of economic agents in the Soviet Union to embark on the transition to a market economy, proves once more the validity of the approach proposed here.

---

15. For example, a presidential decree dated 2 November 1990 calls for the obligatory sale of 40 percent of foreign-currency receipts of Soviet enterprises (at the so-called commercial exchange rate of approximately 1.8 rubles to the dollar) to the centralized fund designated for servicing the Soviet Union's external debt. Only part of the remaining 60 percent (the actual amount an enterprise may retain is determined on a sector-by-sector basis by the central authorities) is available for use by the enterprise.

16. See, for example, the Council of Ministers' regulation dated 24 June 1990 on the use of foreign currencies in domestic trade operations.

Comment

Richard N. Cooper

I am not an expert on the Soviet Union, and I have had enough experience with economic policy formulation and execution to be very uncomfortable about applying general principles to a country without knowing both its institutional setup and the likely behavioral responses to changes in government actions. General principles are critically important, but they can only take the policymaker so far; a multitude of practical details and tactical dynamics remain to be worked out. For these, local knowledge is crucial.

My impression is that the critical difference between the Soviet Union and other Eastern European countries is that in the former there is not yet a real consensus on the aim of achieving a market economy; hence there is not yet a genuine willingness to accept the full implications of a market economy. In most of the other Eastern European countries the arguments focus mainly on the details and tactics of execution, not on the basic objective.

In the Soviet Union there is still lively controversy over the principle of private ownership—together with a lack of understanding of its role in achieving efficiency in a complex economy—and over really letting prices be determined by market forces. There is also an unwillingness to accept the distributional consequences that may flow from both these features of Western economies.

On the assumption that the Soviet Union does want to achieve a market-oriented economy, however, I would argue on general principles that some form of current account convertibility of the ruble is not only highly desirable but should be an integral part of economic reform. That is, the ruble should be made freely convertible by all Soviet enterprises, including new ones, for the importation of goods and services from abroad, and by foreign enterprises for the remittance of profits.

Convertibility would, first, introduce effective competition on price and quality into an economy where monopoly production, at least in manufacturing and mining, is the norm. Subject to consciously determined import tariffs, convertibility would also introduce the world market price structure, something that is necessary to do in the long run, and desirable to do early so as to avoid making another major price adjustment several years hence.

Third, convertibility would greatly increase the availability of wage goods in an economy where the incentive to work is now relatively low. Convertibility would necessarily be achieved only at a substantial depreciation of the ruble

Richard N. Cooper is Maurits C. Boas Professor of International Economics at Harvard University and Chairman of the Federal Reserve Bank of Boston. He is a former Under Secretary of State for Economic Affairs.

from the current official rate. Such a depreciation would give a strong stimulus to exports, both to foreigners taking the initiative to buy in the Soviet Union and to new, autonomous Soviet enterprises. The tariffs that would be imposed on imports would generate badly needed revenue for the government.

Finally, a convertible ruble would quickly reduce and possibly eliminate the so-called ruble overhang, since holdings of financial assets in the Soviet Union are not as high relative to GNP as they are in other countries with roughly comparable income levels. The overhang exists because there are too few consumer goods available relative to the supply of liquid assets at the present time.

Two interesting papers have been presented in this session. I am not sure I grasp either of them fully. A problem facing any analyst at an international conference is that he frequently finds himself addressing issues that are being vigorously debated at home but that are unfamiliar to his international audience, and so the full import of some parts of the papers are lost on relatively uninformed readers such as myself.

I largely agree with Boris Fedorov. Apart from his general pessimism about the prospects for economic reform in the Soviet Union, he advances several propositions. First, convertibility of the ruble is no panacea, and indeed it cannot stand alone. Second, convertibility should be an integral part of a comprehensive economic reform, and if adequately prepared it indeed implies comprehensive reform. Third, the Soviet Union is not prepared either politically or institutionally for this reform at present, but it should take the necessary steps right away to rectify the institutional weaknesses. Fourth, these necessary changes involve making enterprises autonomous and subjecting them to hard budget constraints. Fifth, these changes also presuppose the development of at least a rudimentary financial market, so that enterprises can mobilize savings other than their retained earnings for new investments, and the development of a labor market that will allow workers who are released from enterprises in the interest of greater efficiency to be retrained, relocated, and sustained during the transitional period between jobs. And sixth, it is necessary to reduce greatly the budget deficit and to make monetary policy independent of financing the government.

All of this corresponds to the analysis and recommendations in the report prepared by the IMF and other agencies in fulfillment of the charge given them at the Houston economic summit (IMF et al. 1990); it also corresponds to the report prepared by a group at the International Institute for Applied Systems Analysis (IIASA) for Soviet presidential counsellor S. Shatalin (Peck et al. 1990, 1991). Both of these reports have a strongly similar basic thrust.

The puzzles in Fedorov's paper concern price liberalization and exchange controls. He wants to delay the former and to introduce the latter, which would then be relaxed gradually. Presumably he is seeking a more formal system than presently exists of allocating limited foreign exchange among enterprises and others who have some need for it—in other words, his proposal represents a plea for greater transparency.

The time frame Fedorov envisages is unclear. He writes of the "medium term" and of a "very near future," and in a different context he mentions three to five years. In my view, however, currency convertibility would be very costly without price liberalization, because of the misallocation of resources that would arise if foreign currency could be used, and if exports were encouraged, under the existing price structure. It is very easy to conjure up examples in which the Soviet Union would actually be subtracting value under the current price structure, for example by exporting energy-using products for less than their energy content at world prices. This is not consistent with Fedorov's stated desire for an efficient economy, so I suspect I have misunderstood him. Price liberalization should, at a minimum, accompany a move to currency convertibility, and possibly should precede it by a short interval.

The paper by Andrei Kazmin and Andrei Tsimailo also reflects pessimism concerning at least one aspect of economic reform, namely, getting the budget deficit, and hence the monetary emission of rubles, under control. To create a semblance of a monetary economy, the authors therefore propose to establish a parallel currency, which they call the domestic convertible ruble (DCR). Their paper offers an abundance of detail concerning the introduction and regulation of the DCR. However, two fundamental points remain unclear. First, what is the basis for issuing the parallel currency, and hence what are the limits on its issuance? Second, what is expected to happen to the existing ruble in the meantime?

The authors make it clear that the DCR cannot be issued by the government. They want sound money. But they are not clear on what the principle of issue should be. They mention the possibility of making sound business loans. That is a sensible basis for issuing money, up to a point, but it does not represent the basis for a sound monetary system. The "soundness" of a business loan reflects a judgment about creditworthiness, which is always fallible and hence suspect unless those in charge of making the loans have already established a reputation for not exceeding the requirements of the demand for money in the economy. In other words, a monetary system based on sound business loans is essentially a purely discretionary monetary system, such as exists in many Western countries, but one that will work only where reputations have already been established.

A second basis for issuing the DCR might be in exchange for commodities, such as gold, as has recently been suggested in several quarters. Commodity-based monies have worked historically, usually with gold or silver as the base, provided the supply of the commodity is restrained. However, the use of a commodity basis for money introduces a capricious element into the monetary system, due to variations in the relative price of the commodity or commodities used relative to all other goods and services. Such a system also involves the devotion of real resources to the issuance of the money, since the money is issued against the purchase of commodities, which must be both produced and stored. Commodity-based money was rejected long ago by market-oriented economies in the West.

A third basis for issuing the DCR is foreign exchange. Like commodity-based money, foreign exchange–based money involves the devotion of real resources to augmenting the money supply, since the foreign exchange must be earned through a current account surplus (unless it is borrowed, but borrowing eventually draws down the credit standing of the borrower). Unlike commodity-based money, however, foreign exchange–based money continues to earn seigniorage, since the foreign exchange can be invested in securities on the international market, whereas commodity-based money involves storage costs. Foreign exchange–based money also faces uncertain credibility unless citizens can freely convert the DCR into foreign exchange on demand. If they cannot, they have no basis other than restraint in its issuance for believing that the money is sound, and in this respect the system differs little from a discretionary system that issues money only in a restrained way. The extreme form of foreign exchange–based money with convertibility is of course "dollarization" of the economy, where foreign money actually circulates as domestic money. Dollarization represents a highly credible system, since the local government cannot influence the money stock except indirectly through its overall policies. However, it involves not only the devotion of real resources to earn the foreign currency but also the loss of seigniorage, since interest cannot be earned on circulating notes. Thus, a foreign exchange–based money with full convertibility is strongly preferable to dollarization of the economy.

Those who propose introduction of a parallel currency need to solve this problem of the basis of its issuance. There seems to be a trade-off, in circumstances in which a parallel currency can be seriously contemplated, between the credibility of the new currency and the requirement to devote real resources to its issuance. Resource-conserving mechanisms are likely to lack credibility. Kazmin and Tsimailo implicitly reject foreign exchange–based money in that they call for both official and free (auction) exchange rates for the DCR against foreign exchange, and they call for free convertibility of the DCR into foreign exchange if the DCR has been earned in certain ways. These qualifications fall far short of full convertibility, and furthermore they replicate the different kinds of ruble that now exist.

The second fundamental issue that Kazmin and Tsimailo fail to address is what exactly is to be done with the existing ruble. If the DCR is indeed freely convertible into goods and services and offers at least limited convertibility into foreign exchange, it is likely to be preferred over the existing ruble, both by suppliers and by wage earners. If its exchange rate to foreign currency is officially fixed, that implies a depreciation of the existing ruble against the DCR. Is a market to be developed, or at least tolerated, between the two currencies? It is difficult to see how one can be prevented from emerging, at least implicitly, in price quotations for goods and services. Yet under these circumstances there will be accelerating inflation when measured in ordinary rubles, and an accelerating depreciation of the ruble against foreign exchange, so long as the budget deficit persists. The DCR would eventually crowd out the ruble in most transactions, since suppliers and workers would not want to accept ordinary rubles.

What about taxes? Kazmin and Tsimailo suggest that taxes could be paid in DCRs. But would they be required to be paid in DCRs? If not, taxpayers would certainly prefer to use the depreciating ordinary rubles, since they could gain from any time lag between the tax liability and the payment. Yet if taxes are required to be paid in DCRs, why would anyone accept ordinary rubles in other transactions? Hyperinflation in ordinary rubles would occur very quickly, and the government would find that its payments in ordinary rubles were buying less and less in goods and services. In short, seigniorage would diminish rapidly.

It is difficult to imagine this arrangement surviving without the government trying to exploit the attractiveness of the DCR by issuing some itself. In the absence of this violation of the principles of the system, it must act to cut the budget deficit in real terms, something that Kazmin and Tsimailo argue is impossible to do initially. In other words, the DCR seems to be a device designed to create chaos. It is better to understand the fundamental issues at the outset and address them directly.

Kazmin and Tsimailo deal with this issue by arguing that revenues would increase sharply upon widespread acceptance of the DCR. It is probably true that some revenues (in real terms) would rise as enterprises develop positive earnings and meaningful accounting. But it is extremely optimistic to suppose that this factor alone could close a budget deficit now in excess of 10 percent of GDP, especially in view of the loss of seigniorage.

The viability of the authors' proposal thus hinges on a strong behavioral assumption, namely, that the growth of enterprise earnings combined with improved tax compliance brought about by wide use of the parallel currency would yield an additional 10 percent of GDP in revenues. I am in no position to assess this claim, but the authors do not offer supporting evidence for it, and it sounds extremely implausible.

In conclusion, unless the proposed parallel currency is freely convertible into hard foreign currency, the proposal is not likely to work without substantial fiscal restraint. Yet with fiscal restraint, the ordinary ruble could probably be salvaged. In short, it is difficult to avoid addressing the fundamental issue of the budget deficit, and the parallel currency is not a good way to address it. However, one should not be dogmatic about it—in a world of fourth-best, third-best can appear relatively attractive.

Comment

Guzel Anulova

It has already been stressed at this conference that, in contrast to the other Eastern European countries, the Soviet Union still does not have even a general concept of the convertibility of its national currency. I shall raise a number of the most disputed questions in this area.

The first is the question of creating a parallel currency. Like any human hope for a painless solution to a perplexing problem, the idea of inventing a new chervonets never really dies among some economists in the Soviet Union. Yet my opinion is that a parallel currency, being an artificial construction, cannot survive. To ensure its development into a hard currency would require the same general economic preconditions that would be needed to strengthen the existing ruble. If one could be achieved, so could the other, with equal facility.

The specific proposal advanced by Kazmin and Tsimailo, for a domestic convertible ruble (DCR), could even be dangerous if it were ever attempted. To maintain the implied division into "good" and "bad" money, every step of production and exchange would have to be strictly controlled. Far from being a painless way to a market economy, a parallel currency of the kind they propose would be the surest means available of preserving and strengthening the existing administrative system.

Their proposal is based on maintaining a sharp separation between cash and noncash spheres of monetary circulation. This separation is characteristic of a centrally planned economy, but irreconcilable with the conduct of civilized monetary policy. The authors assert that the quantity of goods would equal the quantity of "good" money because the latter would be issued only against actual purchases by consumers. But this balance is immediately destroyed as soon as one imagines that consumer demand could concentrate on one single item. There is also the problem of credit creation, which is essential for the functioning of enterprises in any developed economy. In an attempt to make their DCR look like money, the authors have to add to their construction one element after another: some part of salaries paid in DCRs, special shops in DCRs, hard-currency auctions against DCRs, and so on. In all these functions the DCR would be an unnecessary and nonviable intermediary between the existing ruble and the dollar. Last but not least, the system the authors propose would undoubtedly produce a huge amount of speculation and additional distortions in the Soviet economy.

Guzel Anulova is a Senior Research Fellow at the Institute of World Economy and International Relations, Moscow.

One may well ask, If the DCR is a nonstarter, what about the famous chervonets of the 1920s, which is considered to have been such a success? My view is that in essence the chervonets was a monetary reform, not a parallel currency, because the sovznak that it supposedly complemented did not fulfill any monetary functions at all.

A second important issue is the appropriate place of internal and external convertibility in the sequencing of policy measures. The latest official Soviet documents stress internal convertibility, interpreted as commodity convertibility or as an improved redistribution of hard currency in the internal economy. However, the term "internal convertibility" as used in some Eastern European countries means rather a freedom of national entities and individuals to exchange local money for hard currency. In small, relatively open economies this form of convertibility serves to attain stabilization, using the exchange rate as a nominal anchor. In the Soviet Union this kind of stabilization is not workable because of the size and closed nature of the economy.

The most important aim of convertibility of the ruble would be to attract foreign investment. In this sense external convertibility, understood as freedom of foreigners or of entities with foreign participation to exchange local money for hard currency and transfer their profits, is much more important for the Soviet Union at present.

What degree of convertibility, if any, is achievable in the Soviet Union? This question is closely connected with the previous one. The Soviet Union does not seem to be a suitable candidate for a shock therapy approach, especially if one considers the problem of the social acceptability of adjustment policy. Moreover, a high degree of convertibility is not necessary at the beginning of the transition period. One can, however, speak of some reasonable, pragmatic elements of convertibility of the ruble that would bring considerable benefits both to the Soviet economy and to its Western partners.

First of all, the guarantee of foreign investors' rights to buy assets, property, and land in the Soviet Union for rubles would be an important step toward convertibility. Another important preparatory measure would be to create some kind of an exchange guarantee fund for Western firms investing on Soviet territory. Some share of any external assistance funds could be used for this purpose (as was done in the framework of the Marshall Plan), replacing consumer-goods purchases in the donor countries. Preparing the ground for convertibility of the ruble would also mean working out appropriate foreign-exchange legislation, streamlining foreign-exchange restrictions, increasing the transparency of the whole system, and creating a network of banks authorized to deal in foreign currencies. This process has started, although slowly, as with anything in the Soviet Union.

Another important issue is whether to impose a ban on currency substitution within the Soviet Union. Many Soviet economists put the blame for the ruble's weakening on the ever-increasing presence of hard currencies in the internal economy. Some people think it is possible to stop this process simply by forbidding the use of hard currencies within Soviet territory. Reflecting this position, in an attempt to stabilize the purchasing power of the ruble some of the latest official Soviet documents declare that the ruble is the only legal tender in the Soviet territory, and that the circulation of foreign currencies as a means of payment is forbidden. A ban on hard-currency trade within the country is also contained in the draft foreign-exchange law that passed the first reading in the Supreme Soviet.

These actions do not seem very realistic. Dollarization of the economy is an evil, of course, but an inevitable evil at the present stage. It is not that the ruble is weakened because of dollarization, but rather that dollarization takes place because the ruble is weak. Dollarization is inevitable because, among other reasons, the first embryonic forms of the market economy need some reliable measure of value. The black market cannot be eliminated through administrative bans in any case. The only choice the state has is to ignore the black market or to legalize trade and payments in foreign exchange.

If it chooses the latter course, the government can better control and tax the pool of hard currencies already in the country. And, of course, it can avoid looking ridiculous, as it does when it attempts to introduce unenforceable bans. On the other hand, the policy of allowing enterprises to retain a share of their foreign-exchange proceeds should be abolished as soon as possible, because the negative effects of such a policy turn out to be much greater than the export incentives created. The surrender of export proceeds by enterprises is relatively more controllable than foreign-exchange transactions among individuals.

A final issue worthy of consideration is whether regulation of foreign exchange should be by the Soviet government or by the republics. The foreign-exchange policy of the Soviet Union was seriously complicated in 1990 by the fact that many republics declared their sovereignty in the area of external economic relations. It is obvious that if every republic imposed its own foreign-exchange restrictions, its own rules on foreign borrowing, and so on, the single market of the Soviet Union would disintegrate. To prevent a further escalation of separatism in foreign-exchange policy, while at the same time giving every republic a voice in important decisions concerning the sources and uses of hard-currency funds, a Union-Republic Foreign Exchange Committee was created. The principle of a single foreign-exchange market as the core of the draft foreign-exchange policy seemed somewhat relaxed. The idea of achieving convertibility through the creation of republican currencies, once rather popular, has lost nearly all its proponents.

All of the problems surrounding the convertibility of the ruble, as well as those of the external economic relations of the Soviet Union in general, are closely connected with both internal political developments and the state of political relations with other countries. We shall hope that the willingness of Soviet authorities to progress toward a market economy will be maintained. All technical problems will then be solved sooner or later.

Comment

Michael R. Dohan

The authors of both papers in this session agree on the need for macroeconomic stabilization and economic reform before currency convertibility is attempted in the Soviet Union. Andrei Kazmin and Andrei Tsimailo believe, however, that the implementation of such policies is at least a few years off. They are concerned about the growing demonetization of the ruble in the meantime and the increasing dollarization of transactions, which they believe could lead to a major disruption of the economy. Kazmin and Tsimailo see a strong similarity between the conditions that prevailed in the Soviet Union in 1922–23 and those prevailing currently. Drawing on the successful Soviet experience with the chervonets, a parallel currency in use from 1922 to 1924 (i.e., during the period of the New Economic Policy), they argue for establishing a similar currency with limited convertibility, similar to the chervonets of the NEP period, for use by firms producing for the market (see also Kazmin 1990).

Does the Soviet experience with the chervonets support this proposal, and does it offer any lessons for the present monetary problems of Eastern Europe, and in particular the Soviet Union? A brief history of the chervonets experiment will begin to provide some answers.

In early 1921, Lenin inaugurated the NEP to reverse the catastrophic decline of the Soviet economy, which had been devastated by civil war and the policies of War Communism. Those policies had attempted to replace the institutions of the former capitalist market system with centralized administrative orders. The NEP was in essence intended to restore the market mechanism without the corresponding political and social institutions. In 1922 the Soviet tax, banking, and financial systems were still rudimentary and unable to collect sufficient revenues and savings to finance the government and investment. As a consequence, the government had to continue printing ever-increasing amounts of Soviet rubles, called sovznaks, to finance the bulk of its expenditures. By mid-1922 the value of the sovznak was falling by about 8 percent per *week* (table 1).

Michael R. Dohan is Associate Professor of Economics and Director of the Social Science Laboratory for Research and Teaching, Queens College of the City University of New York.

Table 1   Soviet Union: price indices for the sovznak and currency in circulation, 1913–24

Year	Price index[a] (1913 = 100)	Currency in circulation (billions of sovznaks)
1913	100	2.4[b]
1918	300	9.3[c]
1921	242,000	1,169
1922	28,800,000	17,539
1923	2,000,000,000	1,994,000
1924	127,500,000,000	225,637,000

a. As of 1 January.

b. Figure is that for 1914.

c. Figure is that for 1917.

Source: Statisticheskii spravochnik SSSR za 1928 (Moscow, 1929), 599.

Under this hyperinflation, enterprises and even the government itself had to use an artificial "1913 goods ruble" (basically a price index) to make contracts, to buy and sell from other enterprises, and to plan budget expenditures. Moreover, the populace was resorting to holding gold, foreign currency, and even old tsarist currency as a store of value and a medium of exchange. In 1922 a currency conversion of 10,000 old sovznaks to 1 "1922 sovznak" was carried out. However, this first currency reform was unsupported by other policy measures; the reform failed and hyperinflation continued. In 1923 a second currency conversion was carried out, this time exchanging 100 of the 1922 sovznaks for each 1923 model; this conversion was equally ineffective (Iurovskii 1928/1990, 70; see also Carr 1952, 350). So, even though the availability of goods was increasing, the sovznak was losing all its monetary functions (Iurovskii 1928/ 1990; see also Kazmin 1990a, 65–72), and this development threatened economic recovery.

The major steps leading to the conversion of all sovznaks into chervonets in May 1924 are shown in table 2. Proposals for a new, more stable currency to replace the sovznak were already being circulated in mid–1921. The introduction of chervonets actually started on 11 October 1922, when Gosbank (the state bank) was given permission to issue the new monetary unit, which was equal to 10 pre–1913 gold rubles and was backed 25 percent by precious metals and 75 percent by short-term paper (Iurovskii 1928/1990, 73). Its initial purpose was to provide a stable unit of account for making loans to enterprises and for interenterprise transactions rather than to create a new currency for hand-to-hand circulation (Carr 1954, 40). Indeed, the monetary authorities did not at all intend for the new monetary unit to replace the sovznak in hand-to-hand

Table 2 Chronology of the chervonets reform, 1920–26

1921	March	Tax-in-kind policy established. Beginning of the New Economic Policy.
1922	April	Decree permitting private ownership of gold and foreign currencies.
	October	Decree permitting Gosbank to issue chervonets as a unit of account.
	November	Conversion of the pre-1922 sovznak and all previous rubles to the 1922 sovznak (at 10,000 to 1).
1923	February	Decree mandating deposit of gold and foreign currency in Gosbank.
	April	Decree permitting private purchase and sale of gold and foreign currencies. Reaffirmation of state monopoly on foreign trade.
	August	Chervonets accounts for 50 percent of currency in circulation.
	October	Conversion of the 1922 sovznak to the 1923 sovznak (at 100 to 1). State budget for 1923–24 is balanced.
1924	February	New Treasury ruble tied to the chervonets is issued. Minting of silver and copper coins. Printing of sovznak ceases.
	March	Redemption of the 1923 sovznak for chervonets at 50,000 to 1.
	July	Decree prohibiting emission of paper money to cover fiscal deficits.

During the year the chervonets is quoted on exchanges in Riga, Kaunas, Tallinn, Harbin, Tehran, Constantinople, and Rome, and on domestic financial exchanges in Moscow, Leningrad, Kharkov, and elsewhere.

1925	Summer	Excellent harvest. Excess credit is extended to buy grain for export. Goods famine appears. Prices are restricted and then reduced by state decree.
	November	Gosbank uses gold reserves to stabilize the ruble.
1926	March	Sale of gold and foreign currency to private persons is discontinued. Gold redemptions are ended.
	July	Export of Soviet coins and notes is forbidden.

Sources: Iurovskii (1928/1990); Manevich (1988); Carr (1952, 54, 58).

circulation, because the Soviet government still needed to print sovznaks in order to finance the large budget deficit. Nevertheless, chervonets (in the form of 10-ruble notes) rapidly entered circulation starting in late 1922 and began to circulate in parallel with the rapidly depreciating sovznak. Soon the chervonets became the preferred store of value, even by the populace, and replaced the artificial "goods ruble" as a standard of account in transactions among enterprises (Carr 1954, 143).

The massive issue of sovznaks throughout 1923, together with the availability of the relatively stable chervonets, continued to accelerate the sovznak's free fall. By August 1923, the chervonets constituted half of the value of currency in circulation, and four-fifths by November 1923. On 10 May 1924 all sovznaks were converted into chervonets, or into newly issued treasury rubles tied to the chervonets, at the rate of 50 billion pre–1922 sovznaks to one chervonets. This ended the brief Soviet experience with a parallel currency.

Given the failure of the two previous conversions, the rapid acceptance and relative price stability of the chervonets were indeed remarkable. In 1924 and 1925 most prices in the Soviet Union were still true market prices in the sense that commodities were available at those prices. The new currency possessed internal commodity convertibility in the sense that it could be used freely to buy and sell goods within the domestic economy, although not for trade and foreign investment (Holzman 1978, 145).

The chervonets reform succeeded because, in contrast with the two previous reforms, it was accompanied by a classic application of "Western, and particularly British, canons of financial orthodoxy" of the 1920s (Carr 1969, 145): balanced budgets, a restrictive credit policy, and a growing stock of gold and currency earned by trade surpluses. By 1923, the War Communism rhetoric that had called for the "dying out of money" and for attacking capitalism through an inflationary monetary policy had been supplanted by a firm belief among most Soviet leaders in the need for a strong ruble and price stability, a stable rate of exchange, and commercially profitable exports.

By mid–1925, however, strong disagreements had emerged between the more cautious "monetarists" and the more impatient "planner-industrializers" in the government over the role of credit policy and currency issue in financing industrialization.[1] G. Sokolnikov, the original architect of the monetary reform, along with others on the right and in Gosbank and in the finance commissariat argued for continued restraint in monetary policy; their opponents on the left, while supporting the need for a stable currency in principle, felt that credit and the money supply could be used more aggressively to finance industrialization

---

1. Carr (1958, 472–89) summarizes this debate.

without causing inflation. The industrializers won the political battle, but history was to prove them wrong.

Despite considerable publicity about the trading of chervonets on domestic and foreign-currency exchanges, the chervonets never achieved more than nominal convertibility for most foreign commercial transactions. The currency convertibility of the chervonets on exchanges abroad appeared to serve mostly tourists, holders of flight capital, and smugglers (Ball 1987, 122–23). The chervonets was quoted and traded primarily in the countries bordering the Soviet Union, such as Latvia, Lithuania, Estonia, Manchuria, Persia, and Turkey. No major international exchanges, except briefly Rome, quoted the chervonets.

The reasons for this are clear: the state monopoly on foreign trade had been reaffirmed in 1923, and Gosbank continued to control the foreign-exchange holdings of enterprises and trading organizations.[2] Except for a few who painfully negotiated concessions, foreigners could not simply come to Russia with rubles, buy products, and export them. Import licenses were even more tightly controlled. In short, there was no real external *commodity* convertibility, and so nominal *currency* convertibility served little commercial purpose. Except for a brief period in 1924 and 1925, these currency markets played little role in the actual conduct of Soviet trade or capital account transactions, other than for those under direct state control.

Even so, these limitations on external commodity convertibility had little impact on the chervonets's function as money within the domestic economy. Oddly, a considerable volume of chervonets financial instruments were traded on official financial exchanges in Moscow, Leningrad, and Kharkov, chiefly by the government and cooperative credit institutions, state enterprises and ministries, and mixed-stock companies that needed or had received foreign exchange (Manevich 1988, 50–54; Patterson 1989, 186). The volume of contracts equaled about 10 percent of Soviet foreign trade in 1924–25. Private traders, however, did not participate in the official financial exchanges, but traded currency unofficially on the unregulated after-hours "Amerikanka" exchange. Even though the chervonets was not officially redeemable in gold, Gosbank bought and sold gold and foreign currencies in both the official and the unofficial markets to regulate the exchange rate of the chervonets.

If foreign trade and foreign capital flows were so carefully controlled, then what was the purpose of making the chervonets convertible into gold and foreign

---

2. In 1923 and 1924, more and more organizations were initially granted the right to engage in foreign trade, which was only "coordinated" by the commissariat of foreign trade. The literature from 1922 to 1925 reports an intense debate about the state monopoly of foreign trade, and these trading rights, usually for exports, were tentative steps toward the loosening of foreign trade. But the basic state monopoly remained in place along with requirements that all state (and cooperative) enterprises deposit their foreign exchange earnings in the state bank or associated banks. (See Carr 1958, 445–54.)

exchange on these domestic exchanges? Domestic currency convertibility was important for the currency reform because it reassured the holders of chervonets that the government intended to maintain the value of this new currency. The populace still remembered the gold rubles of the tsarist period. Thus, even though chervonets could not be used freely to import goods on a commercial basis,[3] this internal currency convertibility played an important psychological role in inducing individuals and enterprises to hold domestic currency and currency-denominated accounts, especially in the wake of three bad experiences with paper currencies.

Economists in the commissariat of finance and in Gosbank in 1923 had envisioned still another, more important role for these exchanges in the emerging market economy of the NEP. Many initially believed that the chervonets could become truly convertible and that the foreign trade monopoly could be relaxed, if not eliminated, in which case the conventional financial and commodity exchanges would play an important role in both domestic and foreign trade. They envisioned a socialist market economy, guided from the commanding heights of finance by indirect credit and fiscal policies. But in the end these visionaries lost.

The beginning of the end came in the summer of 1925, a year that saw the best Soviet grain harvest since 1918, a balanced budget, and rising industrial output. Unfortunately, this success bred a fatal overoptimism, which led to an overexpansion of credit and currency, huge deficits in foreign trade, and higher inflation. Ironically, the initial surge in demand can be traced to the large credits granted in the summer of 1925 to grain purchasers, who were trying to fulfill an ambitious grain export plan. The large planned trade surpluses were to be used in part to increase the reserves of Gosbank to permit a further expansion of the money supply—an inherently inflationary policy. Growing budget deficits, expansion of bank credits for investment, and rising wage costs also contributed to inflation.

Grain prices rose, shortages of consumer goods (the so-called goods famine) emerged in the countryside, prices in the private markets started to rise, and grain procurement faltered. The planned trade surpluses turned into large trade deficits. The Soviet government, fearful of inflation and paralyzed by memories of the "scissors" crisis (the emergence of a gap between prices of agricultural and industrial goods) and hyperinflation, directly attacked the symptom of inflation—namely, prices—and their purveyors, the private traders. Despite the goods famine, they froze wholesale and retail prices in state and cooperative trade

---

3. Limited amounts of chervonets and foreign exchange could be taken or sent abroad, and packages could be received from abroad without tariffs. Thus, some significant portion of private purchases of foreign exchange went to finance such small-scale imports (Loevet-skii 1926/1990b, 124–36).

and started a vigorous policy to restrict private trade (Dohan 1969). Failing to understand the information and allocation functions of prices and profits, they killed the messenger bringing the bad news.

Any pretense at foreign-exchange convertibility of the chervonets in late 1925 and early 1926 quickly collapsed. After fruitless expenditure of gold reserves to prop up the chervonets, the sale of gold and foreign currency to private persons was discontinued in March 1926, and Soviet currency ceased to be redeemed in gold. In July 1926 the export of chervonets, treasury notes, and coins was forbidden. Although some economists had advocated a deliberate devaluation of the chervonets to bring it in line with its relative purchasing power, the government rejected this proposal for reasons of national pride, fear of inflation, and a fear that devaluation would weaken popular confidence in the currency (Loevetskii 1926/1990, 164–75). Instead, the government preserved the nominal gold content while *de facto* devaluing the chervonets completely.

What can and cannot be learned from the successes and failures of this first effort to achieve convertibility of the Soviet currency in a socialist market economy? One lesson is that the current Soviet emphasis on currency reform, and even a parallel, partly convertible currency such as the chervonets, is probably misguided. Simply put, such a reform will fail if other stabilization policies are not also implemented, and if stabilization policies are implemented, then a major currency reform is probably not necessary.

The current monetary situation in the Soviet Union bears some similarities to the situation in 1922 and 1923: budget deficits financed by the printing of currency, some dollarization of the economy, and rising prices. Yet the analogy breaks down precisely because today's ruble still does perform, if imperfectly, the functions of money. Indeed the 1923–24 experience with the chervonets suggests that a second parallel currency would only cause the quick and unwarranted demise of the ruble.

The position of the sovznak in the early 1920s was quite different from that of the ruble in 1991. At that time enterprises and the populace were fleeing from the sovznak into gold and foreign currency as a medium of exchange and a store of value. Commercial transactions denominated solely in sovznaks had become almost impossible even though goods were available in the markets. The sovznak had simply ceased to be money, necessitating the introduction of the chervonets as part of a package of other stabilizing monetary and fiscal policies.

In comparison, the 1991 ruble is still a relatively healthy, functioning internal currency, despite assertions by some to the contrary. Indeed, the ruble remains the principal store of value, so much so that some economists advocate a "currency reform" that would also remove the currency overhang and its alleged inflationary threat. Yet despite this huge overhang, the Soviet populace seems willing to earn rubles and expand their holdings of the currency, at least for the time being. Most goods, although not frequently available at the distortedly low state prices, are usually available for rubles at much higher market prices. Dollarization remains limited, and free market prices are rising far less rapidly than in 1922–23. Budget deficits, expansionary credit policies, and wage inflation, not the currency overhang or an unwillingness to hold rubles as money, are responsible for the surge of inflationary pressures since 1985, and neither currency reform nor convertibility nor a parallel currency will remedy these problems. Indeed, the 1923–24 experience with the chervonets suggests that a second parallel currency would only cause the quick and unwarranted demise of the ruble.

The chervonets episode also sheds light on the important link between convertibility and trade policy. The chervonets never achieved true external convertibility because the state's control over foreign trade was never relaxed. The reasons for this reluctance to abandon the foreign trade monopoly are complex, and include a growing overvaluation of the ruble, the Soviet leadership's lack of understanding of tariffs and exchange rates in managing trade and the trade balance, and the belief that direct planning of foreign trade was more effective in using scarce foreign-exchange resources.

In January 1923, the chervonets, set at the prewar gold content of 10 gold rubles, was probably slightly undervalued, and there was talk about relaxing the foreign trade monopoly. Within a year it became overvalued because rising industrial prices and growing demand made imports very profitable, while higher agricultural procurement prices and export costs made exports unprofitable. This overvaluation and lack of external convertibility did not initially affect the chervonets's internal commodity or currency convertibility, but it prevented any relaxation of the foreign trade monopoly and any possibility of achieving *external* commodity convertibility at the official rate for the chervonets. Of course, the export problem could have been cured by export subsidies (as it eventually was) and the import demand by import tariffs (which were never used in any systematic way). Eschewing a formal devaluation, the government ended gold sales (i.e., internal currency convertibility) but stubbornly stuck with the chosen nominal exchange rate as well as with their policy of price stability and export profitability.

As part of this policy the Soviet government tried to keep agricultural procurement prices from rising, so that grain and agricultural exports would be profitable. To prevent the reopening of the price "scissors" between industrial and agricultural goods, the government also froze and then forced down prices of manufactured goods. This misguided price policy caused even greater shortages of goods in the countryside and was in large part responsible for the disastrous agricultural marketing crises from 1926 to 1928 and, ultimately, for the end of the NEP. In retrospect, the end of internal currency convertibility of the chervonets in March 1926 was merely a symptom of a much more serious problem, namely, the widespread decline of internal commodity convertibility. That problem persists today.

How important are currency convertibility and free trade for establishing market economies in the Soviet Union and the rest of Eastern Europe? Many Western and Soviet economists, including several at this conference, believe that they are a critical component of economic reform. They argue that competition on world markets, both in exports and from imports, is the best way to improve the product quality and the efficiency of domestic industry and to combat inflation caused by monopolistic producers. This may be true for an existing market economy, but there is nothing in the logic of a market system as such that requires free foreign trade and foreign-exchange convertibility for the successful *establishment* of a market economy. Indeed, the Soviet experience in the NEP suggests that free trade and convertibility are definitely *not* essential to the establishment or restoration of a market system.

Some would cite the role of domestic currency convertibility in the chervonets reform as evidence of the need for currency convertibility in the transition to a market economy in the 1990s. But as we saw above, the function of currency convertibility in the chervonets reform had the very specific purpose of inducing the populace to accept a new currency. Once it was accepted as money, the chervonets's domestic convertibility into gold and foreign exchange was no longer significant for its functioning as a domestic currency. More significant was its convertibility into domestic goods and services. The same is true for the ruble in 1991.

The most important lesson to be gleaned from the chervonets episode is that macroeconomic stabilization with stable market-clearing prices and the establishment of a market system is probably a necessary precondition for achieving true convertibility. On this point, Fedorov and Kazmin and Tsimailo seem to agree.

The experience of the chervonets in the 1920s, taken as a whole, suggests first that an austere macroeconomic stabilization policy must be quickly implemented in the 1990s to reestablish market-clearing prices, and second that a market mechanism should be established (including hard budget constraints for enterprises) to achieve true internal commodity convertibility of the ruble. Only then does a policy of currency convertibility become meaningful.

The chervonets monetary reform succeeded because of Sokolnikov's restrictive macroeconomic stabilization policies. Sokolnikov and his advisers knew that the state budget had to be balanced *prior* to completing monetary reform. Otherwise, the government would have had to use the chervonets as the major source of revenue, just as they had been forced to do with the sovznak. A restrictive fiscal policy was therefore introduced, which brought the budget into balance in 1923–25. State expenditures were held in check primarily by taking many state enterprises off the state budget and telling them to operate according to commercial principles and earn a profit. This introduction of hard budget constraints on producers was also vital to the efficient functioning of the market system. The principal method of balancing the budget, however, was to increase revenues through a major reform of the tax system during 1923 and 1924. Measures included increases in fees, new taxes, and conversion of the tax-in-kind system to a monetary tax. State loans, denominated in chervonets, were floated in traditional ways and traded on exchanges, but with less success. The experience with the chervonets suggests that the current failure of the Soviet government to develop an effective system of taxes and financial intermediaries will be a major impediment to fiscal and monetary stability and economic reform in the 1990s.

Soviet monetary policy from 1923 to early 1925 carefully restricted the growth of the chervonets money supply and credits for financing the economy, often to the dismay of less knowledgeable Party leaders. Although legally limited only by the 25 percent gold cover, chervonets were in fact initially issued in much smaller amounts. Indeed, limiting credits to industry in the autumn of 1923 was a major method by which the government forced the monopolistic industrial trusts and syndicates to lower prices to clear existing stocks. Meanwhile the government liberally extended credit for grain purchases in an effort to raise agricultural prices. Both initiatives were part of a credit policy intended to close the scissors between industrial and agricultural prices. That policy was successful in 1923–24.

An equally important lesson is that the failure to maintain stabilizing fiscal and monetary policies can quickly cause the demise of a market system—as happened to the NEP beginning in late 1925. As noted above, the 1924 policy of credit restraint was replaced by excessive expansion of credit to finance grain purchases and industry in mid– and late 1925. The results were catastrophic. The ensuing inflationary pressures were never brought back under control by fiscal or monetary policy, and after the government pursued the misguided policy of forced price stability described above, the resulting goods famine (that is, the domestic commodity and agricultural marketing crisis) in 1926 and 1927 led in essence to the end of the NEP market economy.

The Soviet experience with the chervonets currency reform in the early days of the NEP suggests that, under current Soviet economic conditions and institutions, an attempt to introduce currency convertibility or to create a parallel currency as a method of inducing the populace to hold the ruble is likely to be unsuccessful. Such policies distract from the primary goal of increasing internal commodity convertibility—of providing well-stocked shelves at market-clearing prices—by using fiscal and monetary policies both to restrain aggregate demand and to increase output. Ultimately, it was the domestic goods famine that brought down the NEP market system, not the inability to convert rubles into gold. And it is the modern goods famine of 1990, so similar to that of 1925–27, that is thwarting economic reform today, not the lack of a convertible currency.

In sum, there are two important lessons to be learned from the early success and the ultimate failure of the chervonets and the collapse of NEP. First, macroeconomic stabilization plays a vital role in establishing and maintaining a market system and, eventually, convertibility. Second, currency convertibility per se does not contribute significantly to macroeconomic stabilization and establishment of a market economy, but rather to the more efficient operation of an existing market economy. Ultimately, currency convertibility is the sign of a healthy market economy, not vice versa.

Comment

Richard Portes

I hope that our Soviet colleagues will not misunderstand me when I say that I have very little sympathy now with Soviet economic reform efforts. This is not political. It is rather that the Soviet Union—and even most of those favorable to or working for economic reforms—has learned so little over the past few decades, either from experience in Eastern Europe, or from past Soviet reform efforts, or even from early Soviet history in the 1920s. We all recall Evsei Liberman's proposals and the reforms attempted by Aleksei Kosygin in 1965, the experimental enterprises and all that. There has been painfully little progress since then, not merely in practice but even intellectually.

The extremely elegant presentation by Andrei Kazmin and Andrei Tsimailo should not disguise the fact that Boris Fedorov is correct in pointing to unsound solutions everywhere—the parallel currency is one of them. It is dismaying, not reassuring, that such prominent Soviet economists as Bogomolov and Petrakov are sympathetic to this idea. The glaring inconsistencies of the Shatalin Plan are another sign of the failure to learn some of the basic concepts of system reform common to the conceptual frameworks in Czechoslovakia, Hungary, and Poland, despite their differences.

I can understand why for political reasons Germany and Italy have pushed the European Community and the Group of Seven to take Soviet "reforms" seriously. Unfortunately, that has diverted for six crucial months the attention, the organizational resources, and the talent of all the international institutions

Richard Portes is Director of the Centre for Economic Policy Research, London, and Professor of Economics at Birkbeck College, University of London.

to studying the Soviet economy and reform projects. These studies produced excellent documents that, I believe, fully support my case. Nevertheless, I hope their authors will forgive me for saying that we—the Western analytical and policy community—should now turn our attention away from this country that is so "peculiar" (as the authors' epigraph puts it) that we can do very little for it, to the other countries of Eastern Europe, which we *can* help.

This said, I have an assignment. I begin with Boris Fedorov's paper. I do agree with much of it, and I would stress three points. First, on the roles of convertibility: it is indeed needed to import efficiency and competition, although this is somewhat less so for the large, relatively closed Soviet Union than for the smaller countries of Eastern Europe. Full convertibility is not essential, however, to attract foreign investment; the freedom to repatriate profits will suffice. On the other hand, the Soviet Union may need convertibility even more than the other Eastern European countries for its effect on expectations, that is, as part of a shock treatment that might carry credibility. As Fedorov says, gradualism is no longer a serious option for reforms in the Soviet Union.

Second, Fedorov is right to reject dollarization, multiple currencies for the republics, and permitted retention of hard-currency earnings by exporters. All this favors disintegration along one or another fault line in the economy. This is also one of the objections to any parallel-currency proposal.

Third, it is correct and important that the free market exchange rate will not be a fair indicator of the implicit exchange rate; rather, it will reflect the prices of a few acutely scarce goods. I have argued for some time that this rate will undervalue the currency with respect not only to purchasing power parity, but also to any other plausible equilibrium concept.

I disagree, however, with Fedorov's proposal that the ruble should float (with a daily fixing). The Soviet Union will need a nominal anchor, too. A fixed rate is not just a target for monetary policy or a check on inflation, although these are important. In the Soviet case, when relative prices will change so violently under reforms, stability of the most important single price in the economy is especially desirable, even if the peg must eventually be adjusted. Of course, it is necessary that the peg not be incredible from the outset.

Finally, the paper's treatment of monetary disequilibrium is unsatisfactory. It discusses the stock problem—excess real balances—but does not mention one of the likely ways of dealing with it, namely, a sharp upward adjustment of the price level (as in Poland). Moreover, there is no mention of the flow monetary disequilibrium, which requires cutting subsidies, raising taxes on enterprises, and being tough on bank lending.

The paper by Kazmin and Tsimailo strikes me as "*déja vu* all over again," but with no learning from experience, the Soviet Union's (the chervonets) or the West's (recent analyses of parallel-currency proposals in the EMU context).

Other discussants have dealt with the chervonets story, so I shall focus on other criticisms of their proposals.

The basic premise of the paper is that monetary stabilization is impossible because the Soviet Union cannot quickly eliminate its budget deficit, and the existing tax and credit systems would reproduce the monetary disequilibrium. Yet Poland has demonstrated that this premise is false: the budget switched from a deficit at an annual rate of 9 percent of GDP in mid–1989 to a surplus at an annual rate of 8 percent only a year later.

Moreover, the arguments for a parallel currency do not hold up. The authors say that market relations require a stable currency, and they assert the converse as well, concluding that there is a vicious circle invalidating any attempt to stabilize. But the converse proposition is false.

The authors are right to say that dollarization must be stopped, but wrong to say that a parallel currency could do the job without bringing many of the same disadvantages. As it is, there are already three currencies in Moscow: rubles, dollars, and cigarettes. Four would be excessive—indeed, having more than one loses a lot in economies of scale and transaction costs.

Again, it is true that the commodity inconvertibility of the ruble encourages separatism in the republics, but so would a parallel currency, and even more so any version of special economic zones. The Chinese experience strongly suggests that, far from stimulating radical reforms, these zones are pure enclaves. So either the parallel currency would operate only in these enclaves, in which case it would not affect the monetary system, or we end up with monetary dualism (or pluralism).

If the central bank tries to maintain a fixed exchange rate between the ruble and a parallel currency, we get the chervonets story again. If the rate is determined in a free market, it will be unstable. Moreover, agents who get the parallel currency will convert it into domestic money only to the extent that they need domestic liquidity—then the central bank will be unable to implement any exchange control or exercise any stabilizing influence on the rate. There is a further danger that the parallel currency will facilitate capital exports. And finally, it would seem inevitable in Soviet conditions that a significant proportion of goods would become available only in exchange for the new currency; this would stimulate currency substitution and transform inflation into hyperinflation.

The oddest remark among several in this paper is the contention that a parallel currency would stabilize the economy by eliminating the budget deficit. The authors assert (with no theoretical or empirical basis) that a parallel currency would stimulate output and thereby generate a sufficient increase in budget revenues to close the gap. I do not find this at all plausible.

The parallel currency would go in the wrong direction on the microeconomic level, by creating distortions and transaction costs, and on the macroeconomic level, by making monetary management harder. All variants of this proposal should be rejected.

I conclude as I began: it is time to turn our attention to serious reform programs in countries where our assistance can do some good. The Soviet Union is a great country, with tremendous intellectual and natural resources. It will have to solve its own problems, and aid from the West is essentially irrelevant in that process. When the internal blocks are broken, provided that the reformers pay due regard to past experience with reforms at home and abroad, they will not need our aid, except for technical assistance and limited, sector-specific foreign capital and know-how.

Discussion

Marie Lavigne questioned whether it was worthwhile to spend so much time discussing the gimmick of the parallel currency proposal, and she joined Richard Portes in wondering why so many of the leading Soviet economists had expressed sympathy for the idea. Perhaps it had been thought politically useful to draw on the Soviet Union's own historical experience during the period of the NEP, so as to bolster the case for convertibility. Unfortunately it made a bad case. One reason was that given by Guzel Anulova, namely, that today the ruble is still a viable money, whereas in 1922 the sovznak (and the other currencies then in circulation on the periphery of the Soviet Union) was as useless as the French assignat had become during the French Revolution. In addition, the chervonets was created exclusively for circulation between enterprises, and in fact it prepared the way for the subsequent dichotomy between money for circulation in the producer sphere and that for circulation in the consumer sphere. Finally, Lavigne emphasized that the NEP had not been conceived as a transition from central planning to the market, but (as Lenin himself had said) as a tactical retreat intended to prepare the ground for the shift to a planned economy. The chervonets was a means of centralizing power so as to facilitate that shift. This is quite the opposite of what today's reformers are seeking to achieve. However fascinating the chervonets episode may be as history, it should be dismissed from our thoughts as a possible basis for any convertibility plan today.

Flemming Larsen dissociated himself from Portes's suggestion that the West simply write off the Soviet Union—the rest of the world, he felt, has a lot to contribute to the reform process there. Nevertheless, he did share the sense of frustration that Portes had expressed. The experience of the rest of the world does not seem to carry much weight in the Soviet debate, and certainly not in the reform efforts that are being proposed (let alone those actually implemented). In that regard, he asked the Soviet participants to what extent the recent report issued at the request of the Houston summit (IMF et al. 1990) and the report of the European Commission (1990) had triggered a debate within the Soviet Union. Given that this must be the first time, certainly in many years, that so much attention, analysis, advice, and criticism had been directed from the rest of the world to the Soviet Union, one might well expect that all this would have initiated an extensive internal debate. If it has not, what explains the lack of reaction?

Rouben Indjikian expressed a strong preference for Boris Fedorov's approach to the problem of convertibility over the parallel currency proposal. The process of flooding the economy with increasingly worthless rubles by the central government was leading to widespread barter and a further deterioration of the economic situation. Although its use was illegal and risky, the dollar was increasingly viewed as one of the best available media of exchange and stores of value. But the process of dollarization has nothing to do with moving toward convertibility. A precondition for currency convertibility of the ruble must be reestablishment of its commodity convertibility, which in turn demands comprehensive economic and institutional reforms. Hence Fedorov was right to stress the need for drastic parallel changes in the internal economy and in the foreign sector, including new ways of managing foreign trade and foreign-exchange policy.

However, while the economy does need decisive reform measures, even shock therapy, including quick changes in the whole institutional framework, one should concede that the adjustment cost may be very high. A genuine monetary reform like that in postwar Germany might be inevitable, as the present monetary expansion threatens to lead to hyperinflation. Given its complex institutional and economic requirements, the privatization program proposed in the Shatalin Plan cannot correct the imbalance between the real and the monetary economy even in the medium term. The lack of policies capable of promoting an escape from the current nonsystem is adding to the costs of an eventual transition to the market and increasing the need for Western technical and financial support. Continuing conflicts between the central bureaucracy, which is attempting to sabotage reform and maintain its control over resources, and the republics, which blow hot and cold over reform, only add to the confusion and chaos within the Soviet economy.

Indjikian concluded with several specific comments on Fedorov's paper. He agreed that simply creating currencies for the individual republics would not solve the convertibility problem, but he argued that the reformist zeal of many republican leaders and the additional power they would gain from controlling their own national currencies were becoming the driving forces behind the moves toward republican sovereignty. The center had lost the reformist initiative that it had enjoyed in the early days of perestroika.

On the other hand, several of Fedorov's specific proposals were too cautious and did not follow from the general thrust of his paper. For example, Fedorov had proposed that initially 75 percent of hard-currency earnings should be allocated centrally by the central bank, leaving only 25 percent to be sold through foreign-exchange auctions. Indjikian thought that, from the start, at least two-thirds of these earnings should be distributed through market mechanisms (either by auction or through the interbank market), with the balance to be used by the state to build reserves, service debt, or support projects of national significance. Moreover, after criticizing the system of retention quotas, Fedorov then had tried to integrate it into a system of foreign-exchange management. However, the main problem in moving toward ruble convertibility was not such inadequacies of the technical details, but rather the continuing lack of political will.

Ljubiša Adamovich suggested that expectations for the transition in some of the Eastern European countries might be too high. Capitalism does not function the same way in Chile and in Switzerland, so why should one expect the transition process to be the same in all the formerly centrally planned economies? Yugoslavia used to have a relatively sloppy system of central planning, then it had a rather sloppy system of workers' management, and now it is developing a relatively sloppy market economy. The common denominator is Yugoslavia's easy-going Slavic-Mediterranean life-style. Parts of Yugoslavia function somewhat like Switzerland, but most of the country is rather Latin. Similarly, some Russians are taking advantage of central planning, and tomorrow some of them will take advantage of the market economy. Plenty of Soviet peasants are already exploiting the opportunities that are available, and others will do so if the bureaucratic obstacles, including the absence of currency convertibility, can be dismantled.

Mario Nuti remarked that he also came from a Latin tradition, but he felt that Adamovich's comments had been remarkably complacent in tone given that Yugoslavia was coming apart. His purpose in speaking, however, was to put another nail in the coffin of the parallel currency proposal. One argument put forward in favor of this proposal, both in the Soviet Union and in the West, was that it would restore some seigniorage that had been lost to the Soviet Union through dollarization. It was argued that a currency board that issued a parallel currency at a fixed parity against a Western currency, or gold, could hope to see its currency used in place of the dollar in intra–CMEA transactions and as a means of payment, and so its issue would yield real resources. The flaw in this argument was that it assumes a credibility in Soviet monetary institutions that does not exist. Recall the currency boards that functioned in the British colonies prior to independence: these issued currencies that were convertible into sterling, but they were backed by a reserve ratio of over 100 percent (because they had to allow for the possibility of falls in the price of sterling bonds). A Soviet parallel currency would also need a reserve ratio of over 100 percent, and because of this it would yield negative seigniorage. Thus, the seigniorage argument, which is probably the strongest one for a parallel currency, is also a dangerous fantasy.

The history of Soviet reform, Nuti remarked in conclusion, seems to have involved repeated encounters between the irresistible force of monetary expansion and the immovable object of fixed prices. Any government standing between the two was going to be crushed. To say that price increases are not socially acceptable is to invite the riposte that it is no more possible to protect Soviet citizens against the fallout from monetary explosions than it was to protect them against the physical fallout from Chernobyl.

Replying to the debate, *Boris Fedorov* agreed that the best stimulus to work was the presence of goods in the shops. Goods were in fact still available in the Soviet Union, but many of them were available only in the shadow economy at extremely high prices. A new tax system had been introduced on 1 January 1991; it was not working properly because of the conflicts between the union and the republics, but it was nonetheless a major step forward. Fedorov also noted that monetary reform was becoming a popular cause among populist politicians, but he argued that alone it could not possibly help.

Fedorov explained that he too would like to have an anchor provided by a fixed exchange rate, but he thought that initially, if the Soviet Union did move to the market, there would be no alternative to a flexible exchange rate. He had not spoken in his paper about the need to cut subsidies, but Portes was right to point to this as one of the major issues: indeed, his own attempt to cut subsidies (which consumed more than 30 percent of the budget of the Russian Republic) had been one of the causes of his removal from office. Fedorov concluded by remarking that he thought of convertibility as an instrument in the comprehensive reform package that was needed, rather than as a target.

Andrei Tsimailo said that everyone knew what was needed but everyone could see that comprehensive reform would never be accepted, and so his and Andrei Kazmin's work should be viewed as an attempt to find a practical way to make progress.

Andrei Kazmin said that they had indeed tried to learn from the experience of their Eastern neighbors, but he and Tsimailo had tried to show in their paper that it was not conceivable that the budget deficit could be eliminated as fast in the Soviet Union as it had been in Poland. The inherited structure of the economy, especially the absence of wholesale trade, was a far bigger obstacle to reform than it had been elsewhere. The Soviet Union had to start building wholesale markets while there was still a vast overhang and budget disequilibrium. Portes had challenged the claim that the parallel currency would eliminate the budget deficit, and Lavigne had told them to forget the experience of the chervonets, but Kazmin thought it *was* relevant to recall that in the early 1920s, after introduction of the chervonets, industrial output had increased by 36 percent per year and agricultural output by 28 percent per year, and in consequence the budget deficit had decreased from 42 percent of GNP in 1921 to zero in 1924.

Guzel Anulova expressed her comprehension of Portes's frustration at the lack of a coherent program of reform in the Soviet Union. With regard to the question posed by Larsen, she said that the Soviet press and broad Soviet public opinion had paid far too little attention to the Houston Summit report. It was a pity that the study had not appeared simultaneously with the Shatalin Plan and the government program for reform, when public attention to reform was at its peak. Perhaps the delay in publication was an attempt to avoid the appearance of interference in Soviet internal affairs, but unfortunately it had resulted in the report being too little, too late. She hoped that in the end it might nonetheless prove not to have been too late to contribute to a new level of cooperation in designing an adjustment program for the Soviet Union.

9

Panel Discussion:
Lessons from the Past
and Strategies for the Future

9

Panel Discussion:
Lessons from the Past
and Strategies for the Future

Helmut Kramer

Several of the papers in this volume, for example the paper by Wolfgang Schill (chapter 5) about the special case of East Germany, have raised the question of whether currency convertibility should be envisaged as a policy instrument— that is, a precondition—or as an objective of economic policy and therefore the result of longer-term developments.

The postwar experience in Austria and in several countries of Western Europe shows that progress toward full convertibility of a currency has to be seen as serving both purposes: on the one hand, partial convertibility can be an incentive to adapt to world market signals, whereas on the other, perfect convertibility of the currency should be seen as a final state achieved only after an inevitably time-consuming process of catching up with more competitive economies.

Therefore I would argue that the introduction of ever-higher degrees of convertibility has to be seen as going hand in hand with structural improvements, with the two mutually reinforcing. If there is no credible foundation in the real economy for free conversion of the currency, that lack of credibility could prevent convertibility from working as an incentive, because currency devaluations would tend to enter into a vicious circle. On the other hand, the opening of an economy to world market competition improves the price signals it receives, not primarily by the convertibility of the currency itself but by competitive mechanisms.

This leads me to feel a bit dissatisfied by discussions that present the alternative strategies for introducing market mechanisms into the economies of Eastern Europe in terms of a dichotomy of shock versus sequential therapy. Neither a sudden big bang nor a logical sequence of measures seems to me an appropriate description of the political and economic situations that these countries are facing

Helmut Kramer is Director of the Austrian Institute of Economic Research.

now and that Austria and other countries faced after the war. Both models seem to me to yield solutions that are predetermined by the model assumptions and by rules of the game that have been fixed in advance.

I would prefer to think instead in terms of a model that allows for learning processes and for interactions between policy changes and economic developments. The shock-versus-sequence dichotomy allows no room for feedback from one level to the other, and no room for trial and error. Yet surely whoever is in charge of the economic development of the countries undergoing transition will be able to learn and to adapt earlier decisions.

Turning to the former East Germany in particular, I confess I am a bit skeptical about the prospects for an imminent turnaround. As Schill himself points out, the only degree of freedom that remains to producers in the eastern part of Germany is to lower their labor costs. All the other possible options—exchange rate policy or gradual opening of the economy—have been preempted. The problem is that if one is confronted with a significantly and persistently lower level of wages in one region of a country than in another, one has to expect internal migration of mobile and qualified workers to the higher-wage part of the country. This only worsens investment conditions in the low-wage part. The only way to prevent this is by offering massive subsidies to producers in one form or another for quite a long period.

This leads me to another observation: in most of our models we assume implicitly that the introduction of market prices and the abolition of subsidies, together with convertibility, mean the establishment of world market prices in the economy in question. But is this an adequate description of the real world? It seems rather to be an oversimplification: the trade regime even in Western countries is characterized by a variety of trade barriers that distort competition. Only recently, moreover, steps toward reinforcing competition in world markets in the framework of the GATT have broken down. Generally speaking what I find missing from the discussion are analyses of the mutual interaction of the trade regime to be applied and the degree of convertibility.

For me there is no doubt that the countries of Eastern Europe are faced with buyers' markets for many of their products—including primarily agricultural goods, raw materials, semifinished products, and low-technology consumer goods. In this respect, too, the situation differs from that of postwar Western Europe: at that time the reconstructing countries faced predominantly sellers' markets. This suggests that, unless they apply protective mechanisms, these countries will have extreme difficulties in competing on world markets. This argument seems all the more valid given that the Western countries are obviously not inclined to open their markets substantially or to refrain from all sorts of tariff and of nontariff barriers.

Therefore, I would argue, the introduction of higher degrees of convertibility has to be seen in the context of the prevailing foreign trade regime, of existing trade barriers on both sides. And I am convinced that the dismantling of such barriers cannot be undertaken symmetrically; rather it requires concessions in advance on the part of the Western countries. Otherwise Eastern markets risk being swallowed up by Western producers before any structural improvements they may be able to introduce can have a chance to succeed.

One last and very general remark relates to the earlier discussion between Richard Portes and Friedrich Levcik about the differences in the economic and the political way of thinking about these questions (see chapter 3 discussion). In some of the countries of Eastern Europe, obviously, the political system has tried to integrate economic wisdom by personally conveying high political functions to academic economists. (If this should ever happen in Austria I would be very much alarmed, because it would have to be seen as an extraordinary situation.) Yet the normal state of policy formulation seems to me to follow a model in which political possibilities and constraints as well as economic considerations can be regarded simultaneously.

This means that adequate models for the analysis of transition strategies have to incorporate such political constraints. Reform in the Eastern European countries is basically both a political and an economic problem. Therefore we have to try to introduce at least the most important policy variables and policy constraints into our model building. If this proves impossible to accomplish in a formal way, then economists have to be aware of the fact that restrictions of their models may possibly give misleading answers.

There is some experience reported in the literature about modeling mere policy variables (see, for example, Nordhaus 1975). This kind of modeling results in models that may look different from country to country. Certainly there are basic features similar to most of the countries in question, but equally important, it seems to me, are differences in the cohesion and support that economic policy in the different countries can expect.

Andrzej Olechowski

Like most practitioners, I seldom have time to stop and formalize my thoughts as to the lessons that I should draw from my experience in the making of economic policy. Therefore what I have to say is more in the form of reflections and questions concerning that experience.

My first reflection relates to the sharp devaluation of the zloty that Poland implemented in January 1990. The most striking result of this devaluation was a surprisingly rapid and strongly positive reaction of Poland's exports, which caught us by surprise. Although we cannot explain it fully, the surge in exports is an encouraging indication of the underlying strength of the economy and its management capabilities.

Only in the first month after the devaluation were Polish exports lower than in the corresponding month of the preceding year. In every month since then, exports have been much larger than in the corresponding month a year before. For example, exports were 67 percent higher in July 1990 than in July 1989, and in October 1990 they were 71 percent higher than in the preceding October. Finally, at the end of 1990, exports reached their highest level in the entire postwar period.

We have also seen in Poland some encouraging signs of strengthening confidence in the domestic currency. This increased confidence is due to the introduction of convertibility. Savings by households in zlotys have increased more than savings in foreign exchange—a sharp difference from past experience. However, this rise in confidence in the zloty has not been sufficient to induce households to convert their existing stock of foreign-exchange savings into zlotys. Instead they retained what foreign exchange they had but did not increase it, or increased it less rapidly than they increased their savings in zlotys.

Convertibility also allowed the Polish authorities to eliminate that strange hybrid animal known in Poland as the foreign-exchange shop, which sold for foreign currency goods that were unavailable elsewhere in the country. Since 1 January 1991, all prices in Poland are in zlotys. It is illegal to quote prices other than in zlotys, or to accept foreign exchange as a means of payment. The reaction to this measure was immediately visible on the foreign-exchange market, where the demand for foreign exchange dropped, there being no longer any reason to hold large amounts of foreign currencies.

The introduction of convertibility also eliminated a very important barrier to entry to certain business sectors. Importing immediately became open to anyone

Andrzej Olechowski is First Vice President of the National Bank of Poland.

who wished to enter, and a host of new importers emerged, both wholesalers and retailers. Competition greatly increased as a result. This reform also had an interesting effect, for better or worse, on the security of supply of such essential commodities as oil. For example, when the Soviet Union cut back its oil sales to Poland, the number of private importers of oil and oil products increased, and oil is being supplied without any need for coordination or control by the central authority.

Convertibility has also had an impact on the most important target of all of our activities, namely, the welfare of the individual household. Consumers' freedom of choice has increased enormously. Polish shops are completely different from what they were before. They now stock a variety of products, both domestic and foreign. For most people this is probably the most visible sign of convertibility, and it is an important sign.

Two questions for future policy remain, and they are questions that will be quite familiar by now to those who have followed this debate. One of these is the question of when and how a country should move away from a regime of fixed exchange rates to a situation where exchange rates are decided on the market. The other question is the proper sequencing of convertibility, and how quickly the scope of convertibility should be extended. In Poland in 1991 convertibility will be extended to household transactions. The restrictions imposed on companies in 1990 will be left untouched for the time being, because we still do not know how the recent profound changes in the CMEA payment system will affect Poland's balance of payments. After we have seen the figures for the first quarter, we should be able to decide whether to extend convertibility.

John Williamson

I plan to take advantage of this opportunity to lay out the gist of the conclusions and recommendations that I expect to present in the study, summarizing and synthesizing the results of our deliberations, that I intend to write immediately after this conference ends. This will give you the chance to inform me while there is still time if you think that I have got the sense of the meeting wrong.

It seems to me—and it would accord with a number of the comments that have been made—that the title of my study should be broader than the title we gave to the conference. Accordingly, I provisionally plan to call it *Opening the Eastern European Economies*.

One central point on which there is very little dispute is that convertibility matters. Moreover, its establishment is rightly seen as deserving a higher priority than was accorded to it in Western Europe during the period of postwar reconstruction. The reasons for this priority are that market economies need both prices that reflect scarcity and competitive pressures to enforce them, and by far the quickest way of getting both is to import them by opening the economy up to foreign competition.

A second point on which we seem to be largely agreed is the form of convertibility that deserves such high priority. It is a concept of convertibility that is close to both the "current account convertibility" of the IMF Articles and the "internal convertibility" already being introduced in several Eastern European countries, yet is identical to neither. *Enterprises* gain the right to buy foreign exchange on the official market when needed to finance imports of goods and services, but also take on the duty to sell on the official market any foreign exchange they earn from exporting. This implies both that retention quotas must disappear and that tourist and household transactions (whether for foreign travel or on capital account) may take place on a parallel market. This differs from full current account convertibility in excluding the purchase of foreign exchange for foreign travel at the official exchange rate (a derogation often accepted in the past). Much more significantly, it differs from internal convertibility in including the right to buy foreign exchange on the official market in order to purchase services, which I would want to see interpreted to include the remission of profits earned by foreign investors (such an interpretation goes under the title of "external convertibility" in Eastern European parlance).

A question on which we have not reached agreement is the desirability of introducing convertibility in a single step and simultaneously with other reforms.

John Williamson is a Senior Fellow at the Institute for International Economics.

My own tentative view is that it makes a lot of sense to decontrol prices and establish convertibility as part of a single package. My main reason for favoring this approach is that we seem to lack any convincing principles that could guide sequential liberalization, whereas it is easy to identify second-best problems that may be created by partial liberalization or to point to the danger of monopolistic exploitation of price-setting powers that could result from price decontrol without convertibility. However, I do sympathize with Friedrich Levcik's view (chapter 3) that it is silly to embrace bigger bangs as necessarily better. There may at times be compelling grounds for embarking on macroeconomic stabilization at the same time as microeconomic liberalization, for example because the public will accept the price increases implied by eliminating subsidies only as part of a regime change. But where such factors are absent and stabilization can be achieved first, so much the better.

I have not sensed any violent controversies on the conditions (they are often called preconditions, but it may suffice to establish some of them simultaneously) needed to permit a move to convertibility. At the microeconomic level, currency convertibility only makes sense once the essential features of a market economy are in place. This means autonomous enterprises, hard budget constraints, commodity convertibility, and price decontrol. At the macroeconomic level, currency convertibility requires fiscal discipline, a firm monetary policy, elimination of any monetary overhang, a viable balance of payments position, and an adequate level of reserves.

Perhaps surprisingly, there also seems to be general agreement that the period of reform is not a good time to let the exchange rate float, or at least that one should not float the official rate that applies to exports and essential imports. The main reason for this conclusion is acceptance of Peter Bofinger's contention (chapter 4) that monetary relationships tend to be too unstable during the reform process to permit informed conduct of an autonomous monetary policy, which is the necessary complement to a floating rate. Where we clearly disagree, however, is on the wisdom of treating the exchange rate as a medium-term nominal anchor. It is certainly important to get and keep inflation down to a modest level. But it is also vitally important to ensure that exports are competitive and that enterprises expect exporting to remain remunerative, so as to give them an incentive to invest in export industries. These two contradictory imperatives are in my view best reconciled by combining a crawling peg with a domestic management of demand (and, in an emergency, of wages) aimed at price stability. But the achievement of complete price stability, and locking it in through a fixed exchange rate commitment, is an investment that is best left until the immediate task of reconstruction has been accomplished. It seems to be too rarely recognized that the way a nominal anchor works is by creating uncompetitiveness in tradeable-goods industries of countries with excessive inflation until such time as the resulting unemployment causes wages to fall relative to those abroad.

It is surely not true that everyone here has accepted the logic of Ronald McKinnon's case (chapter 4) for transitional protection. I myself find it perhaps exaggerated (I have difficulty in getting upset about closing down industries that produce negative value added) but nonetheless with a persuasive core (I do worry about too many low-value-added industries being closed down too soon). Even if that is a justifiable worry, however, it may be that some countries in the vanguard of reform, like Poland and Hungary, have already gone so far toward free trade that it would make no sense to backtrack. Nevertheless, transitional protection or its close relative, a dual exchange rate that consigns "inessential imports" to a depreciated rate, seems to me an option that may make sense for countries in the early stages of reform and facing an acute foreign-exchange constraint.

I would not endorse Peter Kenen's quip (chapter 4) that a Central European Payments Union (CEPU) is "a solution in search of a problem." The problem is the possible breakdown of intratrade within Eastern Europe. What is not at all clear to me is that a CEPU is the right way of tackling that problem. Provided that the reforming countries grant each other most-favored-nation (MFN) treatment, in the sense that each of them makes dollars available to importers wanting to buy from another country of the group just as they would to an importer wanting to buy from a convertible-currency country, intratrade can proceed without difficulty. If, beyond that, it is desired to give that intratrade some advantage over trade with the West, then the natural and straightforward way of accomplishing that would be to create a free trade area among the countries involved. This would give an incentive to individual enterprises to prefer importing from partner countries, *ceteris paribus*, without backtracking on the convertibility already established in countries like Poland. Thus, the main policy recommendation that seems called for is that each of the reforming countries grant the others MFN treatment in the sense described above. Only if several countries fail to establish or maintain convertibility might a CEPU be called for.

Finally, it will doubtless not surprise Andrei Kazmin and Andrei Tsimailo to learn that I go along with the other speakers' overwhelming skepticism about their parallel-currency proposal (chapter 8).

My task in the next month will be to incorporate these conclusions (unless modified by debate this afternoon or by further evidence that may come to my attention) into a brief monograph. The last time I attempted a similar task was in November-December 1989, when I was writing *The Progress of Policy Reform in Latin America* (Williamson 1990c) and kept getting distracted by events in Eastern Europe. This time there is also a threat of distractions, from the conflict in the Middle East. One cannot but regret that the distractions this time around are so much less full of promise than they were in 1989.

Boris Fedorov

There is much to be learned from the history of efforts to establish or restore the convertibility of currencies, both from the history of the Western European countries after World War II and from the recent and ongoing history of the Eastern European countries of today. That history contains mistakes as well as successes, so that relying on only one or two examples from the past can be dangerous. Unfortunately it seems at the present moment that the Soviet Union is repeating many of those past mistakes.

One lesson that the Soviet Union has to learn is that the time has run out for debating the relative merits of capitalism and socialism. The time has come for action, where the only criteria for decisionmaking are the rationality and the efficiency of the measures under consideration.

On the other hand, a second lesson, I believe, is that the time for drastic reform is not a time for wild experiments with the economy. There is an abundance of precedents from which to draw lessons—both the recent experience of reform programs in Poland and Hungary and elsewhere in Eastern Europe, and that of earlier times and other regions. This is not to say that there is never anything new under the sun, but even at a time when the economic situation is critical it is still possible to do things that are concrete and practical and offer predictable results.

At the same time there is a need to retain a degree of flexibility in economic management, because in a country as diverse and complex as the Soviet Union it is not possible to plan every detail of economic policy far in advance. There are no absolute prerequisites for any of the reforms being contemplated. The situation changes from moment to moment; what was impossible last month may be possible today. What the Soviet Union most needs now is to get the ball rolling. Once a few steps in the right direction have been taken, the path to be followed will become clearer.

Another important lesson is that the human factor must always be taken into account. Theory may tell us that this or that specific measure will produce this or that result, but even if the political power is there to take such action, the population's limited understanding of the new rules may thwart the intended effects. It will take time for the mentality of the Soviet people to adapt from the patterns established by more than seventy years of socialism. There is at present the danger of a backlash against the implementation of radical reforms, but if

Boris Fedorov is a former Minister of Finance of the Russian Republic.

that danger can be passed, the people's mindset will have been changed irrevocably, and there will be no turning back to the old ways.

There is no well-charted route from socialism and central planning to a market economy, no formula that one can look up in a textbook. Lacking such a clear framework, it takes a strong government to decide on and implement a strategy. At the present time, of course, the Soviet Union lacks a strong government. It is obviously not a solution to have some kind of democratic referendum on what the level of prices should be—no sensible person is going to vote for higher prices on the goods and services he needs. In times of crisis those who take responsibility for leading the country must have the political will to do things that are unpopular.

One repository for this kind of willingness to do what is unpopular but necessary is an independent central bank. The Soviet Union today has 16 central banks—one in each of the republics plus one in the center. This arrangement is not viable. There should be one single, comprehensive monetary policy for the whole of the Soviet Union.

To manage the transition effectively, policymakers must be able to stay ahead of the current situation in the economy, preparing the way for the next set of reforms while the most recent ones are still under way. The present Soviet policymakers are not only not staying ahead of the situation but failing even to keep abreast of it. To swim ahead of or at least with the tide, Soviet policymakers are going to need a lot of help from the market economies, not just in the form of aid but in the form of technical advice and assistance as well, like that now being provided to the other Eastern European economies.

That help, however, should not come without conditions. If I were a banker, I would lend only to those who are ready and willing to do something on their own, and not to those who are merely sitting waiting for help. Help should be conditioned on the presence of a clear strategy indicating where the government intends that the country should go. Otherwise there is the risk that any help on offer will merely serve to maintain the old system in place.

In the Soviet Union at the present time there is a hunger for action. Everyone, from the ordinary people in the street to the ministers and prime ministers of the republics, is waiting for action from the central government, and when the central government takes real, visible action it will have their support. The only question is how and when and who in the central government will make the first move.

Flemming Larsen

The discussions at the earlier sessions of this conference rather overwhelmingly support the introduction of some degree of current account convertibility (for trade, some services, and investment earnings, but not necessarily for tourism) at an early stage of the reform process. The economic arguments for the early introduction of convertibility in Eastern Europe are well known and accepted by most: the need to "import" a realistic relative price structure; the urgency of exposing industry to foreign competition to promote a restructuring of trade toward new markets in the West; and the need to gain credibility for the comprehensiveness of the reform programs.

Political conditions in Eastern Europe also seem to favor an early move to convertibility. These countries are experiencing an exceptional thirst for change and what may well be an unprecedented level of acceptance of reform measures that may well hurt in the short run. The populations of Eastern Europe understandably demand that the reform efforts be of high quality, and they are impatient to see their countries fully integrated in the world economy.

The quest for convertibility constitutes a fundamental departure from what have been some of the most striking failures of the command economy: multiple exchange rates and a pervasive shortage of hard currency. Postponement of convertibility would therefore cause immense frustration. In these circumstances it is not difficult to understand the reluctance of most Eastern Europeans to accept gradualist reform strategies such as a payments union for Eastern Europe.

Several of the papers in this volume have touched upon the question of the costs of reform, including those that may result from convertibility. Statistically, such costs may appear to be large when convertibility leads to sharp price increases and the apparent erosion of real wages. In reality the costs are much smaller than they appear and must be seen against the much larger costs of delaying key reforms. The statistical illusion of large costs can be explained by the distorted starting conditions. In a shortage economy, with artificially controlled prices and suppressed inflation (manifested in a monetary overhang), living standards are poorly measured by the usual indicators of real wages. It is indeed interesting to note that the populations of Eastern Europe worry much less about the short-term loss in real incomes than do many Western observers, who often favor a gradual implementation of convertibility and other reforms.

Notwithstanding these strong arguments for introducing convertibility early in the reform process in Eastern Europe, our discussions at this conference

Flemming Larsen is Head of Division, International Financial and Monetary Matters, European Commission.

have underlined that convertibility is no panacea. The early introduction of convertibility requires decisive action to stabilize the reforming economy; in most Eastern European countries—as indeed in the Soviet Union—a key task must be to absorb a substantial proportion of the monetary overhang that has resulted from years of deficit spending and pump priming. Tight monetary and fiscal policies will be required to dampen inflation as reforms are implemented. Some front-loading of microeconomic reforms will also have to accompany any move toward convertibility: price liberalization and removal of trade restrictions are part and parcel of a reform strategy whose primary objective is the establishment of a competitive, market-oriented economy. Finally, privatization of state-owned enterprises will have to accompany other measures to allow the economy to begin to respond to economic incentives as quickly as possible.

The experience of many developing countries that have attempted similar reforms suggests that all of these conditions are rarely fulfilled, which is often, of course, a reason for postponing the introduction of convertibility. The situation in the Eastern European countries is quite different: both the economic and the political conditions necessary to pursue bold, front-loaded reform programs do indeed seem to be in place. Poland and now also Czechoslovakia have clearly opted for drastic reform strategies, with convertibility as a key intermediate objective. Bulgaria and Romania seem ready to follow suit during the early part of 1991. Hungary and Yugoslavia have been pursuing reforms for many years already and have achieved a high degree of convertibility of their currencies. The Soviet Union will also need a convertible ruble if the population's confidence in the monetary system is to improve; there, however, neither the economic nor the political conditions seem yet to be in place.

How can the international community help to enhance the chances of success of Eastern Europe's bold reform programs? This question can best be answered by considering how a reforming country can meet a crucial external condition for convertibility, namely, the accumulation of an adequate level of international reserves. This requirement follows from the need to ensure a sufficient reserve of "working capital" when all payments are made in hard currency; to prevent an excessive depreciation of the national currency; and, more generally, to boost confidence in the reform program.

An adequate level of reserves can be acquired through various means:

- If there is no external assistance, a country must build up reserves through trade surpluses; this is obviously the most expensive solution because it may require much import compression during the initial stages of the reform program.

- Alternatively, the international monetary system could create reserves and make them available to the reforming country under certain conditions. An instrument that permits international reserve creation exists already in the form of allocations of IMF Special Drawing Rights (SDRs). However, at present there is not a sufficient majority among IMF members in favor of a new general SDR allocation, because many members fear that this would increase inflationary pressures. An allocation of SDRs aimed only at Eastern Europe would, at least in theory, be less inflationary to the extent that the reforms in these countries may be viewed as enlarging the international monetary system. However, in practice it would be difficult to justify an allocation of SDRs for a limited number of countries.

■ Given the drawbacks of the first two options, the most realistic solution would be to rely on borrowed reserves. For this purpose the IMF is again the first port of call, as illustrated by the fact that all six Eastern European countries that are members either have recently concluded agreements with the IMF or are in the process of negotiating new arrangements.

Although the international monetary system in a sense has anticipated the type of assistance Eastern Europe requires, it will be difficult for the IMF alone to fully cover the region's financing needs. This is proving especially true in 1991, as the region is being confronted with an exceptional combination of adverse external shocks.

In addition to the release of pent-up demand for consumer and investment goods, these shocks include the terms-of-trade consequences of the dissolution of the CMEA and the transition to convertible-currency pricing in intra–CMEA trade (the loss from which is estimated at $6 billion for Eastern Europe as a whole vis-à-vis the Soviet Union), together with the economic consequences of the Persian Gulf crisis (including the impact of higher oil prices as well as lower export revenue).

Following the IMF–World Bank annual meetings in September 1990, several changes were introduced in the IMF's lending facilities, including a temporary oil element in the Compensatory and Contingency Financing Facility (CCFF) and increased rates of access under stand-by and extended arrangements. These changes will allow the IMF to finance a large share of the region's financing needs in 1991—including a minimum build-up of reserves. The World Bank is also expected to step up lending to the region in the form of policy-based structural adjustment loans as well as project lending. (Although project commitments by the European Bank for Reconstruction and Development as well as the European Investment Bank are likely to begin in 1991, disbursements from these two institutions are expected to be quite small in the short run.) However, even on the basis of optimistic assessments of the speed of disbursement from the multilateral and regional financial institutions, there is the prospect of a substantial residual financing gap for most of the Eastern European countries in

1991. If left uncovered, this gap could compromise the introduction of convertibility and indeed the entire process of reform.

To close the financing gap, the 24 OECD countries have launched a series of initiatives. The first was the creation of a $1 billion stabilization fund for Poland at the end of 1989; this was recently extended for a second year. Subsequent assistance has included balance of payments loans mobilized through an effort coordinated by the European Commission.

The Commission's involvement dates back to the mandate, extended by the Paris Summit in 1989, to the European Community to coordinate assistance to the newly reforming countries in Eastern Europe. Initially, this assistance was concentrated on various forms of technical assistance and emergency aid. However, in the spring of 1990 the Commission began to signal to the Twenty-Four that the assistance efforts would need to be expanded to cover financial assistance, particularly in 1991, which was shaping up to be a crucial and extremely difficult year for these countries. From the very beginning the need for financial assistance was based on the idea that early introduction of convertibility would be the most logical response to the challenges facing Eastern Europe in the areas of price reform and trade restructuring.

By the end of 1990, a political consensus emerged, in the Community and among the Twenty-Four, on the need for complementary financial assistance in the amount of $4 billion for 1991. This estimate, which was worked out in close cooperation with the IMF, covered the expected needs of four countries—the initial view was that Poland and Yugoslavia might not require complementary assistance in 1991. The initiative of the Twenty-Four is now being implemented.

For *Czechoslovakia,* the objective of collecting pledges for an assistance package totaling $1 billion has virtually been reached. The assistance will be provided in the form of medium-term loans at market terms, untied to imports from the donor countries. The largest contributors are the European Community (50 percent), Japan (20 percent, provided through co-financing of a World Bank structural adjustment loan), Austria (5 percent), and Switzerland (4 percent); most of the other members of the Twenty-Four have also contributed. In addition, the members of the Gulf Cooperation Council have contributed about one-eighth of the overall package.

The package for Czechoslovakia complements an IMF stand-by arrangement (and drawings under the CCFF) approved in early January 1991. Drawings on the IMF will amount to some $1.4 billion in 1991; the World Bank expects to disburse some $225 million. The Twenty-Four package is closely coordinated with the IMF and the World Bank, and the conditions attached to it are similar to those attached to the IMF's stand-by arrangement.

Hungary had already obtained from the Community a balance of payments loan in the amount of 870 million ecus in 1990; a second tranche of this loan amounting to 260 million ecus ($350 million at current exchange rates) is due to be disbursed in February 1991. Japan will also disburse the second tranche of a loan granted in 1990 (again through co-financing of a World Bank structural adjustment loan). Despite these commitments, the IMF estimates that Hungary will have a residual funding gap of $500 million in 1991. The Twenty-Four have agreed to cover this additional need, with the Community alone likely to contribute $250 million.

Bulgaria and *Romania* will be considered next. Negotiations about the use of IMF resources are at an advanced stage, and stand-by arrangements supporting comprehensive, front-loaded reform and adjustment programs are expected to be in place by March or April 1991 (see the epilogue to the paper by Ventseslav Dimitrov, chapter 7). In both cases, moves toward current account convertibility are anticipated at an early stage, and both countries have requested complementary financial assistance from the Twenty-Four. In the case of Bulgaria, such assistance should take due account of the need to obtain a satisfactory debt-restructuring agreement with the commercial banks that hold most of the country's debt.

Poland also faces a large gross financing requirement in 1991. However, negotiations currently under way in the Paris Club to consider Poland's request for debt reduction will have to be completed before the need for complementary assistance—in addition to the extension of the stabilization fund—can be assessed. The debt-restructuring agreement is expected to substantially reduce the need for complementary assistance.

Yugoslavia is facing a sharp deterioration in its external position in 1991 due to a combination of adverse external shocks and a premature relaxation of its domestic stabilization policies. Reserves declined significantly in the latter part of 1990 but remain sufficient to permit the country to confront the worsening external situation, provided its domestic policies are corrected. For the moment there does not seem to be a need for financial assistance from the Twenty-Four.

The *Soviet Union* also does not seem to be candidate for this type of assistance, at least in the short run. Both the Commission's recent study of Soviet reform efforts (1990) and the study led by the IMF (1990) concluded that substantial external balance of payments assistance was not warranted for the moment. This assessment was based on two considerations: the fact that the counterpart of Eastern Europe's large terms-of-trade loss in 1991 is a large gain for the Soviet Union, and the hesitant pace of economic reform within the Soviet Union so far. However, if and when the domestic conditions for reform—including convertibility of the ruble—improve decisively, the issue of external financial assistance may well come up again.

Discussion

Hans Genberg observed that the use of a fixed exchange rate as a nominal anchor implied that monetary policy had to be used *only* as a support to the exchange rate. If monetary policy is to be used for some other purpose, which is possible in Eastern Europe inasmuch as capital mobility is largely absent, then some additional mechanism of monetary control will be needed to prevent pressures from building up on reserves, prices, the balance of payments, and so on. He emphasized that adoption of a crawling peg in no way eliminated the need for complementary macroeconomic policies, and he argued that an endogenous crawling peg—in which the peg is adjusted in pursuit of a target real exchange rate so as to maintain competitiveness—could lead to an accelerating wage-price spiral if wages became formally or informally indexed. That once again pointed to the need for complementary macroeconomic and monetary policies. Genberg also remarked that he saw no particular reason why Poland or any other country should ever feel itself obliged to move to a market-determined exchange rate: the market would determine either the price or the quantity of money but not both, and one solution was no more implied by the market than the other.

Referring to Williamson's assertion that the nominal anchor worked by creating unemployment when an overvaluation had developed, *Susan Collins* pointed out that it was widely believed that the nominal anchor could work in an additional way. The announcement of a nominal anchor in the form of a fixed exchange rate might increase the credibility of macroeconomic policy, and thus reduce the output cost of bringing down inflation. She argued, however, that experience had shown that one could not buy credibility just by announcing the nominal anchor.

Collins suggested that there were three distinct social costs of adjustment programs. First, unemployment may arise from the tight monetary and fiscal policies that some countries may need to introduce in order to reduce inflation. Second, demand for domestic goods may decline in favor of that for foreign goods when the possibility of buying imports arises, and that also will cause unemployment. Third, a transfer of resources from declining to expanding industries will cause more jobs to be lost in the former than are created in the latter in the short run. The importance of each of these three factors will doubtless vary from one country to another, but it is useful to distinguish them and to explain up front that they are likely to occur. The mere existence of such adjustment costs does not, however, imply that a gradual program is better than shock therapy. It may be politically more difficult to sustain support for a program that involves accepting a bit more pain each year than for one that challenges the public to bite the bullet. Collins pointed out that a country whose leaders were open about the social costs of adjustment would need to be able to dangle some carrots as well. Finally, Collins asked whether there were any estimates of the magnitude of these adjustment costs, and she stressed the importance of supporting careful cross-country empirical work in this area, using common definitions.

John Thompson suggested that any country that quickly accepted two of Williamson's conditions for establishing convertibility—price liberalization and trade liberalization—was committing itself to a program of shock therapy. A strategy of aiming to establish those two conditions over a period of two or three years was the essence of a gradualist approach. This was the basis for labeling the policy of Czechoslovakia a case of shock therapy and that of Hungary one of gradualism. Williamson's third and fourth conditions were really one: autonomous enterprises facing hard budget constraints. This was a very long-term objective that was currently satisfied nowhere in Eastern Europe. These criteria were thus too ambitious as minimum requirements.

The problem Thompson saw with a radical opening of the economy was the disproportion between the powerful demand-side signals transmitted to the economy from the rest of the world (such as world prices and interest rates) and the limited ability of the supply side to respond. This imbalance led to a waste of resources and high social costs of adjustment. The problem would be further intensified by adoption of a fixed exchange rate as a nominal anchor in the current circumstances of Eastern Europe. A nominal anchor might make sense when a country's inflation has been brought down to something close to the world level, but the lowest open inflation rate expected in the region in 1991 was about 35 percent, and the problems of repressed inflation in the countries that did not permit open inflation were even more serious.

Thompson noted that full convertibility included freedom of capital movements as well as liberalization of current account operations. Given the liberalizing trends in most market economies, it was unlikely that controls on capital movements could be maintained indefinitely. However, in the experience of the OECD countries, capital account liberalization tended to be gradual, usually beginning with foreign direct investment and ending with controls on short-term capital movements. Thompson also stressed an intermediate stage of exchange controls, where authorities retained some right to review individual transactions. Some speakers had characterized the lack of convertibility as an impediment to foreign investment, but in Thompson's view it was only necessary to liberalize one operation at a time, not to remove all controls for the sake of attracting investment. He recommended that the formerly centrally planned economies begin by liberalizing operations closely related to direct investment, possibly with some rules governing repatriation of earnings. Complete removal of controls would be imprudent until existing distortions are removed from the domestic financial markets.

Jozef van Brabant offered several suggestions for Williamson's report. He cautioned against incorporating Václav Klaus's view that it would be politically unacceptable to have anything less than current account convertibility. This Brabant saw as a red herring: the public, he argued, does not care about such abstractions as convertibility. What people want is to be able to travel and to have a wider choice of goods in the shops. Those objectives can be achieved without a convertible currency. That is not to say that convertibility is unimportant; it should be realized as quickly as possible, but countries that have been insulated from the international economy for so long would incur enormous social costs in moving there quickly. Those costs might be so great as to make convertibility unsustainable.

Brabant agreed with much of what Larsen had said about the need for international assistance because there was a limit to the adjustment costs that could be imposed on the population, but he asked what would happen if inadequate assistance were forthcoming. A large shortfall would lead to the failure of convertibility, and debt levels were already unmanageable in several countries, so that additional borrowing was not hopeful either. The choice might yet be between unbearable adjustment costs and an unfinanceable payments deficit, and in that event he still thought the payments union might come into its own. He too favored a customs union, but of course that needed at least a transferable currency; if there were no convertible currencies, then the payments union could provide at least the transferable currency that would allow a customs union to function.

Andrei Kazmin reverted to the parallel currency proposal. He could understand the skepticism that had been voiced, which he thought arose from a lack of familiarity, but he had found the criticisms unconvincing. Of course it would be wonderful if it were practical to liberalize all prices, to abolish all subsidies, and to give total freedom to all economic agents in a single comprehensive liberalization. But although that might be theoretically possible, there were enormous differences between the financial and monetary systems in the Soviet Union and those in the West, and these could not be wished away overnight. The irrational structure of the Soviet economy and the lack of enterprise autonomy cause 25 percent of output to be wasted and another 50 percent to be of substandard quality. The parallel currency he and Andrei Tsimailo were proposing would establish a new monetary circuit with a direct link between producers and final consumers that would reintroduce appropriate incentives. On the historical precedents, he said that the chervonets was killed by the authoritarian political system, which could not tolerate the existence of a market economy.

Michael Dohan also returned to the chervonets. He argued that there was an important thing to be learned from its death, which was due not to political reasons, as Kazmin had argued, but to bad economics. The beginning of its end occurred in the summer of 1925 with a massive overextension of credit, which led to the goods famine. Desiring to kill the messenger that was bringing the bad news, and not understanding the role of prices, the Soviet government decided to fix prices below market-clearing levels. That, not political conspiracy, ended the chervonets.

One thing that Dohan had observed at the conference was the consensus on the need for macroeconomic stabilization as a precondition for economic reform, price liberalization, and currency convertibility. The end result of a successful stabilization program was the establishment of market-clearing prices—not in the sense of free market prices with their customary efficiency properties, but prices that clear the markets given the composition and level of output. Such prices can only reign in the consumer-goods markets if aggregate demand is reduced to the level of aggregate supply—a change that will not reduce the standard of living since just as many goods are available as before, but will actually increase welfare because of the elimination of queues. How aggregate demand is reduced—whether it involves an agreement on the relation between wages and prices, and whether it takes the form of a wage cut or a price or tax increase—is a political question.

Dohan had read in a number of papers the assertion that real wages fall when prices increase. But that is true only if prices are initially at a market-clearing level. What happens when prices rise in an economy with repressed inflation is not a fall in real wages but the translation of repressed into open inflation. It is misleading to compare a price level at which no goods are available with one at which goods can actually be bought.

Friedrich Levcik said that he found Larsen very hard-line in his views. He asked Larsen whether he thought that the introduction of convertibility demanded just political will, or whether there were some minimum conditions that had to be satisfied before a government should be expected to commit itself to making the currency convertible. Specifically, did he think it was necessary to have a central bank that was relatively independent of the government? Did he see a need for real commercial banks? Did he think the state enterprises needed to be de-etatized first? Do enterprises need to have some independence in their decision-making? In Levcik's view those were all necessary requirements for the introduction of convertibility, and he wanted to know whether Larsen saw no need for any such conditions.

Miroslav Hrnčíř said that he thought Williamson was right to stress the need to import discipline over relative prices from the outside world. He agreed that this was much more important for the economies in transition than it had been in postwar Western Europe. But Williamson had also argued that Eastern Europe should be less dogmatic about fixing the exchange rate and that there might be a case for some form of nonuniform transitional protection. Hrnčíř understood that this was an attempt to reduce the costs of transition, but he still worried about how the protection really could be made transitional and how it could be made rational. The problem is not only one of finding criteria, but also one of resisting vested interests. The tradition in Czechoslovakia had been to protect the least efficient, whereas Williamson was assuming that it would be those with greater medium-run efficiency who would receive protection. The problem would be to avoid misusing transitional protection.

Replying to the debate, *Flemming Larsen* said that it was hard to disagree with Levcik, given the way he had posed his question. In emphasizing the dangers of gradualism and the need to take political perspectives into account, he was agreeing with Klaus's comment (chapter 2) that sequencing is important but is not always in the hands of the policymakers, in the sense that political opportunities that arise should be seized before they slip away. That is consistent with the need to place convertibility in the context of a comprehensive reform program, which is what he thought concerned Levcik. It is also consistent with his own warning of the danger of postponing key reforms, which may delay the time when real benefits start to emerge and create the conditions in which adjustment fatigue can emerge.

Andrzej Olechowski commented that Williamson's postulate of a choice between modest inflation without a recession and zero inflation with a recession came from a different book from that which governed Poland. There the choice was between 50 percent to 60 percent inflation with some growth and 20 percent to 30 percent inflation with no growth. He challenged Williamson's suggestion that countries could benefit from some mild selective transitional protection, since import-competing enterprises got ample natural protection from the inefficiency of the import sector. He also worried about the political nightmare of having to choose which industries to protect. Furthermore, since tariffs were very low in Eastern Europe and it would be difficult to increase them, any additional protection would take the form of quotas and similar nasty measures, which would be difficult to remove again when their justification had gone. On the question of the costs of rapid opening, he expressed the hope that the Polish example might help to establish that they were not in fact that substantial; moreover, he thought that the Czechoslovaks' decision to open rapidly had been influenced by their reading of the Polish evidence that the costs were not very high.

Boris Fedorov agreed that the question of social costs was one of the most important issues. One of the peculiar aspects of the Soviet debate was that many politicians were still promising that there would be no costs at all, and that everyone could be protected 100 percent. That would be impossible, even if the social security system were completely overhauled. Cuts in subsidies were needed, but they had to be a part of an overall macroeconomic policy, which was still lacking. One of the major problems in planning for convertibility in the Soviet Union was that most people in government—in the republics as well as in the union government—continued to think in terms of material production and quantitative targeting. This leads them into arguments over where all the goods are going. The idea of limiting policy to the pursuit of general goals like low inflation and unemployment and improved competitiveness is still not accepted, and hence while specific reform projects will continue to be adopted it is unlikely that a comprehensive, big-bang approach will be implemented, at least for several years yet. The objective economic situation is worse than in Eastern Europe, yet everyone is in favor of indexing wages and pensions, even though the Soviet Union lacks the basic essentials like a relevant price index able to cope with an initial situation of repressed inflation. Clearly the minimization of social adjustment costs will be a primary task for those in charge of economic policy.

John Williamson responded to Olechowski that a choice between growing with a 50 percent rate of inflation and getting inflation down to 20 percent with a big recession was no choice at all. Opting to accommodate 50 percent inflation this year would guarantee its rapid acceleration to a point where there would be no choice but to slam on the brakes and create a massive recession. This had been witnessed innumerable times in Latin America. Had any countries ever succeeded in maintaining a respectable rate of growth for any length of time with inflation above 20 percent? The only cases Williamson could think of were Brazil in 1967–74 (when inflation stabilized at a little above 20 percent) and Indonesia in the late 1960s (which began its spectacular recovery from the antihyperinflation stabilization when inflation was around that level, although it later came down to single figures).[1] But it was difficult to find examples of countries that have combined vigorous output growth with the sort of macroeconomic instability represented by rapid inflation. Macrostabilization did have to come first: Klaus was absolutely right about that. Williamson worried that the excessive devaluation at the beginning of 1990 had prejudiced the chances of stabilizing inflation in Poland, and that Czechoslovakia might have repeated the error a year later. For the moment, he saw no sensible choice but to give priority to reducing inflation in Poland.

Once inflation has been reduced to single digits, a real element of choice arises: whether to press on the rest of the way to price stability at the cost of delaying the revival of growth, or to accommodate a degree of inflation by adopting a crawling peg during the period of reconstruction. The latter would still require macroeconomic discipline: indeed, Genberg was right to say that a crawling peg that offset differential inflation would be a recipe for disaster if it were not accompanied by macroeconomic discipline.

---

1. Additional cases are those of Colombia, which has maintained a healthy growth rate ever since the 1960s with inflation of between 20 percent and 30 percent per year, and Chile, which has grown strongly in recent years with inflation of around 20 percent. Had I picked 30 percent rather than 20 percent as my critical maximum level, I think I would have had no counterexamples.—ED.

Responding to Olechowski's remarks about protection, Williamson emphasized that he advocated only *tariff* protection during the transition; indeed, one
of the main objectives of interim tariff protection was to permit the immediate
elimination of all other import restrictions. He thought it unwise to rely on
natural protection provided by the inefficiency of the import sector, which was
likely to diminish rapidly. If transitional tariff protection were to be introduced,
Hrnčíř was right to point to the need for discipline to ensure that it was indeed
phased out over time, but surely that could easily be provided by committing
the country ahead of time to such a phaseout in the GATT. The West would then
retaliate against exports if the promise were broken, which would be extremely
unpopular with another important domestic constituency, thus providing the
needed discipline.

With regard to Dohan's remarks, Williamson regarded macroeconomic stabilization as a necessary condition—following Richard Cooper's distinction (chapter
8)— rather than a precondition. Surely Soviet Prime Minister Ryzhkov had been
trying to achieve macrostabilization first, by raising prices and thus stemming
the budget deficit; that strategy had encountered political resistance, because (to
use Collins's expression) there were no carrots to offset the sticks. There *is* still
a cost to some people in seeing prices go up even when there is no reduction in
the quantity of goods available; poorer people then lose their ability to buy those
goods that had been available at the lower price by queuing.

Replying to Brabant, Williamson said that he was assuming that at least
Czechoslovakia, Hungary, and Poland would succeed in maintaining convertible
currencies, and there the need was to ensure that they gave enterprises that
wished to import from one another currency facilities at least comparable to
those that wished to import from the West. Any further preferences were best
provided by free trade arrangements. A more serious problem might arise in
maintaining trade with the countries that had *not* yet come close to convertibility:
conceivably a payments union would be helpful in that context.

10

The Economic Opening of Eastern Europe

10

The Economic Opening of Eastern Europe

John Williamson

Few events in this century have been greeted with such widespread acclaim as the revolutions in Eastern Europe in the second half of 1989. Not only did the populations of one country after another throw off the totalitarian yoke that had oppressed them ever since the Second World War, but they did so with the acquiescence (or even the help) of the Soviet leadership, which was somewhat hesitatingly moving in the same direction. Not only did the countries of the region embrace democracy and pluralism, but all set themselves the objective of making the complementary transformation to a market economy. The Cold War was over; a new order was waiting to be born.

The initial euphoria proved to be excessive. Although the new democratic institutions are so far showing encouraging vigor, the region finds itself confronting serious economic disarray and, in several countries, outbreaks of virulent nationalism. The reform movement in the Soviet Union continues to be challenged by the conservatives. Both Yugoslavia and the Soviet Union are facing constitutional crises. For all its current difficulties, however, Eastern Europe is a vastly more hopeful part of the world than it was during the years of the Cold War. There is still a widespread, and in most places dominant, desire to practice democracy, to respect human rights, and to build a market economy.

The present volume is intended to further debate on one aspect of that latter ambition, namely, how to open up the economies of Eastern Europe and integrate them into the world economy—a step that is widely recognized in the region to be an essential element in making a market economy function efficiently. This chapter is based on the conference the proceedings of which appear in preceding chapters. Even before the conference was held, it had become clear that one could not really discuss convertibility independently of the other policy questions that arise in opening an economy to the world—hence the more general title of this chapter.

This chapter was published separately as *The Economic Opening of Eastern Europe*. POLICY ANALYSES IN INTERNATIONAL ECONOMICS 31 (Washington: Institute for International Economics).

363

This chapter covers all of what is conventionally described as Eastern Europe, meaning the Soviet Union as well as Bulgaria, Czechoslovakia, the former East Germany, Hungary, Poland, Romania, and Yugoslavia.[1] It starts by sketching the economic system, especially its external aspects, that prevailed throughout the region (except for Yugoslavia) during the period of high Stalinism in the early 1950s; it then describes the major modifications that had already been introduced prior to 1989 as well as the economic ambitions now driving policymakers in the region. The next section, which is the core of the chapter, discusses the issues that arise in pursuing those ambitions and integrate the countries of the region into the world economy. This is followed by a country-by-country account of the present situation, centered on an assessment of each country's actual and prospective strategy for opening up. A final section summarizes the policy conclusions suggested by the preceding discussion.

Background

The Stalinist Legacy

The Stalinist system of central planning was the very antithesis of a market economy. There were no entrepreneurs using the private property they controlled to try to satisfy needs (as reflected in willingness to pay), seeking the rewards of success and accepting the risks of failure. Instead, virtually all property was publicly owned;[2] managers were responsible simply for producing what they were told by the planners to produce, using the inputs allocated to them for that purpose, much as the managers of a branch factory might operate in a rather centralized capitalist firm.

The planners set prices for both inputs and outputs, but these prices were not supposed to influence the behavior of an enterprise. High output relative to input prices would lead to an enterprise recording a surplus, but this would be taxed away—either explicitly by what were essentially enterprise-specific profits taxes, or implicitly by remaining in the monopolistic state bank where it could not be spent without the planners' permission. (The inability to use money balances at the enterprise's own discretion is termed "commodity inconvertibility.") Conversely, low output relative to input prices would result in an enterprise recording a loss, but this could be financed automatically by borrowing from the state bank at a low rate of interest, if an explicit subsidy was not provided.

---

1. Occasionally Czechoslovakia, Hungary, and Poland are referred to collectively, in distinction from the others, as the "Central European" countries.

2. The major exception was agriculture in Poland and Yugoslavia, which remained largely private.

Table 1 Population, per capita income, and openness to trade of selected European countries[a]

Country	Population (millions)	Per capita income	Exports as a percentage of GDP
Poland	37.9	1,930	22.8
Hungary	10.6	2,240	37.6
Portugal	10.4	2,830	33.5
Greece	10.0	4,020	24.2
Spain	39.0	6,010	19.5

a. Export and GDP data refer to 1988; other data refer to 1987.

Source: Kenen (1991).

The international economic relations of the socialist economies were organized to complement the national plans. Trade with other centrally planned economies was planned on a long-term basis to achieve a "socialist division of labor," meaning international specialization on a product basis and aimed at bilateral balance between countries. Trade with market economies was used to fill gaps and compensate for planning mistakes, with exports consisting of whatever goods were saleable on the world market and could be spared from domestic output.

Several authors have recently asserted that the centrally planned economies were quite open by Western standards. This claim is based on figures such as those shown in table 1. However, the ratios of exports to GDP in that table are constructed by dividing trade measured in dollars by an estimate of GDP that comes from translating local-currency GDP into dollars by applying a market exchange rate, rather than by taking the trade statistics from the GDP figures themselves. The resulting estimates are highly sensitive to the exchange rate used to translate GDP into dollars. Analysts using exchange rates that reflect purchasing power parities (PPP) show GDPs roughly twice as high as those used in table 1, and hence openness ratios only half as big.[3] Those using black market exchange rates get derisorily small GDP figures, and are therefore logically obliged to believe that these economies rival Hong Kong and Singapore in their openness.

By another measure, the planned economies were unambiguously autarkic. Czechoslovakia is reputed to have produced domestically some 65 percent of all categories of industrial goods at the five-digit SITC (Standard International Trade Classification) level—a higher proportion than Japan, despite Japanese GNP

3. See, for example, Marer (1985) or the table on page 19 of *International Economic Insights,* July-August 1990, which gives GNP per capita of about $6,000 per year for both Eastern Europe and the Soviet Union.

being at least twenty times as large. Similarly, East Germany produced a wider range of industrial products than did West Germany. The explanation for this apparent paradox presumably lies in the attempted self-sufficiency of each enterprise: because suppliers suffered minimal sanctions for late delivery of components, every enterprise sought to produce everything it needed for itself (where this was impracticable, it aimed to keep massive stockpiles).

A high proportion of trade in the planned economies consisted of trade within the group (see table 2); this intratrade was much above what would have been expected from the experience of the market economies and reflected the planners' belief in economies of scale. The ideal socialist division of labor would be realized when every forklift truck used from Berlin to Vladivostok was made in a single plant; even though that ideal was never completely achieved, the world's biggest forklift factory was indeed constructed in Bulgaria and came to supply a very large part of that market.

Table 2 CMEA trade, 1987 (millions of dollars)[a]

Country	Soviet Union	Other CMEA	Industrial West	Developing countries	Total
Imports					
Bulgaria	9,284	3,513	2,479	726	16,001
Czechoslovakia	10,158	7,404	4,106	807	22,475
East Germany	11,928	7,232	7,963	902	28,026
Hungary	2,806	1,909	4,070	642	9,426
Poland	2,977	2,007	4,312	759	10,055
Romania	2,766	2,470	1,400	2,500	9,136
Soviet Union	—	61,450	21,940	7,507	90,897
Exports					
Bulgaria	9,722	3,238	1,079	1,696	15,735
Czechoslovakia	9,975	7,379	3,578	1,189	22,121
East Germany	11,085	8,797	7,995	1,319	29,195
Hungary	3,135	1,750	3,517	807	9,209
Poland	3,024	2,076	5,078	1,206	11,384
Romania	2,923	3,084	3,700	2,500	12,206
Soviet Union	—	64,425	22,456	15,446	102,326

CMEA = Council for Mutual Economic Assistance.

a. Data have been converted into dollars using export and import conversion factors.

Source: Comecon Data 1988, edited by the Vienna Institute for Comparative Economic Studies, 1989.

Importing and exporting were undertaken by monopolistic state agencies, which controlled essentially all foreign-exchange operations. These agencies bought goods from domestic enterprises in local currency and resold them abroad for foreign currency, and vice versa with imports. In the process they might have made an accounting gain or loss for the government, but they did not regard that as of any particular consequence. This system provided total protection against foreign competition, although tariffs were very low and formal quantitative restrictions nonexistent.

Trade among the centrally planned economies was organized through the Council for Mutual Economic Assistance (CMEA), often known as COMECON. The CMEA provided the forum for negotiating trade deals as well as the accounting system for recording receipts and payments and the difference between them. These payments imbalances were recorded in one of the world's stranger units of account, the "transferable ruble." The main point about the transferable ruble was that it was not transferable; the proportion of intra–CMEA imbalances netted out by using a surplus against one country to settle a deficit with another was trivial. The reason for the minimal level of multilateral clearing was that no debtor country was willing to give up the credit it had obtained by managing to run a deficit, unless its bilateral creditor insisted that it had found some additional imports it was prepared to take in settlement.

The other major feature of the CMEA was its formula for pricing goods traded among its members. In principle this was a five-year moving average of the world market price. This formula was easily applied to trade in primary products; its application resulted in the Soviet Union subsidizing its partners in the 1970s and early 1980s, after the two oil price shocks, and conversely obtaining some temporary relief against the terms-of-trade loss imposed by the 1986 oil price decline. It was far more difficult to apply the formula to trade in manufactures, since the quality of the goods made in the CMEA region was generally inferior to that of the Western goods used as the basis for the price comparisons. However, there was no objective measure—such as willingness to pay—of the extent of the shortfall. Prices were in practice determined by a process of bargaining; the general view is that the Soviet Union paid more than what would have been the market price for its substantial net imports of manufactures from its partners, since their prices did not make adequate allowance for quality differentials, whereas the prices of primary products averaged out over time to a realistic level. Overall, therefore, the Soviet Union subsidized its CMEA partners.

Trade with the market economies was determined by each country individually. This trade was conducted in convertible currencies.

Pre–1989 Reforms

The socialist ideal, which originally inspired the substitution of public ownership and central planning for private ownership and the price mechanism, was to replace greed by need as the motive force driving economic behavior. Implementation of this ideal foundered on two basic problems. One is that few individuals are prepared to devote the bulk of their lives to doing conscientiously what somebody else decides they should do, rather than what they perceive to be in their own interest given the constraints and opportunities confronting them. Hence the planners, unable to rely on voluntary compliance, had to give orders; naturally the planned reacted by trying to exploit the limited knowledge of the planners so as to maximize their own welfare. This was the origin not only of the fights over norms, but also of the technical stagnation and lack of innovation long suffered by the socialist economies. Reinforcing the lack of motivation of the planned was the increasing corruption of the planners, explained all too well by Lord Acton's dictum that "power corrupts, and absolute power corrupts absolutely." Communists did not prove immune to the temptations of absolute power.

The other fundamental systemic problem arose from the lack of real markets in which prices responded to demand and supply. Friedrich A. von Hayek's conjecture that planners would be unable to dispense with the information provided through the market proved to be correct. The absence of both markets and democratic processes deprived the economy of any socially organized error-correction mechanisms, so that wrong choices of product mix or technology went uncorrected indefinitely. Because capital and natural resources were not privately owned, there was no pressure to recognize their scarcity, nor was there any price that could allocate their rational distribution among alternative uses, let alone between current consumption and investment for the future. It turned out that the alternative to having those decisions motivated by greed was to have them driven by pharaonic grandiosity and bureaucratic inertia, with dismal results for the environment as well as for consumers. Adam Smith (unlike some of his self-proclaimed successors) never idolized greed, but he did argue that it could be harnessed to drive a relatively benign mode of social organization, which looks pretty convincing now that we have seen the alternative.

Economic reforms undertaken from time to time within the socialist system attempted to break the link between social ownership and central planning, keeping the former but weakening or discarding the latter—the idea that underlay the concept of "market socialism" propagated by Oskar Lange (1937). It was largely an attempt to address the problem of inadequate motivation by providing incentives for enterprises to act in more socially benign ways. Such ideas were first introduced in Yugoslavia, the only Eastern European country apart from the Soviet Union where socialism resulted from an indigenous movement rather than from foreign imposition. This history may help explain why, following Marshal Tito's break with Stalin in the late 1940s, Yugoslavia felt free to experiment. Both Czechoslovakia (during the "Prague Spring") and Hungary initiated reform programs in 1968, although the experiment survived only in Hungary.

Despite the unpromising political context, Poland followed suit in 1982. Finally, from 1985 on, the Soviet Union began to pursue *perestroika*.

Details of the new managerial structures varied, from worker self-management in which the workers appointed the managers, to worker-management cooperatives, to enterprises run by the managers. Comprehensive central direction of output was abandoned, so that some scope emerged for enterprises to establish contracts directly with one another, but market freedom remained circumscribed by state orders, and prices were regulated, generally on a cost-plus basis, rather than freed to respond to supply and demand. Cost increases were always ratified, and competition was absent, thus destroying any incentive to keep costs under control. In each case enterprises, or at least some enterprises, were given more autonomy as part of an effort to provide the incentives that were so damagingly lacking in the traditional model, but the reforms did not attempt to address the other systemic problem, namely, the lack of real markets. Kornai (1986) argued that even in Hungary the reforms had not taken the economy over the threshold to a market economy.

The success of these reforms was mixed. The initial impact of all the reform programs, except Soviet *perestroika,* seemed to be distinctly positive, as workers and managers responded to being given the motivation that had previously been lacking. But in each case, except perhaps Hungary, these gains were limited in time, just as the initial rapid growth following the introduction of socialism had petered out. The explanation seems to be partly that worker management contains a series of perverse incentives, notably an inbuilt incentive to invest too little for the future or even to decapitalize enterprises, resulting from the fact that the basic objective of a worker-managed enterprise is to maximize the return per worker. Piecemeal reforms also led to the emergence of acute second-best problems, in which the removal of one distortion while leaving others alone made things worse rather than better. An example of this is provided by the anecdote (related by Jeffrey D. Sachs at the Brookings Panel on Economic Activity in April 1990) about how Poland had become an exporter of semitropical flowers prior to the reforms of January 1990. No central planner would ever have conceived of decreeing an activity with such massive negative value added as the export of semitropical flowers from a country with Poland's climatic endowment; however, Polish enterprises rendered autonomous under reforms, but confronted with energy prices that remained fixed at perhaps 6 percent of the world level, were quite capable of subtracting value in that way.

In the interest of improving motivation, enterprises were increasingly allowed to spend some of their surpluses. Since a substantial proportion of government revenue (typically between 10 percent and 20 percent of GNP) had taken the form of enterprise surpluses that were appropriated by government, this led to increasing fiscal deficits. But this happened in an environment where the government still controlled prices, and indeed tried to avoid price increases, with the result that the fiscal deficits often had their counterpart in excess demand, queues, rationing, rising premiums on the black market, and a monetary overhang.[4] The rising black-market premiums interacted with increased tolerance for small-scale "private" (or cooperative) enterprises to enlarge the scope for diverting goods from official distribution channels to the informal ones. This resulted, at least in the Soviet Union, in the nascent entrepreneurs in the informal sector getting a bad name as profiteers.

Liberalization led to major changes in the traditional CMEA trade and payments regime. Perhaps the principal impulse came from the decision to try to stimulate exports to the non–CMEA area by allowing some enterprises to sell abroad directly rather than go through the state trading agency, and to retain a proportion of their foreign-exchange earnings to spend themselves. Andrzej Olechowski and Marek Oleś (chapter 5 of this volume) report that, in Poland, imports financed from these so-called retention quotas rose from zero prior to 1982 to over 50 percent of total imports by 1989. Currency auctions were instituted in some countries; these could in principle have been fed by the retention quotas but in practice relied almost entirely upon the government releasing part of its dollar earnings.

Reinforcing this movement to decentralize trade was the growth of tourism and the increasing tolerance of nationals going abroad to work and bringing back foreign exchange. Some countries allowed the proceeds to be placed in foreign-exchange accounts in domestic banks, whereas in others they were held under the mattress and increasingly used to finance black-market transactions. Currency substitution and dollarization arrived.

Although the planners no longer exerted the total control of foreign trade that they had in the 1950s, they certainly did not withdraw and allow the market to

---

4. A monetary overhang is said to exist when individuals would choose to exchange their holdings of money for goods at existing prices if more goods were available. It is sometimes argued that the existence of a monetary overhang is inconsistent with that of a black market, since money can always be spent there (Cochrane and Ickes 1991). To this Lawrence Summers has replied that people hold onto money rather than spend it on the black market in the hope that goods may become available in the future at the official prices. At the other extreme, Hinds (1990, 8) has argued that a monetary overhang is almost inevitable in a socialist economy. The planners aim to secure comparable standards of living for people with objective needs that differ because of family circumstances, position in the life cycle, and so on. But salaries cannot be tailored to match the particular consumption needs of each individual, so the government attempts instead to distribute many goods by rationing outside the monetary system (e.g., through the allocation of apartments, or by provision of goods at the workplace). Unless the rationed goods are provided free, the operation of this system requires an excess supply of money; otherwise some people entitled to rationed goods would not be able to afford them. That excess supply, Hinds argues, must cumulate to a monetary overhang. Both the view that a monetary overhang is impossible and the view that it is inevitable appear extreme, and both are contradicted by experience in some of the Eastern European countries.

determine trade flows. In some countries, such as Poland, both exports and imports required administrative licenses. In others, such as the Soviet Union, the planners continued to attempt to control the pattern of trade by deciding the "currency conversion coefficient" at which a particular sector would be allowed to trade. Since there were about 3,000 such coefficients, there was in effect a multiple exchange rate system with about 3,000 different exchange rates, each chosen with the object of inducing enterprises to act as desired without leaving them with an "unfair" rent.

By 1989 it was clear that economic reform within the context of a basically socialist system had failed to nurture efficient international economic relations, just as it had failed to provide an efficient national economic system. GNP in all of the centrally planned economies was officially stagnant but in reality declining: it is now well known that past statistical procedures systematically exaggerated growth rates,[5] and that the real income of Eastern Europe underwent a calamitous decline relative to that of Western Europe in the postwar period.[6] Inflation, either open or repressed, was rampant almost everywhere. Shortages and queues were commonplace. Foreign debt was high in most countries (see table 3). Currency auctions and black-market exchange rates demonstrated a massive unsatisfied demand for Western goods and travel and a chronic lack of confidence in the local currencies. It was in this situation that the political revolutions of autumn 1989 created the opportunity to change direction and to seek to make the uncharted transformation from socialism to a market economy.

Before the transition could be accomplished, however, the region was hit by two major economic shocks. The first was self-induced. At a meeting in Sofia, Bulgaria, in January 1990, the CMEA decided to dismantle itself at the end of the year. Intratrade among the countries of the region would in future be conducted at world market prices and settled in dollars. Apparently the Central Europeans pressed for this change because the old system was inconsistent with the establishment of market-determined prices; the Soviets were only too happy to agree, since they saw no reason why they should subsidize their former

---

5. The major reason stems from the treatment of quality changes. An enterprise that introduced a new, higher-quality product was entitled to charge a higher price for it. Enterprises evaded the price controls by introducing "improved" products, charging a new high price, allowing the old product to go out of production, and then permitting the quality premium of the new product to erode. The statistics show a series of increases in value added as the quality improvements were captured by the reporting procedure, while the alternating declines in quality have been overlooked. It has been estimated that in Czechoslovakia this factor resulted in an exaggeration of real growth (and a corresponding underestimation of inflation) of about 2 percent a year in recent years.

6. For example, Austrians estimate that before the war their standard of living was comparable to that in Czechoslovakia, whereas now they are roughly twice as well off as the Czechoslovaks.

Table 3 External debts of the Eastern European countries, 1990

Country	Net debt (billions of dollars)	Debt per capita (dollars)	Net debt as a percentage of: Non-CMEA exports	Total exports	GNP
Bulgaria	9.8	1,090	468	126	20
Czechoslovakia	6.3	400	111	62	5
Hungary	20.3	1,910	343	244	36
Poland	41.8	1,100	418	314	28
Romania	1.3	60	38	23	2
Soviet Union	43.4	150	139	89	n.a.
Yugoslavia[a]	15.6	660	n.a.	84	34

n.a. = not available.

a. Data are for 1989.

Sources: OECD (1991, Special Feature tables 3 and 7). Debt-exports ratio figures use Economic Commission for Europe estimates of CMEA trade as a proportion of total trade, reducing this ratio by 10 percentage points for each country. Debt-GNP ratios use PlanEcon estimates of GNP. Figures for Yugoslavia are from IMF, *International Financial Statistics,* and World Bank, *World Debt Tables.*

Table 4 Estimated effects of shifting to world prices on the 1989 terms of trade and dollar values of trade balances of five Eastern European countries

Country	Percentage change in terms of trade	Change in trade balances (millions of dollars)
Bulgaria	− 24.0	− 1,617
Czechoslovakia	− 30.9	− 3,585
Hungary	− 36.7	− 2,080
Poland	− 22.6	− 1,480
Romania	− 31.4	− 2,677

Source: Kenen (1991).

satellites' transition to capitalism, and they hoped that their income gain would provide the wherewithal to finance reform at home. Estimates of the impact of the change in CMEA arrangements on the payments balances (and terms of trade) of five countries are shown in table 4. The whole of the gain corresponding to this loss, some $12 billion per year, will accrue to the Soviet Union—or at least it would have if the Soviet Union were still producing enough oil to maintain its previous level of exports. In practice the big shock has come from the collapse of export demand from the Soviet Union and East Germany.

The second shock, or rather series of shocks, came from the oil market. The Iraqi invasion of Kuwait in August 1990 sent the oil price sharply higher, further raising the oil bill of the countries of Eastern Europe excluding the Soviet Union, and conversely increasing Soviet receipts. Actually these effects were much muted by the fact that the CMEA pricing system ended only on 31 December 1990, and within three weeks of that date the oil price fell back sharply (close to its precrisis level) when the outbreak of war in the Persian Gulf was seen not to bring the calamitous impact on oil supply that had been feared.

More serious than the fluctuations in the oil price were two other factors. One was that faltering oil production in the Soviet Union led to drastic cutbacks in oil exports to Eastern Europe: this hurt the Soviet payments position and led to widespread shortages in the other countries, which had become highly dependent on Soviet oil. The other factor was that Bulgaria, Czechoslovakia, Poland, and Romania lost the substantial imports of Iraqi oil that they had been receiving in repayment of debts Iraq had incurred to finance previous imports from them.

These external shocks have certainly complicated the process of transition to a market economy. They have helped to create the difficulties that the region is currently enduring.

New Ambitions

The new regimes in Central Europe and East Germany were unambiguously in favor of moving to a market economy. They wished to see their countries "rejoin Europe" and recognized that the market economy was one of the key elements of the mainstream European tradition. They were quite prepared to run political risks in order to secure a rapid transformation of their countries' economic systems.[7]

It was initially taken for granted in the West that the Central Europeans' desire for a market economy would translate into a preference for a social market economy as practiced by their highly successful neighbors in West Germany, Austria, and Finland, rather than for a more laissez-faire approach. However, it became increasingly clear over the succeeding months that the old Austrian tradition of total skepticism about socialism, embodied in the writings of Friedrich von Hayek and Ludwig E. von Mises, exerts a strong influence on intellectual thought in the region (Lavigne 1991). Perhaps the most eloquent exponent of this approach (certainly the most eloquent in English) is the Czechoslovak Minister of Finance, Václav Klaus, who addressed the introductory session of

---

7. It is still unclear whether economic reform is an electoral asset or an albatross: in the fall of 1990 it looked for a time as though the reformers were going to be routed in the Polish elections, but they are still running Poland at the time of this writing.

the conference (chapter 2). Perhaps the apparent reluctance to embrace the social market economy is explained by the bad connotations in the East of anything labeled "social"—a legacy of the previous regime—or perhaps it reflects a realistic recognition of the dangers of attempting to provide social services more extravagant than the economy can afford.

No such reluctance found expression in the former East Germany, which was swallowed whole by the Federal Republic, with the apparent support at the time of most of its inhabitants. The social market economy will prevail at least there, since the former West Germany is paying for it.

The commitment to a market economy is somewhat less clear in the Balkans. Both Bulgaria and Romania overthrew their Communist regimes in late 1989: the former quickly and peacefully, the latter with difficulty and bloodshed. Both held free elections in 1990, which were in both cases won by parties dominated by former Communists with new labels (the Socialist Party in Bulgaria, the National Salvation Front in Romania). Both have nonetheless declared, in emphatic terms, that they are committed to building a market economy. Implementation of that ambition was much less far-reaching than in their northern neighbors as of January 1991 when the conference was held, but both have acted decisively since then.

Although Yugoslavia pioneered the break with Stalinism, it has now lost its lead over the countries of Central Europe in moving toward a market economy. Worker management remains very much a part of the system, and the country shows little urgency in replacing such cooperatives with privatized concerns. Recent legislation has removed the obstacles to private ownership, but few enterprises have been privatized, and the public sector remains dominant. Yugoslavia is, moreover, a country riven by ethnic disputes, which spill over into disagreements over economic policy. The northern (and richest) states of Slovenia and Croatia are intellectually a part of Central Europe, whereas the Serbian core is a part of the Balkans. An environment of ethnic conflict is not propitious for constructive economic change, which may explain why Yugoslavia is no longer on the cutting edge of reform.

The final Balkan socialist country, Albania, was not represented at the conference, because it showed no sign of wanting to reform when the conference was being planned. That changed in the weeks immediately prior to the conference, but the change happened too late to allow an invitation to be extended. It is not clear as this is written how extensive a reform effort will be mounted.

The remaining country is, of course, the largest of them all, the Soviet Union. It is also the country in which the range of views is broadest and the debate about the desirable direction of policy reform most intense. For several years after the world first learned the word *perestroika*, it seemed that the reforms envisaged were fairly modest, and certainly that they would not go beyond market socialism as it had been practiced in, say, Yugoslavia. However, every reform seemed to stimulate calls for even more extensive changes toward a market economy.

Attention switched from reforming socialism to making the transition to a market economy in late 1989, at very much the same time that the Soviet Union's former allies were also changing course. The Abalkin Plan of November 1989 was the first to propose transition to a market economy, albeit a "mixed planned market economy." Prime Minister Nikolai Ryzhkov presented a program the following month that spoke of developing something called a "regulated market economy"; it was never very clear exactly what this was supposed to mean, but the program at least recognized the need for private property. In 1990 competing programs were presented by the Soviet government and by the president of the Russian republic. Boris Yeltsin, with the latter (the Shatalin Plan) envisaging a 500-day transition to a market economy without any adjectival qualification. These programs were combined in various permutations, until ultimately the Supreme Soviet authorized President Mikhail Gorbachev to proceed on the basis of a set of "Presidential Guidelines" that were supposed to represent a synthesis of the competing plans.[8] But just as the Soviet Union appeared committed to real reform and a torrent of helpful Western advice was published on how to make the transition,[9] a conservative counterattack within the upper echelons of the Soviet hierarchy placed the prospects for further reform in jeopardy. It seems that battles are still to be fought in Moscow before the Soviet Union follows its former allies into the modern world; we can only hope they are fought on the intellectual plane and not with guns and bullets.

If the most important change in economic thinking over the past 30 years is the conclusion that markets work and planning doesn't, the second most important is in attitudes toward the international economy. Thirty years ago it was normal to see import substitution as the key to a backward country catching up with the developed world. Today, in the light of the comparative experience of the export-oriented economies in Spain and East Asia versus the import-substituters of Africa, South Asia, and Latin America, it is standard to favor outward orientation. The countries of Eastern Europe, with the possible exception of the Soviet Union, clearly and sensibly subscribe to the current conventional wisdom: they want to open up their economies and become integrated into the European and world

---

8. An accessible account of the various programs and the debate is contained in chapter V of a special issue of *European Economy* on Soviet reform (European Commission 1990).

9. In addition to the study in *European Economy*, the end of 1990 and the first weeks of 1991 witnessed publication of the report commissioned at the Houston Summit (International Monetary Fund et al. 1990), a study under the auspices of the International Institute for Applied Systems Analysis (IIASA; Peck et al. 1991), and another under the auspices of the World Institute for Development Economics Research (WIDER; Blanchard et al. 1991).

economies. Most of them hope that they can look forward to eventual membership in the European Community. They are nonetheless sufficiently realistic to
recognize that full membership in the Community is a long-term hope rather
than a short-run possibility, and that associate membership is the most that can
be hoped for in the next few years. Since the probability of acceptance by the
Community will be enhanced by opening up rather than pursuing an autarkic
policy, both the recognition of the economic advantages of outward orientation
and the desire for the geopolitical advantages of "joining Europe" point toward
a strategy of dismantling border controls and integrating into the world economy.
The question discussed at the Vienna conference, and pursued in the rest of this
chapter, is how that strategy should be designed.

The Issues

Eastern Europe is not the only area of the world that has sought to integrate
itself into the world economy in recent years: the shift to an outward orientation
has also been marked in Latin America (Williamson 1990). What makes Eastern
Europe distinctive is the magnitude of its parallel transformation from a planned
to a market economy. No reforming developing country has needed to create *ex
nihilo* anything like the full range of institutions of a market economy. Even
where the topics overlap, as with privatization, the scale is vastly different:
privatization in even the most statist Latin American countries referred to at most
a few hundred enterprises producing at most 40 percent of GDP, whereas in the
socialist economies it involves several thousand enterprises producing as much
as 95 percent of GDP.

The total absence of domestic competition or a functioning price system in the
ex-socialist economies has lent a particular urgency to their establishment of
currency convertibility, which therefore occupies a prominent place in the topics
treated here. The staple issues of trade and exchange rate policy are also covered.
Proposals for a payments union, for the introduction of a parallel currency in
the Soviet Union, and for early incorporation of the Eastern European currencies
into European monetary arrangements were also taken up at the Vienna conference and are discussed below. One important topic, the opening to foreign direct
investment, was omitted, except insofar as it bears on the need for currency
convertibility.

Alternative Concepts of Convertibility

"Convertibility" is a word with several meanings. The standard definition is that
a currency is convertible if it "is freely exchangeable for another currency"

(Pearce 1981, 82). In contradiction to earlier usage, convertibility does not today generally imply the right to convert at a fixed exchange rate, but it does imply the right to convert at the legal exchange rate, rather than just at an unofficial or parallel rate (at which the local currency is normally depreciated in comparison with the official rate).

What the standard definition leaves open is *who* should be allowed to exchange the currency freely, and *for what purposes* it should be freely exchangeable. If anyone is allowed to exchange the currency freely for any purpose at the legal exchange rate, then one speaks of "unrestricted convertibility." A currency becomes convertible in this sense only when exchange restrictions on capital exports are abolished, so that residents have the right to export capital in unlimited quantities at the official exchange rate. Nowadays most of the industrial countries have unrestricted convertibility, but this is very recent: France and Italy abolished their last capital controls only in 1990.

The traditional alternative to unrestricted convertibility is current account convertibility. This is the concept of convertibility embodied in Article VII, section 2(a) of the IMF's Articles of Agreement: ". . .no member shall, without the approval of the Fund, impose restrictions on the making of payments and transfers for current international transactions." In other words, anyone—whether a domestic importer or a foreign exporter or investor—should be able to exchange domestic for foreign currency at the official exchange rate to settle any transaction involving the purchase of goods or services from abroad, the payment of interest, or the repatriation of profits. In practice, current account convertibility has often been abridged by placing a ceiling on the sum that individuals are allowed to take out of the country for tourist expenditures (which are included in the current account): the main objective is usually to prevent the tourist allowance being misused as a mechanism for bypassing controls on the export of capital. Some debtor countries have also abridged current account convertibility by suspending the payment of interest on the foreign debt.

It is important to note that the substance of current account convertibility could be denied *de facto* if an abolition of exchange controls were accompanied by an intensification of trade restrictions. It is the joint product of exchange controls and trade restrictions that determines how fully a country's goods markets are integrated into the world market.

Discussion in Eastern Europe typically uses the concepts of internal and external convertibility rather than the traditional Western distinction between unrestricted and current account convertibility.[10] That is, the distinction relates to *who*

---

10. As pointed out earlier, the term "commodity convertibility" is also used, primarily to refer to the right of an enterprise to use its money balances to purchase goods without the permission of a planner. The term is sometimes used more broadly, to include the ability of households to use money to acquire goods, or the right of an enterprise to sell goods at its own discretion rather than to the purchaser earmarked by the planners.

should be allowed to exchange domestic for foreign currency, rather than to the *purpose* for which such exchange should be allowed. Internal convertibility relates to a right of domestic residents to make such exchanges, whereas external convertibility relates to an analogous right for foreigners, interpreted to include foreign investors. Thus, the statement that external convertibility deserves a higher priority (cf. Anulova, chapter 8) is typically justified by arguing that it is important to attract foreign investment and that this requires that the foreign investors be assured of the right to repatriate their earnings.

Which Concept to Use?

The first issue is which concept of convertibility should be pursued in the relevant future, meaning the next five years or so.

Polak (chapter 3) argues that the central purpose of convertibility in an emergent market economy is to permit the importation of competitive pressures and a rational price system from abroad. Breaking up monopolies is a time-consuming process even in those industries where economies of scale would permit efficient operation of several firms—a criterion that will in any case exclude most manufacturing industries in countries other than the Soviet Union (and possibly Poland). Freeing prices without introducing competitive pressures from somewhere is an invitation to the existing enterprises to abuse their monopoly power. Allowing an enterprise the right to buy foreign goods and the foreign exchange to pay for them—i.e., import liberalization plus convertibility—is the quick way of introducing a measure of competitive pressure into the tradeable-goods sector. It ensures that international relative prices will prevail in the domestic economy, give or take a margin for trade restrictions, transport costs, and the imperfections of arbitrage.[11] This in turn ensures that enterprises that face hard budget constraints[12] will encounter incentives to produce and trade in accordance with comparative advantage. Either current account convertibility or internal convertibility will serve these purposes.

---

11. Those margins can be quite wide, as is demonstrated by the well-established fact that the law of one price typically does not hold even within (let alone among) functioning market economies. They would be widened further still if transitional protection along the lines discussed below were to be introduced, or if the currency were drastically undervalued. Even in those circumstances, however, the world market provides some discipline on domestic price setting.

12. The Hungarian economist János Kornai introduced the notion that enterprises in socialist economies were typically confronted by "soft budget constraints," meaning that a failure to cover costs could always be offset by additional subsidies or borrowing rather than posing a threat of bankruptcy. Conversely, a hard budget constraint is one that does limit the enterprise's purchases, ultimately by the sanction of bankruptcy.

A second reason for convertibility is to encourage foreign direct investment. Without the right to remit profits in foreign currency, direct investors have to engage in a set of subsidiary business deals to repatriate their earnings; this acts as a severe deterrent to foreign investment. Current account convertibility permits the repatriation of earnings; capital repatriation can be added without difficulty (as is done in Latin America) by giving investors the right under the exchange control regulations to repatriate any capital that was registered with the central bank at the time of its arrival. Thus, encouraging the inflow of capital does *not* require unrestricted (i.e., capital account) convertibility. Note, however, that internal convertibility does not provide for the right to remit earnings of foreign investment: that requires (one aspect of) external convertibility.

A number of Eastern Europeans, including the architects of the Shatalin Plan for Soviet economic reform, have also argued for the right of households (but not enterprises or financial intermediaries) to convert local currency into foreign exchange on demand and to maintain foreign-exchange accounts. Given the enormous uncertainties that these economies face, it would seem distinctly imprudent to promise such convertibility, which might be prohibitively costly to maintain under adverse circumstances. However, it will be impossible in practice to prevent a parallel market from continuing to function, and so that market (and foreign-currency bank accounts) might as well be tolerated with good grace. One would hope that under normal circumstances the dollar will increasingly command only a small premium on the parallel market, but the premium will be free to rise in response to adverse shocks and thus provide a buffer limiting capital flight.

Unrestricted convertibility would be inadvisable for the Eastern European countries at the present stage, or indeed at any time soon. There is all the difference in the world between tolerating retail use of a parallel market by households wanting to place some of their assets abroad (despite the premium they have to pay for foreign exchange), and facilitating the wholesale export of savings by allowing enterprises and financial intermediaries to buy foreign assets with no financial penalty. Savings are needed at home during the years of economic reconstruction that lie ahead, and capital controls, even if not 100 percent effective, can help to keep them there. The countries of Eastern Europe would be well advised to delay the abolition of capital controls until reconstruction has been achieved, when such a luxury will be affordable.

The following set of arrangements, which are not described exactly by any of the existing terms but which overlap substantially with both current account convertibility and internal convertibility, would effectively address the needs assessed above. Enterprises (including foreign investors) would be allowed to buy foreign exchange at the official rate in order to finance current account transactions; they would also be required to sell their earnings of foreign exchange at the official rate. This would enable them to pay for imports of goods and services and to repatriate profits at the same rate at which they earned foreign exchange through exporting. The export of capital would be subject to exchange controls; permission would be given automatically to repatriate capital upon maturity of a loan or at any time by a direct investor provided that the inflow was registered with the central bank when it arrived, but other capital exports would be prohibited unless the authorities saw some particular national advantage accruing from the transaction.

Households and tourists would have to go to the parallel market to obtain foreign exchange. This recognizes the reality that there will be retail capital export by individuals, mostly as a counterpart to foreign tourist expenditures. And it automatically takes care of the derogation from current account convertibility regarding outward tourist expenditures that was noted above.

"Convertibility" should be interpreted in the sense described above in the remainder of this chapter. Unrestricted convertibility, involving unification of the two exchange markets and withdrawal of the proscription on export of capital by enterprises and institutions, should be postponed until economic reconstruction is complete. In the interim, however, macroeconomic policy should be sufficiently tight to keep the premium on the parallel market modest.

Conditions for Convertibility

It is generally although not universally accepted that a number of conditions have to be satisfied in order to make the establishment of convertibility a prudent act.[13] History abounds with cases, from Great Britain in 1947 to Yugoslavia in late 1990, where necessary conditions were not satisfied and therefore a promise of convertibility had to be withdrawn.

Critics of the notion that certain conditions need to be satisfied if convertibility is to be advised generally have a Hayekian faith that markets can always find the right price for everything, and in particular that a freely floating exchange rate is the best way to determine the value of a currency. As noted earlier, such ideas have a strong foothold in Central Europe. I am not myself persuaded that floating would be a wise policy for the emerging market economies of Eastern Europe, for reasons that will be explained in detail in the discussion below concerning the choice of an exchange rate regime.

Assuming that the exchange rate is not to be allowed to float, the maintenance of convertibility requires that the central bank not exhaust its stock of foreign-exchange reserves. So the question becomes, What are the conditions under

---

13. These conditions are often referred to as "preconditions," but in fact it suffices if some of them are established simultaneously with convertibility; hence they are in reality conditions rather than preconditions.

which the central bank can be confident of avoiding reserve depletion without imposing intolerable costs (in terms of deflation) and while maintaining convertibility? Those conditions fall into two categories, macroeconomic and microeconomic.

First, macroeconomic policy must be such that the foreign-exchange position is manageable. This requires both an adequate *stock* of reserves and a reasonably satisfactory *flow* balance of payments position. The latter needs a competitive exchange rate as well as control over domestic demand; hence any monetary overhang must have been (or be) dealt with, monetary policy must be firm, and fiscal discipline must be in place. In the absence of those conditions, demand for imports will inevitably be so high as to threaten the sustainability of convertibility.

A declaration of convertibility that is not perceived to be sustainable is unlikely to carry credibility. Convertibility that is not expected to last long will provoke an import surge as importers seek to exploit the window of opportunity before restrictions are reimposed. Hence a lack of credibility will confront the authorities with a brutal choice between abandoning convertibility and deflating demand. It was precisely the fear of such a choice being imposed by the balance of payments constraint that made the Western European countries so cautious (after the British experience of 1947) in moving to convertibility in the 1950s.

There is a delicate judgment as to just how satisfactory the balance of payments situation needs to be to justify a move to convertibility. In retrospect it seems clear that Western Europe was excessively timid in delaying convertibility until the danger of the balance of payments acting as a constraint on macroeconomic policy had practically vanished. But that is no excuse for lurching to the other extreme.

The microeconomic condition for convertibility would seem to be that the economy has made the fundamental shift from a planned to a market economy. As long as most decisions on resource allocation are made centrally by the planners rather than in a decentralized way by enterprises and households, it makes no sense to devolve those decisions for one particular activity, namely importing, which is what convertibility would imply. To put the matter another way, currency convertibility without commodity convertibility would concentrate all unsatisfied demands on the foreign sector, where they would add to the demand for imports. And as long as enterprises are not subject to hard budget constraints, those demands could be unlimited (Kornai 1990, 156).

One essential element of the shift from a planned to a market economy is in fact granting enterprises the right to spend money balances as they see fit (commodity convertibility). A second is the establishment of a hard budget constraint, which if violated imposes the ultimate penalty of bankruptcy. A third is that enterprises should be able to set prices for themselves, subject to the sanction of losing customers and thus jeopardizing their continued viability if they set prices above what the market will bear. All three of these changes are essential complements to what is often referred to as "de-étatization"—making enterprises responsible for their own destiny rather than leaving them as agents of the state subject to direction by the planners.

Privatization is another much-emphasized aspect of the move to a market economy, but it is one that I would argue is both less fundamental and less urgent. It is less fundamental because it is at least in principle possible to conceive of a market economy functioning without private ownership, as the vision of market socialism (Lange 1937) showed. Indeed, worker-managed enterprises and worker-management cooperatives have operated in several Eastern European countries—not always as one might have wished, but apparently in some cases efficiently enough to justify following the adage to avoid fixing what is not broken (Jorgensen et al. 1990). And it is less urgent because the *expectation* of future privatization is enough to change the motivation of managers and workers, provided at least that they are promised a share in the proceeds of privatization. As Sir Alan Walters (1991, 29) has recently pointed out, the major efficiency gains from privatization in the United Kingdom under Prime Minister Margaret Thatcher were achieved while the enterprises were being prepared for privatization. It is of course crucial that privatization be expected in the not-too-distant future, for otherwise the attractions of the easy life possible in state industry will dominate; but there is no need to insist on privatizing everything immediately.

A rather different set of preconditions for convertibility is offered by Mario Nuti (chapter 3) in his discussion of the papers by Jacques Polak and Friedrich Levcik:

- Market-clearing prices without excessively inflationary conditions;

- No generalized subsidies on tradeable goods;

- Significant price elasticity of demand and supply.

Nuti's first condition is perhaps a more concise description of the microeconomic and macroeconomic conditions that I have tried to spell out above. His second condition seems to me exaggerated: subsidies may undermine fiscal discipline, and they might conceivably nurture such a reluctance to export that a satisfactory payments position is inconceivable, but I find it more natural to focus on those possible results than on the subsidies per se. His third condition demands a "significant" response to price changes on the ground that in its absence devaluation will not improve the balance of payments but only worsen the terms of trade. In fact, in the small-country case where both foreign elasticities are infinite, devaluation has no effect on the terms of trade and the balance of payments improves provided only that the domestic elasticities are nonzero (the mathematical proof can be found in Williamson 1983, 152), so I would not want to include this condition.

To summarize, convertibility should not be attempted in advance of the fundamental transformation to a market economy. It also requires adequate reserves and the orthodox conditions for macroeconomic stabilization.

The Timing of Convertibility

Few issues have proved as controversial in discussions of the transition to a market economy as that of the speed and sequencing of reform, and this held true at the Vienna conference. Until late 1989 it was taken as axiomatic that any transition would be a long-drawn-out affair, with the changes spaced over many years. Convertibility was regarded as an aim for the next century, which would match the time it took for Western Europe to reestablish convertibility after the Second World War. Then along came the Polish "big bang," in which the Polish authorities announced their intention of making the transition to a market economy in one leap. The establishment of convertibility was one of this set of simultaneous reforms.

Attitudes were transformed overnight. Now, as Levcik (chapter 3) complains, everyone vies to support a bigger bang than his neighbor, and any reluctance to do everything together is taken to be a sign of a lack of virility. All of the three Western reports on Soviet economic reform (the Houston Summit study, the IIASA report, and the WIDER report) conclude that comprehensive reform must involve simultaneous action on a wide front. The Shatalin 500-day program for Soviet reform was criticized for being about 499 days too long. Levcik argues that precipitate haste will inevitably be costly in terms of economic disruption, and that the recessions in Poland and the former East Germany (where industrial output fell by a staggering 50 percent in the first months after unification) give a foretaste of what has to be expected elsewhere unless the current haste gives way to a more measured pace of reform. If the transition proves too costly, it could undermine popular support for reform (as some argue has already happened in the Soviet Union, although others might retort that it is difficult to classify Soviet reform efforts to date as precipitate).

Why should fast reform be costly? One possible reason is that pressure for rapid change may prevent plans from being properly prepared, as Bundesbank President Karl Otto Pöhl argued was the case when the deutsche mark was introduced into East Germany in July 1990.[14] This is clearly an argument for proper preparation, however, and not one for planning that the adjustment should be lengthy and phased rather than implemented in a single, decisive step

---

14. Speech before the European Parliament's committee on economic and monetary affairs, reported in *Financial Times*, 20 March 1991.

once the plans are ready. Nuti (chapter 3) addresses the question of why a one-shot introduction of convertibility might be more costly:

> The faster the rush to convertibility, the higher the cost. A relatively rapid move to convertibility increases the share of low-positive-value-added activities that have to be run down, and increases the impact on the terms of trade, price elasticities being lower in the short than in the longer term. Hence, the faster the move to convertibility, the greater the domestic-currency undervaluation necessary to ensure its credibility.

Nuti's first argument is close to the point argued by Ronald I. McKinnon in his paper for the Vienna conference (chapter 4); as discussed in the section on trade policy below, it can be taken care of by allowing transitional protection. Nuti's second point, however, is questionable, as the preceding section explained: the cost of devaluation in a small economy is not a worsening of the terms of trade (which are largely exogenous) but simply a bigger currency undervaluation. This constitutes his third point, which is very much on the mark. The introduction of convertibility prior to reasonable satisfaction of the conditions enumerated in the previous section will require a highly undervalued currency to maintain confidence, given the need to secure a viable balance of payments position and to check a surge of imports inspired by the fear that convertibility may be temporary. Currency undervaluation is stagflationary, at least in the short run until exports have time to respond, since prices are both pushed and pulled up while the resulting real-balance effect cuts demand.

The conference did seem to make some progress toward a meeting of minds on this issue. Jacques Polak argued that the reason why early establishment of convertibility was crucial to the Eastern European countries was their pressing need "to subject domestic producers to competitive pressures from abroad and, in the process, to 'import' a system of economic pricing" (chapter 3). This implies that convertibility "must not be delayed in time or qualified in scope to any important extent."

Levcik's exposition focused on the conditions that need to be satisfied before convertibility is introduced rather than on the desirability of phasing the process of convertibility. He argued that one could not sensibly introduce convertibility before deregulating domestic prices, and that the latter has its own preconditions, which require time to be put into place. He writes (chapter 3):

> Can domestic price liberalization be introduced at one stroke? It has been done in the former East Germany . . . with disastrous results for the population, although there the adverse effects have been cushioned by huge gifts from the West German government. . . . The other countries of the region can hardly expect any similar level of outside support. Under more realistic circumstances, domestic price liberalization has to involve doing away with price subsidies at each of the circuits mentioned [wholesale, retail, agricultural purchase, and foreign trade]. . . . [T]hese separated price circuits must be linked by unifying, to the extent possible, the existing turnover tax rates (later to

become value-added taxes) and introducing the legal and organizational instruments needed to execute a prudent fiscal and monetary policy. The process of de-étatization and demonopolization of state enterprises, and of establishing a functioning and expanding private sector, ought also to be well under way, to ensure the presence of a sufficient range of independent economic agents when prices are free to be determined by the market. Once the most important preconditions have been met, the bulk of domestic prices ought to be freed at one stroke. . . . [the] introduction of currency convertibility belongs to a later stage of the transformation process.

In fact the conditions that Polak and Levcik specify as necessary for convertibility are not that different. Both agree that domestic prices must be liberalized and budget constraints hardened, and that the macroeconomy must be in reasonable balance, as was argued in the previous section of this paper. Note that the latter condition will limit the degree of undervaluation that is needed, thus addressing the stagflationary danger highlighted by Nuti.

Clearly there do exist some differences between Polak's and Levcik's positions, perhaps most notably as to whether one should delay price liberalization until demonopolization is well under way. However, in the final session of the conference Levcik emphasized that what he regarded as the crucial point was that convertibility was not just a matter of political will but a step with certain requirements. He did not object to introducing convertibility in a single step, and perhaps even simultaneously with some of the conditions he specified, provided that the necessary conditions were satisfied.

My own view is that Levcik is right to emphasize the potential disruption from making many changes simultaneously, but that as argued above there are nonetheless compelling reasons for doing a number of things at the same time. This suggests that one should seek to identify the *smallest* package of measures that is needed to make the fundamental transition from a planned to a market economy without running into second-best problems that might jeopardize the success of reform. The aim should not be a big bang per se, but rather the minimum critical size of bang (Williamson 1991a), or, for short, a "minimum bang."

Such a minimum bang clearly needs to include the microeconomic measures that characterize the transition to a market economy, as discussed in the previous section: the hardening of budget constraints, commodity convertibility, price liberalization, and preferably the other elements of de-étatization. It seems to me that it should also include convertibility and import liberalization, for the reasons that Polak spells out: that this is the only way to secure competitive pressures and a rational price system quickly, and that without those elements price liberalization could make things worse rather than better. Note that this provides a cogent justification for the greater urgency that the Eastern Europeans are displaying in seeking convertibility, compared with what happened in Western Europe in the 1950s. Western Europe at that time already had a functioning market economy with competitive pressures and prices that reflected scarcity, so convertibility was a luxury that permitted consumers to get the best value out of the economy's productive capabilities rather than a necessity to give the market economy a chance to get off the ground.

Does the minimum bang need to contain other components as well? It is now widely understood that few reforms have a chance of succeeding in the absence of macroeconomic stability. Ideally, it may be better to introduce a macroeconomic stabilization package prior to the move to a market economy, but this may not be feasible, for example because the price rises needed to eliminate subsidies and balance the budget would be politically acceptable only as part of a reform package that gives hope of making the transition to a market economy. Hence one has to leave open the possibility that the minimum bang may need to have a component of macroeconomic stabilization to accompany the microeconomic liberalization and external opening. Countries that start off from a situation of crisis (like Poland, Bulgaria, Romania, and the Soviet Union) are far more likely to need a big bang than those that have preserved a functioning economy (like Czechoslovakia and Hungary).

The Payments Union Proposal

When it first became clear that virtually the whole of Eastern Europe was intent on making the historic transition to a market economy but was likely to face severe balance of payments constraints in the process, a number of economists recalled the valuable role that the European Payments Union (EPU) had played in easing payments problems during the postwar reconstruction of Western Europe. The prospective end of the CMEA threatened to intensify the payments constraints faced during the process of reform (except in the Soviet Union). Hence the question soon arose as to whether a mechanism similar to the EPU might be helpful in Eastern Europe. In each case one had an industrial region in need of economic reconstruction, with a relatively high level of intratrade conducted subject to the constraint of bilateral balance, suffering from a shortage of liquid international reserves, and offering good medium-run growth potential given the abundant availability of skilled human resources. If the EPU had done so much to revive the fortunes of Western Europe (Kaplan and Schleiminger 1989), perhaps an analogous institution should be created to serve Eastern Europe in the 1990s.

This proposal has been pursued most forcefully by Jozef M. van Brabant, who presented a paper advocating establishment of a Central European Payments Union (CEPU) to the Vienna conference (chapter 4). His advocacy stemmed from deep skepticism as to whether the Central European countries would succeed in maintaining the convertibility that two of them (Poland and Czecho-slovakia) had already declared and that Hungary is approaching. Moreover, even after making the zloty convertible for imports from the West, Poland had continued to conduct trade with its Central European neighbors through the traditional clearing mechanism, *de facto* penalizing imports from those countries as compared to those from the West. Thus, Brabant saw the Central European countries at best discriminating against one another, and at worst he feared the collapse of their intratrade. Prospects for the maintenance of trade among the other Eastern European countries would seem even more doubtful.

A payments union is an arrangement in which the member countries agree that they will accept one another's currencies in payment for exports, deposit their earnings from those exports with the agent of the union, allow the claims to be consolidated and periodically netted out on a multilateral basis, and then settle the remaining imbalances centrally with the union in a mixture of credit and convertible currencies. So long as settlement is less than 100 percent in convertible currencies, a payments deficit with a fellow member of the union will impose a smaller reserve loss than an equal deficit with a nonmember, thus giving the authorities an incentive to discriminate in favor of imports from fellow members. Of course, since every member will have such an incentive, exports to union members will be stimulated as well as imports enlarged, and *ex post* the deficit with the union need not be larger than it would have been in the absence of a payments union. On average it is the *level* of trade among the members, rather than the size of their imbalances, that one expects to be higher. This can be very helpful in a situation of acute liquidity shortage such as afflicted postwar Western Europe, since it permitted a great deal of liberalization of intra-area trade that would not have been feasible if it had had to be extended immediately to the dollar area as well. As reserves were rebuilt, trade with the dollar area was liberalized and the discrimination was phased out.

Brabant's proposal came in for a good deal of criticism at the Vienna confer-ence, especially from Jacques Polak in chapter 3 and from all three of the discussants in chapter 4 (Peter B. Kenen, Dariusz K. Rosati, and John Flemming). One issue concerned the sharp contrasts between the scope of the EPU in 1950 and the likely scope of an EEPU in 1991. The EPU covered the bulk of the participants' trade and provided much scope for multilateral netting out. In contrast, an EEPU would be limited to a very small proportion of the participants' trade if the payments union excluded the Soviet Union. (If it included the Soviet Union, it would probably face the problem that the Soviet Union would be a structural creditor, given that energy prices were adjusted to the world level on 1 January 1991.) Thus, it was argued, the potential benefits of an EEPU are at best small.

The second criticism was that in order to make an EEPU work it would be necessary for Poland and Czechoslovakia to go back on the liberalization they have already achieved. A payments union provides an incentive for the *authorities* of the members to prefer imports from a fellow member to those from a third party, but that does not automatically translate into an incentive for an individual *enterprise* to prefer imports from a fellow member, and it is the decisions of the enterprises that are relevant in a market economy. Postwar Western Europe had a set of exchange controls that could be differentially liberalized to permit imports from the EPU area that were still forbidden from outside. But Poland and Czechoslovakia have now abolished exchange controls on most current account transactions (and, indeed, controls apply to only a minority of transactions in Hungary), so that establishment of a payments union would seem to require those countries to go backward and reimpose exchange controls. That is unappealing. Much better, several participants argued, would be to institute tariff preferences in favor of one another, if some form of preference to intratrade is desired. But that points to establishment of a customs union or a free trade area (a proposal that will be considered in the section on trade policy below), not of a payments union.

Brabant conceded during the conference discussion that a payments union would be redundant *if* the Central European countries succeed in maintaining their newly established convertibility, *provided* that they treat each other's exports as coming from the convertible-currency area. He obviously retained some doubts on both scores. In fact, it seems that Hungary and Czechoslovakia currently have a bilateral agreement that allows for the settlement of their intratrade in local currency: a Czech or Slovak importer can pay a Hungarian exporter in Czechoslovak korunas, which the latter can present to his bank, receiving Hungarian forints in return. A Czech or Slovak importer presumably prefers to pay in korunas rather than in dollars, because this saves him the trouble of buying dollars, whereas the Hungarian importer is indifferent because he ultimately receives forints in either event. Net imbalances are settled in dollars. Brabant's proposal amounts to extending this arrangement to Poland, multilateralizing it, and allowing the imbalances to be settled in a mixture of dollars and credit. It is not clear that this would do much good, because the scope of the payments union and the incentive to use the mechanism would both be so modest, but it surely could not do any harm.

In March 1991 the Russian republic and the Czech republic announced that they were considering abandoning the CMEA agreement to conduct trade in dollars because this had led to an 80 percent fall in Czechoslovak exports to the Soviet Union. Apparently they are considering a bilateral payments agreement. In early April, Soviet Prime Minister Valentin Pavlov described the switch to hard-currency trade with Poland as a mistake, and newspaper reports indicated that Poland had urged that trade with the Soviet Union should be run on a clearing system. Hence it certainly should not be taken for granted that the move to trading in dollars is definitive.

Nevertheless, this is unlikely to revive the prospects for a payments union. Such a union makes much more sense on technical grounds for countries that do not have convertible currencies than for those that do, but if the Soviet Union is soon to be the only country without a convertible currency, it can hardly have a payments union with itself. In any event, there would be political reluctance to recreate an organization that looked too much like the CMEA. A series of bilateral agreements between the Soviet Union and its neighbors seems much more likely and more appropriate to the situation.

Trade Policy

Most of the controversy about trade policy at the Vienna conference concerned the proposals for transitional tariff protection presented by Ronald McKinnon (chapter 4). Two other propositions that would surely have been highly controversial a few years ago were never questioned. One is that nonprice restrictions on imports should be eliminated rapidly; indeed, formal currency convertibility without such a phaseout would achieve little. The second is that the ultimate objective should be something close to free trade—a uniform tariff of perhaps 10 percent, or participation in the European economic space (either full or associate membership in the European Community or the European Free Trade Association).

McKinnon argued that Poland and the former East Germany had made a mistake in moving so rapidly to a situation of virtual free trade with the West. Many of their firms were simply unable to compete against imports, and industrial output therefore fell precipitously. A bigger real devaluation, even if it can be made to stick, is not necessarily much help, because devaluation increases the local-currency cost of inputs of energy and other raw materials *pari passu* with the raising of the local-currency price of output. The problem, according to McKinnon, is that socialist enterprises responded rationally to the very low prices of energy and other materials under the CMEA system by substituting those for other inputs. Now that the prices of energy and materials have suddenly risen to the world level with the demise of the CMEA, many industrial enterprises find that their material inputs cost more at world prices than the world market value of the goods they can produce. In other words, value added is negative at world prices.

Many economists will react by denying that, even if this is true, it poses any particular policy problem. An enterprise that produces negative value added will benefit society by closing down. McKinnon argues that what this overlooks is that many of these enterprises would be capable of adjusting their factor input mix to the new realities if given time. In a functioning market economy we would expect the managers of any enterprise that would eventually be capable of adjusting to go to their bank manager and seek a loan to tide them over a temporary period of losses, and we would expect bankers to be able and willing to advance loans to enterprises capable of adjusting, thus avoiding inappropriate bankruptcies. But one of the problems in the emerging market economies is the absence of bank managers trained in the art of loan appraisal, so that solution is impractical. Another potential way of tiding companies over would be for the government to give them subsidies, but this would run directly counter to the need to establish fiscal discipline and to harden budget constraints. Much better, McKinnon argues, to grant temporary tariff protection to the sorts of industries that were most subsidized by the low prices of energy and materials in the past, and then phase the protection out gradually over ten years or so. Some firms will go bankrupt anyway, but they will at least get the chance to see whether they are capable of adjusting, rather than be confronted with massive changes that throw a lot of enterprises out of business at the same time.

Although McKinnon accepts that a finely differentiated tariff structure would be undesirable, because it would create opportunities for corruption and other rent-seeking behavior, he argues against the uniform tariff that has been urged by most other Western economists advising the Soviet Union (e.g., the Houston Summit report, the IIASA report, and the WIDER report). His objective is to give temporary but initially substantial protection to the industries that previously got the greatest implicit protection through the low cost of energy and material inputs (he favors withdrawing the subsidy immediately so as to create an incentive to economize on the use of those inputs right from the start). He suggests that this criterion implies "a cascading tariff scaled downward according to the distance from the consumer and the degree of manufacturing complexity." Industrial materials would carry the lowest tariff (say, 10 percent, which might also be the level of the ultimate uniform tariff), followed by capital goods and manufactured intermediate products, then consumer nondurables, and finally consumer durables, on which the initial tariff might be as high as 100 percent.

Both McKinnon's diagnosis and his policy recommendations are controversial. Besides being attacked by Jeffrey Sachs in *The Economist* on 19 January 1991, they elicited several criticisms during the conference. Dariusz Rosati suggested that McKinnon was assuming a semi-Stalinist economy such as that still prevalent in the Soviet Union as his starting point, and argued that conditions in the rest of Eastern Europe were very different. There have been almost no bankruptcies in Poland or Hungary, and certainly nothing like the wave of simultaneous bankruptcies conjured up by McKinnon (although admittedly his diagnosis seems much more apt for the former East Germany). Polish industry has not been overwhelmed by a flood of imports, so this is not a plausible explanation for the Polish recession. The massive devaluation of the zloty provided Polish industry with plenty of protection, at least for a time.

So far as McKinnon's prescriptions are concerned, one has to have a lot of faith in the old infant-industry argument for protection (for the issue is analytically the same, as Rosati points out) to override the standard presumption that industries that consume more than they produce should be closed down as quickly as possible. On the other hand, there is a second and in my view more persuasive justification for transitional protection, which appeals to the desirability of keeping industries with positive but low value added operating in the short run. The capital stock that will be needed by the new export industries cannot be put in place instantaneously. Until it is there, it is better that the labor they will need be employed on activities with positive but low value added than that it should sit idle. Hence the case for "senile-industry protection," which can be phased out gradually to match the arrival of new production capacity in more economic activities.

Even accepting that argument, there may be some apprehensions about the validity of McKinnon's policy recommendations. For example, it is not altogether obvious that his criterion of giving the highest transitional protection to the industries that in the past got the biggest subsidies from the underpricing of energy and materials justifies the particular pattern of cascading that he advocates. Again, it could be asked whether the analysis, even if correct for the Soviet Union with its indigenous supplies of energy and materials, carries over to the other countries of Eastern Europe, which are dependent on imports of primary inputs from the Soviet Union, at prices that (since 1 January 1991) are no longer subsidized. I would argue that the analysis *is* still relevant, since low value added is still better than zero value added, and if negative short-run value added is really justified by long-run gains when the cost is an opportunity cost, then it will still be justified when the cost is an explicit cost of importing. But spelling out the latter case does make one wonder even more whether there will be many cases where the preservation of activities with negative value added is justifiable.

Although McKinnon's proposals were subject to considerable criticism at the conference, they also attracted some support. For example, Gabor Oblath (chapter 6) argued that temporary tariff protection would be preferable to a very sharp devaluation as a way of compensating for the removal of nonprice restrictions on imports, since devaluation is inflationary. One should of course ask why, for a given short-run effect in improving the balance of payments, import tariffs would be less inflationary than devaluation. I would suggest that there are three good reasons. First, tariffs raise revenue and thus improve the country's fiscal position, whereas devaluation has that effect only if the government owns the export industries. Second, devaluation pushes up the prices of all goods, including intermediate goods and necessities, whereas (according to the McKinnon cascading scheme, at least[15]) tariffs are concentrated on less essential goods. Even

15. Actually McKinnon's cascade proposal may be more persuasively rationalized on this ground than by his own argument, which depends upon durable consumer goods requiring proportionately greater inputs of energy and materials than, for example, capital goods.

if these enter the price index proportionately, the different distributional impact may make a given measured inflation less prone to provoke demands for higher wages. Third, the prospect of future declines in the price of durable consumer goods as the tariffs are removed will create an intertemporal substitution effect in favor of delaying consumption.[16]

In asking why Hungary has not followed the path of transitional tariff protection, Oblath suggested that at least part of the explanation lay in the country's relations with the General Agreement on Tariffs and Trade (GATT). Having declared to the GATT when it joined that Hungary had no nonprice restrictions on imports, it was then difficult for the government to tell the GATT that it planned to substitute temporary tariffs for restrictions that supposedly did not exist. Clearly there is a problem of "face," but it is one that the GATT should be attempting to minimize. Unfortunately some Western GATT negotiators seem instead all too pleased to exploit this problem and hold the Eastern European countries to the letter of their obligations. Those of us who believe that countries benefit from free trade in anything but the short run find it lamentable that mercantilist-minded trade officials should deny these countries the option of liberalizing their trade in the most efficient way possible; the effect of their inflexibility may be to raise the cost of transition and possibly jeopardize the long-run political saleability of a rational trade policy. The right policy would be to combine a willingness to accept temporary tariffs with strong commitments to the GATT to phase them out over five or ten years. This would provide an answer to Rosati's fear (chapter 4) that transitional tariff protection could all too easily become permanent, since foreign pressure would ensure that it did not.

As mentioned in the previous section, several participants in the Vienna conference expressed the view that any deliberate attempt to encourage intratrade among the countries of Eastern Europe would be better done through a free trade arrangement (a customs union or a free trade area) than through a payments union. Since the countries of the region were all subject to similar price

---

16. This analysis provides an argument for avoiding a greater devaluation than is needed to produce balance of payments equilibrium without import restrictions *in the medium term*. It relies upon the proposition that exports are limited in the short run by installed capacity. This means that beyond some point further devaluation does little to stimulate exports quickly: indeed, this will be true even in the medium term, since exporters will be skeptical whether a hypercompetitive exchange rate will last long enough to allow them to benefit from investment undertaken now. If further import compression is needed in order to get imports down to the fixed level set by export receipts so as to satisfy the foreign-exchange constraint, then there do appear to be benefits in achieving the reduction by temporary tariffs. But this is no argument for a permanent policy of keeping the currency overvalued and compensating the balance of payments effect by protection, which is subject to the standard objection that it distorts resource allocation, since the domestic resource cost of the marginal imports forgone will exceed that of the marginal exports displaced. Nor does this argument apply to a creditworthy country, which has the less costly alternative of borrowing to tide itself over temporary problems.

distortions in the past, McKinnon's argument for transitional protection does not apply to their intratrade. (Actually Hungary already brought its energy prices closer to the world level in the early 1980s, so this argument has to be qualified. Nevertheless, Romania surely need not fear devastation of its economy by Hungarian exports in a manner analogous to West Germany's takeover of the East German market.)

A free trade agreement among the countries of Eastern Europe could also provide a practical demonstration of their ability to act cooperatively, which could be reassuring to potential Western investors fearful of an intensification of traditional nationalistic antagonisms in the region. And it could make the Eastern European countries appear more attractive partners for acceptance into the European Community in due course. Add to that the competitive benefits of creating an environment in which restructuring can bring intraindustry trade, and the attractions of an early move to establish a regional free trade grouping are considerable. Nonetheless it seems that regional free trade is more likely to come as a by-product of several countries joining EFTA than as a result of an agreement confined to the countries of the region. Given that they show no signs of heeding McKinnon's advice to resort to high transitional tariffs, not much will be lost by the absence of an interim free trade arrangement.

Exchange Rate Policy

Would emergent market economies be best served by a fixed or a floating exchange rate, or by something in between?

There are three powerful arguments against floating in the emergent market economies of Eastern Europe. The first, emphasized by Peter Bofinger (chapter 4), is the difficulty of interpreting the traditional monetary indicators during the transition to a market economy. A floating exchange rate needs to be accompanied by an autonomous monetary policy based on well-defined principles, such as seeking a steady growth of the money supply or of nominal income. Such a monetary policy is impracticable or undesirable when such crucial variables as the demand for money or the propensity to save are liable to change unpredictably as a result of fundamental changes in economic organization. In particular, stabilization of inflation normally induces a desire to build up holdings of domestic money (by a large but uncertain amount), and this should be accommodated rather than allowed to appreciate the currency.

The second argument against floating is that a floating rate can be expected to function efficiently only in the presence of a well-developed capital market, which can allow shocks to be absorbed through changes in asset positions. These countries do not at present have such markets, and it was argued above that they should not at this stage contemplate the liberalization of the capital account that would be necessary to support a floating rate.

The third argument is not confined to economies in transition to the market, but it applies to them as well. This is the unsatisfactory record of floating even in economies that have had an adequate basis for conducting monetary policy and a well-developed capital market: notably, the demonstrated propensity of floating rates to generate periodic severe misalignments that produce large trade imbalances and consequent distortions in the economy. A range of factors can generate such misalignments even when government policies are impeccable: rational and irrational speculative bubbles, and interactions that generate "chaotic" behavior in the foreign-exchange market (see Williamson and Milner 1991, chapter 14.5, for a brief survey). There is scant evidence that markets can be relied on to pick the "right" exchange rate. An overvalued currency, or even the fear that it may become overvalued in the future, can discourage exports. This is liable to be particularly damaging in economies where economic recovery almost has to be export-led, as in Eastern Europe.

Apart from a vague reverence for the market, two main arguments are advanced by those in Eastern Europe who favor floating. One is that governments lack the knowledge to pick the right exchange rate. Obviously no one is going to deny that this is a genuine problem: I suggest below the principle that should underlie the choice of an exchange rate, but it is one that cannot be expected to lead to more than a rough-and-ready answer. The question is whether that answer is more or less reliable than that given by a floating rate. Given the size of the misalignments that have been observed in the past, even where conditions for floating are better than in Eastern Europe, the authorities surely have the ability to do better.

The other argument in favor of floating is that at times there is no alternative. A government without reserves cannot defend a pegged exchange rate, so it should not try. In fact there is an alternative, namely the dual-rate system discussed below, but this too is a second-best reaction to a reserve shortage and not something obviously superior to a floating rate.

Even if one ends up concluding that a floating rate is to be avoided if at all possible, one has to recognize that the classic alternative to a floating exchange rate, namely, a fixed (nominal) exchange rate, has its own problems. Permanent maintenance of a fixed exchange rate requires a willingness to allow the money supply to be determined by the balance of payments: a payments deficit must be allowed to reduce the money supply and raise interest rates, so as to cure the deficit without a change in the exchange rate. In countries where capital markets are undeveloped, there is little scope to vary fiscal policy independently of monetary policy, and hence no domestic stabilization policy will be practicable.

It is true that nowadays there is little faith, such as existed in Western Europe during its postwar recovery, that demand management can stabilize employment. Moreover, there do exist circumstances where a fixed nominal exchange rate with a low-inflation area like the European Community can act as a nominal anchor and ensure price stability. The problem is that those circumstances demand a lot more than is suggested by the current buzzword, "credibility." Inflationary inertia can be caused by forward-looking expectations and a lack of credibility, but it can also be caused by indexation, by backward-looking expectations, or by inconsistent real income claims.[17] A totally credible fixed nominal exchange rate will deal adequately with inflation in the first case, but in the other three cases it will deal with inflation by inflicting a prolonged recession and snuffing out hopes of quickly beginning to catch up with the West.

For these reasons it would seem prudent for the emerging market economies to contemplate exchange rate regimes intermediate between the classic alternatives of fixed rates and free floating. It also seems important to distinguish between the short run when the economy is first opened and the longer term.

The discussion of the transition to a market economy has added an important argument for fixing the exchange rate in the short run. The prices inherited from a regime of central planning typically bear no relation to scarcity, and a main purpose of establishing convertibility is to permit the importation of a price system from abroad. This process will be facilitated by the existence of a fixed exchange rate to provide an anchor for the new price structure. Any country making the move to a market economy—and, as argued above, there do seem to be strong arguments for simultaneously making a number of changes that add up to a discrete change from a planned economy to the market—should probably aim to hold its exchange rate fixed for a while after first liberalizing prices. A country that is at the same time stabilizing a hyperinflation that has taught people to think in terms of dollar prices has an extra incentive to opt for a short-run stabilization of the exchange rate.

The case for seeking to preserve a fixed exchange rate in the long run is much less compelling, at least until such time as these countries may be in a position to contemplate consolidating their future membership in the European Community and its prospective monetary union. Real shocks may arise that require a real exchange rate adjustment—a process that can usually be facilitated by a change in the nominal exchange rate. Moreover, all the signs are that it is going to be difficult for the Eastern European countries to get their inflation rates down to the ecu rate in the next few years. It is no use their imagining that, in anything except the very shortest of runs, they can buy growth by letting inflation rip.

On the other hand, unless one believes that a binding commitment to a fixed exchange rate can be made credible and that credibility can make the costs of disinflation vanish, one has to wonder whether this is the time for the Eastern European countries to make the substantial investment in lost output needed to

---

17. See Williamson (1991b, forthcoming) for some elaboration on this analysis.

achieve the near-zero inflation that the countries of the European Monetary System (EMS) hope will continue to prevail in the ecu area.[18] It is surely more important at this stage to get on with reconstruction and export promotion than to achieve complete price stability. Export promotion, in particular, requires not just a competitive exchange rate, but the assurance that the exchange rate is going to remain competitive in the future. This requires a willingness to devalue when needed to offset differential inflation (i.e. something in the nature of a crawling peg).[19]

Use of a crawling peg to offset differential inflation means that the exchange rate cannot be used as a nominal anchor. The implication is that macroeconomic policy needs to provide an alternative nominal anchor, for example by guiding demand management policy by the rule for the growth of nominal domestic demand proposed in the Williamson-Miller blueprint for policy coordination (Williamson and Miller 1987).

If the exchange rate is to be pegged, one also needs to consider what it should be pegged to. It would be sensible if all the Eastern European countries pegged to the same unit, to promote intratrade and to avoid arbitrary changes in their mutual competitive positions as a result of changes in the exchange rates among the major industrial countries. Except for the Soviet Union, the convertible-currency trade of Eastern Europe is predominantly with Western Europe, and especially with Germany, so that on technical grounds either the deutsche mark or the ecu would offer a suitable peg. The ecu has some political attractions, both in avoiding the political sensitivities that the deutsche mark might raise in certain countries, and in that its use might suggest solidarity with the objective of European integration. The fact that the ecu may be marginally more inflation-prone than the deutsche mark hardly seems a serious drawback: the countries of Eastern Europe will have their work cut out in reducing inflation to the average ecu rate in the next few years. Thus, the ecu seems the most attractive candidate.

There remains one last issue: how to pick the exchange rate at which to peg. The criterion—to reconcile internal and external balance in the medium term—

---

18. For example, France has succeeded in bringing inflation down to the German rate by treating the deutsche mark as a nominal anchor—but at the cost of half a decade of slow growth. Since inflation starts at an even higher level in Eastern Europe, and the economies there are less open, the cost would presumably be higher. This does not mean that the emergent market economies cannot benefit from a temporary peg that helps them import a new structure of relative prices, but it should lead them to take caution against confusing that concept of an anchor with the idea of a nominal anchor as used in discussion of the EMS.

19. I include under this term relatively frequent adjustments in a "fixed but adjustable" exchange rate, so long as the individual changes are small enough to avoid intense speculative pressures and adjustments of the rate are regarded as an act of policy rather than its failure.

is uncontroversial. How to apply that criterion is more difficult. One traditional approach, that of seeking purchasing power parity, is prone to be even more misleading than usual because of the highly distorted preliberalization price structures and the uncertainty as to how large the corrective inflation resulting from liberalization will prove to be. The competitive approach, that of seeking to estimate a fundamental equilibrium exchange rate, relies on some form of macroeconometric model to calculate the real exchange rate that will reconcile internal and external balance in the medium term; however, any such models that may have existed are likely to become irrelevant as a result of liberalization.

Since neither of the standard approaches is helpful, one has to fall back on a more judgmental solution. The key need is to make sure that the exchange rate is sufficiently competitive to nurture long-term restructuring toward export-led growth. It is usually not too difficult to tell whether there are lots of entrepreneurs who perceive export opportunities. Excessive devaluation is costly, as has already been pointed out, since it aggravates short-run stagflation: the price rise induced by devaluation cuts the real value of money balances, and in the short run this effect outweighs the boost to demand from export expansion. Hence the criterion for picking an exchange rate is to make sure that there are plenty of enterprises sufficiently competitive to export and wanting to invest more to expand their export capacity, but to avoid devaluing more than is needed for that purpose.

Dual Exchange Rates

No country has yet adopted McKinnon's recommendation to make the currency convertible at a unified exchange rate but then mitigate the short-run results by levying high tariffs on nonessential imports; however, Romania has recently edged toward a policy with rather similar effects. This policy involves liberalizing the import of nonessential goods, but consigning their purchase to a floating exchange rate that allows the local currency to depreciate relative to the official rate.

The diagrams in figure 1 will help to compare this dual exchange rate system with the proposal offered by McKinnon. The exchange rate x in part A, which depicts McKinnon's proposal, shows the number of units of domestic currency that an exporter receives for $1 of exports. Purchase of $1 of essential imports costs an importer $(1 + t_e)x$ units of domestic currency, whereas the purchase of $1 of nonessential imports costs $(1 + t_n)x$ units, assuming that imports are divided into only these two categories. Part B shows in similar form the dual exchange rate proposal. One dollar of essential imports would be purchased for x_o, the official exchange rate. One dollar of nonessential imports would cost x_p, the exchange rate on the parallel market. The government typically requires that traditional exports be sold entirely on the official market at the rate x_o. If exporters

Figure 1 Local-currency prices of traded goods under alternative schemes. *A*, McKinnon's proposal for differential tariff protection; *B*, dual exchange rates; *C*, equal incentive to export under the two schemes.

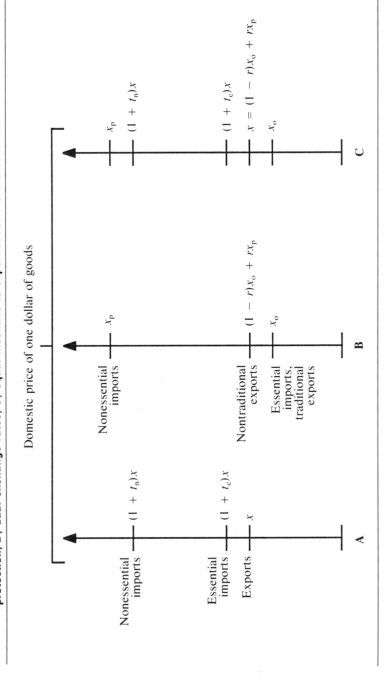

of nontraditional products are entitled to sell a proportion r (the retention ratio) of their earnings on the parallel market, $1 worth of those exports would yield them $(1 - r)x_o + rx_p$ units of domestic currency, a weighted average of the official and parallel rates, as illustrated in part B.

Except to the extent that the central bank is building up or running down reserves, or that there is a net capital inflow or outflow, the total dollar value of exports and imports in the two markets together must balance. However, since the central bank can arbitrage between the two markets, the value of trade need not balance in each of the individual markets. In particular, the central bank can hold the official rate constant by acting as the residual buyer or seller in that market, and transferring any excess supply or demand to the parallel market. If the dollar value of traditional exports plus the dollars sold in the official market by exporters of nontraditional products exceeds the dollar value of essential imports, the central bank will be able to sell its excess dollar receipts in the parallel market. It will make a profit on such an operation, which will help to reduce monetary expansion. This addition to the supply of dollars coming from the enterprises' retention quotas, from foreign tourists, from emigrants' remittances, and so on will help to limit the premium on the rate in the parallel market. (In the converse case where the central bank has a deficit on the official market, which it has to make good by siphoning funds from the parallel market, its operations will add to the fiscal deficit and monetary expansion and will depreciate the parallel rate.)

One key difference between the McKinnon and the dual-rate proposals is that essential imports cost more than nontraditional exports under the McKinnon scheme and less under dual rates. (Obviously one is speaking in each case of an equal dollar value of exports and imports in these comparisons.) If exchange rates and the retention quota are set such as to equalize the incentive to export nontraditional exports under the two schemes (as would be recommended by the analysis of what should determine the level of the exchange rate presented in the previous section), then essential imports must be cheaper under the dual rate (part C of figure 1). The balance of payments constraint then implies that nonessential imports must be more expensive under dual rates. Hence a first ground for choosing between the two schemes is whether it is desired to have a large differential in the prices of the different types of imports—in particular, on how important it is to keep down the price of essential imports, relative to both the price of nonessential imports and that of exports.

A second key difference between the two proposals is that McKinnon envisages several tariff rates to discriminate among different categories of imports, whereas the dual rate is limited to the two-way classification of essential and nonessential.[20] My own view is that something like the four-way classification proposed

20. It might seem that there is a contrary difference on the export side, since the dual-rate proposal accommodates different treatment for traditional and nontraditional exports. But

by McKinnon is desirable, and hence this difference argues in favor of his proposal.

A third key difference is that McKinnon's tariffs must yield net revenue to the government, whereas the public sector could lose money under the dual-rate proposal. That would be highly undesirable. Where a dual rate is employed, the essential imports permitted at the official rate should be restricted to ensure that their value is less than that of the receipts on the official market.

The final key difference is that the parallel exchange rate fluctuates to clear one of the markets under the dual-rate system, whereas the single rate is fixed under McKinnon's proposal. The question that arises is whether the ill effects of fluctuating exchange rates discussed in the previous section apply when only nonessential imports (and a part of the value of nontraditional exports) are subject to them. The answer would seem to be that the effects are sufficiently attenuated to make this a reasonable system to use during a transitional period when seeking to liberalize imports without any cushion of reserves, especially when the authorities have difficulty in deciding where the exchange rate needs to be set.

Support from EMS Membership

In his conference paper, Peter Bofinger (chapter 4) suggests that the Eastern European countries should go much further than fixing their exchange rates, by seeking to join the European monetary union (EMU) that the European Community is aiming to establish. This, he argues, would give credibility to the intention to fix the exchange rate, and thereby lower the cost in terms of lost output of carrying through that intention. Even before they irrevocably fix their exchange rates in EMU, the preceding phase of EMS membership would bring these countries the benefit of access to additional reserves, coupled with the confidence-building effect that would come from the market knowing that devaluation would be possible only when multilaterally agreed by their EMS partners. This would extend to the rest of Eastern Europe the same sort of benefits that, Bofinger argued, East Germany reaped from its monetary union with the West.

I have already argued that the countries of Eastern Europe would be ill advised to commit themselves to a permanently fixed exchange rate in the next few years, since establishment of the necessary degree of price stability is an investment that may require a period of overvaluation and capacity underutilization, and reconstruction is a more urgent task. That argument would be undermined by the countries joining EMU only if one believed that complete credibility guarantees

---

obviously an export tax on traditional exports would allow McKinnon's proposal to replicate that feature readily if it were desired.

costless disinflation. Such an argument is indeed made by Bofinger, but I find it unpersuasive. Accordingly, it would be premature to start thinking about EMU membership for the countries of Eastern Europe, even if this option were likely to be open to them in the next few years.

Moreover, it is surely mistaken to regard monetary union as the key feature that differentiates the experience of the former East Germany from that of the other former members of the CMEA. Of even greater importance are the ability of eastern Germans to move without restriction to the western part of a united Germany, which foreclosed the option of maintaining an adequately competitive exchange rate, and the willingness of the Federal Republic to provide a massive fiscal transfer (Schill, chapter 5).[21] Obviously a halving of industrial production is far less of a disaster if much of the loss in income is compensated by subsidies through the fiscal system. But no such relief is going to be available to the other countries of Eastern Europe, whether or not they enter a monetary union. Since they cannot expect to be bailed out, it is vital that they make sure that their exchange rates remain competitive. Monetary union is too much of a risk at this stage.

Although I do not go along with Bofinger in wishing to see the countries of Eastern Europe contemplate entering an EMU in the next few years, his analysis suggests that they would benefit from early entry into the EMS. Their current reserve shortage does pose a problem in maintaining a pegged exchange rate regime. Moreover, the credibility of their macroeconomic policy commitments could be enhanced by a requirement that devaluations be multilaterally approved within the EMS.

Will the European Community be prepared to welcome new members from Eastern Europe? At the moment it has decided to give priority to deepening rather than widening the Community. That may be natural, but one has to hope that it is a decision that will be reviewed before long. It is far from clear that deepening and widening need be in conflict; a vigorous Community should be able to do both. Nor is it clear what legitimate reason the Community might have for requiring aspiring new members from Eastern Europe to wait a long time before being admitted. These countries are demonstrating that they now meet the Community's ideological criteria (democracy, respect for human rights, and a market economy); if there are other criteria, they should be spelled out so that their legitimacy can be debated in public.

Would the operation of something close to a crawling peg, as recommended above, be consistent with membership in the EMS? In its early years, the EMS did in fact operate rather like a crawling peg. That changed for the existing

---

21. Estimates cited below (in the section discussing the former East Germany) suggest that the transfer is at least 20 percent of the potential GNP of eastern Germany, and probably substantially higher.

members when they decided in 1982–83 to make the EMS a mechanism for reducing inflation. It is already widely recognized that some of the existing member countries may not be able to participate in an EMU from the outset. Similarly, the Community could surely recognize that its new members would need some special dispensations in their early years. One rather reasonable such dispensation would be to allow them to operate for a time according to the principles that the original members initially used.

One hopes that the European Community will have the generosity to welcome the Eastern European countries into membership rather quickly, and the flexibility to enable them to take full advantage of that membership. If and when that happens, they should enter the first stage of the EMS without more ado.

The Parallel-Currency Proposal

In the Soviet Union there has been considerable discussion of a proposal to establish a parallel, convertible currency, rather than to try to make the ruble convertible in the first instance. A paper advocating this approach was presented at the Vienna conference by two economists from the Soviet Academy of Sciences, Andrei I. Kazmin and Andrei V. Tsimailo (chapter 8). The proposal draws support from one of the less unhappy experiences in Soviet monetary history, Lenin's introduction of the chervonets currency under the market-oriented New Economic Policy in the early 1920s. Originally intended to be a stable unit of account during the hyperinflation, chervonets notes (bills, in American parlance) were issued in 1922, backed 25 percent by gold (although not convertible into gold, except for nonresidents). The requirement of gold backing prevented the government using issues of chervonets to finance the budget deficit, so the new currency remained stable in value while the old one depreciated. The increase in output induced by the New Economic Policy and/or the availability of a stable money was so great that the budget deficit vanished by 1924, whereupon the old notes were called in and replaced by new rubles at a ratio of 50 billion to 1. The performance of the chervonets was undermined when stable macroeconomic policies were abandoned in late 1925 (see the account by Michael R. Dohan in chapter 8).

Reinforced by doubts regarding the prospects for a comprehensive reform program in their country, Kazmin and Tsimailo seek a way to make progress by replicating the strategy adopted in 1922. Their suggestion is that the government introduce a new currency, with issue restrictions designed to guarantee its stability, and allow this currency to circulate in parallel with the existing ruble. This "domestic convertible ruble" would be used specifically for financing the wholesale trade that will need to come into being when prices are liberalized and administrative direction of industry is finally abandoned; it would not be available to individuals. The authors argue that monetary emission cannot be halted quickly, or the monetary overhang eliminated rapidly, since output would collapse if subsidies were withdrawn. On the other hand, they assert that a move to the market and the presence of a stable money would so stimulate output that the budget deficit would before long be eliminated without pain. (This reminds one of the economics of joy promised by "supply-siders" in the United States during the Reagan administration.) At that point it would be possible to unify the new parallel ruble and the old ruble.

The parallel-currency proposal received a great deal of criticism at the Vienna conference, and not one whisper of support other than from the authors themselves. All three of the other Soviet economists present were dismissive: Boris Fedorov, the former Minister of Finance of the Russian republic, who presented the country paper on the Soviet Union; Guzel Anulova, who won second prize in late 1990 in the Furth Rouble Prize competition for the best essay on establishment of ruble convertibility; and Rouben Indjikin, who won one of the 1990 Amex Bank essay prizes, also for an essay on the convertibility of the ruble. The proposal received equally little sympathy from Western discussants Richard N. Cooper, Michael Dohan, and Richard Portes, or from contributors from the floor. Richard Portes and Marie Lavigne both expressed dismay that so much intellectual energy was being dissipated in the Soviet Union in debating what they characterized as a gimmick.

Two central reasons for skepticism were presented by Cooper. One concerned the ambiguity of the rules for monetary emission. Kazmin and Tsimailo are very clear that the issuing bank should be forbidden to finance budget deficits, but the positive rule governing emission is obscure. Is the parallel currency to be some form of commodity money? Would it consist of foreign-exchange certificates, issued by what would in effect be a currency board? Or would it be managed by a central bank? If so, on what principles would the central bank operate its monetary policy? To those questions I would add another, which is provoked by the authors' remark about making "special bank loans . . . to enterprises that produce export and consumer goods on a purely commercial basis. . . . [so that] the inflow of the parallel currency would be regulated by the rational demands of economic turnover." Do the authors have in mind the real bills doctrine—the proposition that money should always be backed by short-term self-liquidating bills representing claims to stocks of goods that will shortly come on the market, and that money issued against such claims cannot be excessive? This is a doctrine that periodically reappears in the literature, but it is one that is fundamentally flawed, since it would result in the money supply varying procyclically and would preclude money serving as a nominal anchor.

Cooper's other concern was the impact of creation of a parallel currency on the behavior of the existing ruble. If a part of money demand is diverted to a new asset that cannot be taxed by inflation, but the budget deficit remains unchanged, then the rate of inflation on the old asset will have to increase in order to satisfy the government's budget constraint. Dohan confirmed that creation of the chervonets had indeed led to an acceleration of the inflation rate as measured in sovznaks. Anulova argued that, while today's ruble leaves much to be desired as a currency, it is still far from the state of collapse of the sovznak in 1922, and hence it would not be worth risking such a collapse even if one were confident that the parallel currency would operate as desired.

Are there other reasons that might lead one to doubt whether something that worked in 1922 could be repeated 69 years later? One reason is, perhaps, precisely that it has been done before: this time around people will know what is happening, and the result will presumably be an even more rapid collapse of the old currency. Another possible reason is that faith in monetary normalcy has evaporated since 1922, when monetary debauchery was only eight years old and the public was still ready on the slightest pretext to believe that things were getting back to normal. Yet another difference is that there is no ready-made capitalist class ready to spring back into action the moment it is given encouragement, and in the process resolve the government's fiscal problem. It will be apparent that I concur with the overwhelming sentiment at the conference in regarding the parallel-currency proposal with considerable skepticism.

The Positions of Individual Countries

It is a platitude that the countries of Eastern Europe differ in important respects, and that because of this the strategies that should be pursued will differ from country to country. But platitudes are usually true, which is why they become platitudes, and this one certainly is. Hence it is now time to pass on from examining general arguments about the strategy for opening up to consider what the analysis implies for each of the individual countries.

The three countries that had already established currency convertibility at the time the conference was being planned—Yugoslavia, Poland, and the former East Germany (the "three pioneers")—will be considered first. The "next candidates" for establishing convertibility, Czechoslovakia and Hungary, follow. Then come the "future candidates" of Bulgaria and Romania. The most complex and most important case of all, the Soviet Union, is treated last.

Yugoslavia

By making the dinar convertible on 18 December 1989, Yugoslavia became the first of the Eastern European countries to take this step. As Ljubiša Adamovich points out in his paper (chapter 5), however, in other respects Yugoslavia is no longer pioneering the process of economic reform. On the contrary, most political capital has been expended during the past year in ethnic tensions and feuding among the six constituent republics. Budget constraints remain soft, and much of industry remains subject to the rather unsatisfactory mechanism of worker self-management that was developed in the 1950s.

Convertibility was introduced in Yugoslavia as an element of a stabilization program designed to end hyperinflation. It was hoped that a convertible currency would enable a fixed exchange rate commitment to provide the economy with a nominal anchor that would import price stability. The hyperinflation had developed while the real exchange rate was being maintained at a highly competitive level by a crawling peg. This had provided perhaps the clearest case yet of the long-recognized danger (Dornbusch 1981, Adams and Gros 1986) that pursuit of a real exchange rate target can generate an accelerating rate of inflation if it is not accompanied by a clear commitment of domestic demand management policy to some appropriate nominal anchor. In fact, Yugoslavia allowed ready monetary accommodation of fiscal deficits and enterprise losses, thereby creating the worst possible environment for exchange rate accommodation as well. Some might argue that the massive improvement in Yugoslavia's current account balance, from a bare surplus prior to 1985 to one of almost $2.5 billion (about 5 percent of GDP) in 1988–89, was worth some acceleration in inflation, but the trade-off does not appear to have been an attractive one. Despite the substantial current account surpluses of recent years, Yugoslavia has had difficulty in servicing its debt, even though this debt is rather modest relative to the size of exports or GNP (table 3).

The program inaugurated in December 1989 has often been described as a case of "shock therapy," although the changes were less extensive than those in Poland or East Germany. The measures were focused on macroeconomic stabilization and the establishment of convertibility, supplemented by the lifting of most remaining price and import controls at the beginning of January 1990. Fiscal policy was supposed to reduce the deficit by 5 percent of GNP. Limits were placed on the net domestic assets of the central bank, the discount rate was set at 23 percent per year, and other interest rates were fully liberalized (Coricelli and Rocha 1990). A 60-day tolerance limit on arrears was proclaimed, in an effort to enforce bankruptcy on inefficient state enterprises. A new exchange rate of 7 dinars to the deutsche mark was announced; this represented a depreciation of 15 percent from the rate then prevailing and was to be held fixed for at least six months. Backing up the nominal anchor provided by the pegged exchange rate was an incomes policy that froze wages and a number of public-sector prices, including those of energy, housing, and transport.

Convertibility was more extensive than elsewhere. Enterprises were entitled to buy foreign exchange to settle obligations to foreign suppliers incurred in the course of current account transactions. But in addition individuals received the right to buy foreign currency in unlimited sums and for any purpose, including capital export. Import restrictions were liberalized in parallel.

For the first six months of 1990 the stabilization program appeared to be a considerable success. Foreign-exchange reserves soared, as citizens reacted to the new freedom to convert their dinars into foreign exchange by turning in a lot of their never-converted foreign exchange for dinars. Inflation fell from almost 60 percent per month at the end of 1989 to virtual price stability in the second quarter. Exports were quite strong, although naturally imports increased much more.

The most obvious black spot was a fall of about 10 percent in industrial production in the socialized sector. In addition, wages increased by about 45 percent during the first six months (when they were supposed to be frozen) because of exceptions granted liberally by the governments of the republics and provinces. The dinar was perhaps still not overvalued at midyear, since it had initially been frozen at a highly competitive level. The stabilization might still have been saved at that date if the incomes policy had started to receive support from all levels of government.

Instead, the deepening political crisis and ethnic conflict led to a relaxation of fiscal and monetary policy at the same time that the wage freeze lapsed. Unsurprisingly, inflation reemerged. From 2 percent per month in July and August, it rose to as much as 8 percent in October. Households started to exercise their right to convert dinars into foreign exchange in September, leading Adamovich to muse that, even if not much else was being privatized, convertibility was at least leading to privatization of the foreign-exchange reserves!

The minds of the politicians were elsewhere, but the situation had become unsustainable. In December the dinar was devalued by 28.5 percent (following inflation through the year of almost 80 percent, over twice the rate originally forecast at the time of stabilization). Convertibility was at the same time curtailed by abolishing the right of individuals to shift their capital out of dinars and imposing a limit of DM1,000 (or the equivalent) on the sum that any person could convert for a single foreign journey. With individual republics getting into the money-printing business, it seemed by the time of the Vienna conference that Yugoslavia was far from a model for the rest of Eastern Europe.

The experience of Yugoslavia has three important lessons. One is that capital account convertibility, even for households, is premature in the circumstances of the region. The second is that the exchange rate is not a particularly powerful nominal anchor—and certainly not strong enough to prevail when it is being undermined rather than reinforced by incomes policy.

The third lesson is one in political economy: that a time of political division and ethnic conflict is not an opportune occasion to seek a definitive stabilization. Some minimum level of social cohesion is needed to introduce the hard budget constraints that are indispensable to successful stabilization. If and when Yugoslavia sorts out its constitutional and social problems and resolves that it wishes to remain a nation-state, it will be sensible to return to the agenda of December 1989, although shorn of capital account convertibility and instead making sure that budget constraints are respected.

Poland

Poland was the second Eastern European country to establish convertibility, as part of a package of measures that took effect on 1 January 1990—a package that indisputably constituted a "big bang." The "internal convertibility" that was introduced is current account convertibility circumscribed in two ways: it does not apply to most services (although trade-related services are covered), and it does not apply to nonresidents (thus, the remission of profits from direct investments was not covered[22]).

Prior to its dramatic reforms at the beginning of 1990, Poland was the classic case of a centrally planned economy that had been reformed by abolishing much of the central planning apparatus without hardening budget constraints or reforming the price structure to make sure that the decentralized decision makers were responding to signals that reflected relative scarcities. The foreign trade regime reflected this unsatisfactory compromise between a planned and a market economy. The foreign trade organizations that had monopolized trade under the *ancien régime* still existed, but major exporting enterprises had been given the right to export directly. Both exports and imports still required administrative permission, although exporters received a battery of fiscal incentives to compensate for the overvaluation of the currency, plus generous retention quotas. There seems to be no documentation of the extent to which exports comprised goods with negative value added; however, the presumption is that these were not confined to semitropical flowers.

Poles had gone to the West to work in substantial numbers. This had contributed to a buildup in holdings of foreign currencies. About two-thirds of the money supply consisted of foreign-currency bank accounts, and a flourishing (legal) parallel market allowed such holdings to be converted readily into zlotys when needed to finance consumption. Enterprises had been allowed to retain a part of their export proceeds in foreign-currency accounts, and to buy or sell foreign currency at foreign-exchange auctions, so that foreign exchange was available, at a price, to finance any legal import transaction.

---

22. Legislation to extend convertibility to permit the repatriation of profits by foreign investors is pending as this goes to press.

Although microeconomic irrationality was pervasive, the 1989 collapse was provoked primarily by growing macroeconomic indiscipline (a budget deficit of around 8 percent of GNP). This produced a monetary overhang, a hyperinflation, and a massive premium on the dollar in the parallel market, together with stagnating output and an unserviceable foreign debt. The economic crisis provided the opportunity for Solidarity to negotiate and win free elections and achieve an orderly transfer of power in September 1989. The new government immediately began planning the bold reform program that took effect on 1 January 1990.

The 1 January big bang aimed at both price liberalization and macroeconomic stabilization. Prices were largely freed, energy prices were raised about halfway toward the world level (from a mere 6 percent of that level in 1989), and most subsidies were abolished. These measures were intended to produce a swing in the fiscal balance of some 7 percent of GNP; the actual swing came in at around 11 percent, as a result of an unexpectedly strong surge in revenues and lower-than-expected real wages. Limits were placed on the net domestic assets of the banking system, and interest rates were raised from a monthly rate of 7 percent in December to 36 percent in January. An incomes policy imposed a severe tax on wage increases beyond those sanctioned by an approved rate of partial indexation (the permitted level varied from one month to another, from as little as 20 percent to as much as 100 percent, and was set at 60 percent in the final months of 1990). A requirement that socialized enterprises pay a tax, related to the historic value of their capital stock, in lieu of dividends, was supposed to enforce bankruptcy on insolvent enterprises. Unemployment insurance was introduced. Enterprises were given the right to fire employees.

The zloty was devalued by almost 50 percent from the old official rate, to an exchange rate that was supposed to remain fixed at 9,500 zlotys to the dollar for at least three months; at the same time, as described above, the zloty was made convertible. Retention quotas were abolished; enterprises were obliged to sell all the foreign exchange they earned. Foreign trade restrictions were "almost completely eliminated" (Olechowski and Oleś, chapter 5). This included abolition of the need to get permission to engage in foreign trade, of all quantitative restrictions on imports from the convertible-currency area, and of about half the export quotas. Tariffs were greatly reduced, to an average that is now less than 10 percent. Export incentives were also abolished. In his oral presentation at the conference, Olechowski compared Poland's import regime to that of Hong Kong.

Assessments of the results of this program continue to differ greatly. The facts are that measured output fell drastically (there was a decline of about 30 percent in industrial output by the socialized sector); that inflation also declined, although it picked up again to a monthly rate of around 10 percent in the first two months of 1991; that queues quickly vanished and goods reappeared on the shelves; that the current account developed a substantial surplus (about $1 billion in 1990) due to compressed imports and an impressive 37 percent growth in exports to the convertible-currency area; and that the fixed exchange rate and the convertibility obligation have so far been maintained without strain. The news is good apart from the persistence of inflation and the depth of the recession, so those are the outcomes worthy of discussion.

Karol Lutkowski (chapter 5) argues that at least part of the blame for these two developments lies with the excessive devaluation of the zloty. It was of course difficult to decide the proper exchange rate at which to stabilize at the end of 1989; according to Olechowski, the rate selected was a compromise between the rate favored by the Polish authorities and that preferred by the IMF. It actually represented a larger devaluation than would have resulted from selecting the parallel rate prevailing in November-December 1989, although that rate had been as much as 10,000 zlotys to the dollar in September. It certainly represented a very strong devaluation of the official rate.

The size of the devaluation helped to pull prices upward after their liberalization. This reduced the real value of the money supply sufficiently to eliminate the monetary overhang and deflate demand, which helps account for the recession.[23] The contractionary swing in the budget deficit was presumably also important in that context. In addition, the output loss has been of less consequence than the published figure of a 30 percent decline would suggest, for three reasons (Kemme 1990):

- The output decline was actually less drastic than reported. One reason is that the statistics cover only state enterprises, and the output of the private sector was expanding strongly (by about 25 percent in the first three quarters of 1990). The other reason is that output may have fallen less in the public enterprises than reported because of the new incentive to underreport output (to minimize taxation) rather than to overreport it (to show that plans had been fulfilled).

- Some of the output that was no longer produced was of zero value to the economy, but went into building up stocks that were never consumed or consisted of capital goods that were unusable.

- Final consumption fell less than output declined, partly because there were ample stocks of intermediate goods on which to draw,[24] and partly because

---

23. In the long run a real devaluation is typically expansionary, but in the short run it is well known that the contractionary monetary effect can dominate over the expansionary substitution effect, as seems to have happened in Poland.

24. Socialist enterprises typically accumulate excessively large stocks, both because of the undependability of deliveries and because there are no other stores of value available to them.

of the consumer benefits of eliminating queues (see Lipton and Sachs 1990 for an analysis of this point). It should, however, be recognized that the welfare benefit of eliminating nonprice rationing is not distributionally neutral; it benefits the relatively well off proportionately more than the poor (who at least have the chance of buying goods if they are prepared to stand in line under rationing), thus leaving a presumption that the latter suffered a fall in living standards.

Despite these qualifications, it is generally accepted that Poland paid a stiff price in terms of lost output for its stabilization, and it seems reasonable to presume that the price would have been smaller if policy had not overshot in terms of both the severity of the fiscal adjustment and the extent of devaluation. The latter was also unfortunate for its impact on inflation. Lutkowski argued (and Olechowski echoed the argument) that the exchange rate could not begin to act as a nominal anchor until prices had caught up with the devaluation, which they thought was happening by the last quarter of 1990. (One could actually go further and argue that until the undervaluation had been worked off by inflation the nominal anchor was working—to pull prices upward! Presumably this was aided by the relaxation in monetary policy introduced in the summer of 1990 to limit the recession.) The danger of such a corrective price rise is that it may rekindle inflationary habits that were supposed to have been laid to rest by the stabilization. The return of rapid inflation in the first two months of 1991, despite elimination of the undervaluation, suggests that this did indeed occur. As has happened so often in other countries, the nominal anchor did not hold.

Poland is now faced with the need to steer a delicate course between two classic errors. One is to "go for growth" by accommodating whatever rate of inflation develops (which would include devaluing to offset differential inflation). Experience suggests that such a strategy cannot last for more than two or three years before hyperinflation returns and forces a new and even more difficult stabilization program. The other error is to stick to an exchange rate that increasingly overvalues the currency in the hope that sufficient determination will eventually establish credibility, which will then stop the inflation and validate the fixed exchange rate. This process invariably ends with the currency being devalued in a crisis that leaves governmental credibility in tatters.

It would surely be a mistake for Poland to risk a significant or prolonged overvaluation at the present stage of its transition, facing as it does the need to instill confidence in its new and potential exporters, which is made even more important by the major reduction in exports to its former CMEA partners resulting from the dismantling of the CMEA at the beginning of 1991. If Polish exporters are indeed beginning to find that their competitiveness is seriously eroding, as some reports suggest, it is high time for the government to announce a move to a more flexible exchange rate policy. As always, it will be important that this be accompanied by credible moves to dampen inflation.

The Polish experience to date suggests two lessons. One is that an early move to convertibility is advantageous where it is feasible—that it is right to make it a part of the minimum bang. As Lutkowski writes (chapter 5):

> The commonly accepted conviction in Poland is that the convertibility experiment, together with the radical opening of the economy, has turned out to be the most successful element of the new economic mechanism. . . . [That] stands in sharp contrast with the fears voiced before the start of the reforms, when convertibility was viewed as a particularly risky part of the project.

The second lesson is that it is possible to devalue too much, that this is expensive, and that those who look to the parallel market rate for guidance in setting the official rate run a danger of falling into this trap. Unless it acts soon, Poland may provide another lesson, this time on the dangers of an excessively rigid exchange rate policy.

Poland was on some criteria the most heavily indebted country in the region (table 3), with a debt-export ratio of over 300 percent even if one includes CMEA trade in the denominator, and a debt–GNP ratio of nearly 30 percent using a PPP estimate of GNP (or as much as 65 percent using estimates based on actual exchange rates). However, Poland succeeded in negotiating some 50 percent debt relief with its official creditors in March 1991—a generous settlement by most standards.[25]

East Germany

What was formerly known as the German Democratic Republic, or more colloquially (and accurately) East Germany, acquired a convertible currency on 1 July 1990. Unlike Poland and Yugoslavia, however, East Germany did not make its currency convertible: instead, it traded in its own currency for deutsche marks, as part of a Treaty of Economic, Monetary, and Social Union by which East Germany adopted the legal arrangements, economic system, and money of the Federal Republic of Germany. On 3 October 1990 economic and monetary union was followed by political accession of East Germany to the Federal Republic.

---

25. Four settlements in the postwar period appear to have been more generous: the accord with West Germany in 1953, that with Indonesia in 1970, Bolivia's debt buyback initiated in 1988, and Costa Rica's Brady Plan restructuring negotiated in 1989. Faber (1990) estimates debt relief in the first two cases at about 70 percent and 57 percent, respectively, while Bolivia and Costa Rica got about 89 percent and 60 percent relief, respectively, on their bank debt.

If any reform program has ever deserved the title of "big bang" or "shock therapy," this one did. Wolfgang Schill (chapter 5) calls it an "ultraradical approach." The fact that the East Germans' new money is convertible is a relatively minor aspect of the revolution that swept over those living in the five new Länder. They acquired overnight a whole new set of laws crafted to support a market economy, total free trade with the European Community and near free trade with the rest of the world, access to a developed and functioning capital market, new tax and social security systems, a new price structure, and, last but not least, a new currency. Obviously, important tasks remain to complete the transition to a market economy: Schill describes these as "breathing life into new political, economic, and social structures and . . . overcoming privatization and property problems [which] clearly have a time dimension." He argues that the former East Germany is much better positioned than any other ex–CMEA country to overcome those problems, because it could import so many of the mechanisms essential for the operation of a market economy.

The shock therapy has certainly been disruptive. Industrial production fell by about 50 percent in the wake of monetary union, and by late 1990 over a quarter of the labor force was either unemployed or on short time, with expectations that unemployment had much further to rise. Can the collapse in output be blamed on the exchange rate at which East German marks were converted into deutsche marks at the time of monetary unification? Best estimates were that both wages and productivity in East Germany were between 30 percent and 40 percent of the level in the West, using the 1:1 ratio that was ultimately adopted for converting wage rates (and everything else except for larger money and savings balances, and debts, all of which were converted at 2:1). However, the exchange rate at which East German enterprises had been exporting to the West was 4:1, so it is hardly surprising that they found themselves totally uncompetitive after monetary union. On the other hand, wages in eastern Germany rose briskly after unification, so it seems rather doubtful that a more competitive initial exchange rate would have done anything much except reduce the stock of assets held by East Germans after union.

The central fact about the German case seems to be that East Germany could *afford* to allow its industrial production to collapse by 50 percent. The reason is very simple: the Federal Republic is replacing much of the loss in real income through fiscal transfers. Schill cites an increase in the expected federal budget deficit of over 4.7 percent of GNP between 1989 and 1991. On his estimate that East Germany's potential output was 10 percent of that of the Federal Republic, that is a fiscal transfer approaching 50 percent of the former's potential GDP. Even if one takes East Germany's potential output to have been 15 percent of the Federal Republic's, and if one reckons that as much as a third of the increase in the budget deficit might be due to other causes, the transfer is over 20 percent of potential GDP.

The willingness of the West to subsidize the East in this way is not explained entirely by altruism. Unless Easterners were to be denied the right to migrate to the West by a rebuilt and extended Berlin Wall, wages (and social benefits for those without jobs) had to rise to a level that bore some relation to that in the West. George Akerlof et al. (1991) have recently argued that it would have been much cheaper to subsidize East German wages (although their suggested 75 percent wage subsidy sounds extravagant) and thus limit the loss of employment and output decline than to subsidize unemployment. In fact a number of measures were taken to support nonviable enterprises, including subsidizing exports to the former CMEA area and providing bank guarantees. Nevertheless, the most convincing criticism of German policy is not of the exchange rate at which monetary union occurred, but of the mechanism used to transfer income to the East.

When we were planning the Vienna conference, we debated whether to exclude the former East Germany as *sui generis*. We decided to include it on the ground that what Peter Bofinger was urging could be regarded as an extension to the rest of Eastern Europe of the monetary union that had been offered to and accepted by the East Germans. The shock therapy to which East Germany has been exposed is more drastic than anything that would be involved in joining EMU, since it went far beyond the monetary domain, thus providing some justification for Schill's contention that the experience of East Germany contains no immediate lessons for the rest of Eastern Europe, and certainly provides no model for the other former socialist countries.

On the contrary, what the experience of East Germany does provide is a warning of how just how large the fall in output can be when the changes imposed on an economy are sufficiently drastic. It is one thing to accept such an adjustment strategy when one has a beneficiary willing to pay much of the adjustment cost, although despite that willingness a great deal of dissatisfaction has built up in eastern Germany. But none of the other former centrally planned economies has any hope of getting comparable support if things go wrong. The rest of Eastern Europe must be careful to keep adjustment costs within reasonable bounds. That demands above all a competitive exchange rate.

Czechoslovakia

The Czech and Slovak Federal Republic, as it is now officially known following a vigorous constitutional debate in 1990, established "internal convertibility" of the koruna on 1 January 1991. This was one element of a package of measures that, while distinctly less drastic than the shock therapy applied in either Poland or East Germany, marked a decisive move to the status of emergent market economy.

Prior to the "velvet revolution" of November 1989, Czechoslovakia had for years been one of the most rigidly centralized and highly socialized economies of all. The government of Alexander Dubcek had attempted to break out of that mold during the "Prague Spring" of 1968, but socialism with a human face was destroyed by the tanks of the Warsaw Pact in the summer. For years afterward it seemed that military might had triumphed over the human spirit.

During that period, resource allocation was determined by the plan, and enterprises did as they were told, producing low-quality industrial products for the home market or export to the rest of the CMEA. The role of money was "predetermined by the central plan, with cash flows merely its passive reflection" (Zahradník, chapter 6). The private sector was virtually nonexistent. According to the official figures (table 2), which admittedly exaggerated the weight of CMEA trade because of the overpricing of industrial products sold within the bloc, almost 80 percent of trade was with the rest of the CMEA—a figure exceeded only by Bulgaria. Only at the beginning of 1989 were retention quotas introduced, as it was finally decided to see whether enterprises might export more to the West if they were given some incentive. Czechs and Slovaks were denied permission to work in the West, which helps explain why there was no buildup of dollar holdings, either in bank accounts or under the mattress. Dollarization might have come in time, as more and more enterprises acquired foreign-currency bank accounts, but it had not really started in 1989.

In fact, Czechoslovakia remained a prudently managed economy right to the end of the days of central planning. Open inflation was a mere 2 percent or 3 percent per year (although correcting for the exaggeration of growth might double that), the monetary overhang was quite limited, the budget and the balance of payments were in balance, and foreign debt was under $7 billion (around 60 percent of total exports). The economic managers who took over after the advent of democracy maintained the tradition of prudent macroeconomic management. The budget was tightened and achieved a modest surplus in 1990, and credit expansion was only 1.5 percent. Nevertheless, there was some increase in consumer spending, presumably due to anticipation of future price increases as liberalization occurred; there was some rise in prices (inflation in 1990 was about 10 percent, caused by increases in administered prices); and there was a modest payments deficit with both the convertible-currency area and the CMEA.

Because the macroeconomy was already in reasonable balance, given the tight policies pursued in 1990, Czechoslovakia was in the fortunate situation of not needing to combine its microeconomic liberalization with a macroeconomic stabilization. But it was concluded that liberalization and abolition of the CMEA would necessitate a devaluation of the koruna if a substantial payments deficit, with the threat of a continuous buildup of foreign debt, was to be avoided. The debate on how large the devaluation needed to be is described in Jaromír Zahradník's paper. Calculations based on purchasing power parity (PPP) pointed to an exchange rate of some 8 to 10 korunas to the dollar, but all the evidence suggested that such a rate would be inconsistent with macroeconomic balance; it would have confronted the authorities with a choice between a chronic current account deficit and an underemployed economy. The conclusion that a PPP calculation gives no basis for choosing a rate consistent with macroeconomic equilibrium is hardly news; indeed, one can be quite certain that a country in Czechoslovakia's situation, needing to nurture new export industries and attract foreign investment, will need a more competitive exchange rate than the PPP criterion would yield. The crucial question is how much more competitive it needs to be.

Apparently calculations of the average and marginal domestic resource cost of generating a dollar yielded exchange rates of 16 and 30 to 35 korunas to the dollar, respectively, and debate seems to have closed in on where in that range the exchange rate should be set. The idea of calculating a marginal domestic resource cost for earning foreign exchange is suspect, however, because the marginal export will adjust endogenously to the actual return from exporting, which is influenced by the size of the retention quota and the rate on the parallel market. It gives no indication of where the rate needs to be to achieve medium-term macroeconomic equilibrium.

In the end the exchange rate was set at 28 korunas to the dollar, a figure reached after a 55 percent devaluation in October and a further 16 percent devaluation on 28 December 1990. This rate is close to that which had prevailed on the parallel market: given the presumption noted in the context of the Polish case that the parallel rate will be much weaker than the rate consistent with macroeconomic equilibrium, it is not surprising that some concern was expressed during the conference that Czechoslovakia may have repeated the Polish mistake of devaluing too much. Naturally the discussion of how large a devaluation was needed led to speculative pressures building up in the parallel market, but that should have warned the authorities to avoid being guided by the parallel rate, rather than prompted them to ratify it.

The package of measures introduced on 1 January 1991 was aimed exclusively at microeconomic liberalization. It comprised the abolition of planning commands and the near-abolition of state orders, price liberalization, removal of virtually all nonprice restrictions on imports (although a 20 percent import surcharge was imposed), establishment of current account convertibility for enterprises ("internal convertibility"[26]), and the beginning of privatization. Privatization has started off with small enterprises but has been complicated by the

---

26. Already in 1989 an act allowing joint ventures had provided for full repatriation of profits and capital from foreign investment.

decision to restitute property to former owners. A vigorous debate about using a voucher mechanism to privatize large enterprises (Klaus, chapter 2) has now been decided in favor of such a practice.

Internal convertibility couples abolition of the currency retention system for exporters (who now have to surrender all their foreign-exchange earnings to the banking system) with establishment of the right of any enterprise to acquire foreign exchange when needed to pay for imports. Trade with the ex–CMEA countries other than Hungary (which is settled in korunas) and the Soviet Union (where dollar settlement has been suspended following an 80 percent decline in exports, although no new system has yet been agreed) is settled in dollars. Individual citizens traveling abroad also have access to foreign exchange at the official rate, up to a tourist allowance of 5,000 korunas per year. Once again, Hungary is a special case: there is no limit on the purchase of forints. The parallel market continues to operate, with hard currencies at a premium of around 10 percent. Nonresidents, other than direct investors, still do not have the right to convert korunas freely. Capital transactions remain subject to exchange controls.

It remains to be seen how successful the Czechoslovak reforms will be. The authorities expected some initial pain; the surge in the price level in January was around 30 percent to 35 percent, somewhat larger than had been expected, as a result of both devaluation and price liberalization, but prices fell back a bit in February. The implied fall in the real money supply is bound to intensify the recession in the short run, as will the collapse in exports to the former CMEA markets. The shock of the CMEA price adjustments will also worsen the balance of payments sharply in 1991. I am inclined to agree with the view that devaluation was excessive and that this will make the adjustment more stagflationary than was necessary, especially since Czechoslovakia is the one country in Eastern Europe that had not exhausted its creditworthiness and could probably have borrowed more to help it through the transition.

Nevertheless, the fact that the country started off from a reasonably balanced macroeconomic position gives hope that the transition will be accomplished successfully. That hope could have been thwarted by a poor liberalization program, but the Czechoslovak program was perhaps close to the "minimum bang." The government made its intention of moving to a market economy clear from the start, but it took a year to prepare the program and pass the necessary laws; in the interim action was largely restricted to a reinforcement of stabilization. The government then provided for a set of complementary measures to take effect simultaneously, marking a decisive move to the market economy. Perhaps a smaller devaluation and higher transitional protection could have reduced the costs of adjustment, but the program was sufficiently well balanced to make one feel that if Czechoslovakia fails to make the transition successfully, the outlook for the rest of Eastern Europe is indeed grim.

Hungary

The Hungarian forint is not yet officially convertible, but it has been making progress in that direction for several years. Since the start of 1991, about 90 percent of imports, competing with about 70 percent of industrial production, have been liberalized. This means *inter alia* that enterprises have the right to buy foreign exchange without the need for any special administrative permission in order to pay for those goods when bought abroad. This gradual liberalization is exactly what Levcik commends as a sensible model (chapter 3). Both of the Hungarian participants at the Vienna conference—Lajos Bokros, who wrote the country paper, and Gabor Oblath, who commented on it—are comfortable at this point with the gradualist strategy.

Apart from Yugoslavia, Hungary was the first of the Eastern European countries to start liberalizing. It began to decentralize the management of large enterprises as early as 1968, started liberalizing prices in the same year, and raised energy prices to near the world level in 1982. All of this was still in the context of trying to make a socialist economy function more efficiently, but in 1987 the aim changed to that of introducing—gradually—a market economy. A two-tier banking system was established in 1987, and in 1988 Hungary initiated the privatization of small enterprises and enacted a tax system appropriate to a market economy, including a value-added tax.

Hungary's record of macroeconomic discipline was intermediate between those of Czechoslovakia and Poland: it did run substantial budget deficits but financed them by foreign borrowing. It has maintained debt service punctiliously to the present day, even though the foreign debt is over $20 billion, and the debt-export ratio approaches 250 percent even including CMEA trade. Unsurprisingly, the Polish settlement has sparked a debate on the wisdom of this policy.

It is often argued nowadays, most forcefully by Jeffrey Sachs, that the Hungarian experience shows the perils of gradualism: 23 years after a major reform was started, Hungary has still not achieved a market economy. To this Levcik replies that until 1987 the political leadership had made no real commitment to reform—its policies amounted to a series of pragmatic changes undertaken in response to particular problems as they arose. Interestingly, these piecemeal reforms do not seem to have led to the type of second-best difficulties experienced by other countries introducing partial reforms. This provides perhaps the best evidence that a feasible sequence of partial reforms does exist, and it suggests that exponents of gradualism would be well advised to devote some time to studying the Hungarian experience to understand why Hungary avoided second-best problems. The early rise in energy prices was presumably of key importance in that context.

Nevertheless, a liberalization as gradual as that of Hungary is clearly possible only in an economy that has never been allowed to get out of control. Gradual reform might also have been feasible in Czechoslovakia or East Germany; it clearly was not feasible in Poland. The size of the minimum bang depends critically upon a country's circumstances.

Perhaps one reason why gradualism has worked relatively well in Hungary is that it avoided the mistake of introducing retention quotas. Exporters have always been required to sell all their foreign-exchange earnings to the central bank. However, Hungary plans to create a domestic interbank foreign-exchange market in the second half of 1991, and when that happens, enterprises (as well as individuals, who already have the right) will be allowed to maintain foreign-exchange accounts at authorized domestic banks. Oblath (chapter 6) asked what purpose foreign-exchange accounts are supposed to serve once *de facto* current account convertibility has been achieved—the question is a good one.

Foreign exchange can be bought freely for 90 percent of imports, so that current account convertibility is already close at hand. Tariffs are quite low, averaging 17 percent. Hungary plans to liberalize the remaining 10 percent of imports progressively.

Individual Hungarians are at present limited to a tourist allowance equivalent to $50 per year at the official exchange rate, and the parallel market remains illegal. Cash holdings of hard currency are limited to the equivalent of 5,000 forints, but individuals can deposit unlimited sums of hard currency in a foreign-currency account with an authorized bank, with no questions asked about the origin of the funds. The aims of these "somewhat hypocritical regulations" (as Bokros describes them) are to minimize currency substitution and maximize the flow of hard currency into the central bank.

The Hungarian forint has never been desperately overvalued, and it was devalued a further 15 percent at the beginning of 1991, so as to neutralize the excess inflation accumulated over the previous year. It is pegged to a basket of currencies, and the government appears to be realistic in accepting that the need to offset differential inflation is likely to require further periodic adjustments in the exchange rate. Fiscal policy was tightened in the course of 1990, primarily by withdrawing subsidies. This, together with the devaluation and a tight monetary policy, led to a recession: output fell by some 6 percent, which is significant although less than most other countries of the region have suffered during this period. Inflation spurted to around 29 percent in 1990 and is expected to be 35 percent or so in 1991. The best results of the government's program came in regard to the balance of payments, which went into modest surplus in 1990.

Present Hungarian intentions are to continue avoiding shocks and to maintain gradual (though accelerated) progress toward a market economy. Inflation will be reduced by sustaining the restrictive fiscal policy of the past year. Competitiveness will be preserved by devaluation if necessary. Debt service will be maintained.[27] Further steps will be taken toward currency convertibility, including gradual relaxation of capital controls.

---

27. It remains to be seen whether this determination will survive the demonstration effect of Poland's successful debt reduction. Unless the banks decide to buy off Hungary with a

The main lesson of the Hungarian experience seems to be that gradualism does not deserve the contemptuous dismissal that it has tended to receive in much recent discussion. Under certain circumstances it does provide a feasible road to reform. But this is surely true only where the economy has never been allowed to get out of hand, which excludes a gradualist strategy for most of the countries of the region.

Bulgaria

Bulgaria has only recently launched a serious program of economic reform. It spent the first year after the overthrow of the dictatorship still ruled by a Communist Party; even though the party renamed itself socialist and the relabeling reflected an acceptance of the rules of the democratic game, its heart was not in the economic reforms that it spoke of introducing. Matters changed shortly before the Vienna conference took place: in December 1990 the opposition Union of Democratic Forces (UDF) was given primary responsibility for the conduct of economic policy in a coalition government.

The economic situation this government inherited was a catastrophe. Bulgaria had never attempted a reform program, and so its economy remained extremely highly centralized, dominated by a series of public monopolies. It had the highest proportion of intra–CMEA trade of any country in Eastern Europe: over 80 percent according to the (exaggerated) official measure. This trade was overwhelmingly with the Soviet Union.

Unlike in Czechoslovakia, this unpromising microeconomic inheritance is not compensated by a history of macroeconomic prudence. The government allowed the budget deficit to balloon in recent years, to over 10 percent of GNP in 1990. The financing of that deficit has led to an unmanageable (and, for the last year, unserviced) net foreign debt of close to $10 billion, a debt-export ratio of over 450 percent if one confines the denominator to convertible-currency exports, and a large monetary overhang. In addition, the economy has been buffeted by a series of foreign shocks: interruption of the substantial shipments of oil that Bulgaria was receiving from Iraq in debt repayment, together with a physical reduction in Soviet oil deliveries, reduced Bulgaria's oil supplies by around 40 percent; meanwhile the country experienced a 20 percent terms-of-trade loss from the conversion of CMEA trade to a hard-currency basis at the beginning of

---

more generous extension of new money, it is difficult to believe that Hungarian interests are still best served by punctilious debt service. Alternatively, George Soros (1991) has argued that debt relief would best be provided not by jeopardizing Hungary's impeccable record of debt service but by the European Community providing a long-term loan of 10 billion ecus and making a gift of three years' interest on the loan.

1991 (table 4). Add to that the decay of the central planning mechanism following its loss of legitimacy after the revolution, and it is perhaps not surprising that GNP is estimated to have fallen by some 11 percent, and industrial production to have declined by some 16 percent, in 1990.

Since virtually all prices were still controlled and had not been raised since the 1989 revolution, shortages were ubiquitous. The lev was still chronically overvalued at the official exchange rate, and correspondingly undervalued on the black market. One of the few moves toward decentralization in the course of 1990 was the questionable decision to introduce a 50 percent retention quota for enterprises that exported to the hard-currency area.

The program of the new economic team was described at the conference by the economic spokesman for the UDF, Ventseslav Dimitrov (chapter 7). The new team is committed to a program of thorough liberalization of the economy. Virtually all prices except those of energy were decontrolled on 1 February 1991; the result has been widespread and drastic price increases that largely eliminated the monetary overhang and, in conjunction with drastic expenditure cuts, are intended to reduce the budget deficit by close to 10 percent of GNP. Interest rates have been increased from 4.5 percent to 45 percent. Privatization of small enterprises was planned but has so far been blocked in the National Assembly by the Socialist Party. A tax reform is also planned, to introduce a value-added tax that will permit a lowering of marginal income tax rates (currently up to 90 percent on individuals and 80 percent on profits). The banking system is being stripped of its administrative functions (it traditionally exerted considerable control over productive enterprises through the payments mechanism), and the National Bank of Bulgaria is completing its transformation to the status of a true central bank. A new commercial law, a law on foreign investment, a law on privatization, and action on demonopolization are also planned.

A major liberalization of the external sector was introduced shortly after price decontrol. Many imports are now permitted, the exchange rate was unified,[28] and retention quotas were abolished. Both Ventseslav Dimitrov and Todor Valchev, the new president of the National Bank of Bulgaria, argued at the Vienna conference that Bulgaria was in no position to introduce convertibility immediately—their assertion went unchallenged. Ironically, Bulgaria's subsequent actions came rather close to introducing convertibility. Given the country's lack of reserves and chronic prospective payments deficit, this was possible only because of a decision to float the exchange rate in a new interbank market. (The only conceivable alternative way of liberalizing as much would have been to introduce a dual rate.)

---

28. That is, the three previous legal rates were unified: a parallel "black" market rate still exists, although its premium is now much smaller.

Thus, after a slow start, Bulgaria has now undertaken a dramatic liberalization, although one that has attracted little attention in the West. Even at the time of the Vienna conference, it was unclear whether the brave words would be matched by deeds. Now reform is a reality, and the concerns are quite different. Bulgaria has liberalized prices without either demonopolization or convertibility. Eduard Hochreiter (chapter 7) questioned whether sufficient priority was being given to establishing a nominal anchor capable of countering the strong inflationary forces prevalent even before the price liberalization, and those dangers must be far more severe in the wake of the decision to float the exchange rate and in the absence of any discipline on price setters. Bulgaria is thus likely to provide a nice test case for the conventional wisdom that stabilization must precede liberalization.

The chances are that before long the Bulgarians will need to introduce a stabilization program. A part of the program will need to be a fixing of the exchange rate, but that will be possible only if the country has adequate reserves, which are negligible at the moment. Poland obtained a substantial loan to support its big bang, which included convertibility at a fixed exchange rate, but never had to use it. Bulgaria will need similar support. It is expecting to take out loans totaling about $1.6 billion in 1991, but this money will be fed into the interbank market to finance the imports that are needed to reactivate production; a stabilization loan will need to be additional to this flow support.

Bulgaria's debt also needs restructuring, not because the total level of debt is astronomical by the usual measures—unless the resources formerly used to produce exports to the CMEA area prove useless in a post–CMEA world[29]— but because the short-run liquidity position is unmanageable. Since much of Bulgaria's debt (about 70 percent) is owed to the commercial banks, it is natural to think of a Brady Plan restructuring. Unfortunately the move from the Baker Plan to the Brady Plan was unhelpful to a country like Bulgaria that needs a stretchout of maturities more than it needs debt reduction, so flexibility will be needed to negotiate a suitable package.

Romania

Romania has also made major changes in its economic policy since the Vienna conference, although convertibility remains an aim for the future. It is an ambition that the authorities hope to achieve in about two years' time.

---

29. Table 3 shows Bulgaria's debt-export ratio to be a modest 126 percent if one includes total exports in the denominator, but because of the past concentration of exports on CMEA markets this rises to 468 percent if one restricts the denominator to non–CMEA markets.

Romania has had a tougher time over the past decade than any other country in Eastern Europe. It has the lowest per capita income in the region (apart from Albania), and it suffered a decline in output of about 10 percent in 1990. The monetary overhang is large, and shortages are chronic. There was no hint of economic reform prior to 1989. The country was ruled by a particularly despicable dictator, Nicolae Ceausescu, whose extravagant personal whims added to the economic woes that Romania suffered along with the other centrally planned economies. Not only were Romanian cities surrounded by rings of ugly and dysfunctional apartment blocs and polluting factories, which seem to be a monument left by every socialist regime, but the historic town centers, which everywhere else were carefully preserved (or even lovingly restored) under Communist rule, were being systematically erased to make way for concrete monstrosities at the time of Ceausescu's downfall.

Ceausescu's break with Moscow in the mid–1960s had led to Romania being courted by the West, in disregard of the unsavory nature of the regime. Western bankers helped Romania borrow to the hilt in the 1970s, when the country did not particularly need the money. These loans were then repaid in the 1980s after the debt crisis broke, by squeezing imports to the bone regardless of the cost in terms of consumer welfare.[30] The foreign debt had been entirely repaid by the time Ceausescu was overthrown. The tensions with Moscow had also led to a redirection of trade toward the West, with the result that the share of Romania's trade directed to the CMEA was one of the lowest in Eastern Europe: just over 50 percent even on the official figures.

The Romanian revolution was the last to occur in 1989, and by far the bloodiest. It was engineered by an anti-Ceausescu faction within the Communist Party. The new leaders named their movement the National Salvation Front and went on to win the democratic election held in May 1990. A few weeks later the new regime's democratic credentials were thrown into doubt when the government brought to Bucharest parties of miners who violently broke up an antigovernment demonstration. Romania has since had a hard time reestablishing its reputation as a country aiming to become a pluralist democracy and an emergent market economy.

Nevertheless, the Romanian government's rhetoric remains decidedly reformist, as the paper by Lucian C. Ionescu (chapter 7) confirms. The government has declared that it has firmly opted for a market economy, including privatization and enterprise autonomy. Currency convertibility is treated as an integral part of the process of liberalization. Actions taken since the Vienna conference again

---

30. Romania's experience must be the classic case of misuse of the international capital market to shift absorption to a time when resources are relatively abundant from one when they are relatively scarce.

lend credence to these affirmations: subsidies were withdrawn and prices liberalized on 1 April 1991.

Ionescu discusses in his paper the feasibility of four possible routes to convertibility. The first would involve declaring and defending a fixed exchange rate: he rejects this on the grounds that Romania lacks the reserves to make such a strategy credible, and that an immediate devaluation of the leu of the magnitude required by such a big bang could unleash an unacceptable inflation. The second would involve an Eastern European Payments Union (see Brabant, chapter 4). Ionescu declares sympathy for this strategy, but since he was the only Eastern European to show any interest in it, one has to conclude that Romania would be unwise to rely on being able to choose that route. The third strategy would involve collaboration with the EMS. Ionescu again approves of such an idea, but he affirms, surely realistically, that it would be imprudent to rely on that possibility being available soon enough.

Ionescu therefore concludes that Romania will probably have to fall back onto a fourth strategy, involving a dual exchange rate. An official rate will apply to a limited number of key products, consisting of traditional exports and essential imports, and the alternative rate will apply to all other products and services. This alternative rate will be determined in a new interbank market, which will be fed partly by the retention quotas of enterprises and partly by the reserves. Ionescu envisages a gradual (but relatively rapid) devaluation of the official exchange rate toward the level established in this market.

Policy has already moved toward implementing this approach since the Vienna conference, through the initiation of foreign-exchange auctions. The freedom to buy imports at all, even if only at the severely depreciated rate set in the auctions, is the most important element of convertibility, so this liberalization represents important progress. The premium on the auction (and the parallel) market fell after the initial auctions. When prices were liberalized at the beginning of April, the government also took a first step toward fulfilling the other element of the strategy explained by Ionescu, by devaluing the official exchange rate part of the way toward that on the auction market. The Romanian decision to experiment with a dual rate again provides a fascinating case study from which we should surely be able to learn important lessons in due course.

Romania has no debt in need of restructuring, but it does have a desperate dearth of goods as a result of having starved the domestic economy to repay its debt. It also suffers from a chronic shortage of international reserves, which unless corrected will force it to the undesirable strategy of allowing the exchange rate to float once it is unified. It is right that the West should make sure that the government means what it says about both democracy and economic reform before committing large sums of money, but once those doubts have been resolved there will be no excuse for delay. Romanians have suffered more than their share already.

Soviet Union

Much recent Soviet rhetoric also speaks of making the ruble convertible, albeit often with a timetable of 5 to 15 years. However, there seems to be little confidence that these aspirations will be translated into reality. Reformers like Boris Fedorov (chapter 8) offer a litany of despairing complaints about how little has really changed so far, and about the confusion in official plans. Conservatives (although we had none at the Vienna conference) are presumably equally unhappy; certainly they have reason to be, given the trend toward monetary disintegration of the Soviet Union.

Six years after *perestroika* started, the Soviet economy seems on the verge of collapse. Official estimates of net material product showed a decline of 4 percent in 1990, and the shortage of goods would suggest that the actual decline in output may have been larger; prices officially increased by some 5 percent, but there is a vastly larger repressed inflation that has stripped goods from the shelves; the monetary overhang was estimated at some 250 billion rubles, about 25 percent of GNP, by the Houston Summit report (IMF et al. 1990, 9); oil exports are contracting (the Houston Summit report mentioned a 20 percent decline in 1990, although subsequent PlanEcon figures have shaved this to 7 percent) due to supply difficulties; and the country is failing to service its foreign debt on time, even though its debt is rather moderate compared to that of several other Eastern European countries (the ratio of debt to non–CMEA exports is around 140 percent).

It appears to be universally expected that things will get worse in the Soviet Union rather than better. Gosplan has predicted an output decline of over 10 percent in 1991. Prices increased by an average of around 70 percent on 2 April, but since few prices were liberalized this led to little compensation in the form of increased availability of goods. Moreover, since wages rose to compensate for 85 percent of the loss of purchasing power, the price rise presumably had little effect on the budget deficit. That deficit was larger in the first quarter of 1991 than had been planned for the entire year. President Gorbachev has announced that oil exports are likely to be halved. All this is happening not because the country is investing in a painful but necessary restructuring that will bring benefits in the longer term, but because the old system is collapsing without any coherent alternative model having been substituted for it.

The Soviet Union differs from the countries considered previously in several striking respects. A first difference is that it is a vastly larger country: it has a population of almost 290 million, against the 38 million of Poland and much less in all the others. It is large enough to be able to operate relatively self-sufficiently, if it so chooses. This means that, unlike its former allies, the Soviet Union has a real choice as to whether it accompanies reform (assuming that it does in the end opt for reform) by opening up the economy. A second striking difference is that it has a rich natural resource base, including abundant and accessible energy and material supplies. This means that the Soviet Union should be in less need of external financial support than the other former centrally planned economies.

Other differences are much less favorable. For example, the memory of markets is much more remote (73 rather than 45 years or fewer) in the Soviet Union than in the rest of Eastern Europe; thus, no one in the economically active Soviet population has any experience of operating in a market economy. Moreover, unlike the other countries, the Soviet Union has not yet made an unequivocal political decision that it wants to move to a market economy. Traditional elements, notably the military and the bureaucracy, are unreconciled to abandoning central planning and socialism in favor of a market economy. At the end of 1990 and the beginning of 1991 those elements seemed to be gaining the upper hand in the central government. Then came a renewed burst of hope that the reformers would prevail, sparked by agreement on the principles of a new union treaty in April 1991. One day before the draft treaty was to be signed on 20 August 1991 (and shortly before this volume went to press), convservative elements staged an abortive coup. In its immediate aftermath, the prospects for a decisive move to scrap the old economic order once and for all appear to have improved dramatically.

The other difference from most of the other Eastern European countries lies in the power struggle between the center and the constituent republics (Yugoslavia and to a lesser extent Czechoslovakia face a similar problem). The conservatives charge that one consequence of the reform movement has been to weaken the ties that bind the union together, to a point where the continued existence of the Soviet Union is imperiled. (It is not in fact true that the republican governments in favor of economic reform are the same as those favoring breakup of the Soviet Union, notably because the government of the Russian republic is relatively reformist but also supportive of continued union, but that is beside the point here.)

The lack of a political consensus in favor of reform is well illustrated by Fedorov's account of the wrecking conditions that the bureaucracy tries to insist must be satisfied before convertibility can be introduced:

> Soviet bureaucrats often point to what they see as the absolute prerequisites that must be fulfilled before convertibility can be attained: increased export potential, adequate reserves, proper integration into the world economy, increased efficiency of enterprises, and the development of a qualified work force that is motivated to increase its productivity.

Some of these "conditions," such as integration into the world economy, are consequences of convertibility rather than sensible preconditions. Others, such as efficient enterprises and a qualified work force, are highly desirable whether or not the currency is convertible, but have no obvious relevance to the desirability of convertibility. If the bureaucracy succeeds in turning these into preconditions, the Soviet Union is unlikely to be able to benefit from the advantages of opening up its economy during the transition. Although such an opening may be less essential to efficient reform in the Soviet Union than in the small Central European countries by virtue of the Soviet Union's size, a failure to open up would still hamper the reform program.

Important elements of the strategy suggested as appropriate for the other former centrally planned economies would also seem to fit the case of a Soviet Union that really wished to reform, but a number of significant modifications would be called for. The government would need to spend some months at the outset putting in place the legal, tax, and unemployment insurance systems appropriate to a market economy, for these preconditions are even more absent in the Soviet Union than they were in most of the other economies of the region. In addition, it would need to sort out the constitutional relations between the central government and the republics during this preliminary phase, partly because any new tax system will have to embody an agreed division of revenues (and therefore of spending authority) between the different levels of government, and partly because no program will command credibility until the constitutional issue has been settled. If politically feasible, it would also be desirable to reduce (or, even better, to eliminate) the fiscal deficit during this period.

Within a year or so, one would hope that this preliminary phase would be followed by a decisive, broad-based move to a market economy, on the Czechoslovak model of 1 January 1991. The centerpiece would be general price liberalization. (I agree with Richard Cooper, whose comment in chapter 8 criticizes Fedorov's suggestion that prices be liberalized gradually. One might want to attenuate the impact of price liberalization on the poor, but that is best done by subsidizing and rationing a small basket of basic goods.) Current account convertibility of the ruble (if necessary modified by substantial transitional tariff protection) or a dual-rate system as proposed in Romania should accompany the price liberalization, to provide some external discipline on price setting. Privatization of smaller enterprises might start somewhat before the move to the market but should certainly not be delayed until much after it (as in Czechoslovakia), whereas that of large enterprises would presumably follow along at a pace that would be determined primarily by whether the Soviet Union decides to stick to selling state assets for money or whether it chooses some variant of the voucher scheme.

A Soviet move to the market would need to deviate from the Czechoslovak precedent (which is the most useful point of comparison, since Czechoslovakia has made the most orderly transition from a highly centralized economy) in two major respects. One is that, unlike Czechoslovakia, the Soviet Union has a large monetary overhang. One ill-advised attempt has already been made to deal with this, in January 1991, by suspension of most large-denomination (50- and 100-ruble) notes. One criticism of that step is that it destroyed many of the assets that might have been used by the most entrepreneurial sections of the populace to finance small privatizations. Conversely, the best way to deal with the overhang in the hands of private individuals is to press ahead with small privatization, especially of the housing stock. If that proves insufficient, it might be worth contemplating a quasi-monetary reform, in which those with money holdings in excess of normal liquidity needs are not expropriated but instead receive a claim to shares in large enterprises as these are privatized. If the Soviet Union opts for a scheme where the shares in large enterprises are transferred to mutual funds, claims on which are then distributed to the citizenry at large, one could conveniently give extra claims on those mutual funds as compensation for the money balances eliminated under the monetary reform.

The other big difference from the Czechoslovak case stems from the much larger size of the Soviet economy. McKinnon's argument for transitional tariff protection was developed with the specific case of the Soviet Union in mind. The possibility of supporting several efficient-sized plants that could compete with one another once demonopolization has been achieved makes the prospect of medium-term tariff protection less unappealing than in the small economies of Central Europe. There is also the option of operating with a dual exchange rate during the interim period.

One area in which the Soviet Union has already made important progress is exchange rate policy. In November 1990 the ruble was devalued from its ridiculously overvalued but commercially irrelevant rate of 1.6 dollars to the ruble, to a new commercial rate of 1.8 rubles to the dollar. More important, the thousands of differentiated currency ratios were abolished, so that the exchange rate became for the first time an interesting variable for an enterprise engaged in foreign trade.[31] However, retention ratios remain to distort import decisions toward what is wanted by enterprises that happen to have an export capability, at the expense of what is most urgently wanted by the economy in general. Auctions of foreign exchange allow the most extreme needs for imports on the part of the unprivileged (i.e., nonexporters) to be satisfied, but the distortions remain large. A free interbank market was established in early 1991 with the intention of

31. The original Articles of the IMF contained an apparently anomalous provision whereby a country was exempted from having to seek Fund authorization for a par value change if that change would not affect any internal price. It was included at the insistence of the Soviet delegation at Bretton Woods, at a time when efforts were still being made to induce the Soviets to participate in the Bretton Woods institutions. The intention of the Soviets was, of course, to exempt themselves from having to seek Fund permission to change the exchange rate. This they did by convincing the British and American architects of the new institution, John Maynard Keynes and Harry Dexter White, that their exchange rate was totally unimportant to the operation of the economy!

breaking the state monopoly on foreign-exchange transactions and easing access to imported goods for nonexporting enterprises, as well as diverting part of the black market trading to a legal market. This may represent the beginning of a move toward a dual exchange rate system.

Fedorov asserts that there is no question that the ruble will have to be devalued further, and he guesses that an appropriate rate will lie in the range of 3 to 6 rubles to the dollar. This implies a much smaller devaluation than would a move to the black market or the auction rate (which were both about 25 rubles to the dollar in February 1991). He rightly rejects those as misleading guides.

It may be that all these discussions of Soviet moves to a market economy are just pipe dreams. But not long ago anyone who even entertained such dreams would have been dismissed as an incurable romantic. If in the end the Soviet Union does opt for reform (and it is still declaring its intention of reforming, the West needs to be in a position to respond rapidly and decisively. Following the Houston Summit report and other studies undertaken in 1990 about how the Soviets should reform, we now have a pretty good—and widely agreed—idea of what would constitute a serious Soviet reform program. If and when the Soviet government commits itself to such a program in parallel with political liberalization, the West should welcome the Soviet Union into the Bretton Woods institutions and offer it the financial support needed to get a serious reform program off the ground.

Unless things change a great deal, it seems rather clear that the needed support will be largely up front, covering both imports needed to get the economy functioning again[32] and a stabilization loan to support a move to convertibility. In the longer term, the Soviet Union has all the conditions needed to stand on its own feet: exportable primary products, a low level of debt, and a large enough internal market to make it a potentially attractive location for direct investment.

One thing that the West should surely not do is accept the advice of Richard Portes (chapter 8) and turn its attention away from the Soviet Union on the ground that we can do very little for it. It is true that some of the intellectual hares that have been chased in the Soviet debate, such as the parallel-currency approach, look distinctly unpromising.[33] But the fact is that what happens in the Soviet Union is far too important for the West to stand by and watch with no attempt to help the Soviets sift sense from nonsense.

---

32. For example, my colleague Philip K. Verleger, Jr., tells me that Western know-how and advanced equipment could produce large energy savings and improvements in oil recovery rates at relatively small cost and rather quickly. That would give the Soviet Union additional export capacity with which to start buying the other goods needed for modernization.

33. Much the same could be said of some of the ideas that have dominated debate among academic economists in the Soviet Union's erstwhile competitor in the superpower stakes: just think of the input into discussion of the policy ineffectiveness theorem or real business cycle theory.

Concluding Remarks

The euphoria of early 1990 about the prospects for Eastern Europe has given way to a great deal of pessimism. Output has fallen everywhere, in places dramatically. Inflation is either high or rising or both. Shortages remain rampant in Bulgaria, Romania, and the Soviet Union. Debt looks unmanageable in several countries, even where it is not particularly high by the normal measures. National unity is under challenge in the Soviet Union, Yugoslavia, and even Czechoslovakia. Historic national antagonisms that were forcibly suppressed during the period of Soviet hegemony are arising anew.

This pessimism is almost certainly as exaggerated as the earlier euphoria. Output has indeed collapsed in eastern Germany, but that was the one place that could more or less afford to let it collapse, because the East Germans have a benefactor willing to pay much of the adjustment cost. Elsewhere the decline, while a real setback, is far short of a collapse (so far, although the bottom is not yet in sight, at least in the Soviet Union), and a part of the decline represents the elimination of negative value added.

Although times are difficult, all three Central European states seem on track to make the transition to a market economy. Obviously they still face immense problems: of inflation in Poland, of foreign debt in Hungary, of restitution of private property in Czechoslovakia, of privatization and industrial restructuring everywhere. But an enormous amount has been accomplished in a very short time. Considering the circumstances, social cohesion seems so far to have been maintained surprisingly well. Some of us may regret the signs that these countries are opting for the classic Hayekian version of capitalism rather than for a Western European social market economy, but that is another question.

East Germany presents a very different picture. Its decline in output would have been a catastrophe elsewhere, but its new status as an integral part of Germany ensures that it can hardly fail to make the transition eventually. The most interesting current policy question is whether it would ease the pain of the transition to substitute wage subsidies for the extensive subsidization of unemployment. The key moral for the rest of the emergent market economies is that they must at all costs avoid a comparable overvaluation.

The outcome is obviously much more uncertain in the other four countries, although for different reasons. In Bulgaria and Romania, the big questions are whether the new leaders have the political determination and the technical skill to carry through on the programs they have recently initiated, and whether they will receive the substantial external support that is likely to be necessary if policy reforms are to lead to economic revival before the political viability of the reform process is jeopardized by social unrest. High inflation, perhaps even hyperinflation, is a real danger, and stabilization programs may in due course need strong international support.

In both of the remaining countries, the Soviet Union and Yugoslavia, the outlook is dominated by threats to national integrity. In both countries the prospects for a successful transition to a market economy depend on a new constitutional deal involving a measure of devolution that satisfies the aspirations of the more disaffected regions. The alternatives are all unpleasant: at best, a national breakup that is accepted by all parties relatively quickly; at worst, civil war; in between, ongoing political and ethnic tensions that preclude any chance of fundamental reform, or the imposition of continued central rule by military force. Dismemberment of the central structure would presumably lead to some of the successor states making the transition to the market relatively quickly (the Baltic states and Georgia in the Soviet case, Croatia and Slovenia in the Yugoslav case), provided at least that they find adequate support in the international community. Forced imposition of continued union might eventually lead to economic reform on the Pinochet model, although this seems somewhat unlikely in the Soviet Union, where the military is among the most conservative forces in society.

One of the advantages that the Eastern European countries have over those countries that started to try to develop under a market economy thirty years ago is that it is now widely understood that development is promoted rather than hindered by integration into the international economy. Opening the economy to the outside world is even more important to small countries than to large ones (it will be absolutely critical to tiny successor states like the Baltics and the Yugoslav republics if the Soviet Union and Yugoslavia do break up), but it is valuable even for a country as large as the Soviet Union.

Certainly such opening has been an important element in the reform strategies of all three of the Central European countries in the vanguard of reform. Their strategies have differed somewhat, particularly as regards the pace of their opening—from Poland's big bang, to Hungary's studied gradualism, by way of Czechoslovakia's deliberate stride. There are, at least as yet, no clear lessons as to which of these strategies is to be preferred where there is an element of choice (which there was not in the Polish case), although the Czechoslovak model seems to come closer to the concept of a "minimum bang" than does Hungarian gradualism. But on the whole these countries have reacted rationally to their individual situations: despite the initial overdevaluation in Poland and Czechoslovakia and the current reluctance to face the need to devalue in Poland, their policymakers should be congratulated rather than condemned.

The West should welcome the direction in which Eastern European policies are evolving and should offer prompt and firm support where it is needed, notably to provide countries adequate reserves to establish convertibility once the other prerequisites for this move have been met. The Western countries' record to date has been encouraging. Poland received a $1 billion stabilization loan to help it launch its convertibility experiment, and it has recently achieved a 50 percent debt reduction. All of the Eastern European countries that are members of the IMF have now drawn substantial sums under stand-by programs, which seem to have been preceded by highly constructive policy dialogues. A European Bank for Reconstruction and Development has been created, with capital of $12 billion, and the IMF, the World Bank, and Western governments expect to make loans of some $17 billion during 1991. The Houston Summit report crystallized thought on the actions that the Soviet Union should be expected to initiate before it qualifies for broad-based program support and membership in the Bretton Woods institutions. The Organization for Economic Cooperation and Development created a new department to deal with the transition issue. A substantial academic literature has emerged, most of it encouragingly relevant, rather quickly. Western economies have remained open to exports from the East, with the customary shameful exceptions of agriculture and textiles.

These efforts will be crowned by success only if both East and West stay the course. The success will be universal only if the two countries whose reform programs have been derailed by the conflict engendered by old-fashioned nationalism and old-fashioned communism manage to come to terms with the modern world. It seems a tall order, but no more improbable than the very concept of "transition economics" would have seemed in, say, early 1989.

Acknowledgments

The author acknowledges with gratitude the stimulus provided by the authors, discussants, panelists, and floor participants at the conference cosponsored by the Institute for International Economics and the Austrian National Bank on 20–22 January 1991, as well as by the participants in the study groups held on 24 October 1990, 7 March 1991, and 12 March 1991 (in Vienna). Helpful comments on an earlier draft were provided by Bela Balassa, C. Fred Bergsten, Przemek Gajdeczka, Richard Portes, and several desk economists in the International Monetary Fund, but responsibility for the views and judgments expressed in this chapter is that of the author alone. The publications and support staff of the Institute, notably Michael Treadway and Vilma Gordon, merit particular thanks.

References

Adams, Charles, and Daniel Gros. 1986. "The Consequences of Real Exchange Rate Rules for Inflation: Some Illustrative Examples." *Staff Papers* 33, no. 3 (September): 439–76. Washington: International Monetary Fund.

Aganbegyan, Abel. 1988. *The New Stage of Perestroika*. New York: Institute for East-West Security Studies.

Akerlof, George, André Rose, Janet Yellen, and Helga Hessenius. 1991. "East Germany in from the Cold: The Economic Aftermath of Currency Union." Paper presented at the Conference of the Brookings Panel on Economic Activity, Washington (4–5 April).

Altman, Oscar L. 1962. "L'or russe et le rouble." *Economie Appliquée* 3/4:354–72.

Aslund, Anders. 1989. *Gorbachev's Struggle for Economic Reform*. Ithaca, NY: Cornell University Press.

Ball, Alan M. 1987. *Russia's Last Capitalist: The NEP Men: 1921–1929*. Berkeley: University of California Press.

Barkai, Haim. 1990. "The Role of Monetary Policy in Israel's 1985 Stabilization Effort." *IMF Working Paper* WP/90/29 (April). Washington: International Monetary Fund.

Barro, Robert, and David Gordon. 1983. "A Positive Theory of Monetary Policy in Natural Rate Model." *Journal of Political Economy* 91:589–610.

Bartha, Ferenc. 1989. "Mr. Bartha Presents a Hungarian View on the ECU and its Implications for East-West and Intra-Comecon Monetary Relations." Speech to the "Intergroup European Currency" of the European Parliament, Strasbourg (18 January).

Bauer, Tamàs. 1990. "The Microeconomics of Inflation under Economic Reforms: Enterprises and Their Environment." Paper presented at an EDI–World Bank seminar, Warsaw (12–13 March).

Belkin, V. 1988. "Convertible Ruble: When and Under Which Circumstances?" *Izvestia* 217 (August):3.

Belkin, V., Pavel Medvedev, and Igor Nit. 1989. "Turnover: The Way to Radical Reform." JPRS-UKO-89-002 (24 January).

Belkin, V., A. Kazmin, and A. Tsimailo. 1990. "The Program of the Transition to the Convertibility of the Ruble." *Bank Archiv Zeitschrift für das gesamte Bank- und Börsenwesen* (Vienna) 8:585–94.

Bergsten, C. Fred, and John Williamson. 1990. "Currency Convertibility in Eastern Europe." In *Central Banking Issues in Emerging Market-Oriented Economies*, 35–49. Kansas City: Federal Reserve Bank of Kansas City.

Bishop, Graham, Dirk Damrau, and Michelle Miller. 1989. *1992 and Beyond, Market Discipline Can Work in the EC Monetary Union*. London: Salomon Brothers (November).

Blanchard, Olivier, Rudiger Dornbusch, Paul Krugman, Richard Layard, and Lawrence Summers. 1990. *Reform in Eastern Europe* (the WIDER Report). Helsinki: World Institute for Development Economics Research.

Brainard, Lawrence J. 1990. "Reform in Eastern Europe: Creating a Capital Market." (Amex Bank Prize Essay). In *Finance and the International Economy*, vol. 4. Oxford: Oxford University Press for the Amex Bank Review.

Bofinger, Peter. 1989. "The EMS and Monetary Policy Coordination in Europe." *SUERF Papers on Monetary Policy and Financial Systems* 7. Tilburg, Netherlands: Société Universitaire Européenne de Recherches Financiers.

Bofinger, Peter. 1990a. "Unresolved Issues on the Road to Economic and Monetary Union (EMU) in Europe." *CEPR Discussion Paper Series* 405. London: Centre for Economic Policy Research.

Bofinger, Peter. 1990b. "The German Monetary Unification (Gmu): Converting Marks to D-Marks." *Review of the Federal Reserve Bank of St. Louis* 72, no. 4 (July–August): 17–36.

Bofinger, Peter. 1991. "A Multilateral Payments Union for Eastern Europe." *Banca Nazionale del Lavoro Quarterly Review* 176 (March): 69–88.

Bogomolov, Oleg. 1989. "How to Cure the Economy." *Izvestia* 254 (10 September): 2.

Brabant, Jozef M. van. 1976. "Zur Rolle Mitteleuropas im Rahmen des Rats für gegenseitige Wirtschaftshilfe." *Osteuropa-Wirtschaft* 1:1–20.

Brabant, Jozef M. van. 1987a. *Adjustment, Structural Change, and Economic Efficiency—Aspects of Monetary Cooperation in Eastern Europe*. New York and Cambridge: Cambridge University Press.

Brabant, Jozef M. van. 1987b. *Regional Price Formation in Eastern Europe—Theory and Practice of Trade Pricing*. Dordrecht-Boston-Lancaster: Kluwer Academic Publishers.

Brabant, Jozef M. van. 1989a. *Economic Integration in Eastern Europe—A Handbook*. Hemel Hempstead: Harvester Wheatsheaf and New York: Routledge.

Brabant, Jozef M. van. 1989b. "CMEA Reform and the Formulation of a Constitutional Framework." Paper presented at a conference on The Radical Reform of the CMEA as a Precondition of Cooperation with the EC—Theoretical and Practical Questions, Sopron, Hungary (16–20 November).

Brabant, Jozef M. van. 1989c. "Regional Integration, Economic Reforms, and Convertibility." *Jahrbuch der Wirtschaft Osteuropas—Yearbook of East-European Economics* 13, no. 1: 44–81.

Brabant, Jozef M. van. 1990a. "Ruble Convertibility in the Reform Process—A Sobering Note." In Josef Brada and Michael Claudon, eds., *Reforming the Ruble—Monetary Aspects of Perestroika*, 133–72. New York: New York University Press.

Brabant, Jozef M. van. 1990b. "Transition Economique, Convertibilité, et Investissements Etrangers en Europe de l'Est." In Jean-Daniel Clavel and John Sloan, eds., *Economies en Transition—Le Développement du Secteur Privé*. Brussels: Editions Bruylants (forthcoming).

Brabant, Jozef M. van. 1990c. "Wither the CMEA?—Reconstructing Socialist Economic Integration in the 1990s." New York: author (mimeographed, January).

Brabant, Jozef M. van. 1990d. *Remaking Eastern Europe—On the Political Economy of Transition*. Dordrecht-Boston-London: Kluwer Academic Publishers.

Brabant, Jozef M. van. 1990e. "Toward an Eastern European Payments Union: Questions and Answers." New York: author (mimeographed, October).

Brabant, Jozef M. van. 1990f. "On Reforming the Trade and Payments Regimes in the CMEA." *Jahrbuch der Wirtschaft Osteuropas—Yearbook of East-European Economics* 14, no. 2: 7–30.

Brabant, Jozef M. van. 1990g. *On the Conditions of a Central European Payments Union*. New York: Institute for East-West Security Studies.

Brabant, Jozef M. van. 1991a. "Regional Economic Integration and the Transition in Eastern Europe." In Robert W. McGee, ed., *Eastern Europe in Evolution*. New York: Edward Mellen Publishers.

Brabant, Jozef M. van. 1991b. *Integrating Eastern Europe into the Global Economy—Convertibility Through a Payments Union*. Dordrecht-Boston-London: Kluwer Academic Publishers.

Brabant, Jozef M. van. 1991c. "Assistance to Eastern Europe and European Economic and Monetary Integration." *De Pecunia* (forthcoming).

Brabant, Jozef M. van. 1991d. "The Demise of the CMEA—The Agony of Inaction." *Osteuropa-Wirtschaft* (forthcoming).

Brabant, Jozef M. van. 1991e. "Renewal of Cooperation and Economic Transition in Eastern Europe." *Studies in Comparative Communism* (forthcoming).

Camdessus, Michel. 1990. "Best of Both Worlds." *Financial Times* (London) 20 April.

Carr, E. H. 1952. *The Bolshevik Revolution: 1917–1923*, vol. 2. New York: Macmillan. (Reprinted by W.W. Norton, New York, 1985.)

Carr, E. H. 1954. *The Interregnum: 1923–1924*. New York: Macmillan. (Reprinted by Penguin Books, 1969.)

Carr, E. H. 1958. *Socialism in One Country: 1924–1926*, vol. 1. New York: Macmillan.

Centre for Economic Policy Research. 1990. *Monitoring European Integration—The Impact of Eastern Europe*. London: Centre for Economic Policy Research.

Cochrane, John, and Barry W. Ickes. 1991. "Stopping Inflation in Reforming Socialist Economies." *American Economic Review* (May).

Collier, Paul, and Vijay Joshi. 1989. "Exchange Rate Policies in Developing Countries." *Oxford Review of Economic Policy* 5, no. 3: 94–113.

Collins, Susan M., and Dani Rodrik. 1991. *Eastern Europe and the Soviet Union in the World Economy.* POLICY ANALYSES IN INTERNATIONAL ECONOMICS 32. Washington: Institute for International Economics.

Colombatto, Enrico. 1983. "CMEA, Money and Ruble Convertibility." *Applied Economics* 4:479–506.

Commander, Simon, and Fabrizio Coricelli. 1990. "Levels, Rates, and Sources of Inflation in Socialist Economies." Paper presented at an EDI–World Bank seminar, Warsaw (12–13 March).

Committee for the Study of Economic and Monetary Union (Delors Committee). 1989. *Report on Economic and Monetary Union in the European Community.* Luxembourg: European Community.

Cooper, Richard N. 1990. "Commentary: Currency Convertibility in Eastern Europe." In *Central Banking Issues in Emerging Market-Oriented Economies,* 141–48. Kansas City: Federal Reserve Bank of Kansas City.

Coricelli, Fabrizio, and Roberto de Rezende Rocha. 1990. "Stabilization Programs in Eastern Europe: A Comparative Analysis of the Polish and Yugoslav Programs of 1990." Paper presented to a conference organized by the World Bank and the World Economy Research Institute, Pultusk, Poland (October).

Daviddi, Renzo, and Efisio Espa. 1989. "The Economics of Ruble Convertibility." *Banca Nazionale del Lavoro Quarterly Review* 171 (December): 441–67.

Deutsche Bundesbank. 1990a. "Terms of the Currency Conversion in the German Democratic Republic on July 1, 1990." *Monthly Report* 42, no. 6 (June): 40–45. Frankfurt: Deutsche Bundesbank.

Deutsche Bundesbank. 1990b. "The Monetary Union with the German Democratic Republic." *Monthly Report* 42, no. 7 (July): 13–28.

Deutsche Bundesbank. 1990c. "The Economic Scene in the Federal Republic of Germany in Autumn 1990." *Monthly Report* 42, no. 12 (December). Frankfurt: Deutsche Bundesbank.

de Vries, Margaret G. 1969a. "The Fund and the EPU." In J. Keith Horsefield, ed., *The International Monetary Fund, 1945–1965—Twenty Years of International Monetary Cooperation, vol. II: Analysis,* 317–31. Washington: International Monetary Fund.

de Vries, Margaret G. 1969b. "The Retreat of Bilateralism." In J. Keith Horsefield, ed., *The International Monetary Fund, 1945–1965—Twenty Years of International Monetary Cooperation, vol. II: Analysis,* 297–316. Washington: International Monetary Fund.

Diebold, William, Jr. 1988. "The Marshall Plan in Retrospect: A Review of Recent Scholarship." *Journal of International Affairs* 2: 421–35.

Dietz, R., H. Gabrisch, I. Grosser, P. Havlik, K. Laski, F. Levcik, S. Richter, and H. Vidovic. 1990. "Transition from the Command to a Market Economy." *WIIW-Forschungsberichte* 163. Vienna: Wiener Institut für Internationale Wirtschaftsforschung.

Dohan, Michael R. 1969. "Soviet Foreign Trade in the NEP Economy and Soviet Industrialization Policy." Unpublished doctoral dissertation, Massachusetts Institute of Technology.

Dornbusch, Rudiger. 1981. "Exchange Rate Rules and Macroeconomic Stability." In J. Williamson, ed., *Exchange Rate Rules*. London: Macmillan.

Dornbusch, Rudiger. 1990. "Experiences with Extreme Monetary Instability." Paper presented at an EDI–World Bank seminar, Warsaw (12–13 March).

Economic Commission for Europe. 1990. *Economic Survey of Europe in 1989–1990*. New York: Economic Commission for Europe.

The Economist. 1990. "Industrial Concentration in the USSR." *The Economist* (11–17 August): 67.

Ecu Banking Association. 1990. *Reforms in Eastern Europe and the Role of the Ecu—A Report by the Macro-financial Study Group of the Ecu Banking Association*. Paris: Association Bancaire pour l'Ecu.

Edwards, Richard W., Jr. 1985. *International Monetary Collaboration*. Dobbs Ferry, NY: Transnational Publishers.

Edwards, Sebastian. 1989. "On the Sequencing of Structural Reforms." *NBER Working Paper Series* 3818 (October). Cambridge, MA: National Bureau of Economic Research.

Edwards, Sebastian, and Alejandra Cox-Edwards. 1987. *Monetarism and Liberalization: The Chilean Experiment*. Cambridge, MA: Ballinger.

European Commission. 1990. "Stabilization, Liberalization, and Devolution: Assessment of the Economic Situation and Reform Process in the Soviet Union." *European Economy* 45 (whole issue, December).

Faber, Mike. 1990. "Renegotiating Official Debts." *Finance and Development* (December).

Federal Executive Council. 1989. "Program Ekonomske Reforme i Mere za Njegovu Realizaciju u 1990 Godini." *Jugoslovenski Pregled* 11–12.

Federal Government of the Czech and Slovak Federal Republic. 1990 "Document on the Scenario of the Economic Reform" (in Czech). *Hospodárské noviny* (Prague, 4 September).

Federal Statistical Committee. 1990. *Yugoslav Statistical Yearbook*. Belgrade: Federal Statistical Committee.

Flemming, John. 1990. "Gradualism and Shock Treatment of Tax and Structural Reform." *Fiscal Studies* 11, no. 3 (August):12–26.

Frenkel, Jacob A. 1990. "Commentary: Currency Convertibility in Eastern Europe." In *Central Banking Issues in Emerging Market-Oriented Economies*, 149–56. Kansas City, MO: Federal Reserve Bank of Kansas City.

Garfinkel, Michelle. 1989. "What Is an 'Acceptable' Rate of Inflation? A Review of the Issue." *Review of the Federal Reserve Bank of St. Louis* 71, no. 4: 3–28.

Gianviti, François. 1989. "The International Monetary Fund and External Debt." *Recueil des Cours* 3:213–86.

Gilman, Martin G. 1990. "Heading for Currency Convertibility." *Finance and Development* 27, no. 3 (September): 32–34.

Gold, Joseph. 1971. "The Fund's Concept of Convertibility," *Pamphlet Series* 14. Washington: International Monetary Fund.

Gold, Joseph. 1978. "Use, Conversion and Exchange of Currency under the Second Amendment of the Fund's Articles." *Pamphlet Series* 23. Washington: International Monetary Fund.

Grubel, Herbert G. 1971. "The Demand for International Reserves: A Critical Review of the Literature." *Journal of Economic Literature* 9: 1148–66.

Havlik, P. 1990. "Report on Lecture by S.S. Shatalin at WIIW." *WIIW-Mitglieder-information* 9. Vienna: Wiener Institut für Internationale Wirtschaftsfor-schung.

Hillman, Arye L. 1990. "Macroeconomic Policy in Hungary and its Microeco-nomic Implications." *European Economy* 43: 55–66.

Hinds, Manuel. 1990. "Issues in the Introduction of Market Forces in Eastern European Socialist Economies." *World Bank Report* IDP-0057.

Hogan, Michael J. 1987. *The Marshall Plan—America, Britain, and the Reconstruc-tion of Western Europe, 1947–1952.* Cambridge: Cambridge University Press.

Holzman, Franklyn. 1978. "CMEA's Hard Currency Deficits and Rouble Con-vertibility." In Nita Watts, ed., *Economic Relations Between East and West.* London: St. Martins Press.

Institute for International Finance. 1990. *Building Free Market Economies in Central and Eastern Europe: Challenges and Realities.* Washington: Institute for Interna-tional Finance.

International Monetary Fund. 1989. *Yearbook of Foreign Exchange Restrictions.* Washington: International Monetary Fund.

International Monetary Fund, International Bank for Reconstruction and Devel-opment, Organization for Economic Cooperation and Development, and Euro-pean Bank for Reconstruction and Development. 1990. *The Economy of the USSR: Summary and Recommendations* (mimeographed, December).

International Monetary Fund, International Bank for Reconstruction and Devel-opment, Organization for Economic Cooperation and Development, and Euro-pean Bank for Reconstruction and Development. 1991. *A Study of the Soviet Economy* (the Houston Summit Report, 3 vols.). Washington: International Monetary Fund.

Iurovskii. L. N. 1928. "Chervonets." In *Denezhnaia politika sovetskoi vlasti (1917–1927).* Reprinted in part with commentary by A. I. Kazmin in *Dengi i kredit* no. 7 (1990): 69–79.

Jochimsen, Reimut. 1990. "The Impact of the Monetary Union on the German Economy." *Auszüge aus Presseartikeln* 93, 11–15. Frankfurt: Deutsche Bundesbank (3 December).

Jorgensen, Erika A., Alan Gelb, and Inderjit Singh. 1990. "The Behavior of Polish Firms after the 'Big Bang': Findings from a Field Trip." Paper presented at the OECD Conference on The Transition to a Market Economy in Central and Eastern Europe, Paris (November).

Kaplan, Jacob J., and Günther Schleiminger. 1989. *The European Payments Union—Financial Diplomacy in the 1950s.* Oxford: Clarendon Press.

Kazmin, A. 1989. "Perestroika of the Monetary and Credit Mechanism During the Transition to Market Economy." In A. Agabegyan, L. Abalkin, and V. Belkin, eds., *The Practice of Perestroika of Economic Mechanism,* vol. 2. Moscow: Moskovskii Rabochiij.

Kazmin, A. I. 1990a. "Opyt perekhoda k rynochnoi ekonomike denezhnaia reforma 1922–1924." *Dengi i kredit* no. 9:65–72.

Kazmin, A. I., ed. 1990b. *Finansovoe ozdorovlenie ekonomiki: opyt NEPA.* Moscow: Moskovskii Rabochii.

Keesing, F.A.G., and Paul J. Brand 1963. "Possible Role of a Clearing House in the Latin American Regional Market" *Staff Papers* 10 (November): 397–460. Washington: International Monetary Fund.

Kemme, David M. 1990. "Economic Transition in Poland." *International Economic Insights* 1, no. 3 (November–December): 36–39.

Kenen, Peter B. 1991. "Transitional Arrangements for Trade and Payments Among the CMEA Countries." *Staff Papers* (June). Washington: International Monetary Fund.

Klaus, Václav. 1990. "Policy Dilemmas of Eastern European Reforms." In *Central Banking Issues in Emerging Market-Oriented Economies,* 51–56. Kansas City, MO: Federal Reserve Bank of Kansas City.

Klaus, Václav. 1991. *A Road to a Market Economy.* Prague: Top Agency.

Klaus, Václav, and V. Dlouhy. 1990. Review of *Inflation Stabilization. European Journal of Political Economy* 6.

Kloten, Norbert. 1990. "Zur Transformation von Wirtschaftsordnungen." *Ordo: Jahrbuch für die Ordnung von Wirtschaft und Gesellschaft* 40: 99–127.

Kloten, Norbert. 1991. "Transformation einer zentralverwalteten Wirtschaft in eine Marktwirtschaft, Die Erfahrungen mit der DDR." *Auszüge aus Presseartikeln* 1. Frankfurt: Deutsche Bundesbank (4 January).

Knapp, Manfred. 1981. "Reconstruction and West-Integration: The Impact of the Marshall Plan on Germany." *Zeitschrift für die gesamte Staatswissenschaft* 3:415–33.

König, Reiner. 1990. "The Role of Germany in the New Europe." Paper presented to the International Economic Outlook Conference, sponsored by the WEFA Group, Philadelphia (30 October).

Kornai, János. 1986. "The Hungarian Reform Process." *Journal of Economic Literature* 24, no. 4 (December): 1687–1737.

Kornai, János. 1990. *The Road to a Free Economy.* New York: Norton.

Köves, A., and P. Marer. 1990. "Economic Liberalisation in Eastern Europe: A Conceptual and Comparative Perspective." Paper presented at the Fourth World Congress for Soviet and East European Studies, Harrogate, England (21–26 July).

Kronman, Anthony. 1985. "Contract Law and the State of Nature." *Journal of Law, Economics, and Organization* 1: 5–33.

Lange, Oskar. 1937. "On the Economic Theory of Socialism." *Review of Economic Studies* 4.

Laski, K. 1990. "Concepts of Transition in Socialist Economies." Paper presented to the Workshop on East-West European Economic Interaction, Session XIII, "Economics and Politics of Transition," Tübingen, Germany (10–14 October).

Lavigne, M. 1991. "Economic Reforms in Eastern Europe: Prospects for the '90s." Lecture presented at the Czech Economic Society, Prague (January).

Lerner, A.P. 1936. "The Symmetry Between Import and Export Taxes." *Economica* 111 (August): 308–13.

Levcik, F. 1990. "The Technological Gap in the CMEA Countries: Missing Incentives." In K. Dopfer and K.F. Raible (eds.), *The Evolution of Economic Systems.* London: Macmillan Press.

Lipschitz, Leslie, and Donogh McDonald. 1990. "German Unification, Economic Issues." *IMF Occasional Paper* 75. Washington: International Monetary Fund (December).

Lipton, David, and Jeffrey Sachs. 1990. "Creating a Market Economy in Eastern Europe: The Case of Poland." *Brookings Papers on Economic Activity* 1: 75–133.

Loevetskii, D. A. 1926. *Valiutnaia politika SSSR.* Moscow: Finansovoe Izdatelstvo NKF SSSR. (Portions reprinted in Kazmin [1990b]:112–75.)

Machowski, Heinrich. 1973. "Die Funktion der DDR im RgW." *Deutschland-Archiv* (special October issue): 3–19.

Manevich, V. E. 1988. "O valiutnom paritete i konvertiruenosti chervontsa v 20-kh godakh." *Finansy SSSR* no. 11:50–54.

Marer, Paul. 1985. *Dollar GNPs of the USSR and Eastern Europe.* Baltimore: Johns Hopkins University Press for the World Bank.

Marrese, Michael. 1990. *Rapporteur's Report of the June 1990 ESD Seminars on the Transformation of Planned Economies.* Paris: Economics and Statistics Department, Organization for Economic Cooperation and Development (August).

McKinnon, Ronald. 1963. "Optimum Currency Areas." *American Economic Review* 53: 717–25.

McKinnon, Ronald I. 1966. "Intermediate Products and Differential Tariffs: A Generalization of Lerner's Symmetry Theorem." *Quarterly Journal of Economics* 80 (November): 584–615.

McKinnon, Ronald I. 1973. *Money and Capital in Economic Development.* Washington: Brookings Institution.

McKinnon, Ronald I. 1979. *Money in International Exchange: The Convertible Currency System.* New York: Oxford University Press.

McKinnon, Ronald. 1989a. "The Order of Liberalization for the Soviet Economy." Stanford: Stanford University (mimeographed, April).

McKinnon, Ronald. 1989b. "Stabilizing the Ruble." Stanford: Stanford University (mimeographed).

McKinnon, Ronald I. 1991a. *The Order of Economic Liberalization: Financial Control in the Transition to a Market Economy.* Baltimore: Johns Hopkins University Press.

McKinnon, Ronald I. 1991b. "Financial Control in the Transition from Classical Socialism to a Market Economy." *Journal of Economic Perspectives* (forthcoming).

Mill, John Stuart. 1848. *Principles of Political Economy,* vol. 2. New York.

Milward, Alan S. 1987. *The Reconstruction of Western Europe, 1945–51.* London: Methuen & Co..

Milward, Alan S. 1988. "Was the Marshall Plan Necessary?" *Diplomatic History* 2: 231–53.

Milward, Alan S. 1990. Review of *The European Payments Union—Financial Diplomacy in the 1950s* by Jacob J. Kaplan and Günther Schleiminger. *Economic History Review* 4:767–68.

National Bank of Yugoslavia. 1989. *National Bank of Yugoslavia Bulletin* (November–December).

Nordhaus, W.D. 1975. "The Political Business Cycle." *Review of Economic Studies* 42:169–90.

Nuti, Domenico. 1990a. "Stabilization and Sequencing in the Reform of Socialist Economies." Paper presented at an EDI–World Bank Seminar, Warsaw (12–13 March).

Nuti, Domenico. 1990b. "Internal and International Aspects of Monetary Disequilibrium in Poland." *European Economy* 43:169–82.

Organization for Economic Cooperation and Development. 1990. *OECD Economic Outlook* (July). Paris: Organization for Economic Cooperation and Development.

Patterson, Perry. 1989. "Prospect for Commodity and Financial Exchanges." In J. Tedstrom, ed., *Socialism, Perestroika and the Dilemma of Soviet Economic Reform.* Boulder, CO: Westview Press.

Pearce, David W. 1981. *The Dictionary of Modern Economics.* Cambridge, MA: MIT Press.

Peck, M.J., Wil Albeda, Barry Bosworth, Richard Cooper, Alfred Kahn, William Nordhaus, Thomas J. Richardson, and Kimio Uno. 1990. *The Soviet Economic*

Crisis: Steps to Avert Collapse. Vienna: International Institute for Applied Systems Analysis (December).

Peck, M.J., Petr Aven, and Thomas J. Richardson, eds. 1991. *What Is To Be Done? Proposals for the Soviet Transition to the Market*. New Haven: Yale University Press (forthcoming).

Petrakov, Nikolai. 1990. *People's Deputies: Economy—Today and Tomorrow*. Moscow: Moskovskii Rabochiij.

Portes, Richard. 1990a. "Introduction." *European Economy* 43:9–17.

Portes, Richard. 1990b. "The Transition to Convertibility in Eastern Europe and the USSR." Presented at the Second Varna Seminar on The Way to Convertibility in Central and East European Countries, Varna, Bulgaria (October).

Richter, S. 1991. "Hungary: Recession with First Signs of Adjustment." *WIIW-Mitgliederinformation* 9. Vienna: Wiener Institut für Internationale Wirtschaftsforschung.

Rieger, P. 1989. "Convertibility." In G. Fink and A. Wala (eds.), *New Developments in Banking and Finance in East and West*. Vienna: Austrian National Bank.

Sachs, Jeffrey. 1990. "Eastern Europe's Economies—What Is to be Done?" *The Economist* (13 January): 19–24.

Sachs, Jeffrey. 1991. "Sachs on Poland." *The Economist* (19 January).

Schlesinger, Helmut. 1990. "Die D-Mark in Ost und West." *Auszüge aus Pressartikeln* 88, 5–8. Frankfurt: Deutsche Bundesbank.

Schrenk, Martin. 1990. "Whither Comecon?" *Finance and Development* (September).

Shmelev, Nikolai, and Vladimir Popov. 1989. *The Turning Point: Revitalizing the Soviet Economy*. New York: Doubleday.

Sokil, Catherine, and Timothy King. 1989. "Financial Reform in Socialist Economies: Workshop Overview." In Christine Kessides et al., *Financial Reform in Socialist Economies*, 1–27. Washington and Florence: Economic Development Institute of the World Bank and European University Institute.

Soros, George. 1991. "A Gift for the Hungarian Economy." *Wall Street Journal* (4 April).

Sulc, Z. 1990. " 'Internal' Currency Convertibility" (in Czech). *Hospodárské noviny* 29 (Prague).

Székely, Istvàn. 1990. The Reform of the Hungarian Financial System, *European Economy* 43: 107–23.

Tan, Augustine. 1970. "Differential Rariffs, Negative Value-Added and the Theory of Effective Protection." *American Economic Review* 60, no. 1 (March).

Tew, Brian. 1967. *International Monetary Cooperation, 1945–67*. London: Hutchinson University Library.

Tietmeyer, Hans. 1990. "Wirtschafts und Währungsintegration in Deutschland und Europa. *Auszüge aus Pressartikeln* 78, 8–12. Frankfurt: Deutsche Bundesbank.

Triffin, Robert. 1957. *Europe and the Money Muddle—From Bilateralism to Near-Convertibility, 1947–1956.* New Haven and London: Yale University Press.

Tsimailo, A. 1989a. "What Kind of Convertibility Do We Need?" *Ekonomicheskaya Gazeta* 2 (January):21.

Tsimailo, A. 1989b. "Convertibility: A Result but not a Means." In A. Agabegyan, L. Abalkin, and V. Belkin, eds., *The Practice of Perestroika of Economic Mechanism,* vol. 2. Moscow: Moskovskii Rabochiij.

Walters, Sir Alan. 1991. "Misapprehensions on Privatization." *International Economic Insights* 2, no. 1 (January–February): 28–30.

Wandycz, Piotr S. 1970. "Recent Traditions of the Quest for Unity—Attempted Polish-Czechoslovak and Yugoslav-Bulgarian Confederations, 1940–1948." In *The People's Democracies after Prague—Soviet Hegemony, Nationalism, Regional Integration,* 35–93. Bruges, Belgium: De Tempel.

Wexler, Imanuel. 1983. *The Marshall Plan Revisited—The European Recovery Program in Economic Perspective.* Westport, CT: Greenwood Press.

Wickham, Peter. 1985. "The Choice of Exchange Rate Regime in Developing Countries." *Staff Papers* 32, no. 2: 248–88. Washington: International Monetary Fund.

Williamson, John. 1983. *The Open Economy and the World Economy.* New York: Basic Books.

Williamson, John. 1990a. "Convertibility, Trade Policy, and the Payments Constraint." Paper presented at a conference on The Transition to a Market Economy in Central and Eastern Europe, sponsored by the OECD, Geneva (28–30 November).

Williamson, John, ed. 1990b. *Latin American Adjustment: How Much Has Happened?* Washington: Institute for International Economics.

Williamson, John. 1990c. *The Progress of Policy Reform in Latin America.* POLICY ANALYSES IN INTERNATIONAL ECONOMICS 28. Washington: Institute for International Economics.

Williamson, John. 1991a. "Current Issues in Transition Economics." Paper presented at the J.J. Polak Festchrift Conference, Washington (January).

Williamson, John. 1991b. "On Stopping Inflation." Comment on a paper presented by Miguel Kiguel and Nissan Liviatan at a conference organized by the World Bank and the World Economy Research Institute, Pultusk, Poland (October).

Williamson, John, and Marcus Miller. 1987. *Targets and Indicators: A Blueprint for the International Coordination of Economic Policy.* POLICY ANALYSES IN INTERNATIONAL ECONOMICS 22. Washington: Institute for International Economics.

Williamson, John, and Chris Milner. 1991. *The World Economy: A Textbook in International Economics*. Hemel Hempstead: Wheatsheaf.

Wolf, Thomas. 1985. "Economic Stabilization in Planned Economies." *Staff Papers* 32, no. 1: 78–129. Washington: International Monetary Fund.

Wolf, Thomas A. 1990a. *Market-Oriented Reform of Foreign Trade in Planned Economies*. Washington: International Monetary Fund (April).

Wolf, Thomas A. 1990b. "Reform, Inflation und Anpassung in Planwirtschaften." *Finanzierung und Entwicklung* 27 (March): 2–5.

Wood, Robert E. 1986. *From Marshall Plan to Debt Crisis—Foreign Aid and Development Choices in the World Economy*. Berkeley, CA: University of California Press.

Wyplosz, Charles. 1989. "Asymmetry in the EMS." *European Economic Review* 33: 310–20.

Appendix

Conference Participants

20–22 January 1991

Ljubiša Adamovich
Belgrade University

Heinrich Ambrosch
Zentralsparkasse und
  Kommerzialbank

Hannes Androsch
Vienna

Guzel Anulova
Institute of World Economy and
  International Relations

Birgir Arnason
European Free Trade Association

Ilona Baar
National Bank of Hungary

Stephan Barisitz
International Business Research

André Bascoul
Bank for International Settlements

Gerhard Bauer
Austrian National Bank

Peter Bofinger
Landeszentralbank Baden-
  Württemberg

Jean-Joseph Boillot
Embassy of France, Prague

Lajos Bokros
National Bank of Hungary

Jozef M. van Brabant
United Nations

Lawrence Brainard
International Monetary Fund

Anton Burghardt
Girozentrale

Waltraut Burghardt
Österreichische Kontrollbank

Alison Butler
Federal Reserve Bank of St. Louis

Günther Chaloupek
Kammer für Arbeiter und
  Angestellte

Susan M. Collins
Harvard University

Richard N. Cooper
Harvard University

Doris Cornelsen
Deutsches Institut für
  Wirtschaftsforschung

Raimund Dietz
Wiener Institut für Internationale
  Wirtschaftsvergleiche

Ventseslav Dimitrov
National Assembly, Sofia

Michael R. Dohan
Queens College of the City
  University of New York

Alexander Dörfel
Austrian National Bank

Wolfgang Duchatczek
Austrian National Bank

Boris Fedorov
Moscow

Bertrand Fessard de Foucault
Embassy of France, Vienna

Jarko Fidrmuc
Institut für Höhere Studien

Gerhard Fink
International Business Research

John Flemming
Bank of England

Michael Friedländer
Nomura Research Institute

Helmut Frisch
Technische Hochschule Wien

Christine Gartner
Austrian National Bank

Hans Genberg
Institut Universitaire des Hautes
  Etudes Internationales

Stanislaw Gomulka
Ministry of Finance, Warsaw

Wolfdietrich Grau
Austrian National Bank

Judit Habuda
IFO-Institut für
  Wirtschaftsforschung

Heinz Handler
Österreichische Institut für
  Wirtschaftsforschung

Peter Havlik
Wiener Institut für Internationale
  Wirtschaftsvergleiche

Eduard Hochreiter
Austrian National Bank

Hans Holzhacker
Nomura Research Institute

Franz Hörmannstorfer
Austrian National Bank

Miroslav Hrnčíř
Institute of Economics

Georg Hubmer
Austrian National Bank

Rouben Indjikian
United Nations Conference on
  Trade and Development

Ileana Ionescu
Ministry of Finance, Bucharest

Lucian C. Ionescu
Bucharest

Andrei I. Kazmin
Academy of Sciences of the USSR

Heinz Kienzl
Austrian National Bank

Edith Kitzmantel
Ministry of Finance, Vienna

Terhi Kivilahti
Bank of Finland

Václav Klaus
Ministry of Finance, Prague

Rudolf Klier
Austrian National Bank

Helmut Kramer
Österreichische Institut für
  Wirtschaftsforschung

Michael Krammer
BAWAG

Jan Kregel
University of Bologna and The
  Johns Hopkins University

Günter Krottenmüller
Österreichische Postsparkasse

Thomas Lachs
Austrian National Bank

Ferdinand Lacina
Ministry of Finance, Vienna

Flemming Larsen
Commission of the European
  Communities

Marie Lavigne
European Studies Center at Stirín

Lazar Lazarov
ELAZ Enterprises International

Friedrich Levcik
Wiener Institut für Internationale
  Wirtschaftsvergleiche

Karol Lutkowski
Ministry of Finance, Warsaw

Michael Marrese
Organization for Economic
  Cooperation and Development

Kurt Mauler
Austrian National Bank

Stefaan Missinne
Prince Albert Foundation

Erich Musyl
Office of the Chancellor, Vienna

Domenico Mario Nuti
Commission of the European
  Communities

Alain Nyssens
National Bank of Belgium

Gábor Oblath
Institute of Economic Market
  Research and Informatics

Andrzej Olechowski
National Bank of Poland

Marek Oleś
National Bank of Poland

Alexander Otto
Vienna

Jean-Pierre Patat
Banque de France

Joan Pearce
Commission of the European
  Communities

Theodor Plank
Creditanstalt-Bankverein

Richard Portes
Centre for Economic Policy
  Research

Dariusz K. Rosati
Foreign Trade Research Institute

Karl Werner Rüsch
Austrian National Bank

Sylvia Sabeditsch
Austrian National Bank

Maria Schaumayer
Austrian National Bank

Wolfgang Schill
Deutsche Bundesbank

Klaus Schröder
Forschungsinstitute für
  Internationale Politik

Aurel Schubert
Austrian National Bank

Norbert Schuh
Organization for Economic
  Cooperation and Development

Helmuth Schwap
Zentralsparkasse und
  Kommerzialbank

Hans Seidel
Institut für Höhere Studien

Wanda Skorupa
Erste Österreichische Spar-Kasse-
Bank

Ingrid Stainoch
Austrian National Bank

Jan Stankovsky
Österreichische Institut für
  Wirtschaftsforschung

Werner Studener
Austrian National Bank

Benedikt Thanner
IFO-Institut für
  Wirtschaftsforschung

John Thompson
Organization for Economic
  Cooperation and Development

Andrei V. Tsimailo
Academy of Sciences of the USSR

Todor Valchev
National Bank of Bulgaria

Werner Varga
Creditanstalt-Bankverein

Adolf Wala
Austrian National Bank

John Williamson
Institute for International
  Economics

Andreas Wörgötter
Institut für Höhere Studien

Jaromír Zahradník
State Bank of Czechoslovakia

Peter Zdrahal
Austrian National Bank

Index

Abalkin Plan 375
Abalkin, Leonid 296
Adjustment costs. *See* Output losses
  during transition
Agriculture 51, 56, 81, 102, 255, 325-
  27, 335, 340, 364
Albania 374
Anti-inflation policy. *See also*
  Macroeconomic stabilization;
  Monetary policy
  as condition for convertibility 43
  difficulties facing 122-23, 144, 207,
    354, 358-59
  essentially domestic 199, 212
  exchange rate as target in 126
  frame conditions 35
  in Hungary 228, 246, 248-49
  in Yugoslavia 169, 172, 175
  nominal anchor as part of 148
  real costs of 136
  through ECSB 133
  trade-off with devaluation 199
Article VIII (IMF) 21, 23, 50, 66, 118,
  174, 273, 302
Article XIV (IMF) 273, 302
Auctions, currency
  controls on enterprises and 56
  in Poland 157, 161
  in reforming economies 44
  in Romania 267, 423
  in Soviet Union 288-90, 304, 307,
    333, 427
  under central planning 370-71
Austral Plan (Argentina) 124
Austria 4, 16, 352
Austrian National Bank 16

Balance of payments
  in Czechoslovakia 218, 221, 224,
    236, 237
  in Hungary 228, 240, 247-49
  in Poland 35, 158, 161, 163, 202,
    211
  in Romania 265

in Soviet Union 307
in united Germany 195
in Yugoslavia 169, 175, 353
Bank for International Settlements 64,
  87
Banking reform
  as condition for convertibility 43
  as condition for payments union 271
  in Bulgaria 260, 420
  in East Germany 185
  in Hungary 45, 230, 417
  in Poland 164
  in Romania 269
  in Soviet Union 297, 316
  macroeconomic stabilization and 36
  place in reform process 15
  to enhance central bank credibility
    151
Bankruptcy laws 122, 128
Barter 79, 211, 213, 245, 295, 332
Big bang approach to reform. *See also*
  Shock therapy
  conditions for 227
  definition 35, 355
  elements 35
  German unification as 186, 412
  for Soviet Union 293, 295
  in Czechoslovakia 9-13, 46, 59, 72
  in Poland 3, 35, 46, 58, 72, 161, 231,
    276, 383, 407
  in Yugoslavia 72, 169
  infeasibility of 56
  versus gradualism 21-59, 72, 183,
    253-54, 267, 339, 383-86
Black markets, in currencies 174, 247,
  371
  as misleading exchange rate indicator
    287, 329
  in Bulgaria 254, 256, 278
  in Hungary 228, 247-48
  in Romania 267, 275
  in Soviet Union 287, 306, 317
  in Yugoslavia 174
  monetary overhang and 370

Black markets, in goods 35, 50, 122,
227, 370
Budget reform. *See* Fiscal deficits
Bulgaria 253-63, 272-78, 419-21
commitment to market economy 374
convertibility in 420
economic indicators 258
exchange rates 255, 263, 272, 278,
420
external debt 353, 419, 421
fiscal deficit 419-20, 261, 272
inflation 263
international specialization 255
macroeconomic stabilization 52, 421
monetary policy 273
negotiations with IMF 353
political situation 31, 46
post-1990 reforms 262, 420
pre-1989 economic situation 419
price liberalization 263, 272, 420-21
privatization 254, 256, 273, 278, 420
taxation 420
trade with CMEA 28, 419

CMEA. *See* Council for Mutual
Economic Assistance
Canada–US Free Trade Agreement 111
Capital account convertibility. *See*
Convertibility, capital account
Capital controls 377-80. *See also*
Exchange controls
Capital markets 15, 36, 187, 262, 269,
285, 306, 393. *See also* Stock and
bond exchanges
Cascading tariff regime 110-11, 147,
390-91, 399, 427. *See also* Protection,
transitional
Ceausescu, Nicolae 422
Central American Clearing House 24
Central bank
Eastern European System of Central
Banks 135
enhancing credibility of 128
European System of Central Banks
127, 131-33, 145
in Romania 264
in Soviet Union 286, 287, 289, 290,
297, 333
low credibility in Eastern Europe
122-23
management of debt service 230
need for independence 128, 136, 348
operation of dual exchange rate
system 399
regulation of commercial banks 36,
150, 230

regulation of foreign-exchange
transactions 230, 233
regulation of parallel currency 330
role in maintaining convertibility 357
role in overall reforms 120
Central European Payments Union. *See*
Payments union
Central planning
absence of enterprise-households
links 119
absence of error-correcting
mechanisms 368
bilateral approach to trade 70
declining product quality under 102
differences with Ricardian model 96
effective protection under 97-99
external economic relations under
365
incentive structure 368
negative value added 96-115, 389
price setting under 364
rationale for inconvertibility 67
taxation under 120
trade and payments regimes under 68
wastage of material inputs under 102
Centralization of foreign exchange
in Czechoslovakia 220, 225, 244
in highly indebted countries 232
in Hungary 226, 230, 244
in Poland 162
in Soviet Union 106, 288, 289, 304,
309, 333
Chervonets 54, 302, 316, 318-28, 329,
332, 335, 356, 402, 404
Chile, as model for trade liberalization
104-06
Commercial banks. *See also* Banking
reform
"black holes" in system 150
in Bulgaria 260, 262, 273
in Czechoslovakia 244
in Hungary 233
in Romania 260
regulation by central bank 36, 150,
230
role in financial system 276-77
soft budget constraints and 133
trade in foreign exchange 45
Commodity convertibility. *See*
Convertibility, commodity
Common Agricultural Policy 56, 81
Compensatory and contingency
financing facilities 224, 351
Convertibility
acceptable limits 22

as condition for integration into
world economy 3
as expression of a whole economy
197, 217, 241, 328
comparative advantage and 204
conditions for 35, 39, 50-53, 63, 235,
269, 274, 282, 284, 293, 294, 345,
357, 380-82, 385
costs of, as investment 55
credibility of currency and 275
definitions 4, 66-67, 282, 316, 344,
376-77
external support for 11
foreign investment and 197, 242
gradual versus rapid introduction 4,
16, 21-59, 72, 183, 253-54, 267,
339, 383-86
inflation and 206-07
integration into development strategy
198
obstacles to 217
to gain credibility for reforms 349
to "import" competition 16, 22, 71,
201, 203, 310, 329, 344, 349
to "import" realistic prices 16, 22, 71,
201-04, 310, 344, 349, 378, 384
to increase wage goods availability
310
versus "freely usable currency" 181,
189
Convertibility, and other policies
enterprise reform 50, 71, 345
exchange rate policy 182, 242, 393-
400
fiscal policy 345, 350
import restrictions 23
integration with EMS 36-37, 117
macroeconomic policies 118, 144,
252, 381
monetary policy 126, 197, 235, 284,
345, 350, 380
need to integrate 3, 183
parallel currency 54, 294-309, 402-04
payments union 23-24, 54, 63-95,
388
price liberalization 9-13, 39, 312,
345, 350
privatization 350, 382
role in reform process 3, 15, 183, 363
sequencing of reforms 14, 43, 45,
56, 283, 383
structural reform 37-40
trade liberalization 23, 114, 325, 350
Convertibility, in specific countries
Bulgaria 253, 273, 420

Czechoslovakia 10, 11, 46, 221-25,
234, 235, 238, 243, 413, 415
East Germany 411
Hungary 45, 226, 228-31, 233, 234,
238, 242, 243, 417, 418
Poland 161-64, 199-202, 207, 342,
343, 407, 411
postwar Western Europe 15, 21 33,
85, 181, 235, 239, 268, 339, 347,
381, 386
Romania 265-68, 274, 276, 422, 423
Soviet Union 281-93, 310, 316, 323,
426
Yugoslavia 169, 171, 173, 175, 177-
180, 207, 40
Convertibility, types
alternative concepts 282-84, 376
capital account 23, 67, 114, 178, 245,
355, 406
commodity 22, 50, 68, 97, 294, 300-
02, 308, 333, 345, 364, 377, 381
current account 4, 15, 21, 39-40, 45,
66, 114, 138, 140, 142, 169, 182,
377
for household transactions 32, 50,
129, 178-79, 343
internal versus external 4, 10, 22, 50,
143, 179, 377
Council for Mutual Economic
Assistance (CMEA). See also
Intratrade.
attempts to reform 71
Bulgarian trade with 419
Czechoslovak trade with 218, 414-16
decision to dismantle 351, 371
East German trade with 185
pricing formula used by 367
Romanian trade with 422
payments arrangements after demise
of 116, 239
potential renewal of 113
trade and payments regimes under 70
Crawling peg
accelerating inflation 354
as alternative to fixed exchange rates
190
as nominal anchor 126, 151, 275
as transitional mechanism 277
endogenous 148, 354
EMS membership and 401
for reforming economies 210, 345
to ensure competitiveness 396
Currency auctions. See Auctions,
currency
Currency basket 223

Currency conversion coefficients 70,
126, 287, 371
Currency substitution
countered by parallel currency 54,
299, 303, 330
fixed exchange rates and 275
foreign-exchange accounts and 239
in centrally planned economies 227,
370
in Czechoslovakia 220
in Hungary 230-31, 248
in Poland 158, 200, 203, 231
in small, open economies 126
in Soviet Union 291, 299, 306, 309,
313, 316, 325, 329, 332
monetary instability and 124
Current account convertibility. See
Convertibility, current account
Customs union 141, 150-52, 356, 388,
392
Czechoslovakia 217-25, 234-50, 413-16
absence of strong private sector 51
big bang approach to reform 9-13,
46, 59, 72
bilateral payments arrangements 388
convertibility 10, 11, 46, 221-25,
234-35, 238, 243, 413, 415
devaluation 220, 222-23, 236, 243,
247, 249-50, 414-16
economic indicators 46, 219
exchange rate regime 221-25
external debt 218, 221, 222, 224
financial package for 46, 352
impact of external shocks 220
inflation 10, 208, 218, 220, 225, 236,
247, 414, 416
macroeconomic stabilization 36, 51,
220
pre-1989 regime 218-20, 368, 414
price liberalization 10, 12, 235, 46,
51, 224, 415
privatization 10, 11, 225, 415
reform program 9-14, 413, 416
trade within CMEA 218, 414, 416

De-étatization 38-39, 44, 284, 357, 382
Debt, external
devaluation and 200
in Bulgaria 255, 272, 274, 353, 419,
421
in Czechoslovakia 10, 218, 221, 222,
224
in Eastern Europe 371-72
in Hungary 45, 226, 232, 236, 243,
417
in Poland 89, 155, 200, 353, 411

in Romania 422
in Soviet Union 290, 424
in Yugoslavia 169, 174, 200, 405
payments union and 64, 89
relief 89, 353, 411, 419, 421
setting of exchange rate and 224
Delors Committee 133, 135
Demonopolization 10, 38-39, 40, 231,
255, 284, 286, 420
Depreciation, currency. See Devaluation
Deutsche Bundesbank 184-85, 213
Deutsche mark 169, 186, 212, 223, 396
Devaluation 203
anti-inflation policy and 199
convertibility and 384
dangers of excessive 45, 202, 411
effectiveness 202, 389, 392
external debt and 200
in Czechoslovakia 220-23, 236, 243,
247, 249-50, 414-16
in Hungary 46, 228, 240, 243, 246,
249, 418
in Poland 53, 72, 161-63, 202, 207,
211-12, 342, 359, 408-10
in Romania 276, 423
in Soviet Union 287, 311, 427, 428
in Yugoslavia 72, 174, 177
income effects 409
nominal anchor policy and 127
price liberalization and 144
tariff protection and 203, 390-91
Dollarization. See Currency substitution
Domestic convertible ruble. See Parallel
currency
Domestic demand, growth of, as
nominal anchor 396
Dual exchange rate system. See
Exchange rates, dual
Dubcek, Alexander 414

EPU. See European Payments Union
East Germany 181-96, 211-13, 411-13
adoption of social market economy
374
application of EC tariff 82
collapse of demand for CMEA exports
372
economic indicators 192, 194
elements of reforms 184-88
exchange rate regime 188-90
impact of alternative conversion rates
211, 213, 412
inflation 195
initial effects of unification 191-95,
412
lessons for Eastern Europe 196, 413

monetary policy 132, 184-85, 189-90, 213
monetary union with West Germany 183, 186, 188-90, 195, 411
political transformation 186, 189-198
price liberalization 39, 185
privatization 187-88, 213
special nature of transformation 401
trade liberalization 185
wage subsidies in 429
West German support for reforms 412
Eastern European System of Central Banks (EESCB) 134-35
Economic Commission for Asia and the Far East 24
Economic Commission for Europe 14
Economic Cooperation Administration 25
Economic union, for Eastern Europe 79, 82-83, 88
Ecu, as peg for Eastern European currencies 90, 127-29, 144, 199, 212, 223, 271, 396
Employee stock ownership plans 179
Energy. 98, 147, 151, 218, 369, 389.
See also Oil trade
Enterprise reform. See also Demonopolization, Privatization, Structural reform
as element of structural reform 37
central bank credibility and 122, 128
convertibility and 50, 71, 345
impact on fiscal deficit 120
in Bulgaria 261
in Czechoslovakia 218
in Hungary 52
in Poland 156
in Romania 264-65
in Soviet Union 282, 284-85, 311, 326-27
in Yugoslavia 179
inflation and 120
role of foreign investment 38
Entrepreneurship, attitudes toward 370
Environmental issues 17
Equalization accounts 69, 157
Estonia 299
Ethnic conflicts 172, 177, 199, 334, 374, 430
European Bank for Reconstruction and Development (EBRD) 16, 55, 59, 113, 271, 276, 351, 431
European Commission 332, 352
European Community
Bulgaria and 272
Common Agricultural Policy 81

Czechoslovakia and 11, 17, 224, 352
East German accession to 185
Eastern European membership in 30, 43, 83, 90, 141, 376, 389, 401
external tariff 83
financial assistance to Eastern Europe 17, 352
Hungary and 352
Poland and 199
Romania and 265
support for payments union 88, 141, 143, 271
European Free Trade Association (EFTA) 389, 393
European Investment Bank 351
European Monetary System (EMS). See also European monetary union
Eastern European membership in 127, 131-34, 401
linkages to 58, 90
potential role in transition to convertibility 266
role in payments union 271
Romanian relations with 265, 423
Yugoslav relations with 199
European monetary union 5, 133-34, 395, 400
European Payments Union (EPU) 4, 24-26, 73, 85, 87, 118, 139, 142, 183, 386
European Recovery Administration 25
European System of Central Banks (ESCB) 127, 128, 132-34, 143
Exchange controls 15, 70, 79, 181, 290-91, 330, 355, 416
Exchange rate mechanism. See European Monetary System
Exchange rate regime 393-400
conditions for success 50-53
in Bulgaria 263, 273
in Czechoslovakia 221-25
in East Germany 188-90
in Hungary 230-33
in Poland 157-58, 162-63
in Romania 263-69
in Soviet Union 286-91, 304, 316, 427
monetary policy and 119-25
options for 117-19, 263-64
payments union and 118
Exchange rates. See also Devaluation
between rubles and parallel currency 306
black market as misleading indicator 287, 329
competitive undervaluation 27

deutsche mark as peg for 396
ecu as peg for 127-29, 144, 199, 212,
    223, 271, 396
effects of unifying 107
German monetary union and 188
in Bulgaria 255, 263, 272, 278, 420
in centrally planned economies 227
in Hungary 234
in Poland 157, 159, 161-62, 201,
    203, 212
in Romania 276
in Soviet Union 287, 303, 304, 307
in Yugoslavia 172, 174, 199
nominal targets for 125-28
risk of undervaluation 57
Exchange rates, dual
compared with cascading tariff system
    399
in Bulgaria 278
in reforming countries 346
in Romania 267, 397, 423
in Soviet Union 289, 304, 426-27
role of central bank 399
trade liberalization and 44
versus transitional protection 275,
    397-400
Exchange rates, fixed
alternative to crawling peg 190
as nominal anchor 11, 23, 119, 125-
    28, 144-45, 201, 203, 209-10, 212,
    226, 236, 242, 247, 275, 316, 335,
    345, 354-55, 395-96, 406
circumstances when appropriate 210
costs of defending 394
currency substitution and 275
European monetary union and 395
for Soviet Union 329
implications for monetary policy 354,
    394
in Czechoslovakia 236, 243
in Hungary 243
in Poland 162, 203, 343
in Romania 266
in Yugoslavia 179
inflation and 345, 395
influence on relative prices 205
long-term wage anchor and 275
macroeconomic effects 206
price liberalization and 144, 151
versus floating 393, 395
Exchange rates, flexible 125-26, 190,
    232, 335
Exchange rates, floating 236, 303, 329,
    380, 393-94
Exchange rates, multiple 69-70, 106,
    126, 155

Exchange rates, setting
difficulties in 149-51, 394
external debt and 224
in Czechoslovakia 222, 236, 243
in Soviet Union 303-04
judgmental approach 397
PPP as basis for 106, 222, 244, 347,
    415
Export licensing 156, 371
Export promotion 169, 289, 396
External support for reforms
for Czechoslovakia 11, 46, 222
for Hungary 46
for payments union 89
for Poland 163, 199, 430
need for 11, 16-17
through provision of reserves 350-53

Federal Republic of Germany 90, 198,
    412
Fiscal deficits
convertibility and 345
enterprise reform and 120
in Bulgaria 261, 272, 419-20
in centrally planned economies 227,
    369
in East Germany 191, 195
in Hungary 417
in Poland 155, 330
in Soviet Union 286, 297, 308, 311-
    14, 325, 335, 426
in Yugoslavia 172, 180
Fiscal policy
convertibility and 350
in Bulgaria 257, 263, 278
in Czechoslovakia 9
in Hungary 418
in monetary union 135
in Poland 161, 207
in Soviet Union 296, 323-34, 326,
    350
price liberalization and 39
support for monetary policy 190
500-Days (Shatalin) Plan (Soviet
    Union) 296-97, 328, 333, 335, 375,
    379, 383
Foreign investment
convertibility and 197, 242, 329, 355,
    378
dangers of overreliance on 112
in Bulgaria 254, 420
in Czechoslovakia 244
in East Germany 211
in Hungary 230, 232, 233, 249
in Poland 156, 164
in Soviet Union 290, 292, 306, 316

role in enterprise reform 38
trade liberalization and 111-14
Foreign trade organizations 33, 69, 155-56, 407
Foreign-currency shops 158, 306, 342
Foreign-exchange accounts
  arguments against 379
  for individuals 370
  in Czechoslovakia 218, 221
  in Hungary 230, 233, 238, 418
  in Poland 157, 158, 407
  in Soviet Union 290, 291, 306
  in Yugoslavia 172, 178, 179
Free current accounts 301, 303
Free economic zones 308, 330
Free trade areas 388, 392-93
Fundamental equilibrium exchange rate 397

General Agreement on Tariffs and Trade (GATT) 81-82, 113, 240, 392
German Democratic Republic. See East Germany
Germany. See East Germany, West Germany
Goods famine 323, 327, 357
Gorbachev, Mikhail 375, 424
Gradualist approach to reform. See also Big bang approach to reform, Shock therapy
  case for 40-59
  credibility problem of 56
  dangers 43
  definition 355
  in Hungary 226, 235, 237, 417, 419
  in Soviet Union 299, 329
  versus big bang 21-59, 72, 183, 253-54, 267, 339, 383-86
Great Britain 380, 382
Gulf Cooperation Council 352
Gulf crisis 63, 74, 220, 255, 351

Hard-currency shops 158, 306, 342
Hayek, Friedrich von 373, 380
Households, access to foreign exchange 32, 160, 163, 169, 178, 221, 228, 230, 244, 343-44
Houston Summit report (1990) 147, 311, 332, 335, 375
Hungary 226-50, 417-19
  balance of payments surplus 46, 228
  convertibility 45, 226, 228, 231, 233-34, 238, 243, 417, 418
  devaluation 46, 228, 240, 243, 246, 249, 418
  economic indicators 229

exchange rate regime 230-33
external debt 45, 226, 232, 236, 243, 417, 419
fiscal policy 417-18
gradualist approach to reform 226, 237, 417, 419
inflation 208, 228, 231, 246, 248, 418
monetary policy 228, 240, 418
pre-1989 reforms 368
price liberalization 208, 227, 234, 248, 417
privatization 52, 249, 417
relations with GATT 392
role of banks in currency trading 45
trade liberalization 227, 239, 243, 248-49, 417-18
Hyperinflation. See Inflation

IIASA report (1990) 311, 375
Import licensing 27, 156, 247, 250, 290, 305, 308, 371
Incomes policy 161, 164, 190, 203, 225, 249-50, 405
Inflation
  acceptable level of 358, 359
  as one-time corrective increase 144
  causes 150, 202, 208, 395
  convertibility and 206-07
  enterprise reform and 120
  establishing target rate 124
  fixed exchange rates and 345, 395
  growth in developing countries and 359
  impact of real-sector reforms on 120
  in Bulgaria 263
  in centrally planned economies 121, 227, 371
  in Czechoslovakia 10, 208, 218, 220, 225, 236, 247, 414, 416
  in East Germany 195
  in Hungary 208, 228, 231, 246, 248, 418
  in Poland 120, 155, 158, 161, 200, 203, 207, 231, 408
  in Romania 267
  in Soviet Union 295, 314, 319, 325, 333, 424
  in Yugoslavia 120, 169-74, 207
  monetary overhang and 121, 124
  parallel currency and 330
  price liberalization and 120
  real costs of 122
  repressed 31, 50, 144, 202, 355, 357, 359
Infrastructure needs 16, 38, 76

Interbank currency market 225, 232, 244, 267, 288, 289, 291, 333, 427
Interest rates
  in Bulgaria 260, 263, 272, 420
  in Czechoslovakia 242
  in Hungary 248
  in Poland 211
  in Soviet Union 286, 291
  instability during transition 124
  on payments union balances 64
  under nominal anchor policy 127
International Economic Cooperation Organization 269
International Monetary Fund (IMF)
  Article VIII 21, 23, 50, 66, 118, 174, 273, 302
  Article XIV 273, 302
  approach to stabilization 144
  as universal payments facility 73
  definition of convertibility 21, 66, 181, 344, 377
  distrust of gradualist approach 43
  insistence on convertibility 242
  negotiations with Yugoslavia 174, 180
  opposition of members to SDR allocation 351
  opposition to EPU 25
  recommendations for Bulgaria 263
  recommendations for Poland 409
  role in financing reforms 351
  role in payments union 271
  stand-by arrangement for Poland 201
  stand-by arrangement for Czechoslovakia 225, 352
  technical assistance to Romania 264
Intratrade
  after dismantling of CMEA 371
  among centrally planned economies 366
  breakdown of 74, 245, 346
  extent 75
  licensing and 247
  payments union 24, 28
  prospects for 78
  transitional protection and 393
Iraq 74, 180, 373

Japan 42, 198, 352, 353
Joint ventures. 53, 230, 244, 249-50, 292, 415 See also Foreign investment

Kantors 158, 163
Klaus, Václav 4, 373

Land reform 273

Latvia 300
Legal and regulatory framework 10, 34, 187, 285
Lithuania 300
Lottery tickets, money as 48

Macroeconomic stabilization
  as part of minimum bang 386
  as precondition for other reforms 35, 357, 359
  banking reform and 36
  convertibility and 144, 242, 326
  in Bulgaria 52, 421
  in Czechoslovakia 36, 51, 220
  in East Germany 187
  in Hungary 233
  in Poland 161, 408
  in reforming economies 205
  in Romania 265
  in sequence of reforms 13, 345
  in Soviet Union 293, 327-29
  parallel currency and 324
  preconditions 36
"Market socialism" 41, 368, 382
Markovich, Ante 174-76
Marshall Plan 25, 140
Microeconomic liberalization. See Price liberalization, Trade liberalization
Minimum bang approach to reform
  country-specific 418
  elements 385-86
  in Czechoslovakia 416, 430
  lessons from Poland 411
Mises, Ludwig E. von 373
Monetary overhang
  algebraic expression 49
  alleviated by undervaluation 127
  black market and 370
  convertibility and 50, 345, 381
  exchange rate setting and 150
  in Bulgaria 274, 278, 419, 420
  in centrally planned economies 227, 235, 349, 370
  in Czechoslovakia 414
  in East Germany 186
  in Hungary 228, 235
  in Poland 155, 408
  in Romania 52, 274, 422
  in Soviet Union 52, 286, 295-99, 308, 311, 324, 424, 426
  inflation and 121, 124
  parallel currency and 54
Monetary policy. See also Anti-inflationary policy, Exchange rate regime
  convertibility and 197, 345, 350

credibility of 128
during reform process 119-25, 144, 345
exchange rate policy and 393
in Bulgaria 273
in Czechoslovakia 9, 242
in East Germany 132, 184-85, 189, 190, 213
in Hungary 228, 240, 418
in Poland 131, 161, 207
in Soviet Union 286, 307, 311, 327, 348
in Yugoslavia 172-79
instability of indicators for 123
price liberalization and 39
under fixed exchange rates 354
under system of central banks 134
Money, nature of, in centrally planned economies 48
Most-favored-nation treatment 346

National Bank of Bulgaria 261
National Bank of Hungary 230, 232, 243
National Bank of Poland 157
National Bank of Romania 264, 267
Negative value added
  as special case 145
  doubtful prevalence of 149, 151
  formal demonstration of 101
  in centrally planned economies 96-115, 389
  in Hungary 241, 390
  in Poland 145, 202, 390
  industry closure 149
  versus negative profits 151
New Economic Policy (NEP) 55, 302, 318, 332, 402
Newly industrializing countries, as model for Eastern Europe 198
Nominal anchor
  as element of stabilization program 122
  crawling peg as 126, 151, 175
  devaluation and 127
  domestic demand growth as 396
  fixed exchange rate as 11, 23, 119, 125-26, 144-45, 190, 201, 203, 209, 210, 212, 226, 236, 242, 247-48, 275, 316, 335, 345, 354-55, 395-96, 406
  in Bulgaria 421
  in Hungary 246
  in Poland 161
  in Soviet Union 329, 335
  in Yugoslavia 406

incomes policy and 249
operation of 345, 354

Oil trade 63, 74, 78, 202, 250, 343, 373, 419, 424
Openness ratios 365
Organization for Economic Cooperation and Development (OECD) 16, 352, 431
Organization for European Economic Cooperation 140
Output losses during transition
  in Bulgaria 420
  in Czechoslovakia 220
  in East Germany 188, 191
  in Poland 35, 409
  in Romania 422
  in Soviet Union 424
  in Yugoslavia 169, 171, 176
  under noncredible anti-inflation policy 123

PPP. See Purchasing power parity
Parallel currency 249-309, 402-04. See also Chervonets
  arguments for 298-300, 314, 403
  commodity backing 303, 312
  conditions for success 315
  credibility problems 404
  currency substitution and 54, 299, 330
  existing currency and 312, 314, 403
  foreign exchange as basis 313
  inflation and 330
  method of emission 300, 301, 312, 314, 403
  monetary overhang and 54
  role of central bank 330
  seigniorage under 55, 334
  separatism in Soviet republics and 329-30
  stabilization policies and 324
  technical problems 315
  use in payment of taxes 314
Parallel market 65, 67, 84, 158, 202, 344, 379. See also Black markets
Paris Club 89, 353
Pavlov, Valentin 295, 388
Payments union 63-95, 386-89
  absence of demand for 54, 140, 151, 152
  arguments for and against 27, 28, 54, 64, 73, 89, 94, 118, 141, 143, 150-51, 182, 185, 346, 386-87
  as prerequisite for customs union 152
  asymmetries within 65, 87

basic features 64
capital and credit arrangements 29,
   54, 65, 91
convertibility and 23-34, 63-95
costs of funding 91-94
Czechoslovakia and 388
definition 387
discriminatory features 27
exchange rate regime and 118
expected duration 86
extent of intratrade and 28, 140
external debt and 64, 89
German unification and 90
inclusion of Soviet Union 28, 54, 91,
   94, 140, 149, 271, 387
membership 65, 85
membership in EC and 141, 271
Poland and 388
political obstacles 152
precursors outside Europe 24, 149
problem of structural creditors 24, 29,
   140
role of IMF 271
Romania and 266, 423
settlement and surveillance
   mechanisms 65, 90
support from Western Europe 89
trade liberalization and 65, 94
versus preferential trade arrangements
   360
Perestroika 333, 369, 374, 424
Pöhl, Karl Otto 383
Poland 155-68, 197-213, 407-11
balance of payments 166-67, 202
big bang approach to reform 3, 35,
   46, 58, 161, 231, 276, 383, 407
convertibility 72, 161, 199-202, 207,
   342-43, 407, 411
devaluation 53, 72, 162, 202, 342,
   408-10
economic indicators 164-65
exchange rates 157, 159-62, 201,
   203, 212
external debt 89, 155, 200, 353, 411
fiscal deficit 155, 330
inflation 120, 158, 161, 200, 203,
   207, 231, 408-10
initial results of reforms 163, 207,
   342-43, 407-09
lessons from German unification 198
macroeconomic stabilization 51
negative value added 145
popular support for reforms 203
pre-1990 regime 58, 156, 369, 407
price liberalization 51, 202, 207, 408
privatization 164

trade liberalization 27, 82, 162, 342,
   408
trade with CMEA 164, 202
Prague Spring 414
Price distortions, in centrally planned
   economies 227
Price elasticities 51, 58, 382
Price liberalization
abuse by monopolies 12
conditions 35
convertibility and 39, 312, 345, 350
devaluation and 144
fiscal policy and 39
fixed exchange rates and 144, 151
in Bulgaria 263, 272, 420, 421
in Czechoslovakia 10, 12, 46, 51,
   224, 235, 415
in East Germany 39, 185
in Hungary 208, 227, 234, 248, 407
in Poland 51, 161, 202, 207, 408
in postwar Western Europe 248
in Romania 265, 276, 423
in sequencing of reforms 345
in Soviet Union 284, 288, 292, 296,
   298, 303, 311, 426
in Yugoslavia 179
inflation and 120
place in reform process 15, 35, 249
promotion by payments union 65
rapid versus gradual 39, 59
subsidies and 120
taxation and 39
Privatization
as element of structural reform 37
central bank credibility and 122, 128
convertibility and 350, 382
financial reform and 277
in Bulgaria 254, 256, 273, 278, 420
in Czechoslovakia 10, 11, 225, 415
in East Germany 187-88, 213
in Great Britain 382
in Hungary 52, 249, 417
in Poland 164
in Soviet Union 284, 293, 333, 426
in Yugoslavia 180, 374
need for gradualism 52
of large enterprises 257
of small enterprises 37, 43, 256
voucher scheme for 4
Property rights 37, 225, 256
Protection, transitional 389-93
and infant-industry argument 146,
   391
and shoddy product syndrome 110
arguments for 5, 384, 389
as senile-industry protection 391

capture by vested interests 357
case for 96-115
curbing monopoly power during 110
for Hungary 240
for low-value-added industries 146
identifying viable industries 103
in cases of negative value added 97,
   145, 390
in gradualist approach to reform 45
revenue gains from 391
role of foreign capital inflows 111
through inefficient import sector 358
Purchasing power parity (PPP) 22, 244,
   397, 415

Quantitative restrictions 82, 305, 308

Radical reform approach. *See* Big bang
   approach to reform; Shock therapy
Recession. *See* Output losses during
   transition
Repatriation of profits. *See* Foreign
   investment
Reserves, foreign-exchange
   and convertibility 235, 284, 345, 380
   in Bulgaria 272
   in Czechoslovakia 222, 224, 225
   in Hungary 226, 232
   in Poland 158-59, 201
   in Soviet Union 307
   in Yugoslavia 174, 178, 353
   means of acquiring 350
   payments union and 24, 29
Reserves-imports ratios, 130
Restitution of property 56, 188, 225,
   416
Retention quotas
   absence of, in Hungary 238, 418
   convertibility and 344
   in Bulgaria 420
   in Czechoslovakia 414
   in Poland 58, 157, 408
   in reforming economies 44
   in Romania 267
   in Soviet Union 288, 289, 304, 317,
      333, 427
Retraining 40, 43, 56
Romania 264-71, 274-78, 421-23
   absence of external debt 422
   commitment to market economy 374
   convertibility 265, 268, 274, 276,
      422-23
   devaluation 276, 423
   dual exchange rate system 397
   economic situation 270, 422
   exchange rates 267, 397, 423

inflation 267
mismanagement of reforms 52
negotiations with IMF 353
1990 reforms 265
political issues 31, 46, 277, 422
price liberalization 265, 276, 423
trade with CMEA 422
Ryzhkov, Nikolai 296, 360, 375

Second-best problems 345, 369, 385,
   417
Seigniorage 55, 122, 313, 314
Sequencing of reforms
   and opening of economy 238
   convertibility in 43, 56, 383
   in Bulgaria 421
   in Czechoslovakia 13, 239
   in East Germany 188, 196
   in Poland 343
   in Soviet Union 316
   monetary policy and 136
   price liberalization in 15, 345
   principles for 43
   structural reform in 57
   trade liberalization in 15, 44, 345
Services 217
Shatalin (500-Days) Plan (Soviet
   Union) 297, 328, 333, 335, 375, 379,
   383
Shatalin, S. 296, 311
Shekel Plan (Israel) 123
Shock therapy. 205 *See also* Big bang
   approach to reform
   avoidance by Hungary 226-28, 239,
      242
   costs of 136-37, 175, 200-01, 384
   dangers of 383
   definition 246, 355
   features 227
   impact on enterprises 52
   in Czechoslovakia 9-14, 250, 355
   in East Germany 183-86
   in Poland 46, 173-74, 202
   in Soviet Union 293, 295, 316, 329
   in Yugoslavia 171
Shoddy product syndrome 102
Shortages 50, 175, 207, 218, 227, 235,
   282, 295, 323, 327, 357, 334, 420,
   422-23.
Social market economy 186, 323, 373,
   374
Social security 15, 36, 187, 191
Social values in centrally planned
   economies 34
Socialist division of labor 365

"Soft" budget constraint 33, 121, 177,
206, 208, 248, 311, 327, 345, 355,
364, 378
Sokolnikov, G. 326
Solidarity 156
Soviet Union 281-335, 424-28
attitudes toward free enterprise 310
balance of payments support for 353
change in goal of reforms 375
constitutional issues 333, 425-26
conversion of military sector 297
convertibility 281-93, 308, 310, 316,
323, 426
currency reforms of 1920s 319
devaluation 287, 427, 428
economic characteristics 49, 110, 281
economic conditions 285, 295, 424
emission of currencies by republics
293, 300, 317, 329, 333
exchange rates 287, 303-04, 307
external debt 290, 424
fiscal deficit 286, 297, 308, 311, 314,
325, 335, 426
gradualism versus big bang in 316
impact of disintegration 140
inclusion in payments union 28, 54,
91, 94, 140, 149, 271, 387
inflation 295, 314, 325, 424
membership in Bretton Woods
institutions 428, 431
mismanagement of reforms 52
monetary policy 286, 307, 311, 327,
348
oil production 373
parallel currency for 294-309, 402-04
political issues 46, 310-11, 318, 375,
425, 430
pre-1989 reforms 369
price liberalization 284, 288, 292,
296, 298, 303, 311, 426
privatization 284, 293, 333, 426
reaction to Western advice 332, 335
trade liberalization 290, 302, 307,
333
trade with region 79, 89
Western support for reforms 428
withdrawal of large-denomination
notes 300
Sovznak 302, 316, 318-21, 324-26,
332, 404
Special Drawing Right (SDR) 223, 351
Stabilization lending 16, 163, 266, 352
Stabilization, macroeconomic. See
Macroeconomic stabilization
State Bank of Czechoslovakia 225

Stock and bond exchanges 33, 36, 289,
294
Stockpiling, under central planning 366
Structural reform. See also specific reforms
convertibility and 339
enterprise reform 37
essential to transformation 35
in economies in transition 205
in Yugoslavia 169, 174
price liberalization and 205
privatization and 37
property rights and 37
rational price structure as
precondition 56
Subsidies
convertibility and 50, 382
impact of removal 206
in Bulgaria 255, 262
in Czechoslovakia 9
in East Germany 185, 340
in Hungary 228
in Romania 423
in Soviet Union 286, 296, 329, 335
price liberalization and 44, 120
Switzerland 352
Systemic change. See Structural reform

Taiwan, gradual move to convertibility
198
Tariffication 104, 305, 308
Tariffs 24, 45, 82, 88, 97-101, 104-14,
145-46, 162, 203, 311, 360, 390-91
Taxation and tax reform
convertibility and 43
implicit export tax 98-100, 104-07,
112, 114
in Bulgaria 255-56, 257, 261, 263,
420
in East Germany 187
in Hungary 231, 417
in Poland 157, 161
in Soviet Union 147, 285, 286, 297,
305, 314, 327, 329, 334
macroeconomic stabilization and 36
place in reform process 15
price liberalization and 39
under central planning 34, 120, 364
Terms of trade 83, 372
Tito, Marshal 171
Trade barriers in West 340
Trade liberalization
central bank credibility and 128
convertibility and 325, 350
dual exchange rates and 44
in Bulgaria 420
in Czechoslovakia 10, 235, 415

in East Germany 185
in Hungary 27, 227, 234, 239, 243,
    248-49, 417-18
in Poland 27, 82, 162, 342, 408
in sequence of reforms 15, 345
in Soviet Union 290, 302, 307, 333
in Yugoslavia 169, 179
1970s Chile as model 104
payments union and 65, 94
to import competition 122
Trade unions 40
Transferable ruble 51, 64, 67, 70, 75,
    83, 95, 113, 139, 185, 218, 367
Transitional protection. *See* Protection,
    transitional
Travel and tourism 23, 44, 172, 228,
    231, 245, 306, 344, 356, 370, 377,
    380
Treuhandanstalt 11, 38, 187, 213

Ukraine 300
Unemployment 40, 43, 187, 191
Uniform tariff 104, 389-90. *See also*
    Tariffication
United States 42, 403

Wage policy. *See* Incomes policy
Wages, fixed, as supplementary nominal
    anchor 275
West Germany 90, 198, 412
Western Europe. *See also* European
    Community
    as model for reforming economies 42

postwar return to convertibility 15,
    21, 33, 85, 181, 235, 239, 268,
    339, 347, 381, 386
price liberalization 248
Wholesale market 295, 300, 306, 335
WIDER report (1990) 375
Worker self-management 51, 171, 369,
    374
World Bank 16, 17, 43, 224, 264, 271,
    351, 431

Yeltsin, Boris 375
Yugoslavia 169-80, 197-213, 404-07
    balance of payments difficulties 353
    choice of initial exchange rate 199
    convertibility 72, 169-75, 177-80,
        207, 380, 405
    current state of reforms 173, 404-05
    devaluation 72, 177
    economic indicators 170, 176
    ethnic conflict 172, 177, 199, 334,
        374, 406
    exchange rates 172, 174, 199
    external debt 169, 174, 200, 405
    inflation 120, 169-74, 207
    macroeconomic stabilization 51
    monetary policy 172-79
    political and social issues 171-80, 189
    pre-1989 reforms 171, 368
    price liberalization 51, 179
    private sector 51, 172
    privatization 180, 374
    structural reforms 169
    trade liberalization 169, 179
    worker self-management 51, 374

Other Publications from the Institute

POLICY ANALYSES IN INTERNATIONAL ECONOMICS SERIES

1 **The Lending Policies of the International Monetary Fund**
John Williamson/*August 1982*
$8.00   ISBN paper 0-88132-000-5   72 pp

2 **"Reciprocity": A New Approach to World Trade Policy?**
William R. Cline/*September 1982*
$8.00   ISBN paper 0-88132-001-3   41 pp

3 **Trade Policy in the 1980s**
C. Fred Bergsten and William R. Cline/*November 1982*
(out of print)   ISBN paper 0-88132-002-1   84 pp
Partially reproduced in the book *Trade Policy in the 1980s.*

4 **International Debt and the Stability of the World Economy**
William R. Cline/*September 1983*
$10.00   ISBN paper 0-88132-010-2   134 pp

5 **The Exchange Rate System, Second Edition**
John Williamson/*September 1983, rev. June 1985*
(out of print)   ISBN paper 0-88132-034-X   61 pp

6 **Economic Sanctions in Support of Foreign Policy Goals**
Gary Clyde Hufbauer and Jeffrey J. Schott/*October 1983*
$10.00   ISBN paper 0-88132-014-5   109 pp

7 **A New SDR Allocation?**
John Williamson/*March 1984*
$10.00   ISBN paper 0-88132-028-5   61 pp

8 **An International Standard for Monetary Stabilization**
Ronald I. McKinnon/*March 1984*
$10.00   ISBN paper 0-88132-018-8   108 pp

9 **The Yen/Dollar Agreement: Liberalizing Japanese Capital Markets**
Jeffrey A. Frankel/*December 1984*
$10.00   ISBN paper 0-88132-035-8   86 pp

10 **Bank Lending to Developing Countries: The Policy Alternatives**
C. Fred Bergsten, William R. Cline, and John Williamson/*April 1985*
$12.00   ISBN paper 0-88132-032-3   221 pp

11 **Trading for Growth: The Next Round of Trade Negotiations**
Gary Clyde Hufbauer and Jeffrey J. Schott/*September 1985*
$10.00   ISBN paper 0-88132-033-1   109 pp

12 **Financial Intermediation Beyond the Debt Crisis**
Donald R. Lessard and John Williamson/*September 1985*
$12.00   ISBN paper 0-88132-021-8   130 pp

13 **The United States–Japan Economic Problem**
C. Fred Bergsten and William R. Cline/*October 1985, 2d ed. rev. January 1987*
$10.00   ISBN paper 0-88132-060-9   180 pp

14 **Deficits and the Dollar: The World Economy at Risk**
Stephen Marris/*December 1985, 2d ed. rev. November 1987*
$18.00   ISBN paper 0-88132-067-6   415 pp

15 **Trade Policy for Troubled Industries**
Gary Clyde Hufbauer and Howard F. Rosen/*March 1986*
$10.00   ISBN paper 0-88132-020-X   111 pp

16 **The United States and Canada: The Quest for Free Trade**
Paul Wonnacott, with an Appendix by John Williamson/*March 1987*
$10.00   ISBN paper 0-88132-056-0   188 pp

17 **Adjusting to Success: Balance of Payments Policy in the East Asian NICs,** revised edition
Bela Balassa and John Williamson/*June 1987, rev. April 1990*
$11.95   ISBN paper 0-88132-101-X   160 pp

18 **Mobilizing Bank Lending to Debtor Countries**
William R. Cline/*June 1987*
$10.00   ISBN paper 0-88132-062-5   100 pp

19 **Auction Quotas and United States Trade Policy**
C. Fred Bergsten, Kimberly Ann Elliott, Jeffrey J. Schott, and Wendy E. Takacs/*September 1987*
$10.00   ISBN paper 0-88132-050-1   254 pp

20 **Agriculture and the GATT: Rewriting the Rules**
Dale E. Hathaway/*September 1987*
$10.00   ISBN paper 0-88132-052-8   169 pp

21 **Anti-Protection: Changing Forces in United States Trade Politics**
I. M. Destler and John S. Odell/*September 1987*
$10.00   ISBN paper 0-88132-043-9   220 pp

22 **Targets and Indicators: A Blueprint for the International Coordination of Economic Policy**
John Williamson and Marcus H. Miller/*September 1987*
$10.00   ISBN paper 0-88132-051-X   118 pp

23 **Capital Flight: The Problem and Policy Responses**
Donald R. Lessard and John Williamson/*December 1987*
$10.00   ISBN paper 0-88132-059-5   80 pp

24 United States–Canada Free Trade: An Evaluation of the Agreement
Jeffrey J. Schott/*April 1988*
$3.95   ISBN paper 0-88132-072-2   48 pp

25 Voluntary Approaches to Debt Relief
John Williamson/*September 1988, rev. May 1989*
$10.95   ISBN paper 0-88132-098-6   80 pp

26 American Trade Adjustment: The Global Impact
William R. Cline/*March 1989*
$12.95   ISBN paper 0-88132-095-1   98 pp

27 More Free Trade Areas?
Jeffrey J. Schott/*May 1989*
$10.00   ISBN paper 0-88132-085-4   88 pp

28 The Progress of Policy Reform in Latin America
John Williamson/*January 1990*
$10.95   ISBN paper 0-88132-100-1   106 pp

29 The Global Trade Negotiations: What Can Be Achieved?
Jeffrey J. Schott/*September 1990*
$10.95   ISBN paper 0-88132-137-0   72 pp

30 Economic Policy Coordination: Requiem or Prologue?
Wendy Dobson/*April 1991*
$11.95   ISBN paper 0-88132-102-8   162 pp

31 The Economic Opening of Eastern Europe
John Williamson/*May 1991*
$11.95   ISBN paper 0-88132-186-9   92 pp

32 Eastern Europe and the Soviet Union in the World Economy
Susan M. Collins and Dani Rodrik/*May 1991*
$12.95   ISBN paper 0-88132-157-5   172 pp

33 African Economic Reform: The External Dimension
Carol Lancaster/*June 1991*
$12.95   ISBN paper 0-88132-096-X   82 pp

34 Has the Adjustment Process Worked?
Paul R. Krugman/*October 1991*
$12.95   ISBN paper 0-88132-116-8   82 pp

BOOKS

IMF Conditionality
John Williamson, editor/*1983*
$35.00   ISBN cloth 0-88132-006-4   695 pp

Trade Policy in the 1980s
William R. Cline, editor/*1983*

$20.00	ISBN paper 0-88132-031-5	810 pp
$35.00	ISBN cloth 0-88132-008-1	810 pp

Subsidies in International Trade
Gary Clyde Hufbauer and Joanna Shelton Erb/*1984*

$35.00	ISBN cloth 0-88132-004-8	299 pp

International Debt: Systemic Risk and Policy Response
William R. Cline/*1984*

$30.00	ISBN cloth 0-88132-015-3	336 pp

Trade Protection in the United States: 31 Case Studies
Gary Clyde Hufbauer, Diane E. Berliner, and Kimberly Ann Elliott/*1986*

$25.00	ISBN paper 0-88132-040-4	371 pp

Toward Renewed Economic Growth in Latin America
Bela Balassa, Gerardo M. Bueno, Pedro-Pablo Kuczynski, and Mario Henrique Simonsen/*1986*

$15.00	ISBN paper 0-88132-045-5	205 pp

American Trade Politics: System Under Stress
I. M. Destler/*1986*

$18.00	ISBN paper 0-88132-057-9	380 pp
$30.00	ISBN cloth 0-88132-058-7	380 pp

Capital Flight and Third World Debt
Donald R. Lessard and John Williamson, editors/*1987*

(out of print)	ISBN paper 0-88132-053-6	270 pp

The Canada–United States Free Trade Agreement: The Global Impact
Jeffrey J. Schott and Murray G. Smith, editors/*1988*

$13.95	ISBN paper 0-88132-073-0	211 pp

World Agricultural Trade: Building a Consensus
William M. Miner and Dale E. Hathaway, editors/*1988*

$16.95	ISBN paper 0-88132-071-3	226 pp

Japan in the World Economy
Bela Balassa and Marcus Noland/*1988*

$19.95	ISBN paper 0-88132-041-2	306 pp

America in the World Economy: A Strategy for the 1990s
C. Fred Bergsten/*1988*

$13.95	ISBN paper 0-88132-082-X	235 pp
$29.95	ISBN cloth 0-88132-089-7	235 pp

Managing the Dollar: From the Plaza to the Louvre
Yoichi Funabashi/*1988, second edition 1989*

$19.95	ISBN paper 0-88132-097-8	307 pp

United States External Adjustment and the World Economy
William R. Cline/*May 1989*
$25.00　　　　　ISBN paper 0-88132-048-X　　　　　392 pp

Free Trade Areas and U.S. Trade Policy
Jeffrey J. Schott, editor/*May 1989*
$19.95　　　　　ISBN paper 0-88132-094-3　　　　　400 pp

Dollar Politics: Exchange Rate Policymaking in the United States
I. M. Destler and C. Randall Henning/*September 1989*
$11.95　　　　　ISBN paper 0-88132-079-X　　　　　192 pp

Foreign Direct Investment in the United States
Edward M. Graham and Paul R. Krugman/*December 1989*
$11.95　　　　　ISBN paper 0-88132-074-9　　　　　161 pp

Latin American Adjustment: How Much Has Happened?
John Williamson, editor/*April 1990*
$34.95　　　　　ISBN paper 0-88132-125-7　　　　　480 pp

The Future of World Trade in Textiles and Apparel
William R. Cline/*1987, second edition, June 1990*
$20.00　　　　　ISBN paper 0-88132-110-9　　　　　344 pp

Completing the Uruguay Round: A Results-Oriented Approach to the GATT Trade Negotiations
Jeffrey J. Schott, editor/*September 1990*
$19.95　　　　　ISBN paper 0-88132-130-3　　　　　256 pp

Economic Sanctions Reconsidered (in two volumes)
　Economic Sanctions Reconsidered: History and Current Policy
(also sold separately, see below)
　Economic Sanctions Reconsidered: Supplemental Case Histories
Gary Clyde Hufbauer, Jeffrey J. Schott, and Kimberly Ann Elliott/*1985, 2d ed. December 1990*
$45.00　　　　　ISBN paper 0-88132-105-2　　　　　928 pp
$65.00　　　　　ISBN cloth 0-88132-015-X　　　　　928 pp

Economic Sanctions Reconsidered: History and Current Policy
Gary Clyde Hufbauer, Jeffrey J. Schott, and Kimberly Ann Elliott/*December 1990*
$25.00　　　　　ISBN paper 0-88132-140-0　　　　　288 pp
$36.00　　　　　ISBN cloth 0-88132-136-2　　　　　288 pp

Pacific Basin Developing Countries: Prospects for the Future
Marcus Noland/*January 1991*
$19.95　　　　　ISBN paper 0-88132-081-1　　　　　250 pp
$29.95　　　　　ISBN cloth 0-88132-141-9　　　　　250 pp

Currency Convertibility in Eastern Europe
John Williamson, editor/*September 1991*
$28.95　　　　　ISBN paper 0-88132-128-1　　　　　396 pp
$39.95　　　　　ISBN cloth 0-88132-144-3　　　　　396 pp

SPECIAL REPORTS

1 Promoting World Recovery: A Statement on Global Economic
  Strategy
  by Twenty-six Economists from Fourteen Countries/*December 1982*
  (out of print)   ISBN paper 0-88132-013-7   45 pp

2 Prospects for Adjustment in Argentina, Brazil, and Mexico:
  Responding to the Debt Crisis
  John Williamson, editor/*June 1983*
  (out of print)   ISBN paper 0-88132-016-1   71 pp

3 Inflation and Indexation: Argentina, Brazil, and Israel
  John Williamson, editor/*March 1985*
  (out of print)   ISBN paper 0-88132-037-4   191 pp

4 Global Economic Imbalances
  C. Fred Bergsten, editor/*March 1986*
  $10.00   ISBN paper 0-88132-042-0   126 pp
  $25.00   ISBN cloth 0-88132-038-2   126 pp

5 African Debt and Financing
  Carol Lancaster and John Williamson, editors/*May 1986*
  (out of print)   ISBN paper 0-88132-044-7   229 pp

6 Resolving the Global Economic Crisis: After Wall Street
  Thirty-three Economists from Thirteen Countries/*December 1987*
  $3.00   ISBN paper 0-88132-070-6   30 pp

7 World Economic Problems
  Kimberly Ann Elliott and John Williamson, editors/*April 1988*
  $15.95   ISBN paper 0-88132-055-2   298 pp

  Reforming World Agricultural Trade
  Twenty-nine Professionals from Seventeen Countries/*1988*
  $3.95   ISBN paper 0-88132-088-9   42 pp

8 Economic Relations Between the United States and Korea:
  Conflict or Cooperation?
  Thomas O. Bayard and Soo-Gil Young, editors/*January 1989*
  $12.95   ISBN paper 0-88132-068-4   192 pp

FORTHCOMING

International Adjustment and Finance: Lessons of 1985–1990
C. Fred Bergsten, editor

Equilibrium Exchange Rates: An Update
John Williamson

From Soviet disUnion to Eastern Economic Community
John Williamson and Oleh Harrylyshyn

Korea in the World Economy
Il SaKong

The Dynamics of Korean Economic Development
Soon Cho

Global Oil Crisis Intervention
Philip K. Verleger, Jr.

U.S. Taxation of International Income: Blueprint for Reform
Gary Clyde Hufbauer

Narrowing the U.S. Current Account Deficit: A Sectoral Assessment
Allen J. Lenz

Prospects for North American Free Trade
Jeffrey J. Schott and Gary Clyde Hufbauer

American Trade Politics, second edition
I. M. Destler

The United States as a Debtor Country
C. Fred Bergsten and Shafiqul Islam

The Effects of Foreign-Exchange Intervention
Jeffrey A. Frankel

Sizing Up U.S. Export Disincentives
J. David Richardson

Managed and Mismanaged Trade: Policy Lessons for the 1990s
Laura D'Andrea Tyson

The Greenhouse Effect: Global Economic Consequences
William R. Cline

The Future of the World Trading System
John Whalley

The Globalization of Industry and National Governments
C. Fred Bergsten and Edward M. Graham

Trading for the Environment
John Whalley

Energy Policy for the 1990s: A Global Perspective
Philip K. Verleger, Jr.

International Monetary Policymaking in the United States, Germany, and Japan
C. Randall Henning

The United States and Japan in the 1990s
C. Fred Bergsten, I. M. Destler, and Marcus Noland

The Outlook for World Commodity Prices
Philip K. Verleger, Jr.

The Economics of Soviet Disintegration
John Williamson

Reciprocity and Retaliation: An Evaluation of Aggressive Trade Policies
Thomas O. Bayard and Kimberly Ann Elliott

The Costs of U.S. Trade Barriers
Gary Clyde Hufbauer and Kimberly Ann Elliott

Global Competition Policy
Edward M. Graham and J. David Richardson

A World Savings Shortage?
Paul R. Krugman

Comparing the Costs of Protection: Europe, Japan, and the United States
Gary Clyde Hufbauer and Kimberly Ann Elliott, editors

Toward Freer Trade in the Western Hemisphere
Gary Clyde Hufbauer and Jeffrey J. Schott

The New Tripolar World Economy: Toward Collective Leadership
C. Fred Bergsten and C. Randall Henning

Third World Debt: A Reappraisal
William R. Cline